Virginia Reconsidered

New Histories of
the Old Dominion Virginia

* *

Reconsidered

EDITED BY KEVIN R. HARDWICK AND WARREN R. HOFSTRA

UNIVERSITY OF VIRGINIA PRESS   CHARLOTTESVILLE AND LONDON

University of Virginia Press

© 2003 by the Rector and Visitors of the University of Virginia

All rights reserved

Printed in the United States of America on acid-free paper

First published 2003

9 8 7 6 5 4 3 2

LIBRARY OF CONGRESS CATALOGING-IN-PUBLICATION DATA

Virginia reconsidered : new histories of the Old Dominion / edited by Kevin R. Hardwick and Warren R. Hofstra.

    p. cm.

Includes bibliographical references and index.

  ISBN 0-8139-2227-5 (pbk. : alk. paper)

  1. Virginia—History. I. Hardwick, Kevin R., 1961– II. Hofstra, Warren R., 1947–

F226.5 .V57 2003

975.5—DC21

                           2002153535

Contents

Acknowledgments

* * * * * * * * *T*HAT THIS ASSEMBLAGE OF ESSAYS EXPRESSES high achievement in scholarly quality, written elegance, narrative intensity, potential to engage a wide popular audience, and ability to complement forthcoming texts in Virginia history is owing to the hard work of many people. This volume reflects the judgment of a group of scholars and university professors who teach courses in Virginia history or otherwise have an interest in the teaching and presentation of this history. A working group of these scholars met at the Virginia Historical Society in May 2000 to advise the editors on plans to publish a comprehensive collection of essays focused on the history of the state. This collection thus draws from the practical classroom experience and scholarly wisdom of a substantial number of practicing academic professionals with a stake in the teaching of Virginia history at the university level. The editors wish to acknowledge and thank the following individuals for their contributions during that meeting: John d'Entremont, Randolph-Macon Woman's College; Mary Ferrari, Radford University; Nelson Lankford, Virginia Historical Society; Philip Morgan, then at the Omohundro Institute of Early American History and Culture; the late John Selby, College of William and Mary; James Sweeney, Old Dominion University; Brent Tarter, Library of Virginia; and Robert Vaughan and Andrew Chancey, both of the Virginia Foundation for the Humanities and Public Policy. Richard Holway, of the University of Virginia Press, also participated in this meeting and subsequently guided this collection through a tortuous but rewarding process of additional peer review. Editing notes for the articles we shortened was a laborious task into which Jan Eckert pitched her considerable energies and skills at a very crucial time, and we are deeply thankful to her. We owe a great debt, of course, to all the authors included in this volume and their willingness to put their work before the further scrutiny of public and student audiences. In the final analysis, however, we owe an even greater debt to our own students. Each semester they affirm anew the value of teaching history. In classroom conversations, office hours, and hallway discussions, they confront us with the values reflected in the scholarship of many esteemed colleagues—only a part of whose work is contained in this volume—scholarship that ultimately is part and parcel of a broad, national conversation on American history.

J. Frederick Fausz. Abridged version of "An 'Abundance of Blood Shed on Both Sides': England's First Indian War, 1609–1614," *Virginia Magazine of History and Biography* 98 (Jan. 1990): 3–56. Reprinted by permission of the Virginia Historical Society.

Edmund S. Morgan. "Slavery and Freedom: The American Paradox," *Journal of American History* 59 (June 1972): 5–29. Reprinted by permission of the Organization of American Historians.

Darrett B. and Anita H. Rutman. "The Road." Reprinted from *A Place in Time: Middlesex County, Virginia, 1650–1750*, by Darrett B. Rutman and Anita H. Rutman. Copyright © 1984 by Darrett B. Rutman and Anita H. Rutman. Used by permission of W. W. Norton & Company, Inc.

Jack P. Greene. Abridged version of "Society, Ideology, and Politics: An Analysis of the Political Culture of Mid-Eighteenth-Century Virginia." Reprinted from Jack P. Greene, *Negotiated Authorities: Essays in Colonial Political and Constitutional History* (Charlottesville: University Press of Virginia, 1992), 259–318. Copyright © 1976 by Jack P. Greene, from *Society, Freedom, and Conscience: The Coming of the Revolution in Virginia, Massachusetts, and New York*, ed. Richard M. Jellison. Used by permission of W. W. Norton & Company, Inc.

Woody Holton. "'Rebel against Rebel': Enslaved Virginians and the Coming of the American Revolution," *Virginia Magazine of History and Biography* 105 (Spring 1997): 157–92. Reprinted by permission of the Virginia Historical Society.

Jan Lewis. "'The Blessings of Domestic Society': Thomas Jefferson's Family and the Transformation of American Politics." Reprinted from *Jeffersonian Legacies*, ed. Peter S. Onuf (Charlottesville: University Press of Virginia, 1993), 109–46.

Deborah A. Lee and Warren R. Hofstra. "Race, Memory, and the Death of Robert Berkeley: 'A Murder . . . of . . . Horrible and Savage Barbarity.'" Reprinted from *Journal of Southern History* 65:1 (Feb. 1999): 41–76.

Thomas E. Buckley, S.J. "Unfixing Race: Class, Power, and Identity in an Interracial Family," *Virginia Magazine of History and Biography* 102 (July 1994): 349–80. Reprinted by permission of the Virginia Historical Society.

Elizabeth R. Varon. "'The Ladies Are Whigs': Lucy Barbour, Henry Clay, and Nineteenth-Century Virginia Politics." Reprinted by permission from *Virginia Cavalcade* 42:2 (Autumn 1992), © 1992 The Library of Virginia.

Stephen V. Ash. "White Virginians under Federal Occupation, 1861–1865," *Virginia Magazine of History and Biography* 98 (April 1990): 169–92. Reprinted by permission of the Virginia Historical Society.

Fred Arthur Bailey. "Free Speech and the Lost Cause in the Old Dominion," *Virginia Magazine of History and Biography* 103 (April 1995): 237–66. Reprinted by permission of the Virginia Historical Society.

Elna C. Green. "The State Suffrage Campaigns: Virginia as a Case Study." From *Southern Strategies: Southern Women and the Woman Suffrage Question* by Elna C. Green. Copyright © 1997 by the University of North Carolina Press. Used by permission of the publisher.

Gregory Michael Dorr. "Assuring America's Place in the Sun: Ivey Foreman Lewis and the Teaching of Eugenics at the University of Virginia, 1915–1953." Reprinted from *Journal of Southern History* 66:2 (May 2000): 257–96.

J. Douglas Smith. "'When Reason Collides with Prejudice': Armistead Lloyd Boothe and the Politics of Moderation." Reprinted from *The Moderates' Dilemma: Massive Resistance to School Desegregation in Virginia*, ed. Matthew D. Lassiter and Andrew B. Lewis (Charlottesville and London: University Press of Virginia, 1998), 22–50. An earlier version appeared as "'When Reason Collides with Prejudice': Armistead Lloyd Boothe and the Politics of Desegregation in Virginia, 1948–1963," *Virginia Magazine of History and Biography* 102 (Jan. 1994): 5–46. Reprinted by permission of the Virginia Historical Society.

Funds for the index were provided by a grant from the U.S. Small Business Administration (SBA) Grant Award #SBAHQ-02-1-0012). SBA's funding is not an endorsement of any products, opinions, or services. All SBA funded programs are extended to the public on a nondiscriminatory basis.

Virginia Reconsidered:
New Histories of the Old Dominion

Introduction

* * * * * * * * *W*HEN WE EXPERIENCE VIRGINIA'S HISTORY, WE tend to think of particular places, particular individuals, and particular moments. We come to Virginia's past at sites like Mount Vernon, Monticello, or the Custis-Lee mansion in Arlington. We pause at Jamestown or Martin's Hundred to reflect upon the courage and suffering of the English men and women who first settled there and to ponder how their decision to grow tobacco with impressed labor still, after so many years, shapes American life. At the reconstructed colonial capital of Williamsburg, we encounter the coherent and engaging world that the historical forces set in motion at Jamestown created in the lifeways and political rituals of men and women one and one-half centuries later. We walk Civil War battlefields so carefully maintained by the National Park Service and other organizations, painting in our mind's eye the heroism and tragedy of Manassas, Chancellorsville, Cedar Creek, and Cold Harbor or the poignancy of Appomattox. We imagine long-ago deeds of bravery and desperation as we stroll past lines of cannon and the depressions of old entrenchments facing out across open fields of grass.

Virginia's history is powerfully situated, both in popular and scholarly imaginations, in the stories of men like Christopher Newport, John Rolfe, and Powhatan; or Thomas Jefferson, James Madison, George Washington, and George Mason; or Thomas "Stonewall" Jackson and J. E. B. Stuart, not to mention Winfield Scott and George H. Thomas. It is even more powerfully situated, of course, in the potent conflicts over which such men presided. It is the drama and tragedy of colonial settlement, the Revolution, and the Civil War that come so readily to mind when we reflect on Virginia's history. In telling the stories of those moments, laden with rich significance in our collective memory, we sense the gravity of Virginia's contribution to our present-day life. When we consider Virginia's past, we think of Captain John Smith saving the desperate Jamestown settlement or Patrick Henry proclaiming majestically from St. John's Church in Richmond, "Give me liberty, or give me death!" We think of Robert E. Lee's agonizing decision

I

in April 1861 to decline command of the Union army because he would not make war upon Virginia. In knowing these things, we think we know Virginia.

And of course, in an important sense, we do. The past evoked by such places and such men was real enough, and we learn a great deal that is important by studying it in these locations, in the lives of these figures, in these compelling moments. Virginians have been, and continue to be, prominent among the statesmen whose decisions have done so much to determine America's history. While that is still true today, it was even more true in the nineteenth century, and especially so in the eighteenth. The crises that defined Virginia's statesmen, and were defined in turn by them, all continue to engage the attention of the reading public no less than the interests of professional historians. Nonetheless, the prominence of the conflicts in which these men struggled and which these places embody overshadows other men and women, other places, other moments. The story of Virginia is only half told without these other histories.[1]

It is not simply the case that histories of Virginia which focus only on the lives and decisions of Virginia's prominent public figures are incomplete because they leave out the experiences of so many other Virginians. Such histories are incomplete in another fashion as well, because they leave us, ultimately, unable to understand the actions and decisions of the very leaders upon whom they focus. The fate and the destiny of the Jamestown settlement, for example, were no more powerfully influenced than in the struggle of the Powhatan *mamanatowick* Wahunsonacock (Powhatan) to incorporate the English into his own efforts at empire building and to fight a war with Englishmen when they became more of a threat than an ally. This is the story told by J. Frederick Fausz in this volume. He shows that we cannot comprehend the history of early Virginia if we do not understand this conflict between two rival peoples, each opportunistically seeking their own advantage.

The story of early Virginia is also told in the internal conflicts of settlers who immigrated to the colony. As Edmund S. Morgan notes in his chapter, mid-seventeenth-century Virginia witnessed "the engrossment of tidewater land in thousands and tens of thousands of acres by speculators, who recognized that the demand would rise." Their gains were measured in the losses of others. Consider the story of Arthur Nash and his descendants, so painstakingly reconstructed by Darrett B. and Anita H. Rutman in their contribution to this collection. It took years of struggle, hard work, and not a little good fortune for Arthur to buy land in Middlesex County and decades more for his son John to improve the holding into a viable farm. For Arthur and John, and countless other men like them, the achievement of economic independence, secured by landownership, defined their life struggle. How are we to understand the world of early Virginia without giving due attention—as essays in this volume do—to the aspirations of men like Arthur and John Nash?

Thomas Jefferson, George Washington, Patrick Henry, and other notable Virginians led the American struggle for political liberty and economic independence from Great Britain. They were nurtured within a rich local tradition of political leadership based on social deference, powerfully analyzed in this volume by Jack P. Greene. Personal independence, Greene suggests, had a central place in their political values, no less than in those of men like Arthur and John Nash. But while gentlemen such as Jefferson, Washington, and Henry, and a good many others like them, prepared to lead their society out of dependency in the British Empire, a "small mulatto man," Joseph Harris, stole himself quietly one night in July 1775 from American slavery into British freedom and then helped the king's men attack his previous masters at his hometown of Hampton, Virginia. Harris fought, every bit as much as the Revolutionary leaders we so rightfully celebrate as patriots, to enhance the cause of liberty in Virginia. Harris's struggle for liberty, however, has tended to recede from popular memory, an irony that is poignant when we pause, as Woody Holton invites us to do, to consider it. The decisions of enslaved men and women like Harris surely shaped the political calculus of patriot and British leaders alike, contributing to the evolution of the American Revolution in Britain's largest, wealthiest, and most populous North American colony.

The ideals for which the Revolutionary generation struggled have been a central organizing theme in many narratives of American history and continue to be so today. The struggle for liberty, in all of its various forms, lies close to the heart of Virginia's past. Desire for freedom surely shaped the actions of the African Americans known only as Sarah, Randolph, and London, whose story, and the subsequent stories told about them in later years, are recounted by Deborah A. Lee and Warren R. Hofstra. On the evening of May 12, 1818, these slaves brutally killed their owner, acknowledging that death was preferable to serving him. Die they did by the rope two months later, convicted by magistrates who refused to recognize any authentic motive for their crime. We cannot make sense of the actions of these slaves without giving attention to their understanding of liberty. And just as critically, as Lee and Hofstra demonstrate, we fail to understand something important about antebellum Virginia if we do not recognize the willful blindness of Virginia's planters. We can see clearly what they refused to acknowledge, but only by recovering the humanity of men and women like Sarah, Randolph, and London.[2]

Indeed, most of the essays in this volume address the idea of freedom in one way or another. Jan Lewis's contribution to this volume is also, subtly, about the meaning of freedom and a common struggle to achieve it. Thomas Jefferson, she suggests, grew up in a genteel eighteenth-century world that, at least in theory, rewarded the public-spirited gentleman with fame and the affection of his countrymen. The caustic, rancorous, and constraining reality of early national public life, however, hurled Jefferson back to a more private source of affection, identity, and personal freedom in the adoring love of his daughters and their children. Thomas Jefferson's public life, then, cannot be understood apart from private relationships within his family. Indeed, if we wish fully to understand the story of Virginia, we surely must grasp the aspirations of all Virginians, men and women. Consider, for example, the story of Lucy Barbour, who in the male world of antebellum politics wanted to be heard and struggled "to be counted something in the muster-roll of man." As Elizabeth R. Varon notes, "There was a strong connection between Whig women and reform in Virginia." Lucy Barbour's efforts to inspire Virginia women to erect a statue of Henry Clay, the Great Compromiser, fed into that powerful stream leading to the enfranchisement of American women a long eight decades later.

The patriarchal norms that Jefferson accepted and employed, and against which Barbour struggled, were also the wellsprings of freedom for other Virginians, on occasion in surprising ways. Examine, for example, the remarkable story of Thomas Wright, Sylvia, the woman he loved, and their son Robert, which Thomas E. Buckley has painstakingly pieced together. Although Sylvia was a slave and of "very black" complexion, Thomas Wright, a white man, treated her as his wife, manumitted her children, and proudly designated Robert as his heir. What makes the story remarkable is not that some masters loved their slave mistresses, but rather that Thomas not only took Sylvia as his helpmate in a manner acknowledged by his neighbors in the plantation society of Campbell County but also successfully conveyed his social status as a landed, independent planter to his mulatto son. As Buckley notes, "With his father's considerable assistance and the approval of the white elite, Robert Wright gained entry into Campbell County society and acquired an identity constructed by economic class rather than race." In 1806 Robert married Mary Godsey, a white woman, thus confirming his status as an independent landowner and a man of secure standing in Campbell County. Local white families, some of considerable stature and wealth, by all accounts treated the Wright family as one of their own. Robert secured his freedom in much the same fashion as had Arthur and John Nash, more than a century earlier, as a landed proprietor and head of household.

The efforts of Virginians to define the meaning of freedom shaped the ways in which they understood the Civil War and its aftermath. Consider the experience of Fauquier County planter Edward Turner, recounted by Stephen V. Ash. Men like Turner worked hard, just as had earlier generations of Virginians, to secure their landed independence. But that "people generally are entirely stripped of their subsistence" by occupying armies was not half so devastating as the fact that "excellent and worthy citizens were ... shamefully treated upon the testimony of some unprincipled slave." The war entailed not only dependence and poverty for men like Turner, but it also elevated other people, who formerly had been dependent, and gave them status to confront the authority of Turner and others like him. The Civil War thus represented a double challenge to the identity of Virginia's slave-owning planters, for it threatened their ownership of land and demolished their patriarchal authority over slaves. In the decades that followed the Civil War, the struggle in which black and white Virginians engaged over the meaning of freedom and independence led to the deep divisions of Jim Crow segregation.

The dilemmas with which each and every Virginian has had to struggle emerge nowhere more clearly than in the career of Armistead Boothe. As chronicled by J. Douglas Smith, that career entailed a profound paradox. Boothe was a committed segregationist. But he could not reconcile his commitment to equality and fair play, as well as to individual dignity, with Virginia's Jim Crow statutes. In the aftermath of the 1954 United States Supreme Court decision in *Brown v. Board of Education of Topeka*, which determined that racial segregation in public schools was unconstitutional, Virginia's leaders formulated a policy of "Massive Resistance" to prevent implementation of the Court's ruling. Forced to weigh his public stance on segregation against his most deeply held values, Boothe helped break the logjam of massive resistance and open educational opportunity to all Virginians. In stories such as Boothe's, Virginians today confront the most profound and perplexing contradictions unleashed by the struggle for freedom in a diverse society.

Thirty years ago, in his classic study *American Slavery, American Freedom: The Ordeal of Colonial Virginia*, Edmund S. Morgan argued that the entwined evolution of freedom and slavery was "the central paradox of American history." Morgan was impressed by the degree to which Virginia history speaks to the largest and most important themes of American history. The founders of the United States of America, he noted, devoted themselves to securing ideals of equality and liberty while at the same time holding other men and women as chattel. "The paradox is American," he argued, "and it behooves Americans to understand it if they would understand themselves." Moreover, he pointed out, "the key to the puzzle, historically, does lie in Virginia." Virginians most eloquently and persuasively argued for American freedom during the Revolution, and Virginians disproportionately provided the leadership of the new nation in the crucial years following the struggle for independence. "If it is possible to understand the American paradox, the marriage of slavery and freedom," Morgan argued, "Virginia is surely the place to begin." His understanding of the American paradox has proven powerfully influential to the way recent historians tell the story of Virginia.[3] Indeed, the coherence of Virginia history, as it has emerged in recent decades, stems from the extent to which it illuminates the core issues of American history.[4]

Morgan's concern was to understand the interrelationship of slavery, as the institution had evolved by the eighteenth century, and the concurrent celebration of republican political ideals at the time of the Revolution. He wanted to apprehend the connection between the emergence of America's most cherished public values and the struggle to legitimate the unequal distribution of power and authority in society. The story he tells, an essay-length version of which is included here, is one of idealism transformed by material necessity and opportunism. "Virginia from the beginning was conceived not only as a haven for England's suffering poor," Morgan writes, "but as a spearhead of English liberty in an oppressed world." But over the course of the seventeenth century, the colony became a society itself defined by slavery. By the first decade of the eighteenth century "a system of labor that treated men as things," initially imposed upon white servants, had been transformed into the institutionalized enslavement of Africans. By the mid-eighteenth century Virginians had "achieved a society in which most of the poor were enslaved," and small farmers as well as large planters were "equal in not being slaves." Thus, as Morgan notes, free Virginians readily adopted the language of classical republicanism, which premised virtuous citizenship and political participation on the economic independence afforded by private property. Indeed, because all landowners in Virginia shared such broad common interests, they "could outdo the English republicans as well as New England ones."

The essays included in this volume broaden Morgan's paradox temporally by discussing Virginia's history from 1600 to 1960. And they broaden it thematically as well, describing the articulation of authority and influence throughout a society early defined by individual striving for material success. Virginia's modern historians have tended to center the story of America's core political values on analyses of race, religion, ethnicity, and gender—and ultimately on the contested application of power. Slavery is only one form that the American paradox has taken in Virginia over the years. The tension between freedom and exclusion, and between competing definitions of what it means to be free, in one way or another informs the thinking of every scholar represented in this volume.[5]

The essays herein collectively focus on the projection of power within and across Virginia society. Virginia historians of the last three decades have looked not simply at relationships between classes of people (men and women; African Americans, Indians, and Anglos; workers and bosses; Unionists and secessionists; independent people and dependent people; rich and poor) but also at the fashion in which powerful men and women have constructed and maintained the social and political systems that at any given moment defined Virginia society. The evolution of slavery in late seventeenth-century Virginia, for instance, made it possible for powerful planters to erect a stable social and political order, in the process paving the way for the "Golden Age" of the eighteenth century that figures so prominently at historic sites including the James River plantation houses and Colonial Williamsburg. Impressing blacks into racial slavery relieved tensions among their oppressors, forestalling the kind of political turmoil and rebellion that had characterized the late seventeenth century. The categories available to Virginians by which they could make sense of their social world have been neither static nor fixed in the natural order. They have emerged from the efforts of some Virginians to impose their will and vision upon others. This struggle has been in the broadest sense political.

It is perhaps tempting to place accounts that highlight politically and socially subordinate men and women and their understanding of power, authority, and legitimacy in opposition to the more traditional narratives of political or popular history. To treat the scholarship contained in this volume in that fashion, however, would be a mistake. As Woody Holton argued recently, the American Revolution "reveals that, when Virginia gentlemen launched their struggle to preserve and extend their freedom, they were powerfully influenced by other freedom struggles—movements put together by Indians, debtors, merchants, slaves, and smallholders." Elizabeth Varon has noted the conservatism of the women who strove to affect their social world. "They sought, each in her own way, to resolve an enduring paradox," Varon writes, "to reconcile a commitment to the traditional gender order, in which women deferred to the leadership of men, with a passion for politics and a desire to be heard." Although Holton is alive to social and political struggle structured by class relationships and Varon works in a tradition informed by gender analysis, neither sets the narrative they relate in opposition to the study of the evolution of American public ideals. Quite the contrary, both set out explicitly to deepen our understanding of what Richard Hofstadter famously called the "American Political Tradition." For them, and for the other scholars whose work appears in this volume, the story of American freedom is the story of ideals and people in conflict. Freedom is something that men and women have had to struggle to obtain. Freedom is power, and liberty is also freedom from power. These historians seek to recover subordinate voices, not to replace or reject an accepted political narrative, but rather to expand it.[6]

The best Virginia history, then, speaks to profoundly American issues and does so with sensitivity to the articulation of political power and social authority. For the historians whose scholarship appears in this collection, it is the clash of interests that drives human events forward. In the opening essay J. Frederick Fausz chronicles Virginia's first war between Englishmen and Indians, which started in 1609 and ended in 1614. "The tragic cycle of reciprocal revenge that the First Anglo-Powhatan War initiated," Fausz argues, "made combat the primary method of defending and nurturing cultural identity." In the conflicts that followed, "new generations of warriors would learn from the veterans and victims of each previous conflict." Participants in later Indian wars, in Virginia but also in other colonies, found "the cathartic relief, and brutal simplicity, of violence perversely preferable to the complex process of intercultural understanding." The first Anglo-Powhatan War, then, created the pattern after which later conflicts developed. Certainly after 1614 Anglo-Indian relations would be defined by military and political power. Fausz, like most of the other scholars represented in this volume, centers his account on peoples in contest and struggle.

By the late seventeenth century, Edmund Morgan argues, Virginians had developed a powerful solution to the problem of social exploitation and political inequality among white Englishmen, which had culminated in the belligerence of Bacon's Rebellion. But the enslavement of African Americans only displaced the conflict. Although slavery resolved class antagonism among whites, it effectively premised social order in Virginia on violence and exclusion. The precariousness of this unstable relationship was made forcibly explicit during the Civil War. Because power relationships that define society are exposed most clearly at those precise moments in which they are challenged, the Civil War has proved to be an especially revealing moment in Virginia. Fierce disagreement over its meaning, for instance, shaped how the story of Robert Berkeley's murder would be told. By denying the slave murderers a motive, Virginians at the time of the crime implicitly acknowledged it as a protest against slavery. In the aftermath of the Civil War, however, Berkeley's murder came to be attributed solely to the inherent savagery that supposedly characterized blacks as a race and that white Virginians understood as the antithesis of civil society. Thus, powerful Virginians in the era of Jim Crow segregation put historical narratives to new uses, prefiguring contemporary social and political struggles in the way in which they remembered their past, ultimately writing the guilt of oppression out of their historical memory.

The violence of the Civil War also persisted in the way Virginia leaders "felt their social class threatened by the aspirations of lesser whites and long-oppressed African Americans," Fred Arthur Bailey argues. At a time of Populist protest when both groups clamored for greater economic opportunity and broader political participation, "southern elites once again manned the parapets to defend their status, not on the bloody ground of Gettysburg or Shiloh but in the interpretation of the past." They redefined the Civil War not in Abraham Lincoln's words as a "great battlefield" testing whether any nation "conceived in liberty and dedicated to the proposition that all men are created equal . . . can long endure" but as a constitutional struggle over the rights of states in which moral dilemmas were subsumed by legal disputation. At issue in Bailey's thinking was the contemporaneous question of who would rule Virginia.

This battle for social dominance continued well into the twentieth century. It is revealed in the career of Virginia scientists like Ivey Foreman Lewis, who until 1953 taught popular courses in "eugenics"—the purportedly scientific study of race and cultural transmission—at the University of Virginia. As Gregory Michael Dorr argues, "Eugenics provided generations of educated, self-consciously modern Virginians with a new method of legitimating the South's traditional social order." Backed by the seemingly objective science produced by scholars like Lewis, Virginia lawmakers passed racial integrity legislation, which by strictly defining race outlawed any form of interracial marriage. The Supreme Court of Appeals of Virginia upheld this legislation in 1955, and it was only invalidated by the United States Supreme Court in 1967.

History, like science, is never morally neutral, and its uses reflect contemporary power struggles. Inherited understandings of the appropriate public and private roles of women also acknowledged these struggles. "Virginia, if the dearest of states, is the most conservative. Her men are chivalric, her women domestic," according to Virginia novelist and suffragist Mary Johnson, discussed by Elna C. Green. "She makes progress, too, but her eyes are apt to turn to the past." When woman suffragists organized effectively at the turn of the twentieth century, Green demonstrates, they threatened to invigorate other reform movements. The state's Democratic Party, which represented the conservative interests of planters and industrialists and whose dominance of state politics stemmed largely from limiting the right to vote, opposed the movement. To gain the vote, women had to contend not only with powerful political forces but also with the potent influence of their own past.

The stories told by the historians included in this book insist that public life in Virginia has been profoundly shaped by the actions of a wide variety of Virginians. These essays have value today because they address the enduring struggles that determined our past, and they give us the stock of stories upon which we draw as we define our lives in the present. They have been selected for the quality of these stories and for the varied ways they trace the motivations that inspired all of Virginia's peoples to pursue the implications of freedom. They compose what could be called a new narrative history. After several decades of painstakingly detailed and statistically rigorous accounts of America's little communities and social systems, contemporary historians have returned to the wellspring of their profession: history as the telling of culturally significant stories. Virginia's modern historians draw abundantly on new knowledge of environmental influences, social relations, political arrangements, mental structures, and cultural systems to place the specific experiences and life histories of women and men in richly contextured discourses. The essays included here approach the big stories of Virginia history, and of American history, by recovering and recounting the experiences of individuals, often ordinary people, and exploring how the paradoxes and promises of America unfolded in their lives.

NOTES

1. The focus of Virginia history on the colonial, Revolution, and Civil War periods is amply demonstrated by even a casual survey of the literature. For example, a quick search of Virginia-related essays included in the JSTOR on-line article repository reveals enormous interest in the colonial period and in the Revolution and its aftermath and only slight interest in periods after 1800. Similarly, the steady procession of works on the Civil War in Virginia, which can be followed in the book reviews of the *Virginia Magazine of History and Biography*, reveals the continued fascination that conflict still evokes in contemporary historians, writing for both professional and public audiences. All quotations in this introduction are from articles in this volume unless otherwise noted.

2. For a recent synthesis of American history that places the evolution of liberty as its central theme, see Eric Foner, *The Story of American Freedom* (New York: W. W. Norton, 1999).

3. Edmund S. Morgan, *American Slavery, American Freedom: The Ordeal of Colonial Virginia* (New York: W. W. Norton, 1975), 4–6. Morgan's book has proved powerfully influential not just to Virginia historians but to American historians in general. In a survey answered by more than one thousand historians, the book most frequently mentioned as the most admired was *American Slavery, American Freedom* (David Thelen, "The Practice of American History," *Journal of American History* 81 [Dec. 1994]: 953).

4. We are indebted to John d'Entremont for this observation, which provides one of the themes for his forthcoming synthesis of Virginia history.

5. Edmund S. Morgan, "The First American Boom: Virginia 1618 to 1630," *William and Mary Quarterly*, 3d ser., 28 (Apr. 1971): 198; Morgan, *American Slavery, American Freedom*, 381.

6. Woody Holton, *Forced Founders: Indians, Debtors, Slaves, and the Making of the American Revolution in Virginia* (Chapel Hill: University of North Carolina Press for the Institute of Early American History and Culture, 1999), xxi; Elizabeth R. Varon, *We Mean to Be Counted: White Women and Politics in Antebellum Virginia* (Chapel Hill: University of North Carolina Press, 1998), 9; Richard Hofstadter, *The American Political Tradition and the Men Who Made It* (New York: Alfred A. Knopf, 1948).

J. FREDERICK FAUSZ

An *"Abundance of Blood Shed on Both Sides": England's First Indian War, 1609–1614*

* * * * * * * * THE STORY OF VIRGINIA, OF COURSE, DOES NOT begin with the arrival of English colonists at Jamestown in the early seventeenth century. The history of native peoples can be traced through the continuous evolution of their cultures for at least nine thousand preceding years. During this long epoch the original occupants of the land profoundly altered their environment and built political systems that significantly affected the course of European expansion in the New World. Until recently, however, historians have discounted the agency of Native Americans. Instead, an older tradition of Virginia history implicitly accepted the judgments of the colonists themselves who often thought of the Indians as part of the natural landscape to be acted upon, shoved aside, or otherwise removed to make room for European civilization and progress.

J. Frederick Fausz's account of the First Anglo-Powhatan War brings Indians into the mainstream of Virginia history. The sporadic but intense episodes of violence between Jamestown settlers and the people of the Powhatan chiefdom from 1609 to 1614, Fausz insists, must be seen as a full-fledged war. By depicting the conflict as a clash of equivalent cultures in which both sides fought for the legitimate ends of "political hegemony and territorial control," this ethnohistorian discredits the "hoary myths of Indian ignorance, passivity, or treachery." Fausz's perspective also illuminates and clarifies key events like the Starving Time, the abandonment of James Fort, and the Pocahontas-Rolfe marriage, whose complex meanings have eluded explanations taken only from the viewpoint of Jamestown settlers. The tragedy of the war lay in the cycle of retribution that resulted and in the "missed opportunity for the English and the Powhatans to accommodate cultural differences, to find mutually beneficial relationships worth preserving, and to define the boundaries of limited but inviolable sovereignty that each had as neighbors in Virginia." Thus "England's first Indian war became a primer for future struggles in the forests of America." Ironically, the pattern of endemic violence and vindictive slaughter and plunder would also characterize later struggles within Virginia society such as Bacon's Rebellion treated by Edmund Morgan and Darrett and Anita Rutman later in this volume.

What Fausz achieves in this essay is not the condemnation of one side or the glorification of the other, but a view of history taken from the various perspectives of all the peoples and cultures that shaped it. It is this view that informs each of the essays in this collection and will well serve all students of Virginia history.   * * * * * * * *

* * * * * * * *
IN JUNE 1610 A SHIP FROM VIRGINIA ARRIVED AT LYME REGIS bearing the shocking news that "the Indians hold the English surrounded in the strong place which they had erected there [Jamestown], having killed the larger part of them, and the others were left so entirely without provisions that they thought it impossible to escape, because the survivors eat the dead." Fourteen years later, Virginia's "Antient Planters" who had survived such terrors reported that "most part of the time that Sir Thomas Gates and Sir Thomas Dale governed, we were at warre with the natives, so that by them divers times were many of our people slaine, whose blood . . . Dale neglected not to revenge."[1]

Such events were part of the first—and least known—of England's many colonial wars with American Indians. The First Anglo-Powhatan War (August 1609 to April 1614) evolved gradually from two years of contact between alien peoples with incompatible world views who nonetheless had potential grounds for cooperation. Once begun, however, this conflict quickly escalated into a bitter, vengeful "holy war" for political hegemony and territorial control that neither side could afford to lose. Before England declared its first and most ambiguous military victory in the forests of the New World, the Powhatans had killed between one-fifth and one-quarter of the colonists, forced the temporary abandonment of Jamestown, and severely strained transatlantic lines of supply and communication.

In providing an unprecedented opportunity for Englishmen to assess the effectiveness of their technologically sophisticated firepower against the will power of numerically superior native warriors, this conflict became an important primer for all Indian wars in British America. By promoting intracultural cohesion and intercultural contempt through a vicious cycle of reciprocal atrocities, the First Anglo-Powhatan War sowed the seeds of Virginia frontier conflicts in 1622–32, 1644–46, and 1675–77 that afflicted the colony with twenty years of bloody combat in its first seven decades. Moreover, this seminal event in the formative years of English colonization was witnessed and discussed by the greatest collection of contemporary chroniclers in seventeenth-century Virginia, including John Smith, George Percy, William Strachey, Lord De La Warr, Thomas Dale, Ralph Hamor, Samuel Argall, and Alexander Whitaker—many of whom probably wrote so much about Indians precisely because England's goals were being challenged by the native population.[2]

Despite the rich variety of these sources, modern historians have consistently ignored the First Anglo-Powhatan War. Following three hundred years in which anti-Indian rhetoric posed as history, twentieth-century scholarship has softened the racist opprobrium against the Powhatans too often by avoiding them altogether.[3] . . .

The essay that follows is intended as a corrective to the various "half-histories" of early Virginia that have ignored the critical role of the Powhatans in shaping the English colonial experience and that by doing so have provided insufficient answers to why Jamestown suffered a "Starving Time" during one winter and not others, why martial law was invoked, and why the marriage of John Rolfe and Pocahontas brought "peace" between Indians and colonists (had there been a war?). My thesis is that intercultural hostilities between August 1609 and April 1614 constituted the First Anglo-Powhatan War, because their acknowledged purpose and systematic pattern—as recognized by the combatants themselves—were distinctly different from the sporadic violence that preceded 1609 and followed 1614, and that this conflict significantly influenced the subsequent development of both peoples.

This study has three objectives: first, to delineate, through the kind of detailed narrative description that is almost extinct in scholarly journals, the events and decisions that provoked and perpetuated the First Anglo-Powhatan War; second, to legitimize that conflict as precedent-setting in interethnic relations, as a corrective to recent trends that ignore the seminal role of the Powhatans in favor of the League Iroquois, Virginia in favor of New England, and the seventeenth century in favor of the eighteenth; and third, to challenge the recent ethnohistorical emphases on native accommodationism and the "neutral" process of acculturation without due regard for the systematic aggression that was perpetrated against Powhatan political sovereignty, territorial legitimacy, and cultural integrity.[4]

When 104 Englishmen landed at Jamestown Island on Thursday, 14 May 1607, successful warriors and arrogant leaders from two expansionistic empires began nearly four centuries of uninterrupted Anglo-Powhatan relations. These proud peoples of ascendant destiny were each enjoying a "golden age," and they approached one another with more confidence than fear (they reserved contempt born of familiarity for traditional enemies far better known). English confidence derived from past successes against the forces of Catholic Europe—especially the repulsing of the Spanish Armada in 1588—which produced a convenient, collective amnesia about more recent setbacks to guerrilla forces in Ireland and at Roanoke Island. Despite reports from English eyewitnesses in 1585–86 that the Indians along the James River "would be loth to suffer any strangers . . . and . . . would fight

Table A Military Engagements of the First Anglo-Powhatan War

Map Number	Engagement	Result	Eng. Fatalities (% of force)	
		1609		
1 Aug.–Oct.	Siege at Nansemond	Percy, Martin troops expelled	50	(50%)
2 Aug.–Oct.	Siege at Nonsuch	F. West troops expelled	50	(42%)
3 Sept.?	Ambush of Bermuda Shallop	Ravens and crew slain	10	(100%)
4 Nov.	Ambush of Ratcliffe	Ratcliffe expedition expelled	33	(66%)
5 Nov.	Patawomec Murders	West and crew deserted	0	
6 Nov.–May	Siege of Jamestown	Percy's James Fort garrison reduced	110	(65%)
		1610		
7 9 July	Battle of Kecoughtan	1st English conquest (Gates)	0	
8 Mid-July	Raid on Blockhouse	Attackers repulsed	4	(20%)
9 10 Aug.	Battle of Paspahegh	Percy burned village, took corn	0	
10 11 Aug.	Raid on Chickahominy	Davis burned village, took corn	0	
11 Mid-Aug.	Raid on Warraskoyac	Brewster, Argall took corn	0	
12 Nov.	Appomattoc Ambush	English miners slaughtered	14	(93%)
13 Nov.	Raid on Appomattoc	Brewster, Yeardley avenged ambush	0	
		1611		
14 Winter	Fort La Warr Siege	Lord De La Warr expedition expelled	32	(20%)
15 Feb.?	2d Raid on Blockhouse	Attackers repulsed	2	(10%)
16 29 Mar.	Battle of Blockhouse	Garrison annihilated	20	(100%)
17 June	Battle of Nansemond	2d English conquest (Dale)	0	
18 Sept.–Dec.	Battle of Henrico	3d English conquest (Gates, Dale)	15	(5%)
19 Dec.	Battle of Appomattoc	4th English conquest (Dale)	?	
		1614		
20 Mar.	York River Invasion	Standoff (Dale, Argall)	0	

Estimates only, with strong inferences based on sources and circumstances. English war-related deaths probably exceeded 350 (23% of all immigrants arriving between 1607 and 1614). The Powhatans perhaps had above 250 war-related fatalities.

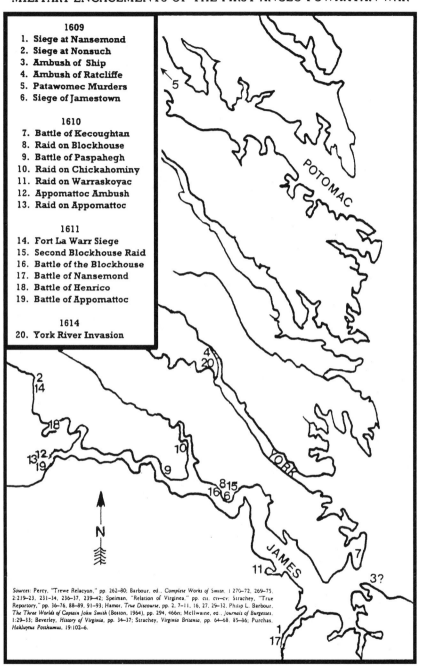

1609
1. Siege at Nansemond
2. Siege at Nonsuch
3. Ambush of Ship
4. Ambush of Ratcliffe
5. Patawomec Murders
6. Siege of Jamestown

1610
7. Battle of Kecoughtan
8. Raid on Blockhouse
9. Battle of Paspahegh
10. Raid on Chickahominy
11. Raid on Warraskoyac
12. Appomattoc Ambush
13. Raid on Appomattoc

1611
14. Fort La Warr Siege
15. Second Blockhouse Raid
16. Battle of the Blockhouse
17. Battle of Nansemond
18. Battle of Henrico
19. Battle of Appomattoc

1614
20. York River Invasion

Sources: Percy, "Trewe Relacyon," pp. 262–80; Barbour, ed., *Complete Works of Smith*, 1 270–72, 269–75, 2:219–23, 231–34, 236–37, 239–42; Spelman, "Relation of Virginea," pp. cii, civ–cv; Strachey, "True Reportory," pp. 36–76, 88–89, 91–93; Hamor, *True Discourse*, pp. 2, 7–11, 16, 27, 29–32. Philip L. Barbour, *The Three Worlds of Captain John Smith* (Boston, 1964), pp. 294, 466n; McIlwaine, ed., *Journals of Burgesses*, 1:29–33; Beverley, *History of Virginia*, pp. 34–37; Strachey, *Virginia Britania*, pp. 64–68, 85–86; Purchas, *Hakluytus Posthumus*, 19:102–6.

very well," the first colonists hoped to find compliant and friendly natives but fully expected to defeat any hostile ones with their advanced weaponry.

Powhatan confidence, in turn, derived from recent conquests of other coastal Algonquians, which reinforced a convenient, collective amnesia about the destructive visits of Spanish conquistadors to the lower Chesapeake in the 1560s and 1570s. Despite prophecies that foretold of a "Nation" of aliens who would invade from Chesapeake Bay and effect "their Subjection and . . . Conquest" in the last of three wars, the Powhatans hoped to find compliant and friendly allies in the alien arrivals but fully expected to defeat hostile ones with their thirty-to-one advantage in manpower.[5]

In the generation before the founding of Jamestown, Wahunsonacock (Powhatan), the paramount chief, or *mamanatowick*, over some fourteen thousand Algonquians in the domain known as *Tsenacommacah*, had vastly expanded an original inheritance of six tribes into some thirty territories by means of alliance, intimidation, and conquest. Such expansion was always eastward, toward the bay, and his recent victories over the Kecoughtans and Chesapeaks on either side of the mouth of the James River gave him strategic access to information on arriving ships and provided rich land and marine resources far removed from strong and dangerous Siouan enemies just west of the fall line. Exercising his power to exterminate or relocate tribal populations, Wahunsonacock had bolstered his "Atlantic strategy" by installing his son, Pochins, as *werowance* of *Tsenacommacah*'s "eastern door" at Kecoughtan and by leaving another grown son, Parahunt, in command at the village of Powhatan, the chiefdom's "western door" and first capital.

The Powhatan chiefdom was the most extensive and powerful Algonquian domain that English colonists encountered along the Atlantic coast in the seventeenth century, but while Wahunsonacock's hegemony was extensive, his power was far from total in either depth or breadth. He was still adding to, and consolidating control within, his empire, for the independent Chickahominies continued to challenge his authority with impunity, and distant "fringe" peoples along the Potomac and on the Eastern Shore were not fully integrated into *Tsenacommacah*. When the English arrived, Wahunsonacock was more concerned with the concrete threats from Monacan enemies to the west and Susquehannock and Massawomeck intrusions from the north than with unknown aliens—a situation that allowed the colonists to establish Jamestown precisely where the Powhatans were fewest and most vulnerable.[6] . . .

At the end of the colonists' first month in the Chesapeake, questions abounded about the benefits and dangers of intercultural cohabitation. The English, despite their published professions of finding only an "idle, improvident, scattered people," discovered that the Powhatans were productive village farmers, and they were at least mildly concerned by the Indians' obsessive curiosity about their firearms. The Powhatans cautiously referred to the colonists as *tassantasses* (strangers)—a purposefully ambiguous term—until their performance as either *wingapohs* (friends) or *marrapoughs* (enemies) could be determined, and they remained most perplexed by the baffling behavior of the white aliens. Because the strangers did not hunt, fish, or clear fields as was expected of Indian men, arrived without women from an unknown world, and died in droves on an abandoned peninsula of "waste ground" while harvesting common timber, the Powhatans could only conclude that the English were an odd, inferior race from a desolate homeland, most similar to the primitive, nonfarming Monacan "barbarians"—except for their awesome ships and sophisticated weapons.[7]

Wahunsonacock could not afford to wait long before determining whether the white men and their muskets could strengthen *Tsenacommacah* through alliance or were capable of subverting it by aggression. Such strategic intelligence on military potential could only be derived under combat conditions; thus, the seeming duplicity and "treachery" of the Powhatans' tactical hostility was less a change in policy than a means to discover what diplomatic hospitality could not. Wahunsonacock's calculated and limited attack to test the English followed numerous parleys that left critical issues unresolved and came only after the colonists signaled their intention to stay by building James Fort—a meaningful military symbol to the Algonquians and an ominous recognition that the aliens mistrusted their generous hosts. On Tuesday, 26 May, while Christopher Newport's exploratory party was away being feted far upriver, Wahunsonacock dispatched some two to four hundred warriors in a "furious Assault" on the still-unfinished fortifications. The "very valiant" attackers killed two colonists and wounded between twelve and fifteen others before ships' cannon and musket fire took a devastating toll at close range.[8] . . .

The tactical hostility of 26 May certainly provided Wahunsonacock with a wealth of information, perhaps more than he wanted. Neither side had ever experienced such an engagement, and if the English were horrified by the awesome offensive capabilities of this "very valiant people," the Powhatans were terrified by the lethal effects of the colonists' firearms. In subsequent skirmishes over the next few weeks, the Powhatans showed respect for those weapons, "not daring to approche scarce within muskett shott," while the English learned to be ever vigilant for the sudden, silent volley of arrows fired from the surrounding forest. After one brief but bloody encounter, the once-confident combatants—equally accustomed to waging colorful, elaborate, open-field battles in massed formations—began to rethink and alter those military tactics. Englishmen were soon cowering behind the crude logs of James Fort, which they had completed on 15 June, while Powhatan bowmen crouched patiently in tall grass waiting to pick off colonists (and in one case a dog) who ventured outside to "doe naturall necessity."[9]

Although European technology could not guarantee survival in America, firearms and large ships—those "miracles of Christendome"—proved invaluable for preserving the English colonists in the Chesapeake. Matchlock muskets were heavy, cumbersome, difficult to shoot fast, and hard to aim accurately, but the psychological effect of their thunderous, smoky discharge and their capacity to inflict painful, lethal wounds at some distance gave the Jamestown colonists a defensive potential that largely neutralized the Powhatans' superiority in manpower. Moreover, the English learned to employ their heavily armed ships as mobile fortresses that were uniquely capable of ravaging several riverine villages in a day and of transporting wounded men, Indian prisoners, and large quantities of corn and other booty back to base. The Chesapeake Bay and its many broad rivers, which divided tribal groups and prevented Powhatan military control, served as avenues of invasion for the well-adapted English sailing vessels.[10]

The exploratory encounter of 26 May was a standoff that chastened both attackers and defenders. The colonists learned the terrors of a massed Indian attack and realized that they possessed neither the men nor materiel necessary for a full-scale war with the Powhatans. Moreover, the cost-conscious Virginia Company wanted assurances of tranquil relations with the Indians before it would fund future voyages or send Christian missionaries.

For his part, once Wahunsonacock discovered how hard it would be to dislodge the intruders from their defensive position, he became more mindful of being caught in a vice between unpredictable aliens to the east and all-too-predictable native enemies to the west. While the colonists were still unaware of his complicity in the attack on James Fort, Wahunsonacock again exercised his diplomatic options in an effort to renew their trust and to procure their terrifying weapons for use against his traditional adversaries.[11] . . .

Throughout the summer and autumn, Wahunsonacock kept the depleted, disease-ridden colonists alive with gifts of food until he had restored their trust and earned a formal recognition of their grateful dependence. His invitation for the English to explore his territories allowed him to capture John Smith in December 1607, and he used this most adventuresome of colonial leaders to symbolize the place of the aliens within *Tsenacommacah*. By means of a ritualized adoption ceremony involving Pocahontas, Wahunsonacock accepted this first Englishman he ever saw into his own family and officially recognized Smith as *werowance* over his newest "tribe" of subservient allies. Offering "Corne, weomen and Country" to the English "as to his owne people," Wahunsonacock ordered Smith to deliver two cannon and a large grindstone as an appropriate tribute and fully expected the colonists' cooperation against his enemies.[12]

The Powhatans' adoption of Smith in January 1608, followed ten months later by the colonists' elaborate "coronation" of Wahunsonacock as a vassal of James I, officially defined the subordinate status of each group according to the traditional customs of the other. Through these misconstrued ceremonies with serious legal implications, both peoples sought to reemphasize their political sovereignty and cultural supremacy in reaction to the increasing interdependence that drew them closer together through a flourishing trade in corn and copper. The whole of 1608 thus became a probationary period of great potential and even greater tension, as Indians and Englishmen probed the limits of trust, loyalty, forbearance, and usefulness in one another. Relations between Wahunsonacock and Smith served as the barometer of intercultural harmony, and although they wrangled constantly (friends should not come armed to meet friends; true friends have nothing to fear if we are armed), the longer they held less astute subordinates in check, the greater were the prospects for day-to-day coexistence and even an enduring alliance. . . .

By late 1608, after a tense year of probationary relations, the English had discovered all of the hostile nations on the periphery of *Tsenacommacah*, and upon realizing how vulnerable the Powhatans were in the larger Chesapeake, they became ever more aggressive toward them. The Powhatans reacted in kind to the colonists' growing insolence by reminding them of their precarious dependency. After the English returned from finally meeting the Monacans in November 1608, the Powhatans at the falls "fayned there were divers ships come into the Bay, to kill them at James Towne. Trade they would not, and finde their Corne we could not." In mid-January 1609 Wahunsonacock entertained a colonial delegation for the last time before going into hiding for five years, and he informed Smith that food and friendship would be increasingly hard to find among the Powhatans. Knowing "the difference . . . [between] Peace and Warre better then any" and convinced by this time that the colonists had come "to invade my people, and possesse my Country," Wahunsonacock challenged the English: "What will it availe you to take . . . by force [what] you may quickly have by love, or to destroy them that provide you food[?] What can you get by warre?"[13]

That remains the key question now as it was then. For two years, these alien peoples had coexisted in relative harmony, forgiving deaths on both sides and preventing violent incidents from triggering a larger conflict, but it seems that the cumulative effect of increased contacts only heightened intercultural tensions and proliferated misunderstanding—specifically making the English more bellicose through a misplaced overconfidence and the Powhatans more bellicose as a reaction to such offensive, disrespectful treatment. Feeding allies was one thing, but the English did not reciprocate as allies should; instead of being the solution to Wahunsonacock's problems with hostile tribes on the periphery of *Tsenacommacah*, the colonists emerged as an additional, even more serious, threat at the very heart of his empire. The short-sighted, short-term success of Englishmen in coercing food from the Powhatans alienated Wahunsonacock by confirming his worst fears and prompted a hostile response to aggression. The Indians had forewarned the colonists about such unacceptable behavior, for the English had recorded Parahunt's admonition to his villagers in May 1607: "Why should you bee offended with [the colonists] as long as they hurt you not, nor take any thing away by force?"[14]

In this atmosphere of growing militancy, nonexistent diplomacy, and volatile tensions, war could have broken out at any time after January 1609. Having lost his credibility with Wahunsonacock, Smith trained a force of hand-picked colonists "to march, fight, and scirmish in the woods . . . [until they] were better able to fight with Powhatans whole force . . . amongst the Trees . . . then the Fort was to repulse 400." He used this personal guerrilla band to intimidate Indian villagers and often boasted how Englishmen derived their "chiefest pleasure" from war. . . .

While Smith was training troops in unconventional guerrilla tactics, renegade "Dutchmen" from James Fort were teaching Powhatan warriors the equally unconventional use of stolen muskets. Having heard that the superiority of English firearms over Indian bows was equivalent to the superiority of Jesus Christ over their native gods, the Powhatans responded by converting to the new weapons, not an alien religion. As Indian warriors became adept in the use of firearms, most of the mystery was eliminated from English technology, and the last reason for keeping the colonists around quickly evaporated. Possessing several muskets, three hundred metal hatchets, and fifty swords, partially as a result of Newport's permissive policies, and provoked into using them by Smith's compensatory aggression, the Powhatans entered the summer of 1609 ready, willing, and able to retaliate against the vexing aliens at the slightest provocation.[15]

That provocation came in mid-August 1609, as the arrival of the Third Supply provided the sparks that finally ignited the flames of full-scale war. Ironically, if that relief fleet had indeed proven to be Spanish rather than English, as the colonists originally thought, war might still have been prevented. Faced with invasion by a powerful enemy they hated and feared as much as the colonists did, the Powhatans reportedly "offer[ed] to fight under our colors." As it was, the Third Supply brought divisiveness, not unity, and exacerbated an already-tense situation.

In a belated move to support Smith's plan for making "the Salvages . . . subject to the English," the Virginia Company had sent reinforcements that included many of his most powerful and vengeful critics, gentlemen who were delighted to inform the haughty, low-born Smith that he had been replaced by Governor Sir Thomas Gates. Neither Gates nor his commission arrived with the others in the relief fleet (being shipwrecked on Bermuda), and the lame-duck Smith, risking tyrannicide if he remained in office illegally and the likelihood of anarchy if he relinquished his authority too soon, bought time by dispersing his unruly rivals far from Jamestown. Although this decision temporarily avoided a political crisis, relieved pressure on the scant provisions at the fort, and forestalled another lethal summer by removing numbers of colonists from the salty, disease-ridden water around the English capital, it proved disastrous for Indian relations. Smith's presumption in sending rude and raucous colonists to eat up the provisions of alienated local tribes was the final provocation that precipitated England's first Indian war.[16]

When Captains George Percy and John Martin encamped one hundred hungry colonists near the villages of the powerful and occasionally aggressive Nansemonds, the Englishmen's fear and inexperience created a volatile situation. After messengers they had dispatched to the Nansemond *werowances* failed to return, Percy and Martin unleashed a vengeful rampage on the Indians, convinced of unsubstantiated native "Trechery." The English "burned their howses, Ransacked their Temples, Tooke downe the Corpses of their deade kings from their Toambes, And caryed away their pearles, Copper, and braceletts, wherewith they doe decore their kings' funeralles." Following this sacrilege and the kidnapping of a *werowance*'s son, Percy and Martin fled to Jamestown, abandoning their men to the horrors of a long and lethal siege by the enraged Nansemonds. Over the next few weeks, the Indians methodically slew "neere halfe" of this encircled garrison— probably forty to fifty men. The "30 good shotte" (musketeers) whom Smith belatedly sent to relieve the beleaguered company told terrifying tales of finding English corpses punctured by a dozen arrows and their mouths stuffed with cornbread in "Contempte and skorne" of hungry aliens.[17]

Similar hostilities erupted simultaneously far upriver. Francis West had settled his company of 120 in a vulnerable palisade "invironed with many intollerable inconveniences"—including a host of angry warriors in the vicinity of the falls. Smith arrived about mid-August and forced *Werowance* Parahunt to "sell" him the nearby village of Powhatan, renamed Nonsuch, a well-fortified site of flourishing maize fields and comfortable lodges that was superior to the one West had selected. Having appropriated this culturally significant village of Wahunsonacock's birth, Smith demanded that the local Powhatans pay "a yearely tribute to King James" to ensure English protection from the Monacans. When West's "disorderly company" of "protectors" moved into Nonsuch, however, they proved to be "worse enimies then the Monocans themselves" by beating the villagers, taking hostages, stealing provisions, and destroying homes. When Parahunt could stand no more of this unprovoked aggression, his warriors struck back and killed at least fifty of West's men in harassing attacks between mid-August and late October.[18]

These bloody confrontations at opposite ends of the James River began a war that no one was skillful enough to prevent or end quickly. Smith, the only Englishman with even the remotest chance of doing so, actually precipitated the violence. Subverted by the company as Council president, scorned by Wahunsonacock as an adopted *werowance*, distracted by Jamestown's political intrigues, and resented as an ineffectual "referee" by all combatants, Smith was sitting atop a symbolic power-keg long before the literal explosion in September that ended his career in Virginia. His departure from the Chesapeake in early October 1609 guaranteed a long and gruesome war, for no Virginia colonist would approach his talents, however flawed, for many years. As the rash actions of Percy, West, and Martin revealed, few Englishmen appreciated the crucial difference between calculated intimidation and limitless atrocities. Like the imperious, arrogant young cavalry officers so often stereotyped in B movies, Percy (son of the eighth earl of Northumberland), West (son of the second baron De La Warr), and Martin (son of the lord mayor of London) were spoiled aristocrats whose incompetence and inexperience, pride and paranoia, cruelty and cowardice, gave the Powhatans a chilling preview of domination by England's best.[19]

Having rediscovered their military confidence and with nothing to lose, the Powhatans quickly launched a determined offensive to destroy or drive out the remaining colonists. No sooner had Smith's ship cleared the James than the Indians "all revolted, and did murder and spoile all they could incounter." Instead of "corne . . . and contribution from the Salvages," reported a colonist, "wee had nothing but mortall wounds." When all of the dispersed Englishmen had retreated to the cramped and hungry confines of James Fort, Wahunsonacock was again able to manipulate them with impunity. In mid-October he sent venison, pledges of peace, and an invitation to trade for maize to Percy, the new president of the Council. When Captain John Sicklemore (alias Ratcliffe) arrived among the Pamunkeys in early November to get the promised corn, however, Opechancanough's warriors ambushed his men from the maize fields and killed thirty-three—two-thirds of the expedition—in the most costly single day the English experienced in the war. While Pamunkey women were skinning Ratcliffe alive with mussel shells, their men attacked his pinnace and almost captured it.[20]

As the terrified survivors of that disaster returned to Jamestown, Francis West and a force of thirty-six colonists sailed to the south shore of the Potomac River and obtained a large quantity of maize in friendly trading with the Patawomecs, Powhatans who often acted independently of Wahunsonacock. Before the English left, however, the veterans of combat with Parahunt's warriors treacherously turned on the Patawomecs, "cutteinge off two of the Salvages heads and other extremetyes." Rather than return to Jamestown to answer for this "harshe and Crewell dealinge" that alienated a hospitable tribe, West and his men sailed the *Swallow* directly to England, thus depriving their fellow countrymen of much-needed maize and native assistance as cold weather closed in on the capital.[21]

These two acts of treachery left the Jamestown colonists in "extreme misery and wante" as they entered their first winter of war. Neither the "100 well trained and expert souldiers" nor the impressive supply of maize, meal, and muskets that Smith had left them could protect England's fragile outpost from the wrath of Powhatan warriors. Although they traditionally spared *werowances*, women, and children in their wars, by this time the Powhatans were determined to destroy the garrison of James Fort root and branch as retribution for all the terror that the aliens had indiscriminately inflicted on their village populations.

Wahunsonacock's warriors completely surrounded and sealed off Jamestown for six months, and from November 1609 to May 1610, this "Starving Time" of siege allowed the Powhatans' lethal allies of famine, disease, and insanity to claim 110 of the 200 colonists in Virginia without risking a direct assault. Living in close quarters, the Jamestown garrison succumbed to foul water, poor sanitation, malnutrition, and constant terror as their enemies stalked the fields and forests, ready to "assault any boat upon the river or straggler . . . by land." Privileged officers and proliferating rodents consumed a disproportionate amount of the stored provisions so that as early as December "famine compelled us wholly to devoure those Hogges, Dogges, & horses that weare then in the Collony, together with rates, mice, snakes or what vermin or carryon soever we could light on . . . and which nature most abhorred." As the months of siege progressed, the frightened, famished colonists even "Licked upp the Bloode" of wounded men and devoured the bodies of the dead. On at least two occasions, impatient cannibals hurried the process along by murdering their countrymen, one a pregnant woman. By the end of the six-month siege, the physically weakened and psychologically ravaged colonists became "so Leane thatt they Looked Lyke Anotamies [skeletons]" and were helpless to prevent their nets from rotting, their boats from drifting away, or their cabins from being torn apart for firewood.[22]

With "Indians kill[ing] as fast without . . . as famine and pestilence did within," the Starving Siege claimed the lives of 65 percent of the Jamestown garrison—over half of the colonists who had been alive at Smith's departure and considerably more than had died in previous Virginia winters. Ironically, the national imperative of the English to establish a permanent colonial capital on American soil gave Jamestown a valuable identity— and an increased vulnerability—because this waste-ground symbolized the larger contest for political and cultural supremacy in Virginia. Indeed, while "all went to Ruine" on Jamestown Island, the Powhatans apparently ignored some thirty Englishmen living at Fort Algernoun near the mouth of the James. Those colonists prospered so well throughout the winter of 1609–10 that they fed surplus seafood to their many hogs.[23]

The Powhatans finally lifted the siege as spring planting beckoned, and Percy immediately decided to abandon Jamestown in favor of Fort Algernoun and the abundant provisions at Point Comfort. As the siege survivors prepared to evacuate James Fort, some 135 long-lost survivors of Governor Gates's shipwrecked *Sea Venture* arrived after a year of being marooned on Bermuda. Observing the "miserie in our peoples faces," Gates announced that Virginia must be abandoned and the colonists returned to England—a decision that was greeted by "general acclamation and shout of joy." On Thursday, 7 June 1610, the colonists buried their cannon and boarded ships for home; only Gates's personal company of musketeers prevented the broken survivors of the Starving Time from burning down the capital that had claimed some 350 English lives and cost the Virginia Company about £20,000 in three years.[24]

After only ten months of organized resistance, the Powhatans had succeeded in expelling the technologically superior invaders from their midst. Wahunsonacock's apparent triumph and Jamestown's seeming demise were short-lived, however, for on 8 June, the fortuitous arrival of Lord De La Warr's relief fleet in the James River—literally only hours from finding Virginia abandoned—prevented a second "lost colony" and forever altered the course of American history. When De La Warr officially assumed his duties as lord governor and captain general of Virginia on Sunday, 10 June 1610, it marked the critical turning point in the First Anglo-Powhatan War. As his fresh troops disembarked at James Fort with their fine livery and forced the dispirited siege survivors to reoccupy their "poore ruinated habitations" with "great griefe," a new, vengeful resolve took root in England's outpost of empire.[25]

De La Warr's administration made a fresh start of the English colony and ultimately doomed Powhatan sovereignty, as revised Virginia Company policies finally became operational after a delay of thirteen months. Bolstered by new investment and the king's confidence, the rechartered company from May 1609 on regarded Indian relations as the key to success or failure of its ambitious American venture. The London directors continued to praise the Chesapeake as an earthly paradise and fully expected the Powhatans to become compliant, civilized Anglican converts, while blaming Virginia's vile reputation as a "miserie, a ruine, a death, a hell" on a few incompetent colonists and malevolent *werowances*. Restating its sacred, patriotic mission to build a "New Britain in another world" and to share "our divine riches" with the Powhatans, the company solicited philanthropic donations "to traine . . . [the Indians] by gentle meanes" and "to make their condition truely more happy." Powerful churchmen and influential courtiers applauded this "holie Cause" and so "inflamed [the] Spiritts" of investors that the company collected some £40,000 to support its policies. Momentum was now with the company, despite the initial horrors of war in the colony, and William Strachey observed that "Virginia was a thing . . . so full of expectaunce . . . as not a Pilgrimage to a romain yeare of Jubile could have been followed with more heat or zeale."[26]

By 1610 the colonization of Virginia had become what Wesley Frank Craven described as "truly a national effort" that integrated royal patronage, large-scale financial support from all classes, conscientious corporate direction, and a growing jingoism that justified war with "savage heathens" to preserve England's power and pride. As the agent of English nationalism in the New World, the Virginia Company diverted its substantial funds for winning over the Powhatans by "mutuall enterchange and commerce" to a punitive campaign for winning against those "implacable foes." Even before the corporate directors learned of the lethal siege of Jamestown, they had abandoned appeasement for a policy of military pacification reminiscent of the ruthless "Romane Legions" that had made the barbarous ancient Britons suitably "tame and civill." Company officials accepted the inflammatory rumor that the Powhatans had murdered the "Lost Colonists," and they recruited veteran officers from the Spanish wars to end the "tirrany" of Wahunsonacock by confiscating his crops and villages, capturing his children and *werowances*, and exterminating his detestable "priests of Baal or Belzebub." Smith's intelligence on the vulnerability of *Tsenacommacah* relative to the semi-independent fringe tribes and hostile peripheral nations gave the English considerable leverage in applying divide-and-conquer tactics to achieve those goals. Ironically, the colonists launched their crusade to destroy savagism in Virginia under a company directive to befriend those Indians "farthest from you and enemies unto those amonge whom you dwell, for you shall have least occasion to have differences with them."[27]

After decades of battling "Catholic terrorism" as God's chosen but threatened people, the self-styled new Israelites of England in the summer of 1610, under the able command of Lord De La Warr, prepared to wage "Religious Warfare" with the Powhatan "miscreants." The "hundred old soldiers" and some fifty others that the lord governor had transported to Virginia increased the colony's population to about 375 persons—sufficient manpower so that "our forces are now . . . able to tame the fury and treachery of the Savages." Citing the example of the Hebrews in war-torn Canaan, De La Warr and Lieutenant Governor Gates assigned all adult males to military companies and work parties of fifty men each, commanded by hand-picked veterans of England's Catholic conflicts. In mid-June the governor instituted the first installment of the *Lawes Divine, Morall and Martiall*, a comprehensive, coercive legal code for promoting civil discipline, political stability, and "warre well managed" in a foreign and hostile environment. Prohibiting commercial and sexual intercourse and all other forms of contact between colonists and Powhatans, the *Lawes* segregated the "civilized" from the "savage" and demanded the colonists' unwavering obedience to church, country, and commanders upon pain of death.[28]

Thus compelled to "fight under the banner of Jesus Christ" against the forces of "Satan, [who] visibly and palpably raignes there more then in any other place of the world," the colonists eagerly vented their long pent-up frustrations on the Powhatans with Old Testament fervor. On Monday, 9 July 1610, Gates initiated the English counteroffensive when his forces suddenly, and without provocation, descended upon the Kecoughtan village near Fort Algernoun. His musketeers killed some twenty men, women, and children, easily inflicting "extraordinary Lardge and mortall wounds" on a high percentage of the population because the unsuspecting Kecoughtans had been lured into the open by the tunes and dancing of Gates's drummer—a traditional Powhatan gesture of hospitality. After slaying or scattering the only villagers who had fed Englishmen all winter, Gates's men looted the Indian lodges. Almost immediately, they began building Fort Charles—the origins of the city of Hampton—to commemorate this first conquest of a Powhatan tribe and to guard the valuable, abundant Kecoughtan maize fields.[29]

One month later, the English expanded their campaign against Jamestown's native neighbors with an attack on the nearby Paspaheghs. In the predawn hours of Friday, 10 August, some seventy colonists, under the joint command of Captains Percy, John Davis, and William West (Lord De La Warr's nephew), launched a surprise attack on Wowinchopunk's village just a few miles from James Fort. They killed about sixteen of their "deadliest enemies" as they emerged from their lodges, thus avenging a recent Paspahegh attack on the Jamestown blockhouse in which four colonists had died. After scattering the survivors, the raiders burned Indian longhouses, harvested their ripened maize, and murdered several captives. Percy reported that his vengeful troops demanded that Wowinchopunk's two children be killed and that, after "Throweinge them overboard and shoteinge owtt their Braynes in the water" on the short sail to Jamestown, they were still not satisfied. Having "seene so mutche Bloodshedd thatt day," the distraught Christian commander had the slain children's mother stabbed to death so that De La Warr could not burn her alive.[30] . . .

These successful summer raids of catharsis and convenience translated England's *ad terrorem* tactics from the Irish wars of the late sixteenth century—specifically the use of deception, ambush, and surprise, the random slaughter of both sexes and all ages, the calculated murder of innocent captives, and the destruction of entire villages—into an American frontier idiom for the first time. These precedent-setting counterattacks neither discriminated between combatant and noncombatant victims nor between hostile and friendly tribes, for of these four Indian groups, only the Paspaheghs represented significant past enmity or a present danger to the English. The Kecoughtans were a threat more symbolic than real; the Warraskoyacs had displayed more "insolence" than aggression; and the independent Chickahominies rarely joined the Powhatans in their wars and then only as well-paid mercenaries. What doomed these tribes as initial targets of English vengeance was their proximity to Jamestown and their flourishing maize fields. The English, in effect, tested their military skills on these relatively unthreatening peoples living within a twenty-mile radius of the colonial capital, and they succeeded in their primary objective of obtaining huge stockpiles of captured corn that would be needed for more ambitious campaigns soon to come. By "cuttinge down and *takinge away* theire corne" in these innovative hostile harvests, or "feedfights," the English immediately removed the threat of another Starving Time, deprived the Powhatans of provisions, and freed colonists from farm fields for use on battlefields.[31]

The summer raids of 1610 quickly shifted the momentum in this war, putting the Powhatans on the defensive and permitting the English to expand their offensives. Within two months of the damaging "feedfights," De La Warr was able to use his well-fed, surplus manpower to pursue a pressing company objective—the "searche for Mineralls and . . . Iron mynes"— while harassing the Indians upriver. In November the governor gathered the garrisons of forts James, Charles, and Algernoun into a force of perhaps two hundred men and launched an ambitious expedition to the falls of the James River.[32] . . .

The Powhatans, like their English adversaries, regarded this conflict as a holy war between powerful, irreconcilable religious beliefs and the political systems they supported. Wahunsonacock and James I headed their respective "state churches," and for both peoples "the service of their God . . . [was] answerable to their life, being performed with great feare and attention." With cultural survival at stake, the Powhatans depended upon their mysterious and malevolent Okee to inspire their *werowances* to victory over the aliens, while the colonists looked to their "God of Battailes" and Christian guns to vanquish the "divel and all the gates of hel against us." Convinced that "God and the Divell will not dwell together" and that the "true order of warre is fitly resembled to true religion," Virginia Company officials encouraged their settlers to seek out and slay the Indian holy men ("Sathans owne brood"), who were considered "most perillous for the English." England's religious allies and enemies in Europe were watching, and it was believed that anything short of total victory over heathen Indians would constitute a "detriment of Christian Religion and a greate prejudice unto this Kingdome"—the greatest calamity for "our state . . . since they lost the Kingdome of Fraunce." For the Powhatans, each military setback came closer to fulfilling the prophecy of subjugation and the unthinkable extinction of their ancient spiritual beliefs.[33]

With both sides committed to becoming the righteous "hand of the weeder" ruthlessly pruning an "outgrowne wildernesse of humaine nature," the marriage between sacred beliefs and secular behavior produced a direct and dramatic escalation in atrocities. Sixteen eleven, the decisive third year of the war, saw the fiercest fighting yet in this conflict, as each side became increasingly desperate for imminent victory and fearful of ultimate defeat. The Powhatans began the year by forcing the withdrawal of De La Warr's army from the falls, after it had spent "three [winter] months doinge little but induringe much" in the futile search for mines. That campaign ruined the governor's already fragile constitution, and on 28 March the physically and emotionally spent baron left Virginia forever. Wahunsonacock took advantage of this last, best chance to crush the enemy by once more attacking Jamestown, where virtually all of the English were again concentrated.[34] . . .

Whatever catharsis the Powhatans derived from this attack, it was a small-scale and short-lived victory—ultimately, the Indians' last triumph in the war. Because the Powhatans were still unwilling to sustain massive casualties in a direct attack on James Fort itself and the English had food reserves to nourish them until spring, Wahunsonacock could not repeat the Starving Siege and thus missed his final opportunity to annihilate the colonists. Huddled fearfully but safely behind their fortifications, the Jamestown garrison held on until critical reinforcements and more aggressive commanders arrived to initiate England's second, and most successful, series of offensives.

On 12 May 1611 Sir Thomas Dale arrived in Virginia as the new deputy governor, and he quickly restored a vital momentum to English plans. His fleet of three ships brought a "greatt store of Armour, Municyon, victewalls," and, most significantly, three hundred "men of war." Immediately doubling Jamestown's population, these well-equipped combat veterans, who had been procured from the anti-Spanish campaigns in the Netherlands after the truce of 1609, finally gave the colony a sufficient quantity of experienced troops that John Smith and the Reverend Richard Hakluyt had long said were essential for victory over the Indians. Personally frustrated with the Powhatans' hostility to Christians, Hakluyt had grown more vengeful by 1609, advising that "if gentle polishing [of the Indians] will not serve, then we shall not want hammerours and rough masons enough, I meane our old soldiours trained up in the Nether-lands, to . . . prepare them to our Preachers hands."[35]

The lethal skills of these "hammerours" nicely complemented the ruthless tenacity of Dale, and compared to those hardened veterans, he found many of the colonists seriously deficient in military skills and discipline. He was unprepared for the dismal capital that greeted him, and he reputedly "pulled Capt. Newport by the beard, . . . threatninge to hang him" for the lies he had helped perpetuate about Virginia's preparedness and prosperity. Dale was especially perplexed (as historians have recently been) to find the residents of Jamestown "bowling in the streetes," neither farming nor fighting. Although modern psychology helps explain how the Jamestown garrison could have been literally immobilized by fear and indecision after the terrors of the blockhouse debacle, the new deputy governor brought coercion, not compassion, to the distraught colonists under Percy. Dale immediately set them to work "in martiall manner and warlike discipline" under expanded articles, and even more punishing applications, of the *Lawes Divine, Morall and Martiall*. Over the next three years, Dale and other officers used this rigid code to justify "the slaughter of his Majestys free subjects by starveinge, hangeinge, burneinge, breakinge upon the wheele and shooting to deathe." Although Dale's punishments were sadistic in the extreme, "the feare of a cruell, painefull and unusuall death" represented desperate but perhaps necessary responses to the colonists' perennial flirtations with insubordination, incompetence, indolence, and intrigue. Modern historians, judging his conduct by the standards of the Bill of Rights rather than by those of a marine boot camp, fail to appreciate that the "drumhead justice" and "Tiranus Government" of the De La Warr–Gates–Dale era addressed crucial concerns for order and survival in a combat zone of a distant war with no precedents or assurances of success.[36]

On the other hand, it is disturbing to read the scathing accounts of free Englishmen who bitterly resisted their cruel treatment as "slaves" of the Virginia Company, and it is instructive to realize how they translated this fear and frustration into cathartic atrocities against their Powhatan enemies. Dale, like Lord De La Warr, Lieutenant Governor Gates, and a host of subordinate officers, had served under the ill-fated Robert Devereux, second earl of Essex, in the brutal campaigns in Ireland. Those experiences conditioned them to believe that "terrour . . . made short warres" and that "all discourse of . . . National Vertue, of Religion, of Libertie, and whatsoever else . . . incourage[s] vertuous men, hath no force at all with the common Souldier." Dale's charge that "not many [of his troops] give testimonie beside their names that they are Christians" echoed Ralph Lane's earlier condemnation of the "wylde menn of myne owene naccione" whom he had commanded at Roanoke Island. One wonders whether such dubious envoys of civility brought an endemic brutality to America that poisoned Anglo-Indian relations, or whether their English officers coerced well-meaning men into a blind hatred of "savages." The elite English commanders who regularly killed or maimed any Powhatan who dared approach James Fort also tortured and executed growing numbers of colonists who sought only to escape to those "implacable foes." The most haunting implication of this tragic first war is that there were probably many reluctant warriors on both sides, with more in common than three centuries of racist rhetoric permit us to appreciate, who were goaded into mutual slaughter by the same group of sadistic zealots.[37]

Compared with his colonial contemporaries, Dale was a brilliant strategist and aggressive tactician who correctly perceived, and exploited, Powhatan vulnerabilities. Although he requested, but never received, an additional two thousand soldiers to crush his "subtile-mischeivous" enemy, he nonetheless proceeded with less grandiose plans to "overmaster" Wahunsonacock by "leav[ing] him either no roome in his Countrie to harbour in, or draw[ing] him to a firme association with ourselves." Because neither side could afford the limitless casualties of "total war," Dale hoped to gain a quick, negotiated settlement by trapping Wahunsonacock in a vice between an enlarged and expansionistic colonial force and the hostile "neighbour Salvadges confining him." His plan was to pacify and fortify the strategic "ends" of the James River—*Tsenacommacah*'s eastern and western "doors"—which would give the English three large and secure garrisons to support raiding parties on several fronts and to prevent massed attacks against any single site until the Powhatans eventually grew weary of this costly war of attrition.[38] . . .

In the first week of August 1611, Gates returned with a fleet of six ships and more than 250 "chosen Men"—especially additional "hammerours" from the Netherlands—and this last large contingent of reinforcements made the colony so strong militarily that the Spanish court expressed alarm about England's intentions. In late September Lieutenant Governor Gates, that "very special soldier," and Dale, the marshal of Virginia, launched their ambitious western campaign against the upriver Powhatans with three hundred well-armed and hand-picked troops. They pushed their way into the territory of the Arrohattecs and began constructing extensive fortifications on Farrars Island, a defensible peninsula of high ground that soon became the "City of Henrico" and ultimately led to the founding of Richmond. . . .

In a brave but futile effort to prevent the English from conquering the "western door" of their domain, the Powhatans provided Gates and Dale's expedition with a rare glimpse of their military élan in its twilight. Among the warriors fiercely defending Henrico was a notable war captain, Nemattanew, the mysterious and mystical "Jack-of-the-Feathers" who later figured prominently in the Powhatan Uprising of 1622. Although most Powhatans went into battle elaborately decorated, smeared with scarlet pigment and brandishing six-foot bows and four-foot arrows, Nemattanew appeared for combat "all covered over with feathers and Swans wings fastened to his showlders as thowghe he meant to flye." This colorful, symbolic armor, like the individualistic heroics and battlefield bravado its wearer displayed, proved to be a military anachronism, destined for defeat at the hands of Dale's faceless mass of steel-coated musketeers, moving methodically against most targets at will.

Always conservative in risking casualties with their limited supply of warriors, Powhatan *werowances* had to deploy their forces ever more cautiously as the engagements of this war became increasingly lethal. Thus, Dale encountered little recorded resistance in December 1611 when he ravaged the main villages of the Appomattocs, located five miles by land and fourteen by water from Henrico. In early 1612, as colonists began to transform this fertile, fortified area of the "New Bermudas" into the most populated region of English Virginia, a company official accurately asserted that "Powhatan . . . remaines our enemie, though not able to doe us hurt."[39]

The extensive and intensive English campaigns of 1611 had proven so successful in altering the original strategic positions of the combatants that both sides welcomed a temporary hiatus in fighting throughout 1612 and much of 1613. Wahunsonacock was on the defensive, unable or unwilling to strike at so many dispersed English garrisons, and he welcomed the respite in order to consolidate his forces among the still-potent Pamunkeys near present-day West Point. The colonists were supreme in their offensive mobility, but having transferred control of the "Kings River" from Wahunsonacock to James I, they wanted to consolidate their conquests and were neither confident nor desperate enough to attack *Tsenacommacah*'s best warriors along the York River.

This cessation of combat demonstrated the pervasive influence that the Virginia Company exerted over the activities of the First Anglo-Powhatan War. Having directed and supplied the colonial offensives in 1610–11, the company entered a period of impotence and indecision in 1612–13 that explains the strange hiatus in the war. The corporate gamble to sacrifice "soe many Christians" and to spend lavishly on men and materiel for a resounding victory had backfired into a damaging scandal. The "extreame slavery and miserye" that the colonists endured under martial law caused the very "name of Virginea" to be "vildly depraved, traduced and derided" throughout the realm, as wealthy investors began "to withdraw those paiments which they have subscribed" to the enterprise. Needing funds for expensive offensives to end the war and needing spectacular victories to generate funds, the company had to resort to public lotteries when stock subscriptions declined markedly in 1612. Although financing was obtained for a final, albeit economical, campaign, the corporate officers were desperate for any quick resolution of the conflict. Trapped by their patriotic hyperbole and the vast promises made to an impatient and increasingly skeptical public, the London directors feared disaster if an Irishlike guerrilla war with arrogant "savages" were allowed to persist for decades.[40]

The two colonists who were most responsible for relieving the company's crisis and resolving the First Anglo-Powhatan War were Sir Thomas Dale and Captain Samuel Argall of Kent. These eventual co-commanders of England's final campaign against the Powhatans employed vastly different, but complementary, tactics in their quest for peace. As the consummate professional soldier, Dale was always the ruthless aggressor, raising the mailed fist against "bad Indians" with military resources that John Smith could not even have imagined. In contrast, Argall was a brilliant navigator, used to riding the waves and meeting different people on strange coastlines; his inclination was to extend a gloved hand of friendly trade and diplomacy to the "good Indians" who would agree to assist the English.

Argall, an expert pilot, who had pioneered a new and faster route to Jamestown, found and named Delaware Bay, and explored the Chesapeake more extensively than any Englishman since Smith, arrived on his third voyage to Virginia in mid-September 1612 as captain of Sir Robert Rich's ship *Treasurer*. On winter trading visits to the Patawomecs, Argall rekindled his friendship with his "adopted brother," Japazaws, *werowance* of Pasptanzie and brother to the "King of Patawomeke," and in early 1613 he persuaded them to assist him in capturing Pocahontas, who was at that time their guest. Anxious for the promised English protection that would allow the Patawomecs to be free of Wahunsonacock's domination (and fearing Argall's anger and Dale's violence if he refused), Japazaws lured Pocahontas into captivity aboard Argall's ship in March 1613; she was the most valuable cargo that the *Treasurer* ever held. The persuasive Argall, who had made the Patawomecs forget West's atrocities, quickly followed up this diplomatic coup by concluding an important alliance in April with the maize-rich Accomacs and Accohannocs of the Eastern Shore, who were willing to associate themselves with the English "because they had received good reports from the Indians of Pembrock [Potomac] River of our courteous usage of them."[41]

By "faire and friendly quarter" and a spotless reputation for keeping promises to Indian leaders, Argall in only two months had significantly constricted Wahunsonacock's empire and severely restricted his options in dealing with the colonists. Contrary to most accounts, however, the paramount chief did not allow fatherly concern for Pocahontas's safety to influence his decision to stand firm against English ultimatums for capitulation. Knowing that the colonists were reluctant to attack the strong core of Pamunkey loyalists (they had never done so in six years), Wahunsonacock toyed with the Jamestown commanders. In his only communication with them during Pocahontas's year-long captivity, he returned seven colonial deserters and several broken muskets as a token "ransome" for his daughter in the summer of 1613 but defiantly refused to pay a large maize tribute or to surrender additional weapons—his battlefield "Monuments and Trophies" of English "shames" in defeat. While his recalcitrance frustrated the colonial leadership, the additional months Pocahontas remained at James-town proved critically important for effecting her conversion to Anglican-ism and in encouraging John Rolfe's affections.[42]

The great stalemate from March 1613 to March 1614 saw the colonists, dispersed among several distant settlements, and the Powhatans, concen-trated in the strong center of a shrinking empire, equally fearful about precipitating what in effect would be an Armageddon between large and well-matched forces of accomplished warriors. No one knows how these wary, pragmatic combatants would have resolved this war on their own, for it required considerable pressure from the Virginia Company to force a fi-nal showdown of arms. Struggling against their declining reputations and diminished resources, the armchair militarists in London demanded a new offensive as the terms of service for both Lieutenant Governor Gates and Marshal Dale neared expiration.

In March 1614 Dale, Argall, and a force of 150 colonists boldly invaded the Pamunkey homeland in the riskiest and most ambitious campaign of the war. They went to deliver an ultimatum to the indomitable Wahun-sonacock: either "establish peace, or continue enemies with us." Sailing up the York River, the English encountered a hail of arrows from an unknown location; being "justly provoked," Dale's troops landed and killed six war-riors, burned forty lodges, and generally made "freeboote and pillage" for the Indians' "presumption in shooting at us."

Tension mounted as the expedition approached the Pamunkeys' capi-tal—the political heart of *Tsenacommacah* where Opechancanough resided with three hundred warriors and where Wahunsonacock could allegedly as-semble "a thousand men together" on short notice. As the English ships came into view, warriors shouted defiantly that they would slaughter the in-vaders as they had Ratcliffe's men in 1609, while the musketeers replied that they "had the hearts and power to take revenge and punish where wrongs should be offered." The men most familiar with the combat capabilities of both groups—those colonial deserters whom Wahunsonacock had recently returned to Jamestown—jumped ship and fled the bloodbath that seemed imminent. As the English troops disembarked near West Point in view of several hundred warriors, however, not a shot was fired. Mutually fearful of unprecedentedly high casualties and concerned for the safety of Pocahon-tas (whom Dale and Argall had wisely brought along), both sides chose discretion over valor. For two days, the best troops from both cultures remained in this posture of confrontation—always threatening, but never committing, violence as they awaited the response of an absent Wahun-sonacock to the English ultimatum. Finally, after negotiating and extend-ing several truces in the expectation of an answer that never came, the colonists suddenly boarded their ships and sailed back to Jamestown un-molested.[43]

The war that had emerged so gradually and escalated so viciously ended with surprising quickness and civility. After four years of reciprocal atrocities that had claimed some five to six hundred lives, the combatants finally achieved a sensible, mutually acceptable settlement that preserved honor short of suicidal slaughter. When Dale abruptly terminated the Pamunkey expedition, he justified his decision by announcing that the men on both sides needed "to prepare ground and set corne for our winters provision." (That was an especially lame excuse, considering that the colonists had seldom grown their own food or allowed Indians to enjoy what they had raised.) Dale saved face by threatening, more characteristically, to return to the Pamunkeys at harvest time "if finall agreement were not made betwixt us" and to "take away all their corne, burne all the houses upon that river, . . . and kill as many of them as we could." Thus, Dale dispensed equal amounts of the lenient diplomacy that Argall was famous for and the harsh militancy that made him marshal of Virginia, but because he already knew of Pocahontas's conversion and of Rolfe's intention to marry her, he did not truly believe that a repeat "invasion" would be necessary. Such intercultural marriages of convenience were customary in both societies, and the military leaders from two traditions could agree that they each had too much to lose not to accept this timely and face-saving method of ending the war without capitulation, a written treaty, or a formal winner.[44]

Thus, the marriage of John Rolfe and the "Lady Rebecca" in the first week of April 1614, and not a climactic military victory, brought an end to "five yeeres intestine warre with the . . . Indians." Following the celebration of this unprecedented event by notables from both societies, a new spirit of cooperation truly seemed imminent. English leaders dropped their demands for the return of captured weapons and captive colonists, while Wahunsonacock held his warriors in check and welcomed the first English delegation in five years.

In this springtime of new beginnings, Dale was cautiously optimistic that peace would allow the colonists "to discover the countrey better" and to "grow in familiarity" with the Powhatans; as the perpetrator of so much destruction, however, he did wonder why the Indians would want to "strive with all allacrity to keep us in good oppinion of them." Ralph Hamor, the colony's secretary, did not have any such reservations, for he believed that the English "hammerours" had sufficiently purged the Powhatans of their "Ingratitude and treasons" and made them ready for conversion by "Champions of Christ." One such missionary, the Reverend Alexander Whitaker of Henrico, reflected on his success in converting Pocahontas and thought it would be "an easie matter" to make the Powhatans "willingly forsake the divell" now that Englishmen were "masters of . . . the Countrey, and they stoode in feare of us."[45]

Despite such optimism, however, the ambiguous peace of 1614, and particularly the Rolfe-Pocahontas marriage, only exacerbated intercultural tensions. Signifying vastly different things to different groups, the wedding failed miserably in making "one people" of "firmly united" colonists and Powhatans, promoting instead division and dissension between London policymakers and Jamestown planters that would leave the Indians completely alienated.

The problem, as Dale correctly perceived, was that a maturing colony finally at peace nurtured the conflicting desires and designs of all Englishmen, whether "their ends be either for God or Mammon." The Virginia Company directors, anxious to cash in on the favorable publicity surrounding the Anglicized Pocahontas, conceived of the colony as a "holy house" for expanded missionary endeavors. In expecting the colonists to maintain close and constant contacts with their recent enemies in order to convert them, however, London officials alienated both planters and Powhatans. The Virginia colonists, anxious to cash in on Rolfe's tobacco experiments, envisioned the colony as a "countinghouse" for expanded economic opportunities that would finally make their wartime sacrifices worthwhile. In cultivating a noxious weed with a ravenous appetite for Indian land, however, the colonists alienated both London moralists and Powhatan militants. In 1622, after eight dangerous and demeaning years of peace in which everyone had a say in their future except them, the frustrated Powhatans finally responded to the twofold assault on their souls and soils with a devastating uprising.[46]

As the significant midpoint between initial hospitality in 1607 and ultimate hostility in 1622, the peace of 1614 represented a tragically missed opportunity for the English and the Powhatans to accommodate cultural differences, to find mutually beneficial relationships worth preserving, and to define the boundaries of limited but inviolable sovereignty that each had as neighbors in Virginia.

The nature of that peace, or truce, by its very ambiguity, however, prevented a rational, bilateral consensus on either the causes or effects of that bloody first war. Although the fighting had ceased, the aggressive arrogance of the English did not; because the final, aborted Anglo-Pamunkey confrontation was inconclusive in determining military supremacy, both colonists and Indians could, and did, rightly claim victory. By assuming that they had won, the Virginia Company and the Virginia colony misinterpreted the Powhatans' grudging tolerance of a few hundred immigrants as a blanket acceptance of all future expansion and mistook the conversion of one Indian girl as proof that thousands more would freely abandon "devil worship." While the English viewed the end of war as an open door to expansion and coercive acculturation, the Powhatans believed that the strong, unscathed core of *Tsenacommacah* would discourage such activities. Wahunsonacock wrongly assumed that the "gift" of his favorite daughter had satisfied his enemies, and he misinterpreted the vague, permissive peace terms as proof of English timidity and a confirmation of his authority. Having never been defeated, the proud and populous Pamunkeys, in particular, reacted with hostility to their subsequent treatment as subject peoples by growing throngs of land-hungry aliens.

It was the Powhatans who were most anxious to respect the military stalemate of 1614 as a permanent peace—content to accept their shrunken empire as it was without further damage or future diminution. Of course, the English regarded 1614 as a preface, not an epilog, to their vast plans for the Chesapeake, and the responsibility for all future Anglo-Powhatan wars must rest with those colonists who sought to accomplish in peacetime what they had not achieved through war. Those first Virginians began an American tradition of violating at least the spirit of treaties or truces with Indians when they developed an expansionistic, agricultural colony only after—and largely because—combat had ceased in 1614. The ensuing proliferation of individual landowners, obsessed with the profits from their farms and oblivious to the consequences for their Indian neighbors, constituted peacetime behavior that was as aggressive and provocative as any military conquest. Establishing a pattern that subsequently became a central component of Anglo-American empire building, the English invaders of *Tsenacommacah* refused to admit that their expansionism was a provocation and consistently portrayed themselves as the innocent victims of retaliatory native "aggression." The international law and holy writ of Europe permitted colonists to occupy the lands of "savage heathens" despite their objections and to defend themselves against "unprovoked attacks" with the righteous wrath of "just," defensive war. The convenient, self-serving conviction that "Christians may not . . . conquer Infidells upon pretence only of their infidelity, *unles upon just cause of wrongs from the Idolaters receved*," thus allowed Europeans, but not Indians, to "slaughter . . . [their] Assailant."[47]

The First Anglo-Powhatan War and the first Anglo-Powhatan peace clearly demonstrated the blatant, consistent English attitude of aggression that precluded creative, intercultural accommodation with the peoples of *Tsenacommacah*. Smith's primary goal had been to make the Powhatans "subject to the English," and in 1612 William Strachey explicitly admitted that the colonial "Envaders" had fully expected to "offend and constrayne" Wahunsonacock. The endemic enmity between the English and the Powhatans occurred because the cultures were too much alike—not different enough—in terms of pride, militancy, and expansionism. Indeed, the colonists who glorified England's heroic repulsing of the Spanish Armada were not surprised by the Powhatans' military resistance, only determined that it should be crushed. The immigrant farmers who enjoyed the fruits of conquest thought it perfectly proper that the Powhatans' "doubtfull" relations with them after 1614 "proceeded from fear without love." Coercion seemed to work, and because history taught that "there never was any Invasion, Conquest, or Far-off plantacion that had success without some partie in the place ytself or neere it," Englishmen adopted a manipulative, divide-and-conquer Indian policy of "warre upon our enemies and kinde usage of our friends" to intimidate and isolate the embittered Powhatans.[48]

The colonists' friendly relations with native nations that served their interests only temporarily obscured the ultimate cynicism of England's plans for conquest. Military intelligence from the Patawomecs, maize from the Accomacs, and later furs from the Susquehannocks all contributed substantially to extinguishing Indian hegemony in the Chesapeake and eventually allowed the English to "encompass the destruction of all the West," as a Spanish prisoner at Jamestown had predicted in 1613. It was no accident that the "kinde usage" of English accommodationism toward their native allies forced the Powhatans into ever more desperate tactics and hastened their subjugation, and that following the demise of the Powhatans, the Patawomecs, Accomacs, and Susquehannocks quickly fell in turn to relentless colonial expansion after they had outlived their usefulness. Although the English subsumed their cultural and racial distaste of "savage" peoples when they were outnumbered or needed something, deep-seated prejudices, like embers in a dying fire, can be stoked into a blazing inferno when needed. After the Anglo-Powhatan wars of 1622–32 and 1644–46 had radically reduced native power, the Chesapeake colonists, overwhelmingly dominant in population, waged their first true race war in 1675–77 and indiscriminately slaughtered their weakened "Friends or Foes, [just] Soe they be Indians." Not surprisingly, the golden age of the Chesapeake gentry had its origins in the simultaneous demise of Indian sovereignty and the rise of African slavery that followed this climactic final conflict, for, as Theodore Roosevelt wrote in *The Winning of the West*, "the most ultimately righteous of all wars is a war with savages," for it establishes "the foundations for the future greatness of a mighty people."[49]

The events and decisions that such self-satisfied rhetoric has too long obscured in American history take on new meaning and significance through a chronological narration and detailed analysis such as this essay has sought to provide. Readers may now appreciate how and why the Powhatans—the first Indians within the limits of the United States to confront sustained English invasion—were provoked into a persistent defense of their world view and lifeways. The recognition and acceptance of the First Anglo-Powhatan War as a bona fide historical event should help discredit the hoary myths of Indian ignorance, passivity, or treachery in the face of invasion and expose the fallacy of English innocence in making that invasion unalterably and consciously aggressive. Change and endure the Powhatans did, and still do. The capitulation of indigenous inhabitants and the destruction of their traditional culture at musket point, however, should never be confused with the voluntary acculturation of later immigrant populations, for who can doubt that the Powhatans had "reason to lament the arrival of the Europeans, by whose means they seem to have lost their Felicity, as well as their Innocence"?[50]

Long after the Powhatan prophecy of their own subjugation had come true and "dwindled them away to nothing," colonist Robert Beverley, a self-styled "Indian" living on a portion of Wahunsonacock's original inheritance, sought to determine why the Indians had developed a "Grudge against" the English and pursued a "National Quarrel" for most of a century. His analysis implied that the common ground that allowed individual Indians and colonists to interact peacefully and profitably in the early days of contact had been eroded by the mutual suspicions of their leaders and was ultimately destroyed by the "Abundance of Blood that was shed on both sides" in the First Anglo-Powhatan War. The indiscriminate killing of innocent civilians with no leverage in official policies forever precluded the trust and friendship that might have developed to spare the "many Christians and Indians [who] fell in the Wars between them." The Powhatans, who had rarely, if ever, slain women or children in their wars before 1607, were appalled by the atrocities done in James I's name and, consequently, never "voluntarilie yealded themselves subjects or servants to our Gracious Soveraigne."

As a company official had predicted in 1612, the shocking carnage from England's "stratagems of warre" had indeed made the colonists "odious to all [the Indians'] posteritie." The tragic cycle of reciprocal revenge that the First Anglo-Powhatan War initiated made combat the primary method of defending and nurturing cultural identity, but, ironically, that combat also became the principal means of acculturating natives and colonists in Virginia. In the decades of destruction that followed 1614, new generations of warriors would learn from the veterans and victims of each previous conflict and adopt the cruelest and most lethal tactics of their enemies, until the common reliance on firearms, mobile guerrilla forces, food raids, scorched villages, and atrocities against noncombatants became the modus operandi of America's frontier conflicts. By making the cathartic relief, and brutal simplicity, of violence perversely preferable to the complex process of intercultural understanding, England's first Indian war became a primer for future struggles in the forests of America, teaching warriors from two worlds tragically myopic lessons in how to survive—but never how to avoid—the ever more terrible wars to come.[51]

NOTES

The Powhatan tribal names in this article conform to current scholarly usage found in Christian F. Feest, "Virginia Algonquians," in Bruce G. Trigger, ed., *Handbook of North American Indians: Northeast*, 15 (Washington, D.C., 1978), pp. 268–69—with the following exceptions: this essay drops the vestigial *k* in *-eck, -ock*, and *-uck* endings, of which the late Elizabethans were so enamored, and prefers *Patawomec* over *Potomac*, in order to avoid confusion between a specific tribe and the generic term for all Indians who lived along that river. The source of the title quotation is Robert Beverley, *The History and Present State of Virginia* (London, 1705), ed. Louis B. Wright (Chapel Hill, 1947), p. 38.

1. Alonso de Velasco to Philip III, 14 June 1610, in Alexander Brown, ed., *The Genesis of the United States . . .* (2 vols.; Boston, 1890), 1:392; "A Breife Declaration of the Plantation of Virginia duringe the first Twelve Yeares . . . By the Antient Planters nowe remaining alive in Virginia" (Mar. 1624), in H. R. McIlwaine, ed., *Journals of the House of Burgesses*, Vol. 1: *1619–1658/59* (Richmond, 1915), p. 32.

2. See Howard Mumford Jones, *The Literature of Virginia in the Seventeenth Century* (2d ed.; Charlottesville, 1968), pp. 1–71. Since Robert Beverley published his *History and Present State of Virginia* (1705), the only accounts to focus on the hostilities in this period have been Darrett B. Rutman, "A Militant New World, 1607–1640: America's First Generation, Its Martial Spirit, Its Tradition of Arms, Its Militia Organization, Its Wars" (Ph.D. diss., University of Virginia, 1959); Richard Lee Morton, *Colonial Virginia*, Vol. 1: *The Tidewater Period, 1607–1710* (Chapel Hill, 1960); and J. Frederick Fausz, "The Powhatan Uprising of 1622: A Historical Study of Ethnocentrism and Cultural Conflict" (Ph.D. diss., College of William and Mary, 1977).

3. Charles McLean Andrews, *The Colonial Period of American History* (4 vols.; New Haven and London, 1934), 1:141–49; Edmund S. Morgan, *American Slavery, American Freedom: The Ordeal of Colonial Virginia* (New York, 1975), p. 72; William S. Powell, "Aftermath of the Massacre: The First Indian War, 1622–1632," *Virginia Magazine of History and Biography* (hereafter cited as *VMHB*) 66 (1958): 44; Wesley Frank Craven, "Indian Policy in Early Virginia," *William and Mary Quarterly* (hereafter cited as *WMQ*), 3d ser., 1 (1944): 71; Nancy Oestreich Lurie, "Indian Cultural Adjustment to European Civilization," in James Morton Smith, ed., *Seventeenth-Century America: Essays in Colonial History* (Chapel Hill, 1959), p. 48; J. Frederick Fausz, "The Invasion of Virginia: Indians, Colonialism, and the Conquest of Cant—A Review Essay on Anglo-Indian Relations in the Chesapeake," *VMHB* 95 (1987): 133–56; J. Frederick Fausz, "Anglo-Indian Relations in Colonial North America," in W. R. Swagerty, ed., *Scholars and the Indian Experience: Critical Reviews of Recent Writing in the Social Sciences* (Bloomington, 1984), pp. 79–105.

4. The *Oxford English Dictionary* defines war as "hostile contention by means of armed forces, carried on between nations, states, or rulers, or . . . the employment of armed forces against a foreign power, or against an opposing party in the state." Because the issue of what constitutes war between two alien cultures continues to be much debated, I employ a broad definition: a discernible pattern of protracted group violence between significant combatant forces for clearly understood political, ideological, cultural, and territorial objectives that are considered purposeful by one group and provocative by another. Anthropologists generally argue that the sporadic, small-

scale raids or ceremonial bluff-displays between feuding bands of hunter-gatherers do not constitute "true" war, which only developed as increasingly competitive and complex agricultural "civilizations" sought to defend or expand their territories (Andrew Bard Schmookler, *The Parable of the Tribes: The Problem of Power in Social Evolution* [Berkeley, 1984], pp. 74–81; Morton Fried, Marvin Harris, and Robert Murphy, eds., *War: The Anthropology of Armed Conflict and Aggression* [Garden City, N.Y., 1968]). Francis Jennings, on the other hand, contends that "there were no innate differences between Indians and Europeans in their capacity for war or their mode of conducting it" (Francis Jennings, *The Invasion of America: Indians, Colonialism, and the Cant of Conquest* [Chapel Hill, 1975], p. 146).

5. Ralph Lane, "Discourse on the First Colony" (1585–86), in David Beers Quinn, ed., *The Roanoke Voyages, 1584–1590,* Works issued by the Hakluyt Society, 2d ser., 104, 105 (2 vols.; London, 1955), 1:261; William Strachey, *The Historie of Travell into Virginia Britania (1612),* ed. Louis B. Wright and Virginia Freund, Works issued by the Hakluyt Society, 2d ser., 103 (London, 1953), pp. 56–57, 63–69, 104–8; Clifford M. Lewis, S.J., and Albert J. Loomie, S.J., *The Spanish Jesuit Mission in Virginia, 1570–1572* (Chapel Hill, 1953), pp. xvii–xviii, 15–21, 28–41, 62–63, 89, 108–11, 183–85.

6. Helen C. Rountree, *The Powhatan Indians of Virginia: Their Traditional Culture* (Norman, Okla., and London, 1989), chaps. 6, 7, epilog; Feest, "Virginia Algonquians," pp. 253–62; Christian F. Feest, "Powhatan: A Study in Political Organization," *Wiener Völkerkundliche Mitteilungen* 13 (1966): 59–83; E. Randolph Turner, "Socio-Political Organization within the Powhatan Chiefdom and the Effects of European Contact, A.D. 1607–1646," in William W. Fitzhugh, ed., *Cultures in Contact: The Impact of European Contacts on Native American Cultural Institutions, A.D. 1000–1800* (Washington, D.C., 1985), pp. 193–224.

7. [John Smith], *The Proceedings of the English Colonie in Virginia* . . . (Oxford, 1612), in Philip L. Barbour, ed., *The Complete Works of Captain John Smith (1580–1631)* (3 vols.; Chapel Hill, 1986), 1:257; John Smith, *The Generall Historie of Virginia, New-England, and the Summer Isles* . . . (London, 1624), in ibid., 2:176; Strachey, *Virginia Britania,* pp. 56, 85, 182, 205.

8. [Gabriel Archer], "A relatyon of the Discovery of our River, from James Forte into the Maine . . . " (May–June 1607), in Philip L. Barbour, ed., *The Jamestown Voyages Under the First Charter, 1606–1609,* Works issued by the Hakluyt Society, 2d ser., 136, 137 (2 vols.; Cambridge, 1969), 1:95–97; Sir Walter Cope to Robert Cecil, earl of Salisbury, 12 Aug. 1607, in ibid., 1:110; John Smith, *A True Relation of . . . Virginia* . . . (London, 1608), in Barbour, ed., *Complete Works of Smith,* 1:31–33. On intercultural conflict, see Lewis Coser, *The Functions of Social Conflict* (New York, 1956), p. 135; Stanley Lieberson, "A Societal Theory of Race and Ethnic Relations," in Pierre van den Berghe, ed., *Intergroup Relations: Sociological Perspectives* (New York, 1972), p. 41.

9. [Archer], "Relatyon," pp. 95–96; Smith, *True Relation,* p. 33; John Smith, *A Map of Virginia* . . . (Oxford, 1612), in Barbour, ed., *Complete Works of Smith,* 1:167; Henry Spelman, "Relation of Virginea" (ca. 1613), in Edward Arber and A. G. Bradley, eds., *Travels and Works of Captain John Smith* (2 vols.; Edinburgh, 1910), 1:cxiv.

10. George Abbot, *A Briefe Description of the Whole World* (London, 1600), p. C2r. According to Smith, without firearms, "our men had all beene slaine," confirming the Virginia Company's appraisal that the Indians' "only fear" was "Shott" (Smith, *Generall Historie,* p. 139; London Council, "Instructions . . . for the intended Voyage to

Virginia . . . " [Nov.–Dec. 1606], in Barbour, ed., *Jamestown Voyages*, 1:52). Expanding upon impact, the soft .60 caliber lead musket balls caused grievous injuries to Powhatan warriors. Strachey reported that the Indians could mend minor sword slashes and arrow punctures, but splintered limbs, "such as our smale shott make amongest them, they know not easely how to cure, and therefore languish in the misery . . . thereof" (Strachey, *Virginia Britania*, p. 110; Humfrey Barwick, *A Breefe Discourse Concerning the force and effect of all manual weapons of fire* [London, 1594]).

11. [Archer], "Relatyon," pp. 95–98; Smith, *True Relation*, p. 33.

12. Smith, *True Relation*, pp. 45–57; Smith, *Generall Historie*, pp. 144–52; George Percy, "Observations gathered out of a Discourse of . . . Virginia . . . ," in Barbour, ed., *Jamestown Voyages*, 1: 143–45. Wahunsonacock and Smith had an unparalleled opportunity to take the measure of one another during the captain's captivity. Smith was impressed with the chief's "grave and Majesticall countenance, as drave me into admiration to see such state in a naked Salvage." He discovered that the Powhatans considered *Tsenacommacah* to be at the center of a flat, platelike world and observed Wahunsonacock's "pride . . . in his great and spacious Dominions, seeing that all hee knewe were under his Territories." At the same time, the *mamanatowick* learned much about James I's empire, the "innumerable multitude of his ships," and the "terrible manner of [English] fighting." Wahunsonacock reputedly "admired" and "feared" James I as Smith had portrayed him, but he seemed pleased to learn that the English hated the Spanish as much as the Powhatans did (Smith, *True Relation*, pp. 53, 55, 57).

13. Smith, *Generall Historie*, pp. 184–85, 196–97; [Smith], *Proceedings of the English Colonie*, pp. 246–47.

14. Percy, "Observations," p. 141.

15. Smith, *True Relation*, p. 85; Smith, *Map of Virginia*, p. 175; [Smith], *Proceedings of the English Colonie*, pp. 250–55, 259–61, 265–66n; Smith, *Generall Historie*, pp. 195–98.

16. [Smith], *Proceedings of the English Colonie*, pp. 268–70. Smith's dispersal of colonists succeeded in May but failed miserably in August because of one critical variable—the disposition of the Powhatans. Carville V. Earle regards "Smith's scheme of dispersal . . . [as] the wisest to date," in terms of avoiding the polluted water of Jamestown, but his contention that "few [colonists] sickened and none died" as a result of Smith's decision totally ignores the 100 or more colonists whom the Powhatans killed (Carville V. Earle, "Environment, Disease, and Mortality in Early Virginia," in Thad W. Tate and David Ammerman, eds., *The Chesapeake in the Seventeenth-Century: Essays on Anglo-American Society* [Chapel Hill, 1979], pp. 107–8).

17. George Percy, "A Trewe Relacyon of the procedeinges and Ocurrentes of Momente wch have hapned in Virginia from . . . 1609 untill . . . 1612," *Tyler's Quarterly Historical and Genealogical Magazine* 3 (1921–22): 262–65; [Smith], *Proceedings of the English Colonie*, pp. 269–70. Smith described the Nansemonds' well-watered homeland of natural defensibility as containing an "abundance of houses and people, . . . [and] 1000 Acres of most excellent fertill ground, so sweete, so pleasant, so beautifull, and so strong a prospect for an invincible strong Citty." In two visits between September and December 1608, the English coerced some 500 bushels of corn from the Nansemonds at gunpoint before "departing good friends" (Strachey, *Virginia Britania*, pp. 43n, 66; Smith, *True Relation*, pp. 79–83, 185; Smith, *Map of Virginia*, p. 146; [Smith], *Proceedings of the English Colonie*, pp. 242–43, 247; Smith, *Generall Historie*, pp. 178–79, 221).

18. [Smith], *Proceedings of the English Colonie*, pp. 270–71; Smith, *Generall Historie*, pp. 90–92; Percy, "Trewe Relacyon," pp. 263–64. Prior to the August attack, the up-river Powhatans had enjoyed peaceful contacts with the English, who ambivalently considered them "a most kind and loving people"—"naturally given to trechery" ([Archer], "Relatyon," pp. 82, 85; [Gabriel Archer?], "The Discription of the now discovered River and Country of Virginia" [June 1607], in Barbour, ed., *Jamestown Voyages*, 1:103–4, 2:465–68; Strachey, *Virginia Britania*, p. 64; [Smith], *Proceedings of the English Colonie*, pp. 238, 263–64).

19. [Smith], *Proceedings of the English Colonie*, pp. 272–74; Biographical Directory, in Barbour, ed., *Complete Works of Smith*, 1:xlii (Martin), xlv (Percy), lii (West). Smith blamed the "losse of Virginia" (which he equated with the Powhatans' decision for war) on the "infinite dangers, plots, and practices" he faced from jealous colonial rivals. Percy, one of Smith's most articulate adversaries, confirmed that the president's departure saved him from certain assassination, and he believed that Smith's powder-burn was sweet revenge after the captain had allegedly refused to supply ammunition to West's beleaguered men at Nonsuch (Smith, *Generall Historie*, pp. 219, 223–25; Percy, "Trewe Relacyon," p. 264).

20. [Smith], *Proceedings of the English Colonie*, p. 275; Percy, "Trewe Relacyon," pp. 265–66; Spelman, "Relation of Virginea," pp. ciii–cv.

21. Percy, "Trewe Relacyon," p. 266; [Virginia Company], *A True Declaration of the estate of the Colonie in Virginia . . .* (London, 1610), in Peter Force, comp., *Tracts and Other Papers, Relating Principally to the Origin, Settlement, and Progress of the Colonies in North America . . .* (4 vols.; Washington, D.C., 1836), 3: doc. no. 1, pp. 15–16. In this latter pamphlet, Virginia Company officials blamed West's actions for having "created Indians our implacable enemies" (p. 16), and two years later they reiterated that "the poore Indians by wrongs and injuries were made our enemies" ([Robert Johnson], *The New Life of Virginea* [London, 1612], in Force, comp., *Tracts*, 1: doc. no. 7, p. 10).

22. [Smith], *Proceedings of the English Colonie*, p. 273; Percy, "Trewe Relacyon," pp. 266–69; "Breife Declaration by the Antient Planters," p. 29; William Strachey, "A True Reportory of the Wreck and Redemption of Sir Thomas Gates . . . " (1610), in Louis B. Wright, ed., *A Voyage to Virginia in 1609 . . .* (Charlottesville, 1964), pp. 62–72; George Donne, "Virginia Reviewed," ed. T. H. Breen, *WMQ*, 3d ser., 30 (1973): 455; Beverley, *History of Virginia*, pp. 37–38. In 1610 Emanuel van Meteren wrote, "[The English] . . . had neglected their sowing-time so their provisions had given out . . . [while] the Indians, seeing that the English were beginning to multiply, were determined to starve them and drive them out" (Emanuel van Meteren, *Commentarien Ofte Memorien . . .* [London, 1610], in Barbour, ed., *Jamestown Voyages*, 2:276).

23. Strachey, "True Reportory," pp. 62–64; Percy, "Trewe Relacyon," p. 268. Although Earle was correct in asserting that fewer colonists literally starved in the "Starving Time" than was previously assumed, he wrongly concluded that the whole episode was "sensationalized and exaggerated." His contention that the colonists had access to some "30,000 pounds" of pork and an abundance of other provisions does not square with eyewitness accounts of meal rationing (one-half can per man per day) and of "Powhatan . . . and his people destroy[ing] our Hogs, (to the number of about six hundred)" (Earle, "Environment, Disease, and Mortality," pp. 108–10; *True Declaration of the estate of the Colonie*, in Force, comp., *Tracts*, 3: doc. no. 1, p. 17; Percy, "Trewe Relacyon," pp. 265–66).

24. Strachey, "True Reportory," pp. 35–36, 49, 53–54, 61–65, 71, 75–77; Percy, "Trewe Relacyon," pp. 268–69; [Johnson], *New Life of Virginea*, in Force, comp., *Tracts*, 1: doc. no. 7, p. 11; William Crashaw, "Epistle Dedicatorie," in Alexander Whitaker, *Good Newes from Virginia* (London, 1613), pp. B1v–B3r.

25. Strachey, "True Reportory," pp. 76–77; Alonso de Velasco to Philip III, 30 Sept. 1610, in Brown, ed., *Genesis of the United States*, 1:418; Whitaker, *Good Newes from Virginia*, pp. B1v–B2v, 21–23; "Breife Declaration of the Antient Planters," pp. 29–30.

26. Strachey, "True Reportory," pp. 77, 84–87; Smith, *Map of Virginia*, p. 176; [Robert Johnson], *Nova Britannia: Offering Most Excellent fruites by Planting in Virginia . . .* (London, 1609), in Force, comp., *Tracts*, 1: doc. no. 6, pp. 6, 13–14, 23–25; *True Declaration of the estate of the Colonie*, in ibid., 3: doc. no. 1, pp. 4–6; Richard Crackanthorpe, "A Sermon . . . preached at Paules Cross . . ." (14 Mar. 1608/9), in Brown, ed., *Genesis of the United States*, 1:256; Virginia Company of London, second charter (23 May 1609), in Samuel M. Bemiss, comp., *The Three Charters of the Virginia Company of London . . .*, Jamestown 350th Anniversary Historical Booklets, No. 4 (Charlottesville, 1957), pp. 28, 54; Fausz, "Powhatan Uprising," pp. 255–65.

27. Wesley Frank Craven, introduction to Robert Gray, *A Good Speed to Virginia (1609)*, Scholar's Facsimiles and Reprints (New York, 1937), p. i; [Johnson], *Nova Britannia*, in Force, comp., *Tracts*, 1: doc. no. 6, pp. 13–14, 20–21, 27; "Instruccions, Orders and Constitucions . . . to Sr Thomas Gates . . . ," in Bemiss, comp., *Three Charters*, pp. 56–63; Strachey, *Virginia Britania*, pp. 58, 90–91, 104–6; Samuel Purchas, *Hakluytus Posthumus, or Purchas His Pilgrimes* (London, 1625), Works issued by the Hakluyt Society, extra series, 14–33 (20 vols.; Glasgow, 1905–7), 19:228; Sir Thomas Dale to "Mr. D. M." (June 1614), in Ralph Hamor, *A True Discourse of the Present Estate of Virginia* (London, 1615), p. 51; Darrett B. Rutman, "The Virginia Company and Its Military Regime," in Darrett B. Rutman, ed., *The Old Dominion: Essays for Thomas Perkins Abernethy* (Charlottesville, 1964), pp. 4–5; Fausz, "Powhatan Uprising," chap. 3. The English justified war against the Powhatans in 1609–10 based on what the formerly tolerant Richard Hakluyt called their "most craftie contrived and bloody treasons" in violating "the lawe of nations"—specifically, the unproven allegations that Wahunsonacock had "miserably slaughtered" the Roanoke colonists, which David Beers Quinn has recently resurrected. The Virginia Company rationalized its aggressive campaign for peaceful conversion by seeing Christianization of the "good" Powhatan majority as the ultimate goal, which the immediate military pacification of the "bad" Powhatan leadership would permit (Richard Hakluyt, *Virginia richly valued . . .* [London, 1609], pp. A3r–A4r; *True Declaration of the estate of the Colonie*, in Force, comp., *Tracts*, 3: doc. no. 1, p. 7; Strachey, *Virginia Britania*, pp. 58, 91; David Beers Quinn, *Set Fair for Roanoke: Voyages and Colonies, 1584–1606* [Chapel Hill, 1985], esp. pp. 358–78; Loren E. Pennington, "The Amerindian in English Promotional Literature," in K. R. Andrews, N. P. Canny, and P. E. H. Hair, eds., *The Westward Enterprise: English Activities in Ireland, the Atlantic, and America, 1480–1650* [Detroit and Liverpool, 1978], p. 178).

28. Pedro de Zúñiga to Philip III, 31 Dec. 1609, 11 Mar. 1609/10, in Brown, ed., *Genesis of the United States*, 1:357, 386; Thomas West, Lord De La Warr, to Robert Cecil, earl of Salisbury, July 1610, in ibid., pp. 413–15; *True Declaration of the estate of the Colonie*, in Force, comp., *Tracts*, 3: doc. no. 1, p. 20; [William Strachey, comp.], *For*

the Colony in Virginea Britannia. Lawes Divine, Morall and Martiall, etc. (London, 1612), ed. David H. Flaherty (Charlottesville, 1969), pp. 9, 12, 15, 20, 27–28, 35, 53–55; "Instructions, Orders and Constitucions . . . to . . . Lord Lawarr" (1609/10), in Bemiss, comp., *Three Charters*, pp. 70–73; Rutman, "Military Regime," pp. 3–13; William L. Shea, *The Virginia Militia in the Seventeenth Century* (Baton Rouge, 1982), pp. 14–17; "Instructions given to Capt. Thomas Holcroft . . . " (29 May 1609), in Brown, ed., *Genesis of the United States*, 1:316–18. The Spanish ambassador to England thought it particularly ominous that the military buildup in Virginia was accomplished with so many troops who had "seen service among the [Dutch] Rebels." He warned his king that the English were "mad about this affair and shameless" in contributing vast sums to a project designed to "kill that King [Wahunsonacock] and the savages, so as to obtain possession of everything" (Pedro de Zúñiga to Philip III, 5 Mar. 1609/10, in Brown, ed., *Genesis of the United States*, 1:244, 246–47).

29. Whitaker, *Good Newes from Virginia*, pp. C2r, 44; Strachey, "True Reportory," pp. 88–89; Percy, "Trewe Relacyon," p. 270; "Breife Declaration of the Antient Planters," p. 30.

30. Percy, "Trewe Relacyon," pp. 271–73; Strachey, "True Reportory," p. 93.

31. Strachey, *Virginia Britania*, pp. 63–69; Percy, "Trewe Relacyon," pp. 272–73, 277; "Breife Declaration of the Antient Planters," p. 32; J. Frederick Fausz and Jon Kukla, eds., "A Letter of Advice to the Governor of Virginia, 1624," *WMQ*, 3d ser., 34 (1977): 126–27; Steven G. Ellis, *Tudor Ireland: Crown, Community and the Conflict of Cultures, 1470–1603* (London and New York, 1985), chap. 9; n. 47, below. Social psychologists find that "the nearer outgroups should be targets of the most ethnocentric hostility," and "the most overtly hated outgroups will be ones that are strong enough to be threatening but weak enough to be successfully aggressed against" (Robert A. LeVine and Donald T. Campbell, *Ethnocentrism: Theories of Conflict, Ethnic Attitudes, and Group Behavior* [New York, 1972], pp. 37, 69). By wrongly assuming that "cuttinge down corne" meant destruction rather than confiscation, Edmund S. Morgan created a nonexistent dilemma: "How to explain the suicidal impulse that led the hungry English to destroy the corn that might have fed them and to commit atrocities upon the people who grew it? And how to account for the seeming unwillingness or incapacity of the English to feed themselves?" (Morgan, *American Slavery, American Freedom*, pp. 74–75).

32. "Breife Declaration of the Antient Planters," p. 30; "Instruccions to Gates," pp. 66–67.

33. Hamor, *True Discourse*, p. 54; [Strachey, comp.], *Lawes Divine, Morall and Martiall*, pp. 10, 84–85, 98–100; *True Declaration of the estate of the Colonie*, in Force, comp., *Tracts*, 3: doc. no. 1, pp. 6, 19, 24, 26–27; [Johnson], *New Life of Virginea*, in ibid., 1: doc. no. 7, pp. 7–9, 15–19, 24; Whitaker, *Good Newes from Virginia*, pp. 22, 25–26, 33, 36; *Virginia Company v. Sir Thomas Mildmay et al.* (Nov. 1612), in Susan Myra Kingsbury, ed., *Records of the Virginia Company of London* (hereafter cited as *Va. Co. Recs.*) (4 vols.; Washington, D.C., 1906–35), 3:36, 38; Sir Thomas Dale to Sir Thomas Smythe (June 1613), in ibid., 2:399; Strachey, *Virginia Britania*, pp. 88–91, 94–106; Fausz, "Powhatan Uprising," pp. 120–80, 255–64, 285–87.

34. Percy, "Trewe Relacyon," p. 275; "Breife Declaration of the Antient Planters," p. 30; "A short Relation made by the Lord De-La-Warre to . . . the Counsell of Virginia" (June 1611), in Purchas, *Hakluytus Posthumus*, 19:85–87.

35. "Breife Declaration of the Antient Planters," p. 31; Percy, "Trewe Relacyon," p. 276; Smith, *Generall Historie*, p. 239; testimony of John Clark (Dale's pilot), 18 Feb. 1613, in David B. Quinn, ed., *New American World: A Documentary History of North America to 1612* (5 vols.; New York, 1979), 5:157; leave of absence granted Dale by United Netherlands, 20 Jan. 1611, in Brown, ed., *Genesis of the United States*, 1:446–47; Hakluyt, *Virginia richly valued*, pp. A4v–A4r. Spanish spies in London reported that the Dale fleet carried 300 men (60 with wives), 8 ministers, 1,000 arquebuses, 500 muskets, 300 corselets, and 500 helmets (Alonso de Velasco to Philip III, 31 Dec. 1610, in Brown, ed., *Genesis of the United States*, 1:442–43).

36. "Breife Declaration of the Antient Planters," pp. 31, 35; "Answere of the Generall Assembly in Virginia to a Declaration of the state of the Colonie in . . . Sir Thomas Smiths government" [Feb. 1623/4], in McIlwaine, ed., *Journals of Burgesses*, 1:21; Hamor, *True Discourse*, pp. 26–28; "Instructions to De La Warr," pp. 72–73; [Johnson], *New Life of Virginea*, in Force, comp., *Tracts*, 1: doc. no. 7, pp. 11–12; Smith, *Generall Historie*, p. 240; Rutman, "Military Regime," pp. 6–17; Karen Ordahl Kupperman, "Apathy and Death in Early Jamestown," *Journal of American History* 65 (1979): 24–40.

37. [Strachey, comp.], *Lawes Divine, Morall and Martiall*, pp. xvi, xviii–xix, xxvi–xxvii, xxxi–xxxvii; Thomas Churchyard, *A Generall rehearsal of warres . . .* (London, 1579), quoted in Nicholas Canny, "The Ideology of English Colonization: From Ireland to America," *WMQ*, 3d ser., 30 (1973): 582; Sir Walter Ralegh, *The History of the World: In Five Books* (2d ed.; London, 1617), p. 148 [2d enumeration]; Sir Thomas Dale to Robert Cecil, earl of Salisbury, Aug. 1611, in Brown, ed., *Genesis of the United States*, 1:506–7; Ralph Lane to Sir Philip Sidney, 12 Aug. 1585, in Quinn, ed., *Roanoke Voyages*, 1:204; Nicholas Canny, "The Permissive Frontier: The Problem of Social Control in English Settlements in Ireland and Virginia, 1550–1650," in Andrews, Canny, and Hair, eds., *Westward Enterprise*, pp. 28–34; C. G. Cruickshank, *Elizabeth's Army* (2d ed.; Oxford, 1966), pp. 159–88, 296–303; J. Frederick Fausz, "Middlemen in Peace and War: Virginia's Earliest Indian Interpreters, 1608–1632," *VMHB* 95 (1987): 41–64. Social psychologists argue that the "greater the discipline of group life, its repressions, privations, and exactions . . . the greater we can expect its aggressiveness to become at the expense of some other group" (LeVine and Campbell, *Ethnocentrism*, p. 117; also pp. 30–35, 57–58, 119–33, 173, 217). See also Morton Deutsch, *The Resolution of Conflict: Constructive and Destructive Processes* (New Haven, 1973), esp. chap. 5. Many more colonists deserted Jamestown than actually succeeded in "going native"—that is, in achieving the crucial second step of being accepted by the Powhatans and fully integrated into their society. It is ironic that while several Englishmen sought to escape the Dale regime by fleeing to Indian lands, "certaine Indians [were] hired by . . . [Dale] to hunt them home to receive their deserts" (Hamor, *True Discourse*, pp. 27, 44).

38. Sir Thomas Dale to Robert Cecil, earl of Salisbury, 17 Aug. 1611, in Brown, ed., *Genesis of the United States*, 1:503–5.

39. Percy, "Trewe Relacyon," pp. 279–80; Hamor, *True Discourse*, pp. 30–33; Smith, *Generall Historie*, pp. 293, 305; Fausz and Kukla, eds., "Letter of Advice," pp. 108–9n; John Rolfe, *A True Relation of the State of Virginia . . .* (Charlottesville, 1971), pp. 7–11; De La Warr, "Relation," p. 89.

40. "Breife Declaration of the Antient Planters," p. 31; "Answere of the Generall

Assembly," p. 21; De La Warr, "Relation," pp. 85–86, 90; [Johnson], *New Life for Virginea*, in Force, comp., *Tracts*, 1: doc. no. 7, pp. 3–4, 19–21; Virginia Company of London, third charter (Mar. 1612), in Bemiss, comp., *Three Charters*, pp. 90–91; Whitaker, *Good Newes from Virginia*, pp. A2r, 33. On lack of support for the company's third charter, see Brown, ed., *Genesis of the United States*, 1:228–29n, 2:542n; Robert C. Johnson, "The Lotteries of the Virginia Company, 1612–1621," *VMHB* 74 (1966): 259–92; Robert C. Johnson, "The 'Running Lotteries' of the Virginia Company," ibid., 68 (1960), 156–65.

41. "A Letter of Sir Samuel Argoll touching his voyage to Virginia" (1613), in Purchas, *Hakluytus Posthumus*, 19:90–94; De La Warr, "Relation," pp. 88–89; Hamor, *True Discourse*, pp. 3–6, 10, 35–37; "Breife Declaration of the Antient Planters," p. 32; Philip L. Barbour, *Pocahontas and Her World* (Boston, 1969), pp. 66–76, 82–89, 96–101, 119–27; Fausz, "Virginia's Interpreters," pp. 48–50; Biographical Directory, in Barbour, ed., *Complete Works of Smith*, 1:xxix (Argall), xxxiii (Dale).

42. Hamor, *True Discourse*, pp. 3, 6, 55.

43. Ibid., pp. 6–9, 52–54; "Letter of Argoll," pp. 93–94.

44. Hamor, *True Discourse*, pp. 10–11, 24, 61–68.

45. Ibid., pp. [A4r], 2, 11, 37–47, 55, 59–60; Whitaker, *Good Newes from Virginia*, p. 40. In giving Pocahontas the christening name of Rebecca, Whitaker sensed the prophetic implications of Genesis 25:23: "And the Lord said to [Rebecca], two nations are in thy wombe, and two maner of people shalbe devided out of thy bowels, and the one people shalbe mightier then the other, and the elder shal serve the younger" (*The Geneva Bible* [1560]; Frances Mossiker, *Pocahontas: The Life and the Legend* [New York, 1976], pp. 164–94).

46. Hamor, *True Discourse*, pp. [A4r], 24, 41, 58, 65, 68–69; Whitaker, *Good Newes from Virginia*, pp. [B4r–D1r], 33, 40, 44; Rolfe, *True Relation of the State of Virginia*, pp. 4–5, 12–14; Smith, *Generall Historie*, p. 259; Kingsbury, ed., *Va. Co. Recs.*, 1:566, 589; 3:219–22, 670; 4:526; Johnson, "Lotteries, 1612–21," p. 258; Fausz, "Powhatan Uprising," pp. 285–370.

47. Sir Walter Ralegh, *The Discovery of . . . Guiana . . .* (1596), ed. Sir Robert H. Schomburgk, Works issued by the Hakluyt Society, 1st ser., 7 (London, 1848), pp. 142–43 (my italics); Ralegh, *History of World*, p. 468 (2d enumeration); *True Declaration of the estate of the Colonie*, in Force, comp., *Tracts*, 3: doc. no. 1, p. 7; Whitaker, *Good Newes from Virginia*, pp. A2r, 33; John R. Hale, *The Art of War and Renaissance England* (Washington, D.C., 1961), p. 54; Michael Walzer, *Just and Unjust Wars: A Moral Argument with Historical Illustrations* (New York, 1977), chaps. 1–2; James Turner Johnson, *Ideology, Reason, and the Limitations of War: Religious and Secular Concepts, 1200–1740* (Princeton, 1975), chap. 2.

48. Smith, *Proceedings of the English Colonie*, pp. 258–59; Strachey, *Virginia Britania*, p. 106; "Breife Declaration of the Antient Planters," pp. 35–36; Whitaker, quoted in Hamor, *True Discourse*, p. 59.

49. "Letter of Don Diego de Molina" (1613), in Lyon Gardiner Tyler, ed., *Narratives of Early Virginia, 1606–1625* (New York, 1907), p. 218; "A True Narrative of the Late Rebellion in Virginia . . . " (1677), in Charles M. Andrews, ed., *Narratives of the Insurrections, 1675–1690* (New York, 1915), p. 123; Roosevelt, quoted in Noam Chomsky, *Turning the Tide: U.S. Intervention in Central America and the Struggle for Peace* (Boston, 1985), p. 87; J. Frederick Fausz, "Merging and Emerging Worlds:

Anglo-Indian Interest Groups and the Development of the Seventeenth-Century Chesapeake," in Lois Green Carr, Philip D. Morgan, and Jean B. Russo, eds., *Colonial Chesapeake Society* (Chapel Hill and London, 1989), pp. 47–98. The Anglo-Chickahominy treaty of 1614, negotiated by Argall soon after the Rolfe-Pocahontas wedding, revealed the ongoing English quest for domination in the Chesapeake. The Chickahominies agreed to become subordinate, tributary allies of the colonists, to recognize the Virginia governor as their *werowance* and the English king as their emperor, to supply 300 to 400 bowmen in the event of war, to pay an annual "tribute" of 1,000 bushels of maize (or 2 bushels per warrior), and to refrain from visiting colonial settlements. The English gave red coats, copper chains, engraved medals of James I, and "eight great Tomahawks" to the ruling elders and encouraged the Chickahominies to call themselves *tassantasses*—"Englishmen" (Hamor, *True Discourse*, pp. 12–15).

50. Beverley, *History of Virginia*, p. 233.

51. Ibid., pp. 29, 38–39, 44–45, 50; "Breife Declaration of the Antient Planters," pp. 35–36; [Johnson], *New Life of Virginea*, in Force, comp., *Tracts*, 1: doc. no. 7, p. 18; J. Frederick Fausz, "Fighting 'Fire' with Firearms: The Anglo-Powhatan Arms Race in Early Virginia," *American Indian Culture and Research Journal* 3 (1979): 33–50. On the prominent veterans of 1609–14 who lived on to perpetuate the practices and prejudices of intercultural warfare, see Fausz, "Merging Worlds," pp. 51–55; J. Frederick Fausz, "Opechancanough: Indian Resistance Leader," in David Sweet and Gary B. Nash, eds., *Struggle and Survival in Colonial America* (Berkeley and London, 1981), pp. 21–37.

EDMUND S. MORGAN

Slavery and Freedom: The American Paradox

* * * * * * * * THIS ESSAY, DELIVERED IN 1972 BY EDMUND Morgan as the presidential address of the Organization of American Historians at its annual meeting in Washington, D.C., represents an early version of an argument Morgan would advance in substantially greater detail in his seminal 1975 book *American Slavery, American Freedom: The Ordeal of Colonial Virginia*. Morgan provides a compelling argument about the evolution of slavery. He explains how Virginia colonists eager to pursue economic betterment freely could bind first their own countrymen into indentured servitude and eventually Africans into perpetual slavery.

Morgan asserts a theme that usefully organizes much of American history, and most certainly the history of Virginia. "The rise of liberty and equality in this country was accompanied by the rise of slavery," Morgan writes. "That two such contradictory developments were taking place simultaneously over a long period of our history, from the seventeenth century to the nineteenth, is the central paradox of American history." Freedom, liberty, independence—all values that, by 1750, Virginians cherished—flourished in the colony precisely because the enslavement of Africans permitted the political equality of white, landowning men. The collective authority exercised by planters created a political culture in eighteenth-century Virginia powerfully rooted in these values. Slavery, then, afforded Virginians the confidence, at the time of the American Revolution, to be among the most vocal proponents of political independence and the republican philosophy that supported American self-government.

The paradox of slavery and freedom, which Morgan develops from analysis of the seventeenth and eighteenth centuries, was not resolved with the end of slavery. The illiberality of slavery and the society that it bred left a long shadow in Virginia, explored in one way or another by all of the essays in this volume.   * * * * * * * *

* * * * * * * *

AMERICAN HISTORIANS INTERESTED IN TRACING THE RISE OF LIB-
erty, democracy, and the common man have been challenged in the past two
decades by other historians, interested in tracing the history of oppression,
exploitation, and racism. The challenge has been salutary, because it has
made us examine more directly than historians have hitherto been willing
to do, the role of slavery in our early history. Colonial historians, in particular, when writing about the origin and development of American institutions have found it possible until recently to deal with slavery as an
exception to everything they had to say. I am speaking about myself but also
about most of my generation. We owe a debt of gratitude to those who have
insisted that slavery was something more than an exception, that one fifth
of the American population at the time of the Revolution is too many
people to be treated as an exception.[1]

We shall not have met the challenge simply by studying the history of
that one fifth, fruitful as such studies may be, urgent as they may be. Nor
shall we have met the challenge if we merely execute the familiar maneuver
of turning our old interpretations on their heads. The temptation is already
apparent to argue that slavery and oppression were the dominant features
of American history and that efforts to advance liberty and equality were
the exception, indeed no more than a device to divert the masses while their
chains were being fastened. To dismiss the rise of liberty and equality in
American history as a mere sham is not only to ignore hard facts, it is also
to evade the problem presented by those facts. The rise of liberty and equality in this country was accompanied by the rise of slavery. That two such
contradictory developments were taking place simultaneously over a long
period of our history, from the seventeenth century to the nineteenth, is the
central paradox of American history.

The challenge, for a colonial historian at least, is to explain how a people
could have developed the dedication to human liberty and dignity exhibited by the leaders of the American Revolution and at the same time have
developed and maintained a system of labor that denied human liberty and
dignity every hour of the day.

The paradox is evident at many levels if we care to see it. Think, for a
moment, of the traditional American insistence on freedom of the seas.
"Free ships make free goods" was the cardinal doctrine of American foreign
policy in the Revolutionary era. But the goods for which the United States
demanded freedom were produced in very large measure by slave labor.
The irony is more than semantic. American reliance on slave labor must be
viewed in the context of the American struggle for a separate and equal station among the nations of the earth. At the time the colonists announced
their claim to that station they had neither the arms nor the ships to make
the claim good. They desperately needed the assistance of other countries,

especially France, and their single most valuable product with which to purchase assistance was tobacco, produced mainly by slave labor. So largely did that crop figure in American foreign relations that one historian has referred to the activities of France in supporting the Americans as "King Tobacco Diplomacy," a reminder that the position of the United States in the world depended not only in 1776 but during the span of a long lifetime thereafter on slave labor.[2] To a very large degree it may be said that Americans bought their independence with slave labor.

The paradox is sharpened if we think of the state where most of the tobacco came from. Virginia at the time of the first United States census in 1790 had 40 percent of the slaves in the entire United States. And Virginia produced the most eloquent spokesmen for freedom and equality in the entire United States: George Washington, James Madison, and above all, Thomas Jefferson. They were all slaveholders and remained so throughout their lives. In recent years we have been shown in painful detail the contrast between Jefferson's pronouncements in favor of republican liberty and his complicity in denying the benefits of that liberty to blacks.[3] It has been tempting to dismiss Jefferson and the whole Virginia dynasty as hypocrites. But to do so is to deprive the term "hypocrisy" of useful meaning. If hypocrisy means, as I think it does, deliberately to affirm a principle without believing it, then hypocrisy requires a rare clarity of mind combined with an unscrupulous intention to deceive. To attribute such an intention, even to attribute such clarity of mind in the matter, to Jefferson, Madison, or Washington is once again to evade the challenge. What we need to explain is how such men could have arrived at beliefs and actions so full of contradiction.

Put the challenge another way: how did England, a country priding itself on the liberty of its citizens, produce colonies where most of the inhabitants enjoyed still greater liberty, greater opportunities, greater control over their own lives than most men in the mother country, while the remainder, one fifth of the total, were deprived of virtually all liberty, all opportunities, all control over their own lives? We may admit that the Englishmen who colonized America and their revolutionary descendants were racists, that consciously or unconsciously they believed liberties and rights should be confined to persons of a light complexion. When we have said as much, even when we have probed the depths of racial prejudice, we will not have fully accounted for the paradox. Racism was surely an essential element in it, but I should like to suggest another element, that I believe to have influenced the development of both slavery and freedom as we have known them in the United States.

Let us begin with Jefferson, this slaveholding spokesman of freedom. Could there have been anything in the kind of freedom he cherished that would have made him acquiesce, however reluctantly, in the slavery of so many Americans? The answer, I think, is yes. The freedom that Jefferson spoke for was not a gift to be conferred by governments, which he mistrusted at best. It was a freedom that sprang from the independence of the individual. The man who depended on another for his living could never be truly free. We may seek a clue to Jefferson's enigmatic posture toward slavery in his attitude toward those who enjoyed a seeming freedom without the independence needed to sustain it. For such persons Jefferson harbored a profound distrust, which found expression in two phobias that crop up from time to time in his writings.

The first was a passionate aversion to debt. Although the entire colonial economy of Virginia depended on the willingness of planters to go into debt and of British merchants to extend credit, although Jefferson himself was a debtor all his adult life—or perhaps because he was a debtor—he hated debt and hated anything that made him a debtor. He hated it because it limited his freedom of action. He could not, for example, have freed his slaves so long as he was in debt. Or so at least he told himself. But it was the impediment not simply to their freedom but to his own that bothered him. "I am miserable," he wrote, "till I shall owe not a shilling. . . ."[4]

The fact that he had so much company in his misery only added to it. His Declaration of Independence for the United States was mocked by the hold that British merchants retained over American debtors, including himself.[5] His hostility to Alexander Hamilton was rooted in his recognition that Hamilton's pro-British foreign policy would tighten the hold of British creditors, while his domestic policy would place the government in the debt of a class of native American creditors, whose power might become equally pernicious.

Though Jefferson's concern with the perniciousness of debt was almost obsessive, it was nevertheless altogether in keeping with the ideas of republican liberty that he shared with his countrymen. The trouble with debt was that by undermining the independence of the debtor it threatened republican liberty. Whenever debt brought a man under another's power, he lost more than his own freedom of action. He also weakened the capacity of his country to survive as a republic. It was an axiom of current political thought that republican government required a body of free, independent, property-owning citizens.[6] A nation of men, each of whom owned enough property to support his family, could be a republic. It would follow that a nation of debtors, who had lost their property or mortgaged it to creditors, was ripe for tyranny. Jefferson accordingly favored every means of keeping men out of debt and keeping property widely distributed. He insisted on the abolition of primogeniture and entail; he declared that the earth belonged to the living and should not be kept from them by the debts or credits of the dead; he would have given fifty acres of land to every American who did not have it—all because he believed the citizens of a republic must be free from the control of other men and that they could be free only if they were economically free by virtue of owning land on which to support themselves.[7]

If Jefferson felt so passionately about the bondage of the debtor, it is not surprising that he should also have sensed a danger to the republic from another class of men who, like debtors, were nominally free but whose independence was illusory. Jefferson's second phobia was his distrust of the landless urban workman who labored in manufactures. In Jefferson's view, he was a free man in name only. Jefferson's hostility to artificers is well known and is generally attributed to his romantic preference for the rural life. But both his distrust for artificers and his idealization of small landholders as "the most precious part of a state" rested on his concern for individual independence as the basis of freedom. Farmers made the best citizens because they were "the most vigorous, the most independant, the most virtuous. . . . " Artificers, on the other hand, were dependent on "the casualties and caprice of customers." If work was scarce, they had no land to fall back on for a living. In their dependence lay the danger. "Dependance," Jefferson argued, "begets subservience and venality, suffocates the germ of virtue, and prepares fit tools for the designs of ambition." Because artificers could lay claim to freedom without the independence to go with it, they were "the instruments by which the liberties of a country are generally overturned."[8]

In Jefferson's distrust of artificers we begin to get a glimpse of the limits—and limits not dictated by racism—that defined the republican vision of the eighteenth century. For Jefferson was by no means unique among republicans in his distrust of the landless laborer. Such a distrust was a necessary corollary of the widespread eighteenth-century insistence on the independent, property-holding individual as the only bulwark of liberty, an insistence originating in James Harrington's republican political philosophy and a guiding principle of American colonial politics, whether in the aristocratic South Carolina assembly or in the democratic New England town.[9] Americans both before and after 1776 learned their republican lessons from the seventeenth- and eighteenth-century British commonwealthmen; and the commonwealthmen were uninhibited in their contempt for the masses who did not have the propertied independence required of proper republicans.

John Locke, the classic explicator of the right of revolution for the protection of liberty, did not think about extending that right to the landless poor. Instead, he concocted a scheme of compulsory labor for them and their children. The children were to begin at the age of three in public institutions, called working schools because the only subject taught would be work (spinning and knitting). They would be paid in bread and water and grow up "inured to work." Meanwhile the mothers, thus relieved of the care of their offspring, could go to work beside their fathers and husbands. If they could not find regular employment, then they too could be sent to the working school.[10]

It requires some refinement of mind to discern precisely how this version of women's liberation from child care differed from outright slavery. And many of Locke's intellectual successors, while denouncing slavery in the abstract, openly preferred slavery to freedom for the lower ranks of laborers. Adam Ferguson, whose works were widely read in America, attributed the overthrow of the Roman republic, in part at least, to the emancipation of slaves, who "increased, by their numbers and their vices, the weight of that dreg, which, in great and prosperous cities, ever sinks, by the tendency of vice and misconduct to the lowest condition."[11]

That people in the lowest condition, the dregs of society, generally arrived at that position through their own vice and misconduct, whether in ancient Rome or modern Britain, was an unexamined article of faith among eighteenth-century republicans. And the vice that was thought to afflict the lower ranks most severely was idleness. The eighteenth-century's preferred cure for idleness lay in the religious and ethical doctrines which R. H. Tawney described as the New Medicine for Poverty, the doctrines in which Max Weber discerned the origins of the spirit of capitalism. But in every society a stubborn mass of men and women refused the medicine. For such persons the commonwealthmen did not hesitate to prescribe slavery. Thus Francis Hutcheson, who could argue eloquently against the enslavement of Africans, also argued that perpetual slavery should be "the ordinary punishment of such idle vagrants as, after proper admonitions and tryals of temporary servitude, cannot be engaged to support themselves and their families by any useful labours."[12] James Burgh, whose *Political Disquisitions* earned the praises of many American revolutionists, proposed a set of press gangs "to seize all idle and disorderly persons, who have been three times complained of before a magistrate, and to set them to work during a certain time, for the benefit of great trading, or manufacturing companies, &c."[13]

The most comprehensive proposal came from Andrew Fletcher of Saltoun. Jefferson hailed in Fletcher a patriot whose political principles were those "in vigour at the epoch of the American emigration [from England]. Our ancestors brought them here, and they needed little strengthening to make us what we are. . . . "[14] Fletcher, like other commonwealthmen, was a champion of liberty, but he was also a champion of slavery. He attacked the Christian church not only for having promoted the abolition of slavery in ancient times but also for having perpetuated the idleness of the freedmen thus turned loose on society. The church by setting up hospitals and almshouses had enabled men through the succeeding centuries to live without work. As a result, Fletcher argued, his native Scotland was burdened with 200,000 idle rogues, who roamed the country, drinking, cursing, fighting, robbing, and murdering. For a remedy he proposed that they all be made slaves to men of property. To the argument that their masters might abuse them, he answered in words which might have come a century and a half later from a George Fitzhugh: that this would be against the master's own interest, "That the most brutal man will not use his beast ill only out of a humour; and that if such Inconveniences do sometimes fall out, it proceeds, for the most part, from the perverseness of the Servant."[15]

In spite of Jefferson's tribute to Fletcher, there is no reason to suppose that he endorsed Fletcher's proposal. But he did share Fletcher's distrust of men who were free in name while their empty bellies made them thieves, threatening the property of honest men, or else made them slaves in fact to anyone who would feed them. Jefferson's own solution for the kind of situation described by Fletcher was given in a famous letter to Madison, prompted by the spectacle Jefferson encountered in France in the 1780s, where a handful of noblemen had engrossed huge tracts of land on which to hunt game, while hordes of the poor went without work and without bread. Jefferson's proposal, characteristically phrased in terms of natural right, was for the poor to appropriate the uncultivated lands of the nobility. And he drew for the United States his usual lesson of the need to keep land widely distributed among the people.[16]

Madison's answer, which is less well known than Jefferson's letter, raised the question whether it was possible to eliminate the idle poor in any country as fully populated as France. Spread the land among them in good republican fashion and there would still be, Madison thought, "a great surplus of inhabitants, a greater by far than will be employed in cloathing both themselves and those who feed them. . . ." In spite of those occupied in trades and as mariners, soldiers, and so on, there would remain a mass of men without work. "A certain degree of misery," Madison concluded, "seems inseparable from a high degree of populousness."[17] He did not, however, go on to propose, as Fletcher had done, that the miserable and idle poor be reduced to slavery.

The situation contemplated by Madison and confronted by Fletcher was not irrelevant to those who were planning the future of the American republic. In a country where population grew by geometric progression, it was not too early to think about a time when there might be vast numbers of landless poor, when there might be those mobs in great cities that Jefferson feared as sores on the body politic. In the United States as Jefferson and Madison knew it, the urban labor force as yet posed no threat, because it was small; and the agricultural labor force was, for the most part, already enslaved. In Revolutionary America, among men who spent their lives working for other men rather than working for themselves, slaves probably constituted a majority.[18] In Virginia they constituted a large majority.[19] If

Jefferson and Madison, not to mention Washington, were unhappy about that fact and yet did nothing to alter it, they may have been restrained, in part at least, by thoughts of the role that might be played in the United States by a large mass of free laborers.

When Jefferson contemplated the abolition of slavery, he found it inconceivable that the freed slaves should be allowed to remain in the country.[20] In this attitude he was probably moved by his or his countrymen's racial prejudice. But he may also have had in mind the possibility that when slaves ceased to be slaves, they would become instead a half million idle poor, who would create the same problems for the United States that the idle poor of Europe did for their states. The slave, accustomed to compulsory labor, would not work to support himself when the compulsion was removed. This was a commonplace among Virginia planters before the creation of the republic and long after. "If you free the slaves," wrote Landon Carter, two days after the Declaration of Independence, "you must send them out of the country or they must steal for their support."[21]

Jefferson's plan for freeing his own slaves (never carried out) included an interim educational period in which they would have been half-taught, half-compelled to support themselves on rented land; for without guidance and preparation for self support, he believed, slaves could not be expected to become fit members of a republican society.[22] And St. George Tucker, who drafted detailed plans for freeing Virginia's slaves, worried about "the possibility of their becoming idle, dissipated, and finally a numerous banditti, instead of turning their attention to industry and labour." He therefore included in his plans a provision for compelling the labor of the freedmen on an annual basis. "For we must not lose sight of this important consideration," he said, "that these people must be *bound* to labour, if they do not *voluntarily* engage therein. . . . In absolving them from the yoke of slavery, we must not forget the interests of society. Those interests require the exertions of every individual in some mode or other; and those who have not wherewith to support themselves honestly without corporal labour, whatever be their complexion, ought to be compelled to labour."[23]

It is plain that Tucker, the would-be emancipator, distrusted the idle poor regardless of color. And it seems probable that the Revolutionary champions of liberty who acquiesced in the continued slavery of black labor did so not only because of racial prejudice but also because they shared with Tucker a distrust of the poor that was inherent in eighteenth-century conceptions of republican liberty. Their historical guidebooks had made them fear to enlarge the free labor force.

That fear, I believe, had a second point of origin in the experience of the American colonists, and especially of Virginians, during the preceding century and a half. If we turn now to the previous history of Virginia's labor force, we may find, I think, some further clues to the distrust of free labor among Revolutionary republicans and to the paradoxical rise of slavery and freedom together in colonial America.

The story properly begins in England with the burst of population growth there that sent the number of Englishmen from perhaps three million in 1500 to four-and-one-half million by 1650.[24] The increase did not occur in response to any corresponding growth in the capacity of the island's economy to support its people. And the result was precisely that misery which Madison pointed out to Jefferson as the consequence of "a high degree of populousness." Sixteenth-century England knew the same kind of unemployment and poverty that Jefferson witnessed in eighteenth-century France and Fletcher in seventeenth-century Scotland. Alarming numbers of idle and hungry men drifted about the country looking for work or plunder. The government did what it could to make men of means hire them, but it also adopted increasingly severe measures against their wandering, their thieving, their roistering, and indeed their very existence. Whom the workhouses and prisons could not swallow the gallows would have to, or perhaps the army. When England had military expeditions to conduct abroad, every parish packed off its most unwanted inhabitants to the almost certain death that awaited them from the diseases of the camp.[25]

As the mass of idle rogues and beggars grew and increasingly threatened the peace of England, the efforts to cope with them increasingly threatened the liberties of Englishmen. Englishmen prided themselves on a "gentle government,"[26] a government that had been releasing its subjects from old forms of bondage and endowing them with new liberties, making the "rights of Englishmen" a phrase to conjure with. But there was nothing gentle about the government's treatment of the poor; and as more Englishmen became poor, other Englishmen had less to be proud of. Thoughtful men could see an obvious solution: get the surplus Englishmen out of England. Send them to the New World, where there were limitless opportunities for work. There they would redeem themselves, enrich the mother country, and spread English liberty abroad.

The great publicist for this program was Richard Hakluyt. His *Principall Navigations, Voiages and Discoveries of the English nation*[27] was not merely the narrative of voyages by Englishmen around the globe, but a powerful suggestion that the world ought to be English or at least ought to be ruled by Englishmen. Hakluyt's was a dream of empire, but of benevolent empire, in which England would confer the blessings of her own free government on the less fortunate peoples of the world. It is doubtless true that Englishmen, along with other Europeans, were already imbued with prejudice against men of darker complexions than their own. And it is also true that the principal beneficiaries of Hakluyt's empire would be Englishmen. But Hakluyt's dream cannot be dismissed as mere hypocrisy any more than Jefferson's affirmation of human equality can be so dismissed. Hakluyt's compassion for the poor and oppressed was not confined to the English poor, and in Francis Drake's exploits in the Caribbean Hakluyt saw, not a thinly disguised form of piracy, but a model for English liberation of men of all colors who labored under the tyranny of the Spaniard.

Drake had gone ashore at Panama in 1572 and made friends with an extraordinary band of runaway Negro slaves. "Cimarrons" they were called, and they lived a free and hardy life in the wilderness, periodically raiding the Spanish settlements to carry off more of their people. They discovered in Drake a man who hated the Spanish as much as they did and who had the arms and men to mount a stronger attack than they could manage by themselves. Drake wanted Spanish gold, and the Cimarrons wanted Spanish iron for tools. They both wanted Spanish deaths. The alliance was a natural one and apparently untroubled by racial prejudice. Together the English and the Cimarrons robbed the mule train carrying the annual supply of Peruvian treasure across the isthmus. And before Drake sailed for England with his loot, he arranged for future meetings.[28] When Hakluyt heard of this alliance, he concocted his first colonizing proposal, a scheme for seizing the Straits of Magellan and transporting Cimarrons there, along with surplus Englishmen. The straits would be a strategic strong point for England's world empire, since they controlled the route from Atlantic to Pacific. Despite the severe climate of the place, the Cimarrons and their English friends would all live warmly together, clad in English woolens, "well lodged and by our nation made free from the tyrannous Spanyard, and quietly and courteously governed by our nation."[29]

The scheme for a colony in the Straits of Magellan never worked out, but Hakluyt's vision endured, of liberated natives and surplus Englishmen, courteously governed in English colonies around the world. Sir Walter Raleigh caught the vision. He dreamt of wresting the treasure of the Incas from the Spaniard by allying with the Indians of Guiana and sending Englishmen to live with them, lead them in rebellion against Spain, and govern them in the English manner.[30] Raleigh also dreamt of a similar colony in the country he named Virginia. Hakluyt helped him plan it.[31] And Drake stood ready to supply Negroes and Indians, liberated from Spanish tyranny in the Caribbean, to help the enterprise.[32]

Virginia from the beginning was conceived not only as a haven for England's suffering poor, but as a spearhead of English liberty in an oppressed world. That was the dream; but when it began to materialize at Roanoke Island in 1585, something went wrong. Drake did his part by liberating Spanish Caribbean slaves, and carrying to Roanoke those who wished to join him.[33] But the English settlers whom Raleigh sent there proved unworthy of the role assigned them. By the time Drake arrived they had shown themselves less than courteous to the Indians on whose assistance they depended. The first group of settlers murdered the chief who befriended them, and then gave up and ran for home aboard Drake's returning ships. The second group simply disappeared, presumably killed by the Indians.[34]

What was lost in this famous lost colony was more than the band of colonists who have never been traced. What was also lost and never quite recovered in subsequent ventures was the dream of Englishman and Indian living side by side in peace and liberty. When the English finally planted a permanent colony at Jamestown they came as conquerors, and their government was far from gentle. The Indians willing to endure it were too few in numbers and too broken in spirit to play a significant part in the settlement.

Without their help, Virginia offered a bleak alternative to the workhouse or the gallows for the first English poor who were transported there. During the first two decades of the colony's existence, most of the arriving immigrants found precious little English liberty in Virginia.[35] But by the 1630s the colony seemed to be working out, at least in part, as its first planners had hoped. Impoverished Englishmen were arriving every year in large numbers, engaged to serve the existing planters for a term of years, with the prospect of setting up their own households a few years later. The settlers were spreading up Virginia's great rivers, carving out plantations, living comfortably from their corn fields and from the cattle they ranged in the forests, and at the same time earning perhaps ten or twelve pounds a year per man from the tobacco they planted. A representative legislative assembly secured the traditional liberties of Englishmen and enabled a larger proportion of the population to participate in their own government than had ever been the case in England. The colony even began to look a little like the cosmopolitan haven of liberty that Hakluyt had first envisaged. Men of all countries appeared there: French, Spanish, Dutch, Turkish, Portuguese, and African.[36] Virginia took them in and began to make Englishmen out of them.

It seems clear that most of the Africans, perhaps all of them, came as slaves, a status that had become obsolete in England, while it was becoming the expected condition of Africans outside Africa and of a good many inside.[37] It is equally clear that a substantial number of Virginia's Negroes were free or became free. And all of them, whether servant, slave, or free, enjoyed most of the same rights and duties as other Virginians. There is no evidence during the period before 1660 that they were subjected to a more severe discipline than other servants. They could sue and be sued in court. They did penance in the parish church for having illegitimate children. They earned money of their own, bought and sold and raised cattle of their own. Sometimes they bought their own freedom. In other cases, masters bequeathed them not only freedom but land, cattle, and houses.[38]

Northampton, the only county for which full records exist, had at least ten free Negro households by 1668.[39]

As Negroes took their place in the community, they learned English ways, including even the truculence toward authority that has always been associated with the rights of Englishmen. Tony Longo, a free Negro of Northampton, when served a warrant to appear as a witness in court, responded with a scatological opinion of warrants, called the man who served it an idle rascal, and told him to go about his business. The man offered to go with him at any time before a justice of the peace so that his evidence could be recorded. He would go with him at night, tomorrow, the next day, next week, any time. But Longo was busy getting in his corn. He dismissed all pleas with a "Well, well, Ile goe when my Corne is in," and refused to receive the warrant.[40]

The judges understandably found this to be contempt of court; but it was the kind of contempt that free Englishmen often showed to authority, and it was combined with a devotion to work that English moralists were doing their best to inculcate more widely in England. As England had absorbed people of every nationality over the centuries and turned them into Englishmen, Virginia's Englishmen were absorbing their own share of foreigners, including Negroes, and seemed to be successfully moulding a New World community on the English model.

But a closer look will show that the situation was not quite so promising as at first it seems. It is well known that Virginia in its first fifteen or twenty years killed off most of the men who went there. It is less well known that it continued to do so. If my estimate of the volume of immigration is anywhere near correct, Virginia must have been a death trap for at least another fifteen years and probably for twenty or twenty-five. In 1625 the population stood at 1,300 or 1,400; in 1640 it was about 8,000.[41] In the fifteen years between those dates at least 15,000 persons must have come to the colony.[42] If so, 15,000 immigrants increased the population by less than 7,000. There is no evidence of a large return migration. It seems probable that the death rate throughout this period was comparable only to that found in Europe during the peak years of a plague. Virginia, in other words, was absorbing England's surplus laborers mainly by killing them. The success of those who survived and rose from servant to planter must be attributed partly to the fact that so few did survive.

After 1640, when the diseases responsible for the high death rate began to decline and the population began a quick rise, it became increasingly difficult for an indigent immigrant to pull himself up in the world. The population probably passed 25,000 by 1662,[43] hardly what Madison would have called a high degree of populousness. Yet the rapid rise brought serious trouble for Virginia. It brought the engrossment of tidewater land in thousands and tens of thousands of acres by speculators, who recognized that the demand would rise.[44] It brought a huge expansion of tobacco production, which helped to depress the price of tobacco and the earnings of the men who planted it.[45] It brought efforts by planters to prolong the terms of servants, since they were now living longer and therefore had a longer expectancy of usefulness.[46]

It would, in fact, be difficult to assess all the consequences of the increased longevity; but for our purposes one development was crucial, and that was the appearance in Virginia of a growing number of freemen who had served their terms but who were now unable to afford land of their own except on the frontiers or in the interior. In years when tobacco prices were especially low or crops especially poor, men who had been just scraping by were obliged to go back to work for their larger neighbors simply in order to stay alive. By 1676 it was estimated that one fourth of Virginia's freemen were without land of their own.[47] And in the same year Francis Moryson, a member of the governor's council, explained the term "freedmen" as used in Virginia to mean "persons without house and land," implying that this was now the normal condition of servants who had attained freedom.[48]

Some of them resigned themselves to working for wages; others preferred a meager living on dangerous frontier land or a hand-to-mouth existence, roaming from one county to another, renting a bit of land here, squatting on some there, dodging the tax collector, drinking, quarreling, stealing hogs, and enticing servants to run away with them.

The presence of this growing class of poverty-stricken Virginians was not a little frightening to the planters who had made it to the top or who had arrived in the colony already at the top, with ample supplies of servants and capital. They were caught in a dilemma. They wanted the immigrants who kept pouring in every year. Indeed they needed them and prized them the more as they lived longer. But as more and more turned free each year, Virginia seemed to have inherited the problem that she was helping England to solve. Virginia, complained Nicholas Spencer, secretary of the colony, was "a sinke to drayen England of her filth and scum."[49]

The men who worried the uppercrust looked even more dangerous in Virginia than they had in England. They were, to begin with, young, because it was young persons that the planters wanted for work in the fields; and the young have always seemed impatient of control by their elders and superiors, if not downright rebellious. They were also predominantly single men. Because the planters did not think women, or at least English women, fit for work in the fields, men outnumbered women among immigrants by three or four to one throughout the century.[50] Consequently most of the freedmen had no wife or family to tame their wilder impulses and serve as hostages to the respectable world.

Finally, what made these wild young men particularly dangerous was that they were armed and had to be armed. Life in Virginia required guns. The plantations were exposed to attack from Indians by land and from privateers and petty-thieving pirates by sea.[51] Whenever England was at war with the French or the Dutch, the settlers had to be ready to defend themselves. In 1667 the Dutch in a single raid captured twenty merchant ships in the James River, together with the English warship that was supposed to be defending them; and in 1673 they captured eleven more. On these occasions Governor William Berkeley gathered the planters in arms and at least prevented the enemy from making a landing. But while he stood off the Dutch he worried about the ragged crew at his back. Of the able-bodied men in the colony he estimated that "at least one third are Single freedmen (whose Labour will hardly maintaine them) or men much in debt, both which wee may reasonably expect upon any Small advantage the Enemy may gaine upon us, wold revolt to them in hopes of bettering their Condicion by Shareing the Plunder of the Country with them."[52]

Berkeley's fears were justified. Three years later, sparked not by a Dutch invasion but by an Indian attack, rebellion swept Virginia. It began almost as Berkeley had predicted, when a group of volunteer Indian fighters turned from a fruitless expedition against the Indians to attack their rulers. Bacon's Rebellion was the largest popular rising in the colonies before the American Revolution. Sooner or later nearly everyone in Virginia got in on it, but it began in the frontier counties of Henrico and New Kent, among men whom the governor and his friends consistently characterized as rabble.[53] As it spread eastward, it turned out that there were rabble everywhere, and Berkeley understandably raised his estimate of their numbers. "How miserable that man is," he exclaimed, "that Governes a People wher six parts of seaven at least are Poore Endebted Discontented and Armed."[54]

Virginia's poor had reason to be envious and angry against the men who owned the land and imported the servants and ran the government. But the rebellion produced no real program of reform, no ideology, not even any revolutionary slogans. It was a search for plunder, not for principles. And when the rebels had redistributed whatever wealth they could lay their hands on, the rebellion subsided almost as quickly as it had begun.

It had been a shattering experience, however, for Virginia's first families. They had seen each other fall in with the rebels in order to save their skins or their possessions or even to share in the plunder. When it was over, they eyed one another distrustfully, on the lookout for any new Bacons in their midst, who might be tempted to lead the still restive rabble on more plundering expeditions. When William Byrd and Laurence Smith proposed to solve the problems of defense against the Indians by establishing semi-independent buffer settlements on the upper reaches of the rivers, in each of which they would engage to keep fifty men in arms, the assembly at first reacted favorably. But it quickly occurred to the governor and council that this would in fact mean gathering a crowd of Virginia's wild bachelors and furnishing them with an abundant supply of arms and ammunition. Byrd had himself led such a crowd in at least one plundering foray during the rebellion. To put him or anyone else in charge of a large and permanent gang of armed men was to invite them to descend again on the people whom they were supposed to be protecting.[55]

The nervousness of those who had property worth plundering continued throughout the century, spurred in 1682 by the tobacco-cutting riots in which men roved about destroying crops in the fields, in the desperate hope of producing a shortage that would raise the price of the leaf.[56] And periodically in nearby Maryland and North Carolina, where the same conditions existed as in Virginia, there were tumults that threatened to spread to Virginia.[57]

As Virginia thus acquired a social problem analagous to England's own, the colony began to deal with it as England had done, by restricting the liberties of those who did not have the proper badge of freedom, namely the property that government was supposed to protect. One way was to extend the terms of service for servants entering the colony without indentures. Formerly they had served until twenty-one; now the age was advanced to twenty-four.[58] There had always been laws requiring them to serve extra time for running away; now the laws added corporal punishment and, in order to make habitual offenders more readily recognizable, specified that their hair be cropped.[59] New laws restricted the movement of servants on the highways and also increased the amount of extra time to be served for running away. In addition to serving two days for every day's absence, the captured runaway was now frequently required to compensate by labor for the loss to the crop that he had failed to tend and for the cost of his apprehension, including rewards paid for his capture.[60] A three weeks' holiday might result in a years extra service.[61] If a servant struck his master, he was to serve another year.[62] For killing a hog he had to serve the owner a year and the informer another year. Since the owner of the hog, and the owner of the servant, and the informer were frequently the same man, and since a hog was worth at best less than one tenth the hire of a servant for a year, the law was very profitable to masters. One Lancaster master was awarded six years extra service from a servant who killed three of his hogs, worth about thirty shillings.[63]

The effect of these measures was to keep servants for as long as possible from gaining their freedom, especially the kind of servants who were most likely to cause trouble. At the same time the engrossment of land was driving many back to servitude after a brief taste of freedom. Freedmen who engaged to work for wages by so doing became servants again, subject to most of the same restrictions as other servants.

Nevertheless, in spite of all the legal and economic pressures to keep men in service, the ranks of the freedmen grew, and so did poverty and discontent. To prevent the wild bachelors from gaining an influence in the government, the assembly in 1670 limited voting to landholders and householders.[64] But to disfranchise the growing mass of single freemen was not to deprive them of the weapons they had wielded so effectively under Nathaniel Bacon. It is questionable how far Virginia could safely have continued along this course, meeting discontent with repression and manning her plantations with annual importations of servants who would later add to the unruly ranks of the free. To be sure, the men at the bottom might have had both land and liberty, as the settlers of some other colonies did, if Virginia's frontier had been safe from Indians, or if the men at the top had been willing to forego some of their profits and to give up some of the lands they had engrossed. The English government itself made efforts to break up the great holdings that had helped to create the problem.[65] But it is unlikely that the policy makers in Whitehall would have contended long against the successful.

In any case they did not have to. There was another solution, which allowed Virginia's magnates to keep their lands, yet arrested the discontent and the repression of other Englishmen, a solution which strengthened the rights of Englishmen and nourished that attachment to liberty which came to fruition in the Revolutionary generation of Virginia statesmen. But the solution put an end to the process of turning Africans into Englishmen. The rights of Englishmen were preserved by destroying the rights of Africans.

I do not mean to argue that Virginians deliberately turned to African Negro slavery as a means of preserving and extending the rights of Englishmen. Winthrop Jordan has suggested that slavery came to Virginia as an unthinking decision.[66] We might go further and say that it came without a decision. It came automatically as Virginians bought the cheapest labor they could get. Once Virginia's heavy mortality ceased, an investment in slave labor was much more profitable than an investment in free labor; and the planters bought slaves as rapidly as traders made them available. In the last years of the seventeenth century they bought them in such numbers that slaves probably already constituted a majority or nearly a majority of the labor force by 1700.[67] The demand was so great that traders for a time found a better market in Virginia than in Jamaica or Barbados.[68] But the social benefits of an enslaved labor force, even if not consciously sought or recognized at the time by the men who bought the slaves, were larger than the economic benefits. The increase in the importation of slaves was matched by a decrease in the importation of indentured servants and consequently a decrease in the dangerous number of new freedmen who annually emerged seeking a place in society that they would be unable to achieve.[69]

If Africans had been unavailable, it would probably have proved impossible to devise a way to keep a continuing supply of English immigrants in their place. There was a limit beyond which the abridgment of English liberties would have resulted not merely in rebellion but in protests from England and in the cutting off of the supply of further servants. At the time of Bacon's Rebellion the English commission of investigation had shown more sympathy with the rebels than with the well-to-do planters who had engrossed Virginia's lands. To have attempted the enslavement of English-born laborers would have caused more disorder than it cured. But to keep as slaves black men who arrived in that condition *was* possible and apparently regarded as plain common sense.

The attitude of English officials was well expressed by the attorney who reviewed for the Privy Council the slave codes established in Barbados in 1679. He found the laws of Barbados to be well designed for the good of his majesty's subjects there, for, he said, "although Negros in that Island are punishable in a different and more severe manner than other Subjects are for Offences of the like nature; yet I humbly conceive that the Laws there concerning Negros are reasonable Laws, for by reason of their numbers they become dangerous, and being a brutish sort of People and reckoned as goods and chattels in that Island, it is of necessity or at least convenient to have Laws for the Government of them different from the Laws of England, to prevent the great mischief that otherwise may happen to the Planters and Inhabitants in that Island."[70] In Virginia too it seemed convenient and reasonable to have different laws for black and white. As the number of slaves increased, the assembly passed laws that carried forward with much greater severity the trend already under way in the colony's labor laws. But the new severity was reserved for people without white skin. The laws specifically exonerated the master who accidentally beat his slave to death, but they placed new limitations on his punishment of "Christian white servants."[71]

Virginians worried about the risk of having in their midst a body of men who had every reason to hate them.[72] The fear of a slave insurrection hung over them for nearly two centuries. But the danger from slaves actually proved to be less than that which the colony had faced from its restive and armed freedmen. Slaves had none of the rising expectations that so often produce human discontent. No one had told them that they had rights. They had been nurtured in heathen societies where they had lost their freedom; their children would be nurtured in a Christian society and never know freedom.

Moreover, slaves were less troubled by the sexual imbalance that helped to make Virginia's free laborers so restless. In an enslaved labor force women could be required to make tobacco just as the men did; and they also made children, who in a few years would be an asset to their master. From the beginning, therefore, traders imported women in a much higher ratio to men than was the case among English servants,[73] and the level of discontent was correspondingly reduced. Virginians did not doubt that discontent would remain, but it could be repressed by methods that would not have been considered reasonable, convenient, or even safe, if applied to Englishmen. Slaves could be deprived of opportunities for association and rebellion. They could be kept unarmed and unorganized. They could be subjected to savage punishments by their owners without fear of legal reprisals. And since their color disclosed their probable status, the rest of society could keep close watch on them. It is scarcely surprising that no slave insurrection in American history approached Bacon's Rebellion in its extent or in its success.

Nor is it surprising that Virginia's freedmen never again posed a threat to society. Though in later years slavery was condemned because it was thought to compete with free labor, in the beginning it reduced by so much the number of freedmen who would otherwise have competed with each other. When the annual increment of freedmen fell off, the number that remained could more easily find an independent place in society, especially as the danger of Indian attack diminished and made settlement safer at the heads of the rivers or on the Carolina frontier. There might still remain a number of irredeemable, idle, and unruly freedmen, particularly among the convicts whom England exported to the colonies. But the numbers were small enough, so that they could be dealt with by the old expedient of drafting them for military expeditions.[74] The way was thus made easier for the remaining freedmen to acquire property, maybe acquire a slave or two of their own, and join with their superiors in the enjoyment of those English liberties that differentiated them from their black laborers.

A free society divided between large landholders and small was much less riven by antagonisms than one divided between landholders and landless, masterless men. With the freedman's expectations, sobriety, and status restored, he was no longer a man to be feared. That fact, together with the presence of a growing mass of alien slaves, tended to draw the white settlers closer together and to reduce the importance of the class difference between yeoman farmer and large plantation owner.[75]

The seventeenth century has sometimes been thought of as the day of the yeoman farmer in Virginia; but in many ways a stronger case can be made for the eighteenth century as the time when the yeoman farmer came into his own, because slavery relieved the small man of the pressures that had been reducing him to continued servitude. Such an interpretation conforms to the political development of the colony. During the seventeenth century the royally appointed governor's council, composed of the largest property-owners in the colony, had been the most powerful governing body. But as the tide of slavery rose between 1680 and 1720 Virginia moved toward a government in which the yeoman farmer had a larger share. In spite of the rise of Virginia's great families on the black tide, the power of the council declined; and the elective House of Burgesses became the dominant organ of government. Its members nurtured a closer relationship with their yeoman constituency than had earlier been the case.[76] And in its chambers Virginians developed the ideas they so fervently asserted in the Revolution: ideas about taxation, representation, and the rights of Englishmen, and ideas about the prerogatives and powers and sacred calling of the independent, property-holding yeoman farmer—commonwealth ideas.

In the eighteenth century, because they were no longer threatened by a dangerous free laboring class, Virginians could afford these ideas, whereas in Berkeley's time they could not. Berkeley himself was obsessed with the experience of the English civil wars and the danger of rebellion. He despised and feared the New Englanders for their association with the Puritans who had made England, however briefly, a commonwealth.[77] He was proud that Virginia, unlike New England, had no free schools and no printing press, because books and schools bred heresy and sedition.[78] He must have taken satisfaction in the fact that when his people did rebel against him under Bacon, they generated no republican ideas, no philosophy of rebellion or of human rights. Yet a century later, without benefit of rebellions, Virginians had learned republican lessons, had introduced schools and printing presses, and were as ready as New Englanders to recite the aphorisms of the commonwealthmen.

It was slavery, I suggest, more than any other single factor, that had made the difference, slavery that enabled Virginia to nourish representative government in a plantation society, slavery that transformed the Virginia of Governor Berkeley to the Virginia of Jefferson, slavery that made the Virginians dare to speak a political language that magnified the rights of freemen, and slavery, therefore, that brought Virginians into the same commonwealth political tradition with New Englanders. The very institution that was to divide North and South after the Revolution may have made possible their union in a republican government.

Thus began the American paradox of slavery and freedom, intertwined and interdependent, the rights of Englishmen supported on the wrongs of Africans. The American Revolution only made the contradictions more glaring, as the slaveholding colonists proclaimed to a candid world the rights not simply of Englishmen but of all men. To explain the origin of the contradictions, if the explanation I have suggested is valid, does not eliminate them or make them less ugly. But it may enable us to understand a little better the strength of the ties that bound freedom to slavery, even in so noble a mind as Jefferson's. And it may perhaps make us wonder about the ties that bind more devious tyrannies to our own freedoms and give us still today our own American paradox.

1. Particularly Staughton Lynd, *Class Conflict, Slavery, and the United States Constitution: Ten Essays* (Indianapolis, 1967).

2. Curtis P. Nettels, *The Emergence of a National Economy 1775–1815* (New York, 1962), 19. See also Merrill Jensen, "The American Revolution and American Agriculture," *Agricultural History*, XLIII (Jan. 1969), 107–24.

3. William Cohen, "Thomas Jefferson and the Problem of Slavery," *Journal of American History*, LVI (Dec. 1969), 503–26; D. B. Davis, *Was Thomas Jefferson An Authentic Enemy of Slavery?* (Oxford, 1970); Winthrop D. Jordan, *White over Black: American Attitudes Toward the Negro, 1550–1812* (Chapel Hill, 1968), 429–81.

4. Julian P. Boyd, ed., *The Papers of Thomas Jefferson* (18 vols., Princeton, 1950–   ), X, 615. For other expressions of Thomas Jefferson's aversion to debt and distrust of credit, both private and public, see *ibid.*, II, 275–76, VIII, 398–99, 632–33, IX, 217–18, 472–73, X, 304–05, XI, 472, 633, 636, 640, XII, 385–86.

5. Jefferson's career as ambassador to France was occupied very largely by unsuccessful efforts to break the hold of British creditors on American commerce.

6. See Caroline Robbins, *The Eighteenth-Century Commonwealthman: Studies in the Transmission, Development and Circumstance of English Liberal Thought from the Restoration of Charles II until the War with the Thirteen Colonies* (Cambridge, Mass., 1959); J. G. A. Pocock, "Machiavelli, Harrington, and English Political Ideologies in the Eighteenth Century," *William and Mary Quarterly*, XXII (Oct. 1965), 549–83.

7. Boyd, ed., *Papers of Thomas Jefferson*, I, 344, 352, 362, 560, VIII, 681–82.

8. *Ibid.*, VIII, 426, 682; Thomas Jefferson, *Notes on the State of Virginia*, William Peden, ed. (Chapel Hill, 1955), 165. Jefferson seems to have overlooked the dependence of Virginia's farmers on the casualties and caprice of the tobacco market.

9. See Robbins, *The Eighteenth-Century Commonwealthman*; Pocock, "Machiavelli, Harrington, and English Political Ideologies," 549–83; Michael Zuckerman, "The Social Context of Democracy in Massachusetts," *William and Mary Quarterly*, XXV (Oct. 1968), 523–44; Robert M. Weir, "'The Harmony We Were Famous For': An Interpretation of Pre-Revolutionary South Carolina Politics," *ibid.*, XXVI (Oct. 1969), 473–501.

10. C. B. Macpherson, *The Political Theory of Possessive Individualism* (Oxford, 1962), 221–24; H. R. Fox Bourne, *The Life of John Locke* (2 vols., London, 1876), II, 377–90.

11. Adam Ferguson, *The History of the Progress and Termination of the Roman Republic* (5 vols., Edinburgh, 1799), I, 384. See also Adam Ferguson, *An Essay on the History of Civil Society* (London, 1768), 309–11.

12. Francis Hutcheson, *A System of Moral Philosophy* (2 vols., London, 1755), II, 202; David B. Davis, *The Problem of Slavery in Western Culture* (Ithaca, 1966), 374–78. I am indebted to David B. Davis for several valuable suggestions.

13. James Burgh, *Political Disquisitions: Or, An ENQUIRY into public Errors, Defects, and Abuses . . .* (3 vols., London, 1774–1775), III, 220–21. See the proposal of Bishop George Berkeley that "sturdy beggars should . . . be seized and made slaves to the public for a certain term of years." Quoted in R. H. Tawney, *Religion and the Rise of Capitalism: A Historical Essay* (New York, 1926), 270.

14. E. Millicent Sowerby, ed., *Catalogue of the Library of Thomas Jefferson* (5 vols., Washington, 1952–1959), I, 192.

15. Andrew Fletcher, *Two Discourses Concerning the Affairs of Scotland; Written in the Year 1698* (Edinburgh, 1698). See second discourse (separately paged), 1–33, especially 16.

16. Boyd, ed., *Papers of Thomas Jefferson*, VIII, 681–83.

17. *Ibid.*, IX, 659–60.

18. Jackson Turner Main, *The Social Structure of Revolutionary America* (Princeton, 1965), 271.

19. In 1755, Virginia had 43,329 white tithables and 60,078 black. Tithables included white men over sixteen years of age and black men and women over sixteen. In the census of 1790, Virginia had 292,717 slaves and 110,936 white males over sixteen, out of a total population of 747,680. Evarts B. Greene and Virginia D. Harrington, *American Population before the Federal Census of 1790* (New York, 1932), 150–55.

20. Jefferson, *Notes on the State of Virginia*, 138.

21. Jack P. Greene, ed., *The Diary of Colonel Landon Carter of Sabine Hall, 1752–1778* (2 vols., Charlottesville, 1965), II, 1055.

22. Boyd, ed., *Papers of Thomas Jefferson*, XIV, 492–93.

23. St. George Tucker, *A Dissertation on Slavery with a Proposal for the Gradual Abolition of It, in the State of Virginia* (Philadelphia, 1796). See also Jordan, *White over Black*, 555–60.

24. Joan Thrisk, ed., *The Agrarian History of England and Wales*, Vol. IV: *1500–1640* (Cambridge, England, 1967), 531.

25. See Edmund S. Morgan, "The Labor Problem at Jamestown, 1607–18," *American Historical Review*, 76 (June 1971), 595–611, especially 600–06.

26. This is Richard Hakluyt's phrase. See E. G. R. Taylor, ed., *The Original Writings & Correspondence of the Two Richard Hakluyts* (2 vols., London, 1935), I, 142.

27. Richard Hakluyt, *The Principall Navigations, Voiages and Discoveries of the English nation* . . . (London, 1589).

28. The whole story of this extraordinary episode is to be found in I. A. Wright, ed., *Documents Concerning English Voyages to the Spanish Main 1569–1580* (London, 1932).

29. Taylor, ed., *Original Writings & Correspondence*, I, 139–46.

30. Walter Raleigh, *The Discoverie of the large and bewtiful Empire of Guiana*, V. T. Harlow, ed. (London, 1928), 138–49; V. T. Harlow, ed., *Ralegh's Last Voyage: Being an account drawn out of contemporary letters and relations* . . . (London, 1932), 44–45.

31. Taylor, ed., *Original Writings & Correspondence*, II, 211–377, especially 318.

32. Irene A. Wright, trans. and ed., *Further English Voyages to Spanish America, 1583–1594: Documents from the Archives of the Indies at Seville* . . . (London, 1951), lviii, lxiii, lxiv, 37, 52, 54, 55, 159, 172, 173, 181, 188–89, 204–06.

33. The Spanish reported that "Although their masters were willing to ransom them the English would not give them up except when the slaves themselves desired to go." *Ibid.*, 159. On Walter Raleigh's later expedition to Guiana, the Spanish noted that the English told the natives "that they did not desire to make them slaves, but only to be their friends; promising to bring them great quantities of hatchets and knives, and especially if they drove the Spaniards out of their territories." Harlow, ed., *Ralegh's Last Voyage*, 179.

34. David Beers Quinn, ed., *The Roanoke Voyages 1584–1590* (2 vols., London, 1955).

35. Morgan, "The Labor Problem at Jamestown, 1607–18," pp. 595–611; Edmund S. Morgan, "The First American Boom: Virginia 1618 to 1630," *William and Mary Quarterly*, XXVIII (April 1971), 169–98.

36. There are no reliable records of immigration, but the presence of persons of these nationalities is evident from county court records, where all but the Dutch are commonly identified by name, such as "James the Scotchman," or "Cursory the Turk." The Dutch seem to have anglicized their names at once and are difficult to identify except where the records disclose their naturalization. The two counties for which the most complete records survive for the 1640s and 1650s are Accomack-Northampton and Lower Norfolk. Microfilms are in the Virginia State Library, Richmond.

37. Because the surviving records are so fragmentary, there has been a great deal of controversy about the status of the first Negroes in Virginia. What the records do make clear is that not all were slaves and that not all were free. See Jordan, *White over Black*, 71–82.

38. For examples, see Northampton County Court Records, Deeds, Wills, etc., Book III, f. 83, Book V, ff. 38, 54, 60, 102, 117–19; York County Court Records, Deeds, Orders, Wills, etc., no. 1, ff. 232–34; Surry County Court Records, Deeds, Wills, etc., no. 1, f. 349; Henrico County Court Records, Deeds and Wills 1677–1692, f. 139.

39. This fact has been arrived at by comparing the names of householders on the annual list of tithables with casual identifications of persons as Negroes in the court records. The names of householders so identified for 1668, the peak year during the period for which the lists survive (1662–1677) were: Bastian Cane, Bashaw Ferdinando, John Francisco, Susan Grace, William Harman, Philip Mongum, Francis Pane, Manuel Rodriggus, Thomas Rodriggus, and King Tony. The total number of households in the county in 1668 was 172; total number of tithables 435; total number of tithable free Negroes 17; total number of tithable unfree Negroes 42. Thus nearly 29 percent of tithable Negroes and probably of all Negroes were free; and about 13.5 percent of all tithables were Negroes.

40. Northampton Deeds, Wills, etc., Book V, 54–60 (Nov. 1, 1654).

41. The figure for 1625 derives from the census for that year, which gives 1,210 persons, but probably missed about 10 percent of the population. Morgan, "The First American Boom," 170n–71n. The figure for 1640 is derived from legislation limiting tobacco production per person in 1639–1640. The legislation is summarized in a manuscript belonging to Jefferson, printed in William Waller Hening, *The Statutes at Large; Being a Collection of All the Laws of Virginia, from the First Session of the Legislature, in the Year 1619* (13 vols., New York, 1823), I, 224–25, 228. The full text is in "Acts of the General Assembly, Jan. 6, 1639–40," *William and Mary Quarterly*, IV (Jan. 1924), 17–35, and "Acts of the General Assembly, Jan. 6, 1639–40," *ibid.* (July 1924), 159–62. The assembly calculated that a levy of four pounds of tobacco per tithable would yield 18,584 pounds, implying 4,646 tithables (men over sixteen). It also calculated that a limitation of planting to 170 pounds per poll would yield 1,300,000, implying 7,647 polls. Evidently the latter figure is for the whole population, as is evident also from Hening, *Statutes*, I, 228.

42. In the year 1635, the only year for which such records exist, 2,010 persons embarked for Virginia from London alone. See John Camden Hotten, ed., *The Original Lists of Persons of Quality . . .* (London, 1874), 35–145. For other years casual estimates survive. In February 1627/8 Francis West said that 1,000 had been "lately received."

Colonial Office Group, Class 1, Piece 4, folio 109 (Public Record Office, London). Hereafter cited CO 1/4, f. 109. In February 1633/4 Governor John Harvey said that "this yeares newcomers" had arrived "this yeare." Yong to Sir Tobie Matthew, July 13, 1634, "Aspinwall Papers," *Massachusetts Historical Society Collections*, IX (1871), 110. In May 1635, Samuel Mathews said that 2,000 had arrived "this yeare." Mathews to ?, May 25, 1635, "The Mutiny in Virginia, 1635," *Virginia Magazine of History and Biography*, I (April 1894), 417. And in March 1636, John West said that 1,606 persons had arrived "this yeare." West to Commissioners for Plantations, March 28, 1636, "Virginia in 1636," *ibid.*, IX (July 1901), 37.

43. The official count of tithables for 1662 was 11,838. Clarendon Papers, 82 (Bodleian Library, Oxford). The ratio of tithables to total population by this time was probably about one to two. (In 1625 it was 1 to 1.5; in 1699 it was 1 to 2.7.) Since the official count was almost certainly below the actuality, a total population of roughly 25,000 seems probable. All population figures for seventeenth-century Virginia should be treated as rough estimates.

44. Evidence of the engrossment of lands after 1660 will be found in CO 1/39, f. 196; CO 1/40, f. 23; CO 1/48, f. 48; CO 5/1309, numbers 5, 9, and 23; Sloane Papers, 1008, ff. 334–35 (British Museum, London). A recent count of headrights in patents issued for land in Virginia shows 82,000 headrights claimed in the years from 1635 to 1700. Of these nearly 47,000 or 57 percent (equivalent to 2,350,000 acres) were claimed in the twenty-five years after 1650. W. F. Craven, *White, Red, and Black: The Seventeenth-Century Virginian* (Charlottesville, 1971), 14–16.

45. No continuous set of figures for Virginia's tobacco exports in the seventeenth century can now be obtained. The available figures for English imports of American tobacco (which was mostly Virginian) are in United States Bureau of the Census, *Historical Statistics of the United States, Colonial Times to 1957* (Washington, D.C., 1960), series Z 238–240, p. 766. They show for 1672 a total of 17,559,000 pounds. In 1631 the figure had been 272,300 pounds. Tobacco crops varied heavily from year to year. Prices are almost as difficult to obtain now as volume. Those for 1667–1675 are estimated from London prices current in Warren Billings, "Virginia's Deploured Condition, 1660–1676: The Coming of Bacon's Rebellion" (doctoral dissertation, Northern Illinois University, 1969), 155–59.

46. See below.

47. Thomas Ludwell and Robert Smith to the king, June 18, 1676, vol. LXXVII, f. 128, Coventry Papers Longleat House, American Council of Learned Societies British Mss. project, reel 63 (Library of Congress).

48. *Ibid.*, 204–05.

49. Nicholas Spencer to Lord Culpeper, Aug. 6, 1676, *ibid.*, 170. See also CO 1/49, f. 107.

50. The figures are derived from a sampling of the names of persons for whom headrights were claimed in land patents. Patent Books I–IX (Virginia State Library, Richmond). Wyndham B. Blanton found 17,350 women and 75,884 men in "a prolonged search of the patent books and other records of the times . . . ," a ratio of 1 woman to 4.4 men. Wyndham B. Blanton, "Epidemics, Real and Imaginary, and other Factors Influencing Seventeenth Century Virginia's Population," *Bulletin of the History of Medicine*, XXXI (Sept.–Oct. 1957), 462. See also Craven, *White, Red, and Black*, 26–27.

51. Pirates were particularly troublesome in the 1680s and 1690s. See CO 1/48, f. 71; CO 1/51, f. 340; CO 1/52, f. 54; CO 1/55, ff. 105–106; CO 1/57, f. 300; CO 5/1311, no. 10.

52. CO 1/30, ff. 114–115.

53. CO 1/37, ff. 35–40.

54. Vol. LXXVII, 144–46, Coventry Papers.

55. Hening, *Statutes*, II, 448–54; CO 1/42, f. 178; CO 1/43, f. 29; CO 1/44, f. 398; CO 1/47, ff. 258–260, 267; CO 1/48, f. 46; vol. LXXVIII, 378–81, 386–87, 398–99, Coventry Papers.

56. CO 1/48 *passim*.

57. CO 1/43, ff. 359–365; CO 1/44, ff. 10–62; CO 1/47, f. 261; CO 1/48, ff. 87–96, 100–102, 185; CO 5/1305, no. 43; CO 5/1309, no. 74.

58. Hening, *Statutes*, II, 113–14, 240.

59. *Ibid.*, II, 266, 278.

60. *Ibid.*, II, 116–17, 273–74, 277–78.

61. For example, James Gray, absent twenty-two days, was required to serve fifteen months extra. Order Book 1666–1680, p. 163, Lancaster County Court Records.

62. Hening, *Statutes*, II, 118.

63. Order Book 1666–1680, p. 142, Lancaster County Court Records.

64. Hening, *Statutes*, II, 280. It had been found, the preamble to the law said, that such persons "haveing little interest in the country doe oftner make tumults at the election to the disturbance of his majesties peace, then by their discretions in their votes provide for the conservasion thereof, by makeing choyce of persons fitly quali-fyed for the discharge of soe greate a trust. . . ."

65. CO 1/39, f. 196; CO 1/48, f. 48; CO 5/1309, nos. 5, 9, 23; CO 5/1310, no. 83.

66. Jordan, *White over Black*, 44–98.

67. In 1700 they constituted half of the labor force (persons working for other men) in Surry County, the only county in which it is possible to ascertain the numbers. Robert Wheeler, "Social Transition in the Virginia Tidewater, 1650–1720: The Laboring Household as an Index," paper delivered at the Organization of American Historians' meeting, New Orleans, April 15, 1971. Surry County was on the south side of the James, one of the least wealthy regions of Virginia.

68. See the letters of the Royal African Company to its ship captains, Oct. 23, 1701; Dec. 2, 1701; Dec. 7, 1704; Dec. 21, 1704; Jan. 25, 1704/5, T70 58 (Public Record Office, London).

69. Abbot Emerson Smith, *Colonists in Bondage: White Servitude and Convict Labor in America 1607–1776* (Chapel Hill, 1947), 335. See also Thomas J. Wertenbaker, *The Planters of Colonial Virginia* (Princeton, 1922), 130–31, 134–35; Craven, *White, Red, and Black*, 17.

70. CO 1/45, f. 138.

71. Hening, *Statutes*, II, 481–82, 492–93; III, 86–88, 102–03, 179–80, 333–35, 447–62.

72. For example, see William Byrd II to the Earl of Egmont, July 12, 1736, in Eliz-abeth Donnan, ed., *Documents Illustrative of the History of the Slave Trade to America* (4 vols., Washington, 1930–1935), IV, 131–32. But compare Byrd's letter to Peter Beck-ford, Dec. 6, 1735, "Letters of the Byrd Family," *Virginia Magazine of History and Bi-ography*, XXXVI (April 1928), 121–23, in which he specifically denies any danger. The

Virginia assembly at various times laid duties on the importation of slaves. See Donnan, ed., *Documents Illustrative of the History of the Slave Trade*, IV, 66–67, 86–88, 91–94, 102–17, 121–31, 132–42. The purpose of some of the acts was to discourage imports, but apparently the motive was to redress the colony's balance of trade after a period during which the planters had purchased far more than they could pay for. See also Wertenbaker, *The Planters of Colonial Virginia*, 129.

73. The Swiss traveler Francis Ludwig Michel noted in 1702 that "Both sexes are usually bought, which increase afterwards." William J. Hinke, trans. and ed., "Report of the Journey of Francis Louis Michel from Berne Switzerland to Virginia, October 2, (1) 1701–December 1, 1702: Part II," *Virginia Magazine of History and Biography*, XXIV (April 1916), 116. A sampling of the names identifiable by sex, for whom headrights were claimed in land patents in the 1680s and 1690s shows a much higher ratio of women to men among blacks than among whites. For example, in the years 1695–1699 (Patent Book 9) I count 818 white men and 276 white women, 376 black men and 220 black women (but compare Craven, *White, Red, and Black*, 99–100). In Northampton County in 1677, among seventy-five black tithables there were thirty-six men, thirty-eight women, and one person whose sex cannot be determined. In Surry County in 1703, among 211 black tithables there were 132 men, seventy-four women, and five persons whose sex cannot be determined. These are the only counties where the records yield such information. Northampton County Court Records, Order Book 10, 189–91; Surry County Court Records, Deeds, Wills, etc., No. 5, part 2, 287–90.

74. Virginia disposed of so many this way in the campaign against Cartagena in 1741 that a few years later the colony was unable to scrape up any more for another expedition. Fairfax Harrison, "When the Convicts Came," *Virginia Magazine of History and Biography*, XXX (July 1922), 250–60, especially 256–57; John W. Shy, "A New Look at Colonial Militia," *William and Mary Quarterly*, XX (April 1963), 175–85. In 1736, Virginia had shipped another batch of unwanted freedmen to Georgia because of a rumored attack by the Spanish. Byrd II to Lord Egmont, July 1736, "Letters of the Byrd Family," *Virginia Magazine of History and Biography*, XXXVI (July 1928), 216–17. Observations by an English traveler who embarked on the same ship suggest that they did not go willingly: "our Lading consisted of all the Scum of Virginia, who had been recruited for the Service of Georgia, and who were ready at every Turn to mutiny, whilst they belch'd out the most shocking Oaths, wishing Destruction to the Vessel and every Thing in her." "Observations in Several Voyages and Travels in America in the Year 1736," *William and Mary Quarterly*, XV (April 1907), 224.

75. Compare Lyon G. Tyler, "Virginians Voting in the Colonial Period," *William and Mary Quarterly*, VI (July 1897), 7–13.

76. John C. Rainbolt, "The Alteration in the Relationship between Leadership and Constituents in Virginia, 1660 to 1720," *William and Mary Quarterly*, XXVII (July 1970), 411–34.

77. William Berkeley to Richard Nicolls, May 20, 1666, May 4, 1667, Additional Mss. 28,218, ff. 14–17 (British Museum, London).

78. Hening, *Statutes*, II, 517.

DARRETT B. AND ANITA H. RUTMAN
The Road

✴ ✴ ✴ ✴ ✴ ✴ ✴ ✴ *T*HE ROAD THAT CONCERNS DARRETT AND ANITA
Rutman ran along the spine of Middlesex County during the last half of the
seventeenth century, connecting its people to one another and to the central places of their lives in church, in chapel, in court, and in taverns. The
road for the Rutmans, moreover, is also a metaphor for the complex networks of intersecting responsibilities and obligations that bound these
people into a community. In its social conditions this community stood
about halfway between the social worlds described by J. Frederick Fausz at
early Jamestown and by Jack Greene for mid-eighteenth-century Virginia.
Martial law and economic coercion clearly defined wartime society in
Virginia in 1609–14. In Jack Greene's Virginia, by contrast, social order
resided within a political culture marked by responsible gentry leadership
and widely adopted patterns of social deference. The world of Middlesex
County also stood about midpoint in the process Edmund Morgan describes in which the seventeenth-century paradox of slavery and freedom
came to be articulated in the republican rhetoric of the American Revolution.

To Darrett and Anita Rutman, however, Middlesex County was *A Place
in Time*, the title of their book in which "The Road" composes a chapter.
Their larger study reconstructs the world of Middlesex from 1650 to 1750,
representing a model of the school of historical thought called the New Social History. Stirred by the cultural and political movements of the 1960s
and the manifest role that the American public played in provoking historical change during these years, younger historians set out to study ordinary
men and women in hopes of connecting their lives, actions, thoughts, and
aspirations to the larger narrative of national history. In writing *A Place in
Time*, Darrett and Anita Rutman analyzed every scrap in the surviving public and private records of Middlesex County and reassembled their notes
into biographies of a remarkable number of people about whom historians
previously knew nothing. Their stories, both individual and collective,
yield stunning insights into the social relations, family life, economic ac-

tivity, and political practice of people otherwise left out of history. In addition, the analysis of the world these people created connects them to the defining events of their day, revealing unexpected conclusions about the causes and course of Bacon's Rebellion and providing grounds for reflection on the meaning Edmund Morgan attaches to this upheaval in the long progress of freedom's struggle with slavery.   * * * * * * * *

* * * * * * * *
As the Dictates of Nature are of Force sufficient for securing the Safety of Particular Beings . . . So the Ties we are under, from the Relation which we bear to Communities, and as we all are link'd together in Society, engage our Care for their Defence, and our Concern for their Welfare. Both the Country where we Live, and the Prince that does Protect us, claim from us a particular Regard for their Interest and Happiness.
—Sir Thomas Grantham, *An Historical Account of Some Memorable Actions . . .*

From the northwest where the county began, the road stretched south and east twenty-two miles as the crow would fly, over thirty-five miles by the course the road actually took, ending only when the land fell away and the waters of the bay began. The road was little more than a broad path, beaten flat by the feet of men and women and the hooves of animals, its red soil so compacted as to discourage all but the hardiest weed from growing. In general, the road kept to the high ground between the rivers. But here and there it dropped into an abrupt declivity to meander in seemingly aimless fashion until a rude timber bridge carried it across a stream or swamp. It was almost as though the first person traversing the ground had searched about for the easiest crossing and all those coming after had followed his track. Sometimes, however, abrupt turnings were the product of manmade, not natural obstacles; for now and again as the road was in the process of becoming a road, some county man, in order to make better use of his land, would block one path with fencing or brush, forcing passersby to beat another.

Dusty in summer, mired by spring rains, laid down with minimal plan, the road nevertheless was part of a reasonable scheme of things. It was the central nerve of the county. The families had originally entered by way of the waterways—the Rappahannock and Piankatank—and the waterways carried their tobacco to markets across the sea. But the road linked them to each other.

As the county formed in late 1668 and early 1669, eighty-three families, just over nine hundred men, women, and children lived on and about the road, and large sections of the county were still unpopulated. In the far northwest, the land to the south and west of the road as far as the Dragon, what would be called Jamaica Land, was virtually empty; the heart of old Lancaster Parish—now the upper precinct—lay between the road and the Rappahannock. Here a spider web of paths and lanes threaded through the woods to join houses to each other, to the road itself, and to the newly built Upper Chapel, high on the ridge between Sunderland and Perrott's creeks. A side road branched northeasterly some five miles below the county line, linking the road to the chapel. Near the juncture, Randolph Seager— Oliver's son—would, late in the 1680s, lay out the county's most prominent racetrack; in 1700 it would be referred to as the "publick Race Ground Commonly Called Seagers."[1] Two miles below, at the Mickleburrough property, the road reached the south branch of Sunderland Creek, the first major barrier across its path. Mickleburrough's bridge carried it across and, two miles further on, the road entered the middle precinct.

Here, in the center of the county, the road branched several times. On the high ground between Rosegill Creek and Dragon Swamp, just above where the courthouse would eventually be built, a path cut abruptly south to cross the Dragon into Gloucester County. At the moment, the route was used only infrequently, for the crossing was dangerous, but there had been talk of building a bridge since 1662, and its construction followed shortly on the formation of the county.[2] A mile beyond this first junction, the road branched again. The main path edged southeasterly toward the Piankatank and on into the lower precinct, traversing an area of alternating hills and swamps—"My Lady's Swamp," "the Beaver Dams"—before emerging onto level ground at the Lower Chapel. Halfway down this course, still another path cut away to a ferry across the Piankatank, the safest way into Glouces- ter before the building of the Dragon Bridge. The second path headed north from the road and onto Wormeley land, now generally called "Rosegill Plantation," turned to parallel the Rappahannock along the heights to reach the Mother Church, then continued on through the Lady Lunsford's "Bran- don Plantation" before looping southward to rejoin the main road just above the chapel.

The Lower Chapel itself stood roughly in the middle of its precinct and here, as in old Lancaster Parish, there was a cluster of relatively small hold- ings joined together by a spider web of subsidiary paths. Through this web, increasingly unrecognizable as anything other than simply another strand, the road stretched eastward, past Skipwith's and Kemp's, finally crossing the "neck of land" that attached the main to Stingray. There on the point it ended.

To a modern traveler along the road, any part of the countryside could only appear desolate, the middle precinct a bit more so than the rest. There the rugged terrain between the main road and the northern loop, an area broken by the headwaters of My Lady's Swamp and the Beaver Dams, was all but empty of people and only vaguely surveyed; small gores of land

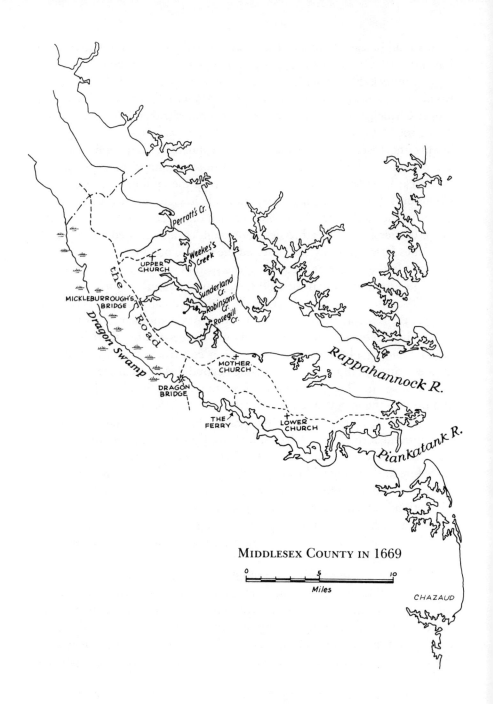

Perrott's Cr.

Weeke's Creek

UPPER
CHURCH

Sunderland
Cr.

Robinson's
Cr.

Rosegill
Cr.

MICKLEBURROUGH'S
BRIDGE

the Road

Dragon Swamp

DRAGON
BRIDGE

MOTHER
CHURCH

THE
FERRY

LOWER
CHURCH

Rappahannock R.

Piankatank R.

CHAZAUD

MIDDLESEX COUNTY IN 1669

0   5   10

Miles

76 * DARRETT B. AND ANITA H. RUTMAN

would still be unclaimed well into the eighteenth century. The northern loop, "the Church path" as it was frequently called, ran for half its length through Rosegill, and while this was the most populated holding in the county—forty-eight tithables in 1668, 10 percent of all the tithables in Middlesex—most were laborers clustered on the several "quarters" of the plantation. The largest of these, that immediately surrounding the Wormeley-Chicheley house, lay on the waterside a mile from the church path. A traveler described it in the mid-1680s as "a rather large village" of "at least twenty houses in a lovely plain along the Rappahannock."[3] But the rest of Rosegill's thousands of acres were woods and natural clearings, broken only here and there by an occasional tenant farm.

In the emptiness of the middle precinct, the paths tended to be routes to places—the road to Mickleburrough's bridge, to the Mother Church, to the Piankatank, to the ferry—in contrast to the upper and lower precincts, where the paths linked families. Everywhere, however, in 1668, the road and its subsidiary paths passed through woods more often than through a landscape improved by man. The experience of a visitor of the 1680s would not have been atypical. Wandering away from his host's home "a simpling"—that is, collecting wild herbs—he soon found himself lost and subsequently wrote home of "gazeing round to spie an opening that is a Plantation."[4]

Even man's improvements would appear rough, crude, desolate to a modern eye, certainly in the spring before the tobacco and corn had grown high enough to hide the stumps among which the planters set their hills. Rail fences surrounded the cultivated fields, the farmers laboriously collecting logs to lay lengthwise as a base for the fence—"great timber trees" one traveler called them, heavy enough "so that piggs may not creep" under and into the crop—then pounding stakes into the ground on either side of the logs so that the stakes leaned against the logs to form forks to carry four or more rails.[5] Tobacco houses were ubiquitous—long, narrow wooden structures in which the tobacco was hung in tiers to dry. In the midst of the railed fields stood the farmers' houses, small framed affairs of unpainted, weathering wood, pleasant enough within (according to another traveler) if the planter were well-enough off to coat his walls with a plaster made from oyster shells and "white as snow," but "ugly from the outside, where only the wood can be seen."[6] More than likely one or the other corner of the house would be sagging. For in a land where stone was scarce, skilled bricklayers few in number and expensive to hire, and capital committed to things conducive to income rather than comfort—to land and laborers and cattle—even the prominent planters eschewed foundation walls. Houses were framed with earthfast posts sunk in the ground and extending upward to the plates supporting the rafters. Or, more commonly as the century progressed, the posts were truncated into piers that held the entire structure above ground. In the first instance, the floor of the house was frequently tamped earth, in the second planks. In either event, deterioration was inevitable. Cedar and cypress posts from the Dragon were the best available, but the best was not always used and even it in time fell prey to dampness or termites or both. Houses, even public buildings, constructed also on wooden piers, were in constant need of repairs, eventually replacement.[7] The glebe house that Christ Church Parish finally provided for its minister illustrates the problem.

Situated in mid-county a half-mile off the road, between the road and Rosegill Creek, the house was probably built by Cuthbert Potter in the late 1650s, conveyed to Alexander Smith in 1666, and sometime before 1673 conveyed by Smith to Richard Robinson who, that year, sold it and four hundred acres to the parish for 20,000 pounds of tobacco. But whoever owned it, minister John Shepherd (Robinson's cousin-in-law) was renting it in 1671 when the vestry allowed him 490 pounds of tobacco to undertake minor repairs. Following purchase, the vestry allowed major work, voting 5,030 pounds of tobacco to reimburse Master Shepherd for the cost, a quarter of the purchase price of the house and land, carefully specifying that he was "to leave The Dwelling house . . . in as good repair at his Departure from the Gleab as now when finished." Twelve years later, with the advent of a new minister, 4,000 pounds of tobacco were required to make the glebe "Tenantable." More repairs were necessary in 1691 and 1693, but it was all a stopgap. In the late 1690s, an entirely new house was built for the minister at a cost of 6,480 pounds of tobacco—an unreasonably high price, the vestry thought—while another 1,000 pounds were apparently sunk in the old house to keep it standing until its replacement was completed. Only ten years later the vestrymen were considering another remodeling, ordering that the house "be forthwith framed and removed out of the place where it now stands and set upon blocks in the Most Commodious place that may be." They decided instead to build anew, planning on spending 18,000 pounds of tobacco. Construction was slow and costs spiraled upward; the builder was ordered paid 18,000 in 1707, 24,000 in 1708, 18,000 for "goeing on with the glebe" in 1709, and 1,600 at completion in 1711. Still, the chimneys needed alteration in 1719 (3,590 pounds of tobacco), and in 1728 the then-minister informed the vestry that "the Mansion house" and outbuildings were "in so ruinous a Condition" that he would have to resign. "The Vestry being very Sensible that in case Mr. Yates Should resign . . . no other Minister would receive the Buildings in the condition they are at present" voted unanimously to undertake to repair the old structure as a makedo until a new one could be built. The record: Over an eighty-year span, one dwelling house was built, twice rebuilt, and replaced completely three times.[8]

In terms of social and economic position within the county, the minister was clearly something more than a Seager yet less than a Wormeley. His income from salary alone (sixteen thousand pounds of tobacco a year) was matched or bettered by only a minority of his parishioners. Hence his glebe house can serve to illustrate the size and style of an above-average planter's home. That which Minister Shepherd took possession of in the early 1670s was described as "a 25 foot Dwelling," implying twenty-five feet long and no more than sixteen to eighteen feet in breadth. In all likelihood, it consisted of a single room on the ground floor and another upstairs under the eaves, the two joined by a ladder or a narrow stairway tucked beside a framed and wattled chimney. A massive fireplace at one end of the ground floor room was Frances Shepherd's kitchen, a corner of the common table the good parson's study, and a curtained bedstead in the corner the couple's bedroom. Children and maidservants slept in the windowless room upstairs, pallets and beds competing for space with the produce and odd "lumber" stored there. Male servants slept in a separate building nearby.

The glebe house built in the 1690s was larger, forty feet long by twenty feet wide, with brick chimneys and ground-floor fireplaces at both ends. The larger size allowed the first-floor room to be divided by a partition separating an "inner room" from the "hall" or "great hall" or "common room," the latter still the setting for cooking, eating, and entertaining, the inner room allowing the minister and his wife a modicum of privacy for sleeping and study. The new house of the early 1700s was not any larger, still forty feet long by twenty wide. But to the front was attached an eight-foot "entry" or "porch" with an additional room above. Heat and light were now provided for the upstairs by larger end chimneys with both first- and second-floor fireplaces and by a "porch chamber" window, perhaps even dormer windows. And the hall no longer doubled as kitchen, a separate building being provided for cooking, another to serve as a dairy.

What is most striking about all of these houses—the glebe houses described and others that could be described—are their small size and the progression over time. The glebe, recall, is comparable to the home of an above-average planter; most other houses in the county were smaller. Indeed, the majority of the families of Middlesex, together with their possessions, crowded into spaces not much larger than a modern two-car garage. But the glebe was gradually enlarged and improved; sundry outbuildings came to surround it, and specific functions—cooking, for example—were removed from the house itself. At least on the level of the middling and better-than-middling planter, this was generally the case.

Beyond these two points, however, we must catch a mental image of the buildings. With their steep roofs, narrow casement windows, towering end chimneys, and grey, weathering look, they summon to mind the adjectives

Common Houses of Middlesex

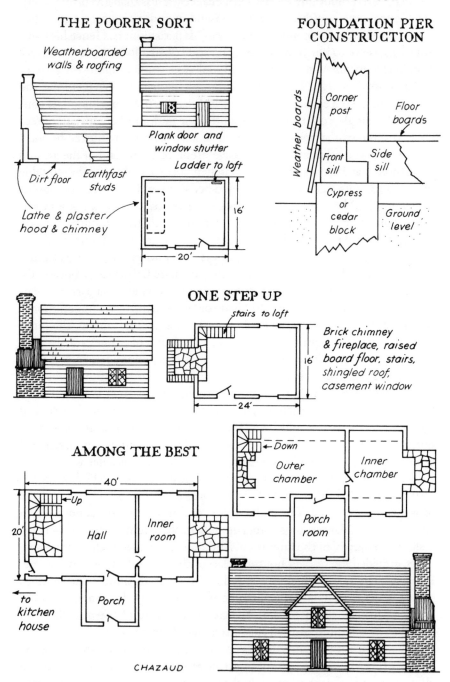

THE POORER SORT

Weatherboarded walls & roofing

Dirt floor

Earthfast studs

Lathe & plaster hood & chimney

Plank door and window shutter

Ladder to loft

16'

20'

FOUNDATION PIER CONSTRUCTION

Weather boards

Corner post

Floor boards

Front sill

Side sill

Cypress or cedar block

Ground level

ONE STEP UP

stairs to loft

16'

24'

Brick chimney & fireplace, raised board floor, stairs, shingled roof, casement window

AMONG THE BEST

40'

←Up

20'

Hall

Inner room

→Down

Outer chamber

Inner chamber

Porch room

to kitchen house

Porch

CHAZAUD

"gothic" and "medieval," and indeed just such have been attached to them by one scholar.[9] The adjectives flesh out our mind's eye view of the landscape of the early county: a winding dirt road, stump-pocked fields, rail fences, tiny buildings medieval and dilapidated in appearance, and the ever-present woods.

There are many ways to glimpse the people of early Middlesex. We can, in our imagination, knock on the door of one of the houses along the road and enter as visitors. If the house were that of Thomas Tuggle and the date 1668, we would find within Thomas himself, his wife Mary, Mary's eleven-year-old son by a previous marriage, John Burke, three of Thomas and Mary's own children—Mary (age seven), Thomas (four), one-year-old Anne—and William Steward, a newly arrived fourteen-year-old obliged to serve Tuggle for ten years. As visitors are likely to do, we might (still in our imagination) engage the older children in conversation. The talk would be constrained but revealing.

School? These particular children had none, although in a few years' time there would be occasional schoolmasters offering one or two years of lessons in reading and ciphering to some of the county's boys. Sports? Games of a sort played now and again, yes, but of formal sports, none. Their day? For the most part, work—John Burke and William Steward in the fields beside Tuggle; and Mary minding the smaller children and helping her mother in the house and vegetable garden, perhaps even going with her to carry plants when the tobacco seedlings were being transplanted or picking worms from the leaves in season. Their futures? A modern American child would undoubtedly talk in terms of choices, even if it were no more than policeman versus fireman. But life for these children did not involve choice. John Burke would answer that he would be a planter, as his stepfather was and his father had been; Mary, that she would be a wife and mother. Aspirations? In a worldly sense, minimal. The children would not talk of traveling or of garnering great wealth or power or fame. Burke might talk of adding to the land he expected to inherit, while young Steward might talk of what his master had accomplished and aspire to do the same. For Tuggle, too, had arrived in Virginia as a servant, leased land on obtaining his freedom, and become a freeholder only in 1662 when he purchased the one hundred acres on which stood the house.

In whatever way they answered such questions about their futures and aspirations, however, the children would answer awkwardly. Life, in their context, was more a matter of being than of progressing. Time simply passed. It was not, as with us, a matter of perpetual revelation but of a cyclic repetition of what was already known. Winter gave way to spring and fall presaged winter again. Sons became fathers who begat sons, a way of thought epitomized by their very names: John Burke carried his father's and grandfather's first name; Mary, her mother's and grandmother's.[10] To these children, questions about their futures predicated on choice and change would make little sense.

Our imaginary conversation with the children of the Tuggle household underscores a fundamental and vital fact about the people of our county. They were, in the scholar's vernacular, more "traditional" in their outlook than "modern," more inclined to accept the world as it was and pass it unchanged through the generations than to expect each passing generation to change the world.[11] It is a point that we will have to keep in mind as we proceed, for it explains much of the lifestyle of the county. But we must keep in mind, too, that while changelessness was part of their mentality, the people of the county did, indeed, live in a milieu that was perpetually changing. It is an equally fundamental and vital point. The historian catches a glimpse of the first in a particular (albeit imaginary) conversation with children; he senses the second when he abandons the particular and becomes ubiquitous.

The Tuggle household of 1668 was one of eighty-three in the county that year, its seven members part of a population of 912. In the immediate background of every inhabitant was change. Fathers and mothers, masters and servants—all remembered and undoubtedly recounted childhoods lived elsewhere and the journeys that had brought them into the county. Over the years immediately ahead, still others would enter, an annual accretion of new faces to be remembered and new personalities to be learned. Continuing immigration, together with natural increase, constantly swept the population upward, the number of people in the county more than doubling by century's end, almost doubling again by the midpoint of the next century. The change implied by growth was not simply quantitative, however, but qualitative as well. The very type of people within the population changed over time.[12]

The families of 1668—the Tuggles on their hundred acres and the Chicheleys on their thousands—lived in a sea of servants. Tobacco profits were a matter of combining land and labor, and bound servants supplied a large part of the latter. Servants were not, of course, spread evenly through the population. Tuggle's one servant boy is to be contrasted with the forty-odd servants working Chicheley land at the same time. But in the aggregate, bound laborers amounted to roughly 45 percent of the population of 1668. Most (just over 38 percent of the total population) were white, preponderately male, and fifteen to twenty-five years old, recruited for their labor from the farms, villages, and city streets of old England. In the Chesapeake, their servitude was temporary. Depending upon the terms of their entry and to some extent their age, they would labor four, five, even as many as ten and twelve years and then, provided always that they lived, merge into the free population.[13] The rest were black, for the most part carried into the

Chesapeake from the slave-based societies of the Caribbean. They, their children, and their children's children were increasingly bound for life to their masters.

In absolute numbers, 334 white servants and 65 blacks labored in Middlesex in 1668, the former outnumbering the latter by five to one. Thirty years later, however, the situation was vastly different. The number of families in the county had risen to 270, and the population to 1,771. Bound labor as a percentage of the population had declined to just under 30 percent, but it was largely black. At the turn of the century, black slaves, the majority imported directly from Africa, outnumbered white servants by four to one.[14]

Slavery would ultimately change the face of our county. For the moment, however, our concern is with white servitude, the dominant labor system through the 1680s. Because of its temporary nature, servitude had wide ramifications in the economy of the county. As bondsmen, the servants profited directly the individual families within which they labored and indirectly, by their labor on the principal export crop, the larger society of families. In all likelihood, the majority did no more than this. The conditions of their lives and, above all, the disease environment of the Chesapeake was such that only a minority survived.[15] But those who did moved into the free society with aspirations for a house and land and wife and children of their own. They had little in the way of capital, only the "freedom corn and clothes" that the law required their masters to give them.[16] But they knew the way of the land and of tobacco culture from their years of service and hence could take up land as sharecroppers or renters. With luck and hard work, at least some eventually amassed enough capital to buy their own land. A few others took a shortcut into the ranks of the landed by marrying the widows of freeholders and assuming control of the property.

There are two ways to look at this process. We could consider it solely from the standpoint of the former servants and note the extent of their opportunity to obtain land. Was it great or small? Did it change over time? And there is much to be said for this strategy.[17] By itself, however, it fails to encompass the whole of the system of which the freedmen were a part. For the former servants themselves constituted an opportunity for others. They sought land, and there were those in the society with land to rent and sell. The point is vital and requires elaboration.

Passing down the road from the northwestern border of the county to its end at Stingray in 1668, we noted where the population was located. Consider now the vacant land. Virtually none of it was unowned. Indeed, in the first flush of the entry into the county in the 1650s and through the early 1660s, up to 80 and 90 percent of the land had come to be claimed by someone, the last major original patent in Middlesex (1,100 acres) being granted in 1674 to George Hooper and John Richens. Only here and there in the tangle of patent boundaries were there still parcels to be claimed, more often than not by discerning and canny residents who could walk the woods to spot areas where boundary blazes failed to meet.[18] Some of this early-patented land would remain in the family of an original patentee and become one of the "great plantations" of the eighteenth century. Wormeley's Rosegill is both the largest and best example of such in Middlesex. But most would be conveyed and conveyed again as early speculators sold or—the most important aspect—as patentees and subsequent purchasers found that in order to develop one part of their holdings they had to rent or sell other parts.

The Nash family holding on Sunderland Creek is an example. On arriving from York County in the 1650s, Arthur Nash, an ex-servant, bought servants of his own and, in partnership with John Needles, made crops on other people's lands until he had enough to buy, purchasing 400 acres from Thomas Pattison in 1664. Arthur died shortly after, but a part of the land was rented out to support his minor son, John. In 1681 John came of age, cleared accounts with his guardian, Matthew Bentley, and took possession of the property. The 2,478 pounds of tobacco he collected from Bentley as the profit of fifteen years running the estate (less the cost of raising young John) was hardly enough to develop his own establishment; hence in 1683 Nash sold acreage to Richard Allen, a former servant of his father's. The next year, in return for title "to one able manservant" and an annual rent of one ear of corn, he signed a long-term lease for another part of the land with Thomas Radley.[19] Still a third part he leased to Christopher Fisher, while in the early 1690s he sold off two small plots of 60 and 40 acres. Ultimately Nash would pass on a fully developed 240-acre plantation to his own children.

The "ancient Jamaica" patent of 1658, which gave its name to the far northwestern section of the county between the road and swamp, is still another example of land that was divided and resold. Originally patented by John Curtis as a speculation and conveyed by him to John Harris, the land (an estimated 1,200 acres) began to be subdivided at Harris's death. Four hundred acres fell to John and Penelope Richens as Harris's heirs, the rest being set aside to satisfy debts. Neighbor Nicholas Cocke, as executor of the estate, apparently paid the debts and held onto the land, selling 200 acres to Robert Porter in 1684. What was left, 646 acres by survey, passed to Nicholas's son Maurice and at Maurice's death in 1696 to Rice Jones, Maurice's sister's son, who in 1704 sold it to William and Robert Daniell, each of whom took half for himself.

Still a third example is the Lindsey patent of 700 acres along the Dragon, to the south and west of Jamaica Land. Patented by John Lindsey in the early 1670s, the land lay idle until conveyed to James Atwood in 1682. Atwood that same year sold 150 acres each to John Bristow and John Micham,

80 acres in 1683 to George Guest (who in turn sold 50 acres to Richard Reynolds and still ended up on resurvey with 100 acres!), and in 1686, 140 acres to Thomas Stapleton. At his death, Atwood left 100 developed acres to his son Richard.

In the far southeastern section of the county, Stingray Point itself was subjected to such subdivision. The whole point—an estimated 800 acres but subsequently proving to be 1,100—was patented by William Brocas in 1654, assigned by his heir, John Jackson, to Sir Henry Chicheley in 1657, and by Cuthbert Potter, as Chicheley's attorney, to William Bawdes in 1661, passing to Bawdes's daughter Mary at his death in 1665. Ultimately William Dudley came into control of the land by marriage to Mary and began selling: 300 acres to Thomas Alloman in 1686 and, all in 1690, 100 acres to Thomas Hill, 50 to Patrick Miller, another 50 to Richard Farrell, and 600 to John Ashburn. Ashburn's 600 acres were again divided when his heir sold off 100-acre plots in 1701 and 1703.

Servants entering the free population on the one hand and a steady process of subdivision on the other—the two phenomena link to form a single system that carried people into every corner of the county, filling in a land of empty patents. Freed servants rented or cropped to obtain the wherewithal to buy, then sold or rented part of what they bought to obtain the wherewithal to develop the rest. Fully three out of four purchasers noted above were freed servants and exemplify the system. So, too, does Thomas Tuggle himself. Finding an unpatented gore of 110 acres near his original 100, he took title to it in 1669 and promptly rented it to another ex-servant, Thomas Oliver, for five hundred pounds of tobacco and three bushels of corn a year plus every fourth hog raised by Oliver from six hogs that Tuggle supplied.[20] The arrangement provided Oliver with a start on the land (as Tuggle's own tenure as a renter had given him a start); the rent Tuggle now received repaid him the patenting costs and provided him the wherewithal to continue improving his original holding.

The decline of the servant body, setting in at least in Middlesex in the 1670s and quickening in the 1680s and 1690s, strained the system.[21] Freedmen buying land found it harder and harder to find still newer freedmen to rent or buy their excess; hence they found it harder to develop their holdings. Moreover, the cost of development itself increased as slaves began to replace servants, the purchase price of the former being two and three times the cost of buying a servant with four or more years to serve. Tuggle conceivably bought ten years of young Steward's labor for two thousand pounds of tobacco; a comparable black at century's end would have cost him five thousand.[22] The inability to develop their lands made the later freedmen far more vulnerable to failure than the earlier. At the same time, those with capital flourished. In the long run, blacks were cheaper since, for those able to purchase them, there was no need for a recurring outlay of capital to replace white laborers completing their terms. Indeed, given that the progeny of the black were also bound, the slave replaced himself. And those flourishing were on hand to buy the partially improved holdings of those failing, turning them into quarters to be worked by ever more black slaves. Stingray Point again is an example. Subdivided by William Dudley in the late 1680s and early 1690s, it was in part reassembled as a single property by William Churchill, who bought out Alloman, Miller, and Farrell between 1699 and 1703.

All the while an inexorable demographic process was at work, ever changing the situation in the county. Men settling the land and taking wives begat children, some of whom, despite a high mortality rate, grew to maturity. One result of the process, when joined with the decline in the number of emigrants from England, was a steadily increasing proportion of native-born in the population. While in 1668 only some 19 percent of the white population had been born in the Chesapeake, that percentage rose to almost 55 percent by the turn of the century, to 77 percent by 1724, and to well over 90 percent by the half-century mark. In personal terms, the luck of the demographic lottery—the element of random chance that determines the fertility of a couple and the survival of its children—was Janus-like in effect. On the one side, young sons and daughters were an asset, additional hands for the fields and housework. But on the other, too many grown sons and daughters could spell disaster for a family's fortunes or for individual children.

John Nash is again a case in point. Having built a plantation of 240 acres, he was, when writing his will, faced with the problem of one plantation and four children, three strong sons and a daughter. To his wife he devised (as by law he was required) a widow's "third"—the "use," or income, of a third of the land during her lifetime. The livestock and slaves of the plantation he carefully distributed among all four children. To his eldest son, Arthur, went possession of the land itself, but Arthur was to take his brothers John and Henry "to live and labour" with him until they reached twenty-one and thereafter to allow each "a competency of living" from the land.[23] Young John died a year after his father. Arthur died the next year, leaving half of the 240 acres to his own wife, Anne, and half to his younger brother Henry, who thus began life with 120 acres.

Still, but for the death of John, Henry might have started with only 60 acres, the fate of the six children of Robert Chowning who shared equally his 350 acres. William Daniell is another example. Arriving in Middlesex in the early 1660s, Daniell amassed 600 acres, which, at his death in 1698, were divided roughly equally among four sons. One of the four, Robert, managed to rebuild to his father's level, amassing almost 750 acres before his own death, but he divided these acres among his own four sons. Of them, only one, another Robert, managed to add land to his inheritance, a

THE CHANGING AGE STRUCTURE OF
THE WHITE POPULATION

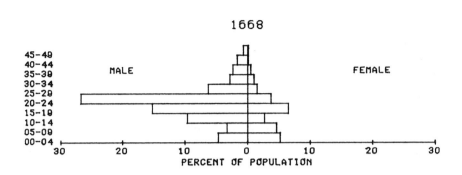

1668

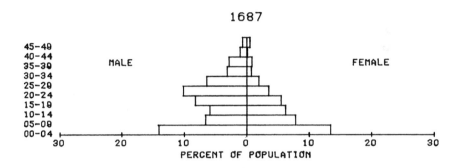

1687

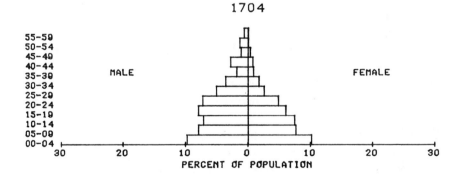

1704

50-acre tract. Marrying twice, this Robert left eleven children, including six sons. The eldest received his father's original inheritance (190 acres). Another received the 50-acre addition. Four received nothing.

Let us return to the Tuggles, the family with which we started this discussion. Late in 1684 Thomas Tuggle died, his wife Mary having preceded him. By then William Steward was gone. Like that of so many other servant boys, Steward's life in the Chesapeake had been short. He died shortly after the date of our imaginary visit of 1668, aspirations unfulfilled. John Burke, too, was for the moment disappointed in his expectations. In writing his will, old Thomas had devised his 110-acre plot to his eldest son Thomas and his original 100 acres to his second son Henry, unborn at the time of our visit. To John Burke, married by then and with an infant son, went only the right to till a particular piece of tobacco ground on the home plantation until Henry "comes att age and no Longer." Tuggle seems to have anticipated his stepson's disappointment. Thomas junior was to head the family, caring for Henry and his unmarried sisters, Mary and Anne; and all four, plus John Burke and his family, were to live together in the Tuggle house "If they Can Live Contentedly together"; otherwise John was to build himself a separate fifteen-foot house on his tobacco land and live apart.[24] As it turned out, John knew (or learned) of an unclaimed gore of land tucked into the curls and swamps of Sunderland Creek. In a series of transactions in 1686, he sold 50 acres of what he thought was 170 in order to obtain the wherewithal (twelve hundred pounds of tobacco) to complete the survey and patenting of the gore, ending up with clear title to 141 acres. On these he would live out his life, fathering in all seven children by three wives before his death in 1699.

All aspects of the early Chesapeake system are exemplified in the story of the Tuggles and John Burke—the progression from servant to renter to freeholder (Thomas senior), the parceling among sons of what fathers accumulated and the disappointment of some (the disposition of Thomas's land and John Burke's failed expectations), and finally, the way of financing a freehold by renting or selling part of it (old Thomas's renting out of his 110-acre plot; Burke's sale of 50 acres to obtain title to 141). In this case, the system left its participants happy. Indeed, in naming his own children, Burke displayed no rancor toward the stepfather who had failed him, only the sense of generational progression that we remarked upon earlier: One son he named Thomas, a second John, and a third for his half-brother Henry, the child's uncle.

We can, however, sense in the story the potentials for personal failure, pinpointing them by a series of "if" propositions. What if old Thomas had not been able to garner as a renter the capital to buy his original land? What if he had not found and been able to patent the gore and hence been forced to divide 100 acres instead of 210? What if John Burke had not found his gore or had been unable to figure a way to obtain it, or had been unable to find a purchaser for the part that allowed him title to the rest? Historians frequently speak of "tensions within society" leading to this or that cataclysmic event. What they are really pointing to is the aggregate of such "if" propositions that circumscribes particular lives, the degree of tension depending upon the frequency with which people faced potentially adverse resolutions.

In the early fall of 1676, armed horsemen cantered along the road. Tumult, riot, and rebellion had come to Virginia.

The troubles had begun far from our county. To the west, from the Potomac to south of the James River, Indians and English were still in contact (as they were not in Middlesex), and the depredations of one upon the other provoked bloodshed. The residents of the inland counties and Virginia's governor, Sir William Berkeley, disagreed as to the best way to counter Indian assaults. Even in the lower counties—those closest to the bay—there was discontent as levies to pay for what proved to be an ineffective defense rose to a point where a man relying on his own labor, possibly supporting a wife and children, was obligated to pay between a quarter and a half of his crop in county, vestry, and colony taxes. Virginians along the freshes of the James River soon found a champion in Nathaniel Bacon, a man "young, bold, active, of an inviting Aspect, and powerful Elocution," who would search out and kill Indians rather than pay for forts and garrisons to guard against their raids.[25]

Bacon's defiance of the governor on Indian matters spiraled into mutiny during the summer of 1676, and then into rebellion. Titling himself "Gen'l By the Consent of the People," Bacon labeled Berkeley "as one, who hath Traiterously attempted, violated and Injured his Majesty's Interest," demanding in the name of the "Commons of Virginia" that Sir William surrender himself and mandating confiscation of the estates of all who supported him. At the same time, he distributed an oath to be sworn to by the inhabitants. They were to acknowledge the legality of all his doings and the illegality of Berkeley's, oblige themselves "to oppose what Forces shall be sent out of England by his Majesty against mee. . . . Divulge what you shall heare at any time spoken against mee . . . [and] keepe my secrets, and not discover them to any person."[26]

Active warfare broke out when Berkeley, having abandoned the mainland counties for the Eastern Shore, recrossed the Chesapeake to seize Jamestown, whereupon Bacon gave up Indian chasing, besieged the town, and ultimately forced Berkeley to retire once again across the bay. Burning Jamestown on the night of September 19, Bacon crossed the York River into Gloucester, both to impose his oath upon the inhabitants and to counter a force of the governor's supporters moving down from the Potomac counties under Giles Brent. No battle was fought, however. Brent's men abandoned him when they heard the fate of Jamestown. The rebellion—led by Joseph Ingram after Bacon succumbed to disease in October—became a matter of isolated skirmishes as the rebels fortified houses here and there along the York and James rivers and the governor conducted a riverine campaign against them, sending flying companies to drive the rebels from their strongpoints or to force their surrender. By mid-January it was all over, with Ingram surrendering January 2 and his remaining captains following his example within the next two weeks or fleeing the colony.

It is impossible to say exactly how much of this turbulence spilled over into Middlesex. Certainly the affair disrupted the county. No courts met between May 1676 and March 1677. At some point, the early records of the vestry were defaced and pages ripped out. Certainly, too, Bacon's oath was administered in Middlesex. In the aftermath of the rebellion, William Dudley's widow petitioned for the restitution of tobacco seized from her husband as penalty for administering the oath, claiming that Dudley had been forced to the act and even then had done so "with a salvo to his allegiance to his Majesty."[27] But when? And where?

Certainly, too, armed men had been abroad in the county. In all likelihood, Brent's "army of the north" forded the Rappahannock upriver and moved down the county's main road, crossing to Gloucester and the battle that was never fought via the Dragon Bridge.[28] And in October or November, according to one account, there was a vague "riseing" of Middlesex men against the rebels, implying that for a time the Baconians were in control. But the loyalists "were no sooner got upon ther feet" than the rebels "resalves to bring them on their knees" again, Ingram sending his second in command "with a party of Horses, to do the worke."[29] Finally, there are tantalizing glimpses of personal confrontations: Minister John Shepherd "Compelled . . . to leave the Parish by meanes and Armed Force of Ill Disposed persons Then in Rebellion," presumably because of his loyalty to governor and king; Ralph Wormeley, Christopher Wormeley, Walter Whitaker, and John Burnham, all imprisoned by the rebels and their property "much worsted": Middlesex's Robert Beverley gaining renown as a commander of one of Berkeley's flying squadrons and eventually leading his horsemen to pacify the county; a letter from the governor, aboard ship on the York River, to Beverley, dated January 18: "Yesterday came on board to me, Boodle, and submitted himselfe, and promised that, this day, his soldiers should lay downe their armes, upon which I gave him his pardon, and promised his soldiers the like."[30] Robert Boodle and his troopers were Middlesex men and among the very last to surrender.

If events within the county are unknown, the nature of Middlesex's indigenous Baconians is not. A series of suits for damages identify at least some of them for us. In one, Christopher Wormeley brought action against the nineteen men of "Captain Boodle's troop," alleging that on the last day of October they had entered upon his plantation "with force and Armes," plundered his house of goods valued at 285*li* 6*s*, and, in camping on his tobacco ground, destroyed a crop worth another 150*li*. John Lewis of New Kent County lodged suits against a number of Middlesex men, but particularly Matthew Bentley as "Commander" of "Fourty or Fifty" men who had quartered themselves on his plantation, consuming "Three hoggs and two Sheepe . . . [and] a great quantaty of my Corne for themselves and horses," and then carried off a variety of supplies for Ingram's forces in Gloucester.[31] In all, twenty-four Middlesex rebels can be positively identified in these suits.

As we scan this list of Baconians in the light of what we know of their lives in the county, a number of things stand out. First, they were not idle, wandering men. Neither were they the brash young. In age, they ranged from twenty to forty, averaging thirty.[32] Two were native-born sons of Middlesex families, eleven others had arrived in the county in the 1660s or earlier, and another four are identifiable as residents as early as 1671. Only three cannot be placed in the county before the rebellion. Of the twenty-four, nine were married, and six of these had children.[33]

Secondly, more of the twenty-four than one would expect from simply a random sample of Middlesex men show in some way a tendency toward trouble making.[34] In 1672 George Anderton had been fined five hundred pounds of tobacco for fathering a bastard child; after the rebellion (1683), he would father another and, in 1687, stand trial for adultery. Robert Knight, although he rode as a Baconian, had been pilloried for refusing to fight Indians when drafted into a Middlesex contingent sent to the frontier. Jeremy Overy was obviously quick to take offense, for he had been plaintiff twice in suits for defamation. Andrew Ross, whose father-in-law and brother-in-law had both been to court on various occasions charged with assaults and swearing, was himself imprisoned on suspicion of felony in 1681. Two years later, Thomas Weatherby would be suspected of attempting to embezzle the estate of orphans left in his care. And still another of the group, George Hooper, had at one point attempted to reduce to servitude an orphan who had chosen him as a guardian.

Thirdly, all were enmeshed in what we have called the early Chesapeake system. Aggregated, they appear as a cross section, a slice of the population encompassing men at all points of the process, from newly freed servants working as tenants and croppers, through the newly landed and the successful, and on to native sons. Eight of the twenty-four can be identified as ex-servants, but that number is a minimum; servitude is a status difficult to establish from the record base; hence there were probably more than eight ex-servants in the group. Fifteen of the Baconians were tenants or share-croppers at the time of the rebellion; seven of these would, after the rebellion, go on to obtain land of their own, six by purchase, one by marriage to the heiress to three hundred acres. Nine owned or controlled by virtue of marriage land of their own, ranging from John Guthridge's half-share in two hundred acres to Matthew Bentley's two thousand plus acres.

Finally, the Baconians were not unknown to each other prior to their participation in rebellion. The connections between them appear in a multiplicity of ways as one scans the records of the county. By way of example (and note that the names of known Baconians are italicized): *John Guthridge* had, before the rebellion, purchased land from Thomas Loe, *Andrew Ross's* father-in-law; Ross was a witness to a land conveyance in which *John Brewer* was involved; Brewer had purchased land from *Jeremy Overy*, who had in turn bought land from the former partner of *Richard Blewford's* father and was a legatee of Thomas Radley, *Barnard Reymey's* landlord and a neighbor and friend of *Matthew Bentley*; Brewer had also been a servant to Humphrey Owen, overseer with Nicholas Cocke of the estate of John Harris, whose principal legatee was *John Richens*; Richens, in partnership with his neighbor *George Hooper*, had patented eleven hundred acres in 1674; *John Brim* was another neighbor of Richens's and a close friend—Brim would name a son "Richens." The string of connections extends and doubles back upon itself: Brim dealt extensively with Thomas Crank, who also dealt extensively with *William Blackford*, who worked land adjoining that of *Matthew Bentley*.

Such interconnections should not surprise us. Riots and rebellions do not emerge from the air but are concocted by men who, in this society, perforce must meet and talk face-to-face. Indeed, Middlesex's small rebellion connects in just such direct fashion to the larger rebellion when we realize that Richard Lawrence—a close confederate of Bacon's, perhaps even, as contempories claimed, his tutelary genius—had sojourned in the county as a surveyor, that one of the properties he surveyed was that of John Richens, and that of all of the county's Baconians only Richens was truly punished. While the rest were pardoned or ignored, Richens was sent to the governor, tried, and banished from the colony.[35]

Aggregations such as we have been indulging in are informative but not particularly enlightening. They summarize the county Baconians as a rather ordinary group of Middlesex inhabitants, somewhat more prone to trouble than the rest. They do not tell us why these ordinary men took up arms, looted Christopher Wormeley's house, and rode off to join Ingram. To put it another way: If we imagine Richard Lawrence, in person or by letter, awakening John Richens to the Baconian cause developing in the south in 1676 and Richens, in his own hall, at church or court, even across a rail fence, haranguing his neighbors, urging action, we are still left with questions. Why did Richens listen to Lawrence? Why did these neighbors listen to Richens? And toward what end did they all act?

Lawrence himself offers a clue. Oxford-trained, a literary man, a leader in the larger events (as none of our Middlesex men were), he left an imprint on the historical record, and what we can learn of his personality might guide us to an understanding of our Baconians. Lawrence was, according to a not entirely unsympathetic contemporary, one who transformed personal frustration into political discontent. "My self have heard him," Thomas Matthew wrote, "Insinuate as if his fancy gave him prospect of finding (at one time or other,) some expedient not only to repair his great Losse, but therewith to See those abuses rectified that the Countrey was oppress'd with." And he goes on to write, "I know him to be a thinking Man, and tho' nicely honest, affable, and without Blemish, in his Conversation and Dealings, yet did he manifest abundance of uneasiness in the Sense of his hard Usages, which might prompt him to Improve that Indian Quarrel to the Service of his Animosities."[36] Richens, too, had frustrations and "Animosities" to be served. His inheritance of four hundred acres had been under constant court challenge from Nicholas Cocke for sixteen years, while his ambitious partnership with George Hooper of 1674 was already failing in 1676. Neither Richens nor Hooper had the capital to develop the eleven hundred acres or the ability to wring capital for its development from the land itself.[37]

The lives of others among the Baconians we have identified display a similar potential for frustration. Robert Boodle and Matthew Bentley had each married a widow of a man of substantial estate and social position—in both cases the deceased had been vestrymen. Marriage gave Boodle and Bentley control of their predecessors' lands but not the social acceptance marked by office. It is not at all implausible that their leadership of Baconian troopers was a surrogate for the offices they did not hold.

For his part, Richard Blewford, a young man of twenty, native-born, could already sense an indifferent future, one not of his own making. His father had been an early entrant into the county, purchasing 217 acres in 1657 and, in partnership with another, 300 in 1663. But bad luck or a lack of ability or both had plagued him. In 1661 the county court declared the elder Blewford "a man not caapeable of an oath"; by 1676 he had lost all but ninety acres and was working those with his sons Richard and Thomas. Ultimately he would surrender all to a son-in-law who undertook to pay his debts, and he would die bankrupt, leaving his widow to the charity of others and Richard to make his way in the world as a renter.[38]

Henry Nichols, too, was native-born, his father the owner of nine hundred acres and well respected in the county. In 1676, at twenty-two, young Nichols was already landed, having inherited two hundred acres from William Pew. Henry's riding with Boodle's troop might well have been nothing more than an escapade inspired by a friend—the Blewford land was immediately adjoining Henry's two hundred acres and in the vicinity of the larger Nichols family holding. Or perhaps it was more. Had the elder Nichols already announced that Henry, the only son, would not be a singular heir, that his three sisters would share in the land? Such would eventually be the case. Did Richard Blewford's more obvious frustration come to define Henry's? Of course, we can only conjecture. The potential for Henry feeling a particular way can be demonstrated, but not the feeling itself.

Still, frustration seems a better key to Bacon's Rebellion, at least in Middlesex, than any other; and tensions seem best defined in terms of the frequency with which people faced potentially adverse resolutions to the "if" propositions of life. In the county, men and women sought to gain (or hold) for themselves and their families that comfortable constancy we sensed in imaginary conversation with the Tuggle children. But the world and their lives were inconstant. Turnings, some requiring conscious actions and decisions, others determined by situations, were myriad, and as many (perhaps more) led away from the goal as toward it. The rebellion—a chronic enigma to historians—seems in Middlesex neither a great cause nor a traumatic uprising of "losers" against "winners," oppressed against oppressors, but simply a venting of frustrations and a release of tension, precipitated by events unrelated to the county's doings and, in the end, negligible in effect.[39]

The rebellion ended in Middlesex as Captain Beverley led the governor's troopers into the county. The Baconians clattered homeward and quietly took up their lives, repairing ignored fences and preparing their seedbeds for another year's tobacco crop. They were neither hanged nor hounded for their actions. On the contrary, the remarkable thing is their immediate reacceptance into the society of the county. Captain Bentley was briefly jailed but released by Beverley. Both Boodle and Bentley were required by the county court to find securities—in effect, bail money—for their "abearing" themselves "Peaceably and quiately towards the Kings Majestie and all his Leige People."[40] Richard Perrott, Jr., Richard Robinson, William Gordon, and Alexander Smith stood bond for the two. Perrott and Robinson were justices of the court, and all were large landholders. At the very next meeting of the justices, Captain Boodle was named a constable for the county. Sued by Christopher Wormeley and John Lewis for trespass, the Baconians lost, but they appealed the jury verdicts to the colony's general court, finding securities among their non-Baconian neighbors for the prosecution of their appeals.[41] Minister John Shepherd, who had been harried from the county by the rebels, stood security for Baconian John Clarke.[42]

Only Richens was, at least for a while, unforgiven. Sent by the county court to the governor and banished, he was back in Middlesex by July, at which time he was arrested and imprisoned without bail, in part for violating his banishment, in part, too, for "uttering publiquely very Scandalous, and abusive Words of this Court and all the Members thereof. And giveing Such threatning Language to the Undersheriff of this County . . . Soe that he was in Dread of his life."[43] In September Richens was sent south to the governor again. There is no record of his reception, but in 1680 he was back in the county prosecuting his by then two-decades-long suit against Nicholas Cocke for the peaceable possession of his inheritance. In 1689 he would die on his land.

The trial of Christopher Wormeley's suit against the Baconians was held on Monday, September 3, 1677, a court day like any other in the early county. Middlesex had no courthouse at the time. The justices met at Richard Robinson's mid-county house, just off the main road between its junction with the church path and the cutoff to the Piankatank ferry, paying Robinson twelve hundred pounds of tobacco yearly "Howse Rent and Candle."[44] Hence it was toward Robinson's that men from all parts of the county moved that morning.

In the upper precinct, justices Richard Perrott and Abraham Weekes, neighbors sharing a neck of land on the Rappahannock between creeks bearing their names, might well have set out together, meeting John Burnham, another justice, and Thomas Haslewood at the Upper Chapel, then riding along the chapel path until it struck the main road. Haslewood was on his way to court to give an accounting of his guardianship of the orphans of William Thompson. At the road, they might have met John Jones coming down from above, on his way to submit a claim to the court for supplying arms to soldiers dispatched from the county to join the garrison at one of Berkeley's forts. Just beyond Mickleburrough's bridge, they might have met John Vause, another justice, and Christopher Robinson, clerk of the court, riding in from their lands on Rappahannock-side. All along their route, the party would have fallen in with, or passed, the old Baconians on their way to trial, fully half of whom (including Matthew Bentley) were from the upper precinct.

Coming toward Robinson's from the other direction, justices Robert Beverley and his step son-in-law Francis Bridge would certainly have ridden together. Bridge and his wife were living at Beverley's. Traveling the lower precinct paths to strike the main road, they might have been joined by Walter Whitaker, the sheriff of the county; John Mann, undersheriff; and George Wooley, whose business at court this day involved the estate of John Hilson, of which Wooley was both executor and principal legatee. At the Lower Chapel, they might have met Christopher Wormeley himself, both plaintiff and justice, whose plantation lay directly north along the Green Glade.

Middle precinct men had less distance to travel. Courthouse and home were one to justice Richard Robinson. William Daniell could ride in from his house near the Dragon Bridge in half an hour. He was attending to prosecute a suit against Thomas Radley. Erasmus Withers, heading to court on the matter of an orphan being bound to him, and Captain Boodle could come up from their lands along the ferry path in about the same time. George Reeves, pursuing separate suits against Daniel Bouton and John Allen, had only a mile along the main road to come, as did Michael Musgrave, who was suing William Wood for trespass.

On business or simply to share the excitement of court day, the people of the county flocked to Robinson's. The assemblage was primarily male, but women and occasionally children were frequently before the court officially, while women and children, at least those from the immediate vicinity, were undoubtedly on hand as onlookers. The county's taverners, closing their ordinaries on court day, set up stalls in the yard or along the road, selling their beer and hard cider. A nearby field became an impromptu race course, for inevitably conversation about horses led to wagering. Milling in the yard, our people met, talked, smoked, and read the potpourri of announcements attached to Robinson's door—intentions to leave the country (did John Ascough, departing for England, owe one money? would he carry letters with him?); proclamations by the governor: notices of stray horses, of distress sales, and of missing heirs; and the rules of the court:

> Noe person presume to move the Court for anything, but by peticion.

> Noe peticion bee presented to this Court but in a faire and legible hand, otherwise the peticion to bee rejected.

> Noe person presume to speake to any busines in Court wherein hee is not onely called and concerned, [but] permitted by the Court.

> Noe person presume to smoke tobaccoe or to be covered in the face of this Court upon the penaltie of lyeing in the stocks one houre or payeing 100 lb of tobaccoe.[45]

Stocks, together with the pillory, stood in the yard awaiting use.

All the while, inside, Robinson would be directing his servants as the hall was rearranged for the session: a table and chairs at one end for the justices; a jurors' bench to the side; and as much open space as possible for litigants, their spokesmen, and spectators to stand in. The spokesmen were sometimes attorneys in a real sense, but too often—despite the rules of the court—simply "busy and ignorant men who . . . pretend to assist their freind in his busines and to cleare the matter more plainly to the court although never desired or requested thereunto."[46] Finally, at ten in the morning, the justices entered to take their seats and the sheriff opened the proceedings by reading their commission from the governor:

To all to Whom these present shall come, Greetings. Know yee that I
have assigned these gentlemen severally and every one of them justices
to keep the peace for Middlesex County, charging them to keep all ordi-
nances, statutes, and acts of assembly set forth for the conservation of
the peace and the good rule and government of the people, to cause to
come before them any or all such that shall threaten or assault any of his
Majesties liege people either in their bodies or burning their houses to
give good and sufficient securityes before you of their peace and good
behavior, to hear and determine all suites and controversies between
party and party, as neare as may bee according to the lawes of England
and lawes and customes of this countrye.[47]

The justices swearing to discharge their duty, the session began.

As the rules indicated, business was brought before the court by petition—perhaps a request from an inhabitant for payment for a service done
the county or to be named executor to an estate; or from a group of inhabitants asking that the justices order the clearing of a road or building of a
bridge; or from one inhabitant charging another with trespass, defamation,
assault, or nonpayment of a debt. But petition was a broad word in the context of the court's rules. A petition could be in the form of a presentment
submitted by the churchwarden on behalf of the vestry charging a servant
girl with having a bastard child or by the county's grand jury through its
foreman charging that an ordinary keeper was selling liquor "at greater
rates than is set by Law" or that a cooper was making hogsheads out of
unseasoned wood. Petitions and presentments were submitted usually in
advance of the session directly to the clerk or to a single justice, either of
whom was empowered to issue a writ to be delivered by the sheriff or sub-
sheriff commanding the presence of an opposite party.

At court the clerk took up the petitions in the order in which they lay in
a pile on the table, ostensibly the order in which they were received, reading each in turn; and the sheriff summoned the parties involved. Petitions
were put over, nonsuited—that is, dismissed with costs of appearance
awarded to a defendant when the complainant or plaintiff was not present
to press his suit—or resolved at the moment, the justices approving or rejecting, awarding or denying damages and costs, directing the sheriff to collect a fine here or inflict physical punishment there. Punishment was swift,
an earlier court having on hand one "Grasher a Neager [to] be a Beadle for
the Whipping of such delinquents as shall be found deserving." Yet leniency
of a sort was not unknown; another court ordered that "Elenor Jackson being very sick and having a Soore brest hir punishment for having a bastard
Childe is Refered to the next Court."

When jurors were needed to make a finding of fact, the sheriff simply selected the needed number from a panel of eligible males he had earlier com-

manded to attend court day, having care only that each one selected had no immediate interest in the case. The resulting panel would not appear impartial to modern eyes; among the jurors hearing the Baconian case at this session were Thomas Dudley, whose father had administered Bacon's oath in the county, and John Jones, whose brother stood attorney for the defendants. But then, among the justices sat the plaintiff, his brother-in-law Robert Beverley, and Beverley's son-in-law Bridge. And "fact" was a relative thing in this small society. What could be demonstrated in law and what was known to the county were two entirely different things, with the latter frequently the more important. The evidence against William Evans, charged with theft, was not such as to "touch his life," but the court nevertheless considered him to be a man of such "bad Character" and the circumstantial evidence against him so "pregnant" that it ordered him whipped in any event. Similarly, the evidence against John and Margaret Hardy offered "not sufficient ground" to proceed, "but for as Much as they appear to the Court to be people of bad Characters," they were remanded to the jail until they could give bond for five pounds sterling each "for their good behavior for one year and a day." Only occasionally was a matter beyond the jurisdiction of the court—when the sum involved was too large or the presentment involved such a "hanious Crime . . . against almighty God" or the king's majesty as to place the perpetrator in hazard of life and limb. Such matters were forwarded to the colony's general court.[48]

Case followed case to the figurative bar of justice. And always a constant coming and going, even of justices, as men traded places with each other, some crowding into court, others pushing outside to smoke, imbibe, relieve themselves against the fence, and talk. Court day! A once-a-month event in the life of the county.

This particular court day was as any other. In the myriad of petitions dealt with by the court lay one from Thomas Tuggle asking that, because of infirmity, he be made "levy free." The court approved it. Yet this court day was also exceptional. As the session opened, four men not of the court entered to sit with but slightly apart from the county's justices: Sir Henry Chicheley, Ralph Wormeley, Nicholas Spencer, and Richard Lee. Sir Henry and his stepson Wormeley were, of course, Middlesex men; Spencer and Lee were from Westmoreland County. But Chicheley was deputy governor of Virginia, and all four were members of his majesty's council of state for the colony; all had been declared, with Berkeley, traitors "against the cominality" by Bacon; and all had suffered Baconian depredation.[49]

Quite conceivably their mutual presence at court was merely coincidental. Spencer and Lee could well have been on their way to or from Westmoreland, breaking their journey at Rosegill. Chicheley, who had business unrelated to the Baconians to attend to at the court, might simply have invited the others to come along. It is equally conceivable, however, that their attendance was purposeful, that they suspected Baconian sympathies were rampant and intended to overawe with their presence the court, jury, and milling populace. Such suspicions might well have been to the point. Berkeley himself supposedly spoke of "not above five hundred persons untainted" by rebellion in all Virginia, while an underlying Baconian sympathy born from common frustrations and tensions could explain the ease with which the Middlesex Baconians slipped back into their normal lives.[50] In any event, the councillors sat through Chicheley's business—the first to be called—and the trial itself, but left immediately thereafter, perhaps simply to go to dinner at Rosegill, perhaps because their task was done when the jury brought in its verdict for Wormeley.

We remark the brief presence of the councillors at this September court to make a point. The rebellion had been born in the stiff, unbending characters of its major actors—Bacon and Berkeley—and carried along by the anxieties and frustrations of common Virginians. Passing, it left a residue of suspicion. But it by no means shattered what had come to exist in the county. Sir Thomas Grantham, a ship captain who had placed his vessel in the service of the governor, subsequently wrote of "the Ties we are under, from the Relation which we bear to Communities" and of being all "link'd together in society"; these "engage our Care" for the defense of "Particular Beings" and our "Concern for their Welfare." The councillors sitting with but apart from the justices hark back to the rebellion; the otherwise ordinary court day epitomizes the ties and common concerns of the society that had emerged along the road, a society, moreover, that commanded allegiance if not always affection. "Concerning my Seeing England I give you many thankes," Alice Corbin, nee Eltonhead, relict Burnham, wrote about this time. Widowed once more when, in 1676, Henry Corbin was killed by Indians, Alice was responding to an invitation from an English brother-in-law to live with him. "But I have not any inclination to leave Virginia whilst I live, though I must confess the last years troubles both with in our selves and those with the Indians hath given but few people reason to fall in love with it, the differences with in our selves being far greater then those without. . . . God be praised [they] are now well composed."[51]

NOTES

1. Middlesex Orders, 1694–1705, 335. For the location of the Upper Chapel, see George Carrington Mason, *Colonial Churches of Tidewater Virginia* (Richmond, Va., 1945), 280–82.

2. William W. Hening, comp., *The Statutes at Large: Being a Collection of all the Laws of Virginia from the First Session of the Legislature in 1619* (Richmond, New York, and Philadelphia, 1809–23), II, 156; H. R. McIlwaine and J. P. Kennedy, eds., *Journals of the House of Burgesses of Virginia* (Richmond, Va., 1905–15), II, 48; Middlesex Orders, 1673–80, 21, 22.

3. Gilbert Chinard, ed., *A Huguenot Exile in Virginia: Or Voyages of a Frenchman exiled for his Religion with a description of Virginia and Maryland* (New York, 1934), 142.

4. Edmund Berkeley and Dorothy S. Berkeley, "Another 'Account of Virginia' By the Reverend John Clayton," *Virginia Magazine of History and Biography*, LXXVI (1968), 421.

5. Ibid., 426.

6. Chinard, ed., *Huguenot Exile*, 119.

7. Cary Carson et al., "Impermanent Architecture in the Southern American Colonies," *Winterthur Portfolio*, XVI (1981), 135–96, is a superb treatment of the subject; Carson, "Doing History with Material Culture," in Ian M. G. Quimby, ed., *Material Culture and the Study of American Life* (New York, 1978), 56–57, is a flawed preliminary statement. H. Chandlee Forman, *Old Buildings, Gardens, and Furniture in Tidewater Maryland* (Cambridge, Md., 1967), 189–200, describes an extant house that originally used tree trunks as piers and includes a photograph of a much decomposed remnant.

8. For obvious reasons, the glebe house is the best documented in Middlesex. Its history can be followed in C. G. Chamberlayne, ed., *The Vestry Book of Christ Church Parish, Middlesex County, Virginia, 1663–1767* (Richmond, Va., 1927). The quotations are from pp. 21, 46, 107–8, 115, 218–19.

9. By H. Chandlee Forman in *The Architecture of the Old South: The Medieval Style, 1585–1850* (Cambridge, Mass., 1948), *Virginia Architecture in the Seventeenth Century* (Williamsburg, Va., 1957), 23, and other works. While perhaps technical misnomers, "medieval" and "gothic" convey the texture of the style.

10. See our *A Place in Time: Explicatus* (New York, 1984), "Child-Naming Patterns."

11. We use "traditional" and "modern" as ideal types delimiting a scale, full well recognizing that societies always fall somewhere between ideals. A good short statement is in Richard D. Brown, *Modernization: The Transformation of American Life, 1600–1865* (New York, 1976), 7–16. Note also the argument against a modern entrepreneurial mindset in James A. Henretta, "Families and Farms: *Mentalité* in Pre-Industrial America," *William and Mary Quarterly*, 3d ser., XXV (1978), 3–32.

12. On the growth and changing nature of the population, see *Explicatus*, "Population Estimates."

13. See generally Abbot Emerson Smith, *Colonists in Bondage: White Servitude and Convict Labor in America, 1607–1776* (Chapel Hill, N.C., 1947), and specifically: Mildred Campbell, "Social Origins of Some Early Americans," in James Morton Smith, ed., *Seventeenth-Century America: Essays in Colonial History* (Chapel Hill, N.C., 1959), 63–89; David Galenson, "'Middling People' or 'Common Sort'? The Social Origins of Some Early Americans Reexamined," *William and Mary Quarterly*, 3d ser., XXXV (1978), 499–524, and "Mildred Campbell's Response," 525–40; Campbell, "'Of People Too Few or Many': The Conflict of Opinion on Population and Its Relations to Emigration," in William Appleton Aiken and Basil Duke Henning, eds., *Conflict in Stuart England: Essays in Honour of Wallace Notestein* (London, 1960), 171–201; Galenson, "British Servants and the Colonial Indenture System in the Eighteenth Century," *Journal of Southern History*, XLIV (1978), 41–66; Galenson, "Immigration and the Colonial Labor System: An Analysis of the Length of Indenture," *Explorations in Economic History*, XIV (1977), 360–77; James Horn, "Servant Emigration to the Chesapeake in the Seventeenth Century," in Thad W. Tate and David L. Ammerman, eds., *The Chesapeake*

in the Seventeenth Century: Essays on Anglo-American Society (Chapel Hill, N.C., 1979), 51–95; and David Souden, "'Rogues, whores and vagabonds': Indentured Servant Emigrants to North America, and the Case of Mid-Seventeenth Century Bristol," *Social History*, III (1978), 23–41. Galenson's *White Servitude in Colonial America: An Economic Analysis* (New York, 1982) appeared too late to be of direct use.

14. On early blacks and the shift to Africans, see Philip D. Curtin, *The Atlantic Slave Trade: A Census* (Madison, Wis., 1969), 118–19, 142–43; Russell R. Menard, "The Maryland Slave Population, 1658 to 1730: A Demographic Profile of Blacks in Four Counties," *William and Mary Quarterly*, 3d ser., XXXII (1975), 29–54; Allan Kulikoff, "The Origins of Afro-American Society in Tidewater Maryland and Virginia, 1700 to 1790," *William and Mary Quarterly*, 3d ser., XXXV (1978), 226–40.

15. On mortality see *Explicatus*. There is no way to establish an exact percentage for those surviving servitude. Edmund S. Morgan, *American Slavery, American Freedom: The Ordeal of Colonial Virginia* (New York, 1975), 180–85, argues that mortality rates in general improved from the 1640s on. Our calculations indicate a radical deterioration in Middlesex in the last quarter of the century. These separate conclusions suggest that servant survival rates in Middlesex were high during the first twenty years of settlement, then declined. It is unlikely, however, that more than 50 percent of arriving servants survived to freedom.

16. Middlesex Orders, 1673–80, 23. Lois Green Carr and Russell R. Menard, "Immigration and Opportunity: The Freedman in Early Colonial Maryland," in Tate and Ammerman, eds., *Chesapeake in the Seventeenth Century*, 208–9, estimate that 40% of those immigrating under indentures died. Formal indentures usually involved a shorter term of servitude than was required of those entering without indentures or as minors and serving according to the "custom of the country." When service categories involving these longer periods are included, the 40% estimate rises to some 60%.

17. The more frequent approach and that of Carr and Menard in ibid.; Menard, "From Servant to Freeholder: Status Mobility and Property Accumulation in Seventeenth-Century Maryland," *William and Mary Quarterly*, 3d ser., XXX (1973), 37–64; Lorena S. Walsh, "Servitude and Opportunity in Charles County, Maryland, 1658–1705," in Aubrey C. Land et al., *Law, Society and Politics in Early Maryland* (Baltimore, Md., 1977), 111–33; Menard, P. M. G. Harris, and Carr, "Opportunity and Inequality: The Distribution of Wealth on the Lower Western Shore of Maryland, 1638–1705," *Maryland Historical Magazine*, LXIX (1974), 169–84.

18. The patenting system flowed from the headright system, i.e., for every "head" transported into Virginia, the person paying the cost of transportation gained the right to fifty acres of land. Robert Beverley, *The History and Present State of Virginia*, ed. Louis B. Wright (Chapel Hill, N.C., 1947), 277–78, described the system as of the turn of the seventeenth to eighteenth century. To paraphrase: (1) The headrights were "proved" by entering a list of persons transported to the clerk of a court and swearing to the truth of the list. They were then forwarded to and certified by the secretary of the colony. Notably, certified headrights ("certificates") circulated almost as money. (2) The applicant selected the land and obtained an official survey. (3) A copy of the survey, with certificates sufficient for the size of the tract, was forwarded to the secretary, who, if there were no objections or contravening patents, made out the patent itself, which was subsequently "passed" by the governor and council. The patent was conditional upon paying a quitrent of twelvepence per fifty acres and "seating" the

land within three years, that is, clearing, planting, and tending an acre of corn or building a house and running cattle for a year. A patent could "lapse" if not seated or it could "escheat" upon the death of the patentee intestate and devoid of "heirs of the body." In both instances, a second party had to act to obtain the lapse or escheat; the loss of the land was, therefore, neither automatic nor inevitable. The patenting of land purchased or inherited as a way of insuring title was a very common phenomenon. This and the multiple entry of headrights makes the use of patents for any other purpose than tracking particular properties very hazardous, and even in tracking, patents considered without a scrutiny of wills and conveyances in county records can be misleading. Extant patents are on file at the Virginia State Library, Richmond; specific patents can be located using the manuscript Index and Abstracts of Patents and Grants, Counties, Nos. 19 (Lancaster) and 21 (Middlesex), or Nell Marion Nugent, *Cavaliers and Pioneers: Abstracts of Virginia Land Patents and Grants* (Richmond, Va., 1934–79). We have invariably gone back to the full patent as the source of the most complete information.

19. Middlesex Deeds, 1679–94, 138. Old Nash's partner, Needles, also earned enough to buy and followed the same course of selling and renting parts of his land.

20. The terms of the lease in this case are embodied in Tuggle's will in Middlesex Wills, 1675–1798, pt. 1, 27–28.

21. In Middlesex subdivision continued well beyond the abrupt decline of the servant body in the 1680s and 1690s; it was not, therefore, a case of exhausting the supply of land when there were still freed servants wanting it, but the reverse. The number of freed servants (demand) gave out before the supply. Sons of those with land replaced the freedmen on the demand side, but this created an altogether different psychological problem.

22. Based upon our own analysis of prices and values from a variety of Middlesex sources and Menard's analysis of values found in Maryland and Virginia inventories as reported in his "From Servants to Slaves: The Transformation of the Chesapeake Labor System," *Southern Studies*, XVI (1977), 372. See also Paul G. E. Clemens, *The Atlantic Economy and Colonial Maryland's Eastern Shore: From Tobacco to Grain* (Ithaca, N.Y., 1980), 62.

23. Middlesex Wills, 1713–34, 80.

24. Middlesex Wills, 1675–1798, pt. 1, 27–28.

25. Beverley, *History*, 78. Wilcomb E. Washburn, *The Governor and the Rebel: A History of Bacon's Rebellion in Virginia* (Chapel Hill, N.C., 1957) remains the best account.

26. "Proclamations of Nathaniel Bacon," *Virginia Magazine of History and Biography*, I (1893–94), 60–61; "A True Narrative of the Late Rebellion in Virginia, By the Royal Commissioners, 1677," in Charles M. Andrews, ed., *Narratives of the Insurrections, 1675–1690* (New York, 1915), 122.

27. "Virginia in 1677–1678 [Sainsbury Abstracts]," *Virginia Magazine of History and Biography*, XXIII (1915), 148–49.

28. Brent's route is surmised from Bacon's, as the latter moved to counter Brent's approach.

29. "The History of Bacon's and Ingram's Rebellion, 1676," in Andrews, ed., *Narratives*, 87.

30. Chamberlayne, ed., *Vestry Book of Christ Church*, 25; "Persons Who Suffered by Bacon's Rebellion. The Commissioners' Report," *Virginia Magazine of History and Bi-*

ography, V (1897–98), 64–70; Hening, comp., *Statutes at Large*, III, 569. Sir Henry Chicheley was also imprisoned, but not in the county. Despite extensive genealogical research on the Wormeley family both by us and others (e.g., *Virginia Magazine of History and Biography*, XXXV [1927], 455–56, XXXVI [1928], 98–101, 283–93, 385–88), there is no evidence of a connection between the two Wormeley families of Middlesex, one stemming from the Ralph Wormeley who settled Rosegill and the other from the Christopher referred to here. The latter makes his first appearance in the county records in 1667. By then he was already married to Frances Armistead, widow of both Justinian Aylmer and Anthony Elliott. (Armistead, Aylmer, and Elliott were all prominent names in the colony and Anthony Elliott a major Middlesex landowner.) Wormeley is not a common name, however, suggesting a connection between the two families. The fact that "Christopher" does not appear in the line from Ralph although it was the given name of Ralph's grandfather, father, and brother hints at a "left-handed" connection displeasing to the Rosegill family. The most obvious possibility is that Christopher of Middlesex was Ralph II's uncle Christopher's illegitimate son. The earlier Christopher had been governor of Tortuga in the 1630s and had come to Virginia following the Spanish capture of that island, settling in York. A justice of the York County Court and member of the colony council, he died in the early 1640s, his widow marrying William Brocas.

31. Middlesex Orders, 1673–80, 61, 77–78, 81, 90.

32. We can at least estimate the age of twenty-one of the defendants. We report the median.

33. It might be argued that Wormeley (whose suit gives us most of the Baconians) could name only those of Boodle's troop he knew and that he would have recognized long-term residents more readily than others. In the nature of seventeenth-century judicial proceedings, however, what was common knowledge of the vicinage was as admissible as particular knowledge. Wormeley need not even have had to be on his property at the time of the raid to cite as defendants those whom common knowledge associated with the trespass. Moreover, in returning their verdict the jury specifically found against "Dr. Robert Boodle . . . with the rest of his Troope." Middlesex Orders, 1673–80, 78.

34. Five separate random drawings of twenty-four Middlesex men resident in the 1670s produced only five men in all whose life histories displayed incidents similar to those in the text.

35. Middlesex Orders, 1673–80, 71.

36. T[homas] M[athew], "The Beginning, Progress and Conclusion of Bacon's Rebellion, 1675–1676," in Andrews, ed., *Narratives*, 40.

37. Eventually their eleven hundred acres would lapse for lack of seating; Hooper would lose his plantation next to Richens's in a debt proceeding.

38. Lancaster Orders, 1655–66, 135.

39. Our agreement with Washburn, *Governor and the Rebel*, 83, and disagreement with the thesis of Book III of Morgan, *American Slavery, American Freedom*, 215–92, is self-evident. The dichotomization of the latter fails to encompass both the totality of the early Chesapeake system we see operating in the county and the nature of the county's Baconians.

40. Middlesex Orders, 1673–80, 60; C.O. 1/40, 129, Public Record Office, London.

41. In the absence of general court records, we do not know the results of the appeals. However, by the time they reached the general court (if, indeed, they did), the official climate was against such prosecutions. If the appeals had gone against the defendants, one would expect the county court records to reflect the fact in executions and distraints for the actual collection of the damages awarded. There are none.

42. There is no evidence from Middlesex to support the description by other authors of a Berkeleian "terror" following the suppression of the rebellion. Notably, such descriptions are documented by recounting the executions of twenty-three Baconian leaders and quoting descriptions sent to England by royal commissioners intent on painting the governor in the worst possible light. See e.g., Thomas J. Wertenbaker, *Virginia under the Stuarts, 1607–1688* (Princeton, N.J., 1914), 200–207. Both of the "lucrative lawsuits" entered in Middlesex by followers of Berkeley intent on enriching themselves—part of what Morgan, *American Slavery, American Freedom*, 274–75, calls "the legalized plundering by which the loyal party were accumulating property at the expense of everyone they could label a rebel," which extended into 1680—are recounted in the text. Robert Beverley, alleged to be one of the chief plunderers, filed neither.

43. Middlesex Orders, 1673–80, 71.

44. Ibid., 45.

45. Lancaster Orders, 1666–80, 208. We have reordered the rules and omitted ellipses for effect.

46. Hening, comp., *Statutes at Large*, II, 478.

47. We have shortened and in part paraphrased the Middlesex commission of May 1684 found in Middlesex Deeds, 1679–94, 144–45.

48. Lancaster Deeds, 1652–57, 213; Middlesex Orders, 1694–1704, 424; 1710–21, 111–12; 1721–26, 6; "Some helps for the Grand Jury of Middlesex," Middlesex Deeds, 1679–94, 672–73. In this early period, the forms of law were only loosely followed. See Henry Hartwell, James Blair, and Edward Chilton, *The Present State of Virginia and the College*, ed. Hunter Dickinson Farish (Williamsburg, Va., 1940), 44–45. Published originally in 1727, the description was written thirty years earlier. The justices' principal guide was Michael Dalton, *The Countrey Justice, Containing the practise of the Justices of the Peace out of their Sessions. Gathered, for the better helpe of such Justices of Peace as have not been much conversant in the studie of the Lawes* (London, 1622) and their knowledge of Virginia's statutes. The description in the text, however, is based upon actual proceedings at the Lancaster and Middlesex courts. These frequently were at variance with both Dalton and statute.

49. The councillors had a customary and legal right to attend and even vote in any county court, although they did not do so ordinarily. Hening, comp., *Statutes at Large*, II, 358, 390.

50. Quoted in Washburn, *Governor and the Rebel*, 109.

51. Sir Thomas Grantham, *An Historical Account of Some Memorable Actions, Particularly in Virginia* (London, 1716), 3–4; "The Corbin Family," *Virginia Magazine of History and Biography*, XXIX (1921), 378–79.

JACK P. GREENE

Society, Ideology, and Politics: An Analysis of the Political Culture of Mid-Eighteenth-Century Virginia

* * * * * * * * VIRGINIANS CONTRIBUTED AN ENORMOUS, AND disproportionate, share of statesmanship and political ability to the American Revolution. "This extraordinary flowering of talents," Jack Greene argues, was no accident. "The high quality of Virginia political leadership derived quite as much from a viable political culture as from the individual talents of its practitioners." The key to understanding that culture, Greene claims, is the character of the Virginia gentry.

By the middle of the eighteenth century, articulate and dedicated plantation leaders dominated the public life of the colony. They exercised power, to be sure, in their own interests. Nonetheless, they expressed a deep commitment to an ethic of "stewardship and order" that afforded widespread legitimacy to their rule. As Greene notes, "the very ideal of government by extraordinary men imposed an enormous obligation upon the ruling group in Virginia," an obligation that they seem to have fulfilled with considerably ability. While it is clearly the case that gentlemen benefited materially from public service, they also served out of a sincere sense of duty and responsibility to their local communities.

The unity of white Virginia, Greene suggests, reflected the harmony underlying plantation society before the 1760s. Despite significant economic inequality between large planters and small, there was remarkably little political conflict. "Deference and respect, not envy and resentment or fear and obsequiousness, were the conventional attitudes of the rest of Virginia society towards the gentry." Slavery and a commitment to tobacco culture ensured that there was little disparity in the class interests of small yeoman planters and the gentleman who owned the best and largest tracts of land as well as the vast majority of Virginia's slaves. Thus in many respects Greene picks up where Edmund Morgan left off. Stability, stewardship, and order existed as viable ideals in the colony because Virginia's large planters had little need to oppress the small.

Simmering beneath the ordered world of Greene's Virginia, however, was the violence that fixed some Virginians in bondage but also erupted frequently in defiant acts of private resistance by the enslaved. This violence at the core of what J. Frederick Fausz called "the golden age of the Chesapeake gentry" originated, he concluded, "in the simultaneous demise of Indian sovereignty and the rise of African slavery." This paradox of order and violence was what disrupted Virginia society during the American Revolution, according to Woody Holton, and threatened to undermine it in the brutal murder of Robert Berkeley, recounted by Deborah Lee and Warren Hofstra. The replacement of slavery by race after emancipation as a contested ordering principle of Virginia society is a theme explored in articles that follow on late nineteenth- and twentieth-century Virginia.

* * * * * * * *

* * * * * * * *
OVER THE PAST TWO CENTURIES, FEW COMMENTATORS ON THE era of the American Revolution have failed to appreciate Virginia's preeminent contribution of political talent to that period, a contribution which has perhaps never been equaled by any other state at any other point in American history. What has been less appreciated and only imperfectly understood, however, is that this extraordinary flowering of talents was not simply an accident of history and that the high quality of Virginia political leadership derived quite as much from a viable political culture as from the individual talents of its practitioners. The brilliant assemblage of gifted politicians associated with Revolutionary Virginia—Patrick Henry and George Washington, George Mason and Thomas Jefferson, James Madison and John Marshall are only the most conspicuous examples—brought much more than their own individual geniuses to the momentous events between 1763 and 1789.

Trained in a functional political system which had been tested and refined by a century and a half of experience and coming out of a tradition of superior political leadership which was of more than two generations' standing, they brought as well an intimate knowledge of day-to-day politics in a society where politics was an old and laudable pursuit. Perhaps of equal importance, they came with a deep commitment to a code of political behavior and a political ideology which was peculiarly well suited to meet the demands of a revolutionary situation. That commitment governed their relationships with one another and with leaders from other places and determined to a remarkable extent the nature of their responses to the successive problems of their generation. To identify the code and the ideology to which they were committed—the rules of the game of politics as it had come to be played in mid-eighteenth-century Virginia—and to elaborate the social circumstances and political conditions that underlay them are necessary first steps toward understanding Virginia's extraordinary contribution to the foundation of the American nation.

The key to any comprehension of the politics of colonial Virginia is that unusual group referred to by contemporaries as the "Virginia gentry." In its largest meaning the term *gentry* referred to a broad and miscellaneous category of people: old families and new, those of great and only modest wealth, mannered gentlefolk and crude social upstarts, the learned and the ignorant. As the dissenter James Reid, an obscure but effective social satirist, said of the gentry of King William County in the 1760s, any person who had "Money, Negroes and Land enough" was automatically considered a gentleman, so that even a person "looked upon as . . . unworthy of a Gentleman's notice because he had no Land and Negroes" could, if he "by some means or other, acquired both," become "a Gentleman all of a sudden." What Reid's remarks underline is that the only common denominator among all of the members of the broad social category of gentry was possession of more than ordinary wealth.[1]

Within that broad category, however, was a much smaller, cohesive, and self-conscious social group, at the core of which were about forty interrelated families who had successfully competed with other immigrants for wealth and power through the middle decades of the seventeenth century and consolidated their position between 1680 and 1730. Initially, their fortunes had been derived from a wide variety of sources—planting, shipping, commerce, land development, public office, the law—but by the early decades of the eighteenth century, plantation agriculture—specifically, tobacco culture—had become the most prestigious economic pursuit. Members of this inner gentry continued to engage in a variety of subsidiary or auxiliary enterprises, and some even spent more of their energies in commerce or at the bar than in managing their estates. But almost all of them were heavily involved in planting, and although by the 1740s and 1750s antiquity of family was also becoming of some consequence, possession of large holdings of land and slaves was perhaps the most visible symbol of membership in the group. Because wealth in a rapidly expanding economy was available to most enterprising men and, especially after 1730, to the lawyers who were needed in large numbers to handle an ever-increasing volume of land and business transactions, the inner gentry was continuously replenished from below and without, and the social structure remained open throughout the colonial and Revolutionary periods. There was always room for the ambitious, talented, and successful from among both new immigrants and scions of the older yeomanry, and frequent marriages between families with new wealth and those of the older gentry meant that assimilation was quick and easy.[2]

The gentry dominated virtually every phase of life in the colony. Its members created with the use of slaves and large units of production a disproportionate amount of the colony's wealth, frequently served as entrepreneurs for smaller producers in their immediate areas, and stimulated the growth of the colony by their activities in land development. In politics, they early assumed leadership, filling almost all posts of responsibility at every level of government from the governor's council and the elective House of Burgesses down to the county courts and the parish vestries. In social and intellectual life, they were the unquestioned leaders, defining the preferred social roles and the dominant values, setting the style of life to which all ambitious Virginians aspired, providing, as the young New Jersey tutor Philip Fithian observed in 1773, "the pattern of all behaviour."[3]

Although the gentry was preeminent in Virginia life and was probably, as the English traveler J. F. D. Smyth noted in the 1780s, more numerous than its counterparts in other colonies, it never constituted more than a small percentage of the total population. If the category is defined as the larger plantation owners and their families—a definition which would include all of the larger merchants and the wealthier and more important lawyers—it probably did not comprise much over 2 to 5 percent of the total white inhabitants, with the inner gentry group comprising no more than a fraction, perhaps a fifth, of the whole category. Beneath the gentry was a numerous miscellany of free white people whom contemporaries customarily divided into two ranks—a very large middle rank consisting of the less affluent planters, independent yeoman farmers, and rural artisans and tradesmen, who together with their families seem to have comprised the bulk of the white population in every Virginia county, and an apparently smaller lower rank of landless overseers and agricultural laborers, many of them young or just out of their indentures, who, according to travelers, were seldom miserable and were fewer "in number, in proportion to the rest of the inhabitants, than perhaps [in] any other country in the universe."[4]

If there was little real poverty among white people in colonial Virginia, there were nonetheless great extremes in wealth, and traveler after traveler was impressed, as was Smyth, by the "greater distinction supported between the different classes of life" in Virginia than in most of the other colonies. Just how this distinction affected the inner dynamics of Virginia society, the relations between various social groups, is not an easy matter to determine. Smyth thought that that "spirit of equality, and levelling principle" which pervaded "the greatest part of America" did not "prevail to such an extent in Virginia," and Fithian testified in the early 1770s that the "amazing property" of the gentry so tended to blow "up the owners to an imagination, which is visible in all, but in various degrees according to their respective virtue, that they are exalted as much above other Men in worth & precedency, as blind stupid fortune has made a difference in their property."[5] . . .

Whether this attitude was matched at the other end of society by that envy of the rich that modern social analysts have come to expect from the poor is less easy to establish. The lower sort, obviously, left few records of their aspirations and resentments, but there was at least some suspicion among the gentry that, as Landon Carter phrased it in response to a poetic election attack on him, there was "something in a good Estate, which those who don't enjoy, will ever hate." There were also some poorer sorts like the Reverend Devereux Jarratt, a carpenter's son, who remembered in his old age that as a small boy he had regarded the "*gentle folks*, as beings of a superior order" and "kept off at a humble distance." Still others who, like the growing group of dissenting Baptists after 1760, found the lifestyle of the more crude and dissolute segments of the gentry thoroughly reprehensible, reviled the gentry as "men brought up in ignorance, nourished in pride, encouraged in luxury, taught inhumanity and self conceit, tutored in debauchery, squandering youth either in idleness, or in acquiring knowledge which ought to be forgot, illiterate, untinctured by sentiment, untouched by virtues of humanity."[6]

Most remaining evidence, however, indicates that deference and respect, not envy and resentment or fear and obsequiousness, were the conventional attitudes of the rest of Virginia society toward the gentry. How many people shared the pride in the gentry exhibited by the York County blacksmith—and erstwhile poet—Charles Hansford is not clear. "Who can but love the place that hath brought forth / Such men of virtue, merit, honor, worth?" rhymed Hansford in 1752:

> The gentry of Virginia, I dare say,
> For honor vie with all America.
> Had I great Camden's skill, how freely I
> Would celebrate our worthy gentry.[7]

Economic inequality does not, however, seem to have resulted in any deep or widespread social or political antagonisms toward the gentry, at least not before the 1760s. A remarkably wide franchise which extended even to tenants who rented the requisite amount of land;[8] a fluid social structure with a vital upper stratum which not only was always eager to receive but also was constantly searching out new talents and new abilities; the mixing of tenants, yeomen, small planters, and gentlemen amongst one another in every section of the colony; and frequent interchanges among people of all social classes at church, court days, horse races, cockfights, militia musters, and elections—all seem both to have precluded the development of a rigidly stratified social system and to have promoted free and easy intercourse among all groups in the society. Moreover, the fact that tobacco was the lifeblood of the entire economy and every segment of society meant that disparity of economic interests among people of various social categories was rare. Richard Bland, perhaps the most impressive political thinker in mid-eighteenth-century Virginia and also a member of an old gentry family, accurately characterized the situation when he wrote in

1745 that he would "always act to the utmost of my capacity for the good of my electors, whose interest and my own, in great measure, are inseparable."[9] . . .

Some of the cement of this relatively harmonious relationship between the gentry and the rest of society was supplied by the related concepts of stewardship and order. Frequent observations by travelers and Virginians alike on the indolence of the lesser gentry and the middle and lower ranks in the colony, with their fondness for society and their addiction to pleasure, suggest that apathy may have been the primary reason why men from those ranks failed to play a more prominent role in political life.[10]

But a factor of enormous importance was the widespread belief among Virginians at all levels of society that government should be reserved for and was the responsibility of enlightened and capable men. "The happiness of mankind," the Reverend David Griffith, Anglican rector of Shelburne Parish, declared in a sermon before the Virginia Convention in 1776, "depends, in a great measure, on the well ordering of society," while order, in turn, depended upon a necessary "subordination in society." However complex the economic and social divisions in colonial Virginia, there were only two orders in politics. All society was divided between the rulers and the ruled, and although the line of separation was neither very sharply nor very rigidly drawn, the habit of equating the rulers with "Gentlemen of Ability and Fortune" had the sanction of a long tradition which stretched back well beyond the original settlement of the colonies to antiquity.[11]

Although the gentry never pretended to have an "exclusive title to common sense, wisdom or integrity" and insisted upon the "right" of all "orders of men" to "assume the character of politicians," men of "High Birth and Fortune," as one anonymous writer, perhaps the Reverend Jonathan Boucher, pointed out in 1774, did have "the solid and splendid advantages of education and accomplishments; extensive influence, and incitement to glory." Because they also had "a greater Stake in the Country" and enjoyed a "larger Property," the Reverend William Stith of the College of William and Mary declared in a sermon before the House of Burgesses in 1752, they were naturally "bound . . . to be more studious of that Country's Good." The conclusion followed almost irresistibly that they were, therefore, the proper persons to entrust with the political leadership of the country.[12]

On the other hand, those in the middle and lower ranks, who, it was assumed, lacked the talent, wisdom, training, time, or interest for politics, were expected, as Lieutenant Governor William Gooch put it in the early 1730s, to live as honest men, mind their own business, fear God, honor the king, make good tobacco, shun those "given to Noise and Violence," and "Submit . . . to every Law." The liberty of the governed depended, in fact, declared the Reverend James Horrocks, also of the college, in 1763, upon "a dutiful Obedience to the Laws of our Country, and those [of] our Superiors, who have the Care of them." The alternative, he suggested, was no less than complete licentiousness, a state in which those handmaidens of the happy state—"Liberty and public Safety"—actually became enemies instead of allies to each other. There was, then, in society no antagonism but, as David Griffith observed, *a mutual obligation . . . between the governed and their rulers.*" That obligation consisted in a reciprocal promise, a kind of covenant, to which all free white inhabitants were party, by which the rulers—those "virtuous and enlightened citizens" whose numbers were small in every community—were to provide good government, and the governed were to obey them.[13]

Government by the "virtuous and enlightened" was not only the ideal but also, to a remarkable degree, the habit of colonial Virginians. Members of the native gentry occupied almost all important appointive posts. Right up to 1776, the crown regularly chose them for all crown offices except the governorship and lieutenant governorship as well as for its twelve-man council, which throughout the middle decades of the eighteenth century was for the most part "composed of some very respectable characters." Similarly, governors invariably selected the gentry for justices of the peace, sheriffs, militia officers, and other positions in county government.[14]

Within the counties, the critical areas where the values of the community were enforced, the gentlemen justices of the peace had complete authority to administer the laws and dispense justice. Particular status and responsibility attached to membership in the quorum, that inner circle of justices designated by the governor from among the most esteemed men in the county, whose presence was required in all "Matters of Importance." Charged with the heavy responsibility of doing "equal Right to all Manner of People, Great and Small, High and Low, Rich and Poor, according to Equity, and good Conscience, and the Laws and Usages of . . . Virginia, without Favour, Affection, or Partiality," all magistrates, and especially members of the quorum, said the handbook which described and directed them in the execution of their responsibilities, were supposed to be "Men of Substance and Ability of Body and Estate; of the best Reputation, good Governance, and Courage for the Truth; Men fearing God, not seeking the Place for Honour or Conveniency, but endeavouring to preserve the Peace and good Government of their Country, wherein they ought to be resident." . . . Moreover, the freeholders regularly exercised their liberty of choice to select gentlemen to represent them in Williamsburg in the elective House of Burgesses, the only institution of government elected by the voters in Virginia and by the 1750s certainly more powerful and perhaps more prestigious even than the royal council.[15]

Because the small size of the council excluded all but a few from a seat on it, the pinnacle of success for most of the politically ambitious among the gentry was a position of leadership in the House of Burgesses. To reach such a position a man had to go through a process of rigorous selection. First, he had to have the approval and the backing of the leading local gentry. Individuals without such approval often sought and occasionally won election, but because of the long and vital tradition of gentry leadership, the sanction of community leaders was usually a decisive advantage. Moreover, the gentry tended to select from among its numbers not the gamesters or the spendthrifts, not those whom the Reverend John Camm, the contentious Anglican rector of Yorkhampton Parish, derisively referred to as "decayed gentry" or James Reid cruelly lampooned as "Assqueers," but the men they most admired; and those they most admired were those who most successfully adhered to the most cherished and deeply held values of the group. The man who was "best esteemed and most applauded," Fithian found, was the one who attended "to his business . . . with the greatest diligence," and it was not only diligence but a whole congeries of related qualities—honesty and generosity, "probity and great Integrity," moderation and humility, courage and impartiality, learning and judgment, "Circumspection & frugality"—that recommended a gentleman to his neighborhood peers.[16]

The broad body of freeholders, the next hurdle on the path to political preferment, seem routinely to have looked for the same qualities. Of course, few candidates, no matter how impressive their other qualities, could expect to secure election if they were personally disagreeable to the voters. Only the most secure candidate did not find it necessary "to lower himself a little" to secure election. "Swilling the planters with bumbo," "Barbecues," and other forms of "treating" paid for by the "friends" of the candidates—for candidates themselves were prohibited by law from engaging openly in such activities—were common practices at elections. "At an election," said one caustic observer, "the merits of a Candidate are always measured by the number of his treats; his constituents assemble, eat upon him, and lend their applause, not to his integrity or sense, but [to] the quantities of his beef and brandy." But character and distinction rather than "Bribery" or a willingness to "cajole, fawn, and wheedle" before the populace seem to have been the characteristics that most frequently recommended men to the electorate.[17]

The freeholders understood, as a popular handbook for justices of the peace put it, both that the House of Burgesses was "one of the main Fundamentals of our Constitution, and the chief Support of the Liberty and Property of the Subject," and that, "considering the great Trust reposed in every Representative of the People in General Assembly," "every Freeholder" should "give his vote for Persons of Knowledge, Integrity, Courage, Probity, Loialty, and Experience, without Regard to Personal Inclination or Prejudice." Enjoined by the election law to choose "Two of the most fit and able Men" among them for their representatives, the free-holders regularly returned the same men whom the leading gentry also found most suitable.[18] . . .

After a man had obtained election, he underwent an even more exacting scrutiny within the House of Burgesses. Of the many called to that body, only a few were chosen for leadership. In the Burgesses, as in most large as-semblies or societies, a few men, as the German traveler Johann David Schoepf found in the 1780s, led the debate and thought and spoke for the rest. The Burgesses was the theater for political talents, and only those who turned in superb performances could expect to secure a leading role. Men with special qualities or skills that set them off from their fellows had a de-cided advantage, and it was usually those with thorough legal training, good education, and clear and refined ideas, an impressive command of language, a brilliant oratorical style, a capacity for business, unusual personal charm, or some combination of these characteristics who played the most active and influential roles, who were singled out by their fellows, the demands of the institution, and their own qualities for the pinnacle of Virginia politi-cal life.[19] . . .

Perhaps the most important element in the gentry's assumption of po-litical leadership was their commitment to the notion built into the concept of stewardship that it was not merely the right but the duty of the social and economic leaders of society to exercise the responsibilities of government. In the best tradition of the English country gentleman, the Virginia gentry labored tirelessly at the routine and tedious business of governing in the county courts, the parish vestries, the House of Burgesses, and various lo-cal offices—offices that were "Attended with a certain Expense and trouble without the least prospect of gain"—not primarily to secure the relatively small tangible economic rewards they derived from their efforts but rather to fulfill the deep sense of public responsibility thrust upon them by their position in society. That all good men should concern themselves with the welfare of their country lay at the very center of the value structure of the gentry, and when George Washington expressed his strong "Sense of Obligations to the People" to do everything in his "power for the Hon'r and Welfare of the Country," upon his first election to the House of Burgesses from Frederick County in 1758, he was merely subscribing to a time-honored belief.[20] . . .

Nor were the gentry's burdens limited to the chores of government. Upon them fell the task of providing social models and moral leadership for their respective communities. As the magistrates for the counties, the gen-try were obligated, Governor Gooch declared, to give the rest of the people "all the Light they" could "into the Intent and Meaning" of the laws, which were "the People[']s Direction in moral Actions." As "Gentlemen and Persons of Distinction," they were expected, William Stith declared in a sermon against gaming in 1752, "by their Example to lead" the "lower people . . . on to every thing, that is virtuous and honest, and with the utmost Severity of the Law to restrain and punish" vice and dishonesty. Nothing would ever affect "the Generality of the People," he added, if it were "contradicted by the Lives and Conversations . . . of their rich and powerful Neighbors." Landon Carter agreed that it was the obligation of the "polite and more considerable part" of society to set "Patterns and examples" for and give "Prudent advice and assistance to" the rest of the community, and he was convinced that there was nothing more commendable than "to let men see our good works that they may take example by them in their conduct to each other and to the happiness and safety of their Country."[21] . . .

How widely diffused and generally accepted these notions were is indicated by the remarks of the Presbyterian divine Samuel Davies, the most influential dissenting minister in Virginia in the 1750s and himself only on the fringes of the colony's establishment, to the Hanover volunteers during the Seven Years' War. Emphasizing the obligation of the gentleman-officers to "enforce Religion and good Morals by your Example and Authority" and to "suppress the Contrary," he argued that "Such a Conduct" would render them "popular among the Wise and Good" and would bring them no other censure than "the senseless Contempt of Fools."[22]

Among the gentry, fathers sought to instill this strong sense of social duty—this powerful commitment to public service—in their sons from a very young age. They took deliberate care to transmit the political values, ideals, and attitudes of the group and to nurture that devotion to the public good that was the mark of all gentlemen of distinction. One of the most important elements in the education of young gentlemen was the constant exposure to the inner workings of governmental institutions and their early involvement in discussions of political and judicial affairs. Their study was purposely oriented toward politics and the law. Because laws, one writer said in the *Virginia Gazette* in 1745, were "the Ties of harmonious Society, and Defence of Life, Liberty, and Property against arbitrary Power, Tyranny, and Oppression," they were obviously worth intensive study. The gentry, wrote one unfriendly observer, "diligently search the Scriptures; but the Scriptures which they search are the Laws of Virginia: for though you may find innumerable families in which there is no Bible, yet you will not find one without a Law-book." "Bring [up] any Subject from Mercer's abridgement [of the laws of Virginia], and the youngest in Company will immediately tell you how far a grin is actionable."[23] . . .

These were aspirations of the highest order, and they suggest still another motive for gentry participation in politics: the opportunities for diversion and distinction in public life. The give-and-take of politics was the most exciting and challenging activity in the life of rural Virginia, and the gentry enjoyed it thoroughly. Even if they proved unequal to the challenge it presented, politics still offered an escape from the isolated and sometimes enervating life of the large plantations. For the most part gentry families were widely dispersed among the counties, and neighboring with equals was neither easy nor frequent. Even men of a bookish turn, like Landon Carter or Richard Bland, longed for the conversation and company of people with similar interests and aspirations. "In Virginia," Landon Carter complained in his diary in 1762, "a man dyes a month sooner in a fit of any disorders because he can't have one soul to talk to."[24]

Yet it was not so much the possibility for diversion that pulled them into politics as the desire to excel. Their fathers and grandfathers—the men who had between 1640 and 1740 established and consolidated the position of the gentry in Virginia life—had fulfilled themselves by acquiring landed estates, enhancing the family name, and obtaining status and wealth in the community. But their extraordinary success in realizing these ambitions meant that members of the third generation, who were just coming into manhood in the 1720s and 1730s, had to look elsewhere to find a proper outlet for their talents. Whereas the desire of the first and second generations to outdistance their fellows had led them primarily into the pursuit of wealth and status and only incidentally into politics, the third generation found that their desire to excel could best be realized in the public sphere; hence they entered into politics with the same avidity and the same devotion that their ancestors had shown in carving out a place for their families in the New World environment. Increasingly in the decades after 1725, politics became the chief road to individual distinction. The public arena was where men could test their mettle in discussion and debate, employ their talents for the benefit of the community as they had been taught they were supposed to, perhaps even attain real praiseworthiness, that elusive and rare quality that set extraordinary men off from the rest of mankind and obtained for them the respect and admiration of society. Perhaps because the stakes were so high, the gentry learned to play the game very well.

At least in part because of the gentry's devotion to politics and because of the relatively high quality of government it provided through the middle decades of the eighteenth century, the concept of stewardship retained its vitality and meaning in Virginia long after it apparently began to break down elsewhere in the British colonies. In Virginia it was not just an anachronistic tradition, an empty ideal which no longer conformed to reality; it was a fact of social life. The result was a relatively harmonious political relationship between the gentry and the rest of society, the central feature of which was the routine acquiescence of the middle and lower ranks in gentry government. "From the experience of nearly sixty years in public life," the politically powerful Edmund Pendleton, one of the foremost lawyers in Virginia, wrote in 1798, "I have been taught to . . . respect this my native country for the decent, peaceable, and orderly behaviour of its inhabitants; justice has been, and is duly and diligently administered—the laws obeyed—the constituted authorities respected, and we have lived in the happy intercourse of private harmony and good will. At the same time by a free communication between those of more information on political subjects, and the classes who have not otherwise an opportunity of acquiring that knowledge, all were instructed in their *rights* and *duties* as freemen, and taught to respect them."[25] . . .

That a group so devoted to politics should have produced so little theoretical writing on political matters has puzzled many later historians. But the imperatives of Virginia political life as well as the values of the gentry dictated that other qualities should be more admired than the speculative. In Virginia, as elsewhere in the English colonies, politics had already assumed that functional and pragmatic character that has been so predominant a feature of subsequent American politics, and Virginians were wary, as Jonathan Boucher noted, of "the false refinements of speculative men, who amuse themselves and the world with visionary ideas of perfection, which never were, nor ever will be found, either in public or in private life." The man of action, the man with a capacity for business who addressed himself directly to problems at hand, rather than the philosopher, was the sort of person Virginians most admired.[26]

Many of the older gentry families and many of the new professional men, especially among the lawyers, had large libraries and seem to have read widely. One English traveler reported in the 1740s that many of the gentlemen were "a most agreeable Set of Companions, and possess a pretty deal of improving Knowledge; nay, I know some of the better sort, whose Share of Learning and Reading, would really surprise you, considering their Educations." But the Reverend Hugh Jones's characterization of Virginians as "more inclinable to read men by business and conversation, than to dive into books" seems to describe the vast majority of the gentry, who, Jones reported, were "generally diverted by business or inclination from profound study, and prying into the depths of things." Virginia's was essentially an oral culture whose predominant orientation was toward action. The gentry valued "mental acquirements" and paid "particular Respect to Men of Learning," but they appreciated other traits, including industry, polish, good character, and affability, even more and preferred that men demonstrate their "clear and penetrating powers of mind" in their deeds or in conversation and speaking rather than in writing. Men with a strong scholarly or speculative bent, such as Landon Carter and Richard Bland or, in a later generation, Thomas Jefferson and James Madison, were not quite the "biological sports" one writer has suggested, but they were the exception rather than the rule among the leading Virginia politicians.[27]

Lack of concern for political theory and speculation did not mean, however, that Virginians did not operate within a clear, if nowhere systematically articulated, framework of assumptions and perceptions about politics and society. This framework was wholly conventional and almost entirely English, albeit it contained a heavy infusion of ideas from the classics. It was drawn from a wide variety of English sources: the Anglican literature of piety, such as Richard Allestree's *The Whole Duty of Man;* popular works of civility, including Henry Peacham's *Compleat Gentleman,* Richard Braithwaite's *English Gentleman,* and Allestree's *Gentleman's Calling;* mainstream English political thought, especially as expressed in contemporary English periodicals, which quickly found their way to Virginia and frequently were pirated by the editors of the several *Virginia Gazette*s; English legal theorists, particularly Coke and, later, Blackstone; seventeenth-century Whig opposition writers like Milton, Harrington, Sydney, and Locke; Tory Augustan or "country" opposition writers, most heavily Addison, Pope, Swift, and Bolingbroke; and—to a much lesser extent—radical Whig thinkers such as Trenchard and Gordon.[28] However derivative in origin and however commonplace in content, this framework of political and social ideas played a powerful role in Virginia politics. It underlay and informed virtually all political behavior. It was, moreover, above debate. No important Virginia politician rose to challenge it at any point between 1720 and 1790, and this consensus was an important factor in both the absence of speculative political philosophy and Virginia's unanimity in the face of the repeated political crises between 1760 and 1789.

At the heart of that framework was the conventional belief in the imperfection of man. Man was not depraved or innately sinful, but he was weak, shortsighted, fallible in his judgments, perpetually self-deluded, prone to favor his own errors, and a slave to his vanity, interests, prejudices, and passions. "*Humanum est errare*" ("to be human is to err") was the Reverend David Griffith's succinct expression of this belief, and the most frequent source of man's errors, he noted in a sermon in 1775, was his "Selfishness and ambition." The pursuit of self was behind man's "insatiable passion of . . . avarice" and his "Fondness for Power incontroulable." His inability to resist those desires, which, as Landon Carter observed in his diary in 1770, "increased like a dropsical thirst . . . the more they are indulged," led him into corruption and ultimately into that state of complete depravity where "power and self aggrandizement" became the sole "object of . . . pursuit," ambition and passion ruled unrestrained, and, as Richard Bland put it in 1764, a man would "trudge, with Might and Main, through Dirt and Mire, to gain his Ends." The natural weakness of all men and the conscious malevolence of some meant that they could never be left entirely to their own devices or to the mercy of one another, for it was virtually certain, as Landon Carter pointed out, that sooner or later some of them would "fall into such Depravations of Mind, as to become more cruel than the most savage Beast of Prey." The good of every individual and of society in general demanded, therefore, that man's weak and evil tendencies be restrained; and the function of government was to protect man from himself and his fellows, to neutralize his passions by checking them against those of other men, to "restrain vice and cherish virtue," and to promote order and happiness by securing the life, liberty, and property of every individual.[29]

This was a large order. Because they were necessarily composed of imperfect men, all governments, no matter how benevolent the intentions of the rulers, could be expected to be fallible, to be continually, if inadvertently, inflicting injustice and injury upon the very society they were trying to serve. It was in the very "nature of men in authority," it seemed to Richard Henry Lee, "rather to commit two errors than to retract one." An even greater difficulty arose from the probability that there would always be some among the rulers who would be unable to resist their grosser passions. That "more determinations of government have proceeded from selfishness and ambitions, than from disinterested and benevolent measures," noted David Griffith, was a lamentable fact of history, and the paramount danger to any state was man's unquenchable thirst for power. Virginia politicians were wary of the possibility that someone or some group might eventually acquire what Richard Bland called a "Leviathon of Power" and introduce the worst sort of arbitrary and despotic polity. Clearly, the governed had to be protected from the baser tendencies of their governors, and the main instrument for their protection was the constitution.[30]

To the Virginia gentry, *constitution* was the most hallowed term in their political vocabulary. The constitution was the guarantor of their rights, liberties, and property. The "most valuable Part of our Birthright as Englishmen," Richard Bland asserted, was the "vital Principle in the Constitution" that "all men" were "only subject to Laws made with their own Consent." That principle provided the primary security for the "liberty and Property for every Person," placed them beyond the reach of the "highest EXECUTIVE Power in the State" as long as they lived in "Obedience to its Laws," and ensured that they would live under a government of impartial laws rather than partial men. For, although laws made by fallible legislators could never be entirely satisfactory to everyone in society, they were infinitely preferable to the "voluntary Mercy" or "charitable Disposition" of men.[31]

Every branch of government was bound by this principle, but the House of Burgesses, as the predominant force in the legislative process and as the agency through which the governed gave their consent to laws, was the "natural" guardian of their rights. It had a special obligation to keep a sharp eye out for any transgressions of the law and to oppose every measure that had "the least tendency to break through the legal Forms of government," because, as Bland argued, "a small spark if not extinguished in the beginning will soon gain ground and at last blaze out into an irresistible Flame." The rule of law had to be absolute. "LIBERTY & PROPERTY" were "like those previous Vessels whose soundness is destroyed by the least flaw and whose use is lost by the smallest hole."[32]

The House of Burgesses itself, of course, was a potential threat to the liberty, property, and basic rights of its constituents. The house, said Edwin Conway, a representative from Northumberland County, in 1737, was like "the *Lion* . . . in the Fable who" was "stronger in Power than any single Subject in the Colony." Precisely because of this great power, both the constituency and the members of the house had to be ever watchful lest a conspiracy of evil or misguided men capture the house and seek to subvert or destroy the rule of law. One protection against such a development was the customary prohibition within the Anglophone world against legislative tinkering with those traditional and fundamental rights of individuals, such as trial by jury and the right to a writ of habeas corpus, that were firmly rooted in English common law and had been guaranteed by the Revolutionary Settlement of 1688.[33]

Another check against the legislature, of course, was the requirement of periodic elections. Although there was no law in Virginia requiring elections at stated intervals, eighteenth-century governors followed English practice and never tried to keep a legislature in existence beyond the seven-year limit. No matter how frequent the elections, however, representatives, by deliberately deceiving and playing upon the emotions of their constituents, could always secure their support for the worst species of legislative tyranny. "In all free governments, and in all ages," Jonathan Boucher observed in 1774, there would always be "Crafty, designing knaves, turbulent demogogues, quacks in politics and imposters in patriotism" who sought to overturn the constitution while pretending to defend it.[34]

The ultimate safeguard against such a threat was a balanced constitution, that "ingenious" contrivance that most of the eighteenth-century British world regarded as the secret of a successful polity. By mixing the various elements of the polity together in such a way as to keep them in a constant state of equilibrium, so that each would serve as a countervailing force against the others and harmful tendencies would thereby be checked or neutralized, a balanced constitution was the device through which imperfect men could live together in a state of relative harmony. Before the 1770s no Virginian spelled out exactly what was balanced by the constitution— whether the governors were balanced against the governed, the gentlemen against the commoners, the prerogative against local interests, or each of the three branches of government (the legislative, judicial, and executive) against one another. But Virginians were thoroughly persuaded that "in every state" it was absolutely "necessary for the publick weal that as just an equilibrium as possible should be preserved." That the preservation of the whole polity depended upon maintaining a proper balance and a distinct separation of functions between its several parts was, as Robert Carter Nicholas declared in 1774, an article of faith, and the fact that the House of Burgesses, even after it had gained the ascendancy in Virginia politics in the mid-1750s, did not attempt a significant extension of its authority over executive affairs after the fashion of its counterparts elsewhere in the colonies is in part a testimony to the continuing devotion of Virginia politicians to the ideal of a well-balanced constitution.[35]

This ideal, with its emphasis upon the subordination of the several parts of society to the interests of the whole, was closely related to another "fundamental . . . Rule of the *English* Constitution": the doctrine of *salus populi est suprema lex*. Landon Carter and Richard Bland employed that doctrine extensively between 1759 and 1764 as a defense, first of Virginia's wartime paper money emissions against the opposition of British merchants and then of the Two-Penny Acts, which enabled people to pay their public obligations in money instead of tobacco in two years of extremely short crops, against the attacks of the clergy, the prime victims of the acts. As defined by Carter and Bland, the doctrine meant simply that anything that was "absolutely necessary for the Good of the Community," that is, the corporate welfare of the society, was "therefore just in itself," other constitutional rules or individual interests to the contrary notwithstanding. Not the disadvantages to a few individuals but "the Advantages . . . to the People in general" were the "principal Consideration with legislatures in forming Laws," Bland asserted in defending the Two-Penny Acts, and Carter thought it was a "great Absurdity" to suggest that the interests of any man or group of men were more important than the preservation of the "community, which they compose." Even the king's prerogative, great and powerful as it was, Bland argued in writing against the crown's disallowance of laws the Virginia legislature thought necessary for the welfare of the colony, could "only be exerted . . . for the Good of his People, and not for their Destruction"; and Carter contended that the constitution itself, which in normal circumstances should be kept "as sacred as possible," might have to be "aided, extended or qualified . . . to support and preserve the Community." Everything had to give way before the public good.[36]

To make sure that the welfare of the entire community would always be its central concern, government, Virginians felt strongly, had to be especially careful not to grant to any group within it—and particularly to no group among the rulers—any special status, privileges, exemptions, or benefits. However salutary such a grant might appear at the time it was given, and however virtuous the men to whom it was given might be, "Ambition and lust of power above the laws" were, as Jonathan Boucher asserted, "such predominant passions in the Breasts of most men, even of men who escape the infection of other vices," that they could never be trusted not to try to turn it to their own selfish ends, perhaps even to attempt the establishment of a despotism, or what Landon Carter disapprovingly called "a mere Aristocratic power," that "Arbitrary and Oppressive" form in which men governed for their own private ends rather than for the common good. So pronounced was the tendency of a few to try to extend their power in any state that the legislature had to be constantly on the alert, Landon Carter declared, to protect the "greater Number of Individuals against an almost certain Oppression from the lesser Number," and the only certain way to prevent the polity from degenerating into an aristocracy was to preserve the absolute equality of all freemen within it. That "Subjects have not Pretence to Immunities, one more than another," was, therefore, a first principle with Virginia political leaders.[37]

The evils of an excessively popular government were similar. The people, as young James Madison, cousin of the fourth president, and later bishop of the Episcopal church in Virginia, said in a Phi Beta Kappa oration at the College of William and Mary in 1772, were "the original Springs of Government." But they entrusted at each election part of their liberty to the men they chose for representatives, thereby giving them a large measure of independence and freeing them from the necessity to cater to the whims or act according to the sentiments of their constituents. Except in cases that "related particularly to the interest of the Constituents alone" and on which he had the "express Instructions of . . . Constituents," a representative had to "be Governed" not by the collective "sentiments of his Constituents" but by "his own Reason and Conscience," so that, in consultation with his fellow legislators, he could act on behalf of the good of the colony as a whole and not simply in the narrow interest of a particular constituency. The alternative, that a representative was bound by the wishes of his constituents in all cases, was unacceptable largely because it placed responsibilities on the people at large that they had neither the breadth of perspective nor the capacity to bear and perhaps even paved the way for their inevitable domination and manipulation by a small band of demagogues who could be expected to play upon the "credulity of the well-meaning, deluded multitude" for their own selfish ends and to introduce, under the guise of democracy, "an Aristocratic Power." The electorate was simply too restricted in its vision and too prone to be misled by men who could appeal to the passions or humors of the moment to be trusted to act in the best interests of the community at large.[38]

To prevent the degeneration of the polity into either aristocracy or democracy and to preserve the constitution in its "due Poise," Virginians depended upon the stewardship of the "real Patriot." A patriot could never be a man who was indolent, "ambitious of power," "proficient in the arts of dissimulation," or governed by "self and gain alone." Rather, he had to be an impartial and disinterested man whose "first principle," his "Ruling Passion," was "love of . . . Country"—a determination "to act under all appointments relative to the Public" and for no "Interest less than that of a whole Country." He had to be a man who would always "view the whole ground and persevere to the last," and one who would constantly adhere rigidly to the commands of the Burgesses' oath and upon "all Things proposed . . . deliver" his "Opinion faithfully, justly, and honestly, according to" his "best Understanding and Conscience, for the general Good, and Prosperity of this Colony, and every Member thereof; and to do" his best "endeavours to prosecute That, without mingling therewith, the particular Interest of any Person or Persons whatsoever." He could not "value" himself upon "Titles and Honors" or other "empty Things . . . of no intrinsic Worth" or "exchange his Duty and Integrity for Civilities" or other blandishments from the hand of power. He had to be, as the epitaph of William Byrd II of Westover declared he was, "the constant enemy of all exorbitant power, and hearty friend to the liberties of his country," an "honest Man" chosen, as an anonymous writer said in the *Virginia Gazette*, "to represent his County, or Borough, from the Knowledge his Constituents have of his Worth. He believes no Party can ever be in the Right, or always in the Wrong: He votes and speaks as he judges best for the Service of his Country, and when the Session ends, returns, like *Cincinnatus*, to the Plough." He could not attach himself to any party because parties, Virginians were convinced, were the instruments of partial men whose devotion to factional ends necessarily robbed them of their independence of judgment and prevented them from considering the welfare of the entire country impartially. Finally, he had to concern himself primarily with keeping "Society moving on its proper Hinges" and to be willing to justify unpopular "public Measures when he thinks them necessary," to renounce the "people when he thinks them wrong," and to "call the first Connexions to an Account" whenever they acted unjustly or injuriously to the public.[39]

The two most essential qualities for the patriot, and ideally for all men, were virtue and independence. Virtue required a devotion to truth, honesty, moderation, and reason, a "Behavior . . . above every Appearance of Evil," and a determination both to guard against one's weaknesses by a constant exercise in self-control—a virtuous man could never be "a Slave to his own Ill-nature"—and to attempt to ennoble one's life by "real Goodness." "Whoever does not take care to govern his Passions, they will soon govern him," wrote James Reid, "and lead him into labyrinths of vice, error, prejudices, and immoralities from whence he will find it very difficult to extricate himself; for in time he will become fortified and impregnable against common sense and the dictates of right reason." "Virtue," the Reverend William Stith asserted, was the "grand Fountain of publick Honour and Felicity," and no man, as Robert Carter Nicholas once remarked, could "be safely trusted" with public office who did "not act upon *solid, virtuous* Principles" and would not "sacrifice every sinister, selfish Consideration" for the "True Interest" of "his Country." Only men who were "conscious of the Uprightness and Integrity of their Actions" and were therefore "not easily dismayed," Richard Bland explained, could be expected to "stand firm and unshaken" against the imperfections of themselves and other men; and Landon Carter was convinced that chaos could frequently be reduced to "order and comfort" by "the appearance only of some good man."[40]

Independence was no less important than virtue. Perhaps because their constant exposure to black slavery impressed upon them how miserable and abject a slave could be, Virginians took great pride ... in thinking that a spirit of personal independence was particularly strong among them. In Virginia, Edmund Randolph later remarked, "a high sense of personal independence was universal": "disdaining an abridgment of personal independence," he declared, was one of the most essential "manners which belonged to the real Virginian planter and which were his Ornament!" Foreign travelers and internal social critics alike were repeatedly impressed with this strong sense of independence among Virginians. A Virginia gentleman, said James Reid, had such overweening pride as to regard anything that seemed to deprive "him of his free agency" as "an imposition which is not to be put up with in a land of Liberty. It would be making him a piece of Clock work, a mere lump of mechanism, and a cypher of no value. It would be changing one who was born a Gentleman into a vile slave, and depriving him of that freedom which nature has vested him with." For the aspiring patriot, independence was especially important. It was, as Landon Carter wrote in 1769, the "base or footstool on which Liberty can alone be protected," and without liberty, without complete freedom to act impartially and independently, no man could fulfill the obligations of the patriotic public servant.[41] ...

... Between 1752 and 1763 the Virginia political system had not only to meet the heavy demands of the Seven Years' War but also to cope with its first serious challenges since Alexander Spotswood's frontal assault on it four decades earlier. The contests over the pistole fee, the legal tender status of wartime paper money issues, and the Two-Penny Acts put the system to a series of demanding tests. In each case, it proved its essential viability, as it demonstrated an ability to cope with political crises while at the same time preserving an overall political stability in the colony and a high degree of unanimity among its leaders and retaining the support of the electorate at large—all testimonies to the caliber of its leadership, the strength of the relationship between the leadership and the constituency, and the vitality of its traditional political ideals. In addition, the three crises vividly underlined for Virginia political leaders the necessity for a vigorous and jealous cultivation of those ideals. In all three controversies, the central issue was the same: some individual or group was trying to extend its power or gain some private advantage at the expense of the whole community. . . .

The most pressing, perhaps, but not all, or ultimately even the most important, sources of anxiety to the Virginia political community were external, however. Throughout the middle decades of the eighteenth century, the internal state of Virginia society was a source of persistent concern. Part of this concern was endemic to a largely one-crop economy and derived from the enduring fear that if the bottom ever fell out of the world tobacco market, Virginia's prosperity would quickly go down the drain. . . .

But the limited success of repeated attempts to encourage agricultural diversification through legislation rendered the colony's economy especially vulnerable to sudden fluctuations in the demand for tobacco. Through most of the period between 1725 and 1775, the world tobacco market was expanding, almost even bullish, the result to a great extent of a growing tobacco market in France. But a major economic downturn at the end of the Seven Years' War vividly reminded Virginians of the disadvantages of too heavy a concentration upon a single crop. Tobacco prices were low and falling, and credit was especially tight. Invariably, in such periods of concentration the normal indebtedness of the planters—in flush times a major economic resource—seemed to be an overwhelming burden. Also, with a large public debt arising out of the heavy military expenditure made by the colony during the war and a contracting money supply caused by the successful offensive of British merchants against the colony's fund of paper currency, the economic picture by 1763 seemed especially bleak.[42]

As Arthur Lee wrote to his brother Philip Ludwell Lee from Britain in November 1763, Virginia was "a country overburdened with debts," both private and public, "threatened with the horrors of a [renewal of] savage War [brought on by Pontiac's uprising in the west]: her produce sinking universally in its value; without funds, trade or Men"—a "truly miserable" situation that required "the utmost Exertions, of the few able & patriotic Men among you, to save the state from sinking." The causes of this seemingly desperate and, unknown to him, short-term situation were numerous. But Lee thought a major part of the problem was traceable to the colony's excessive dependence upon tobacco. "Tobacco, your present Staple," he declared, "seems to be [a] very precarious commodity; its culture appears to be falling continually & shoud the same consumption continue, yet as the Colony becomes more populated, the produce must of course overstock the Markets & reduce its value." It was "therefore incumbent" on Virginians to develop a diversified agricultural economy.[43]

Nor was the excessive vulnerability of a one-crop economy the only evil attributable to "that baneful weed tobacco." It had, said Edmund Randolph, "riveted two evils in the heart of Virginia, the declension of that agriculture which is the most safe and most honorable [i.e., mixed agriculture], and the encouragement of slavery, the most base of human conditions." Furthermore, as was becoming increasingly clear by the 1750s, tobacco was also exhausting "the fertility of our soil" and swallowing "up in its large plantations vast territories, which if distributed into portions were best adapted to favor population."[44]

As Randolph's recitation of the malicious effects of the race for tobacco profits suggests, black slavery, which had expanded so dramatically as a result of increasingly heavy importations of new slaves after 1720, was a second internal source of social unease among white Virginians. Every state has "an internal Weakness, or Distemper," said an anonymous writer in the *Virginia Gazette* on April 3, 1752: "I take the *Slavery* established here to be . . . a greater Fund of Imbecility to the State, than the old English *Villainage*, or the late *Clanship* of Scotland," a "poison," said another writer, which had diffused itself "in a variety of destructive shapes." The mad "Rage" for these "innumerable black Creatures" not only "swallow'd up" all of the liquid resources, the rich "Treasure" bestowed upon the colony by nature and industry, declared an anonymous correspondent in a trenchant allegory in the *Virginia Gazette* in 1738, but it also introduced a powerful internal enemy of incalculable danger. "Having no Enemy from without," said the allegorist, "this simple People are madly fond of securing one in their own Bowels," an enemy, another writer pointed out, who might, if a consistent vigilance were not maintained, at any time rise in conspiracy and end up "cutting our T[hroa]ts."[45]

Along with the "propitious" natural environment, which was too "luxuriant" to "generate the noble art of living upon little," slavery had also discouraged art, industry, and a respect for labor, other observers lamented. Nor was the diminution of the industry of whites the only "ill Effect" slavery had "upon the Morals & Manners of our People." It also gave rise to such "Habits of Pride, and Cruelty in . . . Owners" as to make it unclear whether, as James Reid remarked, a "vicious, rich" slaveowner differed in any respect from "his . . . vicious, poor Negro, but in the colour of his skin, and in his being the greater blac[k]-guard of the two" and to raise the question of whether every such master should not in justice "be punished in hell by his own slaves."[46]

Tobacco and the excessive avarice it generated had thus "stained the country with all the pollutions and cruelties of slavery," and it was almost universally known, as George Mason, the learned Fairfax County planter and future author of the Virginia Declaration of Rights, pointed out in 1765, that "one of the first Signs of the Decay, & perhaps the primary Cause of the Destruction of the most flourishing Government that ever existed was the Introduction of great Numbers of Slaves—an Evil very pathetically described by the Roman historians." Some observers hoped that the evils of slavery might yet be mitigated if further importations of slaves were inhibited by high duties and "proper Encouragement" were offered "to white persons to settle the Country." "The Policy of encouraging the Importation of free People & discouraging that of Slaves has never been duly considered in the Colony," Mason complained, "or we shou'd not at this Day see one Half of our best Lands in most parts of the Country remain unsetled, & the other cultivated with Slaves." But the "blessings" to be expected from such a policy, another writer had bitterly remarked in the mid-1750s, were probably "too great" either "for the consent of a British Mother, or for the Option of a people already Infatuated & Abandoned."[47]

The fear that Virginians were indeed growing increasingly "Infatuated & Abandoned" was still a third—and infinitely the most powerful—internal source of social anxiety. Beginning in the late 1730s, a growing number of Virginians complained about the decline of the old values of industry, thrift, and sobriety; certain signs, they predicted, of the moral declension of Virginia society. Particularly disturbing was the exorbitant growth of luxury. Increasingly, after 1740, travelers and thoughtful members of the gentry alike remarked upon the "extravagance, ostentation, and . . . disregard for economy" in the colony, particularly among the wealthy, and Lieutenant Governor Francis Fauquier expressed alarm in 1762 at the planters' rising indebtedness to British merchants, which he attributed to the planters' unwillingness to "quit any one Article of Luxury." Certain it was that a growing number of gentlemen planters, including William Byrd III, Benjamin Grymes, and other scions of old gentry families, were rapidly bringing "ruin upon themselves by their extravagance" and were able to "screen themselves from ignominy only by the ostentation and allurements of fashionable life," which they could keep up only by plunging themselves ever further into debt.[48]

The ultimate consequences of this rising addiction to luxury were well known. "There are two pernicious Things in the Government of a Nation, which are scarce ever remedied," warned Mentor in the *Virginia Gazette* in 1752: "the first is an unjust and too violent Authority in Kings: the other is Luxury, which vitiates the Morals of the People." Of the two, luxury was more to be dreaded. Whereas "too great an Authority [only] intoxicates and poisons Kings," "Luxury poisons a whole Nation," as it "habitates itself to look upon the most superfluous Things, as the Necessaries of Life; and thus every day brings forth some new Necessity of the same Kind, and Men can no longer live without Things, which but thirty years ago were utterly unknown to them." . . . In his sermon on the peace in 1763, James Horrocks warned his listeners against too "great a Tendency amongst us to Extravagance and Luxury" and admonished them to eschew the "insignificant Pride of Dress, the empty Ambition of gaudy Furniture, or a splendid

Equipage . . . which must undoubtedly serve more for Ostentation and Parade, than any real Use or valuable Purpose."[49]

But luxury was not the only sign of moral decay in mid-eighteenth-century Virginia: drunkenness and swearing seemed to be increasing at an alarming rate, and, beginning in the 1740s, a rampant "spirit of gaming" had broken "forth . . . in ways [equally] destructive of morals and estates." By the early 1750s gaming had become so "very fashionable among the young Men" of the colony that William Stith preached a sermon before the House of Burgesses on *The Sinfulness of Gaming*, and the pages of the *Virginia Gazette* contained numerous warnings on its evil effects. . . . "What a damned situation our Country is in," complained James Mercer in 1754. "No money to be got but at Horseraces & Gaming Tables & that not sufficient to open the Eyes of the People who frequent those places & are worse than selling their Wives & Children." But it was not just that the rage for gambling, as Hansford put it, did "much harm / To some estates; 'tis like a spell or charm"; it also had devastating effects upon the character of the gamesters. The "prevailing Passion and Taste for Gaming[,] . . . Racing, Cards, Dice and all other such Diversions," warned James Horrocks, carried with them a "fatal Tendency" that ate away at the very foundations of Virginia society.[50] . . .

What was infinitely more frightening, however, was the increasing possibility that Virginians were already too far abandoned even to feel any guilt, that they had already proceeded too far along the road to corruption traveled by Rome to avoid the inner decay and destruction that were the ultimate fate of that once mighty empire. Indeed, so prevalent was the addiction to luxury and pleasure that the very character of Virginia society seemed to be changing. "I have observed," wrote "A Gentleman" to the *Virginia Gazette* in 1751, "that the Majority of those that claim" the "term GENTLEMAN . . . have abandoned themselves to such trifling or vicious Practices, and glory in them as their peculiar Badge and Characteristic, that I am afraid the unfashionable Minority who sustain the same Denomination, will not be able to preserve it in its original Reputation, especially since their Number and Influence seem [to be] daily declining. I am already," he added, "somewhat uneasy, when I am complimented with the Character; and indeed could not bear it, did I not take the Liberty to abstract from it the modern Ideas crowded under it, and assure the Company I am not a *Gamester, Cock-Fighter,* or *Horse-Racer* by Trade; that I speak *English,* not *Blasphemy;* that I drink to quench my Thirst, not to quench my *Reason;* &c."[51]

In the new scheme of things, "Learning and good sense; religion and refined morals; charity and benevolence" seemed to have "nothing to do in the composition" of a gentleman. To be sure, there were still a "discerning few" among the gentry in every county in whom "good sense abounds."

Such men were truly "an honour to humanity, a glory to the Colony, and the luminaries of the County." But could this "unfashionable Remnant of Gentlemen of this antique Stamp" possibly stem the tide of fashion, the corrosive "degeneracy in morals which is so conspicuous all around us" and had already struck deep roots in Virginia society?[52]

For that degeneracy, various observers noted, proceeded from the very conditions of life in Virginia, from the ease, affluence, and indulgence and the lax—some said, vicious—"manner of Education" they promoted. "For the Youth" of Virginia, observed one English traveler, "partake pretty much of the *Petit Maitre* Kind, and are pamper'd much more in Softness and Ease than their Neighbours more Northward," with the result that "young Fellows" were "not much burden'd with Study" and, in sharp contrast to their fathers, learned to spend more of their "Time and Money in modish Recreations than in furnishing" their libraries "with valuable Collections, in charitable Distributions, or intellectual Improvements."[53] . . .

How could men thus "brought up" possibly reverse the precipitous moral decline that seemed to have seized the colony? For Virginians, in common with all western Europeans, had been taught—most vividly by the example of Rome—that "revolutions of life" were inexorable: "Obscurity and indigence are the Parents of vigilance & economy; vigilance and economy of riches and honour; riches and honour of pride and luxury; pride & luxury of impurity and idleness; and impurity and idleness again produce indigence and obscurity." Were Virginians really on the downward turn in this irreversible wheel of fortune? "We need only to open our eyes," wrote James Reid, "to behold this in the most glaring colours. The father toils his body, vexes his mind, hurts his soul, & ruins his health to procure riches for his son, who not knowing the trouble of acquiring them, spends them without prudence, and sinks into his original obscurity with contempt, disgrace and mortification."[54]

Clergymen of all persuasions seconded Reid's opinion. During the Seven Years' War, the Presbyterian Samuel Davies developed at great length in a series of blistering sermons the proposition that the war was God's punishment for the colony's sins. The roots of Virginia's troubles, he announced, were its "Riches." Excessive wealth had produced so great a "deluge of Luxury and Pleasure" that wherever one looked he found not virtue but a surfeit of drunkenness, swearing, avarice, craft, oppression, prodigality, vanity, sensuality, gaming, and disobedience to superiors: the catalogue of Virginia's sins was endless. "O VIRGINIA! a Country happy in Situation; improved by Art, and hitherto blessed of Heaven," he cried in 1756, "but now undermined and tottering by thy *own sins*," sins so great that it could be said of the "Men of *Virginia*, as well as those of *Sodom*, *They are wicked, and Sinners before the Lord exceedingly*."[55]

Anglican clergymen from James Blair in the late 1730s to William Stith in the early 1750s and James Horrocks in the early 1760s echoed these sentiments, albeit in the more moderate and less impassioned tones befitting their religious persuasion. "The Vice and Wickedness of a Nation," Stith had counseled the Burgesses in 1752, "are the certain Forerunners and Cause of its Disgrace and Destruction," and both Davies and Horrocks agreed that all signs suggested that the destruction of Virginia was imminent. Davies believed that the situation called for nothing less than "A THOROUGH NATIONAL REFORMATION" marked with "Repentance, Reformation and Prayer," and Horrocks, that a permanent return to the solid virtues of Virginia's forefathers was needed. In such an enterprise, responsibility fell heavily on those men of solid virtuous principles, that increasingly "unfashionable Remnant," which still in the early 1760s dominated both the House of Burgesses and the other major political institutions of the colony. How or even whether they could fulfill that responsibility was a question of crucial importance that Virginia society would soon have to confront.[56]

In the early 1760s—on the eve of the great political and emotional crisis that preceded the American Revolution—the Virginia political community thus faced the future with an uncertain blend of anxiety and confidence. It was anxious over the unhealthy state of the tobacco market, the pernicious effects of black slavery upon white society, the disturbing crisis in moral behavior, and, more than at any time since the very first decade of the century, the colony's constitutional security within an empire whose leaders were showing disturbing signs of a growing disregard for the political welfare of its peripheral members. But it was also confident in the basic stability, responsiveness, effectiveness, and virtue of the Virginia political system and in the colony's long-term future within an empire which enjoyed so great a blessing, so great a security to liberty and property, as the British constitution. Over the next quarter of a century, this peculiar combination of anxiety and confidence would in considerable measure shape the responses of the Virginia political community to a series of political challenges of a magnitude undreamed of in 1763.

NOTES

The earliest draft of this chapter was written in the summer of 1964 for a book Keith Berwick and I planned on the politics of Revolutionary Virginia. I gave it as a lecture entitled "The Conditions and Assumptions of Virginia Politics on the Eve of the American Revolution" at the University of Michigan at Ann Arbor on October 14, 1964, and at the History Faculty Seminar at Dartmouth College, Hanover, N.H., on March 8, 1965. An abbreviated version of the present draft was presented on April 5, 1973, at Miami University of Ohio, Oxford, Ohio, as one of the "McClellan Lectures on the American Revolution" under the title "Virtue and Liberty: A Case Study of the Revolution in Virginia," and, under the present title, at the Anglo-American Conference of Historians in London on July 9, 1976; at the English Institute of the University of Lyon, Lyon, France, March 19, 1977; and at the English Institute of the University of Bordeaux, Bordeaux, France, March 22, 1977. It was one of three papers on eighteenth-century Virginia politics considered at a seminar held in the Department of History at La Trobe University, Bundoora, Victoria, Australia, August 20, 1976.

1. James Reid, "The Religion of the Bible and Religion of K[ing] W[illiam] County Compared," [1769], in Richard Beale Davis, ed., *The Colonial Virginia Satirist: Mid-Eighteenth-Century Commentaries on Politics, Religion, and Society* (Philadelphia, 1967), 48.

2. Bernard Bailyn, "Politics and Social Structure in Virginia," in James M. Smith, ed., *Seventeenth-Century America: Essays in Colonial History* (Chapel Hill, N.C., 1959), 90–115; Jack P. Greene, *The Quest for Power: The Lower Houses of Assembly in the Southern Royal Colonies, 1689–1776* (Chapel Hill, N.C., 1963), 22–24, and "Foundations of Political Power in the Virginia House of Burgesses, 1720–1776," *William and Mary Quarterly*, 3d ser., 16 (1959): 485–506; Robert E. and B. Katherine Brown, *Virginia, 1705–1786: Aristocracy or Democracy?* (East Lansing, Mich., 1964), 7–31; Hugh Jones in Richard L. Morton, ed., *The Present State of Virginia* (Chapel Hill, N.C., 1956), 81.

3. *Journal and Letters of Philip Vickers Fithian, 1773–1774: A Plantation Tutor of the Old Dominion*, ed. Hunter D. Farish (Williamsburg, Va., 1943), 35; Carl Bridenbaugh, *Myths and Realities: Societies of the Colonial South* (Baton Rouge, La., 1952), 1–53, and *Seat of Empire: The Political Role of Eighteenth-Century Williamsburg* (Williamsburg, Va., 1950); Louis B. Wright, *The First Gentlemen of Virginia: Intellectual Qualities of a Colonial Ruling Class* (San Marino, Calif., 1940); Charles S. Sydnor, *Gentlemen Freeholders: Political Practices in Washington's Virginia* (Chapel Hill, N.C., 1952); Daniel J. Boorstin, *The Americans: The Colonial Experience* (New York, 1958), 99–143; and Greene, "Foundations of Political Power," 485–506.

4. See especially John Ferdinand D. Smyth, *A Tour in the United States of America*, 2 vols. (London, 1784), 1:65–69; Thomas Anburey, *Travels through the Interior Parts of America*, 2 vols. (Boston and New York, 1923), 2:215–17; Marquis de Chastellux, *Travels in North America in the Years 1780, 1781, and 1782*, ed. Howard C. Rice, Jr., 2 vols. (Chapel Hill, N.C., 1963), 2:437; and Brown and Brown, *Virginia, 1705–1786*, 32–59.

5. Smyth, *Tour* 1:65–69; Fithian, *Journal and Letters*, 211–12. On poverty in Virginia, see Chastellux, *Travels* 2:437.

6. Landon Carter's Reply to Election Poem, Nov. 1, 1768, Sabine Hall Collection, University of Virginia Library, Charlottesville; *The Life of Reverend Devereaux Jarratt* (Baltimore, 1806), 16; Reid, "Religion of the Bible," 57.

7. Charles Hansford, "My Country's Worth," [1752], *The Poems of Charles Hansford*, ed. James A. Servies and Carl R. Dolmetsch (Chapel Hill, N.C., 1961), 56–57.

8. Brown and Brown, *Virginia, 1705–1786*, 136–50.

9. Bland to Theodorick Bland, Sr., Feb. 20, 1745, *The Bland Papers*, ed. Charles Campbell, 2 vols. (Petersburg, Va., 1840–43), 1:4.

10. See, for instance, Hugh Jones, *Present State of Virginia*, 84; Andrew Burnaby, *Burnaby's Travels through North America*, ed. Rufus Rockwell Wilson (New York, 1904), 53–55; Thomas Jefferson, *Notes on the State of Virginia*, ed. William Peden (Chapel Hill, N.C., 1955), 164; Chastellux, *Travels*, 2:435–36; and Reid, "Religion of the Bible," 45–68.

11. David Griffith, *Passive Obedience Considered* (Williamsburg, Va., [1776]), 6, 12;

William Stith, *The Sinfulness and Pernicious Nature of Gaming* (Williamsburg, Va., 1752), 14–15.

12. Stith, *Sinfulness of Gaming*, 14–15; [John Randolph], *Considerations on the Present State of Virginia* ([Williamsburg, Va.], 1774), 22–23; Jonathan Boucher, *A Letter from a Virginian* ([New York], 1774), 7–8.

13. Sir William Gooch, *A Dialogue between Thomas Sweet-Scented, William Orinoco, Planters, . . . and Justice Love-Country* (Williamsburg, Va., 1732), 17; James Horrocks, *Upon the Peace* (Williamsburg, Va., 1763), 8; Griffith, *Passive Obedience*, 13. For instances of questioning of the political abilities and wisdom of the middle and lower sorts, see James Wood to George Washington, July 7, 1758, in Stanislaus M. Hamilton, ed., *Letters to Washington and Accompanying Papers*, 5 vols. (Boston and New York, 1898–1902), 3:149; [Randolph], *Considerations*, 22–23; Chastellux, *Travels* 2:435–36; and [Boucher], *Letter from a Virginian*, 7–8.

14. Greene, *Quest for Power*, and "Foundations of Political Power"; Sydnor, *Gentlemen Freeholders*; St. George Tucker to William Wirt, Sept. 25, 1815, *William and Mary Quarterly*, 1st ser., 22 (1914): 253.

15. George Webb, *The Office and Authority of a Justice of the Peace* (Williamsburg, Va., 1736), 200–202.

16. John Camm, *A Review of the Rector Detected* (Williamsburg, Va., 1764), 7; Reid, "Religion of the Bible," 56–57; Fithian, *Journal and Letters*, 35; [Randolph], *Considerations*, 22–27; [Gooch], *Dialogue*, 14; Landon Carter's essay on refusal of councillors to join the Association, [1775?], Sabine Hall Collection, University of Virginia Library; Landon Carter to George Washington, Feb. 12, 1756, in Hamilton, *Letters to Washington* 1:195; Robert Carter Diary, July 5, 1723, vol. 12, Virginia Historical Society, Richmond; *Virginia Gazette* (Williamsburg), September 29, 1752. For an insight into the influence of the leading men in a county on the nomination of burgesses, see Theodorick Bland, Jr., to John Randolph, Jr., Sept. 20, 1771, Bryan Family Papers, University of Virginia Library.

17. Sydnor, *Gentleman Freeholders*, 39–59; Reid, "Religion of the Bible," 50–51, 54; Robert Munford, *The Candidates*, ed. Jay B. Hubbell and Douglass Adair (Williamsburg, Va., 1948), 17, 20, 24, 40.

18. Webb, *Office and Authority*, 17–18; *The Acts of Assembly* (Williamsburg, Va., 1752), 51.

19. Johann David Shoepf, *Travels in the Confederation* [1783–84], trans. and ed. Alfred J. Morrison, 2 vols. (Philadelphia, 1911), 1:56–57; Greene, "Foundations of Political Power," 485–506. On the importance of oratory, see Edmund Randolph, *History of Virginia*, ed. Arthur H. Shaffer (Charlottesville, Va., 1970), 192, and *Diary of Colonel Landon Carter of Sabine Hall, 1752–1778*, ed. Jack P. Greene, 2 vols. (Charlottesville, Va., 1965), May 14, 1755, 1:120. For an extended analysis of the ingredients of political leadership in colonial and Revolutionary Virginia, see Jack P. Greene, "Character, Persona, and Authority: A Study of Alternative Styles of Political Leadership in Revolutionary Virginia," in W. Robert Higgins, ed., *The South during the American Revolution: Essays in Honor of John R. Alden* (Durham, N.C., 1976).

20. George Washington to James Wood, [July 1758], *The Writings of George Washington*, ed. John C. Fitzpatrick, 39 vols. (Washington, D.C., 1931–44), 2:251; Munford, *Candidates*, 38; [Mercer], "Dinwiddianae," [1754–57], in Davis, *Colonial Virginia Satirist*, 23.

21. [Gooch], *Dialogue*, 14–15; Stith, *Sinfulness of Gaming*, 14–15; Landon Carter to Purdie and Dixon, Fall 1769, Carter Family Papers, Swem Library, College of William and Mary, Williamsburg; *Diary of Landon Carter*, Nov. 6, 1771, Oct. 6, 1774, Mar. 15, 1776, Feb. 15, 23, 1777, 2:638, 866–67, 1001–2, 1084.

22. Samuel Davies, *The Curse of Cowardice* (Woodbridge, N.J., 1759), 21.

23. "Common Sense," *Virginia Gazette*, Oct. 3, 1745; Reid, "Religion of the Bible," 51–52.

24. *Diary of Landon Carter*, Nov. 23, 1762, 2:242.

25. Pendleton to Citizens of Caroline County, Nov. 1798, *The Letters and Papers of Edmund Pendleton, 1734–1803*, ed. David J. Mays, 2 vols. (Charlottesville, Va., 1967), 2:650.

26. [Boucher], *Letter from a Virginian*, 9–10.

27. "Observations in Several Voyages and Travels in America," [1746], *William and Mary Quarterly*, 1st ser., 16 (1907): 158; Jones, *Present State of Virginia*, 80–82; Fithian, *Journal and Letters*, 211; Landon Carter, *The Rector Detected* (Williamsburg, Va., 1764), 24; Schoepf, *Travels* 1:61–62, 91–95; Horrocks, *Upon the Peace*, 12.

28. See esp. Wright, *First Gentlemen of Virginia*; Robert Manson Myers, "The Old Dominion Looks to London: A Study of English Literary Influences upon the *Virginia Gazette* (1736–1766)," *Virginia Magazine of History and Biography* 54 (1946): 195–217; and Elizabeth Christine Cook, *Literary Influences in Colonial Newspapers, 1704–1750* (New York, 1912), 179–229.

29. Examples of this conception of human nature and the function of government are [Landon Carter], *A Letter to the Right Reverend Father in God, the Lord B——p of L——n* (Williamsburg, Va., 1760), 6, 17, 43; *A Letter from a Gentleman in Virginia, to the Merchants in Great Britain, Trading to That Colony* (London, 1754), 5, 16; *Maryland Gazette* (Annapolis), Oct. 28, 1754; *Letter to a Gentleman in London from Virginia* (London, 1759), 15, 20–21; *Diary of Landon Carter*, Sept. 28, 1770, Sept. 11, 1775, 1:505, 2:940–42; Common Sense [Richard Bland], *The Colonel Dismounted or the Rector Vindicated* (Williamsburg, Va., 1764), 13; [Gooch], *Dialogue*, 13; *Defence of Injur'd Merit Unmasked* (n.p., 1771), 9; [Nicholas], *Considerations on the Present State of Virginia Examined*, 24–25; Griffith, *Passive Obedience*, 6–14, 18–19, 23; speech of Sir John Randolph, Aug. 6, 1736, in *Journals of the House of Burgesses of Virginia*, ed. H. R. McIlwaine and John Pendleton Kennedy, 13 vols. (Richmond, 1905–15), 1727–40, 241–42.

30. [Carter], *Letter to a Gentleman in London*, 20–21, *Letter to B——p of L——n*, 6, 46, 55, and *Rector Detected*, 16, 22; Camm, *Review of Rector Detected*, 16; [Bland], *Colonel Dismounted*, 14; Richard Henry Lee, Introduction to John Dickinson and Arthur Lee, *The Farmer's and Monitor's Letters to the Inhabitants of the British Colonies* (Williamsburg, Va., 1769), i; [Nicholas], *Considerations*, 28–29; [Boucher], *Letter from a Virginian*, 9–10; Griffith, *Passive Obedience*, 12; George Mason to George Washington, Sept. 15, 1756, in Kate Mason Rowland, *The Life of George Mason, 1725–1792*, 2 vols. (New York, 1892), 1:66.

31. [Carter], *Letter from a Gentleman in Virginia*, 29, 35, and *Letter to B——p of L——n*, 29, 35; [Bland], *Colonel Dismounted*, 21–23, and *A Fragment on the Pistole Fee, Claimed by the Governor of Virginia, 1753*, ed. Worthington C. Ford (Brooklyn, N.Y., 1891), 36–37.

32. Bland, *Fragment on the Pistole Fee*, 37–38; [Gooch], *Dialogue*, 13; [Carter], *Let-*

ter from a Gentleman in Virginia, 12, 19, 22–23, *Letter to B——p in L——n,* 44, and *Letter to a Gentleman in London,* 14, 19–20.

33. See Edwin Conway to Mr. Parks, *Virginia Gazette,* June 24, 1737.

34. [Boucher], *Letter from a Virginian,* 7–10.

35. Alexander Spotswood to Sir John Randolph, *Virginia Gazette,* Dec. 10, 1736; speech of Sir John Randolph, Aug. 6, 1736, *Journals of the House of Burgesses of Virginia, 1727–40,* 241–42; [Nicholas], *Considerations,* 24–25; Randolph, *Considerations,* 5–8; *Virginia Gazette* (Purdie), June 27, 1766; [Bland], *Colonel Dismounted,* 14.

36. Richard Bland, *A Letter to the Clergy of Virginia* (Williamsburg, Va., 1760), 15–16, 18; Bland to John Camm, Oct. 25, 1763, in [Bland], *Colonel Dismounted,* ii; and [Carter], *Letter to a Gentleman in London,* 20–21, *Letter to B——p of L——n,* 6–7, 19, 46, 50–51, and *Rector Detected,* 30. For a report of a similar argument by Patrick Henry, see James Maury to John Camm, Dec. 12, 1763, *Journals of the House of Burgesses of Virginia, 1761–65,* liii.

37. [Boucher], *Letter from a Virginian,* 9–10, 15; *Diary of Landon Carter,* May 9, 1774, 2:808; and [Carter], *Letter to a Gentleman in London,* 10, 19, *Letter to B——p of L——n,* 29, and *Rector Detected,* 22.

38. James Madison, *An Oration in Commemoration of the Founders of William and Mary College* (Williamsburg, Va., 1772), 6; [Boucher], *Letter from a Virginian,* 9–10; [Randolph], *Considerations,* 3–5, 22–23; Conway to Parks, *Virginia Gazette,* Nov., 17, 1738; *Diary of Landon Carter,* Oct. 17, 1754, 1:116–17.

39. *Defence of Injur'd Merit,* 7; *Diary of Landon Carter,* Mar. 21, 1752, Jan. 31, 1776, Aug. 8, 1777, 1:89, 2:970, 1121–22; [Carter], *Letter from a Gentleman in Virginia,* 3–5, 21–22, 27, 35, *Maryland Gazette,* Oct. 28, 1754, *Letter to a Gentleman in London,* 6–7, 9, 14, 27, *Letter to B——P of L——n,* 5, 10, 53, *Rector Detected,* 24, and Landon Carter to Councillors, [1774–75], Sabine Hall Collection, University of Virginia Library; Richard Bland's poem to Landon Carter, June 20, 1758, in Moncure D. Conway, *Barons of the Potomack and Rappahannock* (New York, 1892), 138–41; [Randolph], *Considerations,* 7–8; George Washington to Mrs. Mary Washington, Aug. 14, 1755, to Speaker John Robinson, Dec. 1756, and to Governor Robert Dinwiddie, Sept. 15, 1757, *Writings of Washington* 1:159, 532–33, 2:133; Robert Carter Nicholas to Washington, Aug. 18, 1756, Philo Patria [Richard Bland] to Washington, 1756, and John Robinson to Washington, Nov. 15, 1756, in Hamilton, *Letters to Washington,* 1:338, 391, 394–95, 2:1–2; epitaph of William Byrd, n.d., in *The Writings of "Colonel William Byrd of Westover in Virginia Esqr.,"* ed. John Spencer Bassett (New York, 1901), xli; Randolph, *History of Virginia,* 273; Burgesses' Oath, *Virginia Gazette,* Nov. 24, 1738; Sir John Randolph to Alexander Spotswood, ibid., Oct. 29, Dec. 17, 1736; essay on "an honest Man," ibid., Sept. 29, 1752.

40. *Diary of Landon Carter,* Mar. 6, 9, 13, 1752, Feb. 15, 1770, June 6, 1773, May 10, 1774, 1:75–78, 84–85, 357–58, 2:755–56, 808–9; [Carter], *Letter to a Gentleman in London,* 12, 27–28, *Letter to B——p of L——n,* 1, 8, 40; Landon Carter to "My Friend," n.d., and to Councillors, [1774–75], Sabine Hall Collection, University of Virginia Library; Landon Carter to Purdie and Dixon, Fall 1769, Carter Family Papers, folder 3, Swem Library, College of William and Mary; Stith, *Sinfulness of Gaming,* 11–12, 25; [Randolph], *Considerations,* 3; [Nicholas], *Considerations,* 37–38; Bland, *Letter to Clergy,* 9; Burnaby, *Travels* 20; Shoepf, *Travels* 1:55; William Nelson to Washington, Feb. 22, 1753, Landon Carter to Washington, Oct. 7, 1755, in Hamilton, *Letters to Washington*

1:1, 108; Randolph, *History of Virginia*, 178, 193, 197; The Monitor, "On Good Nature," *Virginia Gazette*, Jan. 28, 1737; essay on "an honest Man," ibid, Sept. 29, 1752; Reid, "Religion of the Bible," 55, 60–61.

41. Randolph, *History of Virginia*, 178, 193, 197; Reid, "Religion of the Bible," 55, 60–61; Landon Carter to Purdie and Dixon, Fall 1769, Carter Family Papers, folder 3, Swem Library, College of William and Mary.

42. The best treatment of economic conditions in Virginia at the close of the Seven Years' War is Joseph Albert Ernst, "Genesis of the Currency Act of 1764: Virginia Paper Money and the Partition of British Investments," *William and Mary Quarterly*, 3d ser., 22 (1965): 34–59.

43. Arthur Lee to Philip Ludwell Lee, Nov. 5, 1763, Arthur Lee Papers, 1:2, bMS Am 811F, Houghton Library, Harvard University, Cambridge, Mass.

44. Randolph, *History of Virginia*, 71, 202.

45. *Virginia Gazette*, Apr. 21, 1738, Apr. 1752; Randolph, *History of Virginia*, 96; [Mercer], "Dinwiddianae," 32.

46. Randolph, *History of Virginia*, 216; Mason, "Scheme for Replevying Goods . . . ," Dec. 23, 1765, *The Papers of George Mason*, ed. Robert A. Rutland, 3 vols. (Chapel Hill, N.C., 1970), 1:61–62; *Virginia Gazette*, Apr. 10, 1754; Reid, "Religion of the Bible," 49.

47. Randolph, *History of Virginia*, 202; Mason, "Scheme for Replevying Goods . . . ," Dec. 23, 1765, *Papers of George Mason* 1:61–62; [Mercer], "Dinwiddianae," 30; Hansford, "My Country's Worth," 65–67; "Observations on Several Voyages . . . ," [1746], *William and Mary Quarterly*, 1st ser., 16 (1907): 6–9.

48. Burnaby, *Travels*, 55; Fauquier to Board of Trade, Nov. 3, 1762, CO 5/1330, ff. 339–40, PRO; [Carter], *Letter from a Gentleman in Virginia*, 28–29; Randolph, *History of Virginia*, 279–80.

49. *Virginia Gazette*, Dec. 29, 1752; Horrocks, *Upon the Peace*, 9–10, 14. See also the extended essay on the same theme, "The Virginia Centinal, No. X," in *Virginia Gazette*, Sept. 3, 1756.

50. Randolph, *History of Virginia*, 61; *Virginia Gazette*, Feb. 28, Mar. 28, Sept. 5, 1751; Stith, *Sinfulness of Gaming;* James Mercer to Daniel Parks Custis, May 31, 1754, Custis Papers, folder 1754–55, Virginia Historical Society; Hansford, "My Country's Worth," 62–64; Horrocks, *Upon the Peace*, 9–10, 14.

51. *Virginia Gazette*, July 11, 1751.

52. Ibid.

53. Ibid.; "Observations on Several Voyages . . . ," 15–16; Reid, "Religion of the Bible," 48, 52, 53–57.

54. Reid, "Religion of the Bible," 55–57.

55. Samuel Davies, *Virginia's Danger and Remedy* (Williamsburg, Va., 1756), 12, 16, 20–21, 23, 25, 28, 48, *Curse of Cowardice*, 8, 14–15, 33–34, *Religion and Patriotism* (Philadelphia, 1755), 10–12, 27–35, and *The Crisis: or, The Uncertain Doom of Kingdoms at Particular Times, Considered* (London, 1756), 28–35.

56. Stith, *Sinfulness of Gaming*, 11–12, and *The Nature and Extent of Christ's Redemption* (Williamsburg, Va., 1753), 31; Horrocks, *Upon the Peace*, 9–10, 14; Camm, *Review of Rector Detected*, 20; Davies, *Virginia's Danger and Remedy*, 12, 16, 20–21, 23, 25, 28, 48, *Curse of Cowardice*, 8, 14–15, 33–34, *Religion and Patriotism*, 10–12, 27–35, and *The Crisis*, 28–35. See also "Robert Dinwiddie's Proclamation for a Fast," Aug. 28, 1775, *Virginia Gazette*, Sept. 12, 1755.

WOODY HOLTON

"Rebel against Rebel": Enslaved Virginians and the Coming of the American Revolution

✳ ✳ ✳ ✳ ✳ ✳ ✳ ✳ "T ʜᴇ Rᴇᴠᴏʟᴜᴛɪᴏɴ ᴡᴀs ɴᴏᴛ ᴍᴇʀᴇʟʏ ᴀ ǫᴜᴇs- tion of 'home rule,'" Carl Becker argued famously, early in the twentieth century. "It was also a question of who should rule at home." Many subsequent analyses, influenced by Becker and other Progressive Era historians, have viewed the Revolution as two-sided. It was not simply the struggle of exploited colonies against an increasingly assertive British Parliament and monarch. It was also, as Becker wrote, "a struggle within the colonies between the ruling aristocracies and the unfranchised."

Historians of eighteenth-century Virginia have long emphasized the coherence of Virginia politics, the easy confidence with which Virginia's planters ruled the colony, and the willingness of lesser free men to defer to their planter superiors. Edmund Morgan and Jack Greene, in their selections in this volume, chart the emergence of Virginia's plantation aristocracy and emphasize both the widespread legitimacy of the planters' rule and a considerable commitment to good governance in the colony. As Morgan, in particular, argues, this unity and legitimacy was possible in large measure because white Virginians owned black slaves.

Woody Holton both expands upon and subtly inverts Morgan's thesis. Far from being coherent, unified, and conflict-free, Holton acknowledges, late eighteenth-century Virginia society was predicated upon a constant, fierce effort to deprive thousands of men and women of their freedom. Virginia's slaves nonetheless "struck back often enough to maintain a permanent undercurrent of fear in the minds of most whites."

When the developing Revolutionary crisis revealed fractures in the edifice of white authority, enslaved men and women proved eager to exploit its inherent weaknesses and seek their liberty. Consequently they widened the division between British imperial power and Virginia's planter leadership. When Lord Dunmore, the British governor, offered freedom to Virginia's slaves to disrupt the growing rebellion, he inflamed a political and constitutional conflict that was rife with underlying social tension. His efforts failed spectacularly. Poorer white Virginians, who ultimately feared slave insurrection more than they resented the rule of Virginia's plantation aristocracy, aligned themselves further with the patriot cause. Thus Virginia leaders could embrace radical republicanism in condemnation of imperial "misrule." The egalitarian ideals of the Revolution, with the powerful and enduring rhetoric that has so forcefully and rightly resonated in American culture ever since, therefore served less as a passive reflection of social and political legitimacy in Virginia and more as an active means to cement it. Where slavery nurtured white self-confidence in Morgan's Virginia, it produced anxiety and fear in Holton's. Either way, the radicalism of the Revolution in Virginia served to conserve the established order.

Class conflict in Virginia, conflict over "who should rule at home," thus played a crucial role in bringing about the Revolution. Indeed, Holton concludes, "it may be that Virginia was the colony in which class conflict gave the biggest push to the movement for independence."

*　*　*　*　*　*　*　*

*　*　*　*　*　*　*　*

FOR MORE THAN SIX MONTHS AFTER THE BATTLES OF LEXINGTON and Concord, the fighting between British and patriot troops was confined to the northern colonies. Then on 26 October 1775, a squadron of British naval vessels attacked the town of Hampton, Virginia. The Revolutionary War had come to the South.[1] The battle of Hampton resulted partly from the actions of a "small mulatto man" named Joseph Harris. Only four months earlier, Harris had been a resident of Hampton and the property of another Hamptonian, Henry King, whom he served as a pilot on the Chesapeake Bay. Harris, it was said, was "well acquainted with many creeks on the *Eastern* Shore, at *York*, *James* River, and *Nansemond*, and many others." All in all, he was "a very useful person."[2]

Harris's knowledge gave him an opportunity to gain his freedom. On 8 June 1775, Virginia's last royal governor, John Murray, fourth earl of Dunmore, fearing an attack from the increasingly belligerent patriots, fled Williamsburg and took refuge on HMS *Fowey*. There he set about assembling a small squadron to fight the patriots. To accomplish his designs he needed people who knew the bay, so when Harris slipped off one night in July and presented himself to the skipper of the *Fowey*, he was welcomed and immediately put to work as a pilot. When the *Fowey* left the Chesapeake a short time later, Harris transferred to a tender called the *Liberty*.

On the night of 2 September 1775, a hurricane swept through Tidewater Virginia and drove the *Liberty* ashore near Hampton. On board Harris's vessel when it went aground was Matthew Squire, captain of the *Liberty*'s mother ship, the *Otter*. Harris obtained a canoe from a slave, and he and Squire managed to get across Hampton Roads to the *Otter*, which was anchored off Norfolk. Their escape was fortunate, because white leaders had threatened to execute slaves like Harris who fled to the British. Meanwhile, the beached *Liberty* fell into the hands of the rebels, who helped themselves to the sails and other equipment (including seven swivel guns) and then set the boat ablaze. The *Liberty* "was burnt by the people thereabouts," the *Virginia Gazette* reported, "in return for [Squire's] harbouring gentlemen's negroes, and suffering his sailors to steal poultry, hogs, &c." Captain Squire was furious. He demanded that Hampton at least return the *Liberty*'s stores. The rebel committee that ruled the town said it would be happy to comply with the captain's request—as soon as Squire returned Harris and other black crewmen to their former owners. This Squire refused to do, prompting a patriot newspaper to note with sarcasm the "singular ATTACHMENT AND LOYALTY to his sovereign" of Squire's "Ethiopian director."[3]

Eventually deciding that the contest could not be resolved peacefully, Squire attacked Hampton on 26 October with six small craft. The little squadron came under deadly long arms fire. Some nine blacks and other British sailors were killed, and Squire had to retreat. One of his vessels, the *Hawke*, went aground, and its crew was captured. The white prisoners, including Joseph Wilson, an indentured servant who had escaped from George Washington, were "treated with great humanity," a patriot newspaper reported. The black crewmen were "tried for their lives."[4]

The engagement at Hampton was the first battle of the Revolutionary War south of Massachusetts. Just as the earlier fighting in New England had helped poison relations between Britain and all the rebel colonies, so the battle of Hampton helped embitter white Virginians against their king. Thomas Jefferson reported that the armed confrontation had "raised our country into perfect phrensy." The story of the battle would have been very different if Joseph Harris had not made his dash for freedom. Perhaps Hampton whites would never have come into conflict with Captain Squire at all.[5]

Harris was but one of thousands of enslaved Virginians who found opportunity within the breach that opened between loyalist and patriot whites in 1775. A majority of those who reached British lines ended up worse off than before. Many were killed in battle, and hundreds died of disease. Others were recaptured and subjected to worse working conditions than before, in Chiswell's Mines, which supplied rebel soldiers with lead, or on sugar plantations in the West Indies. In the single year 1776, however, 400 former slaves sailed away from Virginia to freedom. The aspirations and actions of enslaved Virginians during the American Revolution have been ably chronicled by several scholars.[6] Now that the struggle for black freedom during the revolutionary era is coming into focus, we can begin to assess its effect on white Virginians. One result of the slaves' struggle was political: In seeking their own freedom, black Virginians indirectly helped motivate white Virginians to declare independence from Britain.

In August 1774 most white Virginians were angry at Parliament for adopting the acts they called Intolerable. These colonists, however, were content to express their outrage by cutting off trade with Britain. It was a long way from the boycott of 1774 to the revolution of 1776. What happened during the crucial year 1775 to convert mere boycotters into revolutionaries? Some of the factors that turned white Virginians against Britain were geographically or temporally remote; the colonists were incensed that the British army had invaded far-off Massachusetts, and they feared that the king's troops might invade Virginia as well. A third source of the white Virginians' anger was not remote at all; they were irate at Governor Dunmore for first threatening to ally with enslaved Virginians and then, later, actually doing so.

Neither Dunmore's threat in April 1775 to emancipate Virginia's slaves nor his offer of freedom in November of that year to patriots' bondspeople who joined his army would have carried much significance if black Virginians had remained entirely passive during the revolutionary crisis. But slaves were not passive. Perhaps a thousand of them took advantage of Dunmore's offer of emancipation in November 1775. Even before the governor published his proclamation, however, scores of slaves had joined his little army or undertaken their own resistance to white rule. Even earlier, before Dunmore first threatened to offer freedom to the slaves, bondspeople in different parts of Virginia had gathered to discuss how to take advantage of the growing rift among whites. And the opposition of 1774 and 1775 was only the culmination of a tradition of black resistance that was as old as Virginia slavery itself.[7]

Afro-Virginians were most often the victims, not the perpetrators, of interracial violence, but they struck back often enough to maintain a permanent undercurrent of fear in the minds of most whites in the Chesapeake. Although it has been estimated that fewer than 1 percent of enslaved Virginians killed whites in the eighteenth century, it is likely that by the 1760s almost every white person in the eastern counties knew of a free person who had been killed by a slave.[8] At the same time that the black percentage of the population increased, the percentage of slaves who killed whites (as opposed to fellow slaves) also grew.[9]

If individual whites had nightmares about waking up amid flames or feeling the first spasms of a stomach contorted by poison, whites as a group frequently worried about servile insurrection. Slave plots seemed to be especially rife during the Seven Years' War (1755–63).[10] In July 1755 Charles Carter reported to Lieutenant Governor Robert Dinwiddie that enslaved workers in Lancaster County had gathered near his son's home, possibly with a view to allying with the Native American and French foes who had just defeated General Edward Braddock's army near Fort Duquesne. Dinwiddie replied on 18 July. "The Villany of the Negroes on any Emergency of Gov't is w't I always fear'd," he told Carter. "I greatly approve of Y'r send'g the Sheriffs with proper Strength to take up those y't apear'd in a Body at Y'r Son's House." If the slaves were "found guilty of the Expressions mention'd," Dinwiddie said, " . . . an Example of one or two at first may prevent those Creatures enter'g into Combinat[ion]s and wicked Designs."[11] Later in the war, Richard Henry Lee told the House of Burgesses that slaves, "from the nature of their situation, can never feel an interest in our cause, because . . . they observe their masters possessed of liberty which is denied to them."[12]

White Virginians became especially alarmed about their slaves during Pontiac's War, the Indian uprising of 1763–64. For the first time in recent memory, Indians spared the lives of blacks at the settlements they attacked; gentlemen wondered why. "As the Indians are saving & Carressing all the Negroes they take," militia lieutenant William Fleming told Lieutenant Governor Francis Fauquier in July 1763, "should it be productive of an Insurrection it may be attended with the most serious Consequences." The following month, a Virginia clergyman reported that Indians had "carried a great number of women and children, as well as some men, and (for the first time too) a good many negroes, into captivity."[13]

Although the slave-Indian alliance that so frightened white Virginians never materialized, bondspeople continued to plan insurrections after the war. A group in Loudoun County revolted in early 1767 and killed an overseer named Dennis Dallis. Three of them were hanged. In neighboring Fairfax County that same year, enslaved workers poisoned several overseers. "[S]ome of the negroes have been taken up, four of whom were executed about three weeks ago, after which their heads were cut off, and fixed on the chimnies of the court-house," a Boston newspaper reported, "and it was expected that four more would soon meet with the same fate." Frederick County slaves also reportedly plotted a rebellion in the 1760s.[14] In Stafford County in May 1769, some of John Knox's slaves "barbarously murdered" him. Suspicion fell on two fugitives named Phill and Winny, and Knox's brothers offered a reward of £105 for their capture and conviction. Within a month both had been apprehended and put to death, along with one of the "house wenches," who had not initially been a suspect in her master's death.[15] Around Christmas of the same year, the bondsmen on Bowler Cocke's plantation in nearby Hanover County attacked the steward, his assistant, and a neighbor and beat each severely. When a band of whites arrived to suppress the insurrection, Cocke's slaves "rushed upon them with a desperate fury, armed with clubs and staves." The whites saved themselves by shooting dead two of the rebels and nearly decapitating a third.[16]

As Lieutenant Governor Dinwiddie had said in 1755, "any Emergency" that divided white Americans could give blacks the opportunity to launch rebellions.[17] The American Revolution was such an emergency. By Christmas 1774, some enslaved Virginians had begun to discuss how to exploit the widening rift between white colonists and the royal governor and navy. "In one of our Counties lately," James Madison reported in November 1774, "a few of those unhappy wretches met together & chose a leader who was to conduct them when the English Troops should arrive." Enslaved workers in other colonies also met to consider how to profit from the imperial conflict. In St. Andrew's Parish, Georgia, slaves rebelled in December 1774 and killed four whites before they were captured and burned alive. An account of a plot in Ulster County, New York, appeared in the *Virginia Gazettes* in mid-March 1775; the scheme had been uncovered when a white man overheard two enslaved conspirators planning to obtain gunpowder and shot.[18]

The fears that these plots induced in white Virginians were heightened by the rumor that the British government might encourage slave insurrections as a way of suppressing the patriot movement.[19] Late in 1774, William Draper, who had just returned to London from an extended tour of America, published a pamphlet arguing that one way to put down the patriot rebellion would be to "Proclame *Freedom* to their Negroes." Arthur Lee, who was living in London, had obtained a copy of Draper's pamphlet by early December 1774, when he mentioned Draper's "proposal for emancipating your Negroes . . . & arming them against you" to his brothers in Virginia. Lee reported the plan "meets with approbation from ministerial People."[20] James Madison heard in early 1775 that a bill freeing the slaves had been introduced in Parliament. No such bill has been found, but Edmund Burke noted on the floor of the House of Commons in March that many pro-government members favored "a general enfranchisement of [the] slaves."[21] During spring 1775, many Virginians believed that these proposals were about to be implemented. According to a House of Burgesses report, British officials contemplated "a Scheme, the most diabolical," to "offer Freedom to our Slaves, and turn them against their Masters." A similar accusation was made in an anonymous letter that appeared in Alexander Purdie's *Virginia Gazette* in June. The writer alluded to recent rumors of slave conspiracies and then added: "From some hints, it was inferred that the negroes had not been without encouragement from a Gentleman of the Navy"—probably Captain Henry Colins of HMS *Magdalen*.[22]

Enslaved Virginians did not wait for British "encouragement" to intensify their activism. In spring 1775 several groups of slaves in the James River watershed reportedly assembled to plan rebellions. On 15 April 1775 Toney, a slave in Prince Edward County, was charged with insurrection and conspiracy to commit murder; he received fifteen lashes.[23] Three days later whites in nearby Chesterfield County were "alarm'd for an Insurrection of the Slaves," trader Robert Donald reported. Slave patrols were usually somewhat lax in Virginia, but the one in Chesterfield was quickly revived. "[W]e Patrol and go armed—a dreadful enemy," Donald wrote on 18 April.[24] Three more days passed. Then "Sentence of death [was] passed upon two Negroes . . . tried at Norfolk, for being concerned in a conspiracy to raise an insurrection in that town," the *Virginia Gazette* reported. One of the accused blacks in Norfolk was Emanuel de Antonio. The other was called simply Emanuel, and he was the property of Matthew Phripp, the militia lieutenant for Norfolk County.[25] On 21 April, the very day that the two Emanuels were sentenced to die, Edmund Pendleton reported that the free half of Williamsburg's population had been frightened by "some disturbances in the City, by the *Slaves.*"[26]

It is possible that the two Emanuels in Norfolk and Toney in Prince Edward County were not in touch with each other, with the Williamsburg plotters, or with those in Chesterfield County. Many white Virginians, however, thought that the alleged occurrence in different parts of the James River watershed of four slave conspiracies during the third week of April 1775—the largest number in such a short time before Gabriel's Rebellion in 1800—was no coincidence. They believed that what they were facing was not just a few scattered outbreaks but a coordinated attack. Edward Stabler, a Williamsburg Quaker, noted in May that during the previous month "[t]here had been many Rumours here of the Negroes intending to Rise." Although Stabler considered the rumor of a wide-ranging slave conspiracy "without much foundation," it was real enough to terrify many of his fellow citizens. An anonymous newspaper essayist stated in June that "various reports of internal insurrections" had circulated throughout the spring. "Whether this was general, or who were the instigators, remains as yet a secret," he said.[27]

It was in this context of rising aspirations among blacks and mounting fears among whites that Governor Dunmore decided to put Virginia's major ammunition cache out of the reach of patriot militiamen. Early on Friday morning, 21 April, he had a detachment from HMS *Magdalen* remove fifteen half barrels of gunpowder from the colonial magazine in the center of Williamsburg and secure them on the warship. Many white Virginians believed that the governor's timing was no coincidence, that he intentionally removed the powder amid the swirl of rumors of servile insurrection in order to abandon them to the fury of their slaves. Many years later, Edmund Randolph, who had lived in Williamsburg in April 1775, pronounced the transfer of the powder "not far removed from assassination." He concluded that the governor "designed, by disarming the people, to weaken the means of opposing an insurrection of the slaves . . . for a protection against whom in part the magazine was at first built."[28]

In 1774 Dunmore had led an attack against the Shawnee and Mingo nations that forced them to cede all the land east of the Ohio River to Virginia; in March 1775 a patriot convention unanimously praised the earl "for his truly noble, wise and spirited Conduct on the late Expedition against our Indian Enemy."[29] As late as 20 April, despite the anti-British currents sweeping over the American colonies, Dunmore remained what Norfolk merchant James Parker pronounced him in January 1775—"as popular as a Scotsman can be among weak prejudiced people." Overnight the relocation of the gunpowder turned him into a villain. By dawn on 21 April, most of white Williamsburg, having learned of the removal of the powder, gathered on the town green near the governor's palace. Many carried weapons. The people in the crowd meant to force the governor to return the gunpowder, but they agreed to stand down while the town council and provincial leaders first gave Dunmore a chance to give up the powder peacefully. A delegation met with him and surprised everyone by agreeing to let the powder stay on board the *Magdalen*. Returning to the green, the leaders persuaded the crowd to disperse.[30]

Williamsburg lapsed into "perfect tranquility." But then "a Report was spread by his Excellency's throwing out some threats respecting the Slaves."[31] The report was true. On 22 April, the day after he removed the gunpowder, Dunmore reignited the crisis. He gave Dr. William Pasteur, a member of the Williamsburg town council, a message for Peyton Randolph, the Speaker of the House of Burgesses: If any high-ranking British official was harmed, Dunmore "would declare Freedom to the Slaves, and reduce the City of *Williamsburg* to Ashes."[32]

It became clear at once what probably had prompted Speaker Randolph and other white leaders to back off so quickly from their demand the previous day that Dunmore immediately return the powder. They did not want to provoke him to employ a weapon far more lethal than fifteen half barrels of gunpowder, the more than 180,000 Virginians who were enslaved.[33] A day later, Dunmore went beyond whatever subtle hints he may have dropped in his meeting with white leaders; he explicitly threatened to free Virginia's slaves.

Dunmore's posture frightened white Virginians. In Williamsburg, the town fathers doubled the nightly slave patrol. In Amelia, the patriot committee, fearful "for the internal security of the county," ordered "that patrollers in every neighbourhood be constantly kept on duty."[34]

Dunmore's suspiciously timed seizure of the gunpowder and his threat to free the slaves coincided with the battles of Lexington and Concord. White Virginians interpreted the initiatives of General Thomas Gage in Massachusetts and Governor Dunmore in Virginia as part of a concerted ministerial plot to disarm them. The government's scheme seemed likely to have its most dire consequences in the slave colonies. White Virginians debated how best to respond. Provincial leaders in Williamsburg believed the safest strategy was to avoid antagonizing Dunmore. In the countryside, however, independent military companies mustered and prepared to march to the capital. At least seven counties that had not yet formed independent companies hastily did so.[35]

Although the clash at Lexington and Concord was clearly one reason that so many white Virginians turned their attention to military prepared-ness at this time, they were also concerned about events in their own colony. The Sussex County committee explicitly linked its decision to establish an independent company to Dunmore's oddly timed relocation of the gun-powder. The governor, the Sussex committee asserted, had attempted "to render (at least as far as in his power so to do) this colony defenceless, and lay it open to the attacks of a savage invasion, or a domestick foe." His ac-tions made it "absolutely necessary that this county be put into the best pos-ture of defence possible." More than six hundred members of independent companies converged on Fredericksburg by 29 April and made ready to march south to the capital. Among their goals, a Virginia historian recalled many years later, was "to seize the governor and crush at once the seeds of insurrection."[36]

The men who assembled for the march to Williamsburg no doubt ex-pected whites in the capital to be comforted to hear that reinforcements were on the way. Instead, white Williamsburg residents were terrified. The moment colonial treasurer Robert Carter Nicholas and Speaker Peyton Randolph learned that the independent companies had gathered, they began "writing letters over all the country to prevent those meetings," according to Norfolk merchant James Parker.[37] Speaker Randolph warned the Fredericksburg encampment that "violent measures may produce ef-fects, which God only knows the consequence of." His fears were not un-founded. On 28 April, the day after Dunmore learned that the independent companies intended to march against him, he reiterated his threat to raise the slaves. The governor drew a line in the sandy Tidewater soil. He told Pasteur that "if a large Body of People came below *Ruffin's Ferry* (a place about thirty Miles from this City) that he would immediately enlarge his plan, and carry it into Execution." If any whites had dared to hope that Dun-more's earlier warning had been only the product of momentary passion, by repeating it he set them straight. During "this alarming crisis," a group of Williamsburg slave patrollers said, "even the whispering of the wind was sufficient to rouze their fears." The governor underscored that he would not strike the first blow; Pasteur reported that he "more than once did say, he should not carry these Plans into Execution unless he was attacked."[38]

Fearful gentry leaders managed to persuade most of the independent volunteer companies to disband—most, but not all. The Albemarle County volunteers voted on 29 April to march to Williamsburg "to demand satis-faction of Dunmore for the powder, and his threatening to fix his standard and call over the negroes," the company's first lieutenant noted.[39] Apparently the Albemarle troops had second thoughts and turned back, but the company from Hanover County, led by Patrick Henry, decided on 2 May to march on. The Hanover men, who were soon joined by volunteers from other counties, feared that Dunmore's suspiciously timed removal of the gunpowder would lead to "calamities of the greatest magnitude, and most fatal consequences to this colony," presumably including a slave revolt.[40] Speaker Randolph and other leaders tried to persuade Henry's followers that by attacking Dunmore they would provoke him to create the very "calamities" and "fatal consequences" they meant to prevent.[41]

The leaders' assessment of the governor's intentions was correct. As Henry's band headed toward Williamsburg, "several negroes" went to the governor's palace and "made a tender of their services." Dunmore turned them away, but he told Attorney General John Randolph that if the Hanover volunteers attacked him and "Negroes on that Occasion offered their Service they would be received."[42] On 3 May, Dunmore issued a proclamation. He demanded that free Virginians cease all resistance to his authority, and he took the occasion to remind them of their vulnerability to a slave or Indian uprising. This veiled warning may have helped persuade Henry and Receiver General Richard Corbin to reach a face-saving compromise in which Corbin paid Henry for the gunpowder—which remained on board the *Magdalen*.[43]

The powder magazine incident is one of the chestnuts of Virginia history. It marked the first time since Bacon's Rebellion in 1676 that a large number of Virginians had taken up arms to attack a royal governor. It served also "to widen the unhappy breach between Great Britain and her colonies," as the soldiers encamped at Fredericksburg declared. All over the colony, county committees proclaimed that Dunmore had "highly forfeited all title to the confidence of the good people of Virginia."[44] In the midst of the crisis, Patrick Henry recognized that the episode would foster patriotism in Virginia. As the Hanover independent company marched toward Williamsburg, he observed that the removal of the gunpowder "was a fortunate circumstance, which would rouse the people from North to South."[45]

The growth of anti-British sentiment in Virginia in May 1775 is usually ascribed simply to the battles of Lexington and Concord and to Dunmore's decision to seize the gunpowder.[46] But the governor learned from Benjamin Waller, a member of Williamsburg's patriot committee, that Dunmore had forfeited "the Confidence of the People not so much for having taken the Powder as for the declaration he made of raising and freeing the Slaves." Louisa County trader Thomas Mitchell noted "that the Governor's Declaration to give Freedom to the Slaves greatly inflamed the Minds of those who believed it," although not everyone did. It is possible that many patriots only pretended to believe the stories about Dunmore's "stiring up the

Negroes to Rebellion" (as Rawleigh Downman put it in July) because the rumors furnished a good pretext for anti-British activities.[47] Because Dunmore's opponents had backed down, however, no one knew what he would have done if they had called his bluff and attacked him. Patriots may have exaggerated their anger at Dunmore's tactics of intimidation, but they did not invent it.

Racial tensions escalated the imperial conflict in another way as well. One of the charges that whites lodged against Dunmore was that he had chosen to remove the powder at the very moment when reports of slave conspiracies poured into Williamsburg. The slave revolt scare in April 1775 was the crucial context of Dunmore's seizure of the gunpowder. It was not only his decision to "remov[e] the powder from the magazine" but also "the several circumstances attending the same" that angered the Richmond County committee. Others agreed. The Fredericksburg encampment considered the relocation of the gunpowder "ill timed." A South Carolina newspaper described the racial context of the transfer and then observed, "The monstrous absurdity that the Governor can deprive the people of the necessary means of defense at a time when the colony is actually threatened with an insurrection of their slaves . . . has worked up the passions of the people there almost to a frenzy."[48]

Despite the reality of Dunmore's threat to free the slaves and his decision to remove the gunpowder during this tense period, the possibility must be considered that patriots publicly exaggerated their fear in order to cast further odium on the royal governor. White Virginians, however, seem to have been sincere when they said they feared a slave insurrection at the time Dunmore removed the powder. Loyalists such as James Robison, the chief factor for William Cuninghame & Company of Glasgow, agreed with patriots that "an insurrection . . . was dreaded" in Virginia during the spring of 1775.[49] If one suspects that the *Virginia Gazette*'s account of the "conspiracy to raise an insurrection" in Norfolk was only patriot propaganda, one need only consult the minute book of the Norfolk County court, in which the trial of the two Emanuels is recorded.[50] The death of one of the alleged conspirators, Matthew Phripp's Emanuel, can be traced in the Norfolk County tithable lists, from which he disappeared between the taking of the 1774 and 1778 enumerations.[51] The trial of Toney in Prince Edward County is also a matter of record. It is possible that the Williamsburg town council's allegation on 21 April that Dunmore had removed the gunpowder amid "various reports" of slave plots "in different parts of the country" was just rhetoric,[52] but whites' fears as recorded in the private letters of Edmund Pendleton, Edward Stabler, and Robert Donald were almost certainly not fabricated.

If anything, white Virginians may have understated their apprehensions of slave revolt in their public pronouncements. In November 1774, when

James Madison told a Princeton classmate that slaves in the Piedmont had planned to take advantage of the expected British invasion, he judged it "prudent such attempts should be concealed as well as suppressed." A year later, when editor John Pinkney printed a letter from South Carolina in his *Virginia Gazette*, he omitted part of it. "This letter goes on farther," Pinkney informed his readers, "and relates a great deal about the negroes in South Carolina; but we think it prudent to suppress the account." Although nothing was certain in this murky world of "exaggeration, distortion, [and] censorship," it seems likely that white Virginians' anger at Governor Dunmore for taking their gunpowder was intensified by the context in which he took it. The earl seized the stores at the end of the third week of April 1775, when white Virginians circulated more reports of slave conspiracies than they had during any previous week in the colony's history.[53]

Some white Virginians expressed their growing rage at Dunmore in jokes about his relations with black women. There had long been talk about the governor's philandering, but during the summer of 1775, for the first time, his concubines were said to include blacks. On 1 June 1775, Pinkney's *Virginia Gazette* sarcastically predicted that "The BLACK LADIES" would "be jollily entertained at the p[alac]e." A year later, after Dunmore had assembled a mostly black army to battle the patriots, Purdie's *Virginia Gazette* maintained that the diminutive Dunmore and his forces celebrated their landing on Gwynn's Island "with a promiscuous ball, which was opened, we hear, by a certain spruce little gentleman, with one of the black ladies." The next month, Landon Carter of Richmond County heard a story about a patriot cannonball passing between Dunmore's legs. Carter joked in his diary that perhaps the "shot cooled his latitudinous virility for that night at least."[54]

Accounts of the Virginia slave plots, the removal of the gunpowder, and the possibility that Dunmore would ally with slave conspirators soon spread throughout the South. At the same time, the same routes of communication carried reports of the battles of Lexington and Concord and rumors from London about an emancipation bill being proposed in Parliament. All of this news led many southerners of every race and condition to believe that the British government might soon forge some sort of alliance with enslaved Americans. Dunmore's threat on 22 April to "declare Freedom to the Slaves" was ambiguous—perhaps deliberately so. Had the governor meant he would liberate only those slaves he could enlist in the British army—or all of them? Many southerners believed during the late summer of 1775 that Britain might adopt "an Act of Grace" by which enslaved Americans would "be all set free," as Charleston merchant Josiah Smith, Jr., reported on 18 May. A group of Charleston slaves had apparently contemplated a rebellion since April. The news from Virginia, Massachusetts, and London persuaded many South Carolinians that the new governor, Lord William Campbell, who was due to arrive in June, was going to free the slaves and "encourage an insurrection," as the governor himself later reported. The rumor kept white South Carolinians on tenterhooks from early May until 19 June, when Campbell landed without incident.[55]

In North Carolina, too, reports from London, Massachusetts, and Virginia contributed to talk that the British government might soon incite a slave revolt. In early July, when a widespread slave conspiracy was discovered in Pitt, Craven, and Beaufort counties, whites suspected that British officials had conferred with the conspirators about strategy and made certain promises to them. Allegedly the plan was for blacks to start a rebellion on the night of 8 July. They were to kill their owners and then move westward toward the backcountry, where "they were to be received with open arms by a number of Persons there appointed and armed by [the] Government for their Protection," according to Colonel John Simpson of Pitt County.[56]

Many enslaved Americans carried the rumors about British aid for black insurrection one step farther: They believed that the whole purpose of the expected British invasion of the South was to liberate them. In South Carolina, a slave reported that Thomas Jeremiah, a free black fisherman and harbor pilot who hoped to help the British troops link up with rebel slaves, told bondspeople "the War was come to help the poor Negroes." Farther south in St. Bartholomew Parish at about the same time, a black preacher named George told gatherings of slaves "That the Young King, meaning our Present One, came up with the Book, & was about to alter the World, & set the Negroes Free." George was executed.[57] The widespread belief among many black southerners that their freedom was Britain's chief war aim was detected by some whites. John Drayton wrote many years after the Revolution that Arthur Lee's assertion that the London government meant to incite an insurrection was "the more alarming; because, it was already known, [bondsmen] entertained ideas, that the present contest was for obliging us to give them their liberty."[58]

The report that freeing the slaves was one of Great Britain's objectives—perhaps even the primary one—may have been fabricated by black leaders in the hope that it would serve as a self-fulfilling prophecy. If a real slave revolt crystallized around the apocryphal story of a British army of liberation, British statesmen might indeed be drawn into an alliance with the slave rebels.

An additional source of anxiety for white leaders, and of hope for blacks, was the possibility that a large number of poor whites might cast their lots with the slaves and the British. About a month after Dunmore removed the Williamsburg gunpowder and threatened to emancipate the slaves, John Simmons of Dorchester County, Maryland, boasted: "[I]f I had a few more white people to join me I could get all the negroes in the county to back us, and they would do more good in the night than the white people could do in the day." He added, "[I]f all the gentlemen were killed we should have the best of the land to tend."[59] During July, Thomas Cox, a white inhabitant of York County, Virginia, was accused of trying to incite slaves to rebel. He was found innocent of this charge but guilty of breach of the peace.[60]

The deepest fears of white leaders, and the highest hopes of blacks, were not realized. Dunmore did not proclaim a general emancipation, nor did he lead a rebellion of slaves and poor whites. During the summer, however, he began assembling a small fleet to confront the patriots. The governor soon welcomed such fugitive slaves as the pilot Joseph Harris, and the sanctuary that he offered runaways changed the whole calculus of race relations in Virginia. Previously, fugitive slave advertisements appearing in the *Virginia Gazettes* commonly surmised that the escapee had gone to visit family. By September 1775, however, advertisers began to conjecture that their slaves had fled slavery by joining the British.[61]

The story of one fugitive illustrated how the meaning of escape had changed. On 10 February 1775, a fifteen-year-old girl (whose name is not known) was purchased by Virginia's official vintner, Andrew Estave. The teenager may have been one of the many young Virginians who were sold far away from their families as they reached adulthood. In any event, she found life with Estave so intolerable that in her first few months as his property, she ran away three times. Each time the girl was recaptured and suffered forty lashes. The punishment did not have its desired effect, so Estave suspended it and assumed that the fifteen-year-old would be thereby reconciled to her fate. She was not. Early in the summer of 1775, as Estave told readers of the *Virginia Gazette*, another of the women he owned "found my child, together with this cruel and unnatural wretch, concealed behind my barn, among the bushes, with her thumb thrust into the private parts of my poor child." Estave was summoned. "During the confusion," the fifteen-year-old escaped and fled—to the governor's palace in Williamsburg, where she hoped to cast her lot with Dunmore. The governor had himself recently fled to a British warship, and the teenager was soon returned to her master for punishment. First she suffered "eighty lashes, well laid on." Then Estave poured fire embers on her back.[62] Although the teenager's escape attempt was unsuccessful, it is significant that she sought refuge in the building that until recently had symbolized the enforcement, not the evasion, of white rule.[63]

The new opportunities produced by the conflict among white Virginians inspired activism even among those slaves who did not try to reach Dunmore. During the summer of 1775, the number of enslaved workers brought before the county courts for criminal trials reached a record level.[64]

No doubt many white Virginians blamed the crime wave on Governor Dunmore.

In the fall of 1775, Dunmore gave white Virginians additional reasons to hate him and the government he represented. On 15 November at Kemp's Landing south of Norfolk, his outnumbered force, made up largely of former slaves, defeated 170 members of the Princess Anne County militia. Several militiamen were killed, and the rest were put to flight. The patriot commander, Joseph Hutchings, was captured by one of his own former bondsmen.[65] Kemp's Landing persuaded Dunmore that fugitive slaves could be valuable allies indeed. The governor "was so ela[ted] with this Victory," John Page, vice-chairman of the Committee of Safety, reported, that he immediately published his famous emancipation proclamation.[66] About 1,000 slaves escaped their owners and joined Dunmore. Enlisted in an "Ethiopian Regiment" and wearing uniforms that pointed up the hypocrisy of liberty-seeking patriots by proclaiming "Liberty to Slaves," former bondsmen soon made up the major part of the loyalist troops.[67] In order to glimpse the psychological effect of emancipation on the people who reached Dunmore, it may be sufficient to notice the case of a man whites called Yellow Peter. He escaped one day in 1775 or 1776 and was later seen "in Governor Dunmore's regiment with a musket on his back and a sword by his side." He had changed his name to Captain Peter.[68]

Although Dunmore apparently meant to limit his offer of emancipation to able-bodied men (he addressed it to servants and slaves "able and willing to bear Arms"), half of those who joined him and survived the war were women and children.[69] Among them was Francis Rice's slave, Mary. One night in spring 1776, Mary, a resident of Hampton, snatched up her three-and-a-half-year-old daughter Phillis and made a dash for the British lines. The two got in safely, lived through the Revolution, and settled afterward in Nova Scotia.[70]

Still, for the 99 percent of slaves who did not escape to Dunmore, his emancipation proclamation was in many ways a disappointment. During summer 1775, many Virginians anticipated that the British government might make the abolition of slavery a goal of the war. Instead, Dunmore offered freedom only to individuals and formed a conventional army to pursue the limited strategy of taking and holding ground. Even as Dunmore's decision to fight a traditional war destroyed the hopes of many black Virginians, it emboldened whites. To them, a black regiment in the British army was a frightening thing indeed, but it was nothing like a British promise of general emancipation. By August 1776, patriots forced Dunmore's vastly outnumbered army to retreat to New York City.

The relief that white Virginians experienced when Dunmore chose to fight a conventional war did not diminish their anger at him for allying with slaves. As early as May 1775, free subjects had begun literally to demonize their governor. In November, when he published his declaration of emancipation, this process intensified. Citizens denounced Dunmore's "Diabolical scheme" and all "his infernal tribe." "Our Devil of a Governor goes on at a Devil of a rate indeed," Benjamin Harrison commented after reading the Virginia news.[71]

The deterioration in white Virginians' affection for Dunmore was not the only political result of his proclamation. Thomas Jefferson spoke for other white Americans when he stated in the Declaration of Independence that Dunmore's emancipation proclamation was a major cause of the Revolution.[72] Throughout Virginia, observers noted that the governor's pronouncement turned neutrals and even loyalists into patriots. "The Inhabitants of this Colony are deeply alarmed at this infernal Scheme," Philip Fithian recorded in his journal as he passed through the Virginia backcountry in late November. "It seems to quicken all in Revolution to overpower him at any Risk." Richard Henry Lee told Catharine Macauley that "Lord Dunmores unparalleled conduct in Virginia has, a few Scotch excepted, united every Man in that large Colony." Archibald Cary agreed. "The Proclamation from Lord D[unmore], has had a most extensive good consequence," he wrote; white "Men of all ranks resent the pointing a dagger to their Throats, through the hands of their Slaves." Cary noted that by endangering loyalists as well as patriots, Dunmore's decision converted many of the former into the latter.[73]

These patriot writers' comments on the governor's declaration may have reflected some measure of wishful thinking about its effect on undecided and loyalist whites, but Dunmore's pronouncement did transform many neutrals and loyalists into patriots. It even pushed two members of the colony's powerful executive council, Robert "Councilor" Carter and William Byrd III, from the loyalist to the patriot camp. During summer 1775, Byrd had offered to lead British troops. Both he and Carter, however, became patriots after Dunmore confirmed his alliance with black Virginians. Byrd then tendered his services to the patriot forces.[74]

Some of William Byrd's fellow conservatives initially believed that as soon as Dunmore's superiors in London learned about his emancipation proclamation, they would repudiate it and recall him. At the end of 1775, Landon Carter assured his diary that it was "not to be doubted" that Dunmore would soon receive "some missive commission to Silence all his iniquities both male and female." (This was yet another reference to Dunmore's alleged miscegenation.)[75] But the winter of 1775–76 came and went with no evidence that anyone at Whitehall objected to Dunmore's decision to offer freedom to the slaves.

It was not just in Virginia that Dunmore's emancipation proclamation helped alienate whites from Britain. In Maryland, loyalist William Eddis observed that Dunmore's "measure of emancipating the negroes has excited an universal ferment." He speculated that the declaration would "greatly strengthen the general confederacy." Edward Rutledge of South Carolina expected that the "proclamation issued by Lord Dunmore" would tend "more effectually to work an eternal separation between Great Britain and the Colonies,—than any other expedient, which could possibly have been thought of." In Philadelphia, a play depicting Dunmore welcoming black recruits became part of the library of anti-British propaganda. In the play, *The Fall of British Tyranny* by Philadelphia silversmith John Leacock, Lord Kidnapper (Dunmore) congratulates himself on raising "rebel against rebel" and says he expects his emancipation proclamation "will greatly intimidate the rebels—internal enemies are worse than open foes."[76]

Although Dunmore was the only royal governor who made a formal offer of freedom to his colony's slaves before 4 July 1776, other British leaders informally cooperated with bondspeople and thereby helped motivate white Americans to declare independence. In North Carolina in June 1776, patriot James Iredell stated that when royal officials encouraged enslaved Americans "to cut our throats," they "added spurs to our Patriotism."[77]

White Americans also denounced British cooperation with American Indians. Here, too, Dunmore was one of the most popular targets. In November 1775 Dunmore sent his associate John Connolly to Detroit and the Ohio country to recruit an army of Indian warriors that would join forces with the governor's Anglo-black army at Alexandria in spring 1776. Connolly was captured as he rode west through Maryland, and his plot was revealed. It infuriated white Americans. In John Leacock's *Fall of British Tyranny*, Lord Kidnapper muses: "[I]f we can stand our ground this winter, and burn all their towns that are accessible to our ships, and Colonel Connolly succeeds in his plan . . . we shall be able to make a descent where we please, and drive the rebels like hogs into a pen."[78]

As previously noted, a man named Emanuel disappeared from Matthew Phripp's tithables between the recording of the 1774 and 1778 lists. He was one of the two slaves executed in Norfolk in April 1775 "for being concerned in a conspiracy to raise an insurrection in that town."[79] Emanuel was not the only enslaved worker whom Phripp lost in the early years of the American Revolution. Other names also vanished from his tithable list during the war. About most of these people we know nothing, but we do know what became of several of them. When the British army and navy evacuated New York City in 1783, about 3,000 slaves went with them. Before leaving, navy captains made a list of their formerly enslaved passengers. On board the *Danger,* anchored near Staten Island (and not far from the little island where the Statue of Liberty would rise a century later), the compilers of the list recorded the presence of "James Tucker, 55 years, almost worn out . . . Formerly slave to Capt. [M.] Fipps, Norfolk, Virginia; left him in 1776 with Lord Dunmore."[80] When the *Danger* cleared New York harbor, bound for Nova Scotia, James Tucker was on board. He might have been "almost worn out," but he was headed to freedom.

We do not know how James Tucker had spent the years between 1776 and 1783, but it is clear that he was able to wring a larger measure of freedom from the American Revolution than did any of the white colonists who had revolted against British tyranny. If slaves such as Matthew Phripp's Emanuel had not made their own efforts to win freedom in 1774 and 1775, Governor Dunmore might never have published the emancipation proclamation that resulted not only in the freedom of hundreds of Virginians such as Phripp's James but also in the deterioration of relations between white Virginians and the British government.

Although the effect of Dunmore's cooperation with slaves on white Virginians' decision to declare independence is often mentioned by scholars who write about the Revolution, it is generally underestimated.[81] One reason for this minimization is that students of the origins of the Revolution often do not mention enslaved Virginians until November 1775, when Dunmore issued his famous emancipation proclamation. Actually, as several social historians have shown, the governor's declaration culminated a process that had begun much earlier. Slaves had always resisted their condition. In 1774, while Dunmore was still one of the colony's most popular governors, enslaved Virginians began conspiring to exploit the opportunities presented to them by the imperial crisis. The following April, as rumors of the planning of a wide-ranging insurrection circulated, a group of slaves literally knocked on the governor's door and offered to cast their lots with his.[82] And slaves kept knocking all through the summer and into the fall. Andrew Estave's fifteen-year-old bondswoman presented herself at the governor's palace early in the summer, after Dunmore had taken refuge on a British warship. She was recaptured, but other slaves did reach the earl and served him as sailors, raiders, and soldiers.[83] It was not until after the series of black initiatives culminating in the victory at Kemp's Landing on 15 November that Dunmore officially offered freedom to the slaves.[84] The slaves' insurgency played an important role in persuading Dunmore to ally with them—and thus in prodding white Virginians farther along the road to independence.

If black Virginians really did help push whites into independence, how does that change our understanding of the Revolution in Virginia? At least to some extent, we must agree with an anonymous resident of Williamsburg who assessed the situation in November 1775, shortly after Dunmore published his emancipation proclamation. "Whoever considers well the meaning of the word Rebel," he wrote, "will discover that the author of the Proclamation is now himself in actual rebellion, having armed our slaves against us, and having excited them to an insurrection."[85] In modern terms, this author might have said that white Virginians' struggle against Dunmore and his Ethiopian Regiment was not a revolution but a counterrevolution.

The war in Virginia pitted two classes, slave owners and slaves, against each other. At least in this one aspect of Virginia's multifaceted revolutionary experience, therefore, Virginia fits the Progressive historians' interpretation of the Revolution as a dual conflict over both home rule and who would rule at home. For years students of the origins of the American Revolution in Virginia, taking as an article of faith the "relative docility of the poorer farmers" in that colony, found almost no value in the Progressives' hypothesis that class conflict helped cause the Revolution.[86] More recently, the assumption that small farmers were tractable has been challenged.[87] And if enslaved Virginians are considered a class—which surely they must be—then there certainly was class conflict in Virginia during the prerevolutionary period, and that antagonism did help bring on the American Revolution. In fact, judging from the frenzied white reaction to Dunmore's decision to forge an alliance with black Virginians, it may be that Virginia was the colony in which class conflict gave the biggest push to the movement for independence.

NOTES

The author wishes to thank the following groups and individuals for useful comments on earlier drafts of this essay: Fred Anderson, the Bloomsburg University Social Studies Club, Edward Countryman, John d'Entremont, Emory G. Evans, Marjoleine Kars, Staughton Lynd, Michael A. McDonnell, John Murrin, Michael Lee Nicholls, Julie Richter, John E. Selby, Jon Sensbach, Brent Tarter, Thad W. Tate, Fredrika J. Teute, the outside readers for the *Virginia Magazine of History and Biography*, and especially Peter H. Wood. Research for this essay was funded in part by fellowships from the Virginia Historical Society and the Virginia Foundation for the Humanities.

1. Howard H. Peckham, ed., *The Toll of Independence: Engagements & Battle Casualties of the American Revolution* (Chicago and London, 1974), p. 9.

2. George Gray, deposition, 4 Sept. 1775, in William J. Van Schreeven, Robert L. Scribner, and Brent Tarter, eds., *Revolutionary Virginia: The Road to Independence* (7 vols.; Charlottesville, 1973–83), 4:70 (first quotation); George Montague to Matthew Squire, 20 July 1775, in Peter Force, comp., *American Archives: Consisting of a Collection of Authentick Records, State Papers, Debates, and Letters and Other Notices of Publick Affairs . . .* , 4th ser. (6 vols.; Washington, D.C., 1837–46), 2:1692 (second and third quotations).

3. *Virginia Gazette* (Purdie), 8 Sept. 1775; *Virginia Gazette* (Dixon and Hunter), 23 Sept. 1775. Joseph Harris appears on the muster role of the *Otter* during this time; see Admiralty 36/7763, Public Record Office, Kew, England (hereafter cited as PRO), Virginia Colonial Records Project, survey report 8793.

4. Lund Washington to George Washington, 3 Dec. 1775, in W. W. Abbot et al.,

eds., *The Papers of George Washington: Revolutionary War Series* (7 vols. to date; Charlottesville, 1985–), 2:479; *Virginia Gazette* (Purdie), 3 Nov. 1775 (quotation); John Page to Thomas Jefferson, 11 Nov. [1775], in Julian P. Boyd et al., eds., *The Papers of Thomas Jefferson* (26 vols. to date; Princeton, 1950–), 1:257. The fate of the *Hawke's* black crewmen is not known.

5. Thomas Jefferson to John Randolph, 29 Nov. 1775, Archibald Cary to Thomas Jefferson, 31 Oct. 1775, in Boyd et al., eds., *Jefferson Papers*, 1:269 (quotation), 249; Edmund Randolph, *History of Virginia*, ed. Arthur H. Shaffer, Virginia Historical Society Documents, 9 (Charlottesville, 1970), pp. 227–29. George Montague, captain of the *Fowey*, stated that Joseph Harris was free (George Montague to Matthew Squire, 20 July 1775, in Force, comp., *American Archives*, 4th ser., 2:1692). The captain's comment implies that Harris was already legally free before he joined the crew of the *Fowey*. Certainly there were free blacks in prerevolutionary Hampton, but it is not known whether Harris was one of them. Every other reference to Harris indicates he was a fugitive slave. See, for example, Sarah Shaver Hughes, "Elizabeth City County, Virginia, 1782–1810: The Economic and Social Structure of a Tidewater County in the Early National Years" (Ph.D. diss., College of William and Mary, 1975), p. 32.

6. See, for example, Benjamin Quarles, *The Negro in the American Revolution* (Chapel Hill, 1961); Sylvia R. Frey, "Between Slavery and Freedom: Virginia Blacks in the American Revolution," *Journal of Southern History* (hereafter cited as *JSH*) 49 (1983): 375–98; Sylvia R. Frey, *Water from the Rock: Black Resistance in a Revolutionary Age* (Princeton, 1991); Robert A. Olwell, "'Domestick Enemies': Slavery and Political Independence in South Carolina, May 1775–March 1776," *JSH* 55 (1989): 21–48; and Charles W. Carey, Jr., "'These Black Rascals': The Origins of Lord Dunmore's Ethiopian Regiment," *Virginia Social Science Journal* 31 (1996): 65–77. Earlier studies of African Americans in the Revolution include William Tittamin, "The Negro in the American Revolution" (M.A. thesis, New York University, 1939); Herbert Aptheker, *The Negro in the American Revolution* (New York, 1940); and Luther P. Jackson, "Virginia Negro Soldiers and Seamen in the American Revolution," *Journal of Negro History* (hereafter cited as *JNH*) 27 (1942): 247–87.

7. Quarles, *Negro in the Revolution*; Frey, "Between Slavery and Freedom"; Peter H. Wood, "'The Dream Deferred': Black Freedom Struggles on the Eve of White Independence," in Gary Y. Okihiro, ed., *In Resistance: Studies in African, Caribbean, and Afro-American History* (Amherst, Mass., 1986), pp. 166–87; Peter H. Wood, "'Liberty Is Sweet': African-American Freedom Struggles in the Years before White Independence," in Alfred F. Young, ed., *Beyond the American Revolution: Explorations in the History of American Radicalism*, Explorations in the History of American Radicalism series (DeKalb, Ill., 1993), pp. 149–84.

8. Philip J. Schwarz, *Twice Condemned: Slaves and the Criminal Laws of Virginia, 1705–1865* (Baton Rouge, 1988), p. 144. For examples of violence, see Richard Bland and William Fleming, petition, 5 Nov. 1764, James Boyd, petition, 7 Nov. 1764, in John Pendleton Kennedy, ed., *Journals of the House of Burgesses of Virginia, 1761–1765* (Richmond, 1907), pp. 237, 239; Daniel Hamlin, petition, 25 Feb. 1772, in John Pendleton Kennedy, ed., *Journals of the House of Burgesses of Virginia, 1770–1772* (Richmond, 1906), p. 189; Thomas Patterson, petition, 12 May 1774, Committee of Public Claims, report, 13 May 1774, in John Pendleton Kennedy, ed., *Journals of the House of Burgesses of Virginia, 1773–1776 . . .* (Richmond, 1905), pp. 92, 98; Augusta

County Order Book, 11 Apr. 1772, in Lyman Chalkley, ed., *Chronicles of the Scotch-Irish Settlement in Virginia, Extracted From the Original Court Records of Augusta County, 1745–1800* (3 vols.; Rosslyn, Va., 1912–13), 1:167; John Davis, *Travels of Four Years and a Half in the United States of America During 1798, 1799, 1800, 1801 and 1802* (1803; New York, 1909), p. 414; Henry Lee to Richard Lee, 16 Feb. 1767, Richard Bland Lee Letterbook, Custis-Lee Papers, Manuscripts Department, Library of Congress, Washington, D.C. (hereafter cited as DLC); David John Mays, *Edmund Pendleton, 1721–1803: A Biography* (2 vols.; Cambridge, Mass., 1952), 1:22, 35; Freeman H. Hart, *The Valley of Virginia in the American Revolution, 1763–1789* (Chapel Hill, 1942), p. 15; Schwarz, *Twice Condemned*, pp. ix–x, chap. 6; and William Waller Hening, ed., *The Statutes at Large; Being a Collection of All the Laws of Virginia . . .* (13 vols.; Richmond, Philadelphia, and New York, 1809–23), 6:104–12.

9. Schwarz, *Twice Condemned*, p. 143. Edmund S. Morgan draws a connection between slavery and the American Revolution that is very different from the one drawn in this essay. He argues that elite Virginians felt secure enough to embrace republicanism because they had solved "the problem of the poor" by creating "a society in which most of the poor were enslaved." By holding the poorest Virginians in bondage, he says, gentlemen "removed them from the political equation." Morgan's argument is undermined by a growing body of evidence showing that slaves consistently resisted their condition and thus remained, at the same time that they were among their owners' largest sources of income, a "problem" for them. (It also appears that very few Virginia gentlemen embraced republicanism with the enthusiasm ascribed to them by Morgan.) See Edmund S. Morgan, *American Slavery, American Freedom: The Ordeal of Colonial Virginia* (New York, 1975), pp. 381 (first and second quotations), 380 (third quotation).

10. Herbert Aptheker, *American Negro Slave Revolts* (New York, 1943), pp. 18–208; Thad W. Tate, *The Negro in Eighteenth-Century Williamsburg* (Charlottesville, 1965), pp. 109–13; Theodore Allen, "'. . . They Would Have Destroyed Me': Slavery and the Origins of Racism," *Radical America* 9 (1975): 56; Schwarz, *Twice Condemned*, pp. 171–74; Mays, *Edmund Pendleton*, 1:119–20.

11. Dinwiddie advised Carter to keep "Patrollers out for the Peace of Y'r Co[un]ty" and to instruct sheriffs to "seize all Horses used by Negroes in the Night Time" (Robert Dinwiddie to Charles Carter, 18 July 1755, in R. A. Brock, ed., *The Official Records of Robert Dinwiddie . . .*, Collections of the Virginia Historical Society, new ser., 3, 4 [2 vols.; Richmond, 1883–84], 2:104–5). Cf. Mark J. Stegmaier, "Maryland's Fear of Insurrection at the Time of Braddock's Defeat," *Maryland Historical Magazine* 71 (1976): 467–83; Wood, "'Liberty Is Sweet,'" p. 154.

12. Richard Henry Lee, speech, n.d., in Richard H. Lee, ed., *Memoir of the Life of Richard Henry Lee, and His Correspondence With the Most Distinguished Men in America and Europe . . .* (2 vols.; Philadelphia, 1825), 1:18.

13. William Fleming to Francis Fauquier, 26 July 1763, in George Reese, ed., *The Official Papers of Francis Fauquier, Lieutenant Governor of Virginia, 1758–1768*, Virginia Historical Society Documents, 14, 15, 16 (3 vols.; Charlottesville, 1980–83), 2:998; Peter Fontaine to Moses and John Fontaine and Daniel Torin, 7 Aug. 1763, in Ann Maury, ed., *Memoirs of a Huguenot Family* (New York, 1872), p. 372. Cf. Benjamin Johnston, advertisement, in *Virginia Gazette* (Rind), 16 Dec. 1773.

14. *Boston Chronicle*, 11–18 Jan. 1768, quoted in Aptheker, *American Negro Slave Re-*

volts, pp. 198–99; Frederick County militia, accounts, 23 Mar. 1767, Committee of Public Claims, report, 23 Nov. 1769, in John Pendleton Kennedy, ed., *Journals of the House of Burgesses of Virginia, 1766–1769* (Richmond, 1906), pp. 91, 286; Schwarz, *Twice Condemned*, pp. 146–47.

15. Robert Knox and William Knox, advertisement, in *Virginia Gazette* (Rind), 15 June 1769 (first quotation); *Virginia Gazette* (Rind), 20 July 1769 (second quotation).

16. *Virginia Gazette* (Rind), 25 Jan. 1770.

17. Robert Dinwiddie to Charles Carter, 18 July 1755, in Brock, ed., *Dinwiddie Records*, 2:104 (quotation); Aptheker, *American Negro Slave Revolts*, p. 4.

18. James Madison to William Bradford, Jr., 26 Nov. 1774, in William T. Hutchinson et al., eds., *The Papers of James Madison* (17 vols.; Chicago and Charlottesville, 1962–91), 1:130 (quotation); Wood, "'Liberty Is Sweet,'" pp. 161–63.

19. Jonathan Boucher, *A Letter from a Virginian to the Members of the Congress . . .* ([New York], 1774), p. 32; Henry Cruger to Ralph Izard, 21 Mar. 1775, in *Correspondence of Mr. Ralph Izard, of South Carolina . . .* (New York, 1844), p. 58.

20. "Viator" [William Draper], *The Thoughts of a Traveller Upon Our American Disputes* (London, 1774), p. 21; Arthur Lee to [Richard Henry Lee?], 6 Dec. 1774, Lee Family Papers, 1638–1867, Virginia Historical Society, Richmond. Lee continued: "Do not laugh at it, till you are sure it woud be vain. If you apprehend it woud be dangerous take proper precautions against it."

21. William Bradford, Jr., to James Madison, 4 Jan. 1775, in Hutchinson et al., eds., *Madison Papers*, 1:132; Edmund Burke, speech on conciliation with the colonies, 22 Mar. 1775, in Edmund Burke, *Speeches and Letters on American Affairs*, Everyman's Library, 340 (London and New York, 1908), p. 102.

22. House of Burgesses, address to John Murray, earl of Dunmore, 19 June 1775, in *JHB, 1773–76*, p. 256; *Virginia Gazette* (Purdie), 16 June 1775. Cf. Virginia convention of 1775, "A Declaration of the Delegates . . . ," 26 Aug. 1775, in Van Schreeven, Scribner, and Tarter, eds., *Revolutionary Virginia*, 3:501. The rumor that the British government intended to arm enslaved Americans against their masters circulated in other colonies as well. During the critical month of April 1775, Philadelphia Quaker James Kenny reported that "a great Woman in London" had written a Philadelphian saying several members of the House of Lords had informed her of a "secret Plan." "[A]rms &c" were "to be given to all the . . . Negros to act against the Collonie" (James Kenny to Humphry Marshall, 25 Apr. 1775 [typescript], Humphry and Moses Marshall Papers, William L. Clements Library, University of Michigan, Ann Arbor).

23. Schwarz, *Twice Condemned*, pp. 182, 184.

24. Robert Donald to Patrick Hunter, 18 Apr. 1775, in *Buchanan and Milliken* v. *Robert Donald*, 1794, U.S. Circuit Court, Virginia District, Ended Cases (restored), Box 6, Vi.

25. *Virginia Gazette* (Dixon and Hunter), 29 Apr. 1775 (supplement); Norfolk County Minute Book, 21 Apr. 1775, Vi.

26. Edmund Pendleton to George Washington, 21 Apr. 1775, in David John Mays, ed., *The Letters and Papers of Edmund Pendleton, 1734–1803*, Virginia Historical Society Documents, 7, 8 (2 vols.; Charlottesville, 1967), 1:102.

27. Edward Stabler to Isaac Pemberton, 16 May 1775, Pemberton Papers, 27:144, Historical Society of Pennsylvania, Philadelphia (microfilm, Colonial Williamsburg

Foundation, Williamsburg, Va. [hereafter cited as ViWC]); *Virginia Gazette* (Purdie), 16 June 1775. Cf. unnamed merchants, note at the foot of Archibald Cary to James Lyle et al., 12 June 1775, Colonial Office 5/1353, ff. 129–31, PRO (microfilm, p. 401, Lamont Library, Harvard University, Cambridge, Mass.). Certainly a conspiracy this extensive was possible. Twenty-five years later, in 1800, organizers of Gabriel's Rebellion recruited clusters of supporters in counties throughout the Tidewater and Piedmont. See Gerald W. Mullin, *Flight and Rebellion: Slave Resistance in Eighteenth-Century Virginia* (New York, 1972), pp. 140–63; Philip J. Schwarz, "Gabriel's Challenge: Slaves and Crime in Late Eighteenth-Century Virginia," *Virginia Magazine of History and Biography* (hereafter cited as *VMHB*) 90 (1982): 283–309; and Douglas R. Egerton, *Gabriel's Rebellion: The Virginia Slave Conspiracies of 1800 and 1802* (Chapel Hill and London, 1993).

28. Randolph, *History of Virginia*, p. 219. Cf. Sussex County committee, resolution, 8 May 1775, Virginia convention of 1775, "A Declaration of the Delegates . . . ," 26 Aug. 1775, in Van Schreeven, Scribner, and Tarter, eds., *Revolutionary Virginia*, 3:107, 501; John Murray, earl of Dunmore, to William Legge, earl of Dartmouth, 1 May 1775, in K. G. Davies, ed., *Documents of the American Revolution, 1770–1783* (21 vols.; Shannon, Ireland, 1972–81), 9:109.

29. Virginia convention of 1775, resolution, 25 Mar. 1775, in Van Schreeven, Scribner, and Tarter, eds., *Revolutionary Virginia*, 2:376. On Dunmore's War, see Jack M. Sosin, "The British Indian Department and Dunmore's War," *VMHB* 74 (1966): 34–50; Turk McCleskey, "Dunmore's War," in Richard L. Blanco, ed., *The American Revolution, 1775–1783: An Encyclopedia* (2 vols.; New York and London, 1993), 1:492–97; Michael N. McConnell, *A Country Between: The Upper Ohio Valley and Its Peoples, 1724–1774* (Lincoln, Nebr., and London, 1992), pp. 268–79; and Woody Holton, "The Ohio Indians and the Coming of the American Revolution in Virginia," *JSH* 60 (1994): 453–78.

30. James Parker to Charles Steuart, 27 Jan. 1775, Charles Steuart Papers, MSS 5025, National Library of Scotland, Edinburgh (microfilm, Vi); John E. Selby, *The Revolution in Virginia, 1775–1783* (Charlottesville, 1988), pp. 1–2.

31. John Dixon, deposition, quoted in Committee on the Late Disturbances, report, 14 June 1775, in *JHB*, *1773–76*, p. 233 (quotations); Randolph, *History of Virginia*, p. 220.

32. William Pasteur, deposition, quoted in Committee on the Late Disturbances, report, 14 June 1775, in *JHB*, *1773–76*, p. 231.

33. Peter H. Wood, "The Changing Population of the Colonial South: An Overview by Race and Region, 1685–1790," in Peter H. Wood, Gregory A. Waselkov, and M. Thomas Hatley, eds., *Powhatan's Mantle: Indians in the Colonial Southeast*, Indians of the Southeast (Lincoln, Nebr., 1989), p. 38.

34. Benjamin Waller and John Dixon, depositions, quoted in Committee on the Late Disturbances, report, 14 June 1775, in *JHB*, *1773–76*, pp. 232–33; Amelia County committee, minutes, 3 May 1775, in Van Schreeven, Scribner, and Tarter, eds., *Revolutionary Virginia*, 3:83.

35. The counties were Mecklenburg, New Kent, Chesterfield, Louisa, Essex, Henrico, and Nansemond. See Randolph, *History of Virginia*, p. 220; James Lyle and Robert Donald, Thomas Mitchell, Archibald Ritchie, Archibald Bryce, and Andrew Sprowle et al., depositions, quoted in Committee on the Late Disturbances, report,

14 June 1775, in *JHB, 1773–76*, pp. 234–37; Mecklenburg County committee, resolution, 8 May 1775, New Kent County committee, minutes, 3 May 1775, in Van Schreeven, Scribner, and Tarter, eds., *Revolutionary Virginia*, 3:105, 85; Mays, *Edmund Pendleton*, 2:353n; and Dale E. Benson, "Wealth and Power in Virginia, 1774–1776: A Study of the Organization of Revolt" (Ph.D. diss., University of Maine, 1970), p. 173.

36. Cumberland County committee, minutes, 1 May 1775, in Van Schreeven, Scribner, and Tarter, eds., *Revolutionary Virginia*, 3:75; Sussex County committee, resolution, 8 May 1775, in ibid., 3:107; Selby, *Revolution in Virginia*, p. 4; John Burk, Skelton Jones, and Louis Hue Girardin, *The History of Virginia, From its First Settlement to the Present Day* (4 vols.; Petersburg, Va., 1804–16), 3:410.

37. Parker said Nicholas had found "it more difficult to extinguish a flame than kindle it" (James Parker to Charles Steuart, 6–7 May 1775, Charles Steuart Papers [microfilm, Vi]).

38. Peyton Randolph and the "Corporation of the City of Williamsburg" to Mann Page, Jr., Lewis Willis, and Benjamin Grymes, Jr., 27 Apr. 1775, in Van Schreeven, Scribner, and Tarter, eds., *Revolutionary Virginia*, 3:64; Charles Campbell, *History of the Colony and Ancient Dominion of Virginia* (Philadelphia, 1860), p. 609; William Pasteur, deposition, quoted in Committee on the Late Disturbances, report, 14 June 1775, in *JHB, 1773–76*, p. 231; *Virginia Gazette* (Pinkney), 4 May 1775.

39. George Gilmer, diary and memoranda, in Van Schreeven, Scribner, and Tarter, eds., *Revolutionary Virginia*, 3:52 n. 2 (quotation); Albemarle County independent company of volunteers, minutes, [29 Apr. 1775], in ibid., 3:69–70; *Virginia Gazette* (Pinkney), 30 June 1775.

40. It has generally been believed that the Hanover men sought only the return of the gunpowder to the Williamsburg munitions depot. But Hanover's patriot committee said the men marched to Williamsburg because they had heard that white inhabitants of the capital felt "apprehension for their persons and property" (Hanover County committee, minutes, 9 May 1775, in Van Schreeven, Scribner, and Tarter, eds., *Revolutionary Virginia*, 3:111, 179n).

41. *Virginia Gazette* (Pinkney), 11 May 1775, in Van Schreeven, Scribner, and Tarter, eds., *Revolutionary Virginia*, 3:117; George Dabney to William Wirt, 14 May 1805, Patrick Henry Papers, DLC; Campbell, *History of Virginia*, p. 612.

42. *Virginia Gazette* (Pinkney), 4 May 1775; John Randolph, deposition, quoted in Committee on the Late Disturbances, report, 14 June 1775, in *JHB, 1773–76*, p. 232.

43. *Virginia Gazette* (Pinkney), 4 May 1775; Randolph, *History of Virginia*, p. 220.

44. Spotsylvania council, minutes, 29 Apr. 1775, in Van Schreeven, Scribner, and Tarter, eds., *Revolutionary Virginia*, 3:71 (first quotation); Mecklenburg County committee, resolution, 13 May 1775, New Kent County committee, resolutions, 3 May 1775, Gloucester County committee, resolutions, 26 Apr. 1775, Richmond County committee, resolutions, 12 May 1775, Orange County committee, resolutions and address, 9 May 1775, in ibid., 3:124 (second quotation), 85, 61, 121, 112. On 20 April, the day before Dunmore removed the gunpowder, Robert Munford had said that he intended to ask the voters of his county to endorse a loyalist address that he had written. After learning of the gunpowder incident and Dunmore's threat to free the slaves, Munford decided not to present his petition. In fact, he became a major in the patriot army (Robert Munford to William Byrd III, 20 Apr. 1775, in Marion Tinling, ed., *The Correspondence of the Three William Byrds of Westover, Virginia, 1684–1776*,

Virginia Historical Society Documents, 12, 13 [2 vols.; Charlottesville, 1977], 2:806, 806 n. 3).

45. Quoted in George Dabney to William Wirt, 14 May 1805, Patrick Henry Papers.

46. See, for example, H. J. Eckenrode, *The Revolution in Virginia* (Boston and New York, 1916), pp. 49–54; Virginius Dabney, *Virginia: The New Dominion* (Garden City, N.Y., 1971), pp. 128–29; and Warren M. Billings, John E. Selby, and Thad W. Tate, *Colonial Virginia: A History*, A History of the American Colonies in Thirteen Volumes (White Plains, N.Y., 1986), p. 342.

47. Benjamin Waller, deposition, quoted in Committee on the Late Disturbances, report, 14 June 1775, in *JHB, 1773–76*, p. 232; Thomas Mitchell, deposition, quoted in Committee on the Late Disturbances, report, 14 June 1775, in ibid., p. 234; Rawleigh Downman to Samuel Athawes, 10 July 1775, Rawleigh Downman Letterbook, DLC, as quoted in Michael A. McDonnell, "The Politics of Mobilization in Revolutionary Virginia: Military Culture and Political and Social Relations, 1774–1783" (D.Phil. thesis, Oxford University, 1995), pp. 37–38.

48. Richmond County committee, resolutions, 12 May 1775, in Van Schreeven, Scribner, and Tarter, eds., *Revolutionary Virginia*, 3:121; Spotsylvania council, minutes, 29 Apr. 1775, in ibid., 3:71; *South Carolina Gazette and Country Journal*, 6 June 1775, quoted in Peter H. Wood, "'Taking Care of Business' in Revolutionary South Carolina: Republicanism and the Slave Society," in Jeffrey J. Crow and Larry E. Tise, eds., *The Southern Experience in the American Revolution* (Chapel Hill, 1978), p. 282.

49. James Robison to William Cuninghame & Company, 3 May 1775, in T. M. Devine, ed., *A Scottish Firm in Virginia, 1767–1777: W. Cuninghame and Co.* (Edinburgh, 1984), p. 187.

50. The newspaper accounts of the Norfolk insurrection do not mention the leaders' names, and the Norfolk County court did not specify the felony for which Emanuel and Emanuel de Antonio were convicted. One might be tempted to conclude, therefore, that the two Emanuels were not necessarily the leaders of the slave revolt mentioned in the newspaper—that they were hanged for some lesser offense. But we can conclude that the accusation against the two Emanuels was indeed insurrection, because they were hanged only one week after their trial. Under Virginia law, the execution of slaves had to be stayed for at least ten days—unless the condemned were insurrectionists (Hening, ed., *Statutes at Large*, 6:106).

51. Lists for the intervening years have not survived. The other alleged conspirator, Emanuel de Antonio, also disappeared from the Norfolk tithable lists between 1774 and 1778—but so did all of the other slaves owned by James Campbell & Company, a loyalist firm whose principal left Virginia early in the Revolution. See Elizabeth B. Wingo and W. Bruce Wingo, *Norfolk County, Virginia, Tithables, 1766–1780* (Norfolk, Va., 1985), pp. 230, 242, 261.

52. Municipal Common Hall of Williamsburg to John Murray, earl of Dunmore, 21 Apr. 1775, in Van Schreeven, Scribner, and Tarter, eds., *Revolutionary Virginia*, 3:55.

53. James Madison to William Bradford, Jr., 26 Nov. 1774, in Hutchinson et al., eds., *Madison Papers*, 1:130; *Virginia Gazette* (Pinkney), 6 Dec. 1775; Aptheker, *American Negro Slave Revolts*, esp. chap. 7. Several recent retellings of the story do not mention its black participants. See, for example, Billings, Selby, and Tate, *Colonial Virginia*, p. 342; and Rhys Isaac, *The Transformation of Virginia, 1740–1790* (Chapel Hill, 1982), pp. 256–58.

Even Herbert Aptheker, a careful searcher for evidence of slave conspiracies, believed that there was no plot in Virginia in April 1775 (Aptheker, *American Negro Slave Revolts*, p. 204). His skepticism regarding Dunmore's assertion that he moved the gunpowder in order to protect whites from a rumored slave plot was justified, because Dunmore himself acknowledged in a letter to the earl of Dartmouth, the secretary of state, that the plot was not the real reason for the relocation of the powder. The governor, however, sincerely believed the rumor itself, because he stated in the same letter that whites in Williamsburg were "apprehensive of insurrections among their slaves (some reports having prevailed to this effect)" (John Murray, earl of Dunmore, to William Legge, earl of Dartmouth, 1 May 1775, in Davies, ed., *Documents of the American Revolution*, 9:107–8).

54. *Virginia Gazette* (Pinkney), 1 June 1775; *Virginia Gazette* (Purdie), 31 May 1776; Jack P. Greene, ed., *The Diary of Colonel Landon Carter of Sabine Hall, 1752–1778*, Virginia Historical Society Documents, 4, 5 (2 vols.; Charlottesville, 1965), 2:1058 (16 July 1776). Still later Adam Stephen predicted that Dunmore would participate in a rumored British invasion of Virginia "in order to add some more oderiferous beauties to his Ethopian seraglios" (Adam Stephen to Richard Henry Lee, 22 Apr. 1777, quoted in Harry M. Ward, *Major General Adam Stephen and the Cause of American Liberty* [Charlottesville, 1989], p. 168).

55. Robert Beverley to William Fitzhugh, 20 July 1775, Robert Beverley Letterbook, DLC; Josiah Smith, Jr., to James Poyas, 18 May 1775, Josiah Smith, Jr., to George Appleby, 16 June 1775, Josiah Smith Letterbook, Southern Historical Collection, University of North Carolina, Chapel Hill; Wood, "'Liberty Is Sweet,'" pp. 166–68; Wood, "'Taking Care of Business,'" pp. 280–87; Robert M. Weir, *Colonial South Carolina: A History*, A History of the American Colonies in Thirteen Volumes (Millwood, N.Y., 1983), pp. 200–203.

56. Wood, "'The Dream Deferred,'" p. 175 (quotation); Alan D. Watson, "Impulse toward Independence: Resistance and Rebellion among North Carolina Slaves, 1750–1775," *JNH* 63 (1978): 317–28.

57. Quoted in Frey, *Water from the Rock*, pp. 58, 62.

58. John Drayton, *Memoirs of the American Revolution From Its Commencement to the Year 1776, Inclusive; As Relating to the State of South-Carolina . . .* (2 vols.; Charleston, 1821), 1:231.

59. Quoted in Ronald Hoffman, *A Spirit of Dissension: Economics, Politics, and the Revolution in Maryland*, Maryland Bicentennial Studies (Baltimore and London, 1973), p. 147.

60. York County Order Book, 17 July 1775 (microfilm and typescript), ViWC; Schwarz, *Twice Condemned*, p. 183. In July 1775 a rumor circulated in York County that British troops were about to land, and Cox's accusers may have thought he was working with slaves to prepare for the invasion. See William Reynolds to George Flowerdewe Norton, 16 July 1775, William Reynolds Letterbook, DLC. My thanks to Julie Richter for sharing her research on Thomas Cox.

61. Mullin, *Flight and Rebellion*, pp. 132–33. White servants, especially convicts, also ran away and headed to the British naval squadron. See, for example, Francis Smith and James Tutt, advertisements, in *Virginia Gazette* (Pinkney), 2 Nov., 27 July 1775; and John Murray, earl of Dunmore, to William Legge, earl of Dartmouth, 25 June 1775, in Davies, ed., *Documents of the American Revolution*, 9:202–3.

62. This story is based entirely on a newspaper notice that Estave published in order to justify what some of his white neighbors had called his "cruel and inhuman treatment" of the enslaved teenager (*Virginia Gazette* [Pinkney], 20 July 1775). We can only imagine how the story would change if we had testimony from the fifteen-year-old.

63. If the teenager had reached the governor's palace before Dunmore left it, he might have been able to grant her sanctuary (charter of Williamsburg, in *William and Mary Quarterly*, 1st ser., 10 [1901–2]: 87). My thanks to Brent Tarter and John M. Hemphill II for this reference.

64. John Bailey's slaves Phil and Mial "received guilty verdicts in Southampton County conspiracy trials" (Schwarz, *Twice Condemned*, pp. 181, 183 [quotation], 184). On 3 July 1775, William Johnson's slave Gloster was sentenced to death for burglary "but broke out of jail and vanished" (William Johnson, petition, 14 June 1776, Caroline County, calendared in Randolph W. Church, ed., *Virginia Legislative Petitions: Bibliography, Calendar, and Abstracts from Original Sources, 6 May 1776–21 June 1782* [Richmond, 1984], pp. 24–25).

65. Robert Honyman, diary, 2 Jan. 1776, DLC; Selby, *Revolution in Virginia*, p. 64.

66. John Page to Thomas Jefferson, 24 [Nov.] 1775, in Boyd et al., eds., *Jefferson Papers*, 1:265.

67. *Virginia Gazette* (Dixon and Hunter), 2 Dec. 1775. Slaves also answered later calls from British generals. North of Virginia, bondsmen were allowed to join the Continental army in return for their freedom—but only with their owners' permission (Quarles, *Negro in the Revolution*, chaps. 4–5).

68. Edmund Taylor, debt owed to Thomas Banks, 1 Sept. 1776, abstracted in "British Mercantile Claims, 1775–1803," *Virginia Genealogist* 16 (1972): 104–5.

69. John Murray, earl of Dunmore, proclamation, 7 Nov. 1775, in Van Schreeven, Scribner, and Tarter, eds., *Revolutionary Virginia*, 4:334; Graham Russell Hodges, ed., *The Black Loyalist Directory: African Americans in Exile after the American Revolution* (New York, 1996). Cf. Quarles, *Negro in the Revolution*, p. 172; and the list of fifty formerly enslaved "Women [who] embarked at Mill Point" with Dunmore's fleet, printed in the *Virginia Gazette* (Dixon and Hunter), 31 Aug. 1776, and analyzed in Sarah Stroud, "Tracing Runaway Slaves from Norfolk County, Virginia, during the American Revolutionary War" (seminar paper, Randolph-Macon Woman's College, 1995).

70. Hodges, ed., *Black Loyalist Directory*, p. 201. During the American Revolution, many of the enslaved women who ran away took their children with them—an occurrence that was very rare before and after the war (Sara M. Evans, *Born for Liberty: A History of Women in America* [New York and London, 1989], p. 52). For accounts of other black Americans who joined the British and settled after the Revolution in Nova Scotia and Sierra Leone, see Gary B. Nash, "Thomas Peters: Millwright and Deliverer," in David G. Sweet and Gary B. Nash, eds., *Struggle and Survival in Colonial America* (Berkeley and Los Angeles, 1981), pp. 69–85; Ellen Gibson Wilson, *The Loyal Blacks* (New York, 1976); and James W. St. G. Walker, *The Black Loyalists: The Search for a Promised Land in Nova Scotia and Sierra Leone, 1783–1870*, Dalhousie African Studies Series (New York, 1976).

71. Thomas Nelson, Jr., to Mann Page, 4 Jan. 1776, Francis Lightfoot Lee to Landon Carter, 12 Feb. 1776, Benjamin Harrison to Robert Carter Nicholas, 17 Jan. 1776, in Paul H. Smith et al., eds., *Letters of Delegates to Congress, 1774–1789* (23 vols. to date;

Washington, D.C., 1976–), 3:30 (first quotation), 237 (second quotation), 107 (third quotation). A rumored British design to ally with Native Americans was also described as "diabolical" and "infernal" (George Washington to John Augustine Washington, 13 Oct. 1775, Richard Henry Lee to George Washington, 13 Nov. 1775, George Washington to Richard Henry Lee, 26 Dec. 1775, in Abbot et al., eds., *Washington Papers: Revolutionary War Series*, 2:161, 363, 611).

72. Page Smith, *A New Age Now Begins: A People's History of the American Revolution* (2 vols.; New York, St. Louis, and San Francisco, 1976), 1:704; Garry Wills, *Inventing America: Jefferson's Declaration of Independence* (Garden City, N.Y., 1978), pp. 71, 75.

73. Robert Greenhalgh Albion and Leonidas Dodson, eds., *Philip Vickers Fithian: Journal, 1775–1776, Written on the Virginia-Pennsylvania Frontier and in the Army around New York* (Princeton, 1934), p. 135 (28 Nov. 1775); Richard Henry Lee to Catharine Macauley, 29 Nov. 1775, Archibald Cary to Richard Henry Lee, 24 Dec. 1775, in Paul P. Hoffman and John L. Molyneaux, eds., The Lee Family Papers, 1742–1795 (microfilm; Charlottesville, 1966), Reel 2.

74. William Byrd III to Sir Jeffery Amherst, 30 July 1775, in Tinling, ed., *Byrd Correspondence*, 2:812–13; Greene, ed., *Carter Diary*, 2:989 (25 Feb. 1776); Van Schreeven, Scribner, and Tarter, eds., *Revolutionary Virginia*, 5:386n–87n; Selby, *Revolution in Virginia*, p. 66; Thomas Jefferson to William Wirt, 29 Sept. 1816, in *Reminiscences of Patrick Henry in the Letters of Thomas Jefferson to William Wirt* (Philadelphia, 1911), p. 29.

75. Greene, ed., *Carter Diary*, 2:960 (n.d. 1775); John Page to Richard Henry Lee, 20 Feb. 1776, in Hoffman and Molyneaux, eds., Lee Family Papers, Reel 2.

76. William Eddis, Letter 26, 16 Jan. 1776, in William Eddis, *Letters from America*, ed. Aubrey C. Land (Cambridge, Mass., 1969), p. 133; Edward Rutledge to Ralph Izard, 8 Dec. 1775, in *Izard Correspondence*, p. 165; [John Leacock], *The Fall of British Tyranny, or, American Liberty Triumphant: The First Campaign . . .* (Philadelphia, 1776), p. 48. Cf. Gary B. Nash, *Forging Freedom: The Formation of Philadelphia's Black Community, 1720–1840* (Cambridge, Mass., and London, 1988), p. 46; Quarles, *Negro in the Revolution*, p. 20, 20n.

77. James Iredell, untitled essay, June 1776, in Don Higginbotham, ed., *The Papers of James Iredell* (3 vols. to date; Raleigh, 1976–), 1:409.

78. [Leacock], *Fall of British Tyranny*, p. 49. On British cooperation with Indians as a cause of white Americans' growing alienation from Britain, see Wood, "'Liberty Is Sweet,'" p. 169; Selby, *Revolution in Virginia*, p. 92; and *Virginia Gazette* (Pinkney), 3 Aug. 1775. Free colonists were also angry at Dunmore for emancipating and arming convict servants ([Leacock], *Fall of British Tyranny*, p. 45; *Virginia Gazette* [Dixon and Hunter], 17 Feb. 1776).

79. *Virginia Gazette* (Dixon and Hunter), 29 Apr. 1775 (supplement).

80. Quarles, *Negro in the Revolution*, pp. 171–72; Hodges, ed., *Black Loyalist Directory*, p. 198 (quotation).

81. See, for example, Burk, Jones, and Girardin, *History of Virginia*, 4:134n; Eckenrode, *Revolution in Virginia*, p. 73; Dumas Malone, *Jefferson and His Time*, vol. 1: *Jefferson the Virginian* (Boston, 1948), p. 215; Billings, Selby, and Tate, *Colonial Virginia*, p. 343; Clifford Dowdey, *The Great Plantation: A Profile of Berkeley Hundred and Plantation Virginia from Jamestown to Appomattox* (New York and Toronto, 1957), pp. 230–31; Campbell, *History of Virginia*, p. 634; John C. Miller, *Origins of the American Revolution* (Boston, 1943), p. 478; and Dabney, *New Dominion*, p. 131.

Several students of the struggle for black freedom have also asserted that the slaves helped push whites into the American Revolution. See, for example, Quarles, *Negro in the Revolution*, p. 19; Wood, "'Liberty Is Sweet,'" p. 171; and Frey, *Water from the Rock*, p. 78.

82. *Virginia Gazette* (Pinkney), 4 May 1775.

83. Quarles, *Negro in the Revolution*, pp. 20–22; Schwarz, *Twice Condemned*, p. 181.

84. For a similar argument—that enslaved Americans, through their actions, helped push Abraham Lincoln into issuing his Emancipation Proclamation—see W. E. Burghardt Du Bois, *Black Reconstruction: An Essay toward a History of the Part Which Black Folk Played in the Attempt to Reconstruct Democracy in America, 1860–1880* (New York, 1935), chap. 4; and Vincent Harding, *There Is a River: The Black Struggle for Freedom in America* (New York and London, 1981), chap. 11.

85. Unidentified letter, 30 Nov. 1775, in Force, comp., *American Archives*, 4th ser., 3:1387.

86. Marc Egnal, *A Mighty Empire: The Origins of the American Revolution* (Ithaca, N.Y., and London, 1988), p. 302 (quotation). In Virginia, "the classic Progressive conflict of domestic interests appears not to have taken place in the political realm" (Herbert Sloan and Peter Onuf, "Politics, Culture, and the Revolution in Virginia: A Review of Recent Work," *VMHB* 91 [1983]: 262, 264 [quotation]). "[A]lone among the thirteen provinces," Virginia "did not face armed internal dispute during the revolutionary era" (Edward Countryman, *The American Revolution* [New York, 1985], p. 35). Many Progressive historians implicitly acknowledged that the internal conflict thesis did not apply to Virginia, where the ruling class endorsed the independence movement. Instead, Progressive historians studying Virginia emphasized the economic motives that inspired free farmers at all income levels. See Isaac Samuel Harrell, *Loyalism in Virginia: Chapters in the Economic History of the Revolution* (Durham, N.C., 1926), pp. v–vi, 5; and Charles A. Beard, *Economic Origins of Jeffersonian Democracy* (New York, 1949), p. 270. For a revision of this economic interpretation of the Revolution in Virginia, see Woody Holton, *Forced Founders: How Indians, Debtors, and Slaves Helped Turn Elite Virginians into American Revolutionaries* (Chapel Hill, 1999).

87. James Titus, *The Old Dominion at War: Society, Politics, and Warfare in Late Colonial Virginia*, American Military History (Columbia, S.C., 1991); Albert H. Tillson, Jr., *Gentry and Common Folk: Political Culture on a Virginia Frontier, 1740–1789* (Lexington, Ky., 1991), pp. 45–77; McDonnell, "Politics of Mobilization."

JAN LEWIS

"The Blessings of Domestic Society": Thomas Jefferson's Family and the Transformation of American Politics

* * * * * * * * *F*EW MEN OF HIS AGE HAD AS GREAT AN IMPACT on the tenor of public life in the new republic as did Thomas Jefferson. He was among the first to hold the positions of state governor and federal secretary of state and president. As decisive as his terms in these offices were for defining newly assumed constitutional powers, they were also marked by contention, rancor, and at times, outright political hostility. Retaining the deference of his fellow citizens, Jefferson could not always say that they held him in their affections. Thus this founding father turned to his own family and his home, Monticello, for the emotional sustenance needed not only in public service but also for personal well-being. As Jefferson assumed national office, he increasingly looked to Virginia as his political home.

For Jan Lewis the essential Jefferson lies in the contrast he drew between the "love of his family" and the "enmity of political life." The distinction between public and private thus had become by the end of Jefferson's presidency as much a part of American political culture as it is today. For Jefferson the poignancy and emotive power of family life were intensified by the early death of his wife, Martha Wayles Skelton Jefferson, his responsibility for rearing his daughters, and the obligation he in turn thrust on them for maintaining the affective bonds of home.

In setting off the separate spheres of public and private life, Jefferson stood squarely in the middle of a transition in American political and popular culture. In the world of eighteenth-century Virginia politics, so ably described by Jack Greene in this volume, few men prominent in public affairs would have weighed the enjoyment of family against the exercise of office. Most would have viewed family as a vehicle to power, not a retreat from it. The prominence of family, in fact, often overwhelmed individual fame, and the influence women had on the political world was as likely to be elevated by their own parentage as it would be by the social standing of the men they married. By the middle third of the nineteenth century, however, the ideal home had become a domestic realm that women maintained as morally pure. In contrast, men prevailed over the conflict and corruption

164

of public life. According to Elizabeth Varon, ambitious women in the nineteenth century could influence politics in their own right but only through moral reform, art, and culture. During an earlier phase in this transformation in American life, Thomas Jefferson's lifelong project of building Monticello serves as a symbolic projection of a domestic vision on his loving daughters as well as on the Virginia landscape.

Jan Lewis wrote "The Blessings of Domestic Society" before tests of Jefferson family DNA and historical research suggested that Thomas Jefferson likely fathered at least one child with his African-American slave Sally Hemings. Although any relations between Jefferson and Hemings would have begun long after the death of Jefferson's wife, the half-sister relationship between Skelton and Hemings further complicated family matters. The possibility, however, that one of the preeminent founding fathers and the author of the Declaration of Independence sired both a white family and a black family—one in freedom, the other in slavery—lays bare the deeply paradoxical nature of Virginia and American history. As Edmund Morgan and Woody Holton have explained, not only was the common parentage of slavery and freedom nothing new by the time of the American Revolution, but the union of black and white experience also had framed this founding event of the American Republic. Later generations of Americans nonetheless would attempt to radically disassociate black and white in American life. By the twentieth century this effort became so strenuous that racial integrity in Virginia mandated the absolute biological isolation of the races. This was the doctrine that Ivey Foreman Lewis taught for decades at the University of Virginia. In one of the intriguing circles of history, however, it was the endorsement of natural rights in the Declaration of Independence that would lead Armistead Boothe to establish a moderate position in Virginia politics during the 1950s and help bring an end to racial segregation in the commonwealth's schools. The careers of Lewis and Boothe are treated in the closing articles of this volume.

* * * * * * * *

* * * * * * * *
WHY WOULD THOMAS JEFFERSON'S FAMILY BE INTERESTING TO those who are reflecting upon the Jeffersonian legacy? When Jefferson wrote his epitaph, he nowhere mentioned his own family or the families of his fellow Americans: he wanted to be remembered as the "Father of the University of Virginia," as well as the author of the Declaration of Independence and the Virginia Statute for Religious Freedom.[1] He measured his worth in ideas and institutions, not human relationships. Moreover, Jefferson entrusted his legacy not to his family, but to his compatriot and closest ally, James Madison. A few months before his death, realizing that the end could not be far off, Jefferson told his friend of fifty years that it has

"been a great solace to me, to believe that you are engaged in vindicating to posterity the course we have pursued for preserving to them, in all their purity, the blessings of self-government." He asked Madison to "take care of me when dead."[2]

To his immediate posterity, a family that had "blessed me by their affections, and never by their conduct given me a moment's pain," Jefferson bequeathed a debt of over a hundred thousand dollars and memories that would last them all the days of their lives.[3] Years after her grandfather's death, Ellen Coolidge would find herself haunted by the memory of Monticello. "When I dream it is mostly of long past times. Night after night I have been surrounded by the friends of childhood and early youth—my grandfather, mother, brothers, sisters, those whom I dearly loved and who dearly loved me, and who I hope in God's own time to rejoin."[4] So dearly did Jefferson's grandchildren love him that they willingly accepted the huge debt, renouncing in advance the property Jefferson had hoped to be able to leave them, and claiming as their only due a lifetime of love.[5]

That Thomas Jefferson's children and grandchildren loved him deeply we cannot doubt, nor could we question his attachment to them. The letters that they wrote each other bespeak a passion that words could barely contain. He closed his letters to his daughters "with unchangeable and tenderest attachment" and "never-ceasing love," and his daughters Martha and Maria responded "with tenderest and constant love," "with the tenderest love and reverence" and "ardent affection."[6] So strong was the love and so inadequate mere words for expressing it that with almost each letter, the conventional closing would be changed. Even after their marriages and the births of their children, both daughters assured their father that he was the one they loved best. Maria apologized for her "inability to express how much I love and revere you. But you are first and dearest to my heart." Martha used almost the same words, asking her father "to believe yourself *first* and unrivalled in the heart of your devoted child," and as she contemplated his retirement from public office she assured him that "I make no exception when I say the *first* and most important object with me will be the dear and sacred duty of nursing and chearing your old age."[7]

Jefferson cultivated this love by telling his daughters that his happiness depended upon it. In 1799 he told Maria that the "affectionate expressions" in one of her letters "kindled up all those feelings of love for you and our dear connections which now constitute the only real happiness of my life." A year later he reminded his other daughter "how essential your society is to my happiness." Such expressions became the refrain of his letters from the seat of national government. A year before the end of his second term as president, Jefferson told his only surviving child, Martha (Maria had died in 1804), "I long to be among you where I know nothing but love and delight, and where . . . I would be indulged . . . with the blessings of domestic society." "It is in the love of one's family only," he had once told Maria, "that heartfelt happiness is known."[8]

Jefferson loved his daughters and, in due course, their children, ardently and deeply. Perhaps that is reason enough for us to be interested in Thomas Jefferson's family: he towers so over the landscape of American history, and his legacy is so great, that anything that was of such great importance to him must be important to us too. Thomas Jefferson adored not simply his own family, but the very notion of family life. As he explained to Maria just before her marriage to John Wayles Eppes, the event "promises us long years of domestic concord and love, the best ingredient in human happiness."[9] Jefferson believed that true and complete happiness—for him and for everyone—could be found only at home.

These were the sentiments he voiced to his family, but not, as a rule, to the world at large. His views on the family do not form a significant part of his political or social philosophy, yet clearly they were deeply felt beliefs, in some ways an expression of his essential character. Because Jefferson's pronouncement on happiness, which proclaimed its pursuit as one of mankind's unalienable rights, is so central a part of our national heritage, it is perhaps curious that he apparently never discussed the relationship between the happiness he found at home and the public happiness that was a staple of Enlightenment thought. Scholars who have debated what Jefferson meant by "the pursuit of happiness" suggest that it must have been either a social, public happiness, or a more private and individualist pursuit—a euphemism for property. While it seems clear that Jefferson had in mind a social happiness whose achievement was somehow enhanced by good government,[10] his letters to his family indicate that he believed deeply in a sort of private happiness that was something other than the acquisition of property. His correspondence—indeed, his life—with his family reveals that Thomas Jefferson believed in a realm of happiness that his political philosophy did not engage.

It might therefore be argued that Jefferson's family life and the opinions he expressed about it bore no relationship to his public, political writings and actions, and that when he used the term "happiness" in writing to his daughters, the words he had written in the first paragraph of the Declaration of Independence could not have been further from his mind. It is possible that Jefferson segmented his life, drawing a sharp line between the part that was private and the part that was public. But "public" and "private" are always relative rather than absolute terms; they derive their meaning from each other. And at just this time, the relationship between these two realms was being redefined.[11] In rendering a vision of private life, Thomas Jefferson was necessarily constructing the public world, as well.

I

If we want to know what place the family occupied in the Jeffersonian vision of social and political life, we might begin by examining those passages in his letters where he wrote most passionately about the blessings of domestic society. The first time Jefferson said that his happiness derived from his family was in June 1791 when, writing his daughter Maria from Philadelphia, where he was serving as George Washington's Secretary of State, he exclaimed, "Would to god I could be with you to partake of your felicities, and to tell you in person how much I love you all, and how necessary it is to my happiness to be with you."[12] It is not clear what, if anything, occasioned this declaration. All of his previous letters to his daughters[13] had been affectionate by any standard, but it was only after he had returned to the United States from Paris, where he had been serving as ambassador, and entered Washington's Cabinet, that he began linking his happiness to his family.

From 1791 on, however, virtually each of Jefferson's explosions of love for his family was so clearly part of an explicit contrast he made with the public world of politics, that we might reasonably surmise that his 1791 letter to Maria was occasioned by some disappointment in Philadelphia. In January 1792, for example, he wrote Martha that his "reveries" about the happy times they had spent together "in our wanderings over the world . . . alleviate the toils and inquietudes of my present situation, and leave me always impressed with the desire of being at home once more, and of exchanging labour, envy, and malice for ease, domestic occupation, and domestic love and society." Jefferson's biographer, Dumas Malone, reads this letter as Jefferson's first disclosure that he had decided to retire from office. He had grown weary of his conflict with Alexander Hamilton and the rancor of national politics. At the time of his 1791 letter to Maria, Jefferson had become embroiled—not for the last time—in a newspaper controversy about Thomas Paine, and it may well have triggered his longing for the "felicities" of home.[14]

Jefferson, of course, did not resign his office for another two years, and barely two years after that he was back in Philadelphia as vice president. He would not retire from public office until 1809, after two terms as president. Except for several extended visits, his daughters remained in Virginia, where they received their father's ardent letters. Barely had Jefferson returned to government before he was once again telling his daughters, "I feel the desire of never separating from you grow daily stronger, for nothing can compensate me with the want of your society. . . . Continue to love me as I do you."[15] Such expressions, whose effect surely worked to achieve the end that Jefferson explicitly designed—increasing his daughters' attachment to him—continued as long as he held public office.

This construction of public life as a burden and a deprivation had been foreshadowed in a letter Jefferson had written to James Monroe in 1782 when he declined the office of delegate to the Virginia legislature. With his young wife weak after just giving birth and apparently dying in perhaps the same room from which he wrote, Jefferson gave voice to the claims of private life: "I considered that I had been thirteen years engaged in public service, that during that time I had so abandoned all attention to my private affairs as to permit them to run into great disorder and ruin, that I had now a family advanced to years which required my attention & instruction." Here family was, like public service, also an obligation, if a private and inescapably countervailing one. "If we are made in some degree for others, yet in a greater are we made for ourselves. It were contrary to feeling & indeed ridiculous to suppose that a man had less right in himself than one of his neighbors or indeed all of them put together. This would be slavery & not that liberty which the bill of rights has made inviolable and for the preservation of which our government has been charged."[16] Jefferson pitted the claims of society against the rights of the individual; like others at the time, he connected the obligations of family to self-interest, which he believed he had neglected.[17] His conception of the polity, at least for the moment, was individualist.

Jefferson no doubt was disappointed that public life had not been more gratifying. His service as governor had been sharply criticized, and the wounds had not healed. "By a constant sacrifice of time, labour, loss, parental & family duties, I had been so far from gaining the affection of my countrymen, which was the only reward I ever asked or could have felt, that I had even lost the small estimation I before possessed."[18] Jefferson must have anticipated that his public service would bind him to his countrymen by ties of affection; he would willingly have sacrificed his personal interest for this form of love. In its absence, he would return to the pursuit of a private, Lockean sort of happiness. In his letter to Monroe, Jefferson implicitly contrasted a Scottish Enlightenment vision of society, bound together by affection, and a Lockean one, in which "we are made . . . in a greater degree for ourselves."[19] In this schema, the family is merely an extension of the self.

In the years to come, Jefferson would return to public service; he would also rework his ideas about the relationship between the self and society. No longer would he expect affection from his fellow citizens; he would plant and nurture it at home. By the 1790s he had decided that the political world was not simply cold, but downright hostile. In 1798 he told Martha, "For you to feel all the happiness of your quiet situation, you should know the rancorous passions which tear every breast here, even of the sex which should be a stranger to them. Politics and party hatreds destroy the happiness of every being here. They seem like salamanders, to consider fire as their element." He longed to be with her, "in the only scene, where, for me, the sweeter affections of life have any exercise." A few weeks later, he would render the contrast almost in a shorthand: the seat of government represented "every thing which is disgusting," and his "dear family," "every thing which is pleasurable."[20]

The bitterness of political life made Jefferson long for his family. In 1797, he was becoming "more and more disgusted with the jealousies, the hatred, and the rancorous and malignant passions of this scene," and added, "I lament my having ever again been drawn into public view."[21] In 1798, political life was "a dreary scene where envy, hatred, malice, revenge and all the worse passions of men are marshalled, to make one another as miserable as possible."[22] In January 1801, writing from Washington where he was waiting to learn if he had been elected president, Jefferson complained that "here . . . there is such a mixture of the bad passions of the heart that one feels themselves in an enemy's country."[23] A month later he described for Maria "the scene passing here" as "a circle of cabal, intrigue, and hatred."[24] By 1807, Jefferson was "tired of a life of contention, and of being the personal object for the hatred of every man, who hates the present state of things."[25]

Jefferson was willing to serve his country, ultimately at great personal cost,[26] but he no longer expected the affection of the public. Public service might yield the satisfaction of duty performed and perhaps even the esteem of his countrymen, but it would never prove emotionally fulfilling. So often and so passionately did Jefferson contrast the love of his family with the enmity of political life that it is evident that, at some level, he had expected that public service would prove more personally gratifying. Moreover, the two terms, *family* and *politics*, were so closely linked in his mind that he could barely mention one without invoking the other.

How easily Jefferson could slide back and forth between descriptions of the pleasures of family and the tribulations of politics is nicely illustrated by the letter he wrote Martha after learning of his other daughter's engagement to John Wayles Eppes, a young man he knew and esteemed. It was a match that not only would ensure Maria's happiness but would also gratify the entire family: "I now see our fireside formed into a groupe, no one member of which has a fibre in their composition which can ever produce any jarring or jealousies among us. No irregular passions, no dangerous bias. . . ." Jefferson shifted smoothly from imagining his daughter's pleasure to fantasizing about his own, and from there it was only one more quick move to railing against the miseries of a life in politics. "When I look to the ineffable pleasures of my family society, I become more and more disgusted with the jealousies, the hatred, and the rancorous and malignant passions of this scene." And from there, another shift to the unrealized emotional expectations of public service: "I have seen enough of political honors to know that they are but splendid torments; and however one might be disposed to render services on which any of their fellow citizens should set a value; yet when as many would deprecate them as a public calamity, one may well entertain a modest doubt of their real importance, and feel the impulse to duty to be very weak. The real difficulty," the then vice president explained, was "that being once delivered into the hands of others, whose feelings are friendly to the individual and warm to the public cause, how to withdraw from them without leaving a dissatisfaction in their mind, and an impression of pusillanimity with the public."[27] No wonder "the impulse to duty" was so weak: The most that the public could offer was friendliness, and once an individual gave himself over to others there was no quitting, lest he be thought a coward. Better, perhaps, not even to have entered into public service.

When we see how quickly Jefferson could slip from contemplating his daughter's future happiness to reflecting upon his own present misery we might be tempted to conclude that he was simply an enormously self-centered man. Certainly, his relationship with his daughters was sometimes manipulative; there was the implication, especially in his early letters to these motherless girls, that his love was contingent upon their fulfilling his expectations. "The more you learn the more I love you," he told Martha in 1786, "and I rest the happiness of my life on seeing you beloved by all the world." A year later, spurring her on to industry in her studies, he elaborated upon his hopes not so much for her, but himself: "No body in the world can make me so happy, or so miserable as you. Retirement from public life will ere long become necessary for me. To your sister and yourself I look to render the evening of my life serene and contented. Its morning has been clouded by loss after loss till I have nothing left but you."[28] Patsy and Polly, as the young girls were called, were designated not simply surrogate wives, replacements for their departed mother, but the handmaidens of their father's happiness: their primary function in life was to make him happy. No wonder both would later tell their father that they loved him above all else; that is exactly what he had trained them to do.

But even in his patently manipulative 1787 letter to Martha, Jefferson implied that public life might still offer its own rewards; it would be only after his retirement that he would look to his daughters to make his life "serene and contented." His daughters were supposed to compensate him for losses in the private, not the public realm. So even if we choose to consider Jefferson an emotionally needy man who throughout their lives burdened his daughters with the responsibility for his own happiness, we must also recognize that over the years, his thinking about the relationship between the private and public realms changed significantly. The variable in this equation is Jefferson's view of public life.

Even with his wife dying and the criticism he had received as governor still ringing in his ears, in 1782 Jefferson's greatest complaint about public service was that he had lost the "estimation" of the public and neglected his family. It was only after he entered Washington's Cabinet, beginning a period of government service from which he would not completely retire for two decades, that Jefferson voiced his most passionate complaints about the rancor and malignant passions of political life; it was not simply that he had lost the esteem of the public, but that a considerable portion of it seemed to hate him.

II

Like most of the Revolutionary leaders, Jefferson had anticipated that the reward for his disinterested service would be fame. This expectation was an article of the republican faith. Indeed, as Garry Wills has argued, "Fame was . . . a social glue, a structural element, for the republic in its early days." The expectation of fame stimulated leaders to the acts of self-sacrifice that the founding generation called public virtue. As James Wilson had explained it, "The love of honest and well earned fame is deeply rooted in honest and susceptible minds. Can there be a stronger incentive to the operations of this passion, than the hope of becoming the object of a well rounded and distinguishing applause? Can there be a more complete gratification of this passion, than the satisfaction of knowing that this applause is given—that it is given upon the most honourable principles, and acquired by the most honourable pursuits?"[29] A number of historians have noted that George Washington sought this sort of fame, consciously deliberating his actions and contemplating their effect upon his reputation. In this successful effort to secure his reputation Jefferson encouraged him, giving him pointers along the way.[30] Years later Jefferson would describe Washington as virtue incarnate: "His integrity was most pure, his justice the most inflexible I have ever known, no motives of interest or consanguinity, of friendship or hatred, being able to bias his decision."[31] This was the standard—and reputation—by which Jefferson would judge himself.

The republican standard of public virtue promised that if one sacrificed one's interest—which included, as Jefferson's 1782 letter to Monroe had suggested—that of one's friends and family as well—one might earn fame, "the affection of my countrymen." That was the reward for public service that Jefferson asked for and expected. He was confounded when it was not forthcoming. And while the source of his disappointment may in some part have been his own sensitivity to criticism and his emotional neediness, some of it surely must be attributed to the nature of politics in the 1790s.

A quarter of a century ago John Howe described the 1790s as a period of "political violence," one characterized by a "brutality both of expression and behavior." Jefferson, Howe suggests, spoke for many other political leaders when he complained to Edward Rutledge in 1793 that "the passions are too high at present. . . . You and I have formerly seen warm debates and high political passions. But gentlemen of different politics would then speak to each other, and separate the business of the Senate from that of society. It is not so now." Howe attributes the volatility of politics in this era to the republican belief that republican governments were inherently fragile. So great were the risks and so likely the prospect of failure that inevitably "politics was a deadly business, with little room for optimism or leniency, little reason to expect the best rather than suspect the worst of one's political enemies."[32] Political violence, then, was a manifestation of republican ideology.

It was also, of course, an expression of the structure of politics. As Jack N. Rakove has recently suggested, both the Constitution and the process of ratification brought about a politics that was less stable and more popular than its framers anticipated. Turnover in the first Congresses was high, as members left public service to pursue private interests. Newspapers that published the proceedings of Congress not only helped create a national politics, but public opinion and pressure, as well.[33] Anyone who entered service in the federal government expecting to find there a forum for the dispassionate discussion of the issues of the day, isolated from the whims and demands of public opinion, was sure to be disappointed.

And Thomas Jefferson surely was disappointed. He began his service in the new national government equipped with republican expectations of fame at a time when politics was becoming increasingly volatile and violent. In theory fame was supposed to be a manifestation of public esteem, but in practice, especially at a time when the mechanisms of public opinion were unformed, it was established by a gentleman's peers, not the promiscuous public. Jefferson said he craved only the "affection of my countrymen," but what he effectively meant was the esteem of the relatively small group of men who served with him in the public realm, for how could he possibly know what the mass of men thought?

We have already heard Jefferson complaining to his daughters about the malice and venom of politics. Public approbation, or even a secure sense of the public's esteem, was elusive. In comparison to that vague sense of a public whose feelings were warm to the cause, but merely "friendly to the individual," the "jealousies, the hatred, and the malignant passions" of those whom he encountered daily cut him to the bone. Less than five months from his death, Jefferson had "no complaint against the world which has sufficiently honored me," but it was only his family that had "blessed me by their affections, and never by their conduct given me a moment's pain."[34] Jefferson had won his family's love, not his nation's fame.

It was a bargain that the fierce politics of the first decades of the early republic prepared him to make. That public life at the time was violent was no mere figure of speech; in fact, politics could be decidedly dangerous, as the experience of Jefferson's great rival, Alexander Hamilton, abundantly illustrates. The duel that ended his life was but the last and most lethal of a series of violent encounters that punctuated Hamilton's public life. In 1778 and 1779, while serving as an aide to George Washington, he twice came close to dueling.[35] Charles Royster has observed that it was just at this time that dueling, a tradition among European army officers, came into vogue among the young officers of the Continental Army. He explains that dueling "increased because it settled questions of honor in a distinctive, gallant way for men newly self-conscious about their uniqueness and their proper public inviolability." The duel mushroomed in the dank soil of Valley Forge, where anxious and ambitious young men who were strangers to one another were thrown together and compelled to establish their worth and standing in each other's eyes. As Royster notes, the world of the Continental Army officer was intimate and intense; the duel was a product of the volatile attachments this environment nourished. "The opinion of a circle of friends might decide a man's self-respect or disgrace."[36]

The same held true in the political world of the new nation, where men from a variety of backgrounds, eager for fame and anxious to prove themselves the equal in honor to the most honorable members of the new government, were thrown together on terms of intimacy. Former officers such as Hamilton, who had learned the rituals of the duel in the army, or hotheads such as John Randolph of Roanoke, insecure about their status, might find themselves issuing or provoking challenges throughout their careers. On one Saturday afternoon in July 1795, while Hamilton was out strolling with friends along New York's Wall Street, his group encountered a party of Republican rivals, also out for a walk. Words were exchanged, then insults; Hamilton attempted to intervene, he himself was insulted, and then promptly issued a challenge. The stroll resumed; a few minutes later Hamilton and his friends met another knot of Republicans, and more arguments, more insults, and another challenge ensued. One dispute was resolved immediately, but it took a week of negotiations to avert a duel in the other case.[37]

When men such as Hamilton believed that their standing with the public, and hence, their capacity to win fame by serving it, rested upon their honor, "the potential for violence hovered around every public dispute." Robert Wiebe has recently noted that, in order to prevent politics from becoming a virtual bloodbath, gentleman politicians began to devise rules and customs that could channel aggressions yet still protect reputations. One tack was to attempt to identify and isolate a private realm, off-limits to both insult and the necessity of defending one's honor. Nonetheless, "anything that could be justified on grounds of republican principle, no matter how vicious or destructive to an individual's reputation, fell within a public realm and lent itself only to political or legal redress." And, conversely, any attack on a public man's character might be construed as sedition. As St. George Tucker would explain, "The right of character is a sacred and invaluable right, and is not forfeited by accepting a public employment. Whoever knowingly departs from any of these maxims is guilty of a crime against the community, as well as the person injured."[38] Until the line between public and private could be sharply drawn—effectively narrowing the perimeters of public virtue and, hence, reworking the assumptions of republicanism—any word or deed that seemed to call into question a man's public honor could lead to political violence.

Wiebe has suggested that the wars of words waged by pamphleteers and newspaper editors in this period were nothing less than sublimated duels, contests of honor by proxy. Jefferson, for example, who had no taste for physical and life-threatening encounter, did not hesitate to spur polemicists on. "A free press," Wiebe explains, "served deep emotional as well as broad public needs."[39] But as long as politics itself remained intimate and emotionally intense it would retain its capacity for violence, and even pamphlets or articles could provide the stimulus to duels. It was a pamphlet, for example, that led Hamilton to challenge James Monroe to a duel.

The "Reynolds affair" is of particular interest to us for what it tells us about the way in which private affairs could become matters of public interest. The story began in November 1792 when the comptroller of the Treasury sued James Reynolds and Jacob Clingman for attempting to defraud the government by filing false claims. While in jail and after his release—charges were dropped when the pair agreed to make restitution and supply certain information—Reynolds hinted darkly that he was in possession of certain information that reflected very badly upon the Secretary of the Treasury. Eventually this information found its way to Frederick Muhlenberg, a Pennsylvania Republican and Speaker of the House in the First Congress; he then brought it to the attention of two Virginia Republicans, Senator James Monroe and Representative Abraham Venable, who then sought confirmation from Reynolds. In mid-December the Republican delegation went to visit Hamilton; he denied Reynolds's allegations and claimed that Reynolds was blackmailing him for having carried on an adulterous affair with Reynolds's wife Maria. "The result," Hamilton would write later, after the whole sordid affair had become public knowledge, "was a full and unequivocal acknowledgement on the part of the three gentlemen of perfect satisfaction with the explanation and expressions of regret at the trouble and embarrassment which had been occasioned to me."[40] He thought the matter had been laid to rest.

Rumors, however, circulated, and in the summer of 1797 pamphleteer James Thomson Callender made them public. If Hamilton had sought to deflect the accusation of public impropriety—specifically, speculating in public funds—by admitting to the private vice of adultery, Callender would recognize no such distinction. Although Callender believed that Hamilton fabricated the story of an affair with Maria Reynolds to cover up his unseemly financial activities with her husband, the pamphleteer was happy to have it both ways, faulting Hamilton both for defrauding the government and committing adultery. Callender would later spell out his rationale for examining what some suggested were purely private matters: "The world has no business with that part of a public character, unless . . . it shall be connected with some interesting political truth."[41] In Hamilton's case, the relevant issue seemed to be his hypocrisy; "We shall presently see this great master of morality," Callender told his readers, "though himself the father of a family, confessing that he had an illicit correspondence with another man's wife."[42] Hamilton was driven to publish an extended and passionate defense, which would call forth another of Callender's tracts. Hamilton, he charged, "has published ninety-three pages to prove, that he was guilty of conjugal infidelity. . . . This is the man, who, at the same moment, has the hardiness to announce 'a conspiracy of vice against virtue.' Mr. Hamilton should speak with reserve as to the faults of others."[43]

It is worth examining Hamilton's defense in some detail so that we may be able to compare it with the response Jefferson would make when, five years later, Callender turned his acid pen against him. In his defense, Hamilton worked hard to erect a barrier between his private and public lives. The stakes, he argued, were high. The attack upon him was a manifestation of the "spirit of jacobinism. . . . Incessantly busied in undermining all the props of public security and private happiness, it seems to threaten the political and moral world with a complete overthrow." Hamilton assumed that his effectiveness as a political figure—that is, his power—rested on his character. His enemies were attempting to destroy "the influence of men of upright principles." They were engaged in a conspiracy "against honest fame," and their strategy was to "wear away the reputations which they could not directly subvert." One of their tactics was to "stab the private felicity" of the person under assault. "With such men, nothing is sacred. Even the peace of an unoffending and amiable wife is a welcome repast to their insatiate fury against the husband."[44] Invading Hamilton's privacy and upsetting his wife is the final and lowest blow.

Although Hamilton argued that his private life was "sacred," and that his enemies should honor its inviolability, his defense reveals that his primary concern was his "public character" and his fame. His focus was upon the public sphere, and it is clear from the argument he would make several years later in the Croswell case that he believed the press ought to be given wide latitude in discussing the character and behavior of not only public figures, but even "private persons." "If this be not done, then in vain will the voice of the people be raised against the inroads of tyranny." Republican principles legitimated "fair and honest exposure." Anything that was true might be published—except if it were "for the purpose of disturbing the peace of families."[45]

Hamilton recognized a small private sphere whose sanctity should be inviolable, not because it contributed something to the public realm, but, instead, because so clearly it did not. The private realm is without political meaning. It became relevant only when it affected the composure and happiness of the public man. In other words, Hamilton depicted his wife and his family as merely extensions of his self. It is as if Hamilton had said to Callender and his other enemies, "Let there be something of mine that you cannot use to hurt me." His concern for his wife was merely a reflection of his interest in his own "private felicity." Had her happiness been a central preoccupation, he would not so coolly have confessed (or invented, if one follows the alternate interpretation) the details of his adultery with Mrs. Reynolds: "After this, I had frequent meetings with her, most of them at my own house; Mrs. Hamilton with her children being absent on a visit to her father." When all is said and done, however, "There is nothing worse in the affair than an irregular and indelicate amour." If, in the scheme of things, Hamilton's adultery was such a trifle, then it was not so much his "indelicate amour" that must be upsetting to his wife, as public discussion of it, which merely ate at *her* peace, but threatened *him* with eternal shame.[46] Mrs. Hamilton was merely an auxiliary to her husband's happiness; in his mind, he apparently has very little bearing on hers. Hamilton would protect himself by sectioning off a private realm, but in comparison to the wide public arena in which his fame would be won, it was a very small space indeed.

And it was in the public arena that Hamilton attempted to defend his honor. Not only did he publish this extraordinary pamphlet, but he challenged James Monroe to a duel. Once Callender published his pamphlets, Hamilton anxiously sought affirmation from Muhlenberg, Venable, and Monroe that they had been satisfied with his defense five years earlier. Muhlenberg's and Venable's responses were adequately reassuring; Monroe's, however, was not. There was an interview and an extended correspondence. Hamilton issued a challenge; Monroe accepted it; Hamilton backed off. More letters ensued. Finally, Monroe enlisted Aaron Burr and John Dawson to help him either make arrangements for a duel or resolve the matter. Although a duel once again seemed imminent, it somehow—and the record is unclear on this point—was averted.[47]

Less than four years later, Hamilton's son Philip would be killed in a duel. Philip and a friend had been challenged when they loudly mocked a speech critical of the Federalists. Philip accepted the challenge and took a bullet in his side. His mother's grief, an observer at the young man's deathbed said, "beggars . . . description."[48] Just over two years after that, Hamilton himself would engage in his fatal duel with Aaron Burr.

Robert Wiebe has suggested that the first political parties functioned, much like the newspapers, as vessels for containing political violence by making a ritual of it.[49] That assessment is no doubt true for the long run, but for at least the first few years of the First Party System, factional conflict could just as easily stimulate as sublimate violence. Burr had apparently been nursing a grudge against Hamilton for the role he played in denying him the presidency in 1800 and the governorship of New York in 1804, but it was not until the summer of 1804 that Burr thought he had grounds for a duel. Finally Hamilton said something—exactly what is unknown—that "could . . . be taken hold of." Burr issued the challenge; Hamilton accepted, and, like his son, he took a bullet in his side. He had left a letter for his wife, to be delivered only in the event of his death. "If it had been possible for me to have avoided the interview, my love for you and my precious children would have been alone a decisive motive. But it was not possible, without sacrifices which would have rendered me unworthy of your esteem."[50] His honor took precedence over her happiness; or rather, Hamilton believed his honor, his reputation, and his fame were, even more than his love, his essential contribution to her happiness.

III

There is little evidence of Thomas Jefferson's reaction to the death of one of his rivals at the hands of another. It is rather evident, however, that he must have followed Hamilton's discomfiture in the Reynolds affair with some glee. James Monroe had kept him informed, and as early as December 1792 Jefferson made note, albeit cryptically, of "the affair of Reynolds & his wife."[51] A number of years later, however, when Jefferson reflected on Alexander Hamilton and his character, he was able—in a way that Hamilton himself never had been—to separate the public from the private man: "Hamilton was indeed a singular character. Of acute understanding, disinterested, honest, and honorable in all private transactions, amiable in society, and duly valuing virtue in private life, yet so bewitched & perverted by the British example, as to be under thoro' conviction that corruption was essential to the government of a nation."[52] In retrospect, Hamilton's flaws were all in his public and political actions.

Perhaps it was his own experience at Callender's hand that made Jefferson not only more charitable, but also more careful in distinguishing between public and private virtue. By 1802, for reasons that need not detain us here, Callender had moved to Virginia; he had begun editing the Richmond *Recorder*; and turned against Jefferson and the Republicans.[53] In September of that year he began publication of a series of articles attacking Jefferson's reputation. "It is well known," the first of these articles began, "that the man, *whom it delighteth the people to honor*, keeps, and for many years past has kept, as his concubine, one of his own slaves. Her name is

SALLY."[54] The story that Jefferson maintained a sexual relationship with his slave Sally Hemings and fathered a number of her children has been in circulation ever since, never effectively proved or disproved. The veracity of the charges, however, is not what concerns us. Instead, it is the manner in which Callender framed the accusation and the way in which Jefferson and his friends responded to it.

In the Reynolds affair, Callender's ostensible rationale for discussing Hamilton's relationship with Mrs. Reynolds had been Hamilton's hypocrisy. Maria Reynolds's connection to the allegation that Hamilton had speculated in government securities should have been reason enough for examining her relationship with the Secretary of the Treasury. Callender, however, was incensed that a "great master of morality, though himself the father of a family," would commit adultery and confess that he had "an illicit correspondence with another man's wife."[55] Similarly, he accused Jefferson of violating the sanctity of the family. His original charge—later amended—was that Jefferson had brought Sally over to France along with his two daughters. "What a sublime pattern for an American ambassador to place before the eyes of two young ladies!"[56] Other Federalist newspapers would pick up and republish Callender's allegations, elaborating on that theme. The Lynchburg *Virginia Gazette*, for example, judged Jefferson a failed father. "These daughters, who should have been the principal object of his domestic concern, had the mortification to see illegitimate mulatto sisters, and brothers, enjoying the same privileges of parental affection with themselves."[57] A good father protected his daughters and gave them all of his affection.

In focusing on the character of Jefferson's fatherhood, Callender and his followers shifted the ground on which the discussion of character took place. No attempt was made to suggest that Jefferson's relationship with Sally Hemings or his daughters directly affected his capacity for governance or had immediate bearing upon his public virtue. It was simply, as Callender put it, that "the public have a right to be acquainted with the real characters of persons who are the possessors or candidates for office." Hamilton's *New-York Post* would elaborate (somewhat disingenuously, perhaps, considering Hamilton's own experience): "We feel for the honor of our country—And when the Chief magistrate labours under the imputation of the most abandoned profligacy of private life, we do most honestly and sincerely wish to see the stain upon the nation wiped away."[58] Honor, then, was a reward for private, as much as public, virtue.

Several years later, when these and other charges became the subject of debate in the Massachusetts legislature, the committee charged with considering them reported that "the preservation of our Republican Constitutions, and the impartial and faithful administration of laws enacted in conformity to them, depend alone on the knowledge which the people may have of the *conduct, integrity and talents* of those of their fellow citizens, who have been, or may be called to offices of trust and honour."[59] What hitherto might have been defined as private virtue was of public interest. As Callender asked rhetorically, in defense of his revelations, "What virtuous character has been destroyed by this paper? If seduction, and hypocrisy, if the grossest breach of personal friendship, and of domestic confidence, form a department in the new code of morality," then, and only then, would the newspaper he published have been in the wrong.[60] The personal had been rendered political.

Everything in a man's life was relevant, and the Federalist press, in its attempt to discredit the president, cast a wide net. Most of the charges originated with Callender, and they eventually included allegations of both a clearly public and just as clearly a private nature: Jefferson's behavior during the Revolution was cowardly; he had paid back a debt in depreciated currency; he had attempted an affair with Betsey Walker, the wife of his neighbor and friend; he had paid Callender to slander George Washington; he was destroying the navy; he did not believe in God; the Louisiana purchase was unwise.[61] This promiscuous mingling of political and personal accusations served to break down the precarious wall that had separated the public and private realms. In the fall of 1802, as the Federalist papers were filled with allegations, and the Republican press attempted a defense, everyone's character became fair game. The *Richmond Examiner* devoted more space to defaming Jefferson's enemies than to defending the President. It recirculated the tale of the Hamilton-Reynolds affair and insinuated that John Marshall, whom it suspected of supplying information to Callender, himself kept a slave mistress. It alleged that Callender himself was consorting with a black prostitute. It even raised questions about the manhood of Charles Cotesworth Pinckney, a potential Federalist candidate for the presidency, dubbing him "Miss *Charlotte* Cotesworth PINCKNEY" and referring to him repeatedly as "she."[62] In the heated political climate, the sexual behavior of any partisan was grist for the mill.

At the same time that the Republican press was tarring Jefferson's enemies with the brush that had been used on him, it began to frame a different sort of defense, one that would attempt to make impregnable the wall between public and private. To be sure, the press was working at contradictory and self-defeating purposes. While one column was defending the sanctity of Jefferson's personal life, another was violating Hamilton's or Marshall's, without even a pretense to consistency. Yet out of this unstable combination of approaches to the question of a public man's sexual behavior, a new understanding of the relationship between the family and the public world would emerge.

The first element in this new configuration was the assertion that the family ought to be protected from political scrutiny. The *Richmond Exam-*

iner charged, in language reminiscent of that which Hamilton had used in his "Reynolds Pamphlet," that because the opponents of Republicanism could find no fault with its policies or its leaders, "they are driven into the sacred recesses of privacy, to hunt up malicious falsehood and obloquy at the hazard of family repose." In response, the Federalist press repeated the standard republican defense that anything that had bearing on a man's public actions was relevant. Hence, a contributor to the *Boston Gazette* would recoil in horror at "the new principles recently advanced . . . that it is unfair to expose the private vices of a public man" and confess himself "unable to discover upon what basis of morals, or of policy, the axiom can be supported, that the most detestable crimes of which a human being can be guilty, must be overlooked and concealed, if committed by a public man, unless they were committed in his *official capacity*."[63] As in the Reynolds affair, the arguments circled each other warily, like equally matched opponents, neither one capable of winning the round.

IV

As long as the political press saw the family as nothing more than an extension of the man who was its head, there could be no effective defense of its privacy. The harm that came from disrupting a family's repose, after all, was imagined to fall most heavily upon the public man, who was distracted from his important endeavors. Moreover, the lines of influence led entirely in one direction, from a man and his family, through society to the nation. That the nation—as distinct from a tyrant who perverted its will—might harm the family was a novel thought. When the Jeffersonian press asserted the sanctity of the "private recesses" of the family and began to describe the family in ways that would make the preservation of its privacy a positive and necessary good, it was redefining both the family and its relation to the political world. In fact, the political press was not the only or the most important sector of society that was rethinking the family; as a number of historians have shown, at just this time, educators, essayists, and novelists (both male and female), ministers, and political theorists, as well as middle-class and elite men and women on both sides of the Atlantic, were beginning to think in new ways about the nature of family and its relationship to the wider public.[64] Indeed, because the redefinition of the family was hardly their central occupation, it seems more likely that the political newspapers were reflecting, and in the process, politically legitimating, changes that were taking place in both society and thought as they attempted to craft a defense for their slandered leaders.

And so it was that defenders of Thomas Jefferson began to offer his character as a family man as an argument in his defense. If Callender accused Jefferson of carrying on a sexual relationship with a slave woman "before the eyes of his two daughters," the *Richmond Examiner* would respond that the presence of Jefferson's daughters rendered such behavior unthinkable. That a man such as Jefferson, "who is daily engaged in the ordinary vocations of the family, should have a mulatto child" was not possible. "Mr. Jefferson has been a Bachelor for more than twenty years. During this period," the paper explained, "he reared with parental attention, two unblemished, accomplished and amiable women, who are married to two estimable citizens. In the education of his daughters, this same Thomas Jefferson, supplied the place of a *mother*—his tenderness and delicacy were proverbial—not a spot tarnished his widowed character" until Callender started spreading his lies.[65] "The ordinary vocations of the family" precluded the sort of behavior of which Jefferson was accused. The unblemished daughters served as proof of their father's virtue. Family life implicitly was virtuous, and, if anything, required protection from the contamination of politics. One Massachusetts legislator was disgusted by the newspapers' discussions of Thomas Jefferson's character. "He asked, whether any gentleman, who had a family, and whose females or daughters, were in the habit of reading the public papers, would permit a paper containing such matter to come into his house."[66] It was the public—not the tender father—that threatened the sanctity of the family.

And it was at home, and on the basis of his fatherhood, that Jefferson was willing to be judged. Hamilton accepted Burr's challenge because, in the end, he had no other choice. He could not go home because his wife, or so he imagined, would consider him dishonored. Jefferson's passionate letters to his daughters should be understood in this context. It was no exaggeration to say that political life was filled with cabal, hatred, and intrigue. When he told Maria that "it is in the love of one's family only that heartfelt happiness is known,"[67] he spoke from both experience and desire. Yet the family is not naturally or necessarily happy or warm, nor is it the opposite of political life. Jefferson, the tender and delicate parent, made it—or at least saw it—as he needed it to be.

And because he fell back upon the happiness of home, Jefferson offered no public response to the charges of his enemies. They were astounded, taking Jefferson's silence as proof of their charges. Some expected a public denial, perhaps his own version of Hamilton's "Reynolds Pamphlet." The *Boston Gazette* "waited in expectation either that Mr. Jefferson himself would deem it not beneath his dignity, to meet the accusation of a crime so deeply infamous, at least with a pointed denial, or that some of his numerous friends and admirers would have taken the task upon themselves." In 1805 a Massachusetts legislator would accept the charges as true, for after all, they "had been made and repeated for more than four years. . . . They had been published and republished again and again, at the seat of government; avowedly and before the face of Mr. Jefferson. . . . Yet, during this whole time, these charges had not been contradicted, either by Mr. Jefferson or his friends.—this . . . in his mind, amounted to at least a tacit confession." Others speculated about possible duels. The *Richmond Examiner* published a report, later retracted, that Light-Horse Harry Lee had carried a challenge from John Walker to the President.[68] Some sort of response was expected.

Jefferson, however, remained almost completely silent. In 1805 he confessed to his Secretary of the Navy that "when young and single I offered love" to Mrs. Walker. "It is the only one founded in truth among all their allegations against me." In 1803 he wrote out his religious creed, explaining to Martha, "I thought it just that my family, by possessing this, should be enabled to estimate the libels published against me on this, as on every other possible subject."[69] The allegations troubled him, of course, as did the general tenor of the Federalist press. He gave both direct and indirect encouragement to the states to prosecute for libel, telling Pennsylvania's governor Thomas McKean that he had "long thought that a few prosecutions of the most eminent offenders would have a wholesome effect in restoring the integrity of the presses." Although, as Leonard Levy has pointed out, Jefferson's willingness to use not only the state but the federal courts to prosecute seditious libel marked a retreat from the more libertarian theories of freedom of the press developed by Republicans in response to the Sedition Act of 1798,[70] Jefferson himself did not seem willing to pursue his policy vigorously or publicly. He wanted McKean to keep "entirely confidential" his recommendation for intimidating the press in Pennsylvania, and he ordered a halt to the prosecution of a Connecticut minister when he learned that a trial would require a public discussion of the Walker affair. Jefferson's later explanation for terminating the prosecution—"I had laid it down as a law to myself, to take no notice of the thousand calumnies issued against me, but to trust my character to my own conduct, and the good sense and candor of my fellow citizens"[71]—surely casts his motive in the most favorable possible light; undoubtedly he must also have wanted to avoid the embarrassment that a public airing of the allegation that four decades earlier he had attempted to seduce his friend's wife was sure to bring. If we consider Jefferson's prosecutions as yet another means of displacing political violence, it is striking that even in this sublimated version of the duel, Jefferson would try to hold his fire.

V

Certainly, Jefferson's attitudes were shaped by his personality. He was by nature sensitive to criticism and averse to direct conflict. Yet, as was his nature, he transformed his inclinations into maxims, and when they were applied to public affairs, they became part of an emergent political culture. We have already seen how smoothly Jefferson would change subjects in letters to his daughters; evocations of the pleasures of family life would quickly and almost inevitably be transformed into diatribes about the miseries of political life. The object of these letters, in fact, was to shape family life so that it would continue to be an effective counter to the ravages of politics. He would tell his daughters both explicitly and indirectly how to behave in a way that would foster peace and family love. In the letters he addressed to their husbands and sons, Jefferson also would discuss family and political life in tandem, but here his objective was to instruct them how to behave in public so that they would live to enjoy the pleasures of family life.

In 1808, as he was nearing the end of his last term of office, Jefferson wrote his grandson and namesake, Thomas Jefferson Randolph, then studying medicine in Philadelphia, a long and, as Dumas Malone put it, "excessively didactic" letter.[72] Clearly he was worried that his young charge, away from home for the first time in his life, would fall in with a bad crowd. The ostensible purpose of the letter was to inculcate in young Jeff, as the President's grandson was known, the personal habits that would enable him to resist the usual temptations of youth—gambling, drinking, and so forth. But along with injunctions about what not to do, Jefferson also told his grandson exactly how to behave. This advice constitutes Jefferson's political sociology, his doctrine about the way men in public ought to act. Thomas Jefferson wrote his grandson a primer on how to avoid the duel.

First of all, a man had to develop the proper frame of mind. Jefferson counseled "good humor as one of the preservatives of our peace and tranquillity." If he could not summon it naturally, he could always feign it: "In truth, politeness is artificial good humor, it covers natural want of it, and ends by rendering habitual a substitute nearly equivalent to the real virtue." Politeness, in Jefferson's view, was a scaled-down version of public virtue— self-sacrifice for the common good, not so much of the nation, as the society in which a man happened at the moment to be. "It is the practice of sacrificing to those whom we meet in society all the little conveniences and preferences which will gratify them, and deprive us of nothing worth a moment's consideration; it is giving a pleasing and flattering turn to our expressions which will conciliate others, and make them pleased with us as well as themselves."[73] It might well be true, as Jefferson would observe at another time, that "the Creator would have been a bungling artist, had he intended man for a social animal, without planting in him social dispositions," but those dispositions required cultivation and even conscious calculation.

In the context of his wider social philosophy, Jefferson seems to have considered anger and political disputation as variants on self-love, the "antagonist of virtue."[74] The self-sacrifice and self-control required to walk away from an argument, then, constituted virtue. And it was just this form of virtue that Jefferson passionately enjoined upon his grandson. He told him quite directly never to enter "into a dispute or argument with anyone."

To make his point, he attempted a number of tacks: He invoked the example of the revered Benjamin Franklin, "the most amiable of men in society," whose rule was "Never to contradict anybody." He told Jeff that argument was always in vain anyway: "I never yet saw an instance of one of two disputants convincing each other by argument"; if anything, such disagreements only made matters worse. He resorted to philosophy, sharing with his grandson the secret of his own success: "When I hear another express an opinion, which is not mine, I say to myself, He has a right to his opinion, as I to mine; why should I question it. His error does me no injury, and shall I become a Don Quixot to bring all men by force of argument, to one opinion?" And he tried simple scare tactics. He had seen too many antagonists "getting warm, becoming rude, and shooting one another." Disputation, Jefferson warned, could lead to death.

Perhaps Jefferson had in mind the sad example of Philip Hamilton when he told young Jeff not to worry about defending his grandfather's reputation from the "puppies in politics" he was sure to encounter. Jefferson assured his grandson that his character was "in the hands of my fellow citizens at large, and will be consigned to honor or infamy by the verdict of the republican mass of our country, according to what themselves will have seen, not what their enemies and mine shall have said." A public man's reputation rested not on his willingness to defend it by force or even on what a small circle of gentlemen in Washington or Philadelphia conceived it to be. Jefferson's character was a matter of public opinion, not the debating or dueling skills of his kin.

When Jefferson instructed his grandson how to avoid political violence, it is even more probable that he had in mind the duel that Jeff's father had narrowly avoided only two years earlier. In 1806, much to his chagrin, Thomas Jefferson's son-in-law almost entered into a duel with his even more volatile cousin, John Randolph of Roanoke. This was not the first time that there had been trouble between John Randolph and the Jefferson sons-in-law, two Congressmen whom the Speaker of the House seemed to regard as tools of the president. After one minor altercation, Jefferson attempted to mollify the Speaker. He explained that there were "no men on earth more independent in their sentiments" than his sons-in-law; nor would Jefferson even consider talking politics with them. In fact, Jefferson would barely risk political dispute with anyone, even members of his own party, "experience having long taught me the reasonableness of mutual sacrifices of opinion among those who are to act together for any common object."[75] Jefferson had little interest in establishing a political dynasty, let alone a family one, or so he led Randolph to believe.

Such reassurances, however, could not cool tempers that were inclined to inflame, and in 1806 Thomas Mann Randolph and John Randolph came close to a duel. The dispute began, as it so often did, over a trifle—a debate in the House about repealing a duty on salt. The proponents were accused of trying to embarrass the administration; their heated response elicited a counter-response from Jefferson's supporters, including Thomas Mann Randolph, who objected to an opponent's tone. John Randolph, then Chairman of the House Ways and Means Committee and increasingly hostile to Jefferson and his policies, took the floor, making one of his typical speeches, nasty yet somehow vague. Jefferson's son-in-law thought it was aimed at him; he took offense and rose in his own defense, effectively challenging the Chairman to a duel. The Chairman sent a second, the son-in-law chose a second and then backed down, issuing an apology for his insults from the House floor. Other Congressmen, however, assailed the Chairman's leadership, and the newspapers transformed this undoubtedly merited criticism into a conspiracy to ruin John Randolph. Thomas Mann Randolph's character was called into question, and it appeared as if the duel might once again be on.[76]

Jefferson was beside himself with anxiety. He was afraid to write his son-in-law at home, where he had gone after Congress had recessed, for fear his daughter would read the letter and learn of the impending duel. He entrusted his letter to a mutual friend, to whom he complained that the newspapers were encouraging the duel. Jefferson decried the custom of resolving disputes by duels. They were especially inappropriate for men with families, and he was certain that "the mass of men would condemn it in a husband and father of a numerous family." He underscored the point to Randolph himself in a letter written several weeks later when the threat of a duel, mercifully, seemed to have passed. "The young ones indeed would have gotten over it; but to two persons at least it would have ended but with life. This period might have been long with one; with the other short but unceasingly bitter. A sincere affection for you personally, a reliance on you for succeeding to cases which age is unfitting me for, sympathies with a beloved survivor, and tender anxieties for those who would have had to embark in the world without guide or protection, would have filled with gloom my remaining time."[77] In this light, fighting a duel would be an act of supreme selfishness, unforgivable for a man with a family.

The family, then, and not honor, was a man's primary obligation. As Jefferson explained it to his son-in-law, "unnecessary risk . . . indeed is the falsest of honour . . . a mere compound of crime & folly."[78] Hamilton had had it all wrong. It was attention to his familial responsibilities that made even a public man worthy of his family's esteem. And it was in the family that a man could find the certain and unchanging love that the public world denied him. In counseling complacency and coolness in public, Jefferson was attempting to alter the tenor of public life; he was struggling to make politics less personal and emotionally intense. Don't argue, he said; don't fight; do as I do, and think of home. Only by constructing the family as the sole realm where heartfelt happiness might be found could Jefferson divest politics of the passions that threatened always to push it over the edge into violence. Not only was political passion in this age displaced, as Robert Wiebe has suggested, into newspapers, political parties, and similar ritualized and less lethal forms of dispute, but it was also transmuted into the love that was experienced at home. Family life would become more intense as political life became cooler.

VI

This process was just beginning as Thomas Jefferson achieved his long-proclaimed desire to retire from politics, but its effects would be profound. Indeed, it might be argued that a viable, relatively modern politics would not be possible until it became less emotionally intense, that is, less personal. It would be a number of years, of course, before the code of the duel would be replaced entirely by less dangerous means of resolving political dispute, but after the War of 1812, the duel—like other forms of violence—became increasingly confined to certain regions and classes.[79] An effective politics would not be possible until a man could argue a position without risking its being construed as a reflection on another man's honor. By the same token, an orderly politics would have to offer men other sources for constituting their identities. A man accepted a challenge in order to maintain his reputation among a small circle of political intimates; these were the men who validated his identity. Jefferson sought to ground reputation in an even wider sphere, "the republican mass of our country." But this wider public could not be the guarantor of a man's fame until mechanisms of communication were developed for registering public opinion. The newspapers and party organizations that were coming into being while Jefferson served in government and that at first seemed only to exacerbate conflict would eventually bring into political being the sort of mass public to which Jefferson attempted to appeal.

Jefferson knew, however, that although this public might esteem him, it could never bathe him in the sort of affection that as a young man he had seemed to crave.[80] For that he would have to turn to his family. They would provide him with the emotional sustenance that would make his continued participation in public affairs possible, and he in turn would serve his family, first and foremost, by not getting himself killed. He would also endeavor to keep the violence that seemed endemic in politics from spilling over into the home. The wall separating the home from politics could be built higher and stronger, now that there was something to protect. This process, which would define the home and what took place in it as sacred and private would not be accomplished until a number of years later after the newspapers and pamphleteers had examined Andrew Jackson's marriage in the minutest detail, insinuating that his most intimate relationship had profound public implications.[81] And although politics would periodically—especially in the nineteenth century—attempt to scale the wall that was supposed to separate it from the private realm, it turned out that the republican mass of the people in whom Jefferson placed his faith would accept the notion that the public and private spheres were separate and distinct. In the long run, they would demonstrate that they cared relatively little about what their leaders did in "the sacred recesses of privacy."

The connection between public and private virtue was in the process of being severed. It was not so much that the meaning of virtue was feminized as that different standards of behavior for politics and the home developed. The notion of public virtue would still have a specific, if less encompassing content; the specter of corruption, for example, a central republican fear, would continue to haunt American politics in the decades to come.[82] And new standards of personal conduct, particularly for the genteel, would be applied to both men and women concerning their behavior at home. Jefferson, after all, would instruct both his sons-in-law and his daughters, his granddaughters as well as his grandsons, to avoid conflict and disputation at all cost. "Honesty, disinterestedness, and good nature are indispensable to procure the esteem and confidence of those with whom we live, and on whose esteem our happiness depends," Jefferson instructed one grandson.[83] He could easily have given that advice to a granddaughter, as well. Personal integrity and unfailing good humor were qualities that knew no gender.

That is not to say that the new political and familial order that Jefferson worked to achieve would affect men and women in the same way, or even that Jefferson had identical expectations of his male and female kin. If a man's primary responsibility was to provide for his family and to return to it in one piece,[84] a woman's was to create the environment that would sustain masculine identity. The sort of behavior Jefferson enjoined upon women and men was similar: avoid conflict at all cost. But because the primary focus of their endeavors was different, so also, would be the meaning of their actions.

Jefferson counted on women to make family life agreeable, just as he expected men of good sense to keep political life calm. In his expectations of family life, Jefferson shared one of the contradictions of republican thinking; it assumed at one and the same time that family life was inherently conflict-free and that it was only the self-effacement of women that made it so. Like republican theorists of the family, Jefferson believed that a peaceful society was founded in a harmonious marriage, and a harmonious marriage required a deferential wife.[85] When his daughter Martha married Thomas Mann Randolph, her father warned her, "Your new condition will call for abundance of little sacrifices but they will be greatly overpaid by the measure of affection they will secure to you. The happiness of your life depends now on the continuing to please a single person." Several years later, he would offer similar words of advice to Maria. "Happiness in the married state is the very first object to be aimed at. Nothing can preserve affection uninterrupted but a firm resolution never to differ in will and a determination in each to consider the love of the other as of more value than any object whatever on which a wish has been fixed." Married people should never argue or criticize, especially in public, no matter what the provocation. "Much better therefore," he advised, "if our companion views a thing in a light different from what we do to leave him in quiet possession of his view."[86]

Although the words were strikingly similar to those he would address to his grandson several years later, it must be remembered that Jeff Randolph was instructed on how to avoid disputes in public, not at home. It is clear from his letters to his daughters that Jefferson expected husbands to be almost naturally disputatious, and that he placed almost the entire burden of family happiness on women alone. Nor was it just the peace of their immediate families with which women were entrusted; women were responsible for the harmony of all domestic society, that is, of all the homes in which men and women mixed and met. Again and again Jefferson would tell his daughters to suppress their own feelings and spread the balm of affection wherever they went. When her sister-in-law was caught in a scandal of incest and infanticide, Jefferson advised Martha to be charitable. "Never throw off the best affections of nature in the moment when they become most precious to their object; nor fear to extend your hand to save another, less you should sink yourself."[87] Jefferson offered this advice in 1793, well before he himself became embroiled in lesser scandals, yet it suggests how he thought a family ought to respond to a scandal that touched one of its members.

Martha's response would show that she grasped her father's intent: to display affection, even in the face of error, in the interest of maintaining harmony. Several years earlier, not long after Martha's marriage, her widowed father-in-law remarried a much younger woman and gave signs that he would begin a new family, threatening his older children's expectations for inheritance. Jefferson told Martha not to contest the marriage settlement, but instead to conciliate not only her father-in-law and his bride, but the bride's mother, as well. He gave his daughter detailed instructions in how to manipulate her in-laws. "Be you my dear," Jefferson advised, "the link of love, union, and peace for the whole family."[88] Not only the peace of the family, but her material well-being depended upon it. When women maintained domestic order, they were doing nothing less than securing the basis for their society's economic and political stability.

Martha learned her lesson well. If we read between the lines of her response to her father's letter recommending charity toward Nancy Randolph, we can see how she absorbed her father's philosophy and transmitted it to her husband. Martha told her father that under the pressure of the scandal, the "divisions" in her husband's family were increasing daily, but that her husband was succeeding in healing them. Her husband's "conduct," she reported, "has been such as to conciliate the affections of the whole family. He is the Link by which so many discordant parts join. . . . there is not one individual but what looks up to him as one, and the only one who has been uniform in his affection."[89] Under her tutelage, her husband, radiating affection, had become the center of his family. And that was the way it was supposed to be: by "sacrifices and suppressions of feeling,"[90] a woman would cultivate the affections of the family, flattering even its most difficult members like a master politician, but it was always to install a man at its head.

Here was the difference, finally, between the home and the world of politics. The methods for achieving harmony in each were similar: they required forbearance, deference to the wishes of others, flattery even, and the suppression of the will. Yet the rewards for men and for women were necessarily different. Jefferson told both of his daughters that the compensation for their self-effacement would be gratifying, but indirect. He promised Martha that "your own happiness will be the greater as you perceive that you promote that of others," and a decade later he renewed the pledge to Maria: "Go on then, my dear, as you have done in deserving the love of every body; you will reap the rich reward of their esteem, and will find that we are working for ourselves while we do good to others."[91] A woman's work was to promote others' happiness, thereby ensuring her own.

Women, in other words, had to earn love; it was the return for love freely given. For men, it was their due. When Jefferson rhapsodized about the happiness of home, he assumed that his daughters would always love him; he never had to worry about earning their love. He could speak with confidence about the blessings of domestic society because he believed its love was eternal. As he told Maria, "The circle of our nearest connections is the only one in which a faithful and lasting affection can be found, one which will adhere to us under all changes and chances." For women, however, love was contingent; it had to be earned. "Be good and industrious," he told Martha when she was fifteen, "and you shall be what I most love in the world."[92]

The letters that Jefferson wrote later, when he was in Philadelphia or New York or Washington, attending to his nation's affairs, with their affectionate closings and their protestations of never-ceasing love more than implied that his daughters had met his expectations. It should not be surprising that they took him at his word when he said that he despised the rancor of politics and longed for the harmony of home. That was another way of saying that he loved them best. How painful it must have been for Martha, then, in the summer of 1800 when her father returned to Monticello for one of his long-anticipated visits, and she could barely spend "one sociable minute" with him for the crowds of people who came in his pursuit. So distressed was Martha that it took her a full two months before she could write. She complained that her father was "allways in a crowd, taken from every useful and pleasing duty to be worried with a multiplicity of disagreeable ones which the entertaining of such crowds of company subjects one to in the country." It was worse for her than if he had been in Philadelphia, "for at least I should have enjoyed in anticipation those pleasures which we were deprived of by the concourse of strangers which continually crowded the house when you were with us."[93] If, as her father told her, it was only the duties of home that were useful and pleasing, why was he entertaining this disagreeable crowd?

Jefferson answered the letter immediately. He assured Martha, "Nobody can ever have felt so severely as myself the prostration of family society from the circumstance you mention." It was more painful for him than it could have been for her. "Worn down here with pursuits in which I take no delight, surrounded by enemies and spies, catching and perverting every word which falls from my lips or flows from my pen, and inventing where facts fail them, I pant for that society where all is peace and harmony, where we love and are loved by every object we see." No, she had not misunderstood him; yes, he would prefer to be at home. "But there is no remedy." As a public figure, however, he had to bring at least part of the public home. Customs were changing, however, and before long, perhaps, the public might intrude only during the day, leaving the family "to tranquility in the evening." Jefferson concluded by asking his daughter to look on the brighter side and "to consider that these visits are evidences of the general esteem which we have been able [sic] all our lives trying to merit."[94] But it was, of course, Jefferson, and not his daughter, that these crowds of strangers were coming to see, just as it was Jefferson who was the object of their esteem.

Jefferson was, after all, a public man, and his aspiration was to serve the public in a way that would win him, if not fame, at least esteem. That is the hidden text of all of his letters. The complaints about enemies and spies notwithstanding, Jefferson was not about to leave public life. Even when he retired from government service, the crowds would still come to his home.[95] And he enjoyed the public, but he wanted it on his own terms. When he became president, he implored his daughters to come visit. Maria was reluctant; she had lived in the country so long that she was fearful of the capital's more sophisticated milieu. Her father empathized. Between his retirement from Washington's Cabinet and his election as vice president, he too had "remained closely at home, saw none but those who came there, and at length became very sensible of the ill effect it had upon my mind, and of it's direct and irresistible tendency to render me unfit for society, and uneasy when necessarily engaged in it."[96] He had learned his lesson, and she should, too. Society was good.

In most of his letters home, Jefferson drew a stark contrast between the world of politics and home, but there was really a third realm, one that he always assumed but rarely discussed. "Domestic society" was but a smaller, more affectionate distillation of society at large, differing from it more in degree than kind. Indeed, contemporary political thought conceived the family as the smallest of the concentric circles of social organization to which a man belonged. As a man moved from his immediate family, through various degrees of his kin, he entered his neighborhood, and then society, and after that, the nation or government, beyond which extended the universe of mankind at large. Scottish moral philosophers such as Adam Smith believed that man was by nature affectionate and sympathetic; the sort of love that bound him to his family also knit him to everyone else.[97] This is what Jefferson also meant when he said that man was a social animal. Yet political life confounded Jefferson's expectations, or at least hopes, of a universalizing sympathy. It was out of this frustration that he turned back to his family, as well as to his friends. As much as he relied upon his friends, however, Jefferson never developed a vision of friendship that could compare to the one he crafted of the family. His hopes dashed at the political end of the social spectrum, he fell back upon the smallest and most comforting unit he knew, making of the family his model for social relations. Jefferson described the family so passionately that it is little wonder that his daughters thought their father considered it the only place where he could be happy.

Jefferson was no hypocrite; he loved his daughters dearly, and surely it was their love that sustained him in his darkest days. But he also shaped his family—and indeed, the idea of the family—to meet his needs. It was the family that made a modern politics possible, by divesting it of the emotional intensity that led all too often to violence and by giving men alternate sources of identity. On his deathbed, according to Jeff Randolph, his grandfather was still thinking about the rancor of politics. "In speaking of the calumnies which his enemies had uttered against his public and private character with such unmitigated and untiring bitterness, he said that he had not considered them as abusing him; they had never known *him*. They had created an imaginary being clothed with odious attributes, to whom they had given his name."[98] It was a man's family, not those he encountered in public life, who knew who he really was.

VII

We have suggested that the requirements of modern politics would define and erect a wall between itself and the family, but that is not to imply that the family occupied a small or inconsequential space. The family, instead, was the prototype of society, the vast domain where men and women met and mingled and behaved with virtue, good humor, and self-restraint. For the wall that protected the family encompassed society, as well; it was the world of politics—and perhaps that of business—that was isolated by this fictive wall. Anywhere that women went, affection might prevail. Responding to a female friend who had congratulated him on his election to the presidency, Jefferson replied, "The post is not enviable, as it affords little exercise for the social affections. There is something within us which makes us wish to have things conducted in our own way and which we generally fancy to be in patriotism. This ambition is gratified by such a position. But the heart would be happier enjoying the affections of a family fireside."[99] Jefferson had reinterpreted public virtue—patriotism—as ambition and will; it was the affections nurtured in the family that bound society together. These were the best affections of our nature, the fulfillment of the disposition that the Creator had implanted in mankind's breast.

Politics and governance were separate and distinct. But this was the arena in which Jefferson had made his mark, and this was where his legacy, he hoped, would be. He asked Madison to help preserve the blessings of self-government, not those of domestic society. The latter he entrusted to his family. And the wall between the two realms had been built so strong that it could not be breached; it was the wall, finally, that separated women from men. Half a year before his death, Jefferson commiserated with his granddaughter Ellen. She had married a Bostonian and moved north. The ship that was carrying her baggage had been lost, taking with it all of her letters and books. "And your life cut in two, as it were, and a new one to begin, without any records of the former." Moreover, a beautiful writing desk made by the talented slave carpenter John Hemings was also gone. It could never be replaced. Jefferson, however, offered a substitute "not claiming the same value from it's decorations, but from the part it has *borne* in history": the lap desk upon which he had written the Declaration of Independence. He surmised that such objects were beginning to "acquire a superstitious value because of their connection with particular persons" and events, and that in years to come, the desk might have a place in celebrations of the Fourth of July. With that purpose in mind, Jefferson entrusted his desk not to his granddaughter, but to her husband. "Mr. Coolidge must do for me the favor of accepting this. Its imaginary value will increase with the years, and if he lives to my age, or another half century, he may yet see it carried in the procession of our nation's birthday, as the relics of the saints are in those of the church."[100] Near death, Jefferson imagined himself a saint in his own religion. It was a faith that his female kin, too, had helped him create, but from whose rituals they were excluded.

NOTES

I would like to thank Norma Basch, Barry Bienstock, Rhys Isaac, James Oakes, and Peter Onuf.

1. Merrill D. Peterson, *Thomas Jefferson and the New Nation: A Biography* (New York, 1970), p. 988. See also *Malone*, VI, p. 499.

2. Feb. 17, 1826, *LofA*, p. 513.

3. TJ to Thomas Jefferson Randolph, Feb. 8, 1826, Edwin Morris Betts and James A. Bear, eds., *The Family Letters of Thomas Jefferson*, (Columbia, Mo., 1966), p. 470; *Malone*, VI, p. 511.

4. Undated autobiographical fragment, Ellen Wayles Coolidge Correspondence, Alderman Library, University of Virginia.

5. See, for example, Ellen Wayles Coolidge to TJ, Aug. 1, 1825; Francis Wayles Eppes to TJ, Feb. 23, 1826; and Thomas Jefferson Randolph to TJ, Feb. 3 [1826], Betts and Bear, *Family Letters*, pp. 454, 467, 471–72.

6. TJ to Mary (Maria) Jefferson Eppes (henceforth, before marriage, Mary Jefferson; after, MJE), April 11, 1801; TJ to Martha J. Randolph (henceforth, before marriage, Martha Jefferson; after, MJR), Nov. 7, 1803; MJR to TJ received July 1, 1798; MJR to TJ, Nov. 18, 1801; and MJE to TJ, July 2, 1802, in Betts and Bear, *Family Letters*, pp. 201, 249, 166, 213, 232. Martha Jefferson was born in 1772 and married Thomas Mann Randolph in 1790; she bore twelve children, of whom eleven survived to adulthood. Maria Jefferson was born in 1778 and married John Wayles Eppes in 1797; only one of her three children, Francis, survived to adulthood. Maria died in 1804 and Martha in 1836.

7. MJE to TJ, Nov. 18, 1801; MJR to TJ, April 16, 1802, and March 20, 1807, Betts and Bear, *Family Letters*, pp. 213, 223, and 303.

8. TJ to MJE, Feb. 7, 1799; TJ to MJR, Feb. 11, 1800; TJ to MJR, Nov. 23, 1807; TJ to MJE, Oct. 26, 1801, Betts and Bear, *Family Letters*, pp. 173–74, 184, 315, 210.

9. TJ to Mary Jefferson, draft, June 14, 1797, in Betts and Bear, *Family Letters*, p. 148. See, similarly, TJ to MJE, Jan. 1, 1799, p. 170.

10. For a summary of this debate see Jan Lewis, "Happiness," in Jack P. Greene and J. R. Pole, eds., *The Blackwell Encyclopedia of the American Revolution* (Cambridge, Mass., 1991), pp. 641–47.

11. See Jan Lewis, *The Pursuit of Happiness: Family and Values in Jefferson's Virginia* (New York, 1983). Consider also Ruth Bloch, "The Gendered Meanings of Virtue," *Signs*, 13 (1987), pp. 37–58.

12. TJ to Maria Jefferson, June 26, 1791, in Betts and Bear, *Family Letters*, p. 86. Jefferson's association of happiness with home was foreshadowed in the letter he wrote Chastellux on November 26, 1782. Before the death of his wife Martha several months earlier, Jefferson "had folded myself in the arms of retirement, & rested all prospects of future happiness on domestic and literary objects." *LofA*, p. 780.

13. Jefferson destroyed the letters he had exchanged with his wife Martha, who died in 1782. *Malone*, I, pp. 393–98.

14. TJ to MJR, Jan. 15, 1792, Betts and Bear, *Family Letters*, p. 93. *Malone*, II, pp. 431, 363–66.

15. TJ to Mary Jefferson, May 25, 1797, Betts and Bear, *Family Letters*, 145.

16. TJ to James Monroe, May 20, 1782, *LofA*, pp. 777, 779.

17. Hamilton thought that "private attachments" to the family could undermine loyalty to the republic and even lead to oligarchy if a man put the interests of his family ahead of those of the nation ("The Federalist No. 77," in *The Federalist*, ed. Jacob E. Cooke [Middletown, Ct, 1961], pp. 518–19). George Washington agreed. He told Hamilton that it was a blessing to the nation that he was childless: "The Divine Providence hath not seen fit that my blood should be transmitted or my name perpetuated by the endearing, though sometimes seducing, channel of immediate offspring. I have no child for whom I could wish to make a provision—no family to build in greatness upon my country's ruins" (Washington to Hamilton, Aug. 28, 1788, quoted in M. J. Heale, *The Presidential Quest: Candidates and Images in American Political Culture, 1787–1852* [New York, 1982], p. 14).

18. TJ to Monroe, pp. 777–78.

19. See Jay Fliegelman, *Prodigals and Pilgrims: The American Revolution Against Patriarchal Authority* (New York, 1982), especially pp. 9–29; Daniel Walker Howe, "The Political Psychology of *The Federalist*," *WMQ*, XLIV (1987), pp. 485–509; and Garry Wills, *Inventing America: Jefferson's Declaration of Independence* (Garden City, N.Y., 1978), especially part 4. Consider also Perry Miller, "The Rhetoric of Sensation," in *Errand into the Wilderness* (New York: 1956), pp. 166–83.

20. TJ to MJR, May 17, 1798; May 31, 1798, Betts and Bear, *Family Letters*, pp. 162, 161, 164.

21. TJ to MJR, June 8, 1797, Betts and Bear, *Family Letters*, p. 146.

22. TJ to MJR, Feb. 8, 1798, Ibid., p. 155.

23. TJ to MJR, Jan. 16, 1801, Ibid., p. 191.

24. TJ to MJE, Feb. 15, 1801, Ibid., p. 196.

25. TJ to MJR, Nov. 23, 1807, Ibid., p. 315.

26. See, for example, TJ to Thomas Jefferson Randolph, Feb. 8, 1826, Betts and Bear, *Family Letters*, p. 469.

27. TJ to MJR, June 8, 1797, Betts and Bear, *Family Letters*, p. 146. See, similarly, his letter to Maria, June 14, 1797.

28. TJ to Martha Jefferson, March 6, 1786, and March 28, 1787, Betts and Bear, *Family Letters*, pp. 30, 35.

29. Garry Wills, *Cincinnatus: George Washington and the Enlightenment* (Garden City, N.Y., 1984), p. 129; James Wilson, Law Lectures (1791), *The Works of James Wilson*, 2 vols., Robert Green McCloskey, ed. (Cambridge, Mass., 1967), I, p. 405. See also Douglass Adair, "Fame and the Founding Fathers," in *Fame and the Founding Fathers* (New York, 1974), pp. 3–26. See also Jack P. Greene, "Society, Ideology, and Politics: An Analysis of the Political Culture of Mid-Eighteenth-Century Virginia," in Richard M. Jellison, ed., *Society, Freedom, and Conscience: The Coming of the Revolution in Virginia, Massachusetts, and New York* (New York, 1976), pp. 32–34.

30. See, for example, Wills, *Cincinnatus*, chapters 7 and 8, and Gordon S. Wood, *The Radicalism of the American Revolution* (New York, 1992), pp. 205–10.

31. TJ to Dr. Walter Jones, Jan. 2, 1814, *LofA*, pp. 1318–19.

32. John R. Howe, "Republican Thought and Political Violence of the 1790's," *American Quarterly*, XIX (1967), pp. 149, 165; TJ to Edward Rutledge, June 24, 1797, *The Life and Writings of Thomas Jefferson*, Adrienne Koch and William Peden, eds. (New York, 1944), p. 544. Howe excerpts this letter somewhat differently. See also

Marshall Smelser, "The Federalist Period as an Age of Passion," *American Quarterly*, X (1958), 391–419.

33. Jack N. Rakove, "The Structure of Politics at the Accession of George Washington," in Richard Beeman, Stephen Botein, and Edward C. Carter II, eds., *Beyond Confederation: Origins of the Constitution and American National Identity* (Chapel Hill, N.C., 1987), pp. 261–94.

34. Jefferson to Thomas Jefferson Randolph, Feb. 8, 1826, Betts and Bear, *Family Letters*, p. 470.

35. Forrest McDonald, *Alexander Hamilton: A Biography* (New York, 1979), p. 20.

36. Charles Royster, *A Revolutionary People at War: The Continental Army and American Character, 1775–1783* (Chapel Hill, N.C., 1979), pp. 209–11.

37. McDonald, *Hamilton*, pp. 308–9.

38. Robert H. Wiebe, *The Opening of American Society: From the Adoption of the Constitution to the Eve of Disunion* (New York, 1984), p. 100; St. George Tucker, *Blackstone's Commentaries* (1803), pt. II, n. G, pp. 29–30, quoted in Leonard W. Levy, *Emergence of a Free Press* (New York, 1985), p. 327.

39. Wiebe, *Opening*, p. 103.

40. Alexander Hamilton, "Printed Version of 'The Reynolds Pamphlet,'" in Harold C. Syrett et al., eds., *The Papers of Alexander Hamilton*, 27 vols. (New York, 1961–1987), XXI, p. 258. The Reynolds affair is detailed on pp. 121–44, as well as in McDonald, *Hamilton*, pp. 227–30 and ff., and Broadus Mitchell, *Alexander Hamilton: The National Adventure* (New York, 1962), pp. 399–422. My account of this episode relies upon these works.

41. Quoted in Michael Durey, *"With the Hammer of Truth": James Thomson Callender and America's Early National Heroes* (Charlottesville, Va., 1990), p. 94.

42. [James Thomson Callender], *The History of the United States for 1796* (Philadelphia, 1797), p. 205. Callender made his original charges in a series of pamphlets that have not survived; he later published them in book form as *The History of the United States for 1796*. Hence, it is from the book, rather than the original publications, that subsequent histories have been written. Syrett et al., *Papers of Hamilton*, XXI, pp. 121–22.

43. James Thomson Callender, *Sketches of the History of America* (Philadelphia, 1798), p. 91.

44. "Reynolds Pamphlet," pp. 238–39.

45. "Reynolds Pamphlet," p. 239; "People v. Harry Croswell, New York Supreme Court, 1803–1804," in Julius Goebel, Jr., et al., eds., *The Law Practice of Alexander Hamilton*, 5 vols. (New York, 1964–1981), pp. 810, 809, 820.

46. "Reynolds Pamphlet," pp. 239, 251, 267. Hamilton charged that "jacobin newspapers and pamphlets" were "artfully calculated to hold up the opponents of the FACTION to the jealousy and distrust of the present generation and if possible, to transmit their names with dishonor to posterity" (p. 239). Hamilton places most of the blame for his affair on the seductive Mrs. Reynolds. In order to entice him, she presented herself as appealingly weak: affecting an "air of affliction," she had "appl[ied]" to his "humanity" with a tale of abuse and abandonment. But once the affair had commenced, Mrs. Reynolds became dangerously strong: "her conduct made it extremely difficult to disentangle myself. All the appearances of violent attachment, and of agonizing distress were played off with a most imposing art" (p. 252).

47. For a thorough account, see Syrett et al., *Papers of Hamilton*, XXI, pp. 133–38, 316–20; for the relevant correspondence, see pp. 146–346.

48. Mitchell, *Hamilton*, II, pp. 496–99; quotation on p. 496.

49. Wiebe, *Opening*, p. 101.

50. For a thorough description of the duel and the supporting documents, see *Papers of Hamilton*, XXVI, pp. 235–349. Burr is quoted on p. 236. Hamilton's letter to Elizabeth Hamilton [July 4, 1804] is on p. 293. See also Hamilton's "Statement on the Impending Duel with Aaron Burr," [June 28–July 10, 1804], pp. 278–80. Among the reasons not to duel were: "My wife and Children are extremely dear to me, and my life is of the utmost importance to them, in various views." Nonetheless, he had to accept Burr's challenge. "To those, who with me abhorring the practice of Duelling may think that I ought on no account to have added to the number of bad examples—I answer that my *relative* situation, as well in public as in private aspects, enforcing all the considerations which constitute what men of the world denominate honor, impressed on me . . . a peculiar necessity not to decline the call. The ability to be in future useful, whether in resisting mischief or effecting good, in those crises of our public affairs, which seem likely to happen, would probably be inseparable from a conformity with public prejudice in this particular."

51. "Notes on the Reynolds Affair," Dec. 17, 1792, *Boyd*, XXIV, p. 75. See also *Papers of Hamilton*, XXI, p. 136. Michael Durey has recently suggested that it might have been Jefferson who gave Callender the documents that he printed in his exposé of Hamilton. After he, Venable, and Muhlenberg had interviewed Hamilton in December 1792, Monroe had kept the originals, which he later claimed to have sent to a friend, whom Durey claims was Jefferson. (Durey, *Hammer of Truth*, pp. 98–101.) The evidence is circumstantial and inconclusive. Most historians have believed that Callender probably got the documents from John Beckley, the Republican Clerk of the House, to whom Monroe had passed on the originals for subscribing. Whether or not Jefferson saw the documents before Callender published them, it is evident that copies of them, at least, and reports of their contents were well known in Republican circles.

52. "The Anas," Feb. 4, 1818, in *LofA*, p. 671. My interpretation follows that of *Malone*, IV, p. 431.

53. For an account of Callender's career, see Durey, *Hammer of Truth*, esp. chs. 6 and 7; and Fawn M. Brodie, *Thomas Jefferson: An Intimate History* (New York, 1974), ch. 23.

54. Richmond *Recorder*, Sept. 1, 1802, quoted in Durey, *Hammer of Truth*, p. 158. I wrote these lines before Annette Gordon-Reed published her book, *Thomas Jefferson and Sally Hemings: An American Controversy* (Charlottesville: University Press of Virginia, 1997) and before Dr. Eugene Foster performed a D.N.A. test on Jefferson and Hemings descendants. It now seems almost certain that Jefferson was the father of Sally Hemings's children. For my current thoughts on this subject, see Jan Lewis, "The White Jeffersons," in Jan Ellen Lewis and Peter S. Onuf, eds., *Sally Hemings and Thomas Jefferson: History, Memory, and Civic Culture* (Charlottesville: University Press of Virginia, 1999), 127–60.

55. Callender, *History of the United States for 1796*, p. 205.

56. Richmond *Recorder*, Sept. 1, 1802, quoted in Durey, *Hammer of Truth*, p. 158.

57. Reprinted in the Richmond *Recorder*, Nov. 3, 1802, quoted in Brodie, *Intimate History*, p. 353.

58. "From Callender's Recorder," in *Boston Gazette*, Nov. 11, 1802; "From the Boston Gazette," *New-York Evening Post*, Dec. 8, 1802.

59. *The Defence of Young and Minns, Printers to the State, Before the Committee of the House of Representatives* (Boston, 1805), preface.

60. Richmond *Recorder*, Feb. 2, 1803, quoted in Durey, *Hammer of Truth*, p. 163.

61. In 1805 the *New-England Palladium* pulled these charges together in an article entitled "The Monarchy of Federalism" (Jan. 18, 1805). The focus of the article was Jefferson's public character (he was described as "a patriot regardless of his country's welfare, and entirely devoted to raize himself and his partizans upon the nation's ruin"); the editors assumed without explaining the relevance of the Sally Hemings and Betsey Walker stories. For a summary, see *Malone*, IV, pp. 206–35.

62. *Richmond Examiner*, Oct. 2, 1802; Nov. 6, 1802; and Sept. 22, 1802. Republican suspicions about Marshall are discussed in Durey, *Hammer of Truth*, p. 161. For the allegations against Callender, see *Richmond Examiner*, Sept. 22, 1802, and Oct. 2, 1802, and Durey, *Hammer of Truth*, 161–62. The basis for this slur against Pinckney is not entirely clear. Since 1799, allegations had been circulating that, while serving as emissaries to France, he and Marshall had been intimate with a French woman, who bore the already-married Pinckney a child and followed him back to South Carolina, where either Pinckney and Marshall were supporting her or she had been cast off. It is not clear, however, how this story might have been construed as a reflection upon Pinckney's masculinity, unless the mere association with France and South Carolina (where he enjoyed "the Atlantic luxuries of a southern climate") somehow feminized him. The insinuation might have been that as Hamilton's puppet, Pinckney was, like a woman, weak. For the allegations against Pinckney, see Marvin R. Zahniser, *Charles Cotesworth Pinckney: Founding Father* (Chapel Hill, N.C., 1967), pp. 175–76, 208–9, 239–41.

63. *Richmond Examiner*, Sept. 25, 1802; *Boston Gazette*, Dec. 2, 1802.

64. The literature on this topic is vast. One might begin with Fliegelman, *Prodigals and Pilgrims*; Melvin Yazawa, *From Colonies to Commonwealth: Familial Ideology and the Beginnings of the American Republic* (Baltimore, Md., 1985); Jan Lewis, "The Republican Wife: Virtue and Seduction in the Early Republic," *WMQ*, XLIV (1987), pp. 689–721; Lewis, *Pursuit of Happiness*. Changes in the American family are summarized in Steven Mintz and Susan Kellogg, *Domestic Revolutions: A Social History of American Family Life* (New York, 1988), chs. 2 and 3.

65. Richmond *Recorder*, Sept. 29, 1802, quoted in Brodie, *Intimate History*, p. 352; *Richmond Examiner*, Sept. 25, 1802. This vision of Thomas Jefferson's family life was not entirely a creation of the political press; it was the way that his family saw it too. Half a century later, Jefferson's granddaughter would also use it to rebut Callender's charges: "Some of the children earnestly reported to be Mr. Jefferson's were about the age of his own grandchildren. Of course he must have been carrying on his intrigues in the midst of his own grandchildren. . . . His apartment had no private entrance not perfectly accessible and visible to all the household. . . . But I put it to any fair mind to decide if a man so admirable in his domestic character as Mr. Jefferson . . . would be likely to rear a race of half-breeds under their eyes and carry on his low amours in the circle of his family." (Ellen Wayles Coolidge to Joseph Coolidge, Jr., Oct. 24, 1858, Ellen Wayles Coolidge Collection, Alderman Library, University of Virginia).

66. *Defence of Young and Minns*, p. 50.

67. TJ to MJE, Oct. 26, 1801, Betts and Bear, *Family Letters*, p. 210.

68. *Boston Gazette*, Oct. 21, 1802; *Defense of Young and Minns*, p. 53; *Richmond Examiner*, June 25, 1803, and July 2, 1803. For Lee's role in the Walker affair, see Charles Royster, *Light-Horse Harry Lee and the Legacy of the American Revolution* (New York, 1981), pp. 208–9. See, similarly, *New-York Evening Post*, Dec. 8, 1802.

69. TJ to Robert Smith, July 5, 1805, in Brodie, *Intimate History*, p. 375; TJ to MJR, April 23, 1803, Betts and Bear, *Family Letters*, pp. 243–44.

70. TJ to Thomas McKean, Feb. 19, 1803, in Ford, IX, pp. 218–19 (incorrectly cited as IX, pp. 451–52 in Levy, *Free Press*, p. 341); Levy, *Free Press*, ch. X. For Jefferson's views on freedom of the press see also Frank L. Mott, *Jefferson and the Press* (Baton Rouge, La., 1943), and Levy, *Jefferson and Civil Liberties: The Darker Side* (New York, 1973), ch. 3. For freedom of the press in Virginia see Steven H. Hochman, "On the Liberty of the Press in Virginia: From Essay to Bludgeon, 1798–1803," *VMHB*, 84 (1976), pp. 431–45.

71. TJ to McKean, Feb. 19, 1803, Ford, IX, p. 218; Jefferson to Wilson Cary Nicholas, June 13, 1809, Ford, IX, pp. 253–54.

72. *Malone*, V, p. 624; TJ to Thomas Jefferson Randolph, Nov. 24, 1808, in Betts and Bear, *Family Letters*, pp. 362–65. This and the following paragraphs are derived from this letter. See, similarly, Jefferson's letter to his other grandson, Francis Wayles Eppes (May 21, 1816, p. 415): "Above all things, and at all times, practice yourself in good humor. This, of all human qualities, is the most amiable and endearing to society." See, similarly, TJ to Thomas Jefferson Randolph, Dec. 7, 1808, p. 369, and TJ to Charles L. Bankhead, Nov. 26, 1808, *L&B*, XVIII, pp. 253–54.

73. TJ to Thomas Law, June 13, 1814, *LofA*, p. 1337.

74. Ibid.

75. TJ to John Randolph, Dec. 1, 1803, Ford, VIII, pp. 281–82.

76. *Malone*, V, pp. 127–32; Peterson, *Jefferson*, pp. 839–40. For a different interpretation see William Cabell Bruce, *John Randolph of Roanoke, 1773–1833* (New York, 1922), I, pp. 261–65. See also Henry S. Randall, *The Life of Thomas Jefferson* (New York, 1858), pp. 164–67.

77. TJ to James Ogilvie, *L&B*, XVIII, pp. 247–48; TJ to Thomas Mann Randolph, July 13, 1806, Ford, VIII, pp. 459–60.

78. Ibid., p. 459.

79. Wiebe, *Opening*, pp. 327–32. Until that time, however, any dispute between gentlemen risked becoming the occasion for a duel. Although the absolute number of duels fought may have remained relatively small, the number of challenges must have been much greater, and the presence in politics of volatile men such as John Randolph of Roanoke ensured that any debate could easily be interpreted as a slur upon one's personal honor. See *Jeffersonian Legacies*, ed. Peter S. Onuf (Charlottesville, Va., 1993), p. 186. Consider also the accounts of duels printed in the *Richmond Examiner* during the fall of 1803.

80. TJ to Thomas Jefferson Randolph, Feb. 8, 1826, Betts and Bear, *Family Letters*, p. 470.

81. Norma Basch, "Marriage, Morals, and Politics in the Election of 1828," paper presented to the American Studies Association, Anaheim, California, October 1992. I am indebted to Professor Basch for letting me see the expanded version of her paper and for her invaluable insights into the ways in which gender figured in early American politics.

82. Bloch, "Gendered Meanings"; Richard L. McCormick, "Scandal and Reform: A Framework for the Study of Political Corruption in the Nineteenth-Century United States and a Case Study of the 1820s," paper presented to the Shelby Cullum Davis Center for Historical Studies, Princeton University, 1982; Robert V. Remini, *Andrew Jackson and the Course of American Freedom, 1822–1832*, (New York, 1981), vol. II, esp. ch. 2; Rubil Morales, "The Cloudy Medium of Language," M.A. thesis, Rutgers University-Newark, 1992.

83. TJ to Francis Wayles Eppes, May 21, 1816, Betts and Bear, *Family Letters*, p. 415. For similar letters to female kin see TJ to Mary Jefferson, April 11, 1790, p. 52; and TJ to Ellen Wayles Randolph, Nov. 27, 1801, p. 214.

84. For Jefferson's view on proper gender roles, see TJ to Governor William H. Harrison, Feb. 27, 1803, *LofA*, pp. 1117–19; "To the Brothers of the Choctaw Nation," Dec. 17, 1803, pp. 559–60; "Travel Journals," pp. 651–52.

85. Lewis, "Republican Wife." This is not to say, however, that all of Jefferson's attitudes about women and marriage were republican. Jefferson retained a streak of misogyny that was characteristic of an earlier age. See Kenneth A. Lockridge, *On the Sources of Patriarchal Rage: The Commonplace Books of William Byrd and Thomas Jefferson and the Gendering of Power in the Eighteenth Century* (New York, 1992).

86. TJ to MJR, April 4, 1790, Betts and Bear, *Family Letters*, p. 51. Jefferson also instructed Martha that she must now put her husband ahead even of him; this advice, however, she was not able to follow. TJ to MJE, Jan. 7, 1798, pp. 151–52.

87. TJ to MJR, April 28, 1793, Betts and Bear, *Family Letters*, p. 116. Thomas Mann Randolph's unmarried sister, Nancy, had been accused of bearing her brother-in-law Richard Randolph's baby; Richard Randolph was tried and acquitted of the murder of the baby, whose body had never been found, although slaves had reported seeing both it and blood stains at the house where Richard and his wife Judith and her sister Nancy had been staying. Richard Randolph was the brother of John Randolph of Roanoke, and it is possible that his animosity to Nancy and her family exacerbated the political tensions that would grow between him and Jefferson. For a full account of the "Scandal at Bizarre," see Bruce, *John Randolph*, I, pp. 107–23, II, pp. 273–77.

88. TJ to MJR, April 28, 1793, Betts and Bear, *Family Letters*, p. 60.

89. MJR to TJ, May 16, 1793, Betts and Bear, *Family Letters*, p. 118.

90. TJ to MJR, June 22, 1792, Betts and Bear, *Family Letters*, p. 102.

91. TJ to MJR, July 17, 1790; TJ to MJE, February 12, 1800, Betts and Bear, *Family Letters*, pp. 61, 186. See, similarly, TJ to Mary Jefferson, May 30, 1791: "To see you in short place your felicity in acquiring the love of those among whom you live, and without which no body can ever be happy" (p. 84).

92. TJ to Mary Jefferson, Jan. 1, 1799; TJ to MJE, May 21, 1787, Betts and Bear, *Family Letters*, pp. 170, 41–42. See, similarly, Nov. 28, 1783; Sept. 20, 1785; pp. 20, 29.

93. MJR to TJ, Jan. 31, 1801, Betts and Bear, *Family Letters*, p. 192.

94. TJ to MJR, Feb. 5, 1801, Betts and Bear, *Family Letters*, p. 195. As long as he lived, strangers would feel free to visit Jefferson at home; Martha never reconciled herself to this situation. See MJR to Ellen W. Coolidge, Sept. 18, 1825, Coolidge Collection.

95. MJR to Ellen W. Coolidge, Sept. 25, 1825; Ellen W. Coolidge to Henry Randall, 1856, in Sarah N. Randolph, *The Domestic Life of Thomas Jefferson* (1871; reprint, Charlottesville, Va., 1978), pp. 344–45.

96. TJ to MJE, March 3, 1802, p. 218.

97. See n. 19 above; see also Adam Smith, *The Theory of Moral Sentiments*, D. D. Raphael and A. L. Macfie, eds., (Indianapolis, Ind., 1982). In the *Notes on Virginia* Jefferson repeated the Comte de Buffon's charge that because native Americans did not love their women, they did not love their fellow men: "Il ne faut pas aller chercher plus loin la cause de la vie dispersée des sauvages & de leur éloignement pour la société: la plus précieuse étincelle du feu de la nature leur a été refusée; ils manquent d'ardeur pour leur femelle, et par consequent d'amour pour leur semblables." In defending native Americans, Jefferson implicitly accepted the Comte's sociology: "he is affectionate to his children. . . . His affections comprehend his other connections, weakening, as with us, from circle to circle, as they recede from the center." *LofA*, pp. 183–85. Also see Rhys Isaac, "The First Monticello," *Jeffersonian Legacies*, p. 100.

98. Randolph, *Domestic Life*, p. 369.

99. TJ to Catharine Church, March 27, 1801, *L&B*, XVIII, pp. 240–41.

100. TJ to Ellen Wayles Coolidge, Nov. 14, 1825, Betts and Bear, *Family Letters*, pp. 461–62.

EXPANDED CITATIONS

Boyd   Julian P. Boyd et al., eds., *The Papers of Thomas Jefferson*, 28 vols. to date (Princeton, N.J., 1950–)

Ford   Paul Leicester Ford, ed., *The Works of Thomas Jefferson*, 12 vols., Federal Edition (New York, 1904–5)

L&B   Andrew A. Lipscomb and Albert Ellery Bergh, eds., *The Writings of Thomas Jefferson*, 20 vols. (Washinton, D.C., 1903–4)

LofA   Thomas Jefferson, *Writings*, ed. Merrill D. Peterson, Library of America (New York, 1984)

Malone   Dumas Malone, *Jefferson and His Time* (Boston, 1948–81)

VMHB   *Virginia Magazine of History and Biography*

WMQ   *William and Mary Quarterly*, 3d ser.

DEBORAH A. LEE AND WARREN R. HOFSTRA

Race, Memory, and the Death of Robert Berkeley: "A Murder . . . of . . . Horrible and Savage Barbarity"

* * * * * * * * *I*N THE SPRING OF 1818, THREE SLAVES LURED their owner, Robert Berkeley of Frederick County, Virginia, into a cabin on his plantation. What happened there created sensational news throughout Virginia, and its impact has resonated across Virginia history to the present day. The story appeared in a thick local history of the county published in 1909; was recalled by descendants of Berkeley and of neighboring planters in the 1920s, 1930s, and 1940s; surfaced as a ghost story in the 1950s; and was remembered and retold by local residents as recently as 1997.

"Berkeley's own community," Lee and Hofstra point out, "wrestled fearfully with the social contradictions of slavery and race relations in an age still steeped in the republican optimism of a revolutionary generation and caught up in the heady idealism of Christian perfectionism." Those who tried to make sense of Berkeley's murder in the weeks following the capture, trial, and execution of Sarah, Randolph, and London, the perpetrators of the crime, recognized the incompatibility of slavery and their public ideals. They could not, however, confront the reasons behind the crime for fear of exposing their inconsistency in a painfully direct fashion. "The slaves could have no motive," Lee and Hofstra argue, for if the motivations of the slaves were exposed, and their humanity was thus presumed, "slavery itself would be indicted."

As the story passed from generation to generation, however, its meaning changed. "In the evolution of a society's collective memory," Lee and Hofstra write, "traumatic events are commonly distorted to conform to changing social imperatives." Storytellers working within the assumptions of Jim Crow Virginia told the story differently, emphasizing white decisiveness and power, the high character of Berkeley himself, and the barbarity of the slaves. Such a rendering of the narrative fit well with the version of Virginia's history told by proponents of the "Lost Cause," as described by Fred Arthur Bailey in this collection, and was attractive likewise to adherents to the genetic theories of eugenics, discussed by Gregory

Michael Dorr. Only the versions of the story told in the aftermath of the civil rights movement acknowledged the moral agency of the black men and women who were its central actors. * * * * * * * *

* * * * * * * *

ONE SPRING EVENING IN MAY 1818 DR. ROBERT BERKELEY OF Frederick County, Virginia, was bludgeoned to death by the people he held as slaves. These men and women then stuffed his body into a fireplace, kindled a fire, and reduced him to ashes and a small pile of bones. This violent act sent shock waves across the land, but in subsequent investigations, manhunts, trials, and executions no motives ever made public explained the actions of the accused. So deeply, however, did these actions penetrate into the conscience of the whole community that people in Frederick and surrounding counties today still recall stories about the Berkeley murder.

The murder itself exposed the two interdependent worlds of Berkeley's community—one white and one black—and the tensions between them. The nature of those tensions changed during the course of the nineteenth century. And so did collective memories of what happened to Robert Berkeley as whites struggled to regain hegemony over blacks after emancipation through new and virulent forms of racism; through violence, intimidation, and Jim Crow segregation in the law; and through the ideology of the Lost Cause, which like slavery had the effect of stripping blacks of personality, history, and legitimate motives for their actions. In the twentieth century other accounts of Berkeley's murder surfaced. Just as blacks struggled to reclaim dominion over their own lives in the course of the civil rights movement, so a motive for the murder emerged in the regional folklore for the first time, giving authenticity, if not legitimacy, to what enslaved men and women did to Robert Berkeley.

Until his death, Robert Berkeley did little to attract any particular attention or historical notice and lived a life exemplifying the expectations of his class. He was born in 1776 at Airwell in Hanover County to a prominent Virginia family. His parents were Nelson Berkeley and Elizabeth Wormeley Carter. A family historian described him as "a gentle, rather ineffectual personality." Following in an older brother's footsteps, he attended the University of Edinburgh but dropped out for lack of funds before he could earn a degree. He returned to the United States and completed medical studies at the University of Pennsylvania. In 1804 he wrote to Robert Carter of his intention to marry Carter's youngest daughter, Julia. Robert Carter replied coolly, "As a Father of a Family I never recommend either Male or Female in the line of marriage, and my married Issue chose for themselves." Although wellborn, Berkeley possessed little personal wealth at the time of his marriage. Julia, on the other hand, owned more than seventeen hundred acres on the Shenandoah River in Frederick County that had been given to her by her father. Like her older sisters, she also received a dowry of five hundred acres of land, ten slaves, and livestock.[1]

Robert Berkeley moved quickly after his marriage to maximize personal control over his wife's property. First he persuaded Julia to assign him her father's land. Skirting legal protections for women's property in marriage, Berkeley had his wife convey her assets initially to a third party and only subsequently to him. When Julia inherited more land upon the death of her grandparents, the wealthy Benjamin and Ann Tasker of Baltimore, Robert earned the enmity of Julia's brother and advisor, George Carter of Oatlands, by suing him in federal court for interest on the land. Berkeley's neighbors resented his self-interestedness as well and objected to his 1807 petition to redirect a public road through his property. As tithables required to maintain the road, they insisted that it was in "no way calculated for public utility" and that Berkeley, acting "with a view wholly for . . . [his] private advantage," was imposing "an unecesary [sic] burden upon the neighbourhood."[2]

Between 1809 and 1813 Robert Berkeley built a brick house, Rock Hill, on a high bluff overlooking a bend in the Shenandoah River. Its four bays enclosed an unusual central octagonal hall surrounded by four rooms on each of three floors including the basement. Every room had a fireplace and a door to the central hall. An addition to the dwelling included a second staircase. But the house was not sound, according to George Carter, because the addition was "put up in the slightest manner and . . . must fall down shortly." Two detached offices were also in sorry condition. An 1818 inspection revealed that, due to inferior mortaring, addition and offices were "in a rapid state of decay" and could not "stand more than a year or two." Carter observed that "the bricks look well to a superficial observer, but the Bricklayers work is generally very badly executed."[3]

In 1818 Robert and Julia Berkeley appeared contented and prosperous. Robert was forty-two years old, Julia thirty-five, and they were raising nine children after fourteen years of marriage. Robert served as a justice of the peace in Frederick County. The couple held thirty-seven slaves: some that Julia's father gave her, others that Robert purchased, and several more that Robert inherited from his father after the death of his mother in 1813. The Berkeleys employed an Irish overseer, John Robinson, and farmed mostly small grains such as wheat, corn, rye, and oats at Rock Hill.[4]

The gruesome events of Berkeley's murder occurred on the evening of Tuesday, May 12, when the entire family was at home. London, an eighteen- or nineteen-year-old slave whom Berkeley had inherited from his father, summoned him with important news—Randolph was back. London told Berkeley that two men had brought home the runaway slave, who had been missing for several weeks, and were holding him in a cabin. Berkeley, cautious enough to take his pistol with him as he accompanied London to the cabin, apparently never questioned why the men did not come to the house.[5]

Little is known about Randolph, but his actions attest to discontent with his lot in life. He was born a slave in central Virginia, sold at the age of nine or ten to a man in Frederick County, and then to Berkeley at twelve or thirteen. Running away was a common protest against slavery; so was passive resistance. Both were frequent at Rock Hill. Writing to Julia about the Rock Hill slaves, her brother George complained that "a more worthless and idle sett I never saw—Jacob now pretends that he has lost the use of one of his hands, and I believe they will all lose the use of their hands very shortly—as they will find that will keep them from work." Randolph was evidently not alone in his grievances.[6]

London had been sent to fetch Berkeley by another slave, Sarah. Both had full knowledge of what was intended. Like London, Sarah had descended to Berkeley from his father. When Berkeley entered the cabin, Randolph was indeed there waiting—club in hand. The "two men" were nowhere to be seen, but Sarah and Ralph, also a slave, were present as well. Berkeley quickly grabbed the club and demanded Randolph's intentions. With both hands Randolph seized Berkeley, who threatened "to take out his pistol and shoot him." The fugitive slave then tripped Berkeley, grabbed the club, and beat him repeatedly. Berkeley cried to the others for help, first to Sarah and then to Ralph, but neither slave intervened. The blows continued until Randolph presumed that his victim was dead. He stepped outside the cabin, but London soon reported that Berkeley was still groaning. Randolph offered London the club to finish the job. When London declined, Randolph delivered three more blows to Berkeley, and "the groaning ceased."[7]

Although the slaves later revealed that they had plotted the murder in advance, they had apparently not planned how to dispose of the corpse. Randolph "went to the kitchen to consult with" Ralph and fellow slave, Harry, about the matter. Sarah and three other Berkeley slaves, Robin, Barnaba, and Tom, joined in the consultation. Ralph suggested that they put Berkeley's body on a horse and leave him on the road to Winchester, an apparent victim of highway robbery. Alternatively they could hide the body in "a pond in the meadow." Harry proposed burning it.

Court testimony stated that the conspirators burned Berkeley's body because they decided it was the best way to "conceal" the evidence of their crime, but incineration may also have had another, deeper significance for them. Robin disapproved of the decision, stating, "It was too evil to burn him." Too evil? Many Christians believed that, unless the body had a proper burial, the dead could not rise with Jesus on the Day of Atonement. Widespread in Africa was the belief that appropriate funeral rites were necessary in order to usher the dead out of human affairs and into ancestral spirit worlds. In the absence of these rites, burning might ensure that Berkeley would be gone forever, unable to return in any form. Witches, moreover, had been burnt to exorcise evil and its perpetrators. Whether the conspirators knew this is unclear, but the Bible, with which they would have been familiar, was unequivocal on the association of evil with the fires of hell. However evil burning was regarded, Sarah clearly considered it fit punishment for Berkeley, exclaiming, "The Devil is dead and we will burn him!"[8]

The conspirators searched Berkeley's pockets, finding keys and papers that they dropped to the floor. His head was already on the hearth in the cabin where he had been slain, and Randolph with Robin's help pulled the body onto it. They then kindled a fire with coals that London retrieved from the other end of the cabin. Ralph observed that all three of the conspirators seemed "wicked pleased," but none more than Sarah. Randolph, London, and Barnaba assisted her in the slow, grisly task, bringing wood while Sarah fed the fire.[9]

Through the night, as the corpse burned, the conspirators made further plans. Near daylight one of them awakened the slave Fanny and told her of the murder. She came to the cabin and observed the nearly consumed body. They later buried the remaining bones in the clay floor at the corner of the cabin. Sarah kept Berkeley's keys. Randolph threatened that if any of the witnesses told of the crime, he would lay in wait and kill them in the same manner. He then disappeared into the countryside, becoming once more a runaway. It was still not daylight when Fanny returned to the kitchen and assumed her usual duties.

Julia, the children, and John Robinson, the overseer, were ignorant of the night's grisly proceedings. As day broke, the slaves were careful to act as though nothing had happened. They simply explained to Julia that Randolph had run off again pursued by her husband and the two men. Inconvenienced in her household duties by the missing keys but otherwise unconcerned, Julia went about her daily routine. As mistress of Rock Hill and mother of nine young children, there was much to do. Meanwhile, the large number of slaves aware of what had happened the preceding night exhibited remarkable solidarity and composure. For the time being, they commanded the situation.[10]

Even though Berkeley failed to return on Wednesday, his absence provoked little suspicion. Late in the evening John Robinson sent a boy to the manor house for a bag of straw. Robinson had last seen his employer on Tuesday during a visit to the house after planting corn for the day. The boy returned to Robinson, stating that Mrs. Berkeley wished to see the overseer early the next day. When Robinson called on her during the morning of Thursday, May 14, she informed him of her husband's sudden disappearance and the explanation she had been given. Her most immediate concern was that the keys to the household provisions were missing—presumably with her husband—and she asked Robinson to go to the nearby village of White Post for groceries.

Julia Berkeley was clearly a determined and independent woman, but much about her behavior remains inscrutable. According to her brother George, her "judgement is generally strong, and she thinks correctly on most questions." He felt, however, that she had made a crucial mistake in conveying her legacy to her husband. On his unexpected death without a will, Julia could expect only a dower share, a one-third life interest in her own property, under the intestate laws of Virginia. George Carter was infuriated. He handled many of his sister's affairs after the murder and deemed her state as a "forlorn beggar upon the bounty of the law" as "too humiliating indeed to think of." He cautioned another sister, Sophia, against conveying her property out of "Sheer love" to some "avaricious wretch" for his personal gain. Instead, he advised her to "keep it as the palladium of your Liberty" and to spurn the "whining, sordid, sycophant, in the character of the Lover." Although there is no evidence that Carter ever mentioned his brother-in-law directly, his profuse and indignant criticism of his sister's situation bespoke little regard for Berkeley. Nonetheless, Robert Berkeley had won the trust and affections of Julia Carter, and it is surprising that she was not more distressed by his sudden disappearance.[11]

Julia, her brother George, and their twelve surviving siblings had had a difficult and unusual childhood. Their father, Robert Carter, was alternately aloof and domineering. His wife, Frances Ann Tasker of Baltimore, although outwardly congenial, was often disabled by powerful fears of thunderstorms and of disease. Carter's political career began with appointment to the Virginia Council in the late 1750s, but he was a tortured soul who came to avoid public life and seek solace in evangelical religion, converting to the Baptist faith in 1778. Frances had periods of serious illness but bore many children, her last, Julia, in 1783. Carter noted then that his wife, although still cheerful, was an invalid. She, too, became a Baptist in 1786, and the couple sent their two youngest sons, John and George, ages fourteen and nine, to school in Providence, Rhode Island, where they would be removed from the influence of slavery. Frances died the next year, when Julia was only four years old. Doubtful of his ability as a parent, Carter sent his three youngest daughters to Baltimore for their education. Despite the death of their mother, Carter did not allow his young sons to return home from Rhode Island for three more years.[12]

Meanwhile, Robert Carter's curious personal and spiritual journey continued. While the Baptist church softened its antislavery position, Carter publicly supported general emancipation in Virginia. He explored mysticism, joined the Swedenborgian church, and in 1791 formulated a program for freeing his five hundred slaves, which continued through 1812, after his death. Carter's plan for gradual emancipation dramatically increased the free black population of Frederick County and influenced events surrounding his son-in-law's murder. Carter believed that "to retain them in Slavery is contrary to the true principals of Religion & Justice, & that therefore it was my duty to manumit them." Robert Carter also divested himself of most of his property, giving each of his surviving children twenty-five hundred acres of land. Although he had shielded them from the effects of slavery, all of his offspring, including Julia and George, became slaveholders, and the management of slaves proved difficult for them. As George wrote to his sister, "my dear Julia, rest assured, that if I know myself aright, I must know that I do not understand the management of slaves neither do I think you do, or that either of us ever will."[13]

Julia certainly failed to understand events at Rock Hill in the aftermath of the murder, and for a while the slaves' deception was complete. On the morning following the murder, Sarah went to the house on her usual business but with the household keys hidden in her pocket. She found Fanny in the cellar and told her to help look for Berkeley's money. Sarah's sister Thamon had said that he kept it in the sideboard in a black bag. Sarah unlocked the sideboard, and Fanny removed a small bag containing a large sum in bank notes. Taking the money, Sarah locked the sideboard and returned the keys to her pocket.

Despite the murder of their master and their newly acquired wealth, all of the slaves, except the runaway Randolph, remained at Rock Hill and went about their customary occupations. Not until four days later, on Saturday, May 16, was any alarm raised. A neighbor John Rust heard that Robert Berkeley had been missing since Tuesday. The circumstances, and perhaps his own experience, convinced Rust that all was not right. He, himself, was no stranger to interracial violence. A brand on his left hand was punishment for murdering his slave Jacob in 1799. In future years, the ambitious Rust became the owner of all the Berkeley property at Rock Hill and lived in the brick manor house. But four days after Berkeley's murder, Rust alarmed the neighbors and instructed them to meet there. He first informed Julia Berkeley of his apprehensions but then told her not to be alarmed—the neighbors would soon collect to make the search. When several men had gathered, they took London and Barnaba, tied them, and isolated them in separate cabins under guard.[14]

Overseer Robinson soon reported that London had confessed to murder. At that point, the youth was brought before two county magistrates who had arrived at Rock Hill to aid the investigation. "Well London I understand you have told the truth once," one of them said, "let us hear you tell it again." London repeated his confession and further stated that the plot had been agreed upon the preceding Friday night and that when he had gone to fetch his master, he knew full well "the object was to kill him." He also told his examiners that Berkeley's bones were buried in the clay pit at the end of the cabin.[15]

A search revealed the scant remains of Robert Berkeley, and his brass buttons were found among the ashes in the fireplace. Sarah, Robin, Ralph, Thomas, and Harry were arrested, bound, and held separately for questioning. All initially denied any knowledge of the murder but later confessed before magistrates reportedly without "threats, promises or persuasions" upon hearing that the plot had been disclosed by others. Sarah would not give a full confession. After she heard that London broke down, she stated that he had hit Berkeley too. She said no more. Kept that night at the nearby mill of John Newman, a justice of the peace, Sarah made "some noise" and uttered "religious phrases," but her guard "could get nothing out of her, that he could understand." On the way to Winchester, the Frederick County seat, the next morning, someone again questioned her about the murder. She simply replied that "they all knew [about] it," except for her sister's husband, Tom. Meanwhile Randolph remained at large, much to the distress of the white community.[16]

Newspapers spread the alarm throughout the state, announcing "a murder, accompanied with circumstances of the most horrible and savage barbarity." Most accounts attributed the crime to robbery, but one Shenandoah Valley newspaper observed that Randolph, appearing "more savage than the rest" and fearful of the chastisement he would receive as a runaway, "thought this a good opportunity of accomplishing his nefarious views" and "hellish scheme." The press warned that the "principal perpetrator" was still at large but assured its readers that "diligent pursuit is . . . pressing upon him." A "liberal reward" was offered for his capture, but the editor of the Alexandria *Gazette* "hoped that other motives will induce every member of the community to be on the alert in apprehending the murderous monster, and bri[n]g him to that punishment his crime so richly merits." Nine days after the murder, on Thursday, May 21, Randolph was finally sighted at a farm near Winchester.[17]

On May 20, in this atmosphere of anxiety and turmoil, Episcopal clergy from throughout Virginia gathered in Winchester for their annual convention. While important for conducting church business, these meetings also functioned as "genteel revivals" for lay people, and large crowds attended. William Meade, a popular young Frederick County rector who was leading the evangelical renewal of the Episcopal Church in Virginia, delivered the introductory sermon. He was a slaveholder but one so deeply troubled by the peculiar institution that he later freed his own slaves, worked to reform plantation society, and promoted gradual emancipation. Throughout his ministry he reached out to people of color and stressed that all souls were equal in the sight of God.[18]

Although he did not speak of the murder itself, the issues of the day were clearly on his mind as he opened the proceedings. He began by asking a special blessing for "the church in this place and the vicinity thereof." He spoke at length of the revival of the church, the good works of its members, and his hopes for its future. But his peroration dealt with relationships between masters and slaves. Meade claimed that, just as clergymen assume a larger responsibility to God for the spiritual health of their congregations, so, too, do slaveholders bear an added duty for their own households, which included bondsmen and bondswomen. The spiritual instruction of slaves was an obligation "which should press heavily upon the mind of every inhabitant of our state." Religious education, according to Meade, was not likely to produce insubordination, as many feared. "There are differences of color, and disparity of station among men, but the value of the soul is the same in all." He observed that Christians

> should make each plantation a little village, with its schoolhouse and its temple, its pupils and worshippers, its teachers and domestic priests. But even here, in this dark vale of sorrow, we have some cause for rejoicing. The spiritual, as well as temporal condition of this class of our fellow creatures is considerably ameliorated. The light of the sun of righteousness shines sweetly through many of the once darkened souls of the sable sons of Africa; a communion of soul often takes place between the master and his slave, and they both look forward with joy to the time, when soul shall meet soul in the still freer, sweeter, intercourse of Heaven.[19]

William Meade was making the best of the crisis. Within their immediate sphere of influence Christians should work to improve conditions and turn existing evil into future good. Social tensions that led to violence could be resolved in a true Christian community. While conditions of birth produced disparities in station, masters and slaves had mutual obligations. Masters, however, bore the final responsibility for the spiritual health of their households. Although an earthly necessity, social inequity—and the guilt that some Christians felt in the oppression of blacks—should encourage them to anticipate the end of time, when the true unity of souls would be accomplished. In the minds of evangelicals like Meade, sharing Christianity with slaves was an important duty and also the basis of communion between whites and blacks that presumably could have prevented the murder of Robert Berkeley. If the sin of slaveholding was the unthinkable explanation for Berkeley's slaying, then absolution would come with the redemption of both master and slave. About the convention the local newspaper reported that "the public have been gratified, and we trust edified, by powerful displays of pious eloquence; on no occasion perhaps have people evinced more serious attention to divine truths, than on the present; happy indeed will it be if their impression shall prove lasting!"[20]

For some, "divine truths" must have hit home the following day, May 21, when "as tremendous a hail-storm as has perhaps ever been experienced" shook the community. "The storm lasted from five to ten minutes and in less than that time the streets assumed a perfectly white appearance," according to newspaper accounts. "The hail was generally from one inch to an inch and an half diameter; windows were broken, limbs of trees were broken off, and many garden vegetables prostrated to the ground. It is feared that the growing crops have sustained a serious injury."[21]

Despite the storm Randolph was finally apprehended the following day and confined in the Winchester jail. Samuel Hackney, a local free black, aided in Randolph's capture and later received a ten-dollar reward from Berkeley's estate. Randolph had only $1.25 in his pocket. Most of the stolen money was retrieved elsewhere. Seven of the bank notes were found with Will, a slave on a neighboring farm, and four with Thomas Newman, also a free black. A farmworker known as Mr. Oliver located another eighty dollars in the cabin of Sarah's brother-in-law, Tom. But it was Samuel Hackney who uncovered the bulk of the stolen money, $972, in a black bag under the corner of Sarah's cabin. He then found the missing keys beneath a slab at Sarah's front door and received an additional twenty-dollar reward. But curiously, $2,873, the lion's share of the money presumably deposited by Berkeley in the sideboard at Rock Hill, was left there by the calculating slaves.[22]

The trials for the accused slaves began on Monday, May 25, in the old courthouse in Winchester. The venerable building, with its steeple and bell, stood at the east end of the courthouse square enclosed with a post-and-rail fence. "Black Betty," the whipping post, commanded the center of the yard; nearby stood two platforms with pillories. Beneath the projecting gable of the courthouse with its bull's-eye window, large stone steps led into the main entrance. The formal and dignified surroundings setting off the visible instruments of punishment reflected the power of white society whose laws they served. Inside, "nearly opposite the front door," stood the clerk's desk, raised about four feet above the floor. Daniel Lee was the clerk of court. Described by contemporaries as tall, black-eyed, and elegant, an able lawyer and masterful servant of the court, he sat straight and expressionless over his copious papers "kept . . . as if they were bank notes."[23]

On the north side of the building sat the hustings bench for the justices, thirty feet long and raised for a commanding view of the proceedings. Joseph Tidball was the only justice to sit for all sessions in the Berkeley murder trials. Justice John Newman had assisted in the apprehension of the accused, he had incarcerated the slave Sarah in his mill, and he would testify at the trial of Barnaba. Newman would later join fellow justices William Cook and James Davis, also a witness, and John Rust as court-appointed appraisers of the Berkeley estate. Sixteen other justices served during the various trials.[24] These men constituted the upper class of their society, and all but two of those for whom accounts exist held slaves. Their holdings ranged from one to twenty-seven slaves, with an average of nine. Each controlled more wealth than did four out of five other citizens in Frederick County. They lived in comfortable houses in Winchester or on farms in the longer-settled parts of the county. This elite, however, did not always enjoy the unspoken deference of the common people. On at least one occasion residents from the remote regions of the county complained that the justices represented only the wealthier areas and for twenty years had considered their own interests alone. To the accused slaves, however, these traits would have only served to impress upon them further the fearful intimidation of the law.[25]

Augustine C. Smith, a leading Frederick County attorney, served as counsel for the slaves. Widely respected as a scholar, Smith also served the community as teacher and preceptor at the Winchester Academy. His activities extended as well into another area bearing on what the murder of Robert Berkeley meant to his contemporaries. Smith was secretary of the Auxiliary Society of Frederick County for Colonizing the Free People of Colour.[26]

The Frederick County auxiliary was the first affiliate formed to support the efforts of the American Colonization Society, which was established in Washington, D.C., in December 1816. William Meade was one of the society's founders and served as its first manager. The Frederick auxiliary met initially in September 1817, eight months before Robert Berkeley's murder. Within a short time thirty-five subscribers had pledged far more money than had members of any other auxiliary—a sum of six thousand dollars including one hundred dollars from Berkeley himself. Also among the contributors were justices James Baker, James Davis, and David Meade.[27]

The founders of the American Colonization Society regarded their plan to transport free blacks from the United States to a new colony on the west coast of Africa as a benefit to all parties. The rapidly growing number of free blacks, so alarming to whites as possible insurgents against slavery or examples of freedom to the enslaved, would be siphoned off to Africa. There, it was hoped, they would enjoy true liberty, free of the prejudice that kept them in political, social, and economic bondage in the United States. Africa, members believed, would benefit from an infusion of Christianity, commerce, and western civilization. Many early supporters of colonization hoped that it would encourage manumissions and result in a gradual emancipation of slaves.[28]

The members of the Frederick County auxiliary were among the most vigorous of all supporters of colonization. Frederick County was not typical of Virginia plantation culture. Located west of the Blue Ridge in the lower or northern Shenandoah Valley, the county had been settled by a mixture of English planters and African slaves from Tidewater Virginia, Germans from Pennsylvania, Scots-Irish, and Quakers. Wheat, not tobacco, was the primary crop and underlay a market-town economy of diverse trades and services more characteristic of the free-labor North than the slave South. Throughout the eighteenth and into the nineteenth centuries, Anglo-American slaveholders were in a minority, and the population of free blacks was substantial. From 1790 to 1820 it increased dramatically from 3 to 12 percent of the black population.[29]

Julia Berkeley's father, Robert Carter, had himself made a significant contribution to the change in demographics and social tensions when he manumitted seventy-two slaves in Frederick County between 1800 and 1804. "It appears to me (witnessing the consequences) that a man has almost as good a right to set fire to his own building though his neighbors is to be destroyed by it, as to free his slaves," wrote one anxious Frederick County resident claiming to speak for the majority. "I have not heard a single instance among those you have freed meriting your liberality . . . by mixing with those in bondage . . . they disquiet their minds—aid them in procuring false and stupid certificates of their being Mr. Carter's free men—the consequence of which is they seek their fortunes, as they call it, some escape." Augustine Smith, writing on behalf of the Frederick County auxiliary, echoed these sentiments more than two decades later, not long after the murder of Robert Berkeley:

> The free negroes corrupt our slaves by urging them to plunder the community and affording a receptacle to the fruits of their depredations; by also inculcating ideas of freedom and independence, which must terminate in insurrection. Some individuals of this class, we readily admit, by their honesty and industry have surrounded themselves with many of the comforts of life; but, unfortunately, their example is not less dangerous than that of an emancipated vagabond. By witnessing the situation of his affluent brother, the slave contrasts it with his own, pants for liberty, becomes discontented and disobedient, and in order to move in the same sphere with the fraternity of freed-men, at the expence of his integrity mimics the dress and manners of fashionable life. From what has been urged, the expediency of removing this nuisance from the community is clearly inferable, both in relation to their interest and ours; and this end can only be attained by means of the colonizing Society.[30]

While the plan for colonization gathered little support among blacks, the literature of the auxiliary in Frederick County illustrated that whites were deeply troubled by the moral contradictions of slavery. Free blacks reminded not only slaves of freedom but also slave owners that they deprived slaves of that freedom. The organization unequivocally professed "that slavery is an evil no one can deny. All must desire to cure this disease or mitigate its ravages." Auxiliary members were keenly aware of the destructive effects that slavery had on the whole community. It stifled economic growth and debased both whites and blacks. The report quoted Jefferson's famous warning that the "whole commerce between master and slave is a perpetual exercise of the most boisterous passions; the most unremitting despotism on the one part, and degrading submissions on the other." Thus the auxiliary called for local members to "prepare the way for the gradual emancipation and colonization of our slaves." The report boldly proclaimed the equality of the races, citing for proof the Declaration of Independence, Roman philosophy, and the Bible: "God hath made of one blood all nations of men to dwell upon the face of the earth." It also quoted contemporary blacks who asked of those who considered slavery a blessing, "If their declarations be sincere, why not put themselves in our place?"[31]

Robert Berkeley was a member of the auxiliary, but he differed from many supporters in two important ways. First, he failed to perform what Meade described as the Christian duty to educate slaves in religion and scripture. Second, he bought and may have sold slaves, actions that many people in the community found objectionable especially when they broke up families. In 1818 Berkeley held three fewer slaves than he had two years earlier, and sales of some of those individuals could account for the large amount of cash in the sideboard as well as the deep enmity of the blacks at Rock Hill.[32]

These Frederick County evangelicals and colonizationists, many of whom sat on the county bench, understood, in Thomas Jefferson's famous phrase, that they had "the wolf by the ears." The murder of Robert Berkeley was a powerful demonstration to the people of Frederick County that they could neither hang on nor let go. They could expect neither to hold nor to free their slaves and at the same time secure the peace of society. The social tensions in the community that underlay the murder and the general alarm it raised reinforced the colonization auxiliary's argument for the transportation of freed people as the only way out of the dilemma. But few held out hope that this objective could be achieved in the foreseeable future. Fears in the present crisis permeated the auxiliary's concluding argument on the expediency of colonization, which again quoted Jefferson: "I tremble for my country when I reflect that God is just, and that his justice cannot sleep forever. The Deity knows no attribute that can take sides with us in such a contest."[33]

In view of the apprehensions of the community regarding blacks and its ambivalence toward slavery, the trials of the slaves accused in the murder of Robert Berkeley could hardly have been summary proceedings intended only to endorse executions. Whether or not they were inherently fair, the court procedures met every requirement of the law. In the antebellum

South, the code of paternalism required the strong to extend their largess and protection over the weak. Even if the outcome of the trials was foreordained, a strong defense, in this case provided by Augustine Smith, upheld the dignity of the judicial process and assuaged uneasy consciences.[34]

London was the first to stand before the bar when the trials began on May 25. Like each of the accused in turn, he pleaded "nowise thereof guilty." When first taken into custody, he was encouraged to tell all he knew with promise of leniency on account of his youth, but his cooperation with the law earned him no favors and his trial proceeded without any concessions. The trials of Barnaba, Sarah, and Robin followed the next day, Randolph's trial was scheduled for Monday, June 1, and the court continued those of Ralph, Harry, and Thomas to a session held on June 3. On that day Will was tried for "having received seven Bank notes from negro Randolph," and Thomas Newman, the free black, for accepting four of the stolen notes from Will.[35]

The atmosphere in town and county seemed portentous. "In addition to the murder, and other dispensations of Providence, which it has lately fallen to our lot to announce, it devolves upon us to record another visitation with which this place was afflicted," announced the Woodstock *Herald*. On May 31, the Sunday before Randolph's trial, the community was hit by another terrible storm, even more awesome and devastating than the one that had preceded his capture a week and a half earlier. This time, a violent rainstorm flooded the town of Winchester within a few hours. "The flood was awful and tremendous," the *Herald* reported, "the main street had the appearance of a river, the depth of water, in some parts of it, being sufficient to sail a boat of considerable burden."[36]

When Randolph's trial opened, John Rust testified that the accused admitted guilt upon his capture but claimed "he never should have done it, but that he was persuaded to it, by Negro Sarah." The full depth of Sarah's role in the murder remains a mystery, but her strong motivation to end Berkeley's life and her considerable influence over other slaves were apparent throughout the events of the slaying and the trials. In a later confession Randolph stated that the plot to kill Berkeley was formed in July of the previous year and that he became party to it in February 1818 when he returned to Rock Hill from another residence nearby. He remained determined to carry out the plan until he ran away three weeks before the fateful evening. But, according to the confession, hunger drove him back to Rock Hill. Berkeley met him at the cabin where Randolph "told him I wanted something to eat." Berkeley then "asked what I wanted with the stick I had in my hand—I told him it was my walking stick—he told me to give it to him, which I refused, and ondoing so he strove to wrest it from me, when I struck him; and before we gave over the struggle . . . I killed him, . . . through fear that if he got the better of me he would have killed me."[37]

Thus the court proceedings themselves were curiously mute on the issue of what actually motivated Berkeley's slaves to conspire and brutally murder him. Randolph's claim of self-defense was not part of his trial testimony. Adopted, perhaps, as self-justification in the face of imminent execution, it contradicted prior admissions of conspiracy. The jailer, moreover, deposed that Randolph "would not have done it, had it not been for those negroes who were brought from the lower Country." The accused confessed to committing robbery, but no evidence substantiated theft as a possible incentive for murder. In their confessions, Randolph and London expressly denied that they killed Berkeley for his money, although Randolph may have taken a small sum off the body. Fanny testified that she had not heard Randolph make any mention of money, and he in fact had fled before the larceny at the sideboard. Sarah's leadership of the conspiracy and murder suggests that she may have been the victim of sexual exploitation or suffered the severance of an important kinship tie, both leading causes of antagonism between masters and slaves. Retaliation for physical or psychological cruelty and the desire to prevent further mistreatment often motivated blacks to assault whites. Blacks also killed whites out of fear of exile to hard labor and banishment from kin on Deep South cotton or sugar plantations, a common punishment imposed by masters on recalcitrant slaves.[38]

As a returning runaway, Randolph could have been motivated by fear of being sold. George Carter expressed a view that his brother-in-law might have shared: "As long as my slaves choose to remain with me, I feel attached to them, but as soon as they leave me, I consider myself absolved, from every tye of affection. I have determined that . . . [none] of those that have ran off, shall ever live again on my farm." But if Randolph acted to save himself, it is not clear why so many other slaves were willing, even eager, to join into the conspiracy and risk their own lives.[39]

While the number of organized rebellions was limited, slaves often struck out at the oppressive world around them. During the decade beginning in 1810, Virginia executed 185 slaves for capital crimes and compensated their owners for economic loss. "Though in most cases the violence perpetrated by slaves could not have been rationally regarded, by either the slaves or their masters, as attempts at freedom," observes historian Winthrop D. Jordan, "one suspects these incidents must often have involved very little in the way of rationality on either side. Because Negroes were slaves, Negro violence was for both blacks and whites an attack on slavery." Virginia law certainly recognized the connection between acts of violence and insurrection—it equated the conspiracy of slaves to kill a white person with conspiracy to rebel. Extending from 1723 until 1865, Virginia outlawed both types of conspiracies in the same laws and required identical penalties for each.[40]

The court, despite the appearance of equity, was an instrument for enforcing the oppressive code of slavery. The victim in this case was himself a justice and a member of the slave-owning class. Just as Randolph and others were condemned, so Berkeley's character had to be publicly exonerated. Two white witnesses, James Davis and Ezekiel White, "concurred with the other witnesses in stating that the deceased was an uncommonly lenient humane and indulgent master." The Richmond *Enquirer* thought this commendation important enough to include it in its extensive coverage of the trials: "It gives us pleasure, in reference to the character of the deceased, to state (although it was irrelevant to the subject at issue) that the most ample and respectable testimony was exhibited, which placed his character, as a master, in a very exalted point of view. He was represented by several highly respectable witnesses as treating his slaves with the utmost humanity, and, indeed, *excessive* indulgence."[41]

Silence in the courtroom on the issue of motive suggests that whites could not recognize or even consider that murder might mean more than a momentary grievance and represent an assault against the institution of slavery itself. A discussion of motive might have raised the awful prospect that Berkeley's slaves had real, albeit criminal, reasons for murdering their owner, and acknowledging those reasons would call into question the legitimacy or morality of the system that held blacks in bondage. Randolph's disappearances were protest enough. Sarah regarded Berkeley as "the Devil" himself. And according to Samuel Hackney, the free black who helped capture Randolph and find the stolen money, the slave Robin had once declared that Berkeley "was a bad master, and that he would sooner die than serve him."[42] Slaves at Rock Hill had plotted to kill Berkeley for nearly a year, and the conspirators finalized their plans a full five days before the murder. They acted from no blind passion or innate barbarity, but cold logic and single-minded determination. If Berkeley, who was thought to be "humane and indulgent" by whites, evoked violent hatred from his "people"—to a degree that they were willing to die to be rid of him and did just that—then no colonization program, no moral wrangling over the justice of slavery, and no Christian effort to ameliorate the condition of slaves in the communion of souls could absolve whites of guilt or free them from the fear that they like Berkeley might be victim to the psychological and physical violence at the heart of the peculiar institution. It was precisely at this point that the contradictions inherent in the slaveholders' world were unmasked, and the tensions they produced rendered intolerable. The slaves could have no motive, or slavery itself would be indicted.[43]

Thus the court rendered its verdicts: Randolph, Sarah, London, Robin, and Barnaba were guilty and sentenced to hang. No testimony was presented against Ralph, Thomas, and Harry, and they were acquitted. Will pleaded not guilty, but "sundry witnesses" testified against him. Condemned as "a man of notoriously bad character and dangerous to society," he was sentenced by the justices to twenty-four lashes at the public whipping post and committed to custody until owner Henry Peack posted a seven-year bond of one thousand dollars. Thomas Newman, who had possession of some of the stolen money, was acquitted. "Their degree of guilt being much less than that of the others," Barnaba and Robin were recommended to the governor for clemency and transportation. Upon his approval the two were soon taken to Richmond, where they were subsequently sold to the Dry Tortugas.[44]

Following the trials three ministers published lengthy confessions taken from the condemned slaves. More a reflection of the ministers' anxieties than the convicts' guilt, the confessions rendered a slave owner's interpretation of events, proffered reassurance to the community, and provided religious and moral instruction to both blacks and whites. Randolph, Sarah, and London each expressed remorse and agreed that they would never have committed their crime if Berkeley had afforded them religious instruction, as their previous masters had and as William Meade advocated. With her "dying voice," Sarah admonished "those who are, as I have been, in bondage, to bear their sufferings with patience," so that, when they put their trust in Jesus, they can be "happy in any situation, however wretched it may be."[45]

While these confessions exploit religious teaching as a means of slave discipline, they also concede slavery's wretchedness, indict Berkeley for neglecting his Christian duties, and poignantly recognize the humanity and intelligence of the slaves. In their form and substance, these published confessions closely resembled traditional execution sermons in which ministers first acknowledged the reality of evil by relating the crime of the perpetrators to the human propensity for sin and then transcended the evil of sin by directing attention to the hope of salvation, often through the repentance of the condemned. These rituals helped to heal the social fissures created by violent acts and restore harmony to the community. However, in reporting on the murder, the press had embraced a more modern, secular reaction to violence in emphasizing the horror of the crime and the savagery of the perpetrators, thereby distancing them from the community. Nonetheless, the newspapers commended the clergy for their attention to the prisoners and for their efforts to save the souls of the condemned before execution. But Sarah's confession ended poignantly with a prayer that made plain on whose terms salvation and social harmony was to be achieved: "Help me, O Lord Jesus to leave a testimony behind me, that thou hast fully healed my soul, and washed it white in thy own *precious blood*." She, London, and Randolph, the three with the largest roles in the murder of Robert Berkeley and the desecration of his body, were hanged in the courthouse square on July 10, 1818.[46]

An incident of extraordinary power and meaning, Robert Berkeley's murder soon passed into local folklore. It possessed the elements of conspiracy, violence, horror, pathos, and drama that were essential to a good story. But the narrative had inherent problems as well, especially for southern whites. First, Berkeley as a representative of the master class was a humiliating failure. He could neither manage the people of his household nor ensure his or his family's security. Second, the white people in this story appeared dimwitted, if not inept or incompetent. Berkeley was apparently unaware of any unrest among his slaves and walked into a trap. His unusual absence after the murder went unquestioned for days while his killer remained at large in the community for a week and a half. Last, the story provided no consistent motive for the brutal murder. The reasons that Randolph, Sarah, London, and the other conspirators acted with such violence and resolve remained buried beneath the tensions of a community agonizing over the contradictions of slavery.

Meanwhile, the Berkeley family wiped clean its memory of the murder. Surviving correspondence among family members made no mention of the incident. One family historian learned of it only through genealogical research. She remarked that "the family kept silent about this melancholy event. . . . There must have been a tradition of disgrace about it, though the records do not bear this out." Julia Berkeley and her children did not speak of it to the next generation. A granddaughter heard about it only as an adult and then from someone outside the family. By that time, the story had changed.[47]

In its subsequent retellings, the narrative clearly bore the imprint of southern history. To ease the burdens of their past, southern conservatives of the post-Reconstruction South remade and rewrote much of it. They had lost the Civil War, their property, their status, and a great deal of their self-respect. But as they recaptured, or redeemed, their state governments, they also addressed the question of how the history of their difficult times would be told. Many southerners consciously and vigorously rejected a New England–centered version of American history that diminished or, worse, omitted the contributions of the South to the founding of the nation and the forging of its national character. This new movement affirmed southern patriotism and embodied republican virtues in classical architecture and sculpture, while glorifying Confederate heroes and embracing colonial roots. Largely absent from this history was any hand-wringing over the moral dilemmas of slavery that so troubled earlier generations of southerners. Plantation life in antebellum America came to represent a golden age of social harmony and racial peace, and planters were portrayed as much the victims of their social environment as were slaves. Enthusiasts erected monuments on almost every courthouse lawn in Virginia and throughout the South, proudly dedicating them to heroes of the "Lost Cause" in a fight not over slavery but the constitutional rights of states.[48]

Beneath the glorification of southern history, however, was the ugly side of race relations, which reached a nadir during the 1890s and early 1900s. Throughout the South, Jim Crow laws imposed an apartheid regime of segregation on blacks and whites. Hundreds of thousands of blacks lost the right to vote. They were denied equal education and equal access to both public facilities and the political process. Lynchings reached a historical high. As southern history was rewritten, black southerners were written out of any meaningful role in their own past.

It was into this milieu of revisionism and racism that the legend of Robert Berkeley's murder passed. Berkeley's own community had wrestled fearfully with the social contradictions of slavery and race relations in an age still steeped in the republican optimism of a revolutionary generation and caught up in the heady idealism of Christian perfectionism. His murder had laid open these contradictions. History closed them for subsequent generations, who sought a past that endorsed failed efforts to divide the Union and, at the same time, success in dividing the races. In the evolution of a society's collective memory, traumatic events are commonly distorted to conform to changing social imperatives and to restore a positive self-image. New beliefs are the most susceptible to memory distortions, and in the retellings of the Berkeley murder, the most significant alterations occurred around the subject of race relations. For instance, local historian and clerk of the Frederick County Court, Thomas K. Cartmell, spent much of his long career poring over the legal records of his community and in 1909 published *Shenandoah Valley Pioneers and Their Descendants*. He knew about the murder of Robert Berkeley and wrote about it. Nonetheless, he claimed

> no two races ever lived in such harmony as the White and Black races enjoyed in *ye olden times*, before the negro was taught by the fanatics that slavery was a yoke that must be removed, and *he must do his part*. . . . When a slave, he was a trusted friend; now we are taught that the rising generations have many monsters to be hounded by mobs and destroyed. Under the old conditions, no monsters or frenzied communities disturbed the country. . . . Southern people remember no trouble between the two races until after the emancipation proclamation, and subsequent schemes adopted by the Washington government to make allies of the negro race. The negro was then encouraged to take weapons of destruction in his hands and wreak vengeance on his old oppressors.[49]

As the account of the Berkeley murder changed over time, each new version addressed its "problems." Contradictions were corrected to conform to the conventions and compulsions of the present—to the Lost Cause and conservative interpretations of the past. Although the Berkeley family did not talk about the murder, apparently the Rust family did. John W. Rust, great-grandson of Berkeley's neighbor John Rust, who had discovered foul play in 1818, wrote a century and a quarter later "that the tradition in my family is that . . . Berkeley was killed by his slaves because of the fact that he had made a will freeing them rather than for the purpose of robbery." Court proceedings, however, indicate clearly that Berkeley died without a will—not unusual in the case of an unexpected and untimely death. Nevertheless, the fear that freeing slaves by will would encourage them to bring about a master's premature demise was widespread in the nineteenth-century South. It served to discourage manumission in the interests of those who feared the influence of free blacks.[50]

Casting Berkeley in the role of compassionate emancipationist, however, corrected his image as a failed master. Instead he became a noble victim of his own altruism. This version also provides the perpetrators with a motive: heedless of any punishment they killed Berkeley to hasten the execution of his will and gain their freedom. Thus their actions could be made to appear simpleminded or irrational—a view more consistent with perspectives on race in the era of Jim Crow. Rust does not mention in his letter, of course, that black men and women were capable of developing and executing a complex plan and subsequently concealing their actions for the better part of a week in the midst of a southern society that prided itself for its vigilance against internal threats. Interestingly, and perhaps not coincidentally, John W. Rust, as a member of the Virginia Senate in 1938, sponsored legislation for erecting a statue of Stonewall Jackson on the Manassas battlefield, and members of his family were involved in other historic preservation activities memorializing an ideal past of a hierarchical social order and harmonious race relations.[51]

Another version of Berkeley's murder was told by his granddaughter from the account of the Mr. Oliver who had worked for Julia Berkeley for many years during and after the event. In 1929 this granddaughter, an old woman herself, wrote the story as she had heard it from Oliver:

On that fateful night that [Berkeley] was killed, he returned from Baltimore with a lot of money, which he put in the secretary in the hall of the house, and told his wife who was then sick in bed with an infant child. She said that she did not notice his going out of the house, for she had become exhausted from the strain of her anxious waiting for Grandpa's return, and had fallen to sleep and did not wake till the next day. But it was a wonder none of the family was aroused till the next morning, when the man who was overseer of the hands knocked on the door for admittance. The family went to the door and old Mr. Oliver inquired where Dr. Berkeley was and said he had been to the quarters and no one was there. Then they went to the stable and no horses or wagons [were] there, so they went to the kitchen and made an examination and found out from the odor there that something had gone wrong, so he summoned the neighbors and they went on to Winchester Town, and overtook the eight

THE DEATH OF ROBERT BERKELEY * 221

men and one woman traveling to town as fast as they could go, and hung them there that same day. When they returned, they examined the house and found the money gone and the bones of our grandfather in the kitchen fireplace. It was awful to think about. I never heard my mother or Aunt Bettie say a word about it in my life. I learned this from old Mr. Oliver himself.[52]

This version promoted Oliver to overseer and made him the one who alarmed the family and promptly discovered the disappearance of slaves, master, and horses. White neighbors then acted decisively to apprehend the slaves and exact immediate punishment. Julia Berkeley was portrayed sympathetically, ill and asleep, excused from not alarming others about the sudden absence of her husband. The four days between the murder and its discovery were simply omitted. This version of the murder story solves the problem of white ineptitude. Whites were vigilant and quick to act. Like late-nineteenth-century counterparts, they lynched the culprits at the nearest tree. Meanwhile the slaves were again denied any motive for their actions, which were reduced to savage barbarity.

The letter from Berkeley's granddaughter appeared in a 1936 newspaper article by Eliza Timberlake Davis, who had been reared near Rock Hill and knew the story of the murder. Claiming inaccurately that Berkeley purchased the Rock Hill property in 1811 from Stephen Davis, "a nephew of John Davis, the ancestor of President Jefferson Davis of the Confederacy," she noted that "Berkeley employed and owned a large number of slaves. That he believed them to be faithful and trustworthy is assured by the fact that he intrusted his family to their care when it was necessary for him to be away from home." Berkeley, at least, regarded himself as a successful slave master.[53]

In her own account of the murder Davis described Berkeley's return from Baltimore, the "large sum of money" he brought with him, Julia Berkeley's confinement after childbirth, and her anxiety over her husband's absence. On the evening of his return Julia slept while Robert read. Summoned to the slave cabin, "he was seized, bound and placed on blazing logs in the great fireplace. Pleading for mercy, he begged to be released, but was held there by long poles until death ended his agony." The perpetrators immediately went to the manor house to search for money hidden there, about "which they must have learned through the t[r]eachery of a slave." They planned to kill Julia Berkeley "if she awoke, and flashed the lamplight before her eyes; but she slept so peacefully, her arm encircling her baby, that they were moved by some semblance of sympathy for their gentle mistress, and closing the bedroom door, went out, leaving her unharmed." In Davis's account the conspirators took the money, went to the stables, and fled with every horse and vehicle available. The very next morning Oliver sensed a "strange stillness." He found no slaves, but "a terrifying odor hung over the whole place." The alerted household then discovered the empty stables and in a fireplace in the quarters, "the charred bones and bits of burning flesh of the master." The alarm soon spread, and vigilantes "set out in hot pursuit . . . and thirsty for vengeance." They overtook the "terror-stricken" blacks about twenty miles from Rock Hill near Winchester and hanged eight men and one woman that same day.[54]

Here again, whites took decisive action with Oliver in the leading role. They detected the crime and its evidence almost immediately, apprehended the perpetrators, and brought them to speedy justice without trial. "Worn out with the long and anxious vigil until her husband's return," Julia was absolved for failing to suspect foul play. The black men and women, on the other hand, acted more savagely than in any other version. They burned Berkeley alive, holding him in the fire with poles. The slaves stole money, horses, and vehicles, but robbery was not the motive. Nothing can explain the murder but utter and absolute barbarism. Only a small flicker of humanity kept the perpetrators from killing their "gentle mistress" as well.[55]

While Thomas Cartmell was certainly wrong about the interracial tranquility that reigned in Frederick County before the Civil War, blacks, even slaves accused and convicted of murder, were not treated as monsters to be hounded by frenzied mobs and lynched without trial. Although the courts regarded them as a strange admixture of persons capable of wrongdoing and property to be protected from harm, they were accorded the full letter of the law and received concerned ministration from the clergy. In 1818 some slaves were hanged, and others transported, bonded to good conduct under their owners, or acquitted as circumstances seemed to warrant. Slaves may have been powerless in their own world and deprived even of a motive for their actions or an unmediated voice in the community, but they were not considered barbarians subject to summary execution without even the semblance of justice.

In the mid-1950s a ghost story circulated about the Berkeley murder. In this rendition, Julia Berkeley awoke one morning and noticed that her husband had not come to bed the night before. Concerned about his absence, she opened the door to the hall and saw the family dog, large, white, and shaggy, approaching with a man's arm in its mouth. Julia screamed with horror and the realization that the arm was her husband's. This story completely ignores issues of race and motive.[56]

Residents of the area surrounding Rock Hill today relate another version of the Berkeley murder, the only one that supplies a credible motive for the crime. In this rendition, Berkeley had returned weary from a business trip to Baltimore with a great deal of cash. Finding his wife, Julia, ill and resting in bed, he went to visit his infant son in the cabin of a slave wet nurse. Upon entering, he saw the woman seated at the hearth, nursing her own infant while his lay nearby, crying in hunger. In sudden rage, he struck the black child away from the breast of its mother. The blow knocked the baby against the stone hearth of the fireplace with enough force to kill it. Berkeley was slain in that same cabin four days later, his body burned upon the very hearth where the black child died. This is not the tale of Berkeley's murder but a parable of retribution for an unspeakable crime.[57]

The eighty-year-old white woman who told this story had lived near Rock Hill all her life. Her mother sternly warned her never to go near the house. Sensing great evil, she never did. Nonetheless, for decades people ventured near Rock Hill, fearing ghosts but also hoping to find the "treasure" of Berkeley's money. Not well built to begin with, the house was in disrepair at the time of Berkeley's death. For a century or more, treasure hunters had been removing bricks from the foundation. The owner, tired of trespassers and aware of the perilous state of the building, razed the house and bulldozed eight to ten feet of the high, narrow ridge upon which it stood. Nothing remains of Rock Hill except the stories. No treasure was ever found.[58]

Of the various versions of the story of the murder of Robert Berkeley, the last resonates most clearly with modern moral sensibilities. Although assigning the role of wet nurse to Sarah is tempting, no element of the story confirms it. But in identifying a comprehensible motive for the crime, this version differs markedly from the monster narratives, and, moreover, it contains some components of the early accounts that acknowledged a common humanity and a shared capacity for wrongful actions. In addition it satisfies twentieth-century notions of criminal behavior. Motive has come to play a larger and larger role in court proceedings and is often used as a mitigating circumstance in defense arguments. More significantly, this last version also reflects a modern willingness to reshape the memory of slavery from the viewpoint of slaves recognizing the tragic costs of slavery for both whites and blacks. While the woman who told the story was white, it is the only known version that gives the slaves some authority over their own lives and lends authenticity to their actions.

That the story of Robert Berkeley's murder has been told and retold for more than 175 years is testimony to its power, on the one hand, to fathom society's deepest, albeit shifting, tensions over race and, on the other, to order race relations from both personal and cultural perspectives. For the community of men and women, white and black, who experienced the murder and its aftermath, the events of May, June, and July 1818 revealed the two worlds of slave and slaveholder at their most vulnerable point of intersection. The murder, like any act of violence by slave against master, called into question the institution of slavery that made this boundary so brutal while at the same time imposing restraints on both the oppressed and the oppressor.

The world of black men and women cannot be readily reconstructed because few slaves left behind sources that reveal their ambitions or intentions. Their actions at times, however, spoke with exceptional clarity about their inner lives and the contradiction residing there between the capacity for rational action and the repression of personal autonomy. In taking Robert Berkeley's life, Randolph, London, Sarah, and the others demonstrated that they could act to rectify—or seek retribution for—long-standing grievances. Admittedly an act of personal vengeance, the murder also represented resistance to slavery's expropriation of self-will. The men and women Berkeley held in bondage acted brutally but not impulsively or barbarically. They considered their plan for nearly a year before executing it. They actively conspired for at least five days before the murder and carried it out with deliberation and conviction. Even Berkeley's ruthless immolation can be construed as a calculated attempt either to destroy evidence or to denigrate his body and eradicate his memory. After the murder the conspirators acted calmly and collectively to conceal their deed.

To say that in killing Berkeley, his slaves took determined steps to change their conditions is not to exonerate them from the crime of murder but to assert that these men and women were competent in acting from the deepest, if not darkest, human emotions. They were not childlike reflections of human beings arrested in their emotional development either by their nature, as Berkeley's contemporaries widely believed, or by their culture, as some students of slavery have subsequently suggested.[59] Randolph, London, Sarah, and their accomplices may have lashed out with chilling brutality against Berkeley and the slave system he represented, but their actions were hardly inconsistent with the violence that pervaded their society and the cruel discipline at the heart of slavery.

If the world of the slaves was rent by contradictions between a humanity expressed in carefully reasoned, deeply emotive action and a culture that reduced blacks to puerile dependence, then the white world was also contradictory in the humanity it afforded black dependents and in the inhumane degradation of slavery. When confronted with a crime that penetrated to the moral foundations of their social order, whites acted deliberately to bring the accused to the justice of their courts, try them by established legal procedures, and execute punishments dispassionately, not as ostensible vengeance but as moral example. Counsel for the accused, Augustine Smith, also served as secretary for the Auxiliary Society of Frederick County for Colonizing the Free People of Colour, an organization sympathetic with the plight of both slaves and free blacks in a racially divided society. Although concerned primarily with removing free blacks from Virginia, the members of the auxiliary looked squarely into the eye of slavery's incompatibility with an ideology of republican freedom inherited from the revolutionary generation. Moreover, the white clergy took an active interest in the spiritual welfare of the accused. The murder's challenge to Christian conceptions of an ordered community deeply troubled William Meade. He made good use of resulting social stresses to redouble calls for the religious instruction of slaves and to caution masters about observing Christian strictures themselves. Although other clergymen published the confessions of the slaves as a vivid demonstration to all of the perils of rebellion and the dire consequences of neglecting Christian duty, these men also acted quite genuinely to secure the salvation of the condemned.

Through adherence to the forms of justice, recognition of contradictions between slavery and republicanism, and concern for the souls of black folk, white people tacitly acknowledged the humanity of slaves. At the same time these behaviors reveal a more desperate attempt to deny any semblance of their own inhumanity as a master class guilty of exploitation more malevolent than that of the European aristocracy they so recently and righteously condemned. The white world had to reject any implication that the murder constituted an inherent attack on the institution of slavery because to acknowledge legitimate insurrection would be to disavow the moral integrity of white society. The institution of slavery was not only designed to deprive blacks of personal autonomy but also imposed legal and social controls constraining whites so they could simultaneously condemn blacks and affirm their own humanity.

The Civil War and emancipation obliterated these restraints and left white southerners devoid of the certainties of a slave regime. Therefore, whites recast race relations in history through the ideology of the Lost Cause and in the present through the violence and oppression of Jim Crow segregation. The recontextualized accounts of Berkeley's murder surfacing after 1900 thus achieve a tragic irony in the "horrible and savage barbarity" of white behavior. Whites lynch blacks suspected of the murder and are never brought to justice for their crime.

According to the final version of the story Berkeley, in a metaphor for the crime of slavery and the African slave trade, kills a child by striking it from the breast of the mother. He thereby initiates the cycle of violence that culminates in his own murder and the subsequent deaths of the slaves. Although no contemporaneous evidence corroborates Berkeley's misdeed, the moral sensibilities of the late twentieth century, by giving it credence, lend insight into the origins and changing character of a racially divided society.

NOTES

1. Frances Berkeley Young, *The Berkeleys of Barn Elms* (1954; rptd., Hamden, Conn., 1964), 84–87 (first quotation on p. 85); and Robert Carter to Robert Berkeley,

February 10, 1804, Letterbook, 1800–1805, Carter Manuscripts (Manuscript Division, Library of Congress, Washington, D.C.), quoted in Louis Morton, *Robert Carter of Nomini Hall: A Virginia Tobacco Planter of the Eighteenth Century* (Williamsburg, Va., 1941), 229 (second quotation); and Frederick County Deed Book, XXIX, 130–33 (Frederick County Courthouse, Winchester, Va.). Berkeley completed his dissertation at the University of Pennsylvania in 1800 and published it that same year. See Robert Berkeley, *An Inquiry into the Modus Operandi of That Class of Medicines Called Sedatives* (Philadelphia, Pa., 1800).

For research assistance, we would like to thank Lyda Costello Bitto, Holly Hast, Michael Henshaw, Dana Lineberg, Cheryl Locke, Andrew Lowder, Michelle Merchant, Kimberly Miller, Robert Ramsey, and Christopher Williams, all members of the 1993 seminar in Historical Thought and Methods at Shenandoah University. Margaret Yocom and Barry Penn-Hollar read the manuscript and provided helpful commentary. Additional research for this project was supported by a Mellon Research Fellowship at the Virginia Historical Society.

2. George Carter to John Wickham, July 1, November 14, 1808, May 17, 1810, July 22, 1813, May 14, 1814, George Carter Letterbook, 1807–1819, pp. 1, 9, 24, 73, 117 (Virginia Historical Society, Richmond); and petition by Robert Berkeley and counter-petition against Berkeley, 1807, Petitions, 1749–1924, Roads, Mills, Dams, and Bridges, Frederick County Court Papers (Library of Virginia, Richmond).

3. George Carter to Julia Carter Berkeley, June 26, 1818, George Carter Letterbook, 217–21 (quotations on p. 220). William Taylor, a bricklayer who lived at Oatlands for many years, inspected the buildings at Rock Hill at George Carter's request. The house was demolished about 1940. For a sketch plan probably drafted at the time of demolition see Frances Blackwell Trenary, Floor Plan of Rock Hill, Laura Virginia Hale Collection (Laura Virginia Hale Archives, Warren Heritage Society, Front Royal, Va.).

4. Frederick County Minute Book, 1809–1813, p. 289 (Frederick County Courthouse) (hereinafter cited as FMB), also cited in R. E. Griffith Sr., "Notes on Rock Hill," *Proceedings of the Clarke County Historical Association*, III (1943), 45. The inventory taken shortly after Robert Berkeley's death lists thirty-two slaves and does not include five slaves held for trial in Berkeley's murder. See Inventory and Appraisement of the Slaves and Personal Estate of the late Doctr. Robert Berkeley, June 4 and 5, 1818, Frederick County Will Book, X, 594–98 (Frederick County Courthouse); and Leesburg (Va.) *Genius of Liberty*, August 4, 1818.

5. The narrative of Robert Berkeley's murder and the trials of the accused slaves and free blacks can be pieced together from trial testimonies and newspaper accounts. See FMB, 1817–1820, pp. 75–100; Alexandria *Gazette and Daily Advertiser,* May 27, 1818; Leesburg *Genius of Liberty*, June 9, August 4, 1818; Richmond *Enquirer,* June 9, July 17, 1818; and Woodstock (Va.) *Herald,* May 27, June 3, June 10, 1818. The killing of Robert Berkeley bears interesting parallels with other cases of slaves murdering owners. See Melton A. McLaurin, *Celia, A Slave* (Athens, Ga., and London, 1991).

6. George Carter to Julia Carter Berkeley, June 26, 1818, George Carter Letterbook, 217–21 (quotation on p. 219); and Leesburg *Genius of Liberty*, August 4, 1818. For a discussion of day-to-day resistance by slaves see Eugene D. Genovese, *Roll, Jordan, Roll: The World the Slaves Made* (New York, 1974), 597–98; Peter Kolchin, *American Slavery, 1619–1877* (New York, 1993), 157; and Kenneth M. Stampp, *The Peculiar Institution: Slavery in the Ante-Bellum South* (New York, 1956), 86–140.

7. Leesburg *Genius of Liberty*, August 4, 1818; and FMB, 1817–1820, pp. 75–79 (first quotation on p. 75, second and third quotations on p. 76). Conflicting testimony from Ralph and Robin places Ralph asleep in the kitchen at the time of the murder.

8. FMB, 1817–1820, pp. 75–79. For discussions of African and African American ideas about death, the spirit, and the afterlife see Mechal Sobel, *The World They Made Together: Black and White Values in Eighteenth-Century Virginia* (Princeton, 1987), 96, 174, and 214–25; and Sobel, *Trabelin' On: The Slave Journey to an Afro-Baptist Faith* (Princeton, 1988), 70, 82, and 112.

9. FMB, 1817–1820, p. 79–80.

10. For a discussion of slave solidarity see Norrece T. Jones, *Born a Child of Freedom, Yet a Slave: Mechanisms of Control and Strategies of Resistance in Antebellum South Carolina* (Hanover, Mass., and London, 1990), 16–17 and 98–105.

11. George Carter to Sophia Carter, June 26, 1818, George Carter Letterbook, 207–10 (first quotation on p. 208, subsequent quotations on p. 209). For an account of the disposition of Julia Berkeley's property under the estate of her husband see George Carter to Dr. Lyons, July 27, 1818, and Carter to Julia Berkeley, August 30, 1818, George Carter Letterbook, 216, 222; *Robert Berkeley's Heirs* v. *Robert Berkeley's Administratrix*, 1824, Frederick County Court Chancery Papers, 1745–1898 (Library of Virginia); and Frederick County Land Book, I, 334–39 (Frederick County Courthouse) (hereinafter cited as FLB).

12. Hunter Dickinson Farish, ed., *Journal and Letters of Philip Vickers Fithian, 1773–1774: A Plantation Tutor of the Old Dominion* (Williamsburg, Va., 1957), 40 and 183; Morton, *Robert Carter*, 31–61, 205–50, and 270; and Shomer S. Zwelling, "Robert Carter's Journey: From Colonial Patriarch to New Nation Mystic," *American Quarterly*, XXXVIII (Fall 1986), 613–36.

13. Deed of Emancipation, August 1, 1791, Robert Carter Papers, Vol. XI, pt. 1, pp. 1–2 (Perkins Library, Duke University, Durham, N.C.), quoted in John Randolph Barden, "'Flushed with Notions of Freedom': The Growth and Emancipation of a Virginia Slave Community, 1732–1812" (Ph.D. dissertation, Duke University, 1993), 7; George Carter to Julia Carter Berkeley, June 26, 1818, George Carter Letterbook, 217–21 (second quotation); and Morton, *Robert Carter*, 245–69. For more on management of slaves see Genovese, *Roll Jordan Roll*, 3–24; and Jones, *Born a Child of Freedom*, Chaps. 1–4. Genovese emphasizes the complexity of the paternalistic relationship between masters and their slaves, while Jones characterizes master-slave interactions as a continual state of war (pp. 162–93).

14. Frederick County Court Order Book, XXXI, 84 (Frederick County Courthouse); Frederick Superior Court Order Book, III, 335 (Frederick County Courthouse); Samuel Kercheval, *A History of the Valley of Virginia* (5th ed.; Strasburg, Va., 1973), 359; and J. E. Norris, *History of the Lower Shenandoah Valley Counties of Frederick, Berkeley, Jefferson, and Clarke* (Chicago, 1890; Berryville, Va., 1972), 165.

15. FMB, 1817–1820, pp. 76–77 (quotations on p. 77).

16. FMB, 1817–1820, pp. 81–82 and 90 (quotations on p. 81).

17. Alexandria *Gazette and Daily Advertiser*, May 27, 1818 (first, fifth, sixth, seventh, and eighth quotations); and Woodstock (Va.) *Herald*, May 27, 1818 (second, third, and fourth quotations).

18. Arthur Dicken Thomas Jr., "The Second Great Awakening in Virginia and Slavery Reform, 1785–1837" (Th.D. dissertation, Union Theological Seminary,

1981), 94 (quotation); Alexandria *Gazette and Daily Advertiser,* May 27, 1818; and David Lynn Holmes Jr., "William Meade and the Church of Virginia, 1789–1829" (Ph.D. dissertation., Princeton University, 1971), 116 and 203–7. William Meade acted on his antislavery beliefs in emancipating slaves from the estates of two deceased sisters and aiding another sister in freeing her slaves and sending them to Liberia. After manumitting his own slaves, he honored their desire to relocate in Pennsylvania and helped establish them there. See Will of Susan Meade, July 3, 1820, in letter from Ann Randolph (Meade) Page to Mary Lee (Fitzhugh) Custis, August 24, 1830, and William Meade to Custis, April 9, 1823, April 13, 1830, all in Custis Papers (Virginia Historical Society); and Marie Tyler McGraw, "The American Colonization Society in Virginia, 1816–1832: A Case Study in Southern Liberalism" (Ph.D. dissertation, George Washington University, 1980), 78–79.

19. William Meade, *Sermon, Delivered . . . at the Opening of the Convention of the Diocese of Virginia, at Winchester, May 20, 1818* (Winchester, Va., 1818), 10 (first quotation), 22–24 (second quotation on p. 22, third quotation on p. 23, fourth quotation on p. 24). Jan Lewis has explored how recasting the plantation as a Christian community allowed many slave owners to believe that "slavery might be moral if planters loved their slaves." See Lewis, *The Pursuit of Happiness: Family and Values in Jefferson's Virginia* (Cambridge, Eng., 1983), 221–22 (quotation on p. 222).

20. For Meade's thoughts on instructing slaves see William Meade, *Pastoral Letter . . . on the Duty of Affording Religious Instruction to Those in Bondage* (Alexandria, D.C., 1834), 3–5 and 13–16; and Alexandria *Gazette and Daily Advertiser,* May 27, 1818.

21. Woodstock (Va.) *Herald,* May 27, 1818 (quotations); and Alexandria *Gazette and Daily Advertiser,* May 27, 1818, reprinted from the Winchester *Gazette,* May 23, 1818.

22. Estate of Robert Berkeley, FLB, I, 339–45; and FMB, 1817–1820, pp. 82 and 99–100. For more on the relationships among slaves, free blacks, and whites during this period see Brenda E. Stevenson, *Life in Black and White: Family and Community in the Slave South* (New York and Oxford, 1996).

23. William Greenway Russell, "What I Know about Winchester . . . ," edited by Garland R. Quarles and Lewis N. Barton (originally published in Winchester *News,* January–June 1876; reprinted in 1953 as Vol. II of *Winchester–Frederick County Historical Society Papers*), 71–72; and David Holmes Conrad, "Early History of Winchester," *Annual Papers of Winchester Virginia Historical Society* 1 (1931), 223.

24. Russell, "What I Know about Winchester," 71; FMB, 1817–1820, pp. 75–100; and Inventory and Appraisement of the Slaves and Personal Estate of the late Doctr. Robert Berkeley.

25. Frederick County Personal Property Tax Books, 1820 (Library of Virginia); Warren R. Hofstra, "These Fine Prospects: Frederick County, Virginia, 1738–1840" (Ph.D. dissertation, University of Virginia, 1985), tables 1, 4, and 5; and Frederick County, Va., Legislative Petition, December 16, 1816 (Library of Virginia).

26. Conrad, "Early History of Winchester," 191–92, and 194; Norris, *History of the Lower Shenandoah Valley,* 196; and Frederick County Auxiliary Society, *Annual Report of the Auxiliary Society of Frederick County, Va. for Colonizing the Free People of Colour in the United States* (Winchester, Va., 1820), 3 and 36.

27. Frederick County Auxiliary Society, *Annual Report* (1820); P. J. Staudenraus, *The African Colonization Movement, 1816–1865* (New York, 1961), 27 and 70; McGraw,

"American Colonization Society," 78; Augustine C. Smith to Elias Caldwell, April 25, 1819, Peter Force Collection (Manuscript Division, Library of Congress); and Account of the Estate of Robert Berkeley, FLB I, 340.

28. Frederick County Auxiliary Society, *Annual Report* (1820); American Colonization Society, *First Annual Report,* 1817, *Second Annual Report,* 1818, copies in American Colonization Society Papers (Manuscript Division, Library of Congress); McGraw, "American Colonization Society," 53 and 79; and Staudenraus, *African Colonization Movement,* 71–72.

29. Rebecca A. Ebert, "A Window on the Valley: A Study of the Free Black Community of Winchester and Frederick County, Virginia, 1785–1860" (M.A. thesis, University of Maryland, 1986), 5–7; Bureau of the Census, First Census of the United States, 1790, *Return of the Whole Number of Persons within the Several Districts of the United States* (Philadelphia, 1791), 48; and Bureau of the Census, Fourth Census of the United States, *Census of 1820* (Washington, D.C., 1821), 24.

30. Letter of August 5, 1796, Anonymous Letters to Robert Carter, 1784–1796, Carter Manuscripts, as quoted in Morton, *Robert Carter,* 266–67 (first quotation); Frederick County Auxiliary Society, *Annual Report* (1820), 14–15 (second quotation on p. 15); and Ebert, "Window on the Valley," 12–13.

31. Frederick County Auxiliary, *Annual Report* (1820), 13–22 (first quotation on p. 15, second quotation on pp. 15–16, third quotation on p. 13, fourth quotation on p. 19, and fifth quotation on p. 20).

32. Leesburg *Genius of Liberty,* August 4, 1818; Charles P. Poland, *From Frontier to Suburbia* (Marceline, Mo., 1976), 143–44n66; Arthur Dicken Thomas Jr., "'O That Slavery's Curse Might Cease': Ann Randolph Meade Page: The Struggle of a Plantation Mistress to Become an Emancipator," *Virginia Seminary Journal,* XLV (December 1993), 60; and Frederick County Assessment Book, 1816, as cited in Griffith, "Notes on Rock Hill," 43–48. Many slaveholders in the upper South sold slaves during this period, fulfilling a strong demand for slave labor in the lower South after the closing of the foreign slave trade. See Michael Tadman, *Speculators and Slaves: Masters, Traders, and Slaves in the Old South* (Madison, Wisc., 1989). For a treatment of the importance of kinship ties among slaves see Herbert G. Gutman, *The Black Family in Slavery and Freedom, 1750–1925* (New York, 1976).

33. Thomas Jefferson to John Holmes, April 22, 1820, quoted in John Chester Miller, *The Wolf by the Ears: Thomas Jefferson and Slavery* (New York, 1977), 241 (first quotation); and Frederick County Auxiliary Society, *Annual Report* (1820), 22 (second quotation).

34. McLaurin, *Celia,* 68–87, and 118–19; Diane Miller Sommerville, "The Rape Myth in the Old South Reconsidered," *Journal of Southern History* LXI (August 1995), 481–518 (esp. pages 483 and 510); and A. E. Keir Nash, "Fairness and Formalism in the Trials of Blacks in the State Supreme Courts of the Old South," *Virginia Law Review,* LVI (February 1970), 82–84.

35. FMB, 1817–1820, pp. 75 (first quotation), 78, 81–82, 84, 89, and 99 (second quotation).

36. Woodstock (Va.) *Herald,* June 10, 1818 (quotations). Another tragedy had occurred on May 25, when the mail stage from Winchester overturned at Harpers Ferry, killing one female passenger and seriously injuring several others. See Woodstock (Va.) *Herald,* June 3, 1818; and Leesburg *Genius of Liberty,* June 9, 1818.

37. FMB, 1817–1820, pp. 89–90 (first quotation on p. 90); and Leesburg (Va.) *Genius of Liberty*, August 4, 1818 (second and third quotations). One inconsistency in the historical records is the nature of the murder weapon. In London's court testimony (the first and most complete description of the crime) and in the newspapers it is called a club; at Randolph's trial Randolph purportedly admitted to killing Berkeley with a stone; and in the published confessions it was a walking stick.

38. FMB, 1817–1820, p. 90 (quotation); Philip J. Schwarz, *Twice Condemned: Slaves and the Criminal Laws of Virginia, 1705–1865* (Baton Rouge, 1988), 240; and Jones, *Born a Child of Freedom*, 7.

39. George Carter to Edmund McGinnis, May 11, 1814, George Carter Letterbook, 109.

40. Winthrop D. Jordan, *White Over Black: American Attitudes Toward the Negro, 1550–1812* (Chapel Hill, 1968), 393; Ulrich B. Phillips, "Slave Crime in Virginia," *American Historical Review*, XX (January 1915), 337; and Philip J. Schwarz, "Forging the Shackles: The Development of Virginia's Criminal Code for Slaves" in David J. Bodenhamer and James W. Ely Jr., eds., *Ambivalent Legacy: A Legal History of the South* (Jackson, Miss., 1984), 135.

41. FMB, 1817–1820, p. 77; and Richmond *Enquirer*, June 9, 1818.

42. FMB, 1817–1820, p. 79 (first quotation), and 83 (second quotation).

43. Historians have debated whether or not slave owners were guilt-ridden. For the case that they were see James Oakes, *The Ruling Race: A History of American Slaveholders* (New York, 1982), 117–22; for the opposing view see Eugene D. Genovese, *The Slaveholders' Dilemma: Freedom and Progress in Southern Conservative Thought, 1820–1860* (Columbia, S.C., 1992). Many slaveholders in Winchester and Frederick County fit the description of those in John C. Inscoe, *Mountain Masters, Slavery, and the Sectional Crisis in Western North Carolina* (Knoxville, Tenn., 1989). Generally speaking, they allowed their slaves greater freedom and autonomy and more readily acknowledged their humanity than did slaveholders in Tidewater Virginia or the lower South.

44. FMB, 1817–1820, pp. 75, 78, 81, 82, 89, and 98–100 (first and second quotations on p. 99); and Woodstock (Va.) *Herald*, June 3, 10, and July 15, 1818 (third quotation in June 3 edition). It has been attributed to Augustine Smith's ability as an attorney that Barnaba and Robin had their sentences commuted by the governor to deportation. See Griffith, "Notes on Rock Hill," 47. The Dry Tortugas are the western-most islands in the Florida Keys. Discovered by Ponce de León in 1513 and named after tortoises found there, they were later described quite accurately by mariners as dry.

45. Leesburg *Genius of Liberty*, August 4, 1818.

46. *Ibid*. For a discussion of confession and murder narratives see Karen Halttunen, "Early American Murder Narratives: The Birth of Horror," in Richard Wightman Fox and T. J. Jackson Lears, eds., *The Power of Culture: Critical Essays in American History* (Chicago and London, 1993), 66–101. In this essay Halttunen argues that the shift in the function of execution sermons from community ritual to secular narrative isolates the murderer and brings horror into the minds of the people.

47. Young, *Berkeleys of Barn Elms*, 86 (quotation); and account of unnamed granddaughter of Robert and Julia Berkeley, February 2, 1929, in Eliza Timberlake Davis, "The Tragedy of Rock Hill," Richmond *Times-Dispatch*, October 18, 1936, sec. 5, p. 10. Davis's ancestors lived in the vicinity of Rock Hill at the time Robert Berkeley

was murdered. Her father, John S. Timberlake, fought for the Confederacy and iron-ically was imprisoned in the Dry Tortugas during the Civil War. See Stuart E. Brown Jr., *Annals of Clarke County, Virginia* (Berryville, Va., 1983), 306–8.

48. On the emergence of the Lost Cause mentality and its meaning for southern history see Fred Arthur Bailey, "Free Speech and the Lost Cause in the Old Domin-ion," *Virginia Magazine of History and Biography*, CIII (April 1995), 237–66; Catherine W. Bishir, "Landmarks of Power: Building a Southern Past, 1885–1915," *Southern Cul-tures* (Inaugural Issue, 1993), 7; Thomas L. Connelly and Barbara L. Bellows, *God and General Longstreet: The Lost Cause and the Southern Mind* (Baton Rouge and London, 1982); Gaines M. Foster, *Ghosts of the Confederacy: Defeat, the Lost Cause, and the Emer-gence of the New South, 1865 to 1913* (New York and Oxford, 1987); and Charles Rea-gan Wilson, *Baptized in Blood: The Religion of the Lost Cause, 1865–1920* (Athens, Ga., 1980).

49. Thomas K. Cartmell, *Shenandoah Valley Pioneers and Their Descendants: A His-tory of Frederick County, Virginia* (Winchester, Va., 1909; Berryville, Va., 1963), 108 and 520 (quotation). The story of Robert Berkeley's murder as it was passed down from the nineteenth to the twentieth century reflected the evolving collective memory of white southerners struggling to maintain a positive identity after a bitter defeat in war, the destruction of their social institutions, and a contested period of northern control. Some scholars distinguish collective memory, as the social analog of individual mem-ory, from history construed as the analytical reconstruction of events. Conflating past and present, group identity therefore can structure the way people see events. The col-lective memory of a society is consequently subject to the psychological mechanisms of selective omission, fabrication, exaggeration, and embellishment by which individ-uals reconcile self-perceptions of identity with contradictory events in their past. For pertinent literature on collective memory see Maurice Halbwachs, *On Collective Mem-ory*, edited and translated by Lewis A. Coser (Chicago and London, 1992); Nell Irvin Painter, *Sojourner Truth: A Life, A Symbol* (New York, 1996), esp. pp. 247–87; James W. Pennebaker, Dario Paez, and Bernard Rimé, eds. *Collective Memory of Political Events: Social Psychological Perspectives* (Mahwah, N.J., 1997); Barry Schwartz, *George Washington: The Making of an American Symbol* (Ithaca N.Y., and London, 1987); and Yael Zerubavel, *Recovered Roots: Collective Memory and the Making of Israeli National Tra-dition* (Chicago, 1995).

50. John W. Rust to Wilson Gee, October 25, 1943, Laura Virginia Hale Collec-tion (Laura Virginia Hale Archives, Warren Heritage Society). The story that Berke-ley had freed his slaves in his will is also mentioned in Young, *Berkeleys of Barn Elms*, 86–87, without indicating a source.

51. James M. Lindgren, *Preserving the Old Dominion: Historic Preservation and Vir-ginia Traditionalism* (Charlottesville, 1993). John W. Rust represented Arlington, Prince William, and Fairfax Counties and Alexandria City in the senate of Virginia from 1932 through 1938. His father, John R. Rust, served under Stonewall Jackson during the Civil War and was associated with efforts to commemorate members of Jackson's command. See George N. Conrad to John Rust, Nineva, Va., May 16, 1898 (Virginia Historical Society).

52. Account of unnamed granddaughter in Davis, "Tragedy of Rock Hill."

53. *Ibid.*

54. *Ibid.*

55. *Ibid.*

56. Mary Morris, interview with the authors, Winchester, Virginia, November 19, 1997 (notes in our possession). Morris heard the story from her fourth-grade teacher, Roberta Earle, in Warren County, Virginia, in 1954 or 1955. This story further relates that guests who spent the night in the room that was formerly Julia Berkeley's bed-chamber would hear a scratching at the door. When they opened it, they would see the ghost of the shaggy white dog with the arm in its mouth.

57. Wayne Chatfield-Taylor, interview by authors, Warren County, Virginia, April 24, 1994 (notes in our possession).

58. Although the money stolen from Berkeley's sideboard was recovered, the idea developed that Rock Hill harbored a lost treasure. The earliest reference is in Kercheval, *History of the Valley of Virginia*, 359. On the condition of the house and its demolition see Lee J. Fristoe to J[osiah] L. Dickinson, March 27, 1940, and Josiah L. Dickinson to John H. Winn, December 22, 1961, Rock Hill Correspondence (Laura Virginia Hale Archives).

59. Stanley M. Elkins, *Slavery: A Problem in American Institutional and Intellectual Life* (Chicago, 1959), 128–29; Ulrich B. Phillips, *American Negro Slavery: A Survey of the Supply, Employment and Control of Negro Labor as Determined by the Plantation Régime* (New York and London, 1918), 291 and 342. Since Elkins and Phillips, historians have recognized the vital communities that slaves and free blacks created despite and as a result of racial oppression. The rich, vibrant cultures of these communities have profoundly influenced American life but not without the social and psychological costs of slavery's inherent abuses. See John W. Blassingame, *The Slave Community: Plantation Life in the Antebellum South* (New York, 1972); Gutman, *Black Family;* Charles Joyner, *Down by the Riverside: A South Carolina Slave Community* (Chicago and Urbana, 1984); Lawrence Levine, *Black Culture and Black Consciousness: Afro American Folk Thought from Slavery to Freedom* (New York and Oxford, 1977); Nell Irvin Painter, "Soul Murder and Slavery: Toward a Fully Loaded Cost Accounting," in Linda Kerber, Alice Kessler-Harris, and Kathryn Kish Sklar, eds., *U.S. History as Women's History* (Chapel Hill, 1995), 125–46; and Sobel, *World They Made Together.*

THOMAS E. BUCKLEY, S.J.

Unfixing Race: Class, Power, and Identity in an Interracial Family

✳ ✳ ✳ ✳ ✳ ✳ ✳ ✳ *F*ROM THE PERSPECTIVE OF THE TWENTY-FIRST century, what stands out in the story of Robert Wright and his family is not that he pursued a divorce in 1816, but that he was black, that his estranged wife was white, and that friends and neighbors lobbied the legislature in favor of his cause. To his contemporaries race meant less than his standing as a propertied farmer who had assumed the rights and responsibilities of citizenship in his community. Although Buckley "does not argue that the situation of Robert Wright and his family was typical, even of free blacks who held land and slaves," Buckley's essay "demonstrates the complexity of antebellum race relations while simultaneously dramatizing the importance of studying the free black experience in terms of individual, family, and local histories." A century later Virginians not only would take extraordinary steps to prevent unions such as Wright's, but they would also define race so rigidly that one black ancestor—one drop of black blood—would prohibit an otherwise white man from marrying a white woman. More remarkable, this later generation—described by Gregory Michael Dorr in this volume—asserted that because the strict partition of the races supposedly comported with both scientific law and legal principle, Virginia society had always been segregated.

In his essay Thomas Buckley unfixes racial boundaries in the Virginia past. He demonstrates in the case of Robert Wright, his father, Thomas, and their extensive family that identity in antebellum Virginia could be flexible, permeable, and responsive to changing conditions. These conditions, moreover, had more to do with class, wealth, and social standing than they did with race. It was possible to be black, marry or live openly with a white woman, possess land, own slaves, enjoy status, and attract the respect of fellow citizens. Racial essentialism was not inherent to Virginia's social constitution, says Buckley, but a construction of particular times and particular places.

For both Robert and Thomas Wright, interracial unions produced companionate marriages, the possibility of domestic happiness, and offspring

234

who inherited considerable wealth if not pride of place. What Thomas Jefferson found in his love for his family, then, was not restricted to men of his political prominence, nor was it the special preserve of his race. Thus the affections that bound men and women across racial boundaries in the case of the Wright family open unexplored perspectives on Jefferson's relation with his slave Sally Hemings and the irony of analogous black and white households at Monticello. In this light, as well, the murder of Robert Berkeley appears less as a desperate act of depraved slaves and more as a deliberate expression of forlorn hope for a better life.

What for later generations fixed race and identity into unyielding definitions in black and white remains unexplored in Buckley's essay. Stephen Ash's perspective on the experience of white Virginians during the Civil War, however, goes a long way in showing how wartime suffering and defeat produced a gulf of guilt and recrimination separating whites and blacks. In Fred Arthur Bailey's thinking, this gulf grew unbridgeable as Virginians by 1900 closed their minds to the complexity of class, power, and identity in an antebellum world they had clearly lost.   *   *   *   *   *   *   *   *

*   *   *   *   *   *   *   *

IN NOVEMBER 1816 ROBERT WRIGHT, A SLAVEHOLDING FARMER from Campbell County in the Virginia Piedmont, petitioned the General Assembly for a divorce. Because the state courts lacked jurisdiction over divorce in the early nineteenth century, the legislators regularly considered such requests. Wright's petition, however, was unlike any other the assembly had ever received. According to Wright's account, his marriage to Mary Godsey in 1806 had been a happy one. Describing his behavior toward her as "kind and affectionate," Wright acknowledged that Mary had brought him "great domestic comfort, and felicity" until 1814, when William Arthur "by his artful, and insidious attentions" replaced Wright "in her affections." The couple eloped in January 1815, taking with them some of Wright's property including a female slave, but were caught in neighboring Bedford County. Wright reclaimed his possessions, and Mary consented "to return to the Home, and the Husband she had so ungratefully, and cruelly abandoned." Despite her infidelity, Wright maintained that he had again treated his wife with affection, hoping "time . . . would reconcile her to her situation and restore her to Happiness." His hopes proved illusory. Ten months later, Mary and William ran off to Tennessee. Charging her with desertion and adultery, Wright asked the assembly to pass a law ending their marriage.

Thus far the case was familiar. Tales of infidelity, desertion, and scorned love the legislators had heard before. What made Wright's petition unique was his frank admission that as "a free man of color" he had married a white woman and so violated Virginia's law forbidding interracial marriage.

While avoiding a rhetorical style that was either defiant or obsequious, Wright defended the validity of his union and presented his case in matter-of-fact fashion. His free status apparently empowered him with a sense of personal worth and dignity and a claim to equal treatment that he was unafraid to assert publicly. Equally noteworthy were the affidavits submitted with the memorial. Defying the mores historians commonly ascribe to white southerners, more than fifty white citizens of Campbell County ignored Wright's miscegenation, endorsed his request for a divorce, and testified to his good standing in their community.[1]

Wright's legislative petition and the accompanying documents are remarkable on several counts. First, they introduce us to the power relationships and the interaction of race and class, both within an interracial family and between that family and the local community, that operated as discursive processes in constructing the shifting identities of Robert Wright and his family.[2] Second, they suggest a level of openness in interracial sexual relationships and a degree of white acceptance of miscegenation that challenge historical generalizations and traditional stereotypes of both free blacks and the slaveholding society of the early nineteenth-century South.[3] Finally, they contest the commonly accepted view that free blacks operated cautiously on the fringes of southern society. This essay does not argue that the situation of Robert Wright and his family was typical, even of free blacks who held land and slaves, but rather, as Ira Berlin pointed out, that historians must pay attention to exceptions.[4] A scrutiny of Wright's background and his family and community connections demonstrates the complexity of antebellum race relations while simultaneously dramatizing the importance of studying the free black experience in terms of individual, family, and local histories at a time when slavery was vigorously expanding.[5]

In a burst of uncharacteristic liberalism, Virginia legalized manumission by deed or will in 1782. Early in the next decade, however, the Old Dominion retreated from emancipation when a new codification of laws concerning slaves spelled out their status as chattels and forbade free Negroes from entering the state. The revelation of Gabriel's plot in 1800 increased the outcry for harsher laws that would further restrict the activities of both slaves and free Negroes, prevent any more manumissions, and remove the free black population. The assembly responded by requiring newly emancipated slaves to leave Virginia and encouraging the various African colonization societies that sprang up in the next decade.[6] Meanwhile, by the end of the Revolution, the Piedmont held more slaves than the Tidewater. During the next three decades, the state's slave population doubled, while more and more whites joined the slaveholder ranks.[7] Richard R. Beeman has documented the expansion of slavery, with its concomitant commitment to agrarianism, into Lunenburg County and asserted that by 1830 the peculiar institution provided "the central point of definition for the Southside's white citizens."[8]

In nearby Campbell County, the same social and economic system provided the context for the Wright family. Fortunately, an abundance of sources makes it possible to reconstruct the interplay between family members. In addition to the divorce petition and the data available from deeds, wills, and census and tax records, a series of legal battles after Robert Wright's death left a rich deposit of court papers detailing his economic affairs as well as family and community relationships. A few years ago Michael P. Johnson and James L. Roark demonstrated the usefulness of family papers in tracing the experience of free African Americans in the antebellum South.[9] A reconstruction of the history of the Wright family indicates the wealth of information available in legislative petition collections and legal files squirreled away in state archives and county courthouses.[10]

Thomas Wright, a white man from a large family in Prince Edward County, bought an extensive plantation in Bedford County from Charles and Sarah Caffrey in July 1779 for 1,500 pounds of tobacco. Amounting to 389^1/$_2$ acres of prime farmland, the property straddled Beaver Creek just a few miles before the stream flows into the James River. Two years later that section of Bedford became part of newly established Campbell County, and in 1784 the town of Lynchburg was founded up the James River, a few miles southwest of Wright's plantation.[11] While struggling to establish himself financially during these years, Wright became estranged from his brothers and sisters. Shortly before he purchased the farm, his father, John Wright, had died, leaving a wife and at least seven children. His will details an extensive estate with bequests of varying sizes. Thomas was assigned one of the smallest portions, a monetary gift of £30 to be paid by his brother James within five years. This legacy was only a pittance, given the financial outlay required to purchase the land on Beaver Creek, but evidently he never received it. Later, in "his drinking fits," a resentful Thomas Wright swore that none of his relatives would ever inherit his property and vowed that he would rather give it to one of his neighbors or the county poor.[12]

Instead of these potential beneficiaries, however, Wright ultimately switched his attention and affection to the mulatto family he established along Beaver Creek. To his new home, Wright had brought several slaves, including a young woman, Sylvia, and her two children, Prudence and Anna, whom he had purchased from the Cabell estate four or five years before.[13] Sylvia was apparently of full African descent, because someone who knew her well later described her as "very black." At the time of her purchase, she was pregnant again and in 1775 gave birth to a son, James. Sometime during the following years, Thomas Wright began to cohabit with her. On 30 June 1780, almost a year after they moved to the Beaver Creek plantation, she bore a mulatto son, Robert, and over the next decade and a

Table: The Descendants of Sylvia Wright

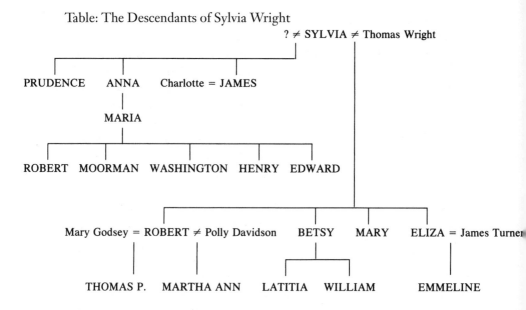

half came three mulatto daughters: Betsy, Mary, and Eliza. Although Thomas Wright never formally married the mother of his children, they "lived together as man and wife." They also prospered. Within the economic ranks of Campbell County, Wright could be considered at least a modest planter. Nor did his miscegenous relationship with Sylvia injure his standing in the community. Rather than censuring or fining him, the county court periodically assigned him to survey roads and serve on juries, and he numbered among his friends some of the most important men in the community.[14]

As the years passed, Thomas Wright took increasing interest in his family and particularly his son. On 1 September 1791, when Robert was eleven years old, Thomas escorted the boy he called "his Robin" to the Campbell courthouse and recorded his manumission, which was to become effective on his twenty-first birthday in 1801.[15] The timing of this civil declaration was crucial in Robert's development. He was old enough to grasp the importance of the status being conferred on him, and the public nature of the announcement must have reinforced his own feelings of self-worth while giving him a keen appreciation of the value of his freedom and a profound gratitude toward his father, qualities that would mark his adult life. About this time, Thomas Wright began telling his friends that Robert would be his heir. Thus, the boy grew up with the sense of entitlement that came from being the only son of a well-to-do and doting father. Far from treating him as a slave, Thomas kept Robert in his home, carefully saw to his education in business as well as academic subjects, and gave him a horse to ride to school. His classroom companions and playmates at home were white boys such as William Hawkins and Stephen and William Perrow, whose fathers also possessed good-sized farms and slaves. Described variously as "light" and as a "bright" mulatto, Robert basked in the approval of a father who proudly pointed him out as one of the "strongest negro fellows" in the county.[16]

Eventually, Thomas Wright also provided for the freedom of his other children. On 14 April 1800 he filed papers for the manumission of his three daughters: Betsy, sixteen, Mary, fourteen, and Eliza, seven, as well as for Maria, three, the daughter of Anna, who was part of Sylvia's first family. Each girl would become free at the age of eighteen. The next February, Wright also manumitted Anna, twenty-eight, and James, twenty-six, "being fully persuaded that freedom is the natural right of all mankind." His belief in natural rights, however, did not induce him to liberate all his slaves. At his death Wright still owned at least five.[17]

In reality, he may well have freed Anna, James, and Maria because of his devotion to Sylvia and her influence over him. The provisions of his will indicate the nature of their relationship as well as his love for both Sylvia and their son. According to reliable witnesses, Wright originally planned to leave the bulk of his estate to Sylvia for the rest of her life. Robert and several of the senior Wright's friends, however, persuaded him that Sylvia would be incapable of managing the property and was not interested in the land. It would be far better, they argued, to leave most of the estate in Robert's hands with the understanding that he would provide financially for his mother's comfort as well as for the rest of the family. Thomas Wright concurred with this paternalism. As one of his closest associates and neighbors, Colonel Daniel B. Perrow, later attested, although Wright was "much attached" to Sylvia and extremely solicitous for her care, he also "had great Confidence in Robert before and at the time of his Death."[18]

When Thomas Wright died in late 1805, he left "the sole and exclusive use and enjoyment" of his plantation house and two acres around it to "Sylvee a woman of colour formerly my slave but since emancipated and with whom I have had children." She also received as her "absolute property forever" all furniture in the house, two milk cows of her own choosing, and whatever money Thomas possessed at the time of his death. The will further specified that Anna's daughter, Maria, should serve Sylvia until she became free at the age of eighteen. To his "natural son Robert Wright," Thomas gave the plantation land, slaves, stock, and equipment, as well as any other real estate or personal property he owned. Moreover, the house and acres in Sylvia's possession would revert to Robert after his mother's death. Apart from the land, the personal estate in the house and on the farm was appraised at almost £500.[19] Wright chose his executors carefully. Undoubtedly, he realized the unusual nature of his will, and he knew his white brothers and sisters and their descendants expected to claim his property.

Three "trusty friends," Daniel B. Perrow, Charles Gilliam, and Lawrence McGeorge, served as his executors. Perrow was especially prominent in the county that he represented for eleven terms in the state assembly and later served as sheriff.[20] He and the other executors ensured that Sylvia and Robert took uncontested possession of the estate.

Thus, with his father's considerable assistance and the approval of the white elite, Robert Wright gained entry into Campbell County society and acquired an identity constructed by economic class rather than race. Almost a year later he displayed and reinforced his position when he married Mary Godsey, a white woman. Because Mary was underage, her mother gave her consent for the marriage license in October 1806, though the county clerk never recorded the marriage.[21] It is not difficult to imagine the minister arriving for the wedding only to discover that the bride and groom were an interracial couple, performing the ceremony under the social constraints of the occasion, and then covering himself with the law by destroying the certificate. If miscegenation under any circumstances had been unacceptable in Campbell County, Wright's neighbors should have demonstrated their disapproval by hauling the couple before the county court for violating the law, or at least shunned them. In all the abundant legal records, however, no evidence exists that either then or later anyone publicly objected to their marriage.[22]

Robert brought his wife to a house located close by his mother's, and the next seven or eight years were probably the happiest of his life. An energetic worker like his father, he was adept at farming. Judging from the tax assessments and the comments of overseers, his acreage ranked among the best in the county. The plantation produced substantial crops of wheat, tobacco, oats, hay, and corn, along with burnt lime. The work was sufficient for seven laborers, most of whom were apparently slaves. Wright fitted easily into the slaveholding ranks and seemingly was not troubled by owning slaves or purchasing them as he thought necessary.[23] His tastes were those of his class and age. In his free time he hunted in the nearby hills or gambled at cards with his friends. Like his father and many other Virginians of the day, he had a penchant for the bottle and drank freely and often. George MacKey, a white stonemason who boarded with him, considered Wright "industrious" around the farm but also noted that he indulged in "frequent Frolicks."[24]

Fulfilling the promises he had made to his father, Robert assumed responsibility for the care of his mother and siblings. Sylvia Wright provided the most difficult challenge. When she discovered that Thomas had altered his original will and given the plantation directly to Robert, she was upset. Evidently, she wanted her economic independence and resented his intervention in the matter of the will and subsequent financial control, which effectively undercut the identity she had constructed as the "wife" of the deceased Thomas. Neighbors noticed that mother and son had "frequent misunderstandings," but Sylvia later admitted that Robert had "honestly fulfilled his agreement" with his father and given her a "decent Support."[25]

Another change in the will may also have displeased Sylvia. At one time Thomas Wright had considered leaving fifty acres of his plantation to James, her elder son, whom he had also freed. But Robert dissuaded his father from breaking up the tract on Beaver Creek and promised that he would purchase land elsewhere for James. A few months after his father's death, he bought fifty-six acres in neighboring Bedford County for his half brother to farm but retained the deed himself to ensure that no one would "cheet [James] out of the land." Robert's half sister Anna had died some time earlier, and when her daughter Maria received her freedom at the age of eighteen, Robert sent her to live with her uncle James in Bedford and provided money for her support.[26] Robert also took responsibility for his mulatto sisters and met their needs as best he could. Betsy, the eldest, was raised in Lynchburg, mainly under the supervision of Sarah Winston Cabell, and later had two children, Latitia and William, without benefit of marriage. Although accused of being a drunkard and a "notorious prostitute," Betsy Wright would be a force to be reckoned with in the family and the courts for years to come. Betsy's reputation for loose conduct may have been the reason Sylvia kept her two youngest daughters at home. Mary died unmarried before her mother, while Eliza married James Turner, a free black shoemaker.[27]

By all accounts, Robert Wright played the role of gentleman farmer and *paterfamilias* well. His father had trained him for that position, and apparently he enjoyed it. After eight years of marriage, his wife gave birth in December 1814. Robert proudly named his son Thomas Pryor Wright, thus identifying him with his own father and his father's family. Within a few weeks, however, Mary rejected both her husband and their mulatto child and ran away with William Arthur. Though she initially returned home in response to her husband's pleading, Mary's elopement at the end of 1815 left Robert "very much exasperated against her" and plunged him into a bitterness from which he never recovered.[28] The cuckolded husband acted out his anger and humiliation. Convinced that his neighbors had assisted in the escape, he confronted Catherine Stockton, who deposed that Wright had threatened her "with a gun to make me talk and drew his fist to break my head." She finally went to court to make Wright "keep the peace." His suspicions were confirmed, however, when he discovered that James Wiley, one of his old gambling companions, had helped the couple elope. Robert cursed him soundly and repeatedly.[29]

The mulatto farmer soon formed a liaison with another white woman. In the fall of 1816, Polly Davidson moved into his home with the cordial approval of her father and other members of her family. George MacKey,

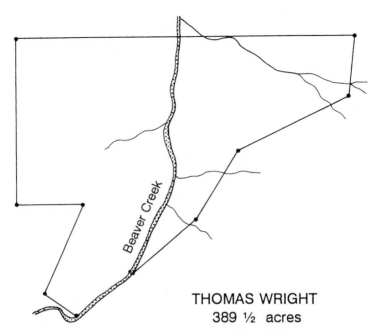

THOMAS WRIGHT
389 ½ acres

In July 1779, Thomas Wright purchased a 389.5-acre plantation in Bedford County from Charles and Sarah Caffrey. This plat of the property on Beaver Creek is derived from the Campbell County Surveyor's Book, 1827–1924.

who "lifted her off of her horse" the night she arrived, testified later that her father on his visits "never" expressed any reservations about the relationship his daughter had formed. Robert Wright himself told Catherine Stockton "that all the relatives of . . . Polly were pleased at her living with him." For the Davidsons, who owned no slaves and little property, this association meant an economic boost. To facilitate the new relationship, Wright also used raw economic power. On the day Polly moved into his house, Robert gave her a bond for $1,000 and, according to some sources, promised her half of his property if she bore his children. Her brother William became Wright's overseer on the plantation, and her clergyman brother may even have performed an informal marriage ceremony without benefit of license.[30]

Although Wright's divorce petition did not mention Polly Davidson, it indicates the depth of his feelings and the need to reassert his own self-worth and the identity constructed through bonding with his father and affiliation with the white, landowning, slaveholding class in the county. Wright presented himself to the General Assembly as "a free man of color," his wife as "a free white woman," and Arthur as "a free white man." In stressing the eloping couple's free status, Wright emphasized the importance of his own. Freedom was the common denominator that made him their equal, while his wife's desertion and adultery without provocation on his part made Wright more sinned against than sinning. The Wrights had obtained a proper marriage license, and an authorized clergyman, William Heath, had officiated at the ceremony. Although admitting that the minister who performed an interracial marriage and the white party who contracted it could be punished under the law, Wright argued confidently that the wedding had been "to all intents and purposes valid and binding between the parties," because such penalties did not render it null and void. Given these circumstances, he wanted a divorce.[31]

The request in itself was unusual, for legislative divorces were extremely rare. Few Virginians applied, and far fewer had their appeals granted. Out of 107 divorce petitions between 1786 and 1815, the assembly acted affirmatively on only fifteen. Ironically in the case of Robert Wright, the most compelling reason a white husband could offer for a divorce in 1816 was proof through the birth of a mulatto child that his wife had been sexually involved with a Negro.[32] By acknowledging that his marriage had been interracial, Wright may have hoped to assure a divorce.

In a ringing endorsement of his request, the local white community rallied behind Wright and testified to his honorable position in their society. Lewis Franklin, Charles Gilliam, and Stephen Perrow, respectable farmers and slaveholders, signed their names at the bottom of his petition and, in a separate affidavit, asserted that as Wright's neighbors they had known him well for a long time. He behaved "with propriety," they told the legislature. Vouching for the accuracy of his statements, they asserted that he had "allways treated his wife with kindness." In still another petition, more than fifty other men testified to the General Assembly that they "have been well acquainted with Robert Wright . . . for many years past, and do with pleasure certify that we consider him an honest, upright man, and good citizen." From the "information" they had gathered about his marital problems, they believed that his petition was a truthful account. Most of these men were middling farmers, but a few possessed extensive plantations of more than a thousand acres. About half owned slaves, and at least two were justices of the county court.[33] In short, they were broadly representative of the local community that regarded Wright as one of its own.

The scene is easily imagined. The men gathered outside the buildings at the county seat on one of the autumn court days. Franklin, Gilliam, and Perrow were well-known, respected members of the community. Perhaps one of them read Wright's petition aloud, noted their own endorsements, and encouraged the other men to sign the briefer statement. They could explain to those who were unfamiliar with his marital situation what his wife had done. The three were credible witnesses. Wright himself may well have appeared, as he did at court days. His economic status in the community, his capable management of the property he had inherited from his father, and the way he conducted himself in their society had helped the mulatto farmer forge strong relationships with his white neighbors. They gave him and his cause their public support.

Despite the widespread local approval, however, the House of Delegates rejected Wright's divorce petition out of hand without even referring it to committee.[34] Affidavits and testimonials from western Campbell County counted for little in Richmond. Although Wright could be married to a white woman in his community, he could not be married to her in law.

Neither of the supporting documents that accompanied the petition mentioned race, yet both Wright and the local community were fully aware of his racial identity. All the legal documents drafted after his death repeatedly labeled him "coloured" or "black" or "negro." County records do not indicate that he ever held any civil position or served on a jury. When he traveled outside Virginia, he was careful to carry on his person a certified copy of his emancipation papers.[35] Yet Robert Wright was in fact a split subject. For many if not most important purposes, class and economic condition, rather than race, constructed his identity. The tax records provide one significant index. The personal property tax list from his section of the county in 1816 counted 2,171 slaves over twelve years of age and seventy-two free Negroes over sixteen. Wright was not included, however, as either a free black or a mulatto in 1816 or in any preceding year. For tax purposes, he was considered to be white. Only in 1817 and 1818, after the divorce petition and during the last two years of his life, did the tax assessor write an "M," for mulatto, next to his name.[36]

That change may have occurred because a new person filled the assessor's office; but it also may represent Wright's altered position in the neighborhood. When he and Mary Godsey had married, the local community had ignored their violation of the law against miscegenation. At least some in the county, however, disapproved of his public adultery with Polly Davidson. One of Wright's boarders recounted that the couple lived together "as though they had been man & wife in the utmost harmony." Polly was in full charge of the "Domestick affairs" in the home.[37] Although certain neighbors were sympathetic to Robert's plight and accepted this relationship, referring to Polly as his "wife" and as "Polly Wright," others condemned her character and insisted that her position as Robert's "concubine" rendered her "notorious in the neighbourhood."[38] Wright's strained relations at this time with his father's old friend and executor, Daniel Perrow, probably resulted from the latter's open disapproval of such "cohabitation." Though Robert had once sought the elderly colonel's advice and consulted with him on business, he no longer did so.[39] Indeed, Robert may well have expected the assembly to reject his petition but hoped that a good-faith attempt to obtain a divorce would gain community acceptance for the relationship he and Polly had formed. Polly may also have wanted the divorce in order to legitimize her position as Robert's wife.

In this uneasy atmosphere created by both Robert's continuing bitterness over Mary's desertion and the hostility of at least a portion of the community, a misunderstanding arose in the spring of 1818 between Robert and his closest friend, Stephen Perrow. Raised on neighboring farms, the two had played and gone to school together and had inherited their fathers' plantations about the same time. Though Robert was older by perhaps as much as seven years, one of the boarders in his home thought that the two men "appeared as greate as Brothers."[40] Perrow had strongly supported the divorce petition and, after Robert's death, would serve as Polly's closest adviser; but in early 1818 a slave told him and Fleming Duncan that Robert had cursed them for letting their hogs run wild in the woods and called them "no better than theives." Duncan wanted to confront Wright, but Perrow persuaded him that because this tale was simply "negro's news, Robin would deny it—that he knew Robin better than he did, & to let him alone." The incident, however, was repeated around the neighborhood. Ultimately someone informed an "astonished, and distressed" Wright during the April court days that Stephen Perrow and others among his peers no longer considered him a friend. Although Robert acknowledged the "dispute" between himself and Daniel Perrow, he was unaware of any other hostile neighbors and was particularly upset by the report that Stephen Perrow was "unfriendly to him." Unwilling to believe it, Wright immediately sought out Perrow and happily reported to Gilliam the next day "that everything was perfectly explained, . . . and they were on the most friendly terms."[41]

Yet Wright's emotional distress was evident to his friends. Lewis Franklin witnessed Robert's crying when he and Perrow were discussing Robert's affairs at the courthouse in September.[42] The reason for Wright's unhappiness was probably not a business matter, because his economic status at this time was excellent. Stephen Perrow may have been warning his friend that he was in danger of being presented to the county court for adultery. Evidently Colonel Daniel Perrow, Campbell's recently retired sheriff, had seriously considered such an action. He later testified that Stephen Perrow had told him he might do so himself, but the colonel thought the younger man had made this statement just to keep him from taking that step. The emotional pressure intensified. Although his neighbors thought Wright was in good health, he began to have premonitions of approaching death. While staying overnight with Franklin, he remarked on the sickness in his family and stated "that he should die before long." He expressed the same belief to another old family friend, John Gardner. Both men later testified that Wright had also told them he had made his will, and Gardner added that Wright had named Stephen Perrow and Arthur Litchfield as his executors.[43]

Less than a month later, on 14 October 1818, Robert Wright died. He left a sizable estate in land, slaves, and crops with a promise of another plantation home, farm animals, and additional property to go to his heirs after the death of his mother.[44] A series of legal battles and appeals to the General Assembly ensued that embroiled the entire Wright family—white, black, and mulatto—involved the conflicting testimony of numerous friends, neighbors, and acquaintances, and employed a flock of lawyers off and on for more than fifty years. These conflicts revolving around the Wrights further demonstrate the status and treatment of a free black family and the way in which its members asserted their rights, used the law, and interacted with one another and the white members of an antebellum Virginia community.

On the evening before Wright died, his home was crowded with family members and friends. As Robert lay unconscious in his bedroom, Stephen Perrow showed a will in Robert's handwriting to several people who later said they had read it.[45] According to most versions of the testimony, Wright had planned to divide his property. His infant son, Thomas P. Wright, would receive the larger section of land on the north side of Beaver Creek; the property on the south side, where his home was located, would go to Polly during her lifetime and then to any child she might have within nine months of his death. If she did not bear his child, then when she died the house and land would revert to his son.[46] After Robert's death, however, the will could not be located, and Polly Davidson maintained that Robert's sister Betsy had destroyed it. She explained that while Robert was dying, Betsy had come to her in another room and "asked for the keys to the Beaureau where the will & other Papers were Kept in the Room in which Robert lay & went directly & opened or unlocked the same." Later, Polly discovered "the will & one hundred Dollars in money were missing & she thought Betsy Wright had taken them."[47] In support of Polly's story, Catherine Stockton swore that shortly after Robert's death, she had been on a road outside Lynchburg and heard Betsy boast to several other blacks that she "had stolen . . . Robert's will, and all the money he had and had conquered all the white folks."[48] A month after Robert's death, the county court sent Betsy, her daughter Latitia, and brother-in-law James Turner to jail until they produced the will but later ordered their release.[49]

In the spring of 1819, Robert's putative will became the subject of a lawsuit filed by Polly Davidson against Samuel Fleming, whom the county court had appointed temporary curator of Wright's estate until the will was settled.[50] For more than a year both sides gathered affidavits from family members and neighbors. Stephen Perrow led the struggle to establish Polly Davidson's claim, while Fleming assembled witnesses who tried to throw doubt on Polly's credibility and Stephen Perrow's friendship with Robert Wright. As accusations of lying and deceit were hurled back and forth, the neighborhood along Beaver Creek became badly fractured. Members of the Perrow family, for example, wound up on opposing sides. Daniel Perrow, whose wife was Elizabeth Fleming, supported Samuel Fleming's case against his cousin Stephen Perrow.[51] Sylvia, Betsy, and the rest of Robert's black and mulatto family supported Fleming. Certainly they stood to gain if Thomas P. Wright inherited all of his father's property immediately. Betsy in particular took a hand in guiding affairs. Fleming and "*Relatives Interested*" paid their lawyer, James B. Risque, $50 in advance and promised him another $300 if he won the suit.[52]

Before the case could be settled, however, the white members of the Wright family filed a cross suit in April 1820 charging that Robert Wright had never been legally emancipated and was therefore a slave and incapable of inheriting any property from his father in 1805. Because Thomas Wright had never married, they asserted that his legal heirs were his brothers and sisters and their descendants. They asked the court to set aside Thomas Wright's will and give them his property.[53] Even though the county clerk maintained that he could not find any evidence of Robert Wright's manumission, the court decided the statement in Thomas Wright's will that "he had '*duly emancipated*' him" was sufficient evidence of Robert's freedom and therefore his capacity to inherit his father's property. His white cousins wound up paying court costs.[54] They then appealed twice to the legislature to award them the property on the grounds that Robert had died "Intestate and unmarried." Both times the assembly turned them down.[55]

While these appeals were still in process, Polly Davidson lost her lawsuit. In *Davidson* v. *Wright*, a Bedford County court ruled "that Robert Wright did not make or execute such will as alleged," and the Lynchburg Superior Court of Chancery then awarded the entire estate to Thomas P. Wright.[56] After almost seven years of litigation, Samuel Fleming and Robert Wright's mother and siblings had emerged triumphant. Meanwhile, Fleming had been systematically robbing the estate and adding to his own personal wealth.[57] Wright had left extensive holdings in land, slaves, horses, stock, plantation equipment, and "a most excellent crop" in his fields and barns, as well as money and bonds worth as much as $500. As Stephen Perrow later testified, Wright had been a capable manager with few debts. Soon after taking over the property, however, Fleming told Perrow that even though the estate had "a Balance of upwards of $500, . . . it made no difference as the estate was going to hell and he might as well have it as any one else."[58]

As curator, Fleming hired a succession of overseers to manage the

Wright plantation. Their affidavits testify both to the excellent quality of the farm and its yield as well as the various ways in which the curator bilked the estate. Fleming regularly sold or took home for himself crops, lamb, pork, wool, cows, horses, beds, and other movable property, but revenues rarely appeared on the balance sheet. He also charged the estate $1 for each trip he made to the plantation, while bragging to the overseer that he made such charges even when he did not appear.[59] Although Sylvia and Betsy Wright would later prove keen enough to defend their own interests in court, no complaints came either from them or from any other member of the Wright family. Fleming may well have been buying them off. Certainly he used estate funds to support Sylvia and the other Wrights, including Betsy's daughter, Latitia, who took care of young Thomas. They continued living in the old plantation house.[60]

Fleming's temporary curatorship ended with the conclusion of the suits over the will in 1825. In what was later proven to be an extraordinary fraud, he drew up a claim against the estate of $726.72, which he transferred jointly to German Jordan, a local tavern keeper, and Richard G. Haden, a deputy sheriff. Then, after selling his own plantation on Beaver Creek, Fleming pocketed his gains both legal and criminal and moved to Tennessee.[61] The county court next designated William Thompson, Jr., as curator, but when he discovered that Betsy Wright objected to his appointment, Thompson did not apply for the papers.[62] Instead, toward the end of 1825, Jordan had himself appointed first the estate's administrator and then Thomas P. Wright's guardian. The boy was eleven years old.[63]

If Fleming had swindled the estate, Jordan wasted it. After renting out the land and the slaves, he auctioned off the stock, crops, and other movable property. He also accepted without challenge several claims against the estate, including one by Haden of $600. Asserting insufficient funds to settle the estate's debts, Jordan then sold the slaves over a three-year period between 1826 and 1829, some for a price far below market value.[64]

Complaints from his securities eventually spurred the court to relieve Jordan of his control over the estate. At young Thomas Wright's request, William Gough, who had recently purchased a large plantation next to the Wright property, became the boy's guardian. Gough retained Samuel and Maurice H. Garland, two prominent Lynchburg attorneys, and the next year brought suit in Lynchburg's Superior Court of Law and Chancery against Fleming, Jordan, and their securities. The inventory made shortly after Jordan became administrator had listed eleven slaves, horses, stock, crops, plantation utensils, and furniture worth $3,667. With the exception of Suckey, an old slave woman valued at nothing, it was "*all gone.*" The attorneys blistered Jordan and Haden for their "high handed frauds & speculations." Jordan, they asserted, had "cheated the child out of all his estate but the land, and it's God mercy" that had not been sold also.[65]

After detailing the defendants' misdeeds, the Garland brothers suggested that "perhaps" Sylvia Wright and Jordan had shared "a secret understanding." In proposing that Sylvia had a hand in looting her grandson's property, the two lawyers spoke from firsthand knowledge, for they had represented her in two successful claims against the estate after Jordan became administrator. Sylvia had first sued Jordan in March 1826, demanding that he support her out of the estate. She claimed an annuity on the basis of her relationship with Thomas Wright and promises made after his death. Without mentioning that she had been a slave and that no marriage had taken place, Sylvia asserted that "in early life she associated herself with Thomas Wright . . . and until his death they lived together in harmony as man and Wife." Sylvia depicted their relationship as a partnership. Although initially "they were both porre, having no property," by their own "industry and economy they had acquired a considerable real and personal estate." After Thomas's death, first Robert Wright and then Samuel Fleming had fulfilled her expectations, but Jordan had reduced her to "a helpless and distressed Condition for the Ordinary Comfort of life and dependant upon Charity." She asked for "support for life" and threatened that without it "she must become chargeable upon the county."[66]

In his response as defendant, Jordan did not appeal to the provisions of Thomas Wright's will, challenge Sylvia's interpretation of events, or note her original status as Wright's slave. Nor did he mention that just a few months earlier, she had purchased furniture and stock at the estate auction. In short, Sylvia was no pauper; but because Jordan offered no contest, the court ordered him to pay her from estate revenues $100 a year in quarterly installments.[67] She took him to court the following year, charging that Robert had borrowed a sizable sum in 1806 and never repaid it, "altho' often required." Jordan did not even appear, and an estate slave was sold to satisfy her claim.[68]

Jordan's failure to defend his ward's estate was not the result of incompetence. In caring for his own interests, he was extremely astute and fast becoming a wealthy man. The case against him proceeded through several sessions until, after evaluating the commissioner's reports on the estate and the affidavits, the court held Jordan responsible "for the fair cash value of the slaves" who had been "improperly sold." This sum, together with the claims against his guardian accounts, amounted to $2,340.41, which he paid to the estate in March 1833. Even this sizable amount, however, did not seriously cut into his holdings.[69]

Meanwhile, Thomas P. Wright approached his majority. Although his early education had been intermittent, he later attended a school conducted by Thomas and Bartlett Baugh. The boy had bills for books as well as "slate, paper and inkpowder" and pocket money "to buy [a] Knife" and "sundries for Christmas." Sometimes he boarded at school, but his guardian also paid

Sylvia "for boarding, washing and mending" and Latitia for "making Clothes."[70] When he became twenty-one on 17 December 1835, Gough paid him in cash $2,540.17, a hefty sum, which with the farmland he inherited might be expected to offer bright prospects.[71] Unfortunately, the young man was enmeshed in debts as well as in another lawsuit, brought by his grandmother against the estate for the annuities that Gough had ceased paying. His guardian had been fending her off for several years, and it must have been with great relief that Gough signed off that responsibility and removed himself from the Wright family affairs. In order to gain his inheritance, however, the grandson had to assume the lawsuit. He made a deed of trust with Charles Mosby and Maurice Garland, selling them the land he had inherited on the understanding that he could continue to reside there and take the profits as long as he paid his grandmother's past and current annuities. If they were not forthcoming, then the trustees could seize and sell his land.[72]

There were other debts, both large and small, so Wright formed a series of eight more deeds of trust with Mosby and Garland to pay a total of $2,361.91. Finally, he agreed that the trustees could auction the land, and Edward Hunter purchased the Wright plantation in 1836 for almost $4,000. Hunter's deed stipulated "that Sylvia Wright the grand mother of Thomas P. is to retain the house" together with the lot and rights to water from the spring and "sufficient wood to burn and timber to repair the house and keep up her fences." After she died, Hunter would receive the house and acres around it.[73]

Thomas Wright had other problems as well. Evidently he was something of a hell-raiser. In August 1835, before he turned twenty-one, he was presented in the Lynchburg Hustings Court for "swearing Twenty profane oaths" and fined $16.60. The next month he appeared before the same court for a breach of the peace, and in November the Campbell court prosecuted him for "beating" another man. Meanwhile, he continued to pile up debts of various sizes, possibly from gambling. In June 1836 the county authorities jailed him as an "insolvent debtor."[74]

Sylvia Wright died in January 1838. Despite the years she had spent with lawyers and lawsuits, she left no will. Betsy and Thomas both filed deeds turning over their share of her estate to Betsy's daughter Latitia. Thomas Wright explained that his cousin had "rendered . . . important services in his infancy and childhood which have never been paid to her, and which [he] is now desirous to make good."[75] He also may have been trying to keep his creditors from swallowing up whatever he inherited from Sylvia's estate. The court named Allen L. Wyllie as administrator, but before the estate could be divided, Latitia died. Because Thomas had already yielded his claim, Betsy and her son William filed a lawsuit maintaining that they and Emmeline Turner, the daughter of Betsy's deceased sister Eliza, were the only three living descendants entitled to Sylvia Wright's estate. They asked the court to order a sale of Sylvia's slaves and a tripartite division of her property. Wyllie and the court concurred, and the three shares each amounted to about $600.[76]

During the following summer, however, in neighboring Bedford County, James and Maria Wright, another son and granddaughter of Sylvia Wright, learned of Sylvia's death and came forward to assert their rights.[77] When Betsy denied any relationship to them, James and Maria explained the existence of Sylvia's first family before her sale to Thomas Wright and the provision that Robert Wright had made for them. Betsy's son William took exception to James Wright's affidavit in the case not only because James was "a party to the suit" but also because he was "a negro." Affidavits by white men in Bedford County, however, supported James and Maria's story. John Overstreet, for example, recalled how Robert had called James his "half Brother" and remembered "too yellow women at James Wrights on visits & said James was their brother." More witnesses came forward, including Stephen Perrow, who supported James and Maria's claims.[78] A court commissioner ultimately concluded that Sylvia had seven children: the first three were "of a black complection," while the last four possessed "a light complection, born whilst she and her master Thomas Wright, cohabited as man & wife, and recognized by him as his children." In 1852 the court eventually ordered a division of Sylvia's estate into five equal shares for Betsy, James, Maria, and William Wright and Emmeline Turner.[79]

Responding to this decree, Betsy reappeared in court. The previous decade and a half had been traumatic for the almost seventy-year-old woman. According to several neighbors, she had been badly burned in a fire in the early 1840s and spent almost two years confined to a rented, unfurnished home in Lynchburg, where her bed was "a parcel of rags." Frequently freezing in the winter's cold without wood for a fire and lacking even basic necessities, she existed on whatever food her friends and son William brought her. Then William had died, leaving her even more alone. By the end of the decade, Betsy resided in Lynchburg's poorhouse.[80] Despite her problems, however, Betsy's amended bill of complaint showed an extraordinary capacity for deception. Although still denying that James and Maria were her half brother and niece, she accepted the court's verdict that they were her relatives and thus claimed their estates. According to her story, they had both died unmarried and childless, as had her son William and niece Emmeline Turner. Thomas P. Wright had died as well. Announcing that she was "the sole survivor of the whole family, and sole heir of all the rest," Betsy demanded "full and complete justice." Moreover, she hounded the court to act "*speedily* (for she is a tenant of the Poor house and with her just rights involved in this case, could be made comfortable, if not happy, the remnant of her days)."[81] Her persistence paid off. Although not entitled to the legacies of either James or Maria—James had lived with a woman he acknowledged as his wife, and Maria had five living children—Betsy received $450 from Wyllie in 1853 and several lesser amounts in later years. Although probably never finding either comfort or happiness and evidently remaining a "pauper," she certainly enjoyed longevity. When the last case was settled and the court accepted the final report of its commissioner in 1873, Betsy was almost ninety years old.[82]

The saga of the Wright family, however pathetic in its denouement, provides a valuable opportunity to examine the personal, social, and economic changes within an interracial family over three generations; the interaction of white, mulatto, and black relatives; and their relationships with the local white community. The most immediately arresting reality is that race did not fix identities. Indeed, the incidence of miscegenation on the part of men and women of both races met a tolerant, even supportive, reaction from one slaveholding Virginia community. Neither white father nor mulatto son felt compelled to disguise or deny the intimate liaisons they formed across the color line. For more than a quarter century, Thomas Wright lived with Sylvia out of wedlock; yet in conversation with friends and through his will, he made clear his love for the mother of his children and the happiness their union had brought him. As best he could, he constructed for her the identity of a wife. In her later years Sylvia treated their relationship as if it had been in fact a legitimate marriage and an economic partnership. For both, it obviously meant much more than the mating of a white master and a black slave.

Nor did Thomas Wright's open concubinage with Sylvia diminish his stature in the local community. Moreover, he successfully transferred his respected position in society to his son, who then reached beyond his parents to marry a white woman and live with her as his wife for ten years. So integral was this marriage to his identity that neither in his reported exchanges with his neighbors nor in his petition to the General Assembly did he ever apologize for his conduct, display embarrassment, or express remorse for violating a supposed taboo. Mary Godsey and Polly Davidson also crossed the racial line publicly and did so with the consent and even approval of their families. Moreover, all evidence indicates that the local community accepted the match between Robert and Mary. In short, everyone immediately concerned and their white neighbors behaved as if interracial marriage was normal and that the legislation prohibiting miscegenation in Virginia did not or should not exist.

Why did this happen—both for father and son? Most obviously, the respectable positions both men occupied in Campbell County were related to their economic standing as prosperous slaveholding farmers as well as to their public behavior. Class status was directly related to wealth in land and slaves. For this place and time in the culture of patriarchy, money counted far more than race in fixing social position. As a member of the planter class and the beneficiary of his father's transference of power, Robert Wright could openly defy even such a potentially explosive prohibition as that against interracial sexual intercourse and still find acceptance in his local community. Although his neighbors clearly knew Robert was a mulatto, they chose not to construct his identity primarily on that basis.

The role he assumed within the family after his father's death fit the patriarchal model he undoubtedly imbibed from Thomas Wright's example and tutelage and reinforced his identity. He fulfilled what was expected of the male head of the household. He supported his mother and provided for his black and mulatto siblings and their children. Thomas Wright also trained his son for the position he would fill in the neighborhood. He bequeathed to him not only his estate but also the patronage of powerful friends in the white community. They ensured that Robert inherited the property without challenge. White men of similar social and economic standing became his closest friends and associates. Slaveholders and lesser planters like himself, some had been schoolmates and boyhood companions. In addition to doing business with one another, they hunted, gambled, and drank together. As he shared their values, the mulatto farmer moved easily and naturally in their society. He ate at their tables and spent nights in their homes, and when his wife abandoned him, he turned to them for the assistance and support they readily provided. Only when he openly introduced Polly Davidson into his home and began living with her as his wife did a portion of the community recoil in disapproval. But the opprobrium resulted from the couple's public adultery, not from their miscegenation. Even then, Stephen Perrow and other close friends continued to sustain him.

Robert Wright's sense of entitlement to move freely and openly in white society was not unique in his family. Nor perhaps was it entirely a result of his father's training or genes. As the legal records make evident, both black and mulatto members of his family displayed a tough assertiveness in confronting members of the white community as well as one another. Undeterred by considerations of race or gender, Sylvia and her daughter Betsy did not hesitate to use the court system to demand what they claimed as their rights. Their legal opponents were usually white males. In case after case throughout the antebellum period, the two women pushed and shoved to advance their interests. Hiring the best lawyers in Lynchburg, they won more often than they lost. Indeed, they sometimes appear greedy. In the struggle to enhance her own economic security after Robert's death, Sylvia played into the hands of Samuel Fleming and German Jordan and thus jeopardized the inheritance of her grandson. Then again, watching the young Thomas P. Wright grow to maturity, she may have recognized his weaknesses and foreseen his inability to maintain his affairs.

Together with her son William, Betsy turned repeatedly to the courts to secure her claims. Described by one of their securities as "idle, dissolute, & extravagant as far as they could obtain either credit or means to be so," the mother and son were continually in debt despite the money they received. Even with her later physical and financial problems, Betsy emerges as the least appealing family member, particularly in her attempt to deny her free black relatives their right to share in Sylvia's estate. Her defeat in that case was a result of the sturdy resistance offered by James and Maria Wright in concert with their white supporters. But that was the only court fight Betsy lost. In substantial measure, her frequent successes depended on her determined persistence. An exhausted Allen Wyllie, appointed by the court in 1838 to administer Sylvia's estate, wrote twenty years later that he had paid more money than he should have to settle the matter and satisfy "my anxiety to be cleared of the Wright[s]."[83]

The legal battles of Sylvia and Betsy Wright reinforce the inescapable conclusions drawn from Robert Wright's life: that emancipated slaves and free blacks did not necessarily live circumspectly on the margins of southern society, and that identities for southern blacks before Emancipation could be constructed on bases other than race. Indeed, the story of the Wright family exemplifies the variety and complexity that underlay the status and position of free blacks in the South in the generations before the Civil War.

NOTES

The author wishes to thank Martha Hodes, Susan Miller, Joseph Tiedemann, and the outside readers at the *Virginia Magazine of History and Biography* for their comments and suggestions on earlier drafts of this essay. A Loyola Marymount University Research Grant and an Andrew W. Mellon Fellowship from the Virginia Historical Society supported the research for this project.

1. Petition of Robert Wright, 16 Nov. 1816, Campbell County, Legislative Petitions, Records of the General Assembly, Record Group 78, Virginia State Library and Archives, Richmond (hereafter cited as Vi). For the pertinent law of 1792, see Samuel Shepherd, ed., *The Statutes at Large of Virginia, 1792–1806: Being a Continuation of Hening* (3 vols.; Richmond, 1835–36), 1:134–35. Catherine Clinton provides a typical perspective on pre-Civil War southern attitudes toward interracial sexual relations in "'Southern Dishonor': Flesh, Blood, Race, and Bondage," in Carol Bleser, ed., *In Joy and In Sorrow: Women, Family, and Marriage in the Victorian South* (New York and Oxford, 1991), pp. 52–68. See also Sally G. McMillen, *Southern Women: Black and White in the Old South* (Arlington Heights, Ill., 1992), p. 27. Martha Elizabeth Hodes challenges this view in "Sex Across the Color Line: White Women and Black Men in the Nineteenth Century American South" (Ph.D. diss., Princeton University, 1991).

2. For an explanation of this use of the documents, see Joan W. Scott, "The Evidence of Experience," *Critical Inquiry* 17 (1991): 773–97. The author is indebted to Susan Miller for suggesting this line of investigation and pointing out this article.

3. Extensive discussions of interracial sexual relationships may be found in A. Leon Higginbotham, Jr., and Barbara K. Kopytoff, "Racial Purity and Interracial Sex in the Law of Colonial and Antebellum Virginia," *Georgetown Law Journal* 77 (1989): 1967–2029; Joel Williamson, *New People: Miscegenation and Mulattoes in the United States* (New York, 1980); David H. Fowler, *Northern Attitudes towards Interracial Marriage: Legislation and Public Opinion in the Middle Atlantic and the States of the Old Northwest, 1780–1930*, American Legal and Constitutional History (New York, 1987); and Bertram Wyatt-Brown, *Southern Honor: Ethics and Behavior in the Old South* (New York and Oxford, 1982), pp. 307–24. See also Thomas Brown, "The Miscegenation of Richard Mentor Johnson as an Issue in the National Election Campaign of 1835–1836," *Civil War History* 39 (1993): 5–30.

Until recently, historians have tended to ignore or minimize the incidence of miscegenation on the part of white women. See, for example, Catherine Clinton, *The Plantation Mistress: Woman's World in the Old South* (New York, 1982), pp. 209–22; Karen A. Getman, "Sexual Control in the Slaveholding South," *Harvard Women's Law Journal* 7 (1984): 115–52. For a contrasting view, see Eugene D. Genovese, *Roll, Jordan, Roll: The World the Slaves Made* (New York, 1972), p. 422; Herbert G. Gutman, *The Black Family in Slavery and Freedom, 1750–1925* (New York, 1976), pp. 82, 389, 614–16; Gary B. Mills, "Miscegenation and the Free Negro in Antebellum 'Anglo' Alabama: A Reexamination of Southern Race Relations," *Journal of American History* 68 (1981–82): 16–34; and Hodes, "Sex Across the Color Line."

4. Ira Berlin, *Slaves Without Masters: The Free Negro in the Antebellum South* (New York, 1974), p. xvii. Berlin's work remains the premier study of southern free blacks between the Revolution and the Civil War, although Wright's case challenges several of his conclusions about their status and treatment. See also Loren Schweninger, *Black Property Owners in the South, 1790–1915*, Blacks in the New World (Urbana and Chicago, 1990); A. Leon Higginbotham, Jr., and Greer C. Bosworth, "'Rather than the Free': Free Blacks in Colonial and Antebellum Virginia," *Harvard Civil Rights–Civil Liberties Law Review* 26 (1991): 17–66. Older, though still useful, are John Henderson Russell, *The Free Negro in Virginia, 1619–1865* (1913; New York, 1960); and Luther Porter Jackson, *Free Negro Labor and Property Holding in Virginia, 1830–1860* (New York and London, 1942).

5. Though some of their conclusions are not applicable to the situation of Robert Wright and his family, Michael P. Johnson and James L. Roark have produced a model study in *Black Masters: A Free Family of Color in the Old South* (New York and London, 1984). See also their essay, "Strategies of Survival: Free Negro Families and the Problem of Slavery," in Bleser, ed., *In Joy and In Sorrow*, pp. 88–102. For the use of the terms *black, mulatto,* and *Negro,* see Johnson and Roark, *Black Masters,* pp. xv–xvi.

Other recent family and local studies include T. O. Madden, Jr., *We Were Always Free: The Maddens of Culpeper County, Virginia: A 200-Year Family History* (New York, 1992); Lee H. Warner, *Free Men in an Age of Servitude: Three Generations of a Black Family* (Lexington, Ky., 1992); and Thomas N. Ingersoll, "Free Blacks in a Slave Society: New Orleans, 1718–1812," *William and Mary Quarterly* (hereafter cited as *WMQ*), 3d ser., 48 (1991): 173–200. For a collection of older local histories, see Elinor Miller and Eugene D. Genovese, eds., *Plantation, Town, and County: Essays on the Local History of American Slave Society* (Urbana, Chicago, and London, 1974).

6. William Waller Hening, ed., *The Statutes at Large; Being a Collection of All the*

Laws of Virginia . . . (13 vols.; Richmond, 1809–23), 11:39; Shepherd, ed., *Statutes at Large*, 1:122, 239; Robert McColley, *Slavery and Jeffersonian Virginia* (2d ed.; Urbana, Chicago, and London, 1973), pp. 71–72; Douglas R. Egerton, *Gabriel's Rebellion: The Virginia Slave Conspiracies of 1800 and 1802* (Chapel Hill and London, 1993).

7. Richard S. Dunn, "Black Society in the Chesapeake, 1776–1810," in Ira Berlin and Ronald Hoffman, eds., *Slavery and Freedom in the Age of the American Revolution*, Perspectives on the American Revolution (Charlottesville, 1983), pp. 49–82. See also Philip D. Morgan and Michael L. Nicholls, "Slaves in Piedmont Virginia, 1720–1790," *WMQ*, 3d ser., 46 (1989): 211–51; Peter J. Albert, "The Protean Institution: The Geography, Economy, and Ideology of Slavery in Post-revolutionary Virginia" (Ph.D. diss., University of Maryland, 1976).

8. Richard R. Beeman, *The Evolution of the Southern Backcountry: A Case Study of Lunenburg County, Virginia, 1746–1832* (Philadelphia, 1984), p. 218.

9. Johnson and Roark, *Black Masters*; Michael P. Johnson and James L. Roark, eds., *No Chariot Let Down: Charleston's Free People of Color on the Eve of the Civil War* (Chapel Hill, 1984).

10. The petition collections have only begun to be tapped. For examples of their use for the eighteenth century, see Raymond C. Bailey, *Popular Influence upon Public Policy: Petitioning in Eighteenth Century Virginia*, Contributions in Legal Studies (Westport, Conn., and London, 1979); and Ruth Bogin, "Petitioning and the New Moral Economy of Post-Revolutionary America," *WMQ*, 3d ser., 45 (1988): 391–425. In his published dissertation, *Race Relations in Virginia & Miscegenation in the South, 1776–1860* (Amherst, Mass., 1970), James Hugo Johnston quoted extensively from petition collections, but this work must be used with care, because it contains numerous inaccuracies.

11. Indenture between "Charles Caffrey and Sarah his wife . . . and Thomas Wright," dated 2 July 1779, recorded 26 July 1779, Bedford County Deed Book 6, pp. 253–56 (microfilm), Vi (unless otherwise noted, all county and tax records are at the Virginia State Library and Archives, Richmond). The amount was initially judged to be 370 acres, but a later survey raised that estimate (Campbell County Surveyor's Book, 1827–1924, 27 Mar., 3 Apr. 1828, p. 13 [microfilm]).

12. Will of John Wright, 18 Mar. 1775, Prince Edward County Will Book 1, pp. 218–19 (microfilm); inventory of the estate of John Wright, 19 June 1779, Prince Edward County Will Book 1, p. 226 (microfilm); affidavit of Daniel B. Perrow, 5 Feb. 1821, in *Wright* v. *Wright* [Fleming], Superior Court of Chancery (see Circuit Superior Court of Law and Chancery), Lynchburg District, file #525, Vi; affidavit of John Gardner, 5 Feb. 1821, in "Davidson v. Wright [Fleming]," Superior Court of Chancery (see Circuit Superior Court of Law and Chancery), Lynchburg District, file #578, Vi. These two cases were so closely related that many of the papers from the second case, file #578, are found in file #525.

13. Answer of James Wright, 9 June 1840, affidavit of Stephen Perrow, 21 Sept. 1841, in *Wright* v. *Wright*, Circuit Superior Court of Law and Chancery, Lynchburg District, file #1886, Vi. Their previous owner was probably Dr. William Cabell, who had died in 1774 and left almost his entire estate to his son, Nicholas (Alexander Brown, *The Cabells and Their Kin* [Boston and New York, 1895], pp. 62, 64). On an issue arising out of his father's estate, Nicholas Cabell brought suit against Thomas Wright in November 1785 (Campbell County Order Book 2, 1785–86, p. 232).

14. Affidavit of William Hawkins, 6 July 1840, answer of James Wright, 9 June 1840, affidavit of Stephen Perrow, 21 Sept. 1841, commissioner's report in *Wright* v. *Wright*, affidavit of John Overstreet, 13 Apr. 1841, file #1886; Campbell County Order Book 1, 1782–88, pp. 247, 255; Campbell County Order Book 2, 1785–86, p. 63; Campbell County Order Book 3, 1786–91, p. 64; Campbell County Order Book 7, 1801–4, p. 7.

15. Affidavit of John Gardner, 5 Feb. 1821, file #578; Campbell County Deed Book 3, p. 110 (microfilm).

16. Affidavit of John Gardner, 5 Feb. 1821, file #578; affidavit of Stephen Perrow, 8 Sept. 1831, in *Wright* v. *Jordan*, Circuit Superior Court of Law and Chancery, Lynchburg District, file #1174, Vi; affidavit of William B. Perrow, 6 Oct. 1820, file #525; affidavit of William Hawkins, 6 July 1840, affidavit of James Turner, 1 Mar. 1842, file #1886; affidavit of Jesse Thornhill, 29 Aug. 1821, file #578.

17. Campbell County Deed Book 5, 14 Apr. 1800, 9 Feb. 1801, pp. 85, 240 (microfilm); Campbell County Personal Property Tax Records, 1805 (microfilm). Sylvia's eldest child, Prudence, had injured her knee; Wright sent her to a doctor in New London to be healed. During her recovery, Prudence married a slave of Nathan Reid and, because she refused to be separated from her husband, Wright sold her to Reid. Thus, Prudence was the only one of Sylvia's seven children who remained in slavery (answer of James Wright, 9 June 1840, affidavit of James Wright, 2 June 1840, file #1886).

18. Bill of Sylva Wright, Copy [of] Record, *Sylva Wright* v. *Wrights Adm.*, file #1174; affidavits of Elizabeth Gilliam, 11 Dec. 1825, and Daniel B. Perrow, 14 Mar. 1826, Copy [of] Record, file #1174. Thomas Wright's father had made a similar provision for his wife (will of John Wright, Prince Edward County Will Book 1, p. 218).

19. Will of Thomas Wright, signed 24 Oct. 1805, proved 9 Dec. 1805, Campbell County Will Book 2, pp. 226–27 (microfilm); inventory of the estate of Thomas Wright, 14 Apr. 1806, Campbell County Will Book 2, pp. 265–68.

20. Campbell County Will Book 2, p. 226; Ruth Hairston Early, *Campbell Chronicles and Family Sketches: Embracing the History of Campbell County, Virginia, 1782–1926* (1927; Baltimore, 1978), pp. 480–81.

21. Petition of Robert Wright, 16 Nov. 1816, Campbell County, Legislative Petitions, Records of the General Assembly, RG 78. The marriage bond was dated 9 October 1806. The bride is named as Polley Godsey on the license (Campbell County Marriage Bonds and Consents, 1782–1853, 9 Oct. 1806 [microfilm]). See also Shepherd, ed., *Statutes at Large*, 1:132, 134–35. In a later court case, the clerk testified that the certificate had never been returned (affidavit of John Alexander, 28 Dec. 1828, Campbell County, Legislative Petitions, Records of the General Assembly, RG 78).

22. Robert Wright's "light" or "bright" appearance may have made the marriage more acceptable, at least to some.

23. Campbell County Land Tax Records, 1806–18 (microfilm); report, 24 Mar. 1832, in *Wright* v. *Jordan*, file #1174; affidavits of Robert Walthall and James Daniel, 8 Sept. 1831, file #1174; affidavit of Elizabeth Gilliam, Copy [of] Record, file #1174. Wright owned between six and eight slaves over twelve years of age (Campbell County Personal Property Tax Records, 1806–18 [microfilm]). For slaveholding among Virginia's free black population, see Philip J. Schwarz, "Emancipators, Protectors, and Anomalies: Free Black Slaveowners in Virginia," *Virginia Magazine of History and Biography* 95 (1987): 317–38.

24. Affidavit of Daniel B. Perrow, 7 Oct. 1820, file #578; affidavit of George MacKey, 1 May 1821, file #525. For MacKey's occupation, see affidavit of Samuel Fleming for continuation, 18 Oct. 1820, file #525.

25. Affidavit of William B. Perrow, 6 Oct. 1820, file #525; affidavit of Elizabeth Gilliam, 11 Dec. 1825, bill of Sylva Wright, Copy [of] Record, *Sylva Wright* v. *Wrights Adm.*, file #1174. For examples of free black women who did control property, see Loren Schweninger, "Property Owning Free African-American Women in the South, 1800–1870," *Journal of Women's History* 1 (1990): 13–44.

26. Bedford County Deed Book 12, pp. 92–93 (microfilm); affidavits of John Overstreet and William Hawkins, 6 July 1840, affidavit of James Wright, 2 June 1840, file #1886. Both remained in Bedford County. The lack of a firm title did not keep James from remaining on the property after Robert's death, and when James died years later, his widow Charlotte rented out the land. They had no children. Maria had five sons and named her eldest Robert (answer of John C. Noell, 11 Nov. 1853, file #1886).

27. Affidavit of James Turner, 1 Mar. 1842, file #1886; affidavit of Patterson Gilliam, 8 Oct. 1820, file #525; Campbell County Marriage Bonds and Consents, 1782–1853, 31 May 1809 (microfilm); *Recognizance, Comm.* v. *Davidson etc.*, 13 July 1832, Old Suits, Campbell County Courthouse, Rustburg, Va.

28. Affidavit of William B. Perrow, 6 Oct. 1820, file #525. Thomas P. Wright's date of birth can be gauged by a deed he made on 17 December 1835 when he reached twenty-one (Campbell County Deed Book 20, pp. 159–60 [microfilm]). His mother, Mary Godsey Wright, married William Arthur in Tennessee, and the couple eventually settled near Knoxville and lived to an old age. William farmed and later became a miller (affidavit of Betsy Wright, Apr. 1822, in *Davidson* v. *Wright*, Judgments, 1825, Bedford County Courthouse, Bedford, Va.; U.S. Census Bureau, Seventh Census, 1850, Anderson County, Tenn.; U.S. Census Bureau, Eighth Census, 1860, Knox County, Tenn. [microfilm]).

29. Affidavit of George MacKey, 1 May 1821, affidavit of Catherine Stockton, 7 Oct. 1820, file #525.

30. Affidavit of George MacKey, 1 May 1821, affidavit of Catherine Stockton, 7 Oct. 1820, affidavit of William B. Perrow, 6 Oct. 1820, file #525; statement of Richard Stratham, 14 June 1819, file #1174; Campbell County Personal and Land Taxes, 1816 (microfilm). A Reverend Samuel Davidson appears on the tax rolls for Campbell County that year, and Samuel Davidson was one of the signers of the divorce petition. Robert Wright must have remained on good terms with Polly's family, because the three witnesses to his purported will were Polly's father, brother, and brother-in-law: James Davidson, William Davidson, and Charles Caffrey (deposition of James Williams, 24 Dec. 1819, file #525).

31. Petition of Robert Wright, 16 Nov. 1816, Campbell County, Legislative Petitions, Records of the General Assembly, RG 78. On the issue of validity, see Higginbotham and Kopytoff, "Racial Purity and Interracial Sex," p. 2007. For Wright's use of the term *man of color*, see Berlin, *Slaves Without Masters*, pp. 180–81. Berlin asserts that the term was "rarely" used in the Upper South.

32. These petitions and legislative action on them are in the *Journals of the House of Delegates of Virginia* (Richmond, 1827–28), 1786–1815. The texts and accompanying documents of most of these petitions are available by county and date in the collection of Legislative Petitions, Records of the General Assembly, RG 78. If the

assembly passed a divorce bill or provided for another venue for the petitioner, those laws are in Hening, ed., *Statutes at Large;* Shepherd, ed., *Statutes at Large;* and, for bills passed after 1806, the annual *Virginia Acts of Assembly.*

33. Petition of Robert Wright, 16 Nov. 1816, Campbell County, Legislative Petitions, Records of the General Assembly, RG 78; Campbell County Personal Property and Land Tax Records, 1815–17 (microfilm); Early, *Campbell Chronicles and Family Sketches,* pp. 412–13, 480–81.

34. *Journal of the House of Delegates,* 16 Nov. 1816, p. 26.

35. Affidavit of John Gardner, 5 Feb. 1821, file #578.

36. Campbell County Personal Property Taxes, 1806–18 (microfilm). It is intriguing that tax records in the 1830s also fail to list Sylvia Wright as a free Negro or Thomas P. Wright as a free mulatto. Nor did the federal census of 1850 tag Betsy Wright with the telltale "M," "B," or "FN" next to her name. These sources do identify other persons as such, and the tax records also total the number of free blacks. Perhaps in some parts of the South people of color who owned or had owned a significant amount of property were not ordinarily labeled by race, because their economic status placed them in a higher stratum of society. If so, the identification of wealth among free African Americans in the pre–Civil War South becomes a much more complicated task (Campbell County Personal Property Taxes, 1831–38 [microfilm]; U.S. Census Bureau, Seventh Census, 1850, Campbell County [Lynchburg], Va., p. 97 [microfilm]).

37. Affidavit of John Hoar, 9 Oct. 1820, file #525.

38. Affidavit of John McAllister, Jr., 9 Oct. 1820, affidavit of William Thompson, 6 Oct. 1821, affidavit of Predhem Moore, 7 Apr. 1820, affidavit of William B. Perrow, 6 Oct. 1820, file #525.

39. Affidavit of Daniel B. Perrow, 5 Feb. 1821, affidavits of Patterson Gilliam, 1 Apr., 8 Oct. 1820, file #525.

40. Affidavit of George MacKey, 1 May 1821, file #525. The census of 1850 lists Stephen Perrow's age as sixty-three. If this figure is accurate, he was born about 1787 (U.S. Census Bureau, Seventh Census, 1850, Campbell County, Va., p. 204 [microfilm]).

41. Affidavit of Jared Gilliam, 7 Oct. 1820, affidavit of Patterson Gilliam, 1 Apr. 1820, file #525.

42. Affidavit of Lewis Franklin, 19 Feb. 1820, file #578.

43. Ibid.; affidavit of John Gardner, 19 Feb. 1820, file #578.

44. The date of his death is stated in the bill of complaint of Polly Davidson, file #525. An inventory of his estate in 1826 listed eleven slaves, three of them children. The total value, not including the land, was $3,667 (inventory of the estate of Robert Wright, Campbell County Will Book 5, p. 22 [microfilm]). Sylvia lived on almost twenty years after her son's death. Her estate was not probated until February 1838. Its value, apart from the house, was $738.49 (estate of Sylvia Wright, Campbell County Order Book 23, p. 7 [microfilm]; inventory of the estate of Sylvia Wright, Campbell County Will Book 8, p. 190 [microfilm]).

45. Affidavit of James Williams, 4 Dec. 1819, affidavit of Nancy Caffrey, 19 Feb. 1820, file #525; affidavit of William Davidson, 19 Feb. 1820, file #578.

46. Bill of complaint of Polly Davidson, affidavit of Predhem Moore, 7 Apr. 1820, file #525; affidavit of John Gardner, 19 Feb. 1820, affidavit of Lewis Franklin, 19 Feb. 1820, file #578; affidavit of George MacKey, 1 May 1821, file #525. At the time of

Robert's death, Polly was in fact far advanced in pregnancy and within a few days gave birth to a daughter, Martha Ann, who died while still a baby.

47. Affidavit of Arthur Litchfield, 1 Apr. 1820, file #525. In her formal statement, which she drafted in 1821, Polly said the will disappeared "by means unknown" (bill of complaint of Polly Davidson, file #525).

48. Affidavit of Catherine Stockton, 7 Oct. 1820, file #525.

49. Campbell County Order Book 13, pp. 165, 176 (microfilm); *Risque* v. *Wright's Estate*, file #1174. The records do not state the reason for their release.

50. Curator's bond, 9 Nov. 1818, *Wright* v. *Jordan*, file #1174. A hearing is recounted in the affidavit of William B. Perrow, 6 Oct. 1820, file #525.

51. Answer, 13 Sept. 1819, file #525; affidavit of Daniel B. Perrow, 7 Oct. 1820, file #578; affidavit of William B. Perrow, 6 Oct. 1820, file #525; Early, *Campbell Chronicles and Family Sketches*, pp. 480–81. When the case initially appeared in Bedford County, Polly Davidson was suing with her "next friend Stephen Perrow," while Daniel B. Perrow and William Perrow were listed as defendants after Samuel Fleming (Common Law Order Book 3, 15 Apr. 1824, p. 100, Bedford County Courthouse, Bedford, Va.).

52. "The Estate of Robert Wright to J. B. Risque Due," file #1174.

53. Bill of complaint, 10 Dec. 1828, Campbell County, Legislative Petitions, Records of the General Assembly, RG 78. See also "Rough, Wright v. Fleming," file #525; answer of S. Fleming, 10 May 1820, answer of Polly Davidson alias Polly Wright, 9 Oct. 1820, file #578.

54. *Davidson* v. *Wright* and *Wright* v. *Fleming*, 10 Dec. 1828, Campbell County, Legislative Petitions, Records of the General Assembly, RG 78. Apparently the clerk neglected to consult Campbell County Deed Book 3, p. 110 (microfilm).

55. Petition of Samuel Wright and others, 6 Dec. 1827, 28 Dec. 1828, Campbell County, Legislative Petitions, Records of the General Assembly, RG 78.

56. Verdict, 14 Apr. 1825, notes of plaintiff's counsel, 20 Oct. 1825, notes of defendant's counsel, n.d., in *Davidson* v. *Wright*, file #578.

57. Note the increase in Fleming's personal property between 1818 and 1825 in Campbell County Personal Property Taxes, 1818–25 (microfilm).

58. Affidavit of Stephen Perrow, 8 Sept. 1831, file #1174.

59. Affidavits of John Akers, 14 Nov. 1831, James Daniel, 8 Sept. 1831, Mary K. Smith, 4 Mar. 1832, Pleasant Bagby, 14 Nov. 1831, George Byrd, 4 Mar. 1832, Robert Walthall, 8 Sept. 1831, John Jones, 17 Sept. 1831, file #1174.

60. Some of Fleming's accounts are in Campbell County Will Book 4, p. 361 (microfilm). The accounts do not mention Sylvia Wright, but in her later suit against German Jordan, she stated that Fleming paid her an allowance (bill of Sylva Wright, Copy [of] Record, *Sylva Wright* v. *Wrights Adm.*, file #1174; Campbell County Deed Book 21, p. 392 [microfilm]).

61. Assignment of claims, file #1174; Campbell County Deed Book 15, 5 Oct. 1825, pp. 198–201 (microfilm). Stephen Perrow maintained that Fleming offered to transfer the account to him "for a Negro Girl worth at that time about $200," but Perrow "refused to trade for it because I did not believe it just" (affidavit of Stephen Perrow, 17 Sept. 1831, file #1174).

62. Campbell County Will Book 5, 14 Aug. 1826, p. 346 (microfilm); affidavit of William Thompson, Jr., 14 Nov. 1831, file #1174.

63. Administrator's bond, 18 Nov. 1825, bill of complaint, 18 May 1830, *Wright* v. *Jordan*, file #1174. In December 1825 Jordan transferred his share of Fleming's claim to Haden. Despite earlier warnings from Perrow and Robert Walthall, the last overseer, that "the claim was unjust," Jordan paid Haden the full amount that Fleming maintained the estate owed him (affidavits of Stephen Perrow and Robert Walthall, 8 Sept. 1831, bill, 18 May 1830, file #1174). Responding to the bill of complaint, Jordan stated that he learned there were questions about the claims only after he had paid them (answer of German Jordan, file #1174).

64. Notes and account of sale, affidavit of Allen L. Wyllie, 16 Feb. 1832, affidavit of Stephen Perrow, 22 Sept. 1832, file #1174.

65. Campbell County Order Book 17, p. 358 (microfilm); "Inventory . . . of the Estate of Robert Wright Decd," file #1174 (also in Campbell County Will Book 5, p. 277 [microfilm]). This estimate, of course, did not include the value of the land and buildings, or the home and property of Sylvia Wright. See notes of plaintiff's counsel, June 1832, file #1174.

66. Notes of plaintiff's counsel, June 1832, file #1174; bill of Sylva Wright, Copy [of] Record, *Sylva Wright* v. *Wrights Adm.*, file #1174.

67. Order of Campbell County March Court, 1826, amount of sale, receipts, Silvey Wright, 29 Nov. 1826, 14 Jan. 1828, file #1174. When Jordan failed to pay the annuity in 1829, she took him back to court (Campbell County Order Book 19, 14 Sept. 1829, p. 44 [microfilm]).

68. Copy [of] Silvry Wright's record, *Wright* v. *Jordan*, file #1174.

69. Decree of court, 22 June 1832, file #1174; [Chancery] Execution Book, 1831–51, Circuit Superior Court of Law and Chancery, Lynchburg City Records, p. 21, Vi; guardian account, 9 Dec. 1833, Campbell County Will Book 7, pp. 234–35 (microfilm). Tax records show that Jordan steadily accumulated both land and slaves. By 1836, he owned seven lots at the courthouse, 1,154 acres of land, and nineteen slaves over the age of twelve. In 1850 his real estate was valued at $15,000 (Campbell County Land and Personal Property Taxes, 1825–50 [microfilm]; U.S. Census Bureau, Seventh Census, 1850, Campbell County, Va., p. 166 [microfilm]).

70. Receipts for tuition and boarding, 8 Apr., 14 May 1825, 9 Dec. 1826, [9] Dec. 1827, file #1174; Campbell County Will Book 6, pp. 462–63; Campbell County Will Book 7, pp. 151, 234 (microfilm).

71. Campbell County Will Book 7, pp. 399–400; Campbell County Order Book 21, p. 262 (microfilm).

72. Campbell County Deed Book 20, 17 Dec. 1835, pp. 159–60 (microfilm).

73. Indentures, 22 Dec. 1835, 5, 13 Jan., 2, 9, 10, 24 Feb. 1836, Campbell County Deed Book 20, pp. 161–63, 179–80, 189–90, 194–97, 210–11, 236–37; Charles Mosby and Maurice Garland to Edward Hunter, deed, 15 May 1836, Campbell County Deed Book 21, pp. 16–17 (microfilm); "Land for Sale," *Lynchburg Virginian*, 31 Mar. 1836, p. 4.

74. Chancery and Law Order Book, Lynchburg Hustings Court, 1835–38, 18 Aug., 23 Sept. 1835, pp. 18, 23, Lynchburg Courthouse, Lynchburg, Va.; Campbell County Order Book 21, 9 Nov. 1835, June 1836, pp. 248, 325, 326 (microfilm).

75. Campbell County Deed Book 21, 23 Jan. 1838, pp. 392, 410 (microfilm).

76. Bill of complaint, answer of Allen L. Wyllie, file #1886; Campbell County Order Book 23, p. 122 (microfilm); advertisement of "Slaves for sale," file #1886; inven-

tory of the estate of Sylvia Wright, Campbell County Will Book 8, p. 190 (microfilm); report of the commissioner, filed May Court 1839, file #1886. Because Emmeline Turner was a person "of unsound mind," the county court appointed Wyllie to administer her affairs, a task he later said gave him "a great deal of Trouble" (Allen L. Wyllie to C. Dabney, 16 June 1838, file #1886).

77. Appointment, 31 Aug. 1839, *Wright* v. *Wright*, file #1886; petition of James Wright (signed also by Maria Wright), Sept. 1839, file #1886.

78. "The amended bill of complaint of . . . Betsey Wright and William Wright," [12 Nov. 1839], answer of James Wright, 9 June 1840, answer of Maria Wright, 9 June 1840, affidavit of James Wright, 2 June 1840, affidavits of John Overstreet, 6 July 1840, 13 Apr. 1841, affidavit of William Hawkins, 14 Apr. 1841, affidavit of Stephen Perrow, 21 Sept. 1841, file #1886. Two affidavits supported the story of Betsy and William Wright (see the affidavits of James Turner and Lavina Baker, 1 Mar. 1842, file #1886). Turner was Betsy Wright's brother-in-law.

79. Commissioner's report, [9 Sept. 1845], order, Circuit Court for the Corporation of Lynchburg, 17 Nov. 1852, file #1886; Circuit Superior Court of Law and Chancery Order Book 7, p. 341 (microfilm).

80. Affidavits of Samuel Pleasants, W. V. Millspaugh, and Adeline Dorsey, 27 Sept. 1853, file #1886; U.S. Census Bureau, Seventh Census, 1850, Campbell County [Lynchburg], Va., p. 97 (microfilm).

81. Second amended bill, 2 Feb. 1853, *Wright* v. *Wright et al.*, file #1886.

82. Answer of John C. Noell, 11 Nov. 1853, affidavits of Nicholas W. Owen and Lucy Tanner, 31 Oct. 1854, memo in *Wright* v. *Wright*, 10 May 1858, report of the commissioner, 24 May 1873, final decree, June Term, 1873, file #1886.

83. The separate answer of Timothy Fletcher, [27 Apr. 1853], Allen L. Wyllie to C. Dabney, 16 June 1858, file #1886.

ELIZABETH R. VARON

"The Ladies Are Whigs": Lucy Barbour, Henry Clay, and Nineteenth-Century Virginia Politics

* * * * * * * * HISTORIANS HAVE LONG HELD THAT WOMEN played no formal role in American politics during much of the nineteenth century. Insofar as the public life of the eighteenth century had been rooted in family dynasties, women profoundly influenced political affairs, if not by governing, then by conferring wealth and power upon their husbands and households. The "cult of true womanhood," so dominant in the next century, however, consigned women to the home and the moral education of children. Only men participated in the public life of campaigning, voting, and holding office. Only men made laws and shaped policy.

Elizabeth Varon comes to a very different conclusion by examining not politics per se but political culture as the sum of all public behavior. Women of the 1840s, according to Varon, not only influenced voting and public office, but they transformed the political culture of their day without upsetting the delicate gender balance that underlay it. In a notable example in 1844, Virginia women organized under Lucy Barbour's leadership to form the Virginia Association of Ladies for Erecting a Statue to Henry Clay. The lifesize image of the great Whig Party leader that finally graced Richmond's Capitol lawn in 1860 would, they asserted, provide a moral example for Virginia politicians and schoolchildren alike. Art and symbolism would lobby for effective government. The women of the Mount Vernon Ladies' Association of the Union were pursuing identical goals at the same time by preserving George Washington's home as a public memorial. These accomplishments transformed "republican motherhood" into "Whig womanhood," says Varon. Erecting monuments, preserving historic shrines, and promoting social reform transcended the private nurturing of political leaders in the home as the medium of women's influence on public life.

Thus by the 1850s women played defining roles in the new rituals of American mass politics. What was transformative in the 1840s and 1850s, however, would become normative by 1900 when many women in Virginia public life supported conservative views on free speech and suffrage, a development explored in essays appearing later in this volume.

* * * * * * * *

* * * * * * * *

LUCY BARBOUR, OF BARBOURSVILLE, ORANGE COUNTY, WAS A little surprised when, on the evening of 17 November 1844, her granddaughters asked her what women could do to honor Henry Clay, the leader of the Whig party. Clay had just lost his third bid for the presidency of the United States. Although Virginia women could neither vote nor hold elective office, they maintained an avid interest in politics and thus, after discussing a few ideas with the young women, Barbour wrote to John H. Pleasants, editor of the *Richmond Whig*, proposing that the Whig women of Virginia present "some token of respect" to Clay. It was hardly an idle suggestion. Barbour was a member of Virginia's social elite. Her husband, James, who had died two years before, had been one of the most prominent Whigs in Virginia, serving as governor, United States senator, and secretary of war. Lucy Barbour herself had earned a reputation in Richmond and Washington, D.C., as a learned and gracious hostess. For years, both had counted Henry Clay among their closest friends.[1]

Barbour knew that her suggestion would raise eyebrows. "I know our sex are thought by many unstable as water," she remarked to Pleasants, "but I hope, after crowding the Whig festivals, and manifesting so much enthusiasm, few will be found so hollow-hearted as to refuse a small sum to aid so good—I had almost said, so holy a cause." The editors of the *Richmond Whig* agreed to adopt Barbour's scheme as their own and printed her letter in the newspaper's 19 November issue. The editors of the *Richmond Enquirer*, supporters of the Democratic party, wasted no time in ridiculing the plan to honor Clay: "It seems this great hero, who has figured in some of the great events of this country, is no longer able to wield a lance in his own defence," and concluded by asking, "has it come to this, that the 'gallant Harry' has been turned over to the tender mercies of the ladies?"[2]

In an equally sharp response published in the *Richmond Whig*, Barbour reminded Virginians—especially Democrats—that women "are the nursing mothers of heroes, statesmen, and divines; and, while we perform a task so important," she added, "we mean to be counted something in the musterroll of man." By 6 December, the *Richmond Whig*, which by then had suggested the tribute to Clay take the form of a statue, was boasting that Barbour's appeal had "gone through the State like wildfire." Three days later, a group of women met at Richmond's First Presbyterian Church and formed the Virginia Association of Ladies for Erecting a Statue to Henry Clay. The statue was to be funded by membership subscriptions—none more than a dollar each—from women; men, for their part, could make donations, but could not become general members.[3]

The women elected Barbour as president of the association, appointed John Pleasants secretary and prominent Richmond businessman William H. Macfarland treasurer, and selected a male board of directors that included many of the commonwealth's most prominent Whigs. The women also organized numerous auxiliaries and began the work of soliciting donations. Barbour was careful, though, to explain that "in associating ourselves for this purpose, we do not enter the political arena nor pass the limit assigned to our sex." Less convincingly, she added that the organization's admiration for Clay was "independent of the party-politics of the day."[4]

Barbour made no other published appeals on behalf of the Clay Association. Advanced age and declining health—she was sixty-nine in 1844—compelled her to rely upon the group's vice-presidents and directors. Other voices would carry on the debate. But Barbour's words merit a close reading, for they reflect not only her own experience but also a transformation of political culture. Barbour had chosen three justifications for her project: that honoring Clay was a natural extension of women's enthusiastic support for the Whig party, that women deserved recognition for their vital role as mothers, and that honoring Clay in no way interfered with male political prerogatives. But how could women identifying themselves with a particular party claim not to be elbowing their way into the political arena? It was not, however, the contradiction it seemed.

Barbour was, in fact, reconciling established ideals with new practices. During her childhood in the era of the American Revolution, the ideal of motherhood reflected the virtues of the new republic. Women played a key political role in the new nation, instilling in their sons civic virtues and a respect for the new, free, and republican form of government. During the 1800s, however, women found themselves turning toward domestic rather than civic roles. The concept of "republican motherhood" gave way to "true womanhood," in which women presided over a distinctly private and narrower sphere of home and family while the public world of business and politics became the exclusive preserve of men. The home thus served as a haven for those virtues attributed to the female—piety, purity, domesticity, compassion, and submissiveness—and as a shield from the corrupting influences of commercialism and party politics.[5]

Yet, despite such perceptions, Virginia women blurred distinctions of gender. In Fredericksburg, Norfolk, Petersburg, and Richmond, for example, women created a "benevolent empire" of schools, orphanages, asylums, Bible and temperance societies, and other charities designed to address social ills. Benevolent women easily explained such activity as a natural extension of their domestic duties and moral qualities. The rituals of mass politics, however, provided a more direct challenge to separate male and female spheres. In Virginia, the Whig party initiated the trend. Stung by their loss in the 1836 presidential campaign, the Whigs decided that in order to win in 1840 they needed to "agitate the people"—and that the people included women. The resulting campaign, described by one historian as "a rollicking songfest," took mass politics to a new level.[6]

Around the nation, the Whigs invited women to attend political speeches, rallies, and meetings of the "Tippecanoe and Tyler, Too" clubs in support of the party's candidates, William Henry Harrison and John Tyler. Women prepared food and elaborate decorations for political meetings. Sometimes women addressed meetings through male proxies who read their statements. On occasion, women even made public speeches or wrote pamphlets in support of the Whigs. The party also provided a dazzling array of campaign paraphernalia specifically aimed at women. Buttons, pitchers, sugar bowls, cups, plates, glassware, hairbrushes, quilts, and stationery all featured the candidates' names, pictures, or slogans.[7]

Granted, women's participation was limited—they could not vote; they could not even participate in the selection of delegates to Whig state conventions. Both men and women nevertheless took the latter's Whig partisanship very seriously. Women as early as 1836 had worked as political partisans. For example, a September issue of the *Staunton Spectator* featured a poem by "a young lady" addressed to the Whig candidate William H. Harrison. By the 1840 presidential campaign, women's partisanship was frequent enough to merit occasional anecdotes in Virginia newspapers, such as the story of the young Whig lady who refused to marry her "Locofoco," or Democratic, suitor. Moreover, Virginia women in their diaries and correspondence frequently proclaimed their Whig allegiances, interpreted political issues, and described their new participation in election canvasses. In 1840, Mary Steger, of Richmond, wrote to a friend: "I never took so much interest in politics in my life," she confessed, adding, "the fact is you have to know something about them for nobody here thinks of anything else."[8]

The height of the 1840 campaign to enlist Virginia women in the Whig cause was Daniel Webster's October "Remarks to the Ladies of Richmond." Twelve hundred women turned out at the Log Cabin, the local Harrison campaign headquarters, to hear Webster—second only to Clay in Whig circles—pay his respects. Of the crowd, the *Richmond Whig* commented that "the better part of creation were and are, almost unanimously Whig." In a reinterpretation of the concept of "republican motherhood," Webster stated that for sound government to prevail, women must teach their sons that "the exercise of the elective franchise is a social duty, of as solemn a nature as man can be called to perform." Men especially, he remarked, needed to be reminded of the "perpetual obligations of conscience and of duty."

Three Virginia Whigs—James Barbour, Benjamin Watkins Leigh, and James Lyons—followed, enthusiastically endorsing his comments.[9]

Henry Clay himself apparently agreed that women had a distinctive role in party politics. Speaking in Lexington, Kentucky, in 1842 Clay expressed great pleasure at the large numbers of ladies in the audience, "always an absolute guaranty of order, decorum and respect." To Clay, Harrison's election had proved the utility of women's support for Whig candidates: "we all know and remember how, as in 1840, they can powerfully aid a great and good cause, without any departure from the propriety and dignity of their sex."[10]

The lesson was not lost on Virginia's Whig leaders. For the 1844 canvass the party stepped up its appeals to women. Women attended Clay-campaign events in droves, prompting the *Richmond Whig* to declare again that "the Ladies are Whigs, almost universally." Virginia writer Mary Virginia Hawes Terhune—best known by her pen name, Marion Harland—in her autobiography recalled that even as a child of thirteen she was a violent Whig partisan and champion of Clay. In 1844, at her father's instigation, Whigs invited the women of her county to a political rally. It was, she believed, the first such invitation, one that set tongues to wagging and virtually guaranteed the county for Clay.[11]

Such examples confirmed to Whig politicians that the approval of women provided a moral sanction to the party's cause. Women attending the speech of a local Whig politician in Goochland got so excited they "could scarcely forbear SHOUTING!" "If we doubted before," the *Richmond Whig* remarked, "now we know the Whigs must be right and will be more than conquerors." On occasion Whig women also gave moral instruction. One, Miss Martha A. Peake, of Albemarle County, submitted a letter to the September 1844 meeting of the Central Clay Club of Charlottesville. Read aloud by a club member, her letter called for caution in victory: "forget not that those whom you have vanquished are your brothers, subjects of the same government, struggling as ardently and as honestly, as you, for what they believe, with mistaken judgment, in my poor opinion, to be the true path to national honor, happiness and glory."[12]

That a woman concluded her gentle remarks with so unmistakable a barb was significant. By the 1840s, with so many women driven by political allegiance—attending Whig festivals, taking their views home, and influencing husbands and sons—there was no doubt that partisan conflict, the fear of the Founding Fathers, had reached new heights. By then, too, perhaps as much as 90 percent of the country's population professed either the Whig or Democratic faith. It was clear to Virginians that the advent of regular competition between the two parties had profoundly transformed electoral politics.[13]

It is in light of such change that Lucy Barbour's public statements should be understood. Barbour, in effect, was recasting the eighteenth-century concept of republican motherhood into a new ideal corresponding to political reality—Whig womanhood. As Barbour saw it, women engaging in party politics purified the political process, making it less corrupt and destructive. Barbour at the same time reassured men that women were not seeking a direct role in nominations and elections. Rather, the Whig women of Virginia wished only to exert a benign influence over an increasingly contentious political culture.

Virginia Democrats were hardly reassured. They rarely invited women to party functions. Moreover, the Democratic presidential candidate in 1840, Martin Van Buren, made no effort whatsoever to appeal to women's interests. By 1844, however, local Democrats had decided to strike back. In August the *Richmond Whig* reported that at a Loudoun County debate a Democratic orator "commenced assailing the ladies for attending political meetings." In both elections the Democrats did little to claim women's support. While some Virginia women evidently supported the Democratic party, they had few public opportunities to express their preferences. Besides, Democrats saw little use in making appeals to women—women, after all, could not vote. Serena Dandridge, an Essex County Democrat, wrote to a friend that the Whigs lost the 1844 election because they had "too many women & children in their ranks."[14]

With the formation of the Clay Association, the debate over women's participation intensified. In December 1844 the editor of the Democratic *Lynchburg Republican* attacked the association, suggesting with derision that "the name of every lady who mingles in this great work of generosity and patriotism will be handed down to posterity as a *partisan* lady" and asking, "Is not this whole movement conceived in a spirit of rebellion?" The Whig *Lynchburg Virginian* defended Barbour and her coworkers. "The Whig ladies of Lynchburg, and the Whig ladies of Virginia," wrote one correspondent, "consider themselves at least as well qualified to judge of their own acts as the Locofoco editor, who has undertaken to lecture them, & to instruct them in the rules of female propriety and obedience, and female patriotism."[15]

In 1845 the *Lexington Gazette* similarly defended the association, pointing out that "the sneering democratic gentry who ridicule the idea of ladies meddling with politics, would not be so bitterly sarcastic if they could have a little of this meddling on their side of the question." Whig ladies themselves took up the defense. A female correspondent to the *Richmond Whig* in December 1844 remarked that women had a duty to honor Clay, since he had been "shamefully neglected by his countrymen." Of the newly elected Democratic president, James K. Polk, she had nothing good to say: "The more insignificant a man is, the greater are his chances, with the Democracy, for attaining exalted honors." Susan Doswell, president of the Hanover County auxiliary, added that the Clay statue would teach children "to distinguish the true difference between exalted worth and . . . cringing sycophancy."[16]

The Democratic attacks on the Clay Association died down within a few months, while Whig newspapers continued to publicize the ladies' association. In November 1845, barely a year after Barbour's appeal, the association commissioned Joel Tanner Hart to design and execute a marble statue. Chosen on Clay's own recommendation as "an artist of uncommon merit," Hart was to be paid five thousand dollars for the project. Hart visited Clay's Kentucky home, Ashland, in 1846 to begin work on the sculpture.[17]

By early 1846 the association had raised six thousand dollars. A surviving subscription book, with donations listed by county, Accomack through Nelson, includes the names of 2,563 donors. Not surprisingly, Virginia counties with a reputation for voting Whig furnished the greatest number of supporters—Fauquier, Hardy, Jefferson, Nansemond, Norfolk, and Ohio. Henrico led with 436 contributors. Of the statewide total, at least 2,236 were women. Contributions also came from Georgia, Massachusetts, Mississippi, and Vermont.[18]

Why did so many Virginia women support the Whig party? Whig political culture combined three elements with appeal to Virginia women: social elitism, a reforming zeal, and an emphasis on statesmanship over partisanship. The Whigs considered themselves the party of "property and talents." Whig women such as Judith Page Walker Rives, vice-president of the Albemarle County auxiliary, believed men of wealth and culture should run the state. Her husband, William Cabell Rives, for example, had served as a Virginia legislator, United States representative and senator, and minister to France. Renowned in her own right as an author, Judith Rives in her 1861 memoirs recalled her husband's early career and remarked that "in those days, education, talent, a noble nature, and even advantages of birth and fortune, instead of being disqualifications for the public service and favor, were considered the best requirements." Perhaps more to the point, Marion Harland recalled that as a child she thought it "monstrous" that poor-white Democrats should have the same political rights as wealthy Whig gentlemen.[19]

As the guardians of culture, Whigs were interested in moral reform, public education, and benevolent societies. There was a strong connection between Whig women and reform in Virginia—for example, seventeen association subscribers from Henrico County were members of the Female Humane Association, of Richmond, which provided shelter and education for destitute girls. Lucy W. Otey, an auxiliary president, was an 1845 founder of the Lynchburg orphan asylum; and Ann Clagett, an association member, was director of the Alexandria Orphan Asylum and Female Free School Society in 1847.[20]

As important, the Whigs embraced statesmanship. Democratic president Andrew Jackson and his successor Martin Van Buren were, in contrast, viewed as too partisan and authoritarian. Whigs, on the other hand, sought to preserve the traditions of the Founding Fathers, especially Thomas Jefferson, thus rising above partisanship and sectionalism in the interests of national unity. Henry Clay—"the Great Pacificator," the man who steered the Union through the Nullification Crisis of 1832—was the very personification of the ideal. He designed his American System of economic diversification expressly to unite the nation through commerce. Indeed, Clay's favorite word was *harmony*, and it was his record as a peacemaker that likely attracted Virginia women to his cause.[21]

In short, Clay embodied on the political stage the very qualities women did on the domestic one—moral virtue, love of harmony, and the willingness to compromise. Clay's reputation for gallantry and social grace further endeared him to women. The fact that he was also a native son of the Old Dominion made him all the more appealing to Virginia women. He acted the part of the attentive southern gentleman to perfection, in Petersburg in April 1844, for example, impressing the ladies with his "manliness and chivalry of character."[22]

But while Clay won over the female population in 1844, he did not win over the voters. In the rush of national expansion, Clay alienated many by opposing the annexation of Texas. Two years later, in 1846, he tried to prevent the war with Mexico: that year the Clay Association's fund-raising drive received no more than an occasional mention in the press. For the 1848 presidential race the chastened Whigs chose the hero of the Mexican War, Zachary Taylor, but the campaign never attracted the popular enthusiasm of 1840 or 1844.

After forging a temporary solution to the problem of slavery with the Compromise of 1850, Clay died in June 1852. His loss contributed to the demise of the Whig party, which in the 1850s split along sectional lines. It is ironic that just as the Whig party was coming apart, its campaign innovation—the inclusion of women in the rituals of mass politics—was becoming commonplace. On occasion, even Democratic women took to public speaking: at a Norfolk meeting in 1852 a certain Miss Bain urged a crowd of gentlemen to support the Democrat, Franklin Pierce, for president.[23]

But even as the Whig party disintegrated, the Clay Association carried on its work. From 1846 until 1859 its primary task was somehow to prod Joel Tanner Hart, who had taken up residence in Europe, to finish the statue. Hart's first model for the sculpture had been lost at sea en route to Florence, the first of many delays. Prone to distraction, mired in poverty, and plagued by poor health punctuated by bouts of cholera and typhoid fever, Hart proved a difficult case. Several testy exchanges followed. Finally, in 1859, Hart completed his work. The sculpture arrived in Richmond on 28 January 1860. A few days later, a large crowd of citizens pulled the statue on wheels to a temporary site at Mechanics' Hall.[24]

In February, the female officers of the Clay Association successfully petitioned the General Assembly for permission to place the statue in front of the Capitol portico. On the date of the unveiling—12 April, Clay's birthday—stores closed, business ceased, and crowds filled the streets and the windows and balconies above to get the best view of the grand procession. Military companies, regimental bands, orators, official dignitaries, and distinguished guests all passed under the flags that decorated Main Street up to Capitol Square. There an estimated twenty thousand spectators waited.[25]

Both the composition and the size of the crowd were noteworthy. The Clay statue ceremony united, if only briefly, a city that had been torn apart by sectional politics, especially the debate over states' rights. Eight years after his death, Clay symbolized compromise, patriotism, and the hope for peace. With crowds of women gathered around the speakers' stand, orator Benjamin Johnson Barbour, Lucy Barbour's son, began his comments by remarking, "Genius and patriotism have always found their truest and purest human reward in the love and sympathy of Woman." President James Buchanan and Martin Van Buren, both Democrats, sent their congratulations to the Whig women of Virginia. The celebration lasted several days, but by the next week the statue had ceased to be news. The *Richmond Whig* was busy drumming up support for John Bell, the Constitutional Union party's presidential candidate. The city's ladies were enthused, but Bell, who stood for sectional compromise, lost. Six months later, Virginia seceded from the Union.[26]

The story of Virginia's Whig women is much at odds with the image of the southern lady that has so long captured the historical imagination. Because organized feminism came so much later to the South than to the North, antebellum southern women have long been regarded as less politically astute and involved than their northern counterparts. A few southern Whig women have drawn the notice of historians. Perhaps the most renowned is Mary Minor Blackford, of Fredericksburg, an eloquent opponent of slavery and an activist for the American Colonization Society, which provided freed slaves with passage to Liberia. But Blackford and women like her often appear in historical scholarship as outside the mainstream. Whig women like Lucy Barbour provide further evidence that perhaps they were not.[27]

During the Civil War, some members of the Clay Association used their new-found experience in assisting various Confederate benevolent societies. Others clung to the role of peacemakers until the last moment, only reluctantly accepting secession. The sectional crisis destroyed the Whig party. But the central focus of Whig womanhood—that party politics was the business of women as well as men—survived the war. After 1865, as before, thousands of Virginia women turned out for campaign events. Some of Virginia's most prominent women of the postwar era remembered the glory days of the Whig party: author and reformer Orra Langhorne, suffragist Elizabeth Van Lew, and writer Marion Harland—all had been raised in Whig families. The next generation of female reformers—Lila Meade Valentine, Mary-Cooke Branch Munford, and Janie Porter Barrett, for example—were born long after the Whig party had disappeared. The passage of time, however, in no way diminished their debt to Lucy Barbour.[28]

The Whig women's memorial to Henry Clay remained in Capitol Square—housed in an ornate iron pavilion on the slope northeast of the Bell Tower—until 1930 when it was moved to the Old Hall of the House of Delegates on the Capitol's second floor. There it stands today, perhaps a reminder on behalf of the Whig women of Virginia that statesmanship and compromise for the sake of the greater good are still virtues.[29]

NOTES

1. *Richmond Whig*, Nov. 19, 1844; Charles D. Lowery, *James Barbour, A Jeffersonian Republican* (University, Alabama: University of Alabama Press, 1984), pp. 9–16, 39–40, 52–53, 178–79, 196.

2. *Richmond Whig*, Nov. 19, 1844; *Richmond Enquirer*, Nov. 29, Dec. 2, 1844.

3. *Richmond Whig*, Dec. 13, 1844. Letters and articles from December 1844, which describe the formation of the Virginia Association of Ladies for Erecting a Statue to Henry Clay, were printed as part of the coverage of the unveiling of the Clay statue in the *Richmond Whig*, April 12, 1860.

4. *Richmond Whig*, Dec. 13, 1844, and April 12, 1860.

5. On republican motherhood and true womanhood, see Sara Evans, *Born for Liberty: A History of Women in America* (New York: Free Press, 1997), pp. 57–67.

6. On Virginia women's benevolence, see Elizabeth R. Varon, *We Mean to Be Counted: White Women and Party Politics in Antebellum Virginia* (Chapel Hill: University of North Carolina Press, 1998), chs. 1–2; on the 1840 campaign in Virginia, see for example the *Staunton Spectator*, Sept. 10, 1840, and *Fredericksburg Political Arena*, March 24, Sept. 22, 1840.

7. Robert Gray Gunderson, *The Log-Cabin Campaign* (Lexington, Ky.: University Press of Kentucky, 1957), pp. 4, 7–8, 135–39.

8. *Staunton Spectator*, Sept. 1, 1836; *Richmond Yeoman*, Sept. 10, 1840; Mary Pendleton (Cooke) Steger to Sarah Harriet Apphia Hunter, Sept. 13, 1840, Hunter Family Papers, Virginia Historical Society, Richmond.

9. *Richmond Whig*, Oct. 9, 1840.

10. Robert Remini, *Henry Clay: Statesman for the Union* (New York: W. W. Norton), pp. 539, 544, 578, 613, 633–43, 650–58.

11. *Richmond Whig*, April 26, May 2, 1844; Marion Harland, *Marion Harland's Autobiography* (New York: Harper & Brothers, 1910), pp. 121–29.

12. *Richmond Whig*, April 26, May 2, Sept. 3, 1844.

13. Lawrence Frederick Kohl, *The Politics of Individualism: Parties and the American Character in the Jacksonian Era* (New York: Oxford University Press, 1989).

14. *Richmond Whig*, Aug. 13, 1844; *Washington Globe*, Nov. 1, 1844; Serena Catherine (Pendleton) Dandridge to Mary Evelina (Dandridge) Hunter, Dec. 11 [1844], Hunter Family Papers, VHS.

15. *Lynchburg Republican*, Dec. 22, 1844; *Lynchburg Virginian*, Dec. 26, 1844, and Jan. 2, 1845.

16. *Lexington Gazette*, Jan. 9, 1844; *Richmond Whig*, Dec. 13, 1844, Feb. 12, 22, 1845.

17. W. Harrison Daniel, "Richmond's Memorial to Henry Clay: The Whig Women of Virginia and the Clay Statue," *Richmond Quarterly* 8 (Spring 1986).

18. Virginia Association of Ladies for Erecting a Statue to Henry Clay, Subscription List, c. 1845–46, Virginia Historical Society, Richmond.

19. Autobiography of Judith Rives, Virginia Historical Society; Harland, *Marion Harland's Autobiography*, p. 122.

20. *Constitution and By-laws of the Female Humane Association* (Richmond, 1843), p. 1; Legislative Petitions, Lynchburg, Jan. 2, 1846, and Alexandria, Feb. 19, 1847, Archives Division, Library of Virginia.

21. On Clay, see Remini, *Henry Clay*.

22. *Ibid.*, pp. 539, 544, 578, 613, 633–43, 650–58.

23. *Norfolk Southern Argus*, Sept. 23, 1852.

24. *Richmond Whig*, April 12, 1860; Daniel, "Richmond's Memorial."

25. *Ibid.*

26. *Ibid.*

27. On Mary Blackford, see Varon, *We Mean to Be Counted*, pp. 45–56.

28. *Ibid.*, pp. 169–77.

29. Daniel, "Richmond's Memorial."

STEPHEN V. ASH

White Virginians under Federal Occupation, 1861–1865

✶ ✶ ✶ ✶ ✶ ✶ ✶ ✶ MORE BOOKS ARE PUBLISHED ON THE CIVIL War than on any other single subject in American history. Despite this outpouring of scholarship, little is known about the largest and perhaps most profoundly affected population in Virginia: white civilians. Their experience between 1861 and 1865, according to Stephen Ash, constituted another civil war. This was a war fought out in the towns and the countryside, not between hostile armies but between occupying forces and their opponents, between Union and Confederate sympathizers, between black and white Virginians, and between the rich and the poor. For many white Virginians the war precipitated chaos upon the land. Tensions sometimes broke out into violence but most commonly took the form of property confiscation, social exclusion, political disfranchisement, or simply robbery, intimidation, and bullying. Insofar as the war aggravated social discord, it was as much a conflict about who would rule at home in Virginia as it was about who would rule over Virginia.

The disruption, upheaval, and partisan conflict in Stephen Ash's Virginia stands in vivid contrast to the stability and order of the Virginia during the late colonial period that Jack Greene described. The coherence of mid-eighteenth-century political culture that rested on the deference of poor Virginians for gentry leaders and the responsibility the gentry assumed for the general welfare was shattered with seeming finality by the thousand resentments that emancipation and military occupation bred in Virginia's first families. Lost forever was the resolution of slavery's paradox with freedom that to Edmund Morgan allowed Virginians to lead the American cause in the defense of natural rights during the Revolution. At the conclusion of the Civil War, Virginia's traditional leaders struggled mightily to restore their political hegemony, but as Fred Arthur Bailey demonstrates later in this volume, they did so eventually at the expense of the values for which the Revolution had been fought. Inequality in modern Virginia, however, in the end could not withstand the mighty force that Revolutionary principles unleashed, as the course of the civil rights movement demon-

strated. Thus the Civil War stands out in Virginia history not as a detached—although compelling—event but as a crisis in the larger story of
freedom's struggle in the commonwealth. In this struggle the actions of
those in whose power it lay to shape events cannot be understood apart
from the collective responses of the many whose lives those events shaped.

* * * * * * * *

* * * * * * * *

SCANNING THE RAVAGED LANDSCAPE OF THE OLD DOMINION DUR-
ing the Civil War, some of the Yankee invaders discerned—and applauded—the avenging hand of God. A Union army chaplain who beheld
desolation and disorder on the Peninsula southeast of Richmond concluded
that "great and sore judgments are on the guilty land. The Lord seems to
be sending a thorough revolution, turning things all upside down." Some
months later, near Fredericksburg, he offered a prayer of thanksgiving:
"Righteous art Thou, in all Thy ways, O Lord. The towering pride of old
Virginia, is being fearfully humbled." Other northerners rejoiced in the evidence of human rather than divine retribution. "Virginia has acted meaner
than South Carolina even," declared a federal soldier who with his comrades
was enthusiastically plundering farms, "and I go for teaching her a lesson
that she will remember." Even those more inclined toward pity than exul-
tation blamed the calamity on the victims themselves. "It will take years of
prosperity to put Virginia in any thing like her former condition," a northern officer wrote. "Her sensible inhabitants must bitterly lament the folly
that carried her into rebellion."[1]

Lamentations could indeed be heard in the Old Dominion during those
years wherever the blue-clad troops marched. Though Virginians might
dispute the Yankees' notions about vengeance, pride, guilt, and folly, they
could not deny that the northern invasion was a fearful cataclysm. Yet not
all Virginians had reason to lament. Blacks in the occupied regions, while
suffering cruel hardships, reaped the immense reward of freedom. Few
whites, on the other hand, reaped anything to compensate for the violence,
destruction, privation, and chaos they endured. The Yankee invasion did in
fact precipitate, as the keen-eyed chaplain noted, "a thorough revolution,"
and this essay examines the ordeal of the white men and women caught up
in it.

Virginians endured enemy occupation longer, and on a larger scale, than
any of their Confederate brethren. At no time, in fact, was Confederate Virginia wholly free of Union soldiers, for the federal army never relinquished
Fort Monroe, situated at the tip of the Peninsula. By the end of 1861 the
Yankees held not only the lower Peninsula but also Alexandria and Fairfax
counties (just outside Washington, D.C.), and the Eastern Shore. In 1862
they extended their control to the upper Peninsula; to Norfolk, Suffolk, and

Portsmouth in the southeastern part of the state; to the Lower Shenandoah Valley; and to the counties surrounding Fairfax, as far south as the Rappahannock River. Moreover, although they stationed no large forces there, they sent frequent raiding and foraging expeditions into the Northern Neck and other Tidewater counties north of the Peninsula. Confederate offensives forced the Yankees to abandon the Valley and the counties around Fairfax several times, but only temporarily. By the last months of the war Union forces held sway in all of these areas and furthermore had advanced to the outskirts of Richmond and Petersburg.[2]

Even early in the war, before any military incursions brought the enemy to their doorsteps, many white Virginians evinced deep anxieties. Like white southerners elsewhere, they were convinced that the Union armies—composed, they presumed, of the dregs of the North's corrupt, mobocratic society and whipped into a frenzy by Republican demagogues and abolitionist zealots—intended a war of plunder, emancipation, and annihilation. Many citizens were further alarmed at the prospect of internal conflict in the newborn Confederacy, fomented by die-hard Unionists and other disaffected southerners, black as well as white. Aristocrats, in particular, feared that slaves, free blacks, and poor whites might join hands with the northern invaders to overthrow the South's ruling class.[3]

In Virginia these apprehensions were aggravated by the exposed position of the state and the certainty that the enemy would make the Old Dominion a prime objective. Just three weeks after the outbreak of war a man living near Alexandria warned of armed Yankees massing along the state's borders: "not regular and disciplined soldiers," he asserted, "but fanatics and lawless ruffians ready for every outrage and violence." Farther up the Potomac, in Loudoun County, citizens pleaded for enough Confederate troops to forestall a Yankee invasion rendered likely by the presence of a "large Union element" in the county. A group of Winchester residents deplored the "defenseless condition" of the Lower Valley and reasoned that "if devastation and plunder are to form a part of the system of this war, this is certainly an inviting field for it. This was selected as the theater of John Brown's raid, and if the destruction of slavery . . . is an object with our enemy, as it is proclaimed to be . . . , these Northern troops will be apt to follow the footsteps of [Brown]."[4]

In the regions most at risk, citizens and civil and military authorities took special precautions. Whites organized patrols to intercept slaves escaping to the Yankees. Some planters removed their bondsmen to safer districts, a course of action endorsed by Governor John Letcher and General R. E. Lee. The governor also ordered the formation of committees of safety in the endangered counties, empowered to "scrutinize all strangers or suspicious characters" and arrest those suspected as "spies and disloyal persons." The Confederate commander in the Northern Neck urged that the "disaffected element" (who, he implied, were those without property) be driven out at bayonet point or forced into the rebel ranks. On the Peninsula a Confederate officer worried that free black and poor white fishermen along the James River might serve the enemy as guides. "I shall order these free negroes to be arrested," he decided, ". . . and the fishing skiffs to be destroyed—those of low white men as well as those of the negroes. Some of the whites are as dangerous as the negroes."[5]

When invasion seemed imminent, anxiety gave way to panic. Visions of looting and savagery, spawned by old stereotypes about the barbaric Yankees, seized white imaginations. As northern troops approached Winchester in March 1862, for instance, a witness described the townsfolk as "all crazy—perfectly frantic for fear [that] . . . the Yanks [will] nab them." Consequently, in every invaded region many whites hurriedly gathered their belongings and took to the road, abandoning homes and farms to seek refuge behind rebel lines. The village of Hampton, for example, lying within easy striking distance of Fort Monroe, was deserted by nearly all its white residents in May 1861. Two months later a northern journalist in Centreville, not far from Washington, D.C., observed that "the mass of the people, men, women, and children had fled,—their minds poisoned with tales of the brutality of Northern soldiers." Hampton and Centreville were extreme examples, however, for in most invaded areas the majority of whites—loath to leave their property unprotected or dismayed by the prospect of refugee life—elected to remain at home and face the consequences.[6]

To the immense relief of all, the advance legions of the Yankees failed to live up to their infamy. In fact, in this early stage of the war the North pursued a remarkably restrained and conciliatory policy. Persuaded that most southern whites were reluctant rebels who if handled gently could be won back to the Union, military commanders strictly forbade any pillaging, abuse of peaceful civilians, or meddling with slavery. Upon commencing the invasion of the Eastern Shore in November 1861, Major General John A. Dix informed the inhabitants that his soldiers "will go among you as friends. . . . They will invade no rights of person or property; on the contrary, your laws, your institutions, your usages will be scrupulously respected." On the Peninsula the following year Major General George B. McClellan reminded his soldiers that "we are not engaged in a war of rapine, revenge, or subjugation" but a purely military and political struggle that "should be conducted by us upon the highest principles known to Christian civilization."[7]

Subordinate officers in the field generally carried out this policy in good faith. The commander of the 28th Pennsylvania Infantry, for example, halted his men as they entered Lovettsville in Loudoun County and, as one of them recorded, "made a few remarks, admonishing us to act as Gentlemen and not as the Seceshionist[s] termed us, Brutes, Robbers &c." An

Ohio officer in the Shenandoah Valley town of Woodstock averred that "I try to make all [citizens] I come in contact with feel as if we were not conquerors, that we did not feel exultant, . . . that we had no desire to play the tyrant." Enlisted men, on the other hand, often declined to take such high moral ground. As a Union general at Fort Monroe noted in June 1861, "The volunteer troops seem to have adopted the theory that all property of the inhabitants was subject to plunder." Such misconduct was kept to a minimum, however, through the rigorous enforcement of discipline by military commanders determined to woo Virginians back to the Union.[8]

Propitiation proved futile. To the chagrin of many well-intentioned Yankees, white Virginians (with some exceptions) greeted them as blood enemies. The same officer who tried to placate the citizens of Woodstock confessed ruefully that "the tenor of society here is hostile to us. *I may say hatefully so.*" "The women," he added, "are almost universally bitter Secesh and spit it out with venom." Many other northerners likewise noted the outspokenness of Virginia women, who—once it was apparent that the Yankees were not an unbridled horde of savages—took advantage of the invaders' Victorian code of gentlemanly behavior to taunt them as no man would dare. They "seized every opportunity to display their hate and bitterness," said a federal cavalryman in Williamsburg. "They would even pass by our wounded and suffering with an air of scorn." Females had no monopoly on hostility, however. "The men are just as mean as the women," one soldier remarked, "but a little more discreet."[9]

Disillusioned, the northern occupiers quickly abandoned optimism and conciliation. "[T]he more I see of these rebels the more I hate them," declared an artillery officer in the Valley in March 1862. "Notwithstanding all efforts we make . . . they still believe we are abolitionists and murderers and the Lord knows what all and they are so infernal impudent in the[ir] treason that it is enough to make one mad." The following year General Dix, who in 1861 had sent his soldiers into the Eastern Shore as "friends," concluded that the strategy of occupying every captured town was foolish. "There was an excuse for scattering our forces while there was reason to believe that the people of the South would rally around them as nucleus for the restoration of the Union," he wrote, but "this hope is now gone." The hardening northern attitude was exemplified by Major General G. K. Warren. "From my experience with the people of Virginia," he said in 1864, ". . . I think them entitled to no consideration."[10]

Having renounced the carrot, military authorities took up the stick and replaced leniency with coercion. This new policy was most readily accomplished in the larger towns, where permanent garrisons were stationed and federal power was omnipresent and unchallengeable. The commandant at Alexandria, for example, abruptly ended months of indulgence toward the town's vociferous secessionists in February 1862, when he arrested an Episcopal clergyman for seditious preaching and threatened to imprison any-one else, male or female, who uttered rebel sentiments. "Within a few days," a Unionist resident noted with satisfaction, "an almost entire stop has been put to all outward expressions of disloyalty in the town." Two weeks later the commandant jailed thirty citizens "on suspicion of complicity . . . with the Rebels." The following year, convinced that Alexandria's seces-sionists were plotting a coup, federal authorities ordered all who would not take an oath of loyalty and post bond for good behavior—men and women alike—to turn over their houses to the provost marshal and leave town. In Norfolk and Portsmouth, authorities not only punished or banished recal-citrant rebels but also took control of the churches, expelled secessionist ministers, and brought in loyal ones to fill the pulpits.[11]

Yankee rule in Virginia's occupied towns was not, however, simply an iron-fisted military despotism. While with one hand army officers subju-gated the rebellious townsfolk, with the other they carried on municipal functions necessary for public order and health. Stepping into the void left by the deposed civil officials, they collected taxes, maintained streets and gaslights, organized schools and fire departments and night watches, tried and sentenced lawbreakers, operated jails, fed the poor, regulated markets and harbors, licensed saloons and brothels, and rounded up stray dogs. By 1863 civil administration was at least partly restored in some towns under the aegis of the federally sanctioned Unionist state government located in Alexandria and headed by Francis H. Pierpont. Thus, although the major-ity of citizens in the occupied towns remained muzzled, disfranchised, and subject to strict War and Treasury Department regulations governing con-quered rebel territory, and although the streets and shops and churches were crowded with blue-coated troops and other strangers, life there as-sumed something like normality. "[T]he town is very lively," observed an Alexandria man in 1862. "I walked down King Street this evening, and found . . . the stores and public houses all brilliantly lighted, places of amusement open, &c."[12]

In the countryside, by contrast, where the great majority of Virginians lived, order and normality rapidly disappeared. Because the Union army could not garrison every village and patrol every crossroads, rural whites remained hostile and unsubdued. Some, anticipating the eventual redemp-tion of their homeland by the Confederate army and determined to harass the invaders until then, formed bushwhacker gangs to waylay Yankee de-tachments. "Every house . . . is a nest of treason," wrote a federal com-mander in northern Virginia in 1863, "and every grove a lurking place for guerrilla bands." "Regiments of the line can do nothing with this fur-tive population," another officer complained, "soldiers to-day, farmers to-morrow, acquainted with every wood-path, and finding a friend in every house. . . . [W]e are not safe in bands of 3 or 4; every one betrays us."[13]

The implacable resistance of rural whites goaded the Yankees into ever more draconian measures. By 1862 exasperated officers began to turn a blind eye to pillaging by their soldiers. "Our men are becoming regardless of any thing belonging to the enemy," a regimental commander wrote, adding (with an ironic allusion to the inveterate plight of southern blacks) that "we are in effect adopting the doctrine that the Secesh have no right[s] that white men are bound to respect."[14]

Official retribution likewise grew harsher. In 1862 Major General John Pope provoked outrage among northern Virginians when he declared that all secessionist men must either swear allegiance to the United States and post bond for good behavior or remove themselves to Confederate-held territory, and, further, that local residents would be held responsible for guerrilla attacks and be required to repair the damages or pay indemnity. Pope's edicts were mild compared to subsequent measures. In 1863 the army warned residents of Prince William County that wherever guerrillas were encountered the homes of nearby residents "will be burned to the ground and their property confiscated." In late 1864, annoyed by guerrilla attacks on the Manassas Gap Railroad, military authorities ordered that all disloyal inhabitants within five miles of the track be arrested or expelled and their houses destroyed. Civilians thereafter found within that zone would be regarded "as robbers and bushwhackers," and if more attacks on the railroad occurred, "an additional strip of ten miles on each side will be laid waste, and that section of county entirely depopulated." Such threats were absolutely sincere. A few weeks later Major General Philip Sheridan ordered that the entire area between the railroad and the Potomac River—including most of Loudoun County—be ravaged. "This section has been the hot-bed of lawless bands," he told a subordinate. "[Y]ou will consume and destroy all forage and subsistence, burn all barns and mills . . . , and drive off all stock in the region. . . . The ultimate results of the guerrilla system of warfare is the total destruction of all private rights."[15]

Sporadically inflicted violence and ruin could not pacify the seething countryside, however. Such random punishment—in contrast to the ineluctable enforcement of obedience in the occupied towns—in fact only stiffened the will of white Virginians to resist and intensified their hatred of the Yankees. "I have been so cruelly treated by the enemy," wrote a planter on the Peninsula in 1864, "that I can never have any thing more to do with them. They have murdered my first born, burned my houses, meat & bread[,] stole and carried of[f] my stock[,] indeed robbed me of all I had. . . . I can but think they desire possession of our lands . . . and to reduce us to want and begary." Many other rural Virginians were likewise thoroughly convinced of the invaders' sinister purpose. "They have hated us without a cause and are striving to exterminate us by slow degrees," declared a Fauquier County woman in 1863. "They are like the cat with a mouse. Whenever we accumulate a little, they come and take it from us, and their faces show that they have no mercy." The appearance of black troops roused the most frantic apprehensions. "A new phase seems to have been put upon the warfare of the enemy," a James City County man said in 1864. "He has not only mustered into his service the ignorant negro, naturally cruel and hard hearted, but instead of employing him in legitimate warfare, it seems his purpose to turn loose his fierce and unbridled passions, that murder, pillage, rape, and arson may follow in his wake."[16]

The unremitting strife in the countryside—along with the mere presence of large armies in the state for four years—had profound consequences for rural Virginians. The most obvious was physical devastation. All who gazed upon the regions where troops had passed were struck by the utter desolation. As early as October 1861 a Union soldier in Fairfax County observed that "the country between here and Washington is in a sorry condition, the fences all burnt up, the houses deserted, the crops annihilated, and everything showing the footprints of war." Another soldier described Stafford County, winter quarters of the Army of the Potomac in 1862–63: "Buildings were levelled; fences burned; . . . the wagon trains and batteries cut new thoroughfares across the estates; the feet of men, and hoofs of horses and mules, trampled fields of vegetation into barren wastes; every landmark was destroyed." Late in 1864 Culpeper County residents reported that their district was "overrun and so despoiled and devastated by the public Enemy . . . that it now resembles more a wide waste than the beautiful and productive region it formerly was." Union troops had marched through every section of the county, residents said, "destroying what they could not consume."[17]

The repeated seizure or destruction of stored provisions, standing crops, livestock, and fencing, and the consequent unwillingness or inability of farmers to continue planting and harvesting, left fields bare and larders empty and brought rural Virginians to the edge of starvation. Edward Turner, a Fauquier County planter, witnessed a typical Yankee visitation in 1862: "All day long the soldiers continue to destroy property. . . . Many hundreds of sheep, cattle and hogs & . . . poultry are destroyed. People generally are entirely stripped of their subsistence," he said. "One-half of the people of this truly unfortunate country have been robbed to destitution & the other half have nothing to spare for their relief." In 1864 a Stafford County man smuggled a letter to the rebel governor in Richmond describing the plight of "the suffering poor on this side of the lines. Many of us . . . will actually starve for Bread unless we can get some help. . . . [T]he yankees took from us our stock, corn, &c &c and . . . we could not make more than one third enough [crops] to last us, and are now suffering."[18]

Plundered and starving, and in some cases forcibly evicted, thousands fled the invaded rural areas. Some communities were wholly depopulated;

and even in those where inhabitants remained, many stayed fearfully at home or hid in the woods to avoid the pervasive dangers. Once-bustling neighborhoods and villages appeared eerily abandoned. "I am riding all day & scarcely meet a single individual on the road," Edward Turner noted in his diary on 27 December 1862. "The country is almost deserted. On former & happier times Christmas week was a time of general hilarity. . . . At present there is scarcely to be seen a sign of human life, much less of human enjoyment. At the cross roads & public stands you look in vain for the usual throng, you listen in vain for the sounds of mirth. A solemn silence reigns on all the surrounding ruin."[19]

Strangled by the immobility or flight of their constituency, the institutions that bolstered rural society—churches, schools, local government—withered and died. "[T]he churches are fast going to ruin," Turner wrote. "No schools public or private in the country." The Quakers of Hopewell Meeting in the Shenandoah Valley sadly recorded in 1864 that "our meetings have not been regularly held . . . our section being a vast camp, & subject to all the interuptions & annoyances of military occupation." In Loudoun County the clerk of Ebenezer Baptist Church took up pen and minute book in July 1865 to report that "the Church has not met together for up[w]ards of three years and the cause thereof was the ware in thes[e] United States." That same month, and in that same locale, the clerk of the county court took up his own pen and book. "[O]wing to the continuance of the war," he explained, "no Court was held in this County from February, 1862, until July, 1865."[20]

As the instruments of order and community atrophied, anarchy seized the countryside. Bandit gangs materialized, preying on defenseless rural folk already scourged by the Union army. A Culpeper County man described his community in 1864 as "greatly annoyed by the Enemy, both native and Yanky, we are annoyed by a pascel of [Confederate] deserters, who are laying about and stealing evry horse they can lay their hands upon. I know not what is to become of us, unless something can be done to Rid us of such a vile pest." Many of the bandits were something worse than larcenous pests. A band that roamed Fairfax and Prince William counties was accurately described as a "gang of thieves and murderers," and another in rural Nansemond County was denounced by the Portsmouth provost marshal as "a lawless band of marauders who have committed all kinds of atrocities," including the cold-blooded killing of a woman who refused to hand over her money. The Union occupiers were too busy fighting rebels and guerrillas to do much about bandits, however, and consequently the rural areas remained, to the end of the war, turbulent and dangerous.[21]

The occupied towns—guarded, regulated, and provisioned by federal garrisons—were mostly spared the violence, chaos, and privation that battered the countryside. They were not, however, spared the political and social upheaval that also appeared in the churning wake of invasion. Just as many white Virginians had feared when the war began, Yankee occupation fractured the status quo along its fault lines and enabled Unionists, poor whites, and slaves alike to rise up and defy their oppressors.[22]

In the panicked weeks following the outbreak of war, Virginia's secessionists had terrorized the steadfast minority who remained loyal to the Union. Those not actually forced to flee for their lives were brutally silenced. Privately, however, the Unionists prayed for redemption, and, as rebel forces retreated, many openly welcomed the northern invaders. A federal officer reported from Loudoun County in 1862 that "joyous manifestations of fealty to the old Government have greeted us," and another officer there told of meeting "a number of [local] citizens and refugees from the mountains, who . . . considered us deliverers, and many of the families wept for joy. Many had been driven from their homes, and dare not return, on the pain of death."[23]

Where the federal presence seemed only temporary, Unionists often avoided public displays of loyalty for fear of later retaliation by their neighbors. (Some, however, secretly aided the Yankees.) Where occupation seemed secure—especially in the larger towns and on the Eastern Shore—many Unionists openly allied with the invaders and avenged old wrongs. The very day the northern army marched into Alexandria in May 1861, for instance, Unionists pointed out houses vacated by secessionist refugees and watched with satisfaction as these buildings were seized for officers' quarters. A Unionist in Winchester "caused all the houses to be searched" by the Yankees, as one rebel resident bitterly recounted, "and did everything he could against the [secessionist] citizens." On the Eastern Shore, Unionists prevailed on the provost marshal to crack down on rebel preachers and their disloyal congregations.[24]

Overt Unionism was risky everywhere, however, for the fortunes of war could bring sudden turnabouts. For example, while attending church during the temporary absence of the town's garrison, the Winchester Unionist mentioned above was seized at gunpoint by Confederate scouts and carried off. A subsequent federal retreat from that town sent other Unionists, in the words of one resident, "flying back to Martinsburg." Moreover, in the rural areas where guerrillas roamed, Unionists faced continual harassment and sometimes death.[25]

Yet even in the countryside, a few of the boldest struck back. In 1863 the Alexandria provost marshal reported that a group of Fairfax County Unionists who "have suffered very much from Guerrillas, . . . have now determined to act in self defence. Seven of them attacked a band of nearly twice their number last night and though armed only with shot guns, they succeeded in wounding three and driving the whole party from the neighborhood, capturing one." Impressed by such spontaneous reprisals, and moved by the pleas of rural Unionists everywhere for protection, federal authorities proceeded to organize and arm loyal home-guard units and then to unleash them against the guerrillas and their sympathizers, thus challenging secessionist power and adding another dimension to the bloody and destructive conflict that convulsed the countryside of occupied Virginia.[26]

A challenge of a different sort—and with a more revolutionary potential—reared up from the depths of white society. Poor whites in Virginia had been swept along in the secession excitement of 1861, and most had patriotically joined the war effort on the home front or in the ranks. Subsequently, however, they endured great hardships and lost faith in what seemed more and more to be a war fought by the poor in the interests of the rich. In the occupied regions, where hardships were multiplied, poor whites in large numbers abandoned the Confederate cause. Most expressed their disillusionment not through vehement Unionism, however, but through quiet apathy. A federal soldier who spoke to a long-suffering poor white woman in northern Virginia, for example, wrote that "she had but little sympathy for the South or North either. She cared but little how the war ended, [just] so it ended soon."[27]

Some poor whites, on the other hand, gave vent to deep anger and vengefulness directed at the perceived authors of their woes—that is, the zealous secessionists, especially the rich and powerful ones. A planter on the Peninsula complained that "we are very much troubled in this co[unty] with [Confederate] deserters . . . men of the low class. . . . [T]hey get their living by pilfering from those who have gone to do battle." Another Tidewater planter reported that "hundreds of deserters have returned & taken the oath of allegiance to the enemy & consequently are ready to act as spies. . . . They have already carried in [to the Yankees] lists of the names of gentlemen [who are] rabid secessionists." In northern Virginia a Union officer noted the enmity between "the poor class and the wealthy or aristocratic class. The poor ones are very bitter against the others; charge them with bringing on the war, and are always willing to show where the rich ones have hid their grain, fodder, horses, &c. Many of them tell me it is a great satisfaction to them to see us help ourselves from the rich stores of their neighbors."[28]

Encouraged by such examples, some Unionists sought to mobilize the poor and enlist them as allies in the reconstruction of a loyal government. "Increase the ill-feeling between the rich and poor in your occupation of all towns in the Valley," a Shenandoah County Unionist advised the federal authorities, ". . . impress the poor with the idea that the rich are the cause of all their miseries, and divide the wealth of the rich with the poor." A Unionist on the Eastern Shore published an appeal "to the Mechanics, Tenants and Laborers" in which he urged them to stand up against the "overbearing small-potatoe aristocracy who have governed you most despotically. . . .

Now is the time to trample under foot this petty despotism . . . and drive the . . . leaders of the rebellion, out of their places of honor and trust, and send them into obscurity."[29]

As it nervously eyed the increasingly defiant poor whites, Virginia's elite was overwhelmed by an even more radical challenge from another source: enslaved blacks. Despite the federal high command's initial conservatism concerning slavery, the presence of the Union army and navy opened avenues of liberation for Virginia's slaves. Even in the earliest days of the war, some bondsmen fled to the Yankee lines or to patrol boats on the Chesapeake and were allowed to remain as laborers; as the war progressed, Union policy gravitated toward full emancipation, and troops in the field were ordered to encourage slaves to desert their masters. With or without such encouragement, blacks in the occupied regions abandoned their owners in droves. A resident of Charles City County reported in 1863 that at least half the county's slaves had absconded, including seven-tenths of the able-bodied men. By late 1864 fewer than seventy-five slaves aged eighteen to fifty remained in Culpeper County, where the prewar slave population had been six thousand.[30]

Slaveowners had long predicted that slavery would not survive a Yankee invasion, in part because they believed northerners were bent on abolition but also because they doubted the loyalty of their slaves. Nevertheless, masters professed shock and disillusionment at the perfidy of their "ungrateful" bondsmen. Tidewater planter Colin Clarke proclaimed his "utter, thorough & deep disgust with the whole race" after a number of his slaves left and the rest refused to work. "[T]hey have all proved themselves to be so false & lying that I confess I have lost all faith in every negro," he said. "There is not *one negro* in *all the South*, who will remain faithfull . . . not one." "Let them go," declared an indignant Fauquier County woman whose servants were preparing to flee, "yes the last one provided we may never be harrassed with the same unfaithful ones again. . . . The very sight of one provokes me."[31]

While slaveowners railed at the "disloyalty" of those who ran off, they also voiced deep anxieties about those who stayed. "They are *all* lyars & scoundrels," Colin Clarke insisted. "Those who remain have an *object of their own.*" A plantation mistress who had seen some of her slaves leave during a Yankee raid confessed that "I feel entirely changed & in a state of insecurity all the time—& I do not sleep soundly . . . unless there is some gentleman in the house. My pistol is loaded, . . . it is a great comfort to me. . . . [I now] look on the creatures [the remaining slaves] as a wretched set of demons." Such fears were magnified in the occupied towns, where runaway blacks mingled with those still under their masters' control. "I am afraid of the lawless Yankee soldiers," a Fredericksburg woman confided in her diary in 1862, "but that is nothing to my fear of the negroes if they should rise against us." A Portsmouth man fretted about the fugitive slaves congregating in his town. "[I]dle impudent and thievish," he called them, " . . . and liable to be led to acts of disorder and violence by rabid Abolitionists. Lord in mercy protect and deliver us."[32]

Protect He did, but deliver He did not. The nightmarish visions of a bloody slave uprising never materialized, for the black men and women of Virginia sought freedom without vengeance. In other respects, however, invasion and emancipation did turn the world of the once-omnipotent master class all topsy-turvy. Humiliation and debasement accompanied the loss of power and property. Ladies and gentlemen of leisure suddenly found themselves unable to command the labor they had long taken for granted. One mistress who lost her slaves was dismayed by the prospect of "a life of labour & servitude. . . . I felt that my time of ease was over, & I must labour for my daily bread. . . . I put my hands to work—& actually fed the horses myself."[33]

More galling still was the realization that in some respects the "bottom rail" was now on top. On the last day of 1862 planter Edward Turner of Fauquier County recorded among the noteworthy events of that year that "Any lying negro who felt disposed to do so could involve in the most serious difficulties the first men in the land. . . . [E]xcellent and worthy citizens were stripped of property & otherwise shamefully treated [by the Yankees] upon the testimony of some unprincipled slave." Moreover, whites who continued to treat blacks highhandedly were often sharply rebuked. A Portsmouth youth who slapped a female servant for being "impudent" was reported by the woman and jailed by federal authorities; when his mother went to the provost marshal's office to remonstrate, she too was put behind bars. A man on the Eastern Shore met the same fate after he contemptuously dismissed an order to allow his former slave to reclaim her belongings and then "fell to beating the girl with a club and tearing her dress." In Gloucester County, planter Colin Clarke fumed at his own helplessness, surrounded as he was by unruly blacks who, he believed, were informing on him and whom he could not remove because they had been declared free and "we would be guilty of *kidnapping* . . . & be *subject* to the *Penitentiary*." "I feel so degraded," Clarke confessed, "whilst in the power of the Yankees violence & the negros insolence."[34]

Surely the ultimate degradation befell slaveowner William H. Clopton of the Peninsula. Clopton, a secessionist, was sarcastically described as a "high minded Virginia Gentleman" by the Union officer who arrested him in 1864.

> He has acquired a notoriety as the most cruel Slave Master in this region, [the officer reported,] but in my presence he put on the character of a Snivelling Saint. I found half a dozen *women* among our [slave] refugees,

whom he had often whipped unmercifully. . . . I laid him bare and [placed a] whip into the hands of the Women, three of Whom took turns in settling some old scores on their masters back. A black Man, whom he had abused[,] finished the administration of Poetical justice. . . . I wish that his back had been as deeply scarred as those of the women, but I abstained and left it to them.[35]

The struggle for southern independence ended abruptly in April 1865 with the fall of Richmond, the flight of the Confederate government, and the surrender of Lee's army. For white Virginians in the occupied regions, these climactic events ended all hope of Confederate redemption and thus brought about what years of Yankee mayhem and retaliation had not: the collapse of the will to resist.

As federal troops marched unopposed into every major town and the whole state became an occupied territory, Virginia's rebel citizens resigned themselves to defeat and guerrillas laid down their arms. (This surrender permitted the occupation forces to turn their attention to banditry, which was quickly suppressed.) Union commanders applauded the rapid restoration of peace. "The secessionists here," wrote an officer in the Shenandoah Valley just two days after Lee's surrender, "have apparently given up all idea of a Confederacy and appear to be inclined to commence anew." Another who rode through Loudoun and Fairfax counties at that same time "found the citizens quite sociable—the formerly cold and distant secession element quite anxious that we would accept some token of their hospitality. . . . I think the political health of this department is rapidly improving."[36]

The citizens themselves readily abjured rebellion and publicly announced the restoration of their "political health." On 27 April the city councilmen of Fredericksburg formally resolved that whereas "the War is at an end" and Virginia was again "subject to the Government & laws of the United States," they would "submit to said Authority & laws, and as quiet & orderly Citizens, acknowledge the powers that be." In May a group of Warren County residents likewise proclaimed it "our duty to submit to and support the constitution and laws of the United States, and . . . we hereby declare our purpose to obey the laws of that Government, and in all things to perform the duties of good citizens thereof."[37]

Convinced that Virginia was pacified, federal authorities during the spring and summer of 1865 disbanded their field armies, deactivated the Unionist home guards, halted large-scale foraging and punitive destruction, lifted trade restrictions, and turned administrative and police duties over to city and county civil governments, which had been quickly reorganized under the Pierpont administration, installed in Richmond. As danger subsided in the countryside, rural folk resumed their old routines, and courthouses, schools, churches, and marketplaces sprang back to life. Destitution and hunger persisted, but the army issued emergency rations in huge amounts. During August, for example, twenty-nine thousand white and black Virginians received rations each day.[38]

The curtailment of violence and devastation, the end of military rule, the rapid resurrection of institutions, and the slower but perceptible resuscitation of the war-blighted economy persuaded many that the wounds of war would soon heal. And so they would, some of them. But the bitter political and social conflicts that erupted during the war did not abate with the stacking of rebel arms at Appomattox. Indeed, the advent of peace rallied the former secessionists, elites, and slaveowners who had been put to rout under Yankee occupation and revived their determination to prevail.

Encouraged by the naively conciliatory policy of Governor Pierpont, who allowed most of them to take part in the summer elections for local offices and routinely endorsed their applications for pardon under President Andrew Johnson's amnesty program, Virginia's former Confederates launched a formidable offensive to subjugate the old Unionists and exclude them from the reconstructed government. "[N]o Sooner then wee commenced the Election," an outraged Williamsburg Unionist told Pierpont in June, "wee were over whelmed with a party of Lawyers Captains & conscript officers with their Rebel uniforms on . . . [who] voted their Red hot Cecesh Brothers in without a single Exception . . . taking the Oath as if it was nothing moore than a Glass of Lemonade while . . . the last Treasonable & Cecesh Expresion had scarcely died upon their Lips." A King and Queen County Unionist declared in July that "I am still an object of persecution. Some [former Confederates] threaten that they intend to kill me, others boast that they intend to give the . . . union men Hell, so soon as the blue Jackets are removed." A Fauquier County resident warned that "these men are now willing to take any kind of oath so as to get into power again, which God forbid, for there will be no justice for the small minority of Loyal citizens, who have been driven from their homes, beggars among strangers, for four long years. . . . We [Unionists] are even now suffering outrages and if there is not some protection given us we will be compelled to leave our homes again."[39]

As Unionists fought desperately against the frontal assault of the former rebels, poor whites likewise found themselves the target of a mighty counteroffensive. Upper-class Virginians, alarmed by the wartime unrest and opportunism among the poor, moved quickly in the postwar months to reassert their leadership in society and to reestablish their control of local government. Particularly threatening to elite hegemony was the Union army's policy of distributing food and other provisions to the needy. A northerner who interviewed an official of the Spotsylvania County court in September 1865 heard him complain vehemently about the "shiftless whites" on the federal dole: a degenerate rabble, he called them, "steeped in vice, ignorance, and crime. . . . [T]hey go clothed like savages, half sheltered, and half fed,—except that [the] government is now supporting them." Insisting that "the system [of provisioning] encourages idleness, and does more harm than good," this official suggested disingenuously that "all these evils could be remedied, and more than half the expense saved the government, if it would intrust the entire management of the matter" to local authorities.[40]

A revealing episode occurred in Appomattox County, where Union military officials had instructed the sheriff to distribute rebel army horses and other abandoned Confederate property to the poor. Instead, according to a Yankee officer, the sheriff "exceeded his authority, and with an armed force of citizens and paroled prisoners takes horses from what he terms common people and turns them over to . . . wealthy planters. Said common people have been organizing and arming a force for their own defense." Violence was averted only because the officer intervened, arrested the sheriff, disarmed his posse, and made certain that all the property was given to the poor.[41]

While poor whites and Unionists struggled to defend themselves, the forces of reaction opened a third front against Virginia's blacks. Former masters conceded the end of slavery, but nothing more; they were determined that blacks would remain their hewers of wood and drawers of water. Moreover, they insisted that blacks were inherently vicious and destructive creatures who must be rigorously controlled, if not through slavery then by other means. Although the army and the newly created Freedmen's Bureau could generally prevent or punish the most heinous abuses, former slaveowners and other whites reacted violently to every assertion of even minimal rights by blacks—an attitude exemplified by a newly elected constable in a Tidewater county who announced in July 1865 that "he has fixed himself to whip every negro who crosses his path, and he intends to make them see Hell."[42]

No other issue in the postwar months unified white Virginians so broadly. "The great subject of discussion among the people everywhere was the 'niggers,'" a northerner wrote after touring the state in August and September 1865.

> The mass of the people, including alike the well-educated and the illiterate [and, he might have added, Unionists as well as former rebels] generally detested the negroes, and wished every one of them driven out of the State. The black man was well enough as a slave; but even those who rejoiced that slavery was no more, desired to get rid of him along with it. . . . [T]he master-race could not forgive him for being free; and that he should assume to be a man, self-owning and self-directing, was intolerable.[43]

White Virginians in 1865 thus faced the future, paradoxically enough, both united and divided—united by race, divided by class and politics. Loosed in the maelstrom of war, these compelling issues of color, caste, and principle were not interred at Appomattox. They persisted; and in the postwar years they evolved and intersected in ways that would come to define the era of Reconstruction. The cannons and muskets rusted silently, and the furled battle flags gathered dust; weeds grew over the massive earthworks and the shallow graves of the slain, and stout new fences enclosed the freshly luxuriant fields of tobacco and wheat. But the war went on.

NOTES

The author gratefully acknowledges the assistance of Paul H. Bergeron of the Andrew Johnson Papers Project, University of Tennessee, Knoxville; Brooks M. Barnes of the Eastern Shore Public Library, Accomac, Virginia; and Thomas M. Moncure, Jr., of Falmouth, Virginia. Research for this essay was conducted with the help of grants from the American Council of Learned Societies and the Mellon Fellows program at the Virginia Historical Society.

1. A. M. Stewart, *Camp, March and Battle-field; Or, Three Years and a Half with the Army of the Potomac* (Philadelphia, 1865), pp. 145, 262; Oliver Willcox Norton to his family, 4 Oct. 1861, in Oliver Willcox Norton, *Army Letters, 1861–1865 . . .* (Chicago, 1903), p. 26; Alvin Coe Voris to Lydia Allyn Voris, 23 July 1862 (copy), Alvin Coe Voris Papers, Virginia Historical Society, Richmond (hereafter cited as ViHi).

2. This essay excludes from consideration that section of Virginia that became the state of West Virginia in 1863. Vincent J. Esposito, ed., *The West Point Atlas of American Wars* (2 vols.; New York, 1959), vol. 1, is useful in tracing the ebb and flow of federal occupation.

3. White southerners' views on the character and intentions of the Yankees are discussed in Randall C. Jimerson, *The Private Civil War: Popular Thought During the Sectional Conflict* (Baton Rouge and London, 1988), pp. 124–29; J. William Harris, *Plain Folk and Gentry in a Slave Society: White Liberty and Black Slavery in Augusta's Hinterlands* (Middletown, Conn., 1985), pp. 130–31, 134; James L. Roark, *Masters Without Slaves: Southern Planters in the Civil War and Reconstruction* (New York, 1977), pp. 15, 21–22, 26–27, 64–65, 75–76.

4. U.S. War Department, *The War of the Rebellion: A Compilation of the Official Records of the Union and Confederate Armies . . .* (70 vols.; Washington, D.C., 1880–1901) (hereafter cited as *OR;* all references are to ser. 1), 51: pt. 2, pp. 66–67; ibid., 2:915–16; ibid., 52: pt. 2, pp. 58–59.

5. Betsy Fleet and John D. P. Fuller, eds., *Green Mount: A Virginia Plantation Family During the Civil War: Being the Journal of Benjamin Robert Fleet and Letters of His Family* (Charlottesville, 1962), p. 138; Thomas McCandlish to John Letcher, 27 Apr. 1862, Virginia Executive Papers, Virginia State Library and Archives, Richmond (hereafter cited as Vi); F. N. Boney, *John Letcher of Virginia: The Story of Virginia's Civil War Governor,* Southern Historical Publications, No. 11 (University, Ala., 1966), p. 161; *OR,* 11: pt. 3, pp. 669–70; John Letcher, proclamation, 24 Apr. 1862, Virginia Executive Papers; *OR,* 5:994; ibid., 11: pt. 3, pp. 561–62.

6. Kate S. Sperry, Diary, 7 Mar. 1862, Vi; Robert Francis Engs, *Freedom's First Generation: Black Hampton, Virginia, 1861–1890* (Philadelphia, 1979), pp. 4, 20; Charles Carleton Coffin, *Four Years of Fighting: A Volume of Personal Observation with the Army and Navy* . . . (Boston, 1866), p. 26. See also J. M. Drake to his father, 25 June 1861, Federal Soldiers' Letters (Miscellaneous), Southern Historical Collection, University of North Carolina, Chapel Hill (hereafter cited as NcU).

7. *OR*, 5:431–32; ibid., 11: pt. 3, p. 364. See also ibid., 2:38, 5:747, 11: pt. 1, p. 74; Susie May Ames, "Federal Policy Toward the Eastern Shore of Virginia in 1861," *Virginia Magazine of History and Biography* (hereafter cited as *VMHB*) 69 (1961): 440–43, 446–56.

8. William Henry Harrison Fithian, Diary, 1 Mar. 1862, Special Collections, University of Tennessee, Knoxville (hereafter cited as TU); Alvin Coe Voris to Lydia Allyn Voris, 1 May 1862 (copy), Voris Papers; *OR*, 2:663.

9. Alvin Coe Voris to Lydia Allyn Voris, 1, 4 May 1862 (copy), Voris Papers; F. Colburn Adams, *The Story of a Trooper* . . . (New York, 1865), pp. 383–84, 407; Oliver Willcox Norton to his sister, 23 May 1862, in Norton, *Army Letters*, p. 79. See also Henry N. Blake, *Three Years in the Army of the Potomac* (Boston, 1865), pp. 28, 32–33, 87–88; Amanda Virginia (Edmonds) Chappelear, Diary, 17 Mar. 1862, ViHi; Joel Cook, *The Siege of Richmond: A Narrative of the Military Operations of Major-General George B. McClellan* (Philadelphia, 1862), pp. 153–54; James Thomas Ward, Diary, 5 Jan., 13 Feb. 1862, Library of Congress, Washington, D.C. (hereafter cited as DLC).

10. Harry C. Cushing to his mother, 30 Mar. 1862, Harry C. Cushing Letters, Special Collections, TU; *OR*, 18:649; ibid., 33:266.

11. James Thomas Ward, Diary, 7, 9, 10, 13, 28 Feb. 1862; H. H. Wells to J. P. Slough, 18 Apr., 31 May 1863, Letters Sent by Provost Marshal, Alexandria, Va., Records of the United States Army Continental Commands, 1821–1920, RG 393 (hereafter cited as RUSACC), vol. 4, E-1526, National Archives, Washington, D.C. (hereafter cited as DNA); H. H. Wells to J. H. Taylor, 17 June 1863, Letters Sent by Provost Marshal, South of the Potomac, ibid., E-1457; Benjamin F. Butler to William F. Smith, 9 July 1864, in Benjamin F. Butler, *Private and Official Correspondence of Gen. Benjamin F. Butler, During the Period of the Civil War* (5 vols.; Norwood, Mass., 1917), 4:578; General Order No. 3, 11 Feb. 1864, in Walter L. Fleming, ed., *Documentary History of Reconstruction* . . . (2 vols.; Cleveland, 1906), 2:223; Christ (Episcopal) Church, Norfolk, Vestry Minutes, 6 Nov. 1863, Vi; G. MacLaren Brydon, "The Diocese of Virginia in the Southern Confederacy," *Historical Magazine of the Protestant Episcopal Church* 17 (1948): 394–95.

12. James Thomas Ward, Diary, 25 Jan. 1862; see also *Alexandria Gazette*, 5 Sept. 1862. Examples of the municipal duties assumed by the military are in H. G. O. Weymouth to Edward W. Smith, 7 Jan. 1865, United States Army Provost Marshal, Portsmouth, Va., Letterpress Book, 1864–65, Duke University Library, Durham (hereafter cited as NcD); T. C. Harris to O. S. Mann, 12 Apr. 1865, T. L. Clarke to J. H. Liebman, 4 Sept. 1862, J. R. Gould to J. H. Liebman, 6 Aug. 1862, Reports Received, Department of Virginia and North Carolina Provost Marshal Records, RUSACC, vol. 1, E-5175; H. H. Wells to J. H. Taylor, 16 Apr., 28 July 1864, ibid., vol. 4, E-1457; Special Orders, No. 8, 17 Jan. 1863, Orders Issued by Provost Marshal, South of the Potomac, ibid., E-1461; Benjamin F. Butler to Abraham Lincoln, 1 Aug. 1864, and Special Order No. 50, 22 June 1864, in Butler, *Private and Official Cor-*

respondence, 4:578, 589–90; *Alexandria Gazette*, 9 Jan., 25, 28 June 1864; Wilton P. Moore, "Union Army Provost Marshals in the Eastern Theater," *Military Affairs* 26 (Fall 1962): 123–26. The complex issue of federal trade regulations is discussed in Ludwell H. Johnson III, "Blockade or Trade Monopoly? John A. Dix and the Union Occupation of Norfolk," *VMHB* 93 (1985): 54–78. Evidence of the resumption of civil government under Unionist control is in Norfolk Hustings Court Order Book, 1862–65, Vi; Portsmouth City Council Minutes, 1862–65, Vi; Fairfax County Court Minute Book, 1863–65, Vi. On Pierpont's "Virginia Restored Government," see Charles H. Ambler, *Francis H. Pierpont: Union War Governor of Virginia and Father of West Virginia* (Chapel Hill, 1937), esp. pp. 213–80. An acrimonious power struggle ensued between the civil officials of the Pierpont government and the army occupation authorities. See Lenoir Chambers, "Notes on Life in Occupied Norfolk, 1862–1865," *VMHB* 73 (1965): 135–38; Richard S. West, Jr., *Lincoln's Scapegoat General: A Life of Benjamin F. Butler, 1818–1893* (Boston, 1965), pp. 263–72; Spencer Wilson, "Experiment in Reunion: The Union Army in Civil War Norfolk and Portsmouth, Virginia" (Ph.D. diss., University of Maryland, 1973). F. H. Pierpont spelled his surname "Peirpoint" until 1881, when he adopted the New England spelling (Ambler, *Francis H. Pierpont*, p. 3).

13. *OR*, 29: pt. 2, p. 423; ibid., pt. 1, p. 90. See also ibid., 42: pt. 1, p. 684. Residents of the Eastern Shore, cut off from the Virginia mainland and without hope of Confederate redemption, were an exception to the general restiveness of rural whites under federal occupation. On the relatively quick and easy pacification of that region, see E. T. Crowson, "The Expedition of Henry Lockwood to Accomac," *West Virginia History* 36 (1974–75): 202–12.

14. Alvin Coe Voris to Lydia Allyn Voris, 13 July 1862 (copy), Voris Papers.

15. *OR*, 12: pt. 2, pp. 51–52; ibid., 25: pt. 2, p. 511; ibid., 43: pt. 2, pp. 348, 679.

16. J. M. Willcox to Susannah P. Willcox, 25 July 1864, James M. Willcox Papers, NcD; Lucy Johnson Ambler, Diary, 2 Aug. 1863, Ambler-Brown Family Papers, NcD; Cyrus A. Branch to William Smith, 15 May 1864, Virginia Executive Papers. See also Cornelia Grinnan to the duke of Argyll, 12 Sept. 1863, Vi.

17. Oliver Willcox Norton to his family, 4 Oct. 1861, in Norton, *Army Letters*, p. 26; Blake, *Three Years in the Army*, pp. 162–63; petition No. 368, Nov. 1864 (enclosing resolution of Culpeper County court, 21 Nov. 1864), Memorials and Petitions, Legislative Records (Confederate), War Department Collection of Confederate Records, RG 109, E-175, DNA.

18. Orlin M. Sanford, "A Virginian's Diary in Civil War Days," *Americana* 18 (1924): 362, 364; John R. Evans to William Smith, 7 May 1864, Virginia Executive Papers. See also *OR*, 51: pt. 1, pp. 1137–38. The hesitancy of farmers in occupied areas to plant or harvest is documented in Simon A. McCartney to J. P. Conn, 24 May 1864, Federal Soldiers' Letters (Miscellaneous); William P. Smith to Christopher Tompkins, 10 Mar. 1863, William Patterson Smith Papers, NcD; Alvin Coe Voris to Lydia Allyn Voris, 23 July 1862 (copy), Voris Papers.

19. Sanford, "A Virginian's Diary," p. 366. For further evidence of depopulation and the restriction of mobility in the rural areas, see H. B. White to Nannie White, 5 June 1862, H. B. White Papers, NcU; Margaret Tilloston (Kemble) Nourse, Diary, 4 Apr. 1862, ViHi.

20. Sanford, "A Virginian's Diary," p. 360; Hopewell Meeting of Friends (Fred-

erick County, Va.) Monthly Meeting Record Book, 5 Oct. 1864, 7 Mar. 1866, Vi; Ebenezer Baptist Church, Loudoun County, Minute Book, July 1865, Vi; Loudoun County Court Minute Book, July 1865, Vi. Other examples are in Luray (Main Street) Baptist Church, Page County, Minute Book, 1862–65, esp. 5 Apr. 1862, 5 Apr. 1863, 2 Oct. 1864, Vi; Thumb Run Primitive Baptist Church, Fauquier County, Va., Minute Book, 1862–65, Vi; Edward Hamilton Phillips, "The Lower Shenandoah Valley During the Civil War: The Impact of War upon the Civilian Population and upon Civil Institutions" (Ph.D. diss., University of North Carolina, Chapel Hill, 1958), chaps. 6–8.

21. L. Y. Field to William Smith, 30 May 1864, Virginia Executive Papers; H. H. Wells to J. H. Taylor, 2 Mar. 1865, RUSACC, vol. 4, E-1457; J. L. Cunningham to T. H. Harris, 19 May 1865, United States Army Provost Marshal, Portsmouth, Letterpress Book.

22. Some occupied towns suffered a good deal of destruction, particularly when first entered by Union troops. See, for example, the descriptions of Fredericksburg and Fairfax Court House in Blake, *Three Years in the Army*, p. 157, and Adams, *Story of a Trooper*, p. 289.

23. H. W. Flournoy, ed., *Calendar of Virginia State Papers . . .* (11 vols.; Richmond, 1875–93), 11:370–71; *OR*, 5:733–34; ibid., 19: pt. 2, pp. 25–26.

24. *OR*, 25: pt. 1, p. 13; [Judith W. McGuire,] *Diary of a Southern Refugee, During the War* (1867; New York, 1868), p. 20; Kate S. Sperry, Diary, 14 Jan. 1864; George C. Tyler to Benjamin F. Butler, 25 Mar. 1864, in Butler, *Private and Official Correspondence*, 3:576–78; circular, 12 July 1864, Orders, Special Orders, and Circulars Issued by Assistant Provost Marshal, Onancock, Va., RUSACC, vol. 4, E-1701.

25. Kate S. Sperry, Diary, 14 Jan., 10 May 1864. The harassment or murder of rural Unionists is documented in the John Sailor case, MM 557, Court Martial Files, Records of the Office of Judge Advocate General (War), 1809–1938 (hereafter cited as ROJAG), RG 153, E-15, DNA; James A. Tait to E. G. Parker, 12 Feb. 1863, H. H. Wells to John P. Slough, 14 Nov. 1863, RUSACC, vol. 4, E-1457.

26. H. H. Wells to Samuel P. Heintzelman, 20 July 1863, H. H. Wells to Rufus King, 9 Oct. 1863, H. H. Wells to J. H. Taylor, 14 Oct., 17 Nov. 1863, 5 Mar. 1864, RUSACC, vol. 4, E-1457.

27. Oliver Willcox Norton to his sister, 8 June 1863, in Norton, *Army Letters*, p. 160. See also Theodore Lyman to Elizabeth Russell Lyman, 30 May 1864, in George R. Agassiz, ed., *Meade's Headquarters, 1863–1865: Letters of Colonel Theodore Lyman from the Wilderness to Appomattox* (Boston, 1922), p. 133; Edward Morley to Sardis and Anna Morley, 1 Nov. 1864, Edward Williams Morley Papers, DLC.

28. Daniel Jones to John Letcher, 6 Nov. 1862, Virginia Executive Papers; Colin Clarke to Powhatan Page, n.d. (ca. May 1862), Maxwell Troax Clarke Papers, NcU; *OR*, 21:776.

29. *OR*, 25: pt. 2, pp. 526, 541; J. G. Potts, *Address to the People of the Counties of Accomac and Northampton in General, and Particularly to the Mechanics, Tenants and Laborers* (Baltimore, 1862), pp. 3–4.

30. Engs, *Freedom's First Generation*, pp. 20, 68–70; John M. Gregory to James A. Seddon, 7 Mar. 1863, in Ira Berlin et al., eds., *Freedom: A Documentary History of Emancipation, 1861–1867*, ser. 1, vol. 1: *The Destruction of Slavery* (Cambridge, London, and New York, 1985), 1:751; petition No. 368, Nov. 1864, Memorials and Petitions, Leg-

islative Records (Confederate), War Department Collection of Confederate Records. For a review of Union policy on slavery in Virginia, see Berlin et al., eds., *Freedom*, 1:59–70, 159–67.

31. Colin Clarke to Maxwell Clarke, 23 Aug. 1863, 10 Aug. 1862, Clarke Papers; Amanda Virginia (Edmonds) Chappelear, Diary, 19 Apr. 1862.

32. Colin Clarke to Maxwell Clarke, 15 Aug. 1862, Clarke Papers; Charlotte Wright to Mary Ward, 9 July 1864, Ward Family of Richmond County, Va., Papers, DLC; Betty Herndon Maury, Diary, 25 Apr. 1862, DLC; Overton and Jessie Bernard, Diary, 25 Dec. 1862, NcU.

33. Charlotte Wright to Mary Ward, 9 July 1864, Ward Family Papers.

34. Sanford, "A Virginian's Diary," p. 368; Overton and Jessie Bernard, Diary, 2 Jan. 1863; J. W. Strong to Frank White, 14 Mar. 1864, Letters Sent by Assistant Provost Marshal, Onancock, Va., RUSACC, vol. 4, E-1700; Colin Clarke to Maxwell Clarke, 5 May 1863, 16 Sept. 1862, Clarke Papers.

35. Edward A. Wild to Robert S. Davis, 12 May 1864, in Berlin et al., eds., *Freedom*, 1:96–97.

36. *OR*, 46: pt. 3, p. 714; ibid., pt. 1, p. 1308. Further evidence of the demise of rebel morale is in ibid., pt. 3, pp. 1006, 1205; *Alexandria Gazette*, 27 May 1865; and Eliza Chew (French) Smith, Diary, 3, 12 Apr., 4 July 1865, ViHi. The rapid collapse of Confederate military and political authority in April and early May 1865 is documented in *OR*, 46: pt. 3, p. 1295; and Alvin A. Fahrner, "William 'Extra Billy' Smith, Governor of Virginia, 1864–1865: A Pillar of the Confederacy," *VMHB* 74 (1966): 87. The generally peaceful occupation of the whole state in the days and weeks after Lee's surrender is illustrated in Mark K. Greenough, "Aftermath at Appomattox: Federal Military Occupation of Appomattox County, May–November, 1865," *Civil War History* 31 (1985): 5–23; and James I. Robertson, Jr., "Danville Under Military Occupation, 1865," *VMHB* 75 (1967): 331–48. On the suppression of banditry, see *OR*, 46: pt. 3, p. 1166.

37. Fredericksburg City Council Minutes, 27 Apr. 1865, Vi; resolution of Warren County citizens, 15 May 1865, Francis H. Pierpont Executive Papers, Vi.

38. W. W. Winship to R. D. Pettit, 4 May 1865, W. W. Winship to Lieutenant Machesney, 4 June 1865, W. W. Wells to C. H. Ware, 17 Sept. 1865, RUSACC, vol. 4, E-1457; *Alexandria Gazette*, 12 Apr., 9 May 1865; Ambler, *Francis H. Pierpont*, p. 275; Penelope K. Majeske, "Virginia After Appomattox: The United States Army and the Formation of Presidential Reconstruction Policy," *W. Va. History* 43 (1981–82): 101–3, 112–16; James E. Sefton, *The United States Army and Reconstruction, 1865–1877* (Baton Rouge, 1967), p. 9.

39. Richard G. Lowe, "Francis Harrison Pierpont: Wartime Unionist, Reconstruction Moderate," in Edward Younger et al., eds., *The Governors of Virginia, 1860–1978* (Charlottesville, 1982), pp. 39–41; William R. Davis to F. H. Pierpont, 11 June 1865, D. D. Bulman to F. H. Pierpont, 23 July 1865, Philip A. Tracy to F. H. Pierpont, 21 June 1865, Pierpont Executive Papers. See also William Bartlett and D. B. Krazor to F. H. Pierpont, 15 June 1865, William A. Defflemyer to F. H. Pierpont, 24 July 1865, ibid.; John Richard Dennett, *The South As It Is, 1865–1866* (New York, 1965), pp. 5–6. Between June and December 1865 Johnson granted pardons to 2,497 Virginia former Confederates (information provided by Andrew Johnson Papers Project, University of Tennessee, Knoxville).

40. J. T. Trowbridge, *The South: A Tour of Its Battlefields and Ruined Cities* . . . (Hartford, 1866), pp. 133–35.

41. *OR*, 46: pt. 3, pp. 1156–57; Greenough, "Aftermath at Appomattox," pp. 6–7.

42. Roark, *Masters Without Slaves*, pp. 96, 106–7; D. D. Bulman to F. H. Pierpont, 23 July 1865, Pierpont Executive Papers. See also William Nalle, Diary, 25 Aug. 1865, ViHi; Charles Phillips and George W. Southworth cases, MM 2655, ROJAG; Engs, *Freedom's First Generation*, pp. 86–87; John T. O'Brien, "Reconstruction in Richmond: White Restoration and Black Protest, April–June 1865," *VMHB* 89 (1981): 259–81.

43. Trowbridge, *The South*, pp. 228–29.

FRED ARTHUR BAILEY

Free Speech and the Lost Cause in the Old Dominion

✱ ✱ ✱ ✱ ✱ ✱ ✱ ✱ LATE TWENTIETH-CENTURY VIRGINIA HAS SEEN
numerous public controversies over the meaning of the Civil War. For
many Virginians today the Confederacy represents slavery, racism, and oppression. For others, Virginia's participation in the war is cause for reflection on individual liberty, patriotism, duty, defense of home and family, and
pride of place. Thus the memorialization of Virginia's Confederate past in
song, flags, license plates, statues, plaques, and other symbols has been the
occasion of bitter disputes, as various groups continue to struggle to define
the meaning of Virginia's past today.

As Fred Arthur Bailey demonstrates, this is by no means a recent phenomenon. Late nineteenth- and early twentieth-century Virginia also witnessed a struggle over the meaning of the Civil War. At a time in which
Virginia's traditional "best families" faced unprecedented challenges from
the "aspirations of lesser whites and long oppressed African Americans,"
Bailey argues, they rallied to defend their status. By asserting political
control over the history taught in the state's colleges and public schools,
Virginia's Confederate patriotic societies reaffirmed "the southern aristocracy's authority as the dominant force in the region's political, social, and
economic life."

Proponents of the Lost Cause ideology sanitized the Old Dominion's
heritage of the troubling paradox of slavery and freedom. In the process
they produced a revisionist account of antebellum plantation society characterized by racial harmony and willing black complicity in white supremacy. The cause that was lost in the Civil War was restricted to the
constitutional defense of states' rights. Lost Cause advocates blamed racial
agitation after the war not on the moral or political agency of the former
slaves but rather on northern interference in southern affairs. Thus they
fixed social boundaries between the races that earlier generations of Virginians would never have recognized.

Strikingly, white women mobilized their moral authority in support of
the Lost Cause. "Steeped in the Victorian belief that women were the nat-

ural preservers of tradition," the heirs to Virginia's plantation aristocracy "urged their wives and sisters to perpetuate those antebellum values that justified enlightened rule by the state's elite families." Virginia's era of Jim Crow was thus complexly defined not just by race and racial oppression but also by prevailing understandings of the appropriate public and private roles of men and women and of the proper structure of public authority.

In the successful effort of Virginia's Confederate patriotic societies to assert and defend their view of the past, Bailey demonstrates the cultural adaptability and political tenaciousness of the plantation aristocracy whose rise has been chronicled by Edmund Morgan and Jack Greene. He also shows convincingly, in much the same way as Warren Hofstra and Deborah Lee have, that the stories a people tell of their past govern the way they understand themselves in the present. ⁂ * * * * * * *

* * * * * * * *

"WE HAVE PLEDGED OURSELVES TO SEE THAT TRUTH IN HISTORY shall be taught," promised Kate Noland Garnett, chairman of the history committee of the Virginia Division, United Daughters of the Confederacy, in 1907. There "shall be no doubt in the minds of future generations as to the causes of the war, and why Southern men were forced to take up arms to defend their homes from the invading North." She praised two distinguished sons of the Old Dominion as allies in this mission, the late Dr. Hunter Holmes McGuire and Judge George L. Christian, whose historical pamphlets had been distributed throughout the country and whose arguments, she asserted, could not be assailed by northerners.[1] Garnett, McGuire, and Christian were only three of the many Virginians who enlisted in a grand crusade to secure in the hearts and minds of the region's young those victories denied in the defeat of 1865 and at the same time to immunize southern children against democratic reforms then threatening the South's ruling class.

In Virginia, the United Daughters of the Confederacy, the United Confederate Veterans, and the Sons of Confederate Veterans cooperated in an earnest campaign to "have used in all Southern schools only such histories as are just and true."[2] They combined with like-minded organizations across the South to condemn the perceived sectionalism of northern historians, to establish lists of approved and disapproved books, and to produce literature congenial to their perception of history. Once established as the arbiters of southern thought, they expunged offending works from schools and libraries, silenced dissident teachers, and indoctrinated southern children with antebellum aristocratic social values.[3] They would not be satisfied, proclaimed Maude Blake Merchant of Chatham, Virginia, before the UDC's general convention, "until all the world admits that the Confederate soldiers were loyal, brave, patriotic, gallant men, justified in their construction of constitutional right . . . [and] every text-book so teaches our children."[4]

The Virginia campaign for historical revisionism was a microcosm of events that swept the South during the waning years of the nineteenth century and the opening decades of the twentieth. The intensity of this campaign and the fact that the Confederate societies' concept of "national history" conformed to a defense of elite southern institutional and social values suggest far more than a simple corrective of historical perspective.[5] In Virginia, and throughout the South, the region's "best families" felt their social class threatened by the aspirations of lesser whites and long-oppressed African Americans. Southern elites once again manned the parapets to defend their status, not on the bloody ground of Gettysburg or Shiloh but in the interpretation of the past. They sought to inculcate into schoolchildren their historical ideology, a tinted account that was supposed to ensure that all southerners would respect their properly ordained leaders.

The Confederate patriotic societies were engaged in an intellectual quest to reaffirm the southern aristocracy's authority as the dominant force in the region's political, social, and economic life. Class stratification had shaped the antebellum South. A small elite of slave-rich planters and related professionals—attorneys, physicians, and merchants—controlled the region's institutions. They molded a culture based on the premise of man's innate inequality and assumed that social order was best served when every individual resided in his proper place. Ensconced at the top of virtually every southern community, the best families were rarely challenged by less-favored whites and almost never threatened by African slaves.[6]

Aristocrats led the South out of the Union in 1861, confident that subsistence farmers and impoverished laborers would follow them in their bloody conflict. Initially they were correct, but in time the realities of suffering prompted many white families of modest means to question their role in a war fought so that others might own slaves. This skepticism dealt southern elites a severe ideological blow. If proper social order mandated the subordination of most men—white as well as black—then the common soldier's flight from faith raised a major challenge to traditional class relationships.[7]

Confederate defeat made it difficult to reassert upper-class hegemony after the war. In the century's last decades, discontented black and white agrarians repeatedly denounced the elites' governance just as northern historians harshly judged the antebellum planter class. The menaced southern patricians responded vigorously by preaching the linked doctrines of class stratification and white supremacy. Although they had reestablished their personal fortunes and their political influence at the demise of Reconstruction, the elites could no longer count on the acquiescence of small farmers and artisans. The Grange movement, the Farmer's Alliances, and the Populist party crusade were evidence of powerful discontent with the southern oligarchy.[8]

At the same time, northern patriotic organizations and historians developed interpretations of the antebellum epoch that confirmed the fears of southern patricians. Representing Union veterans, the Grand Army of the Republic viewed their Civil War experience as the climactic struggle to establish an American democratic millennium. They saw themselves as heroic crusaders, citizen-soldiers engaged in a struggle against the corrupt forces of class distinction as epitomized by the South's slaveowners. Although their campaign was designed to destroy the slavocracy, these veterans showed little empathy for African Americans. To the northern white veterans, freedom for the slaves was an incidental result of the quest to defeat the villainous southern aristocrats.[9]

Northern historians, who shared this millennial cosmology and who were caught up in their own worship of Anglo-Saxon democracy and national progress, also questioned the "self-evident worth" of patrician rule. Southern aristocrats were offended by what they interpreted as northern attacks on the South but which in reality were harsh critiques of a particular group of southerners—the aristocrats themselves. In thick tomes, James Ford Rhodes, James Schouler, and John Bach McMaster prosecuted the planter class, condemned its antique social and economic philosophies, exposed its inhumanity toward slaves and other whites, and placed upon it the onus of war guilt. "The pride of the slaveholder" would not accept legislative limits on the expansion of the peculiar institution, pontificated Schouler. He wilted before "the rays of a disapproving civilization that beat down too hot for him." Planters were accused of misusing their antebellum suzerainty, of hoarding southern wealth, and of impoverishing other whites. "The ruling class of Virginia," criticized McMaster, "was not at all disposed to be taxed for the education of the children of poor whites." This system bred discontent, argued Rhodes, because "poor whites of the South looked on the prosperity of the slave-holding lord with rank envy and sullenness; his trappings contrasted painfully with their want of comforts."[10]

At the century's end, these poor whites—and blacks—rebelled against the dominant upper classes. Significantly, the crusade for an elite southern interpretation of American history commenced at the height of the Populist movement. From Virginia to Texas, this biracial alliance of small farmers mounted a serious threat to the South's establishment. Patricians met the challenge and defeated the Populists in the election of 1896 by blatantly appealing to white fears of black domination. Again secure in their control of state legislatures, white elites enacted laws to abort the incipient black-white coalition. Throughout the South poll taxes, literacy tests, and all-white Democratic primaries virtually eliminated black suffrage and significantly reduced the rolls of white voters as well.[11] The South's elite recognized, however, that to avoid future conflicts, restrictions on civil rights must be intellectually and emotionally acceptable—at least to southern whites. Thus, the region's children had to be taught to "think correctly," to appreciate the virtues of elite rule, to fear the enfranchisement of blacks, and to revere the Confederate cause. History properly presented would perpetuate Old South values in the ensuing generations.

Virginia elites fully appreciated the magnitude of the class struggle in the post–Civil War South. The state's Reconstruction-imposed constitution of 1869 granted suffrage not only to African American men but also to large numbers of previously disenfranchised whites. From the late 1870s to the end of the 1890s, these nonelites united under the rubric "Readjusters" to threaten the power of the long-established elite families. Throughout their decades-long struggle, both the plebeian reformers and their patrician enemies wrangled in electoral campaigns characterized by fraud and demagoguery. At the century's end, however, Virginia's families of the first rank had reestablished their ascendancy and in 1902 had secured a new constitution promulgated without being submitted to a popular vote. Designed to limit officeholding to only the "right kinds of people," it excluded most black voters and at the same time disqualified large numbers of their allies among the impoverished whites. Just beginning a long and distinguished career in government, state senator Carter Glass boasted that this action ended "the darkey as a political factor" and made it impossible for the "unworthy men of our own race . . . to cheat their way into prominence."[12]

Even as Glass cavalierly dismissed democracy, others among his social peers felt compelled to justify "rule by the few" to themselves, to their fellow Virginians, and to those nonsoutherners who might be tempted to criticize. In *Preserving the Old Dominion: Historic Preservation and Virginia Traditionalism*, historian James M. Lindgren has carefully chronicled the ideological foundations of those wealthy patricians who created the Association for the Preservation of Virginia Antiquities. Their preoccupation with their heritage—represented in the visual splendor of restored Jamestown, Yorktown, Williamsburg, and other sites—constituted more than an antiquarian's interest in the past. In the 1890s their conservative social agenda appealed to those politicians and philanthropists who shared their fear that unworthy social groups threatened the commonwealth's stability. "Throughout history, preservation movements have been closely tied to the cultural politics of their day," Lindgren argued. The Old Dominion's "preservationists disputed the claims of African-Americans and popular-class radicals who demanded that Virginia alter its ancient ways." By restoring the architectural heritage of colonial aristocrats, the state's best families reminded people of the "Old South's civility and decorum." Even as these tradition-minded Virginians saved the past of mortar and stone, others of their class built new structures with the printed word and developed intellectual models of the antebellum South, the Civil War, and the ensuing decades that would presumably influence future generations to "right thinking actions."[13] Dominated by Virginia's patrician leadership, the state's Confederate associations crusaded for history rightly taught.

The Confederate patriotic societies commenced their campaign for "impartial, national history" in the mid-1890s with Virginians marching in the advance guard. Prominent in the initial efforts were three citizens of central Virginia: real estate developer John Cussons, physician Hunter Holmes McGuire, and attorney George L. Christian. McGuire and Christian had impressive links to Virginia's first families, and Cussons, an English immigrant and colonel in the Army of Northern Virginia, invested his considerable wealth in the creation of the resort community of Glen Allen, a village just north of Richmond.[14]

Cussons, McGuire, and Christian wrote scathing critiques of northern histories, dominated the history committee of Virginia's Grand Camp of Confederate Veterans, and pressed for a reorganization of the state's school board. In 1898 they achieved the third goal. They presented to the board a list of condemned books and had the satisfaction of seeing most of these works banished from the classroom.[15] This was only the first victory in a long-term crusade for a suitable interpretation of the South's past. Virginia's Confederate societies engaged in a battle without quarter; the reward for success was the inculcation of elite class values into the state's youth. "I fear," Christian said in 1898, "that some of our children, misled by the false teachings of certain histories . . . may have some misgivings" concerning the South's righteousness in 1861.[16]

The apprehension that future generations might lose their fidelity to southern mores galvanized the Confederate societies. The crusade of Cussons, McGuire, and Christian against northern historical interpretations began in earnest in 1897 with the publication of Cussons's pamphlet *A Glance at Current American History*, which was reprinted three years later under the more strident title *United States "History": As the Yankee Makes and Takes It*. For more than thirty years, Cussons charged, northerners "have been diligent in a systematic distortion of the leading facts of American history—inventing, suppressing, perverting, without scruple or shame—until our Southland stands to-day pilloried to the scorn of all the world." He laid full blame on the Grand Army of the Republic, the representatives of a Yankee race rooted in Puritan traditions. Enamored with Virginia's cavalier heritage, this English immigrant scorned Puritans and their descendants. "Self-styled as the apostle of liberty," Cussons argued, the Puritan "has ever claimed for himself the liberty of persecuting all who presumed to differ from him. Self-appointed as the champion of unity and harmony, he has carried discord into every land that his foot has smitten. Exalting himself as the defender of freedom of thought, his favorite practice has been to muzzle the press and to adjourn legislatures with the sword." Faithful to their ancestors, the history committee of the Grand Army of the Republic—along with allied historians—strove to manipulate the past, to "render the [Confederate soldier] more odious than history has thus far depicted him, and at the same time to put the yankee in such a position that the world will be compelled to admire him!"[17] Ironically, Cussons set in motion southern forces of oppression that over the next quarter century committed every sin he charged to New England's Calvinistic lineage.

Largely pleased with the restructuring of Virginia's state board of education in 1898 and with its subsequent adoption of histories congenial to southern elite interpretations, Cussons and his compatriots nonetheless rebuked the board for retaining on its approved list John Fiske's *History of the United States for Schools*. Almost immediately J. William Jones, a respected Richmond minister and Confederate apologist, issued a strongly worded protest. He proclaimed that the book "Should not be Used by any Honest Teacher, North or South, . . . Should not be Allowed in any Southern School or Home," but should be castigated for its slanderous utterances attributable "to Nothing Save a Mind Imbued with Hatred" for the South and its people. Fiske, asserted the minister, praised New England's revolutionary heroes while ignoring the patriotism of Patrick Henry and the legislative leadership of the Virginia House of Burgesses, blamed the South for slavery without noting its existence in all the colonies or its promotion by New England shipping barons, glorified "abolitionist agitators" while sneering at "the recklessness of the Southern leaders," and blessed the Emancipation Proclamation without revealing that it robbed "the Southern people . . . of millions of dollars' worth of property . . . guaranteed by the Constitution."[18]

Hunter McGuire's report to Virginia's Grand Camp of Confederate Veterans in 1899 was only slightly less vituperative than Jones's polemic. Largely an embellishment of the earlier pamphlet, McGuire's critique especially condemned those passages in which Fiske cast aspersions on southern aristocrats. Stonewall Jackson's physician called attention to such phrases as "'Demands of slave-holders,' [and] 'Concessions to slave-holders'" and maintained they presented a distorted "picture of an aggressive South and a conciliatory North." Such shameful rhetoric, according to McGuire, not only demonstrated Fiske's "inability to write a true history of the sectional strife" but also made "his book unfit to be placed in the hands of Southern children."[19]

McGuire bestowed his imprimatur on several "impartial," "truthful" histories—all by writers from former slave states—but southern authorship was no guarantee of his or the Confederate societies' approval. Appended to his lengthy review of Fiske were two tightly written paragraphs harshly imprecating the *History of Our Country* by Texas educators Oscar H.

Cooper, Harry F. Estill, and Leonard Lemmon. McGuire indicted these authors for making too much of an effort to be neutral on key issues leading to the Civil War, for failing to assert the North's evident guilt in forcing the South out of the Union, and for devoting inadequate attention to the exploits of Confederate heroes—especially Virginia worthies. "The book is all the more pernicious because its authors pose as Southern men," he lectured. "Such may be the truth, but they certainly do not teach the truth."[20]

Bowing to persistent pressure from Virginia's Grand Camp, Governor Andrew Jackson Montague in May 1902 ordered the removal of Fiske's *History of the United States* from the state board of education's sanctioned textbooks. He committed a political *faux pas*, however, by replacing it with Cooper, Estill, and Lemmon's *Our Country*. When George Christian reported this travesty to the Grand Camp, the enraged assembly immediately censured both the governor and the board. The state superintendent of public instruction, who was present at the meeting, took the podium, apologized to the convention, and pledged *Our Country's* swift removal.[21]

However powerful the Confederate veterans' political voice, as the century's first decade waned, fewer old soldiers rallied to the cause. McGuire died in 1900, Cussons became immersed in legal battles, and each year hundreds more marched to their final muster. Only Christian remained, zealous as an arbiter of historical truth. Until his death in 1924, he continued as an influential member of the Grand Camp's historical committee and served prominently as a trustee of the Virginia Historical Society.[22]

Conscious of his own mortality, Christian took comfort that the scions of Virginia's first families also cherished his cause. In 1899, when the young attorney and state legislator Beverley B. Munford presented an address fervently defending the constitutionality of secession, Christian praised his effort. The judge reflected that "an old Confederate, shot to pieces in defense of our cause, as I was, is an extremist in his views. . . . [I]t does my heart good, to see those of a younger generation, defend that cause, with . . . zeal and ability." Active in the Sons of Confederate Veterans, Munford typified that organization's commitment to a suitable past.[23] Although he and his fellow neo-Confederate patriots felt a keen need to present history from a southern, elitist perspective, necessity forced them to concentrate their attentions on economic and political pursuits, creating the institutions of debt peonage and segregation that recast the Old South's stratified society. Instead, steeped in the Victorian belief that women were the natural preservers of tradition, this generation urged their wives and sisters to perpetuate those antebellum values that justified enlightened rule by the state's elite families.

The United Daughters of the Confederacy gladly embraced the responsibility of properly instructing Virginia's youth. These resolute women organized Children of the Confederacy chapters, stocked libraries with books favorable to their image of the South, secured scholarships to train would-be teachers in history's proper presentation, and, most important of all, scrutinized school books to remove every tarnish of Yankee bias. "The young of our Southland demand your loving interest," averred Minnie Campbell Eller, president of the Virginia UDC, in 1911. "It is your duty as Daughters to teach them to know the truth, and learn of the bravery of those who wore the gray."[24]

The Old Dominion's first chapter of the Children of the Confederacy was organized at Richmond in 1912, and within five years impressionable youths assembled regularly in Fredericksburg, Charlottesville, Culpeper, Bristol, and two dozen other Virginia communities. The goal of the Children of the Confederacy was to immerse boys and girls between the ages of eight and eighteen in the rituals of the Lost Cause. Most chapters counted between twenty and forty-five members, but a few boasted more impressive numbers. Roanoke had ninety-five enrollees, one Richmond chapter reported 198, and Staunton, largest of all, bragged of their 640 children, two of whom were admitted on the day they were born. These youths sang the haunting anthems of the Confederacy, entertained hoary survivors of the Civil War, and decorated the graves of the honored dead. Apart from other activities, "properly taught" history lessons highlighted each meeting.[25]

The Virginia UDC required all members of the Children of the Confederacy to "make a thorough study" of the *U.D.C. Catechism for Children* by Cornelia Branch Stone, a Texas Daughter and former president of the general convention. An adult leader intoned the forty-eight questions as children responded to each in unison, giving answers that glorified the South's past and justified the Confederate cause. "What was the feeling of the slaves toward their masters?" asked the mentor; the children dutifully responded: "They were faithful and devoted and were always ready and willing to serve them." "How did [the slaves] behave during the war?" "They nobly protected and cared for the wives of soldiers in the field, and widows without protectors; though often prompted by the enemies of the South to burn and plunder the homes of their masters, they were always true and loyal." In October 1917, Roanoke's William Watts Chapter of the Children of the Confederacy considered itself honored when Stone visited their meeting, "gave a delightful talk," and donated books to their small library.[26] The Children of the Confederacy directly reached a relatively small number of adolescents, but these would serve as future leaders in the Confederate patriotic societies.

Determined to influence Virginia's young beyond the organization's membership, the UDC expanded its efforts into overseeing literature for school and public libraries. Essay contests were designed to encourage student research and writing, with rewards granted to those who best articulated the virtues of the Confederate cause. As late as 1913, however, the state's appalling lack of public libraries and the paucity of elementary and high school reference materials frustrated these activities. To assist the schools, local chapters donated encyclopedias and other books from bibliographies carefully prepared by the UDC's state headquarters, and in those few communities with public libraries zealous Daughters scrutinized the collections to remove unacceptable works. When Norfolk's Pickett-Buchanan Chapter found several objectionable volumes in the city's Carnegie Library, they demanded their immediate removal. The trustees demurred, however, feeling the books too valuable to destroy. Instead, they pledged to mark through the offending passages in red ink, to note in the margins their own displeasure with the authors' views, and to suggest "the names of several histories where the truth is told."[27]

Across the South, the UDC appreciated the powerful influence teachers had on malleable youths. Thus, the Virginia Daughters, along with their sisters in other states, pressured colleges and normal schools to offer teacher training scholarships to be administered by the UDC. The Virginia women secured their first scholarship in 1909 and by 1920 boasted their possession of "forty-four . . . with eight others controlled by [local] Chapters."[28] Recipients of these awards graduated with a thorough indoctrination in elite southern values and became devoted apostles of history as prescribed by their sponsors.

Triumphant in the creation of the Children of the Confederacy, in the oversight of libraries, and in the training of teachers, the Virginia UDC achieved even greater successes in censoring public school textbooks and in replacing them with others more flattering to their version of historical truth. From the organization's inception, its bylaws empowered its state historian to "examine such histories of this country as are in use in the schools and report the results . . . to the chapters . . . and to this Division for such action as they may deem proper." Thus, in 1916, state historian Essie Wade Butler Smith reminded her sisters that the "most vital problems confronting" the UDC were "the selection of proper text books. . . . The far-reaching influence of the histories in the hands of the children and the ideas instilled by the [school] readers in the grades cannot be over-estimated." All local chapters, she commanded, "are expected to take an active interest . . . and to report from time to time the result of text book investigation."[29]

The Virginia Daughters strongly objected to interpretations that cast doubt on the aristocracy's virtue. "In all the histories written by Northern men," railed UDC historian Kate Noland Garnett in 1902, "the South is put wholly in the wrong, and no Southern child could read histories without inferring that the Confederate leaders and soldiers were 'traitors' of the deepest dye." She vehemently opposed accounts that indicted the Confederate soldier as a "defender of slavery" and questioned his fidelity to the Constitution. "Let the truth be so instilled into the minds of our children," she admonished, "that no question shall ever be raised in the future as to the purity of the motives of the South, or the justice . . . of our cause."[30]

The response of southern school boards to the Confederate societies' demands created a lucrative market for textbooks with pro-Confederate interpretations, and publishers—northern and southern—rushed to meet this need. From Boston to Chicago, printing houses stocked conflicting versions of the past, each catering to a sectional ideology. The New York–based D. C. Heath and Company assured Virginia's governor in 1904 that their *History of the United States* by Waddy Thompson, son of a former governor of South Carolina, conformed to the state board of education's criteria. The chapters on the Civil War had been "read and approved by the late General John B. Gordon," and "the whole manuscript [had] been read by the Right Reverend Thomas F. Gaylor," Episcopal bishop of Tennessee, whose official connection with the Confederate Veterans Montague knew well.[31]

Although northern publishers hired authors with impeccable southern credentials and secured endorsements by former Confederate generals and politicians, they were at a competitive disadvantage with southern presses, which could rely on patronage generated by sectional loyalty. The B. F. Johnson Publishing Company, headquartered in Richmond, was the largest of these regional publishers and boasted of its extensive catalog of histories, literary anthologies, and school readers free from the taint of New England partisanship. "Sometimes sectional prejudice is shown by the Grammars and Arithmetics," warned the company's president in 1899. He assured the Confederate societies that although "many of the Readers as well as Histories in use in our schools . . . ought to be banished," B. F. Johnson issued only "text-books in which . . . the authors and teachers in the South [are] given that position to which their good work has justly entitled them."[32]

In 1904, the school board of Franklin County learned firsthand that arithmetic books could convey unacceptable sectional values. Examining a copy of the Southworth-Stone arithmetic textbook, published in New York, one curious teacher noted that on one page a problem had a paper strip pasted over it. Printed on the strip was a question challenging students to determine the number of histories found in a library of 567 volumes with one in ten being a history. Peeling away the pasted strip, the teacher learned to her horror that the original question read: "In a school room containing 567 white children, every tenth child is colored. How many children in the school?" Learning of this incident, the *Richmond News Leader* raged at this Yankee attempt to indoctrinate Virginia children with "the idea of mixed schools and social equality." Only southern presses fully appreciated regional sensitivities, it editorialized, and preeminent among these publishers the B. F. Johnson Publishing Company "stands today guarding the Southern schools against the Northern school book monopolies."[33]

From Maryland to Texas, authors sympathetic to the Confederate cause produced textbooks suitable for southern consumption. By 1904, Maude Blake Merchant announced with pride that "owing to the efforts and influence of the United Daughters," every state of the late Confederacy had adopted sound histories.[34] Virginians contributed to this expanding body of literature. Among them three individuals—Mary Tucker Magill, Susan Pendleton Lee, and Beverley B. Munford—profoundly influenced thousands of the Old Dominion's youths by creating an enduring and canted historical paradigm, a grand epic that taught their readers to respect elite rule, fear the Negro race, and distrust Yankees.[35]

Virginia's elementary schoolchildren learned "historical truth" from *Magill's First Book in Virginia History*. Having grown up in the Shenandoah Valley, Magill reminisced at length on her youthful adoration of the valiant Confederate soldier. Infusing into her young readers patrician values, she revealed to them that there is a word to describe the finest qualities of southern manhood; "it is chi-val-ry." This characteristic had motivated the ancient knights, who made vows to "protect the weak, particularly women," to be "noble and brave," to "die [rather] than turn their backs on an enemy," and to "fear God and honor their country and be generous to their enemies." Such, she reflected, were a "good many soldiers in the Confederate army who had all the spirit of these knights of old." As noble warriors, these men valiantly fought for honor and constitutional rights. Slavery had little to do with their holy quest. From the earliest colonial times, she explained, Virginians had "never liked it, and remonstrated" with the king for its removal, but for monetary reasons he forced it on the colony. "This was not bad for the slaves," however. "In their own country they were can-ni-bals, or man-eaters, and very degraded in every way. They were much better off in this country, where they were taught . . . about God and about other things . . . good for them."[36]

If Magill grounded Virginia's young people in the fundamental values of the elite South, Susan Pendleton Lee influenced children well beyond her native state. As early as 1895, the United Confederate Veterans' historical committee praised "the history of the United States, by Mrs. Susan P. Lee, of Lexington, Va., . . . as filling the requirements of histories that should be used in our schools," and within the decade it had been adopted in school systems across the South. Her status as the daughter of one Confederate general and the widow of another, and as the author of a popular pro-Confederate history, made her an honored member of Virginia's United Daughters of the Confederacy.[37]

Lee's *School History of the United States* was a stirring litany of southern virtue and Yankee duplicity. Acknowledging that American slavery began at

Jamestown in 1619, she argued that it was forced on the South by money-hungry merchants from England and New England. "Massachusetts Puritans . . . had . . . no conscientious scruples about selling and buying either Indians or negroes," she wrote; unfree labor existed in all the colonies. To be sure, the peculiar institution thrived in the warmer environs of the South, a region similar in climate to the Africans' homeland, while it gradually dissipated in the frigid North. Envious of the South's slave-generated prosperity, the North's people eagerly listened to frenzied abolitionists who produced documents "filled with false representations of the wretched condition of the slaves and accounts of the cruelty of their masters." Chief among the antislavery leaders, William Lloyd Garrison ignored the Bible's approval of human bondage and the Constitution's sanction of it. Lee quoted the abolitionist's dictum that the Constitution was an "agreement with death and a covenant with hell." On the other hand, southern men, she assured her readers, revered the Bible and the nation's fundamental documents and knew in their hearts "that the negroes in bondage were the best clothed, best fed, best cared for, and happiest class of laborers in the world."[38]

In Lee's mind, the North was guilty of causing the Civil War. She chided northern statesmen for blindly following the abolitionists' lead, setting "aside the rights of the South regardless of law and justice." The ensuing conflict was not about slavery, she emphasized, but rather a southern defense of its constitutional right to maintain its own cultural values without interference from an intruding national government. Lee assured her young contemporaries that from "the Potomac to the Rio Grande" the southern people—"the lowly and the well-born, old men and beardless boys"—marched forth in a burst of "generous patriotism." They were stalwart in fighting a Yankee foe devoid of honor. She castigated Lincoln's Emancipation Proclamation as an attempt to foster slave rebellion, condemned William T. Sherman for crimes against humanity, and cursed the Union's prisoner-of-war camps, where brave southern men encountered "hardship, privation, and cruelty [that] either tortured or destroyed them."[39]

However virtuous the Confederate cause, in the end Susan Pendleton Lee's South succumbed to the North's overwhelming numbers and then endured the nightmare of postwar retribution. Faced with the destruction of their farms and robbed of two billion dollars in property by the Emancipation Proclamation, southern men confronted the future with the same resolute determination that had marked their crusade against the North. But, lectured Lee, their "whole system of labor was destroyed. The negroes, who, in the main, had been loyal . . . while the war lasted, were . . . rendered worthless by their sudden and violent emancipation." A vengeful North further exacerbated these conditions by depriving "the intelligent, cultivated white population" of the vote while imposing on them a political system dominated by carpetbaggers ("fugitives from Northern justice"), scalawags (disloyal southerners), and ignorant Negroes. It was, Lee wrote with passion, "political hell." Justly responding to their oppressors, the South's "best men" organized the Pale Faces, the Knights of the White Camellia, and the Ku Klux Klan to protect "white women and defenceless families," to "keep the negroes from voting," and to retaliate against "the misrule and dishonesty everywhere prevalent." These efforts triumphed, and by 1876 a redeemed South had largely restored its old political systems. Once "[r]id of the burden of caring for and supporting the negroes [who were] incapable of work during childhood, sickness and old age," the southern people, Lee reflected, had demonstrated a "capacity . . . for restoring their shattered fortunes and re-establishing their State governments, [that] must command the respect even of those most hostile to them."[40]

Having been thoroughly indoctrinated by Magill in their elementary grades and by Lee in their early high school years, students in the Old Dominion polished their historical studies by reading Beverley B. Munford's *Virginia's Attitude toward Slavery and Secession*. Born too late to participate in the Civil War, Munford gained prominence in the Sons of the Confederate Veterans and as a member of the state senate led the crusade against northern textbooks in 1898. "Our children shall be taught the history of this country from the pen of authors thoroughly informed" and in "sympathy for the cause to which the people of the South plighted their faith," he pledged. Consumed with a passion to teach Virginia's youth "correct history," Munford produced his own account, an extended defense of the peculiar institution in antebellum Virginia.[41]

Published in 1909, Munford's work was meant as "a contribution to the volume of information" from which future historians could "prepare an impartial . . . narrative of the American Civil War, or to speak more accurately—the American War of Secession." Written with the precision of an attorney's brief, the book's three hundred pages argued that Virginia piloted the crusade to suppress the international slave trade, that prominent Virginia leaders—George Washington, Thomas Jefferson, James Madison, James Monroe, John Marshall, and many more—spoke in opposition to slavery, and that Virginians marched in the van of those colonizing Africa with manumitted slaves. In the end, however, the inability to compensate slaveowners, the concern for the Africans' moral welfare in a free society, and the fear of anarchy engendered by Santo Domingo's "carnival of blood" and the horrors of the Nat Turner Insurrection frustrated emancipation. If "slavery was at war with the ideals upon which Virginians had founded their commonwealth," Munford reasoned, then the tyranny of an oppressive national government was even more repugnant. Thus, in 1861 Virginia departed the Union, not out of any defense of the peculiar institution, but out of solidarity with the South's crusade for state sovereignty. Firmly opposed to federal coercion, he argued that "the people of Virginia took a stand, pre-determined by the beliefs and avowals of successive generations, and im-pelled by . . . their supreme incentive . . . to maintain the integrity of principle."[42]

The work was popular with Virginia's establishment. The state senate thanked Munford for "fairly representing Virginia in the light of history," and the state board of education promptly mandated the book as required high school reading. Tested on it, one enlightened youth proudly essayed, "I have been firmly convinced of the right of the Southern States . . . and feel that I can now break down the arguments of any Yankee on the subject of the American War of Secession."[43]

Munford's work perfectly articulated Virginia's patrician definition of the past, and for that reason it was strongly criticized by William Edward Dodd, a University of Chicago history professor who had recently left his chair at Randolph-Macon College in Ashland, Virginia. The son of a North Carolina yeoman, Dodd devoted his entire academic career to exposing the antidemocratic policies of the South's establishment.[44] Called upon to cri-tique *Virginia's Attitude toward Slavery and Secession* for the *American Histor-ical Review*, he was offended by the volume. "I could not find it in my heart to pronounce it valuable," he wrote a colleague, because the author "never once touched the core of the subject." To go to the "eve of the Civil War contending that nobody of influence and power in the Old Dominion fa-vored slavery," read Dodd's review, "shows a lack of knowledge . . . dis-paraging to the author's claims. Yet this is just what Mr. Munford attempts to do." Unfairly selective in its presentation of the topic, the work was clearly deficient; "many important facts and conditions [were] omitted en-tirely." Never once, for example, did Munford respond to the accusation that Virginia was a slave-breeding state, a charge supported by "Governor William B. Giles's published statement (in . . . 1829) that 6000 slaves were exported from Richmond and Norfolk each year" and by the "effective propaganda of Thomas R. Dew . . . in defense of . . . raising negroes for the Lower South." The book, Dodd summarized, "is too much of a defense to be final or convincing."[45]

The bitterness evident in Dodd's review went far beyond a mere distaste for intellectual sophistry. This former Virginia professor was one of several academicians who had learned or would soon learn that offending the Con-federate societies placed their careers in jeopardy. Appalled by the arbitrary removal of Fiske's *History of the United States* from the state board of edu-cation's reading list in 1902, Dodd—then at Randolph-Macon College—boldly criticized Virginia's Grand Camp of Confederate Veterans in the *Nation*, a magazine not noted for its sensitivity to the South's upper class. Appealing to a national audience, he detailed the difficulties of teaching his-tory in the South and concentrating on the specific requirements of pleasing the region's elites. "The ruling classes of society are usually responsible for the kind of teaching the young receive," he maintained, "and this particularly applies to collegiate training." Complaining that southern "public sentiment [was] controlled by men who were either participants in the great Civil War" or by their sons, he condemned their demand that all history teachers subscribe to the linked ideas that the South was morally correct in seceding from the Union and that the Civil War had nothing to do with slavery. "No investigation, no honest unbiased work can be hoped for," he lamented, "when such a confession of faith is made a [consideration] of fitness for teaching or writing history."[46]

Dodd immediately became the focus of a heated controversy. Inferring ideas not fully expressed in the article, one Virginia professor declared that any "Southern man who would say that . . . he would not have followed Lee and Jackson, ought to be kicked out of a Southern School"; George Christian demanded Dodd's expulsion from the classroom; and, as Dodd later remembered, "a leading Richmond paper asked that I be dismissed from Randolph Macon because I was a disloyal Southerner." Although his college's trustees supported him in the name of academic freedom, Dodd had been severely chastised. He reported to the American Historical Association's 1903 convention that a "man who [takes] a perfectly dispassionate attitude" toward the South's past is "apt to be met not only with disapproval, but with things even more disagreeable."[47]

Both his own difficulties and those of his North Carolina friend and colleague John Spencer Bassett stimulated Dodd's observations. A Trinity College professor and editor of the *South Atlantic Quarterly*, Bassett published in 1903 a provocative statement lauding Booker T. Washington as "the greatest man, save General Lee, born in the South in a hundred years." The state's conservatives vilified Bassett in the press, sent him menacing letters, and pledged to boycott his school. Bassett then tendered his resignation from Trinity College. Dodd entered directly into the conflict by encouraging Randolph-Macon students to pass a resolution supporting Bassett and by writing a strongly worded personal letter, which was shared with Trinity's board. The trustees turned down the resignation, but the damage was done, and in 1906 Bassett left North Carolina for the more open climate of New England's Smith College. Learning two years later that a much-harassed Dodd was considering a move to the University of Chicago, Bassett urged him on. "Don't linger in Va. on account of any sentimental attachment to the South," he warned. "I have never regretted my own change."[48]

Before leaving the South, however, Dodd fired a parting volley at one of Virginia's intellectual nabobs. Reviewing Thomas Nelson Page's *The Old Dominion: Her Making and Her Manners* for the *American Historical Review*, he censured the author's class assumptions. Dodd found in the book "nothing new or fresh" but rather a panegyric celebrating a "traditional Virginia" populated by "colonial lords and ladies, or close imitators." He appreciated Page's analysis of the American Revolution "with all its bitterness, class hatred and shrewd political manoeuvers" but pointed out that the author's heroes were "gentlemen [and his] villains . . . outside the charmed circle." In his original manuscript, Dodd had personalized his attack: "[T]hrough all Mr. Page has ever written [runs] . . . the judgment and the language . . . too frequently akin to those of a confirmed snob." Chided gently by the *Review*'s editor, Dodd softened the last phrase to read: "too frequently those of one who supposes character to be absolutely determined by status."[49] Dodd possessed a keen intellect and pugnacious personality, traits that would serve him well in the University of Chicago's Byzantine politics and later as American ambassador to Adolf Hitler's Germany.[50] Lesser men and women more readily cowered before the Confederate societies.

In the spring of 1911, tiny Roanoke College in Salem, Virginia, became the target not only of the Old Dominion's Confederate partisans but also of like-minded zealots across the South. When a prominent Salem judge and Civil War veteran discovered that Professor Herman J. Thorstenberg required students to read Henry William Elson's *History of the United States of America*, he clamored for the book's immediate removal and demanded that the teacher's lectures be monitored.[51] The Confederate societies considered Elson's textbook a thoroughly objectionable work because it illuminated the sexual indiscretions of masters with their female slaves, termed the nation-rending conflict a "Slaveholders' War," and praised Lincoln as "the Providential instrument . . . guiding the nation through the wilderness of threatened disunion."[52]

The college's trustees met in emergency session, requested that Thorstenberg "voluntarily" withdraw Elson's work, and prayed this resolution would appease the Confederate societies. It did not. Across the state, veterans' camps and UDC chapters railed against the trustees' disloyalty to the South. The Petersburg *Index-Appeal* warned that although the textbook had been banished, the professor who chose it still "assigns the topics of study." The Lynchburg *News* cautioned that Virginia's progeny was endangered "because of the views of a single professor." The Bristol *Herald-Courier* admonished the trustees to suggest to the instructor that "his resignation would be accepted." Observing that Thorstenberg, like abolitionist John Brown, came from Kansas, the *Danville Register* pontificated that if only southern men and women were selected "as teachers . . . there [would] be no likelihood of such false instruction."[53]

Within weeks the controversy had spread beyond Virginia's borders. Confederate societies from Baltimore, Maryland, to Marshall, Texas, registered their displeasure, and again newspapers joined the chorus. The New Orleans *Picayune* professed to favor free speech but declared that southern children should not attend classes where they will "see and hear their fathers and grandfathers vilified and slandered in textbooks and lectures." The Charlotte, North Carolina, *Observer* propounded that "no institution in this country . . . should touch Elson's 'History . . .' with tongs." The *Florida Times-Union* of Jacksonville wailed, "Not only do we object to books which instill . . . heresies, we insist that teachers who hold such views are unfit to instruct Southern children. . . . Put out the bad books and refuse to employ the teachers."[54]

Thorstenberg protested that Elson's history was commonly used throughout the country and in fact had been adopted by at least twenty other southern colleges. This intelligence sparked a wave of hysteria as Confederate societies everywhere demanded that their schools and libraries remove "such damnably false literature as this Elson's history." The universities of North Carolina, Georgia, and Texas purged the offending textbook from their curriculums.[55] In 1912 Thorstenberg tendered his resignation from Roanoke College and left the South for good.[56]

Doubtless most Virginia instructors readily sympathized with elitist interpretations of the past, and certainly all recognized the realities associated with teaching history in the South. Even so, controversy could unexpectedly envelop the soundest schools. The Chatham Episcopal Institute near Danville courted the patronage of daughters from the Old Dominion's best families and carefully molded them into dignified young ladies. In April 1920, however, President C. O. Pruden learned that his faculty, most of them northern-educated women, had invited a lecturer to speak on the topic of Harriet Beecher Stowe as a Christian hero. Knowing that upperclass southerners considered the author of *Uncle Tom's Cabin* a villain of the highest order, he was incensed that his own teachers would put at risk the reputation of a school long "allied by its traditions to the Southern ideal." Eleven of the sixteen instructors resigned and were promptly replaced by teachers well-grounded in the southern historical model.[57]

Virginia's elites controlled the avenues of educational development and by doing so established an intellectual environment suited to their social and political agendas. Historian Thomas Perkins Abernethy, the scion of Alabama patricians, lectured at the University of Virginia from 1930 to his retirement in 1961. He assured his students that although "the plantation is gone and the planter is no more, his place at the head of Virginia society has been taken by the professional man and the man of independent means. . . . The old standards of conduct still prevail. The Squirearchy rides to the hounds, drinks mint juleps, and still sets the social and cultural tone of the State. It still rules Virginia."[58]

Virginia's Confederate patriotic societies and their supporters in the state's education establishment had successfully created a past suited to their particular needs. Well-crafted history lessons inoculated children against interpretations dangerous to the aristocratic class. Southern elites created the documents by which the region's development was traditionally assessed. They published articles portraying their view of southern society, delivered memorial addresses glorifying the Confederate crusade, wrote memoirs preserving their interpretations of the state of race relations, and published textbooks embracing their campaign. Thus, southern whites absorbed values desired by the region's first families: a veneration for the Confederate cause, an intense resistance to black civil rights, and a deferential spirit toward their "proper" leaders. Historical truth, as defined and dictated by the Confederate societies, ensured that southerners would retain cultural values ultimately detrimental to the progress of their own native land. It remained for a second civil war, the racial conflicts of the 1950s and 1960s, to disrupt Virginia and the South's patrician sovereignty.

NOTES

An earlier version of this essay was presented at the annual meeting of the Southern Historical Association in Orlando, Florida, on 13 November 1993.

1. *Minutes of the Twelfth Annual Convention of the Virginia Division United Daughters of the Confederacy, . . . 1907* (Pulaski, Va., [1907]), p. 37. The reports of Hunter McGuire and George Christian to the Grand Camp of Confederate Veterans were published in Hunter McGuire and George L. Christian, *The Confederate Cause and Conduct in the War Between the States* (Richmond, 1907).

2. "Constitution of the Virginia Division of the United Daughters of the Confederacy," in *Minutes of the Annual Convention of the United Daughters of the Confederacy, . . . 1903* (Lynchburg, Va., [1903]), p. 81.

3. Fred Arthur Bailey, "The Textbooks of the 'Lost Cause': Censorship and the Creation of Southern State Histories," *Georgia Historical Quarterly* 75 (1991): 507–33.

4. Mrs. W. C. N. Merchant, "Report of the Historical Committee, U.D.C.," *Confederate Veteran* 12 (Feb. 1904): 63–65 (quotation on p. 64).

5. Historians of twentieth-century southern thought have paid scant attention to this Confederate crusade to reinterpret the past. In 1971 Herman Hattaway argued that on the whole the United Confederate Veterans "served Clio well" by publishing "historical works, encouraging a more wide-spread interest both in writing and reading [history], and aiding the preservation of accurate historical data." Acknowledging that "the organization inculcated some views considered unobjective today," he nonetheless praised the veterans' efforts as a useful corrective to the skewed northern interpretations. More recently, Gaines M. Foster explored the importance of the Lost Cause mentality in the South from 1865 to 1913. To him, the Confederate celebration in books, monuments, and memorial days was less a "revival of rabid sectionalism" and more the championing of common regional values that provided the southern people stability throughout the trying transition from the Old to the New Souths. Both scholars were struck by the former Confederates' appeal to national reconciliation and their insistence that history must be written devoid of a northern or a

southern slant. The intensity of the Confederate campaign, however, suggests neither a simple corrective of historical perspective nor a cultural crutch during a period of social trauma. See Herman Hattaway, "Clio's Southern Soldiers: The United Confederate Veterans and History," *Louisiana History* 12 (1971): 213–42; Gaines M. Foster, *Ghosts of the Confederacy: Defeat, the Lost Cause, and the Emergence of the New South, 1865 to 1913* (New York and Oxford, 1987), p. 8. Angie Parrott's "'Love Makes Memory Eternal': The United Daughters of the Confederacy in Richmond, Virginia, 1897–1920," in Edward L. Ayers and John C. Willis, eds., *The Edge of the South: Life in Nineteenth-Century Virginia* (Charlottesville and London, 1991), pp. 219–38, touches on many of the themes of this essay.

6. The issue of class relationships in the antebellum South has long been debated by southern historians. Early in this century William Edward Dodd argued in *The Cotton Kingdom: A Chronicle of the Old South*, The Chronicles of America Series, 27 (New Haven, 1919) that planters dominated the region's social, political, and economic institutions. A generation later one of his graduate students took exception to this interpretation. In his seminal work *Plain Folk of the Old South* (Baton Rouge, 1949), Frank L. Owsley assumed that the southern yeomen were rarely class-conscious and that social harmony existed between them and the aristocrats. Several students of the South support his view: Blanche Henry Clark, *The Tennessee Yeomen, 1840–1860* (Nashville, 1942); Herbert Weaver, *Mississippi Farmers, 1850–1860* (Nashville, 1945); Clement Eaton, "Class Differences in the Old South," *Virginia Quarterly Review* 33 (1957): 357–58; Forrest McDonald and Grady McWhiney, "The Antebellum Southern Herdsman: A Reinterpretation," *Journal of Southern History* (hereafter cited as *JSH*) 41 (1975): 166; Bruce Collins, *White Society in the Antebellum South* (London and New York, 1985). Some recent scholars have pointed to latent class antagonisms associated with the antebellum and Civil War eras: Emory M. Thomas, *The Confederacy as a Revolutionary Experience* (Englewood Cliffs, N.J., 1971), pp. 102–5; Paul D. Escott, *After Secession: Jefferson Davis and the Failure of Confederate Nationalism* (Baton Rouge and London, 1978), pp. 94–134; Phillip S. Paludan, *Victims: A True Story of the Civil War* (Knoxville, 1981); Orville Vernon Burton, *In My Father's House Are Many Mansions: Family and Community in Edgefield, South Carolina* (Chapel Hill and London, 1985); Steven Hahn, *The Roots of Southern Populism: Yeoman Farmers and the Transformation of the Georgia Upcountry, 1850–1890* (New York, 1983); Fred Arthur Bailey, *Class and Tennessee's Confederate Generation* (Chapel Hill, 1987). To these should be added the older work of Roger W. Shugg, *Origins of Class Struggle in Louisiana: A Social History of White Farmers and Laborers during Slavery and After, 1840–1875* (Baton Rouge, 1939).

7. Frank L. Owsley, "Defeatism in the Confederacy," *North Carolina Historical Review* 3 (1926): 446–56; Georgia Lee Tatum, *Disloyalty in the Confederacy* (Chapel Hill, 1934); Escott, *After Secession*, pp. 94–134; Bailey, *Class and Tennessee's Confederate Generation*, pp. 99–104; James L. Roark, *Masters Without Slaves: Southern Planters in the Civil War and Reconstruction* (New York, 1977). Stephen V. Ash's "Poor Whites in the Occupied South, 1861–1865," *JSH* 57 (1991): 39–62, explores at length the disloyalty of impoverished southerners during the Civil War crisis.

8. See Jonathan M. Wiener, *Social Origins of the New South: Alabama, 1860–1885* (Baton Rouge, 1978); Hahn, *Roots of Southern Populism*; Paul D. Escott, *Many Excellent People: Power and Privilege in North Carolina, 1850–1900* (Chapel Hill, 1985); Bailey, *Class and Tennessee's Confederate Generation*; Stephen V. Ash, *Middle Tennessee Society*

Transformed, 1860–1870: War and Peace in the Upper South (Baton Rouge, 1988). A useful study of agrarian agitation in Virginia is William DuBose Sheldon, *Populism in the Old Dominion: Virginia Farm Politics, 1885–1900* (Princeton, 1935).

9. Stuart McConnell, *Glorious Contentment: The Grand Army of the Republic, 1865–1900* (Chapel Hill, 1992), pp. 181, 187, 189, 198, 215. As early as 1900, Union veterans, meeting in Chicago, deplored the southern histories that "were written with the purpose of perpetuating in the minds of the children the sectional prejudices of the days of 1861." To this accusation the United Confederate Veterans' camp in Danville, Virginia, responded: "In our histories we are earnestly striving for the truth, the whole truth, and nothing but the truth. . . . If we can only get the facts before the grand tribunal, the public opinion of the world, we fear not the result of its decision." See "Crisp Resolutions Adopted in Virginia," *Confederate Veteran* 8 (Sept. 1900): 396.

10. James Schouler, *History of the United States of America, Under the Constitution* (rev. ed., 7 vols.; New York, 1894–1913), 6:51; John Bach McMaster, *A History of the People of the United States, from the Revolution to the Civil War* (8 vols.; New York, 1883–1914), 5:366; James Ford Rhodes, *History of the United States from The Compromise of 1850 to the Final Restoration of Home Rule at the South in 1877* (8 vols.; New York, 1893–1919), 1:345.

11. C. Vann Woodward, *Origins of the New South, 1877–1913*, in Wendell Holmes Stephenson and E. Merton Coulter, eds., *A History of the South*, 9 (Baton Rouge, 1951), pp. 321–49; Jack M. Bloom, *Class, Race, and the Civil Rights Movement* (Bloomington and Indianapolis, 1987), pp. 39–43, 57–58; Alexander Saxton, *The Rise and Fall of the White Republic: Class Politics and Mass Culture in Nineteenth-Century America* (London, 1990), pp. 362–64.

12. Raymond H. Pulley, *Old Virginia Restored: An Interpretation of the Progressive Impulse, 1870–1930* (Charlottesville, 1968), pp. 1–16, 84–85 (quotation), 90; James Tice Moore, *Two Paths to the New South: The Virginia Debt Controversy, 1870–1883* (Lexington, Ky., 1974).

13. James M. Lindgren, *Preserving the Old Dominion: Historic Preservation and Virginia Traditionalism* (Charlottesville and London, 1993), pp. 1–3, 7, 56.

14. Stuart McGuire, "Sketch of the Life of Hunter Holmes McGuire, M.D., L.L.D." (typescript), pp. 67–72, Hunter Holmes McGuire Papers, Virginia Historical Society, Richmond (hereafter cited as ViHi); Wyndham R. Meredith, "Judge George L. Christian," *Proceedings of the Thirty-Fifth Annual Meeting, The Virginia State Bar Association, . . . 1924* (Richmond, 1924), pp. 88–92; James R. Short, "The Strange Lodge of *Wau-zee-hos-ka:* A Tale of Honor Upheld and a Dream That Died," *Virginia Cavalcade* 5 (Winter 1955): 30–33.

15. McGuire, "Sketch of Hunter Holmes McGuire," pp. 67–69.

16. George L. Christian, *The Confederate Cause and Its Defenders, An Address Delivered before the Grand Camp of Confederate Veterans of Virginia* (Richmond, 1898), p. 4.

17. [John Cussons], *A Glance at Current American History* (Glen Allen, Va., 1897), pp. 3, 4–5, 20, 23; [John Cussons], *United States "History": As the Yankee Makes and Takes It* (Glen Allen, Va., 1900), pp. 13, 45–46, 52–53.

18. John Fiske, *A History of the United States for Schools . . .* (Boston, 1894); [J. William Jones], *Fiske's False History: Its Errors and Intentional Untruths Exposed* (n.p., 1898), pp. 1, 2, 4, 6.

19. *Proceedings of the Twelfth Annual Meeting of the Grand Camp Confederate Veter-*

ans, Department of Virginia, . . . *1899* (Richmond, 1899), p. 32. The report of the historical committee of Virginia's Grand Camp also appears in Hunter McGuire, "School Histories in the South," *Confederate Veteran* 7 (Nov. 1899): 500–509, and in McGuire and Christian, *The Confederate Cause and Conduct in the War,* pp. 1–32.

20. Oscar H. Cooper, Harry F. Estill, and Leonard Lemmon, *History of Our Country: A Text-Book for Schools* (Boston and London, 1895); *Proceedings of the Grand Camp Confederate Veterans, 1899,* pp. 33–34.

21. Virginia State Board of Education, minutes, 28 May 1902, Library of Virginia, Richmond (hereafter cited as Vi); *Proceedings of the Fifteenth Annual Meeting of the Grand Camp Confederate Veterans, Department of Virginia,* . . . *1902* (Pulaski, Va., 1903), pp. 32–33; Richmond *Times,* 24 Oct. 1902, p. 1.

22. McGuire, "Sketch of Hunter Holmes McGuire," p. 69; Short, "The Strange Lodge of *Wau-zee-hos-ka,*" pp. 30–33; Meredith, "George L. Christian," p. 88. A millionaire from publishing and real estate ventures, Cussons developed the picturesque town of Glen Allen to conform with his image of a small utopia. He constructed a sixty-room resort lodge surrounded by a magnificent deer-stocked park and then established next to it a comfortable village populated by carefully selected white citizens appreciative of his paternalism. When he demanded concessions from the village to widen roads and install drainage ditches, however, the community banded against him. In retaliation, he threatened to sell his remaining lots to Richmond's impoverished blacks, as a gesture to the loyalty of the antebellum slave. Neighbors sued, but the issue became moot with Cussons's death in 1912. See "Old Confederate Who Is Conducting a Bitter War: One Man's War Against All in a Village He Owns," proof sheet from *New York World,* 29 Oct. [1908], ViHi; John Cussons to Clarence [Archibald Bryce], 12 Feb. 1911, and undated newspaper clippings, John Cussons Papers, ViHi.

23. George L. Christian to Beverley B. Munford, 28 Oct. 1899, Munford Family Papers, ViHi. For a sketch of Munford, see Anne Hobson Freeman, *The Style of a Law Firm: Eight Gentlemen from Virginia* (Chapel Hill, 1989), pp. 6–32.

24. *Minutes of the Sixteenth Annual Convention of the Virginia Division United Daughters of the Confederacy,* . . . *1911* (Richmond, [1911]), p. 47.

25. *Minutes of the Seventeenth Annual Convention of the Virginia Division United Daughters of the Confederacy,* . . . *1912* (Richmond, [1912]), pp. 165–66; *Minutes of the Twentieth Annual Convention of the Virginia Division United Daughters of the Confederacy,* . . . *1915* (Richmond, 1915), p. 160; *Minutes of the Twenty-Second Annual Convention of the Virginia Division United Daughters of the Confederacy,* . . . *1917* (n.p., [1917]), pp. 282, 286, 289, 290–91, 295, 299–300.

26. *Minutes of the Virginia Division UDC, 1917,* pp. 284, 292; Cornelia Branch Stone, *U.D.C. Catechism for Children* (n.p., 1904), p. 5. Staunton's UDC chapter reprinted Stone's *Catechism* for the education of the Old Dominion's children. See Parrott, "'Love Makes Memory Eternal,'" p. 235.

27. *Minutes of the Fifteenth Annual Convention of the Virginia Division United Daughters of the Confederacy,* . . . *1910* (Suffolk, Va., 1910), pp. 50–52; *Minutes of the Eighteenth Annual Convention of the Virginia Division United Daughters of the Confederacy,* . . . *1913* (n.p., [1913]), pp. 79–80; *Minutes of the Virginia Division UDC, 1917,* p. 150.

28. Mrs. Cabell Smith (Essie Wade Butler Smith), Sarah B. Graham, and Alice Whitley Jones, comps., *History of the Virginia Division United Daughters of the Confederacy, 1895–1967* (n.p., [1967]), pp. 6–7; *Minutes of the Twenty-fifth Annual Convention*

of the *Virginia Division United Daughters of the Confederacy,* . . . *1920* (Petersburg, Va., 1920), p. 56.

29. *Minutes of the Fifth Annual Convention of the Virginia Division United Daughters of the Confederacy,* . . . *1899* (Pulaski, Va., [1899]), p. 21; *Minutes of the Twenty-first Annual Convention of the Virginia Division United Daughters of the Confederacy,* . . . *1916* (Richmond, 1916), p. 125. In 1912, the state UDC amended its bylaws to include school readers among the books scrutinized. The revised statement read: "The Historian shall . . . examine such histories and readers of this country as are in use in the schools and report the result of such examination" (*Minutes of the Virginia Division UDC, 1912,* p. 203).

30. *Proceedings of the Eighth Annual Convention of the Grand Division of Virginia United Daughters of the Confederacy,* . . . *1902* (n.p., 1902), pp. 66–67.

31. Waddy Thompson, *A History of the United States* (Boston, 1904); D. C. Heath and Company to Andrew Jackson Montague, 2 Mar. 1904, Andrew Jackson Montague Executive Papers, 1902–6, Vi.

32. B. F. Johnson to Alexander S. Salley, Jr., 22 Nov. 1899, Alexander S. Salley, Jr., Papers, Caroliana Collection, University of South Carolina, Columbia. For a discussion of the influence the B. F. Johnson Publishing Company possessed with the Virginia state board of education, see C. J. Parker to J. G. De R. Hamilton, 23 Oct. 1911, J. G. De R. Hamilton Papers, Southern Historical Collection, University of North Carolina, Chapel Hill.

33. *Richmond News Leader,* 7 May, 11 Apr. 1904. In 1915 the Virginia UDC resolved: "We lay before you the justice of supporting our own publishing houses. . . . The Daughters really owe many thanks to the B. F. Johnson Company" (*Minutes of the Virginia Division UDC, 1915,* p. 126). See also *Minutes of the Fourth Annual Session of the Mississippi Division of the United Daughters of the Confederacy,* . . . *1900* (Macon, Miss., 1900), p. 13.

34. Merchant, "Report of Historical Committee, U.D.C.," p. 63.

35. Mary Tucker Magill, *Magill's First Book in Virginia History* (1890; Lynchburg, Va., 1908); Susan Pendleton Lee, *Lee's Advanced School History of the United States* (Richmond, 1896); Beverley B. Munford, *Virginia's Attitude toward Slavery and Secession* (New York and London, 1909).

36. Magill, *Virginia History,* pp. 153–54, 184–85.

37. Stephen D. Lee, "Report of Historical Committee," *Confederate Veteran* 3 (June 1895): 167; James R. Winchester, "Gen. William Nelson Pendleton," ibid. 4 (Aug. 1896): 263. In 1900 the Mississippi UDC praised "Mrs. Susan Pendleton Lee . . . [for] doing much to cancel the false impressions hitherto made upon the younger generations, by the Northern versions of Southern history" (*Minutes of the Mississippi Division UDC, 1900,* p. 12).

38. Lee, *School History of the United States,* pp. 29–30, 86–87, 279, 289, 314–15.

39. Ibid., pp. 280, 353, 358, 362–63, 435, 439, 516–17.

40. Ibid., pp. 532, 539, 542, 546–47, 549–52, 572–73.

41. "Report: Before the Virginia State Board of Education in the Matter of the Readoption for Four Years of 'Virginia's Attitude toward Slavery and Secession' by Beverley B. Munford," [1919], Westmoreland Davis Executive Papers, 1918–22, Vi; Beverley B. Munford to Armistead C. Gordon, 6 Nov. 1906, Armistead C. Gordon to Beverley B. Munford, n.d., Armistead C. Gordon Papers, ViHi; W. Gordon McCabe,

eulogy of Beverley B. Munford, in "Proceedings of the Virginia Historical Society in Annual Meeting held December 29, 1910," *Virginia Magazine of History and Biography* (hereafter cited as *VMHB*) 19 (1911): xv–xvii.

42. Munford, *Virginia's Attitude*, pp. vii, 15–33, 60–76, 82–103, 164, 176–77, 304.

43. Reamuer Coleman Stearnes to Beverley B. Munford, 17 Jan. 1910, Beverley B. Munford to J. Taylor Ellyson, 10 Mar. 1910, Munford Family Papers; "Report: Before the Virginia State Board of Education in the Matter of the Re-adoption of 'Virginia's Attitude.'"

44. Wendell Holmes Stephenson, *The South Lives in History: Southern Historians and Their Legacy* (Baton Rouge, 1955), pp. 28–57; Fred A. Bailey, "William E. Dodd: The South's Yeoman Historian," *North Carolina Historical Review* 66 (1989): 301–20.

45. William E. Dodd to Frederic Bancroft, 17 Apr. 1910, Frederic Bancroft Papers, Columbia University, New York, N.Y.; William E. Dodd, review of *Virginia's Attitude toward Slavery and Secession*, by Beverley B. Munford, in *American Historical Review* (hereafter cited as *AHR*) 15 (1909–10): 631–33.

46. William E. Dodd, "The Status of History in Southern Education," *Nation* 75 (7 Aug. 1902): 109–11. Writing to the *Richmond News*, 2 Nov. 1902, Dodd charged that Virginia's Grand Camp of Confederate Veterans simply asked, "'Who is the author?' The answer being 'A Yankee,' the matter was settled and the public made no protest."

47. John H. Latane to William E. Dodd, 9 Aug. 1902, William E. Dodd to Harry P. Judson, 30 Nov. 1920, William E. Dodd, "Autobiography" (handwritten manuscript, c. 1932), William E. Dodd Papers, Library of Congress, Washington, D.C.; *Annual Report of the American Historical Association for the Year 1903* (2 vols.; Washington, D.C., 1904), 1:26; New Orleans *Times-Democrat*, 31 Dec. 1903. Revised, Dodd's address to the American Historical Association appeared as William E. Dodd, "Some Difficulties of the History Teacher in the South," *South Atlantic Quarterly* 3 (Oct. 1904): 117–22.

48. John Spencer Bassett, "Stirring Up the Fires of Racial Antipathy," *South Atlantic Quarterly* 2 (Oct. 1903): 299; John Spencer Bassett to William E. Dodd, 9, 24 Nov., 3 Dec. 1903, 17 Dec. 1908, Edwin Mims to William E. Dodd, 21, 22 Nov., 8 Dec. 1903, Dodd Papers; Wendell Holmes Stephenson, *Southern History in the Making: Pioneer Historians of the South* (Baton Rouge, 1964), pp. 105, 126–30.

49. William E. Dodd, review of *The Old Dominion: Her Making and Her Manners*, by Thomas Nelson Page, in *AHR* 14 (1908–9): 182–83; J. Franklin Jameson to William E. Dodd, 10 Aug. 1908, Dodd Papers.

50. For discussions of Dodd as ambassador to Germany, see Robert Dallek, *Democrat and Diplomat: The Life of William E. Dodd* (New York, 1968); Fred Arthur Bailey, "A Virginia Scholar in Chancellor Hitler's Court: The Tragic Ambassadorship of William Edward Dodd," *VMHB* 100 (1992): 323–42.

51. W. W. Moffett to J. A. Morehead, 23 Feb. 1911, Elson Textbook Controversy Papers, Henry H. Fowler Collection, Roanoke College Library, Salem, Va.; William Edward Eisenberg, *The First Hundred Years: Roanoke College, 1842–1942* (Salem, Va., 1942), pp. 261–65; Mark F. Miller, *"Dear Old Roanoke": A Sesquicentennial Portrait, 1842–1992* (Macon, Ga., 1992), p. 134.

52. Henry William Elson, *History of the United States of America* (1904; New York, 1926), pp. 548, 604–5, 610, 740.

53. J. A. Morehead to W. W. Moffett, 2 Mar. 1911, E. L. Greever to J. A. More-

head, 4 Mar. 1911, Elson Textbook Controversy Papers; *Roanoke Times*, 8, 16 Mar. 1911 (clippings), Petersburg *Index-Appeal*, n.d., quoted in Washington, D.C., *Herald*, 25 Apr. 1911 (clipping), Lynchburg *News*, 21 Apr. 1911 (clipping), Bristol *Herald-Courier*, 28 Mar. 1911 (clipping), *Danville Register*, n.d., quoted in Roanoke *Evening World*, 16 Mar. 1911 (clipping), Elson Textbook Controversy Scrapbook, Fowler Collection.

54. R. R. Smith to Herman J. Thorstenberg, 3, 6 Mar. 1911, Elson Textbook Controversy Papers; Marshall, Texas, *Messenger*, 10 July 1911 (clipping), New Orleans *Picayune*, 25 Mar. 1911 (clipping), Charlotte, N.C., *Observer*, n.d., quoted in *Roanoke Times*, 3 May 1911 (clipping), Elson Textbook Controversy Scrapbook; "Virginians Aroused About False History," *Confederate Veteran* 19 (Apr. 1911): 148; "Faculty of Roanoke College 'Defended,'" ibid. 19 (May 1911): 194–96; "That Detestable Elson Book," ibid. 19 (July 1911): 316; *Report of the United Confederate Veterans' Historical Committee* (n.p., 1911), pp. 11–15; Jacksonville *Florida Times-Union*, 31 Mar. 1911. As controversy swirled around Thorstenberg and Roanoke College, the Jacksonville *Florida Times-Union* and the Florida Confederate societies were hounding Professor Enoch M. Banks out of the history department at the University of Florida. See Fred Arthur Bailey, "Free Speech at the University of Florida: The Enoch Marvin Banks Case," *Florida Historical Quarterly* 71 (July 1992): 1–17.

55. Rebecca Cameron to J. G. De R. Hamilton, 13 June, 4 Sept. 1911, Hamilton Papers; Rebecca Cameron to Francis P. Venable, 20 May, 2 June 1911, Francis P. Venable to Rebecca Cameron, 22, 24 May 1911, University of North Carolina Papers, Francis P. Venable Administration, University of North Carolina Archives, Chapel Hill; *Minutes of the Fifteenth Annual Convention of the United Daughters of the Confederacy North Carolina Division, . . . 1911* (Newton, N.C., [1912]), p. 24; David Crenshaw Barrow, chancellor of the University of Georgia, to Nathaniel Harris, [1912], Elson Textbook Controversy Papers; George W. Littlefield to Eugene C. Barker, 15 Apr. 1911, Eugene C. Barker to S. E. Mezes, 12 Apr. 1911 (enclosed in Eugene C. Barker to George W. Littlefield, 17 Apr. 1911), Eugene C. Barker Papers, Eugene C. Barker Center, Austin, Texas.

56. Miller, *"Dear Old Roanoke,"* p. 134.

57. *New York Times*, 28, 29 Apr. 1920; *Danville Register*, 20 Apr. 1920.

58. Thomas Perkins Abernethy, "The Social Scene in Virginia," n.d. (typescript), Thomas Perkins Abernethy Papers (#6464-a), University of Virginia Library, Charlottesville.

ELNA C. GREEN

The State Suffrage Campaigns:
Virginia as a Case Study

* * * * * * * * *T*HE SAME IMPULSE THAT MOBILIZED VIRGINIA'S
Confederate patriotic societies to assert control over the state's history im-
pelled many conservative Virginians to oppose suffrage for women. As Elna
C. Green describes, Virginia's Democratic Party of the early twentieth century, after a bruising struggle to beat back threats from the Republican,
Readjuster, and Populist parties of the late nineteenth century, asserted firm
control over state politics that would last well into the 1960s. Virginia's constitution of 1902, for example, disfranchised vast numbers of black voters
and poorer white Republicans from the mountain districts. "As the agent of
railroads and planters, industrialists and business groups," Green writes,
"the Democratic Party acted as conservators of the economic and political
status quo." Expanding the electorate to include women would, party leaders feared, increase support for broader reform platforms and might even
lead to enlarged political rights for black Virginians. Even in the second
decade of the twentieth century, with progressive reform movements in full
swing, "Virginia's political and economic elites would have none of it."

Race, implicit in so much of the discourse that defined Virginia politics in the twentieth century, circumscribed public discussion of woman
suffrage as well. Virginia antisuffragists, Green notes, "wielded race and
racism" to mobilize support. "By the time the state legislature debated
another state suffrage amendment in 1916," Green argues, antisuffrage
activists had established "white supremacy [as] a prominent part of the
discussion." Suffragists, too, defended white dominance of Virginia public
affairs. They responded not by calling for racial reform in the state but
rather by "denying that white supremacy" would be threatened by woman
suffrage. As leading suffragist Lila Meade Valentine put it, "The state constitutions provide amply for restricting the shiftless, illiterate vote." Valentine went on to assert that "white women" were just as interested as "white
men in maintaining white supremacy."

The Virginia woman suffrage movement thus developed in an inhos-
pitable political environment. The efforts of women such as Valentine,

Anna Whitehead Bodeker, Orra Langhorne, and Mary Johnston, however, expanded on the accomplishments of the earlier Whig political activists like Lucy Barbour. By 1912 Virginia sustained a woman suffrage movement of sufficient strength and breadth that opponents of the vote for women felt compelled to organize formally. The Virginia woman suffrage movement ultimately failed to secure Virginia's ratification of the Nineteenth Amendment because suffragists faced the monolithic strength of the state's Democratic Party, which had a deep stake in a restricted franchise. As Green notes, in the Progressive Era, and indeed for a good many years after, "the Democratic Party generally got what it wanted."   * * * * * * * *

* * * * * * * *

I agree with you that as far as the present work in Virginia is concerned questions of Federal amendments are largely academic. I don't, however, believe that it is always going to be so. Its a pity to see any division among our workers — and yet, as suffragists grow more numerous, some division along lines of temperament and judgement is bound to occur.

Revolutions have to trot along with all kinds of revolutionaries — with bodies within bodies.

Mary Johnston to Lila Meade Valentine, 10 May 1915

Virginia's suffragists lamented the conservatism of their home state regularly and publicly. And Virginia had earned its reputation for conservatism, particularly in the area of women's rights. The Old Dominion was the last state in the Union to grant married women the right to own property in their own names and had a similarly lackluster record in supporting higher education for women.[1] Orie Latham Hatcher, a teacher who had seen something of the world outside of the South, complained that Virginia, especially Virginia's men, still held tenaciously to old social ideals: "Nowhere else in the South except in Charleston, after all a small world to itself, has a certain conception of what a woman should be and do persisted so fervently as in Virginia."[2] Novelist Mary Johnston made a similar assessment: "Virginia, if the dearest of states, is also the most conservative. Her men are chivalric, her women domestic; since the eighteenth century no heavy wave of immigration has touched her shores. She has no large cities, she has a lovely country, wood and field and flood, she has great memories. She makes progress, too, but her eyes are apt to turn to the past."[3]

Virginians did indeed regard woman suffrage skeptically. In fact, opponents of the reform had organized earlier and more effectively than those in most other southern states. Consequently, the state's suffragists moved cautiously. As a case study of suffragism in the South, then, Virginia is ripe with opportunities. Narrowing the scope of the story of suffragism and antisuffragism to one state provides the chance to reassemble the disparate pieces discussed in previous chapters. And Virginia provides a good example of what a contest between a notably large suffrage movement and a notably strong antisuffrage movement entailed. It also permits the close examination of the divisions between suffragists regarding ideology and tactics and how those divisions shaped the suffrage contest in the South.

Virginia: The Early Years

Since at least the 1840s, Virginia's elite women had been practicing partisanship in politics. Although excluded from voting and from officeholding, Virginia women had closely followed party politics and expressed political opinions, generally of the Whiggish variety. Openly partisan sentiments by Whig women appeared in Virginia's newspapers beginning in the 1840s, and women regularly attended political gatherings as well. The state's Whig Party welcomed the support of women and appropriated the image of female nonpartisanship to its political advantage.[4]

In a parallel (but entirely separate) trend, black women in Virginia also found ways to express their political opinions in the years before their enfranchisement. African American women in Richmond, for example, organized political "secret societies" such as the Rising Daughters of Liberty. Part of the vast network of social organizations that undergirded black social life in the postbellum South, these organizations helped to raise money, organize political rallies, and urge blacks to register and vote. Black women also participated in political meetings and rallies, such as the mass meeting held in March 1867 in Richmond to oppose the reelection of the incumbent mayor of the city. And in 1880 women in one of the most important black churches in the city petitioned the deacons to grant them the right to vote in church affairs. The event was so tumultuous that city police intervened to quiet the disorder.[5] Not surprisingly, black women's political activities generally supported Republican or Independent candidates and agendas.

For black and white women alike, political partisanship was steeped in reform politics. Reform-minded women in the late nineteenth century had often been trained or reared in this Whiggish political culture. Partisanship and reformism united under the banner of the Whig Party and then later under that of the Republican Party (although by the twentieth century it would move again, to the Democratic Party). Women were drawn to the Whigs because the party advocated many policies that middle-class women reformers supported: moral reform, public education, and support for benevolent societies. Two of the state's best known suffragists of the late nineteenth century, Elizabeth Van Lew and Orra Langhorne, both came from Whig/Republican families.[6]

Indeed, Virginia's nineteenth-century suffrage movement was very much linked to the Whig/Republican reform effort. Like other such early efforts, the nineteenth-century suffrage movement in Richmond revolved around a single dedicated leader: Anna Whitehead Bodeker. Anna Whitehead was the daughter of a factory superintendent in Richmond who had moved his family from New Jersey in the 1830s. She married a local druggist, Augustus Bodeker, a German immigrant and successful businessman who also served in the House of Delegates during Reconstruction.[7] Although it remains unknown just how and when Anna Bodeker came to support woman suffrage, by 1870 she had committed herself to suffrage activism. Her first action was to bring Paulina Wright Davis, the nationally known suffrage leader, to Richmond to speak to a small group of local civic leaders at her home on 26 January 1870. The meeting apparently fueled an impassioned discussion. At the end of the parlor meeting, Bodeker announced that she planned to form a suffrage organization in the city.[8]

Paulina Davis, greatly pleased with her initial foray into the former capital of the Confederacy, returned home convinced that she had found a southern woman capable of leading the suffrage movement in the South. Davis praised Bodeker's abilities in the pages of the *Revolution*, asserting that Bodeker "might reach the whole south." An indicator of the national leadership's early interest in harnessing the South, other national suffrage leaders soon answered Bodeker's call for assistance. Matilda Joslyn Gage, an organizer for the National Woman Suffrage Association (NWSA), traveled to Richmond several months later to help put together a state suffrage association.[9]

After a public meeting at Bosher's Hall on 5 May 1870, a small group of Richmonders declared themselves the Virginia State Woman Suffrage Association and elected Anna Bodeker as president. Among its leading members were prominent Republicans such as Judge John C. Underwood, Ralza M. Manly, the Freedmen's Bureau's superintendent of education, and Elizabeth Van Lew, the "notorious" Reconstruction postmistress who had been a Union sympathizer and suspected Union spy. (Van Lew was also known for paying her taxes every year under protest, pointing out that as a citizen who could not vote, she was effectively taxed without the right of representation.[10]) The same year it officially organized, the new suffrage association affiliated with the National Woman Suffrage Association, sent delegates to the 1870 national convention, and requested further assistance from the national leadership.[11]

Still feeling optimistic about the opportunities for suffrage activity in Richmond, the NWSA sent some of its most powerful speakers to the city in the next several months to help bolster the fledging state association. Susan B. Anthony, calling Bodeker's request for assistance the "first call from the South for missionaries," personally appeared in Richmond in December 1870. Anthony attempted to appeal to the southern audience with an argument grounded in Reconstruction realities: it was unfair for the government to allow black males to vote but not allow women to do so. Anthony's visit was followed by Lillie Devereaux Blake's, in January 1871. In March, while the state assembly was in session, the Virginia Woman Suffrage Association brought Paulina Wright Davis, Isabella Beecher Hooker, and Josephine S. Griffing to town for several public appearances.[12]

These meetings, and the newspaper coverage that they generated, spurred a great deal of discussion in Richmond about the "woman question." Letters to the local newspapers indicated that people were thinking and talking about woman suffrage, many perhaps for the first time. The opposition appeared in greater numbers, of course, like "Daughter of Virginia" who protested that women's rights threatened the "overthrow of our political fabric."[13] But comments like this one failed to put an end to the debate. Undoubtedly Anna Bodeker's unsuccessful attempt to vote in an 1871 election set tongues wagging again all over Richmond.[14]

However, all this activism and attention did not result in the rapid growth of a suffrage movement. Nor did the Virginia Woman Suffrage Association gain any legislative victories. The association appears to have been firmly linked with carpetbaggers and black Republicans in the public mind, and thus it had difficulty gaining support from most whites in Richmond. Anna Bodeker, discouraged by the meager results that had come from all her efforts, ceased her activism after 1872. The Virginia State Woman Suffrage Association disappeared soon thereafter.[15]

It would be nearly twenty years before Lynchburg's Orra Langhorne, an avid suffragist, stepped in to fill the void left by Bodeker's retirement. Langhorne, the daughter of a Unionist and slaveholding "abolitionist," held liberal views on race and spoke them freely, despite the disapproval of her neighbors. She supported the Republican Party, called herself a radical, and was a longtime supporter of the Hampton Institute.[16]

For several years, Orra Langhorne acted alone: she petitioned the Virginia legislature for voting rights for women,[17] and she regularly attended the National American Woman Suffrage Association (NAWSA) conventions as the sole "delegate" from Virginia.[18] Finally, in 1893, she attempted to revive the suffrage movement by establishing a second state suffrage association, centered in her home in Lynchburg. Its activities were quite limited, geographically and otherwise.[19] Perhaps the two most notable events from these years were the appearances of celebrated national suffrage leaders, both undoubtedly as a result of Langhorne's involvement in the NAWSA. The first of these occurred in 1895, when Susan B. Anthony spoke at the opera house in Culpeper, on her way home from the Atlanta NAWSA convention.[20] The state constitutional convention of 1901 was the setting for the second of these "celebrity" appearances. Carrie Chapman Catt appeared before the convention during its meeting to draft the "disfranchisement" constitution. She asked that woman suffrage be included in the new document.[21] Orra Langhorne's death in 1904, however, put another temporary halt to suffrage activity in the state. Langhorne's work was notable, but Virginia was completely dependent upon her personal efforts alone. The suffrage movement would not be revived again in Virginia until 1909.[22]

In the time between the founding of the first suffrage organization in 1870 and the permanent one to emerge in 1909, Virginia experienced two "revolutions": a political coup d'état and an economic transformation. The state's conservative Democrats, challenged by the agendas of Republicans, Populists, Readjusters, and other shades of Independents, responded with election "reforms" that restored their control of the state government. A secret ballot law helped effectively to disfranchise illiterates (who tended to vote with the opposition); the electorate thus reduced, the Democrats felt confident enough to call a constitutional convention to restrict the electorate more permanently. The convention produced a constitution so controversial that rather than subject it to a public referendum, it was "proclaimed" in effect instead.[23]

At the same time that the Conservatives were reshaping the electorate in their own image, their economic policies were helping to remake urban Virginia as well. Cities were booming, railroads were expanding, factories were appearing. The cities of Norfolk, Portsmouth, and Petersburg experienced real estate booms so intense that the tax assessors were having difficulty figuring tax bills.[24] Norfolk's city boosters formed the "200,000 League," whose goal was to increase the city's population to 200,000 by promoting manufacturing. While the city did not reach the 200,000 mark until World War II, manufacturing did employ 30 percent of the city's residents in 1910 and transportation and trade employed another 30 percent.[25] Richmond, the state's largest city, reached the 100,000 mark by the turn of the century. Its population and its prosperity relied greatly on manufacturing and extensive commercial trade.[26]

These tremendous strides in industrial development were facilitated by the governing elite's belief in unregulated business development as the best solution for the state's economic backwardness. Railroads, real estate developers, and industrialists were allowed free rein in Conservative/Democratic administrations. The state did create a virtually powerless railroad commission in 1877, but that would be the extent of state regulation for decades.[27]

The New Virginia produced great profits for those who survived the competition and the unpredictable economic cycles. Men like Lewis Ginter, James Dooley, and Jed Hotchkiss made their fortunes in various concerns and joined the state's economic elite. Their businesses hired thousands, who joined the state's industrial proletariat. In the mushrooming cities and towns, an urban middle class appeared to provide goods and services to workers who now seldom grew their own food or built their own homes.

Virginia's urban and industrial growth sparked both the rise of trade unionism and the birth of progressive reform groups, two parallel responses to the successes and failures of the New South. In 1900, an estimated 3,900 workers in Virginia were members of trade unions; by 1910 the number had grown to 8,500, and the figures reached a high of nearly 47,000 at the end of World War I.[28] Industrial unrest erupted periodically, such as a large coal miners' strike in 1895, as the newly conscious classes of the New South learned to interact in new ways.[29] Similarly, urban reform associations began to agitate for numerous improvements in the quality of life in Virginia. Although the beginning of the progressive reform movement in Virginia has been dated as late as 1902,[30] in fact, progressive reform organizations had been active in the late 1870s and early 1880s. The state's first local chapter of the Woman's Christian Temperance Union (WCTU) formed in Lincoln in May 1878; the Richmond chapter was organized in 1882. And by 1883, eight unions joined together to form the state WCTU, with Mrs. R. D. Wilson of Loudoun County as the state president.[31] Other manifestations of the emergent progressive sentiment included the establishment of the YWCA in Richmond in 1887; the founding of the Hampton, Virginia, Locust Street Social Settlement in October 1890, by Janie Porter Barrett; the founding of the Richmond Neighborhood Association in 1912, by Ora Brown Stokes; and the opening of the Nurses' Settlement, a visiting nursing service and settlement house in 1901.[32] As progressive reformers elsewhere, those in Virginia began demanding legislative action on behalf of change. The state's first child labor law was passed in 1890, under the sponsorship of Mary-Cooke Branch Munford.[33]

The women, both black and white, involved in "social work" confronted the poverty, disease, illiteracy, and unemployment of Virginia's growing cities. As women of the middle class, with leisure time and extra resources at their disposal, they were able to join reform groups. As religious women, steeped in the language of "mission" and "service," they felt that they had an obligation to do so. When they gained experience in these reform endeavors, they often came to see the need for woman suffrage, out of a desire to serve others or to secure their own equality.

Veterans of the white women's voluntary associations and progressive reform movement were responsible for the reestablishment of the suffrage movement in Virginia. The movement stirred back to life in the spring of 1909, when the Richmond Woman's Club hosted a visit from Kentucky suffragist Laura Clay. Her appearance there helped to spur the establishment of yet another suffrage organization. Despite the skepticism of the local newspaper, which predicted that this, as had all previous efforts, would fail,[34] Ellen Glasgow and twenty other members of the Woman's Club established the Equal Suffrage League of Virginia (ESL) in the fall of 1909. The founders included white women of great standing in the community, such as Lila Meade Valentine, women of distinguished southern lineage, such as Lucy Randolph Mason, women of current fame, such as artist Adele Clark, and women leaders of progressive reforms, such as Kate Waller Barrett.[35]

Selected as president at the very first meeting, Lila Meade Valentine dominated the Virginia suffrage movement for the next decade. Valentine had come from Richmond's social and economic elite and had married well.[36] By the time of her election as president of the ESL, Valentine was a seasoned veteran of women's voluntary associations with connections to the many Progressive Era reform movements then making their way into Richmond. She had spoken before city councils, served on state committees for various causes, including education reform and public health, and helped organize fund-raising drives. Although Valentine's impeccable credentials benefited the suffrage movement by giving her access to leaders of government, business, and education, her conservatism hampered the movement. She ruled the ESL with an iron will, stamping out dissent and purging opposition within its ranks. From the outset, the new league disavowed militancy and radicalism. One of its first press announcements rejected the suggestion that the suffragists would bring militant "suffragettes" like the Pankhursts to Richmond and emphasized the group's patience and willingness to proceed slowly, if surely, toward its goal.[37]

Although Valentine would leave her mark on the ESL, hers was not a one-woman movement. Many other important local leaders emerged both to assist and to challenge Valentine's leadership in the drive for enfranchisement. In Norfolk, Jessie Townsend and Pauline Adams were outspoken and dedicated motivators who helped to build one of the largest city associations in the state. Townsend, the wife of a realtor, was a local suffrage leader who also held state offices occasionally. Pauline Adams, who was born in Ireland, was an attorney (the first woman attorney in the city of Norfolk) and had been a city suffrage leader since the ESL's inception. However, both Townsend and Adams grew restless and frustrated with the ESL and Valentine's conservative leadership; Townsend joined the Congressional Union for a time, and Adams ultimately joined the National Woman's Party, a group with which she was jailed for picketing the White House.

For these local leaders and others, such as Elizabeth Langhorne Lewis of Lynchburg and Louise Taylor Letcher of Lexington, the goal of the first years of organization was recruitment; and they converted women, one by one, to the cause. Mary Johnston recorded in her diary in 1910 that she was "doing a deal of suffrage propaganda. There is here little opposition, a great deal of curiosity, a vague unrest, a few already over, others trembling on the verge. At any rate and at last woman is in the pulpit."[38]

Recruitment could be slow going, as a set of documents from 1912 illustrates. First, Lila Valentine wrote to Merrie Sugg of Guinea, Virginia, who was known for her local mission work. She inquired after Sugg's opinion about suffrage, sent some literature, asked her to forward names of anyone she knew who might be interested, and then asked if Sugg could make arrangements for a public talk by Mary Johnston. Sugg responded with caution, though not with outright hostility. "I have not given this subject serious attention," Sugg wrote, but she did acknowledge that she had once talked to her local legislator about it. He informed her of his opposition to woman suffrage because "the women of the county are opposed to it, and he did not like to vote against their wishes in the matter. I told him I was not opposed to it, but I did not like to offer advice in the matter. He asked me to talk with some of the leading women about it, as in my mission work among the Baptist women of the county, I am acquainted with all parts of the county." And as to Mary Johnston's speaking, Sugg advised, "There is no hall in this immediate neighborhood. I believe there is a small hall at Guinea, our post office. . . . Bowling Green, the county seat would be the best place for it, and I refer you to Mrs. O. P. Smoot, Bowling Green." She added, "P.S. Since writing this letter, I have been looking over some of the woman suffrage literature sent me, and I am favorably impressed."[39] The end result: one possible convert, another name to contact in another small town, and more work to be done.

Suffragists knew instinctively to tap the network of women's voluntary associations to garner new members. In 1916, local leader Elizabeth L. Lewis recommended that organizers focus on securing members "from all the Church associations for women, from all civic and temperance associations, educational bodies and industrials plants."[40] Surprisingly, the women's colleges in the Lynchburg area proved more difficult to reach than Lewis anticipated. Sweet Briar's president, although herself a suffrage supporter, refused to allow Mary Johnston to give a suffrage speech to her students in 1911, permitting her to speak to the faculty only. And Randolph-Macon Woman's College very nearly canceled a scheduled suffrage talk, but it ultimately allowed the event to go on.[41] (Randolph-Macon eventually produced a large college suffrage league; Sweet Briar students remained unorganized.)[42]

Despite the need to recruit as many members as possible, the white suffrage league never reached out to the black middle-class women who might have been their "natural allies." By the early twentieth century, cities like Richmond were populated by a vigorous and substantial black middle class, with women who were the equals to Lila Valentine in voluntary association activity, club work, and progressive reform experiences. Ora Brown Stokes had gleaned organizational expertise from her many years of work with the Negro Organizational Society of Virginia, the Virginia Federation of Colored Women's Clubs, and Baptist missionary societies. (And unlike Lila Valentine, Stokes had also received graduate education from the University of Chicago.) Maggie Lena Walker, now widely known as the first black woman bank president in the United States, also had done years of volunteer work for the National Association of Colored Women, the Virginia Federation of Colored Women's Clubs, the Richmond Council of Colored Women, the National Association for the Advancement of Colored People (NAACP), and the International Council of Women of the Darker Races. But the racial code kept black and white urban middle-class women from joining forces behind a movement that they all supported.

And it does appear that many African American men and women in Virginia supported woman suffrage. As early as 1871, the Richmond press noted the attendance of "three colored men" at a local woman suffrage meeting.[43] Although black women in Virginia did not organize a separate suffrage organization and speak openly or often of their suffragism, when women were finally given the vote in 1920, they marched to the local courthouses to register; they voted when allowed to do so; and they organized the Virginia Negro Woman's League of Voters.

For white suffragists in Virginia, reaching women outside of the biggest cities was critical to the success of the movement, but it was also one of the most difficult tasks confronting the endeavor. Suffragists had little hope for, and expended little energy on, recruiting rural women. Even in small towns, suffragists occasionally found it difficult to compete for the attention of the public. For example, Elizabeth Lewis complained that the low turnout for her suffrage meeting at Drake's Branch in 1916 was "owing to the absence of a number of the representative people who had gone that day to Richmond to see 'The Birth of a Nation.'"[44]

But the diligent and exhaustive work of Mary Johnston, Elizabeth Lewis, and Lila Valentine began to pay off.[45] In 1916, Virginia had 115 local leagues, including 23 organized in that year alone.[46] The Randolph-Macon Woman's College ESL, led by the daughter of Nellie Nugent Somerville, state suffrage leader from Mississippi, had 150 members in 1914.[47] And by 1919, membership had reached 30,000, making it most likely the largest state association in the South. The ESL also had secured endorsements of suffrage from the State Teachers' Association, the State Federation of Women's Clubs, and a number of other women's groups.[48]

In addition to recruiting new members, Virginia suffragists believed that their most important task was to educate the public on enfranchisement issues. As Elizabeth Langhorne Lewis lamented, "it seems that for a few years to come this educational work must proceed in the South before the movement will be sufficiently general to promise legislative action."[49] And in order to educate properly the public, they needed positive publicity. The league sent more than 6,000 press releases a year to the state's newspapers (although few editors supported suffrage and therefore seldom used them).[50] In October 1914, the league began publishing *Virginia Suffrage News*, financed personally by Alice O. Taylor, a local suffragist in Richmond.[51] The ESL also made the usual appearances at county and state fairs, gave talks at conventions, and held public meetings with prominent state and national speakers.

Many of those suffrage talks were accompanied by fund-raising. Both the state and the local suffrage leagues were chronically short of funds and had to use creative measures at times to come up with extra cash. The comments of Jessie Townsend, local leader of the large and active Norfolk league, on fund-raising are telling. "Well," she wrote, "I believe we went about it in a truly feminine way, the way women have raised things since time immemorial, a little here and a little there, everlastingly at it. A member who had a vacuum cleaner rented it out to other members so much a day, the proceeds going into the treasury of the league." Other members sold cakes and breads. And of course, she added, "we passed the hat at most of our evening gatherings."[52]

The message that Virginia suffragists wished to convey was two-fold: women ought to be the legal equals of men and women with the ballot would be catalysts of reform. In 1912, the state convention of the ESL adopted a set of resolutions that effectively defined the Virginia suffragists' agenda. Notably, there was no mention of race or the desire to increase the white electorate. Several items demonstrated their interest in women outside their own class, including a call for an eight-hour work day, the abolishment of child labor, and equal pay for equal work. Several other resolutions, including support for women's equal guardianship rights over their children, advocacy of a single standard of morality, and demand for equal educational opportunities for women "from the kindergarten through the university," revealed their larger feminist vision. Their final plank called for international arbitration, making clear that these women believed that diplomacy and international politics were appropriate areas of interest for women. The domestication of politics included international affairs.[53]

The ESL's resolutions affirm that Virginia suffragists, like the progressive movement itself, accepted the premise that solving modern social problems required the government's intervention. Most of their demands for reform, such as education for all children and a public health initiative, called for legislative actions. As Lucy Randolph Mason wrote, "a divine discontent [had] opened their eyes to the cruel wrong, injustice and human waste of our present social system, to the responsibilities of the individual to society, and to the powerlessness of a class debarred from participation in government."[54] Suffragism was part of a larger agenda that responded to "the changed social and economic order of the present."[55]

Considering the comfortable middle-class lives they lived, a remarkable number of Virginia's suffragists worked to reach organized labor in the state. As early as February 1911, Mary Johnston and Lila Valentine spoke to the Richmond Central Trade Union Council. Johnston's speech linked the causes of organized labor and woman suffrage: women and working people have been the "under dogs" for ages, she argued, and they are rising together now. "We helped you at the Capitol a year ago [in a fight against proposed labor legislation]," she continued. "Could we not have helped you more effectively with the ballot?" The council officially endorsed woman suffrage at the meeting, and several members spoke in favor of the reform.[56] Valentine eventually backed away from her association with labor unions, but Johnston continued to see women's causes and labor's causes as kindred.[57]

Johnston was not alone in her interest in labor. For example, in a letter to Johnston, a local suffrage activist wrote, "I hope very soon now to be able to report you some progress in affiliation between our League and the Labor people. . . . Indeed, we can best forward our work, by never losing sight of its main purpose for a moment, and at the same time, by aiding as far as we possibly can in the educational and social reform work going on around us."[58] And a Richmond suffragist wrote to Jessie Townsend in 1915 that "we have been speaking before labor unions and are glad to see that you are planning the same thing. The labor people are our friends and their names to the petition would help us greatly."[59] Perhaps most dedicated of all in linking the suffrage and labor questions, however, was Lucy Randolph Mason. In a widely quoted address to Virginia's middle-class women, the future labor organizer chided women of leisure: "We have no right to stand idly by and profit by the underpaid and overdriven labor of people bound with the chains of economic bondage."[60] Such a statement makes it difficult to see that Mason's support for woman suffrage and other progressive reforms actually stemmed from her desire to exert middle-class control over the new industrial proletariat. Female "paternalism" was not apparent in her later career with the CIO either.[61]

Nor can this interest in reaching the South's new industrial labor force be dismissed as just rhetoric, for actions often followed the words. In fact, members of the Hampton local suffrage league reported that they personally attended a meeting of the local Carpenter's Union "where new members and signatures to our petition were obtained."[62] Roanoke suffragist Lillie Barbour arranged for Lila Valentine to speak to the Garment Workers in Danville, because she was "confident the Garment Workers there will adopt Equal Suffrage."[63] And in Lynchburg, the suffragists' interest in labor was reciprocated: seventeen garment workers joined the local ESL in 1914.[64]

Lila Valentine, fearful of the taint of radicalism, soon began to work to limit the amount of contact the ESL made with labor unions. When Alice Taylor and Jessie Townsend tried to recruit a labor union official to be an officer in the Norfolk league, Valentine moved quickly to prevent it. "I am inclined to think it far better to keep entirely clear of other organizations," she asserted. We of course want their endorsement, and we can assist them from time to time by backing up certain welfare measures espoused by them at the Legislature, but we must maintain a strictly non-partisan attitude toward them as towards political parties."[65] Valentine grew even more worried about the great sympathy for socialism shown by some leading suffragists such as Alice Tyler, an active suffragist from Richmond who believed that "if we really love our fellow humans, all of us, you and I and all—are socialists at heart, dont you think so? And some day what is in the heart will become manifest in words and actions. The world's way is towards socialism I think, and we are in the way I know."[66] A socialist speaker had appeared at a Richmond ESL meeting in 1912, giving a talk entitled "Why I am a Socialist,"[67] and Valentine began to fear that the public would associate suffragism with socialism. She warned Jessie Townsend that "our very good friend, Mr. Clinedinst, Factory Inspector, said that he noticed in the Suffrage Shop window in Norfolk Socialist literature and that he would strongly advise that it should not be in the shop, as it savors of partisanship and as Socialism itself is a most unpopular policy amongst the rank and file."[68]

Likewise, Valentine went after her old friend, Mary Johnston. Johnston had never hidden her affinity for socialism from her friends, although she did try to keep it from becoming a hindrance to the suffrage cause.[69] In 1911, Johnston had agreed to be guest of honor at a dinner in Baltimore in honor of socialist leader Max Eastman. In that same year, she had attended her "first socialist meeting" in Richmond, where Eugene Debs was speaking.[70] She regularly attended socialist meetings and speeches in the city. Valentine grew increasingly nervous about Johnston's politics, and in 1912 she asked Johnston point blank if she was a socialist. Johnston replied, "I have never become an enrolled member of the Socialist Party. (You have in that party, you know, to sign your card and pay your dues.) I may never actually join it as an organization. But I call myself a socialist, and to all practical purposes I am one."[71]

Valentine had concluded that the only route to enfranchisement was a moderate one, and she worked diligently to stamp out dangerous radicalism from her ranks. "The more I study the situation in Virginia, the more convinced I am of the necessity of quiet, educational propaganda with an entire elimination of the spectacular for the present at least. The latter method simply shocks the sensibilities of most people without convincing them of the truth of our movement."[72] She made it clear to all that militancy, radicalism, and socialism were to be avoided because they endangered woman suffrage. To that end, Johnston never joined the Socialist Party and kept her political views to herself.

Valentine also worked to keep the racial politics of the New South out of the suffrage movement. Southern reformers had used racism successfully as a strategy in support of other programs, such as Prohibition, and suffragists easily could have used that example in their own crusade.[73] But Virginia's suffragists believed that the racial settlement of 1901 was final and the question therefore moot.

The first hearing of the woman suffrage question took place at the 1912 meeting of the state legislature. The local press acknowledged "the seriousness of the occasion, [that] the feeling that here might be an hour to make history for the commonwealth and to mark the beginning of an era, was in the air." It reported, "Women who work, women who write, women who keep house, women who have nothing else to do, and women who have everything else to do, pleaded for the ballot. Men who believe their cause is just stood with them. . . . Ministers of the gospel and representatives of laboring organizations helped."[74] Kate Bosher, Elizabeth Lewis, and Lila Valentine addressed the legislature, but it was Mary Johnston's speech that received the most attention. She pointed out that thousands of Virginia women work for pay, thousands are self-supporting and supporters of others. "Virginia women are in the economic world to stay," yet, Johnston continued, "the gentleman will rub his hands, smile and say, 'My dear ladies, if you'd just consent to stay where your great-grandmothers were.' To which, Johnston wished to reply, 'When you, gentlemen, come to committee properly bepowdered, pigtailed and snuff-boxed, when you again discuss embargo and whether or no we shall purchase Louisiana, then will we, too, return to where our great-grandmothers were.'"[75] Although the Committee on Privileges and Elections issued an open invitation for response, no one rose to speak in opposition to the amendment. The House voted 88 to 12 against the state amendment. The Senate, the *Times-Dispatch* reported, laughed at the announcement by a Richmond senator that he wished to submit suffrage petitions for consideration, and it did not vote on the question during this session.[76]

The Antisuffragists Organize

The 1912 legislative debate over woman suffrage stirred its opponents to action. Antisuffragists announced their intention to organize that February, denouncing the "atheistic impulse of suffrage" which denied that "women's place has been appointed by God as the mother of the family and the mistress of the home."[77] Mary Johnston noted in her diary: "This week sees the announcement of the long looked for Anti-Suffrage Association. A battle royal's coming."[78] The suffragists tried to take the announcement in stride. In fact, Kate Wise decided that "the organization of the opposition in Richmond is a good sign, they can no longer stigmatize the suffragists because of public work, and with opposition comes greater endeavor on the part of adherents to the Cause."[79]

In one of the first southern states to organize, the antisuffragists set up headquarters in Richmond and began to recruit members. The Virginia Association Opposed to Woman Suffrage soon claimed a membership of more than 2,000 women; and several branch associations developed throughout the state.[80] The organization set rules for voting and membership and published their constitution and bylaws.[81] They set out to write and distribute antisuffrage literature, to publicize the fact that prominent women opposed woman suffrage, and to secure names on petitions opposing suffrage. The first state president, Jane Meade Rutherfoord, was a club woman and mainstay of the women's patriotic societies in Richmond. Quite advanced in age, Rutherfoord retired to an honorary presidency by 1916 and was succeeded by Mary Mason Anderson Williams. Williams came from the wealthy Tredegar Ironworks family of Richmond. Other state leaders also came from Richmond's most prestigious families, such as Mary Miller Cary, whose husband's family had been sending members to the legislature since the seventeenth century. Although these leaders were well known in the state, only one was renowned outside of Virginia: the writer Molly Elliot Seawell. Best known for her novel *Throckmorton*, the prolific Seawell published more than forty books and articles before her death in 1916. Her antisuffrage polemic, *The Ladies' Battle*, published the year before the state antisuffrage organization had formed, won her acclaim and instant leadership in the new movement.[82]

The association held its first open meeting in March 1912. Mary Johnston and other interested suffragists attended. Johnston recounted a few details of the event in her diary: "This evening to the Jefferson [for] the first antisuffrage open meeting. Miss [Minnie] Bronson, Miss [Emily] Bissell speaking. We all went. A crowd. Mr. [Edward] Valentine, John Rutherford [sic], Eugene Massie on the platform. Judge [George L.] Christian introducing speakers. Poor speaking, but a curious dramatic evening."[83] As the *Times-Dispatch* reported, it was "the first time in the history of the Commonwealth a band of Virginia women gathered in public meeting to denounce to the world a movement which has infolded five sovereign States and is knocking at the legislative doors of as many more." Emily Bissell, a nationally known antisuffrage speaker, claimed that only one in ten women actually desired the right to vote, while the rest were either opposed or ambivalent. As the voice of all antisuffragists, she challenged suffragists to prove that more than a tiny fraction of American women desired such a momentous change in the polity.[84]

In general, the antisuffragists in Virginia operated in the same fashion as other antisuffragists did: they used the same publicity techniques, utilized the same arguments and evidence, and relied on the weight of their names to impress the public with the gravity of their opinions. They rented a booth at the state fair and distributed literature to the crowds.[85] However, the state's antisuffragists did come up with one unique innovation: they arranged for the free distribution of antisuffrage literature at several bookstores in Richmond.[86] And at least one anti in Virginia was willing to debate the suffrage question in public; Caroline Preston Davis, the field secretary for the VAOWS, challenged the ESL to a debate before the Sweet Briar College Current Events Club. Most antisuffragists avoided this kind of activism, however, because of its overtly political nature and its "unseemliness" for women who were attempting to uphold traditional womanly influence.[87]

Virginia's antisuffragists, much like antisuffragists everywhere, preferred to let women take the lead in the movement, while men organized as a support group. Some of Richmond's most prominent men were members of the state's support group, the "Men's Advisory Committee." James D. Crump was arguably the leading banker in the city; Eppa Hunton Jr. came from a family of politicians and had served as a delegate to the state convention that voted to secede from the Union; Dr. Stuart McGuire, son of famed Confederate surgeon Hunter McGuire, was a leading doctor in the community. Other men on the advisory committee bore names that evoked images of plantations, the Confederate States of America, and the First Families of Virginia: Cabell, Valentine, Pinckney, Rutherfoord, and Anderson. Like other such advisory groups, the male antisuffragists generally stayed in the background, lending their names to letterheads, chairing meetings, and writing literature, but women remained the cornerstone of the antisuffrage organizational effort.

Unlike Virginia suffragists, the VAOWS took advantage of the race issue as the debate grew heated. The idea of the black vote seemed to produce a knee-jerk reaction from white Virginians. Antisuffrage literature began to pound hard at the threat of "negro domination." The antisuffragists injected race into the debate, and it eventually moved to the forefront. By the time the state legislature debated another state suffrage amendment in 1916, white supremacy was a prominent part of the discussion.[88] For example, antisuffragists produced and widely circulated a broadside entitled "Virginia Warns Her People Against Woman Suffrage," which cited 1910 census figures to demonstrate that "the colored people would have absolute and immediate control of" twenty-nine counties.[89]

Meanwhile, the suffragists insisted that white supremacy was not, and could not be, at stake. Lila Meade Valentine defended their position: "A bogey—a mere bogey this. This is not such danger. The state constitutions provide amply for restricting the shiftless, illiterate vote. To assume that only the women of the negro race would be sufficiently interested in citizenship to register and vote is to gratuitously insult the white women of the South. To assume that white women would be less interested than white men in maintaining white supremacy is equally wide of the mark."[90] Although they did not disavow white supremacy, mainstream white suffragists in Virginia did not use it as a weapon. Their strategy of denying that white supremacy was an issue should be seen as the moderate approach.[91] Even a progressive like Mary Johnston used the statistical argument occasionally. "We are asking for the enfranchisement of women on the same terms with men," she asserted. "That means that just as you have closely restricted the negro male voter, so will the amended Constitution closely restrict the woman vote. A few educated, property owning colored women will vote, but not all the mass of the colored women."[92] In fact, the statistical argument became the foundation of official suffrage response to the threat of the black vote. In 1919, the ESL published a "Brief for the Federal Suffrage Amendment," which provided a comprehensive listing of arguments and evidence to refute the states' rights/black voter position.[93] Lila Valentine reminded Jessie Townsend to keep a copy of the Virginia constitution on hand whenever she lobbied any legislator, so she could "prove our statements."[94]

At the same time that race entered the public debate on woman suffrage, the contest was complicated by the developing factionalism of the suffragists. Virginia's suffragists held opinions ranging across the spectrum on issues of race, class, and gender. The ESL, as the state's NAWSA affiliate, desired to be the only suffrage organization in the state. But the ESL did not represent every viewpoint, and dissenters began to look for more congenial associates. Two new suffrage organizations, the Southern States Woman Suffrage Conference (SSWSC) and the Congressional Union (later the National Woman's Party), appeared in Virginia at almost the same time and began to compete with the ESL for members and support.

As state suffrage leaders, both Lila Valentine and Mary Johnston knew Kate Gordon of Louisiana, and both responded to her call for a regional suffrage organization by joining the SSWSC. Neither Valentine nor Johnston was willing to renounce the federal amendment approach as a possible option, but for the time being, they were still working for a state constitutional amendment and therefore could join the SSWSC without reservation.[95] But the relationship between the SSWSC and the ESL deteriorated rapidly, as Kate Gordon seemed determined to dictate a racial agenda in her organization. Women who were members of both organizations found themselves squeezed and pressured by the opposing forces. The SSWSC was scheduled to meet in Richmond in December 1915, and by October, Virginia suffragists were already growing nervous about Gordon's increasingly reckless use of racial rhetoric. Mary Johnston wrote Lila Valentine,

"I, no more than you, like the matter or the tone of Kate Gordon's utterances. [crossed out: Those upon the negro question, for instance, are so opposed to] In many instances they are so opposed to my own moral and mental convictions, silent and expressed, that standing to the outsider as they must do for the opinion of the Conference as a whole, I am coming to feel that I cannot much longer leave my name upon its letter heads. . . . Apparently she sees the universal situation through the window pane of Louisiana politics."[96]

Johnston eventually resigned without fanfare as vice-president of the SSWSC, although she did attend the Richmond convention. As did other mainstream southern suffragists, Johnston disagreed with Gordon on both tactics and ideology. While she never publicly challenged the state's disfranchisement laws, Johnston did argue that "as women we should be most prayerfully careful lest, in the future, that women—whether colored women or white women who are merely poor, should be able to say that we had betrayed their interests and excluded them from freedom."[97] By the time of the SSWSC convention in Richmond, Lila Valentine, in an effort to preserve unity in the suffrage ranks, remained one of the few southern suffragists still in the waning SSWSC.[98]

The SSWSC folded, but a second alternative suffrage group proved more long-lived and ultimately posed more of a challenge to the state's suffrage leadership. A state chapter of the Congressional Union provided a home for suffragists who wanted more emphasis placed on passing the federal amendment and more activism on its behalf. Many members of the ESL had been growing impatient with the cautious leadership of Valentine, including several Virginia women who had participated in the March on Washington in January of 1913.[99] Some had grown restive enough to join the Congressional Union (CU). Sophie Meredith of Richmond, vice-president of the state ESL, led the movement to establish a state branch of the CU. (Meredith was an unlikely radical, however. Her husband, Charles V. Meredith, was a prominent Richmond attorney most well known as the legal representative of the Richmond Liquor Dealers Association in its fight against Prohibition.[100] He had also been a member of the state's constitutional convention of 1901.)[101]

Lila Valentine did everything possible to prevent this rival organization from forming. She tried to convince her coworkers that "to organize a new State League in Virginia would be a tactical blunder. It would mean the confusing of the issue in the minds of the newly converted, and of those more numerous thousands to be converted. It would mean the duplication of machinery already existing, which is bad business from a practical point of view." Furthermore, she reminded Virginia's suffragists that the state leaders, "with the exception of Mrs. Charles V. Meredith, all agree that it would be unwise to further the organization of the Congressional Union in

Virginia."[102] Despite Valentine's opposition, the Congressional Union successfully organized a Virginia chapter.

Mary Johnston and Lucy Randolph Mason both attempted to mollify the factions. "I don't believe it will really or for long hurt things if Mrs. Meredith does decide to have her League," Johnston wrote to Valentine, "though perhaps she will be content with a Congressional Committee."[103] For her part, Mason encouraged tolerance of the militants, remarking that, while each faction "must work in its own way," there was "no reason why we cannot sympathize with all the workers—even those who smash windows, for great has been their provocation."[104] Nevertheless, the tensions between the two groups of suffragists continued to fester. In May 1915, Lila Valentine exploded in wrath at the discovery that CU members had been using the ESL's office and files without permission: "I find they have used our Headquarters after our office hours to further their propaganda. They made use of our typewriter and our card index of city and State members to send out the call to the Conference. . . . Such a proceeding we consider dishonorable in the extreme and if I had no other reason against the existence of their Union in Virginia, this very unscrupulous method of attaining their ends would constitute a strong one."[105]

After failing to halt the formation of the CU, Valentine then tried to limit the appeal of the new group by making it difficult for women to join both the CU and the ESL. In 1916, the ESL issued a new statement of principles and resolutions: "That in order to make plain our position, no person shall be a member of the Executive Council of the Equal Suffrage League who holds an official position in any suffrage organization which does not endorse the policy of the Equal Suffrage League of Virginia."[106] This effectively served as a purge of the Congressional Union.

Renamed the National Woman's Party (NWP) in 1917, the more militant suffragists began picketing the White House. Lila Valentine continued her counteroffensive against the militant faction, announcing that the ESL "condemns the folly of the fanatical women who are picketing the White House." She pled with the public not to "condemn the suffrage cause as a whole because of the folly of a handful of women."[107] Lucy Mason, on the other hand, urged tolerance of the picketers.

Despite the active hostility of Lila Valentine, other Virginia suffragists supported the CU/NWP, both in philosophy and in actions. While none of the Virginia members were as famous as Sue Shelton White of Tennessee, the CU/NWP did attract a number of Virginia's leading suffragists, including Elizabeth (Mrs. Dexter) Otey of Lynchburg, the daughter of Elizabeth Langhorne Lewis, whose "defection" from the ESL disturbed many in the organization. In December 1915, the CU established a state membership committee, whose directive was to recruit new members. Chaired by a Miss J. S. Jennings of Richmond, the committee made steady progress. In December 1915, the Congressional Union had 127 Virginia members; by the end of 1917, the total was up to 401. The increasing militancy of the CU/NWP did not seem to hurt recruitment: in March 1918, after the picketing of the White House began, 54 more Virginia women joined the National Woman's Party. By the end of the year, the total had risen to 504.[108]

In 1916, perhaps in an effort to prevent further defections by the more militant suffragists, the ESL withdrew its longstanding moratorium on open-air and street meetings, tactics previously considered too radical to be effective in Virginia.[109] In fact, the ESL reported that "street meetings have been held in many of the larger cities of the State with most satisfactory results."[110] Although Valentine would undoubtedly have denied it, the successes of the more radical faction effectively pushed the ESL to accept some of their tactics.

Virginia's NAWSA affiliates also found themselves moving toward support of the NWP's central goal: the federal amendment. In 1916, the state legislature considered and once again rejected a state suffrage amendment. Although the number of legislators voting for the amendment had increased since the 1914 defeat, the 40 to 52 vote in 1916 gave suffragists little hope for the immediate future of suffrage through a state amendment. The Virginia state constitution was extremely difficult to amend. It required approval by two consecutive legislatures and then a public referendum before an amendment became law. Under the circumstances, Virginia suffragists turned to the federal constitutional amendment as the best hope for their enfranchisement.[111] At the state convention in 1917, the Virginia ESL unanimously pledged its support for the federal amendment.[112] The ESL was henceforth committed to the same goal and some of the methods of the NWP.

The Ratification Contest

The turn toward the federal amendment carried a burden, however: the states' rights counteroffensive, the issue of the black vote.[113] And the antisuffragists wasted no time launching an attack, publishing a tract called "The Virginia General Assembly and Woman's Suffrage." The pamphlet concisely summarized the antisuffrage position on the federal amendment:

We are asked to—

Help trample and destroy the soul and purpose of the principle of State rights;

Disrupt and disturb to confusion and danger our local and State political and social conditions and the peaceful and contented relations of the races;

Double the number of uncertain and dangerous votes and put the balance of political power at the mercy of 165,000 colored women;

And for what?

To gratify the whims or satisfy the pleadings or escape the importunities of a small minority of women.[114]

Still, the suffragists stuck resolutely to their statistical argument. Valentine argued that the federal amendment would not—in fact could not—enfranchise masses of black women, for it "leaves absolutely intact all the other qualifications which the State Constitution provides for a voter." Therefore, even though some black women would vote, "white men and women together" would continue to be in the majority as before.[115]

The Equal Suffrage League decided not to campaign during the 1918 legislative session, since most members of the association were engaged in war work, running Liberty Loan drives, organizing Red Cross benefits, and operating wartime canteens. But equally important, the suffragists were waiting for the outcome of the congressional debate over the Nineteenth Amendment. They felt that it would be a tremendous waste of time and effort to work on a state amendment, dissipating resources needed later for a campaign to ratify the federal amendment.

After Congress sent the Anthony Amendment to the states for ratification, Virginia's legislature considered the measure on two separate occasions. The first time was during the summer of 1919, in a special session called to consider good-roads laws. At the direction of the NAWSA and in keeping with Carrie Chapman Catt's "winning plan," the Virginia ESL agreed to attempt to delay introduction of the federal amendment as long as possible in order to avoid a badly timed rejection vote. Catt and the ESL believed that a federal amendment would have a better chance of ratification in 1920, after more states had agreed to the measure and a new legislature would meet. The ESL obtained the cooperation of Woodrow Wilson and Governor Westmoreland Davis, who agreed not to pressure the legislature to introduce the amendment too soon.[116] NWP activists, however, believed that any opportunity to consider ratification should be taken, and they arranged for the introduction of the amendment. Within days, the House passed a rejection resolution, while supporters of the amendment managed to postpone the issue in the Senate.[117]

With lowered expectations, Virginia's suffragists prepared for the second ratification contest that would be held during the 1920 regular session of the legislature. The ESL appointed a ratification committee in charge of conducting the campaign. Appeals from powerful men outside the state began pouring in, as politicians like Woodrow Wilson and A. Mitchell Palmer pressured the state's legislators to ratify. When the legislature convened in

January 1920, an impressive body of suffrage supporters waited for them in Richmond, as both civic and political leaders spoke on behalf of the federal amendment.[118] The stakes were so high, tempers were flaring. Just prior to Carrie Chapman Catt's speech on behalf of ratification in the House of Delegates, "small memoranda" had appeared on the desks of the delegates claiming that Catt believed in "free love" and advocated interracial marriages. Her response that "there was a liar in Virginia," although accurate, served to inflame suffrage opponents.[119]

Two of the federal amendment's strongest opponents, Robert F. Leedy of the Senate and Thomas Ozlin of the House introduced a joint resolution rejecting it. The rejection resolution was adopted in the Senate by 24 to 10 and in the House by 62 to 22. One week later Senator J. E. West introduced a resolution to submit to the voters a state amendment. This passed the Senate by 28 to 11. A similar bill, submitting a state amendment to the voters, passed the House by 67 to 10. However, because of the peculiarities of the Virginia constitution, the state amendment would have to pass again in the assembly of 1921 before its submission to the public for approval. Thus "this vote was merely an empty compliment."[120]

Finally, the legislature voted on a third suffrage measure, which had been introduced by Senator Mapp. In order to avoid holding an emergency session later, Mapp's Qualifications Bill set up the machinery for enrolling women in the electorate should the federal amendment be ratified after the legislative session ended. It would go into effect only in the event the federal amendment received the necessary 36 ratifications. The Mapp bill passed the Senate 30 to 6, and the House 64 to 17.[121]

Resounding as the defeat of the federal amendment was, the roll call votes warrant closer scrutiny, for the question of motivation remains. Did the Virginia legislature register opposition to women voting, or to black women voting? Should the defeat of the Nineteenth Amendment be credited to the power of conservative views on gender, or to the force of white supremacy? Why did some legislators vote for one form of woman suffrage, but against another? It is not always easy to determine just exactly what moves a given representative to cast a specific vote. In the case of a single vote, it may not be possible to interpret motive. For example, John C. Blair's lone vote against the Nineteenth Amendment could have been an expression of antisuffragism, or it could have been a vote for states' rights and white supremacy. But when a delegate votes more than once, motivations can be determined more easily.

Twenty-five senators and delegates can be considered with some certainty to be antisuffragists. They voted solidly against any form of woman suffrage. They voted against both the federal and the state suffrage amendments, or they voted against both the federal amendment and the Mapp Qualifications Bill.[122] Senator Leedy, archenemy of woman suffrage in any form, believed that even the Qualifications Bill was a mistake, for "it will go out over the country that Virginia has receded from her position in this matter."[123] Another seven legislators voted against both state and federal amendments, but then approved of the Mapp bill. At the other end of the spectrum, fifteen legislators recorded their support for woman suffrage in whatever form it might take, by voting for both the federal and state amendments and then for the Mapp Qualifications Bill as well.[124] In the middle of these two positions, another group of legislators took the states' rights stance. At least sixteen men voted to reject the federal amendment but then voted in favor of the largely meaningless state suffrage amendment.[125] The Equal Suffrage League believed that these men were really antisuffragists in disguise and condemned those who insisted on a state amendment in 1920 because they supposedly had long opposed any form of woman suffrage: "The very people who are now clamoring for state action fought this state amendment publicly. . . . Those who urge state rights are frequently insincere. *They do not want suffrage at all!* The Association Opposed to Woman Suffrage is now demanding a state amendment, yet for eight years they *have been blocking that identical program.*"[126]

The suffragists' assessment may have been correct in general, but in a few cases, their judgment may have been too harsh. While it could be argued that some of these men were actually antisuffragists who voted for a worthless state amendment in order to woo future women voters, at least two of them had records of supporting state amendment in the past. R. O. Norris, representing Lancaster and Richmond Counties, had voted in favor of the state amendment in 1914 and in 1916; and Robert A. Russell, of Campbell County and Lynchburg, had voted for the state amendment in 1916.

In the votes that took place from 1912 to 1920, there was always present a small core of prosuffrage legislators. In 1912, 12 men voted for woman suffrage; in 1916 the number rose to 40; and by 1920, 95 legislators supported the (moot) state amendment. When the federal amendment was considered, however, the number dropped to 32. Conversely, there was also always present a substantial number of men who opposed woman suffrage in any form. In 1912, 88 votes were cast against the state amendment; in 1916, there were still 52 opponents; and in 1920, 21 legislators continued to oppose the state amendment, even in the nonbinding vote.

Virginia's suffragists, like their coworkers in the rest of the country, blamed the ubiquitous liquor lobby for their defeat. Lila Valentine wrote that "the only possible explanation behind the action of the house is liquor money. . . . The speaker himself was noticeably under the partial influence of liquor. Ozlin and Hudgins are partners of a Richmond German lawyer. Boschen, another bitter opponent, is notably German. Stuart, the other patron of the anti resolution, is the ex-governor's nephew, and I cannot account yet for his action."[127] But, as in other states, the suffragists' conviction that the "liquor lobby" stood behind the antisuffrage movement was only partially true. Virginia had passed a state Prohibition bill in 1914 and had ratified the federal Prohibition amendment in January 1918, both of which occurred before a single woman could vote in the state.[128] Opposition to woman suffrage based on fear of women supporting Prohibition, then, was no longer a viable argument. By 1920, the liquor question was not a central issue, even if liquor interests continued to oppose woman suffrage.

More important to most legislators were the fear of the black vote and the fear of the reform vote. Antisuffragists had pounded away on the "negro domination" theme repeatedly, knowing how well it had worked in past political campaigns. Democrats had used the race issue against William Mahone and the Readjusters in the 1880s. Conservatives had raised the "old spectre of Negro supremacy" against the Populists in 1893, despite the fact that there were no blacks in the Assembly at the time. The technique had worked again in 1900, when Democrats successfully used "negro domination" as a reason to call a constitutional convention and then as an excuse not to put the resultant constitution up for a referendum of approval.[129] This time-honored "racial strategy" worked in 1920 as well. The Democratic Party, which had spent a generation working to reduce the electorate to a manageably predictable size, had established an effective monopoly of public offices in Virginia.[130] The party saw woman suffrage as a threat to its past handiwork. As the agent of railroads and planters, industrialists and business groups, the Democratic Party acted as conservators of the economic and political status quo. Together, the planters and the industrialists had directed the economic development of the state in the postbellum period, and together they had benefited from the policies of the Democratic Party and the state government.[131] Admitting women, black or white, into the electorate threatened to increase the reform vote, and Virginia's political and economic elites would have none of it.

Woman suffrage sentiment had grown sufficiently strong in Virginia to produce a large and vigorous suffrage association. Other progressive reform movements, such as child labor restriction, had attracted support from a large number of the state's urban middle classes. But woman suffrage and other reforms failed in Virginia because of the power of the Democratic Party, which was backed by the money and assistance of planters, railroads, and industrialists. Thanks to the disfranchisement of poor Virginians, both black and white, the Democratic Party generally got what it wanted in the Progressive Era. The opposition could rarely mount a serious political challenge under these circumstances.

Epilogue

In 1920, Puralee Sampson, a fifty-eight-year-old black housewife in Richmond, was a suffragist. Her name never appeared in the newspaper, she never spoke at any suffrage rallies, she never joined a suffrage club. She is unknown to suffrage historians and has been historically invisible. Yet Puralee Sampson was so eager to vote that she went immediately to city hall to register when given the chance. She registered successfully on September 4, 1920, the first black woman to do so in the First Precinct of Madison Ward—and perhaps the first black woman to register in the entire city.[132]

Others followed: Blanch H. Wines, a thirty-year-old domestic worker, Katie D. Pratt, a fifty-three-year-old nurse, Rosa Y. DeWitt, a forty-three-year-old teacher, and others like them all registered and paid their poll taxes the first week the registration books were opened. Black leaders in Richmond did what they could to encourage women to take advantage of their new privilege: large public meetings were held at the Elks Home and St. Lukes Hall to give black women instruction on how to register. Maggie Lena Walker visited city hall several times, demanding that more officials be employed to speed up the registration process and reduce the time black women had to stand in line.[133] Ora Brown Stokes, utilizing the organizational strength of the Richmond Neighborhood Association, petitioned the registrar of voters to appoint black deputies to assist in registering the large numbers of black women desiring to vote.[134] Largely silent in the long debate over woman suffrage, these black women nevertheless expressed their opinions quite firmly at registration time. By the time the books closed, 2,410 black women had successfully registered in Richmond alone.[135]

Not surprisingly, white women registered in larger numbers. And the state suffrage association, no longer needing to agitate for ratification, converted itself into the Virginia League of Women Voters with Adele Clark as president. Like the suffrage association that preceded it, the new league was for whites only. (Clark later recalled that the suffragists "never had the nerve" to enroll black women in the LWV.)[136] Black women therefore formed their own voters league, the Virginia Negro Women's League of Voters, with Ora Brown Stokes as president. Unlike white women, who generally joined the dominant Democratic Party, most black women aligned themselves with the Republicans. Several prominent black women in Richmond joined the National Colored Republican Women.[137]

Yet this initial enthusiasm for political participation dwindled rapidly. Continuing opposition by white conservatives kept the numbers of black voters at a minimal level. Maggie Lena Walker ran for office in 1921 on the "lily-black" Republican ticket, hoping to become the superintendent of public instruction. She and an entire slate of black Republicans lost. While a few white women gained political offices and moved up the ranks of the

Democratic Party during the 1920s, the experience of black women in politics was quite different. On election day, 1925, Maggie Walker noted the following in her diary: "Out early today.—and voted an entire Democratic ticket. Why.—no reason.—just voted the ticket.—One party is as good as the other."[138] The promise of change by enfranchisement went unfulfilled.

Yet, even though they were disillusioned by the outcome of the enfranchisement of women, both black and white suffragists continued their respective club work and reform activities. It appeared that women's voluntary associations, and not politics, would continue to be the source of change in the postratification South. Women's clubs and missionary societies continued their efforts to provide services and assistance to the poor of their communities, including the continuing support of the Federation of Colored Women's Clubs for the reformatory for girls in Hampton. Coming together in a coordinating group called the Virginia Women's Council of Legislative Chairmen of State Organizations, women's groups in the state lobbied the legislature on dozens of measures during the 1920s.[139] Moreover, black and white suffragists laid plans for future cooperation. Maggie Walker noted in November 1920 that Adele Clark, "white—political leader" contacted her. Clark wanted to work together with Walker "to plan the study of citizenship."[140] Thus the interracial cooperation movement of the 1920s emerged, with veteran suffragists (black and white) taking the lead.

NOTES

1. Suzanne Lebsock, "A Share of Honour": Virginia Women 1600–1945 (Richmond: Virginia State Library, 1987), 100–102.

2. Orie Latham Hatcher, "The Virginia Man and the New Era for Women," The Nation 106 (1 June 1918): 650–51. Hatcher had recently resigned her teaching position at Bryn Mawr in order to lead the effort to increase higher educational opportunities for women in her home state of Virginia (Lebsock, "A Share of Honour," 125). On Hatcher see Belinda Bundy Friedman, "Orie Latham Hatcher and the Southern Women's Educational Alliance," Ph.D. diss., Duke University, 1981.

3. Mary Johnston, "The Woman's War," Atlantic Monthly 105 (April 1910): 559.

4. See Elizabeth Regine Varon, "'We Mean to Be Counted': White Women and Politics in Antebellum Virginia," Ph.D. diss., Yale University, 1993, ch. 3.

5. Peter J. Rachleff, Black Labor in the South: Richmond, Virginia, 1865–1890 (Philadelphia: Temple University Press, 1984), 31, 40, 97.

6. Varon, "'We Mean to Be Counted,'" epilogue; and Elizabeth R. Varon, "'The Ladies are Whigs': Lucy Barbour, Henry Clay, and Nineteenth-Century Virginia Politics," Virginia Cavalcade 42 (Autumn, 1992): 80–82.

7. Sandra Gioia Treadway, "A Most Brilliant Woman: Anna Whitehead Bodeker and the First Woman Suffrage Association in Virginia," Virginia Cavalcade 43 (Spring, 1994): 167–68.

8. Ibid., 168–69.

9. Ibid., 169–71.

10. Lebsock, *"A Share of Honour,"* 102. See also the biographical sketch of Van Lew by Hans Trefousse in Edward T. James et al., eds., *Notable American Women: A Biographical Dictionary* (Cambridge, Mass.: Belknap Press, 1971–80), 4 vols.

11. Carol Jean Clare, "The Woman Suffrage Movement in Virginia: Its Nature, Rationale, and Tactics." M.A. thesis, University of Virginia, 1968, 5; Anne Hamilton Stites, "The Inconceivable Revolution in Virginia, 1870–1920," M.A. thesis, University of Richmond, 1965, 56; and Treadway, "A Most Brilliant Woman," 171.

12. Carol Clare, "Woman Suffrage Movement in Virginia," 3; Stites, "Inconceivable Revolution in Virginia," 61; Treadway, "A Most Brilliant Woman," 172–75.

13. From the *Richmond Whig*, 1 March 1870, quoted by Varon, "'We Mean to Be Counted,'" 474.

14. Treadway, "A Most Brilliant Woman," 175.

15. Carol Clare, "Woman Suffrage Movement in Virginia," 5; Marjorie Spruill Wheeler, *New Women of the New South: The Leaders of the Woman Suffrage Movement in the Southern States* (New York: Oxford University Press, 1993), 17; Treadway, "A Most Brilliant Woman," 176.

16. See Charles Wynes's sketch in his introduction to Orra Langhorne, *Southern Sketches from Virginia, 1881–1901*, Charles E. Wynes, ed. (Charlottesville: University Press of Virginia, 1964).

17. Stites, "Inconceivable Revolution in Virginia," 63.

18. Elizabeth Cady Stanton, et al., eds., *History of Woman Suffrage (HWS)* (Rochester and New York: Fowler and Wells, 1889–1922), 3:964.

19. Ibid.

20. Ibid. Langhorne's sister lived in Culpeper.

21. *HWS* 6:669.

22. Carol Clare, "Woman Suffrage Movement in Virginia," 6.

23. J. Morgan Kousser, *The Shaping of Southern Politics: Suffrage Restriction and the Establishment of the One-Party South, 1880–1910* (New Haven: Yale University Press, 1974), 171–81; Joel Williamson, *The Crucible of Race: Black-White Relations in the American South Since Emancipation* (New York: Oxford University Press, 1984), 234–41.

24. Allen Wesley Moger, *Virginia: Bourbonism to Byrd, 1870–1925* (Charlottesville: University Press of Virginia, 1968), 131.

25. Carl Abbott, *The Evolution of an Urban Neighborhood: Colonial Place, Norfolk, Virginia* (Charlottesville: University of Virginia Institute of Government, 1975), 4–6.

26. Moger, *Virginia*, 131.

27. Raymond H. Pulley, *Old Virginia Restored: An Interpretation of the Progressive Impulse, 1870–1930* (Charlottesville: University Press of Virginia, 1968), 94–95.

28. George Talmage Starnes and John Edwin Hamm, *Some Phases of Labor Relations in Virginia* (New York: Appleton-Century, 1934), 125.

29. Moger, *Virginia*, 155.

30. Pulley, *Old Virginia Restored*, 93.

31. Elizabeth Hogg Ironmonger and Pauline Landrum Phillips, *History of the Woman's Christian Temperance Union of Virginia and a Glimpse of Seventy-Five Years 1883–1958* (Richmond: Cavalier Press, 1958), 24–40.

32. On the YWCA, see Mrs. Ralph R. Chappell and Mrs. J. W. S. Gilchrist, "A History of the YWCA of Richmond, Virginia, 1887–1937," *Fiftieth Annual Meeting of the Young Women's Christian Association* (Richmond: n.p., 1938). On the Locust Street Social Settlement, see Janie Porter Barrett, *Locust Street Social Settlement* (Hampton, Va.: n.p., 1912); on Ora Brown Stokes, see sketch in Darlene Clark Hine, ed., *Black Women in America: An Historical Encyclopedia* (Brooklyn: Carlson, 1993). On the Nurses' Settlement, see Elna C. Green, "Settlement Houses and the Origins of Social Work in the South," paper presented to Berkshire Conference, 1990.

33. Moger, *Virginia*, 155.

34. *Times-Dispatch* (Richmond, Va., 1912–1920), 13 November 1909.

35. Sara Hunter Graham, "Woman Suffrage in Virginia: The Equal Suffrage League and Pressure-Group Politics, 1909–1920," *Virginia Magazine of History and Biography* 101 (April 1993): 229–30; Carol Clare, "Woman Suffrage Movement in Virginia," 9–11; Trudy J. Hanmer, "A Divine Discontent: Mary Johnston and Woman Suffrage in Virginia," M.A. thesis, University of Virginia, 1972, 7.

36. Lloyd C. Taylor, "Lila Mead Valentine: The FFV as Reformer," *Virginia Magazine of History and Biography* 70 (October 1962): 471–81.

37. Hanmer, "Divine Discontent," 9; *Times-Dispatch*, 14 November 1909. Despite Valentine's record of conservatism and caution, Raymond Pulley called her "the state's most militant suffragette" (*Old Virginia Restored*, 150).

38. Diary entry for 5 July 1910, Mary Johnston Papers, Box 21, typescripts of diaries, Manuscripts Division, Alderman Library, University of Virginia (UVA), Charlottesville.

39. Merrie Sugg to Lila Valentine, 18 June 1912, Adele Clark Papers, Alice Tyler Correspondence, Special Collections and Archives, James Cabell Library, Virginia Commonwealth University (VCU), Richmond.

40. Elizabeth L. Lewis, 1916 annual report, Equal Suffrage League (ESL) Papers, Box 3, Virginia State Library and Archives (VSLA), Richmond.

41. Hanmer, "Divine Discontent," 21–22.

42. A search of the Sweet Briar school newspaper and yearbooks found no mention of woman suffrage being discussed openly on campus. The Current Events Club discussed the war, but not woman suffrage.

43. *Richmond Dispatch*, 8 March 1871.

44. Elizabeth D. L. Lewis to Lila Valentine, 11 October 1916, ESL Papers, Box 1, Correspondence, VSLA.

45. In 1913, for example, Valentine reported that she had given 100 public addresses on woman suffrage that year (*HWS* 6:666). Anne Stites speculates that the death of Elizabeth Van Lew in 1900 removed a powerful psychological obstacle to woman suffrage in Virginia ("Inconceivable Revolution in Virginia," 77).

46. Stites, "Inconceivable Revolution in Virginia," 113.

47. 1916 Yearbook (annual report), 14, Adele Clark Papers, VCU.

48. *HWS* 6:668.

49. 1915 annual report of Lynchburg ESL, ESL Papers, Box 3, VSLA.

50. Graham, "Woman Suffrage in Virginia," 232, 242.

51. Carol Clare, "Woman Suffrage Movement in Virginia," 32.

52. Norfolk league annual report (undated), ESL Papers, Box 5 (folder 290), VSLA.

53. Pamphlet entitled "Resolutions adopted by the Equal Suffrage League of Virginia in Convention at Norfolk, Virginia, October 25, 1912," Adele Clark Papers, ESL Correspondence, VCU. Mary Johnston chaired the resolutions committee (Hanmer, "Divine Discontent," 34).

54. Quoted by Hanmer, "Divine Discontent," 7.

55. *Times-Dispatch*, 14 November 1909.

56. Hanmer, "Divine Discontent," 18–19; *Times-Dispatch*, 11 February 1911.

57. Wheeler, *New Women of the New South*, 74.

58. Alice M. Tyler to Mary Johnston, 23 July 1910, Mary Johnston Papers, Box 7, Manuscripts Division, Alderman Library, UVA.

59. Alice O. Taylor to Mrs. Townsend, 23 January 1915, ESL Papers, Box 1, Correspondence, VSLA.

60. Lucy Randolph Mason, "The Divine Discontent" (no city listed: ESL of Virginia, n.d.), Box 7, ESL Papers, VSLA.

61. William Link has characterized southern progressive reformers, both male and female, as "paternalistic" (see William A. Link, *The Paradox of Southern Progressivism, 1880–1930* [Chapel Hill: University of North Carolina Press, 1993], 192).

62. Hampton local league, Report, December 1915, ESL Papers, Box 3, Local Leagues, VSLA.

63. Lillie Barbour to Mrs. B. B. Valentine, 7 April 1913, ESL Papers, Box 1, Correspondence, VSLA.

64. See membership list, ESL of Lynchburg, September 1914, ESL Papers, Box 4, VSLA.

65. Lila M. Valentine to Mrs. (Jessie) Townsend, 25 February 1915, ESL Papers, Box 1, Correspondence, VSLA. See also Alice O. Taylor to Mrs. Townsend, 2 February 1915, ibid. Norfolk and Richmond were the two cities with the largest labor organizations in the state during these years. See Starnes and Hamm, *Some Phases of Labor Relations in Virginia*, table 23.

66. Alice M. Tyler to Mary Johnston, 1 July 1910, Mary Johnston Papers, Box 7, Manuscripts Division, Alderman Library, UVA.

67. See Mary Johnston diary entry for 27 February 1912, Mary Johnston Papers, Box 22, Manuscripts Division, Alderman Library, UVA.

68. Lila Valentine to Mrs. C. B. Townsend, 2 July 1915, ESL Papers, Box 1, Correspondence, VSLA.

69. Johnston had once refused a request to declare publicly her support for socialism saying it "would, I think, be disastrous to my immediate cause without doing much good to yours" (quoted by Wheeler, "Mary Johnston, Suffragist," 107).

70. Hanmer, "Divine Discontent," 19, 25.

71. Mary Johnston to Lila [Valentine], 18 August 1912, Mary Johnston Papers, Box 7, Manuscripts Division, Alderman Library, UVA.

72. 1914 quote from Wheeler, *New Women of the New South*, 74.

73. Donald G. Mathews and Jane Sherron De Hart, *Sex, Gender, and the Politics of the ERA: A State and the Nation* (New York: Oxford University Press, 1990), 15.

74. *Times-Dispatch*, 20 January 1912.

75. Ibid.

76. *Times-Dispatch*, 13 January 1912.

77. Hanmer, "Divine Discontent," 29–30.

78. See diary entry for 29 March 1912, Mary Johnston Papers, Box 22, typescripts of diaries, Manuscripts Division, Alderman Library, UVA.

79. Kate Ellis Wise to Alice M. Tyler, 22 March 1912, ESL Papers, Box 1, Correspondence, VSLA.

80. *The Woman's Protest* (New York, N.Y., 1912–18), June 1914, 15.

81. Virginia Association Opposed to Woman Suffrage, *By-Laws* (Richmond: n.p., n.d.), copy found in VSLA.

82. On Seawell, see *Woman's Who's Who of America* (New York: American Commonwealth Company, 1916). For a recent analysis of Seawell's most famous novel, see Thomas L. Long, "Gendered Spaces in Molly Elliot Seawell's *Throckmorton*," paper presented at the Virginia Humanities Conference, April 1994.

83. See diary entry for 27 May 1912, Mary Johnston Papers, Box 22, typescripts of diaries, Manuscripts Division, Alderman Library, UVA.

84. *Times-Dispatch*, 28 March 1912.

85. Interview with Adele Clark, *Times-Dispatch*, 3 July 1949.

86. Copies of several pamphlets in Adele Clark Papers, VCU, contain information on the free distribution of literature at local bookstores.

87. Neither the school newspaper nor the records of the Current Events Club indicate that this debate ever occurred. Since there is no mention in the records, it is impossible to tell whether the suffragists refused the challenge or whether the Sweet Briar administration refused to host the debate.

88. Suzanne Lebsock, "Woman Suffrage and White Supremacy: A Virginia Case Study," in Nancy A. Hewitt and Suzanne Lebsock, eds., *Visible Women: New Essays on American Activism* (Urbana: University of Illinois Press, 1993), 65, 72.

89. This broadside is found in several archives and libraries. One copy is in Governor A. H. Roberts Papers, Box 26, Tennessee State Library and Archives (TSLA), Nashville, Tennessee.

90. Undated pamphlet, "Answer to Anti-Suffragists," Adele Clark Papers, VCU.

91. Lebsock, "Women Suffrage and White Supremacy," 65. Lebsock used editorials and letters to the editors in the Richmond papers to measure public opinion on white supremacy and woman suffrage. She found that only a small fraction of editorials made explicit mention of race ("Woman Suffrage and White Supremacy," 67).

92. From undated speech quoted by Hanmer, "Divine Discontent," 48.

93. Sara Hunter Graham, "Woman Suffrage in Virginia," 247.

94. Lila Valentine to Mrs. (Jessie) Townsend, 10 April 1915, ESL Papers, Box 1, Correspondence, VSLA.

95. Wheeler, *New Women of the New South*, 151–52.

96. Mary Johnston to Lila [Valentine], undated [October 1915?], Mary Johnston Papers, Box 7, Manuscripts Division, Alderman Library, UVA; Hanmer, "Divine Discontent," 47.

97. Quoted by Wheeler, "Mary Johnston, Suffragist," 109.

98. Wheeler, *New Women of the New South*, 156–57.

99. Stites, "Inconceivable Revolution in Virginia," 128. Adams and Townsend marched, as did Mary Johnston. Lila Valentine did not.

100. C. C. Pearson and J. Edwin Hendricks, *Liquor and Anti-Liquor in Virginia, 1619–1919* (Durham, N.C.: Duke University Press, 1967), 181n, 276.

101. Meredith went on to become a charter member of the Congressional Union,

became local chair of the National Woman's Party, and sponsored Alice Paul's visit to Richmond in 1918 (Stites, "Inconceivable Revolution in Virginia," 130).

102. Lila Meade Valentine to Members of ESL of Va., 1 June 1915, Mary Johnston Papers, Box 1, Manuscripts Division, Alderman Library, UVA; Wheeler, *New Women of the New South*, 152.

103. Mary Johnston to Lila Valentine, 10 May 1915, ESL Papers, Box 1, Correspondence, VSLA.

104. Quoted by Sidney R. Bland, "'Mad Women of the Cause': The National Woman's Party in the South," *Furman Studies* 26 (December 1980): 86.

105. Quoted by Wheeler, *New Women of the New South*, 244 n. 57.

106. 1916 Yearbook (annual report), 18, Adele Clark Papers, VCU.

107. From copy of Lila Meade Valentine's untitled press release of 2 July 1917, ESL Papers, Box 1, Correspondence, VSLA; Wheeler, *New Women of the New South*, 76.

108. Virginia membership lists and monthly reports, National Woman's Party Papers, ser. 2, sec. 9 (reel no. 87), Library of Congress (LC).

109. Charlotte Jean Shelton, "Woman Suffrage and Virginia Politics, 1909–1920," M.A. thesis, University of Virginia, 1969, 40.

110. 1916 Yearbook (annual report), 14, Adele Clark Papers, VCU.

111. Graham, "Woman Suffrage in Virginia," 240.

112. *HWS* 6:667.

113. Shelton, "Woman Suffrage and Virginia Politics," 47.

114. Advisory Committee Opposed to Woman Suffrage, "The Virginia General Assembly and Woman's Suffrage," undated pamphlet in Southern Pamphlet Collection, Rare Books Division, University of North Carolina-Chapel Hill.

115. Quoted by Graham, "Woman Suffrage in Virginia," 246.

116. Wheeler, *New Women of the New South*, 174; Carol Clare, "Woman Suffrage Movement in Virginia," 45.

117. Wheeler, *New Women of the New South*, 174; *HWS* 6:670.

118. *HWS* 6:671. Speakers included state auditor Roswell Page, U.S. Representatives Thomas Lomax Hunter and Howard Cecil Gilmer, Dr. Lyon G. Tyler, Carrie Chapman Catt, Elizabeth Langhorne Lewis, Kate Waller Barrett, and Lila Valentine.

119. Wheeler, *New Women of the New South*, 32.

120. *HWS* 6:672.

121. Ibid.

122. In this and the following paragraphs, roll call votes were obtained from the journals of the House and Senate for 1920. "Pairs" have not been included in the totals; only votes that were actually cast have been included. The House roll call vote for the state amendment was not recorded, and so those figures are missing from the following discussion. The twenty-five solidly antisuffragist legislators were: M. B. Booker, W. B. Cocke, J. T. Deal, W. H. Jeffreys, R. F. Leedy, W. T. Oliver, E. T. Bondurant, W. H. Buntin, T. C. Commins, J. H. Crockett, P. Dickerson, J. W. Guerrant, W. T. Hicks, J. R. Horsley, J. M. Hurt, C. C. Hyatt, W. M. McNutt, B. E. Owen, W. H. Robertson, W. B. Snidow, J. W. Stephenson, J. W. Stuart, J. B. Beverly, H. J. Taylor, G. G. Turner.

123. *Times-Dispatch*, 5 March 1920.

124. They are W. C. Corbitt, R. O. Crockett, R. L. Gordon, J. H. Hassinger,

G. W. Layman, G. W. Mapp, J. M. Parson, J. Paul, S. G. Proffit, E. L. Trinkle, J. E. West, N. L. Henley, B. F. Noland, F. Williams, and R. H. Willis.

125. The states' rights suffrage voters were: W. L. Andrews, H. F. Byrd, N. B. Early, S. L. Ferguson, W. A. Garrett, C. O. Goolrick, J. Gunn, T. Hening, S. W. Holt, M. R. Mills, J. D. Mitchell, R. O. Norris, G. T. Rison, A. W. Robertson, R. A. Russell, and J. B. Woodson.

126. "Brief for the Federal Suffrage Amendment," Box 4, Legislation Committee Records, ESL Papers, VSLA.

127. Unsigned letter to Carrie Chapman Catt, 5 September 1919, ESL Papers, Box 1, Correspondence, VSLA.

128. See Pearson and Hendricks, *Liquor and Anti-Liquor in Virginia*, ch. 14.

129. Moger, *Virginia*, 64, 110; Pulley, *Old Virginia Restored*, 72–88.

130. Pulley, *Old Virginia Restored*, 111–12.

131. Moger, *Virginia*, 64, 83.

132. Voters Registration Books, "Colored Female," 1st Precinct, Madison Ward, Richmond City Records, Voter Registrations, 1920, VSLA.

133. Maggie Lena Walker Diaries, 12, 17, 20, 23, 28 September 1920, Maggie Lena Walker National Historic Site, Richmond, Virginia.

134. Lebsock, "Woman Suffrage and White Supremacy," 84.

135. At the same time, 2,402 black men were registered (compared to 10,645 white women and 28,148 white men). Figures quoted by Lebsock, "Woman Suffrage and White Supremacy," 97 n. 57.

136. Quoted by Lebsock, "Woman Suffrage and White Supremacy," 89.

137. See "List of National Colored Republican Women Arranged According to States," undated (copied from an original in the Nannie Burroughs Papers, LC), in "Documents Pertaining to the Public Career of Maggie Lena Walker," Maggie Lena Walker National Historic Site, Richmond. Names on the list from Richmond were: Maggie Lena Walker, Catherine B. Johnson, Emeline Johnson, Margaret R. Johnson, Lillian H. Payne, and Ora B. Stokes.

138. Maggie Lena Walker Diaries, 3 November 1925, Maggie Lena Walker National Historic Site, Richmond, Virginia.

139. Lebsock, "A Share of Honour," 124.

140. Maggie Lena Walker Diaries, 20 November 1920, Maggie Lena Walker National Historic Site, Richmond.

GREGORY MICHAEL DORR

Assuring America's Place in the Sun: Ivey Foreman Lewis and the Teaching of Eugenics at the University of Virginia, 1915–1953

* * * * * * * * THE STORY OF IVEY FOREMAN LEWIS, A RE-spected professor and administrator at the University of Virginia for almost forty years, affords a remarkable window into the intellectual world of mid-twentieth-century Virginia's best-educated and forward-thinking men and women. As Gregory Michael Dorr demonstrates, the career of Dr. Lewis, Miller Professor of Biology at Virginia's flagship university, combined "institutional and social conservatism, religious liberalism, and educational Progressivism" with a scientific argument that legitimated racism, justified segregation, and influenced educational and health policy in the state for much of the twentieth century. "Ivey Lewis's career," Dorr writes, "is a case study revealing links among eugenic discussions about 'race,' scientifically justified white supremacy, and the later actions of educated whites who battled desegregation."

The eugenics movement, which emerged out of Social Darwinism and the science of genetics, reflected efforts to place assumptions about human potential on a scientific foundation. Eugenicists argued that human progress depended upon better breeding. Thus eugenics was premised upon essentialist definitions of race and was popularized by fears that racial amalgamation threatened to dilute the character of "superior" races. Eugenicists throughout the United States argued that the superiority of white northern European peoples—particularly Anglo-Saxons—was threatened by intermarriage with immigrants from other parts of the world. Southerners regarded miscegenation between whites and blacks as the primary threat. Thus Virginia tightened the legal definition of race in 1910 and two years later created the Bureau of Vital Statistics to collect statistical information on Virginians, establish their racial identity, and prevent men and women from crossing the color line in marriage. The Racial Integrity Acts of 1924 and 1930 imposed the "one drop rule," which defined as black any Virginian who had even a single black ancestor.

Lewis's teaching directly influenced generations of socially and politically prominent Virginians who absorbed his ideas in what were, accounts suggest, compelling and memorable courses. His pedagogy, moreover, was powerfully illustrative of the habits of mind of numerous contemporaries, including, as Dorr discusses, Edwin Anderson Alderman, the distinguished president of the University of Virginia. Lewis's story is thus valuable not just in its own right but also for the insight it sheds on the culture and society that molded it.

Lewis's scholarship and the content of his courses certainly reflected a Progressive Era emphasis on rationality, efficiency, science, and governance by enlightened elites. But Lewis synthesized these elements with a distinctively southern concern for racial purity, lending a strongly conservative bent to his scientific faith in human progress. Like the southern leaders who mobilized to support their particular understanding of the Civil War, as described by Fred Arthur Bailey, or who opposed woman suffrage, as portrayed by Elna Green, conservative Virginia intellectuals like Lewis defended long-established hierarchies of race, class, and gender. Deeply entrenched views on these subjects help explain why many Virginians fought school desegregation with what they termed "Massive Resistance." As Dorr notes, the ideas of men like Lewis, embedded in the curriculum of the University of Virginia, permitted educated Virginians "to reconcile their traditional southern identity . . . with their increasingly important identity as modern, progressive Americans."   *   *   *   *   *   *   *   *

*   *   *   *   *   *   *   *

In 1949 Charles W. Clark, a colonel in the Mississippi National Guard, confessed to his former biology professor, "The present pushing by the negro has me extremely worried. I cannot well remember the post–World War I period, but it seems to me that the negroes were pushing then; and that in dealing with its problem the South had articulate support from some first class people in other sections of the country— notably the author Lothrop Stoddard." Alarmed by African American civil rights militancy, Clark sought to discredit blacks, reporting that during World War II, he had seen "plenty of them [blacks], both in and out of combat" and, compared to white soldiers, blacks "were just what one would expect—niggers!" Convinced of the biological inequality of races, Clark complained that a recent news article had asserted "that all races are 'genetically equal,'" scoffing, "whatever that may mean." He viewed the article as a political reaction to the Holocaust and exclaimed, "Truly the backswing from Mr. Hitler over to the opposite extreme is something to behold!" The suggestion that the races are biologically equal aroused in Clark fears that "the worst is yet to come."[1]

While Charles Clark's reaction may be seen as a confirmed racist's reflex response, closer examination of his letter suggests a more complex origin. Clark's letter hints at how higher education allowed elite southerners to reconcile their traditional southern identity—limned in terms of racial, class, and gender hierarchies—with their increasingly important identity as modern, progressive Americans.[2] Clark's references to Lothrop Stoddard, Hitler, and genetics harked back to his undergraduate training at the University of Virginia where he learned "scientific" white supremacy. At Virginia, Clark—like students before and after him—had studied the doctrines of eugenics, a science dealing with the improvement of hereditary qualities, and, specifically, with human racial purity.

For thirty-eight years, from 1915 until 1953, Virginia students studied eugenics with Clark's correspondent, Dr. Ivey Foreman Lewis. As Miller Professor of Biology and Dean of the University of Virginia, Lewis taught that heredity governed all aspects of life, from anatomical form to social organization. Throughout his career, Lewis never wavered in his advocacy of eugenics. While the bulk of scientific opinion changed, Lewis continued teaching heredity and writing about educational theory based upon principles developed in the 1910s.[3] Many of Lewis's devoted students adopted his racialist thinking, and some of them then shaped the opinions of white Virginians—and white southerners in general—about race and society. Term papers written by students in Lewis's classes and his subsequent correspondence with them, especially from the years surrounding the 1954 Supreme Court decision, *Brown* v. *Board of Education*, preserve glimpses of how his students and associates accepted the eugenicist's lessons that race-mixing meant the destruction of civilization. Ivey Lewis's career is a case study revealing links among eugenic discussions about "race," scientifically justified white supremacy, and the later actions of educated whites who battled desegregation.[4]

Beginning in the Progressive Era, eugenics provided generations of educated, self-consciously modern Virginians with a new method of legitimating the South's traditional social order. Modern eugenics began in 1883, when Sir Francis Galton, cousin of Charles Darwin, coined the word to denote "the science of improving the stock."[5] Galton's British followers promoted "positive eugenics" by encouraging procreation among the best stock. American eugenicists emphasized race along with class, and then genetics and "negative eugenics." After three scientists—experimenting independently and simultaneously in plant hybridization—rediscovered Mendelian genetics around 1900, American eugenicists explained social mobility as a function of genetics.[6] In their eyes, the coincidence of "favorable" genes from otherwise "inferior" parents accounted for the careers of American self-made men *and* the existence of "superior strains" within races. Eugenicists assumed that success was a recessive hereditary factor; therefore, most people were doomed to mediocrity or failure. Occasionally, however, two mediocre people might produce a successful offspring. Since races were also ranked by heredity, only rarely would the best of a low race equal the best of a high race. Although American eugenics maintained its own class dynamic, race remained a focus for American eugenical policy. British eugenicists' class bias reflected the stable class structure of British society. Americans emphasized race—a hierarchy that most people wanted to maintain—while they lessened the emphasis on class as a concession to the American democratic tradition.[7] American eugenicists extended Galton's association of "genius" and success even as they adopted his belief that other races were intellectually inferior to whites. Assuming intelligence to be the Mendelian trait that determined success, eugenicists applied intelligence tests as measures of underlying genetic worth. Thus, by definition, smart successful people (who were almost all white) had good genes, and ignorant failures had bad genes.

The marriage of Mendelian genetics and intelligence testing "proved" what scientists had long suspected: heredity produced qualitative differences between classes and races that transcended culture or environment.[8] As a result, American eugenicists accepted positive eugenics but also vigorously promoted negative eugenics—the elimination of "defective germ plasm" through sterilization, immigration restriction, institutional segregation, and bans on interracial marriage.[9]

Though Virginia's scientific racism had originated in Thomas Jefferson's 1785 *Notes on the State of Virginia*, eugenics was viewed, in the early years of the twentieth century, as cutting-edge racial science—as opposed to outmoded theories based on craniometry and rudimentary comparative anatomy.[10] Eugenicists' race- and class-based explanation of the social order fed Americans' growing nativism and racism and echoed white southern rhetoric regarding racial purity. Simultaneously, eugenics eased the merging of Virginians' regional identity with a new overarching identity of so-called pure, 100 percent Americanism. Scholars at elite northern institutions emphasized whiteness and Anglo-Saxon heritage in defining the "American race."[11] This definition resonated with the traditional white southern identity. Southern eugenicists applauded their northern compatriots who argued for the preservation of this distinctly American race. Fears of miscegenation and the resulting offspring alarmed northerners and buttressed southern concerns about both African Americans and the eugenically tainted "shiftless, ignorant, worthless class of anti-social whites of the South."[12] Eugenicists characterized the American melting pot as "race suicide."[13] Subsequently, American eugenicists, North and South, advanced notions of racial purity, using their theories about race mixing to shape public policy. Southern eugenicists drew analogies between racial segregation and northern measures like limiting immigration, institutionalizing mental patients, and passing restrictive marriage laws.

Confronting the tensions between Old South traditions and New South dislocations, eugenics mediated between Progressive liberalism and the self-consciously "backward" Agrarian reaction.[14] Eugenics provided a potential solution for nettlesome social problems—a way to dispense with poor white trash and the so-called Negro Question while ushering in modern liberal-industrial society in one motion. As a modern science, eugenics legitimized dominant social prejudices by justifying widely held beliefs on the basis of apparently objective, scientific observations.[15] The racism of eugenics reinforced the social hierarchy that elevated the elite, extolled sedate whites as fit, and considered troublesome whites, poor whites, and all others to be genetic defectives in need of control. The eugenicists' appeal to scientific expertise to achieve "social efficiency" mirrored both liberal and conservative reform movements during the Progressive Era.[16] Eugenic theories reconciled many whites to invasive state intervention in defense of whiteness. Although eugenic legislation challenged traditions of local control, it sounded many of the major chords of southern society: white supremacy, paternalism, and the myth of a predatory, atavistic African American population. Many Americans believed that, through government action in support of eugenic policies, the nation's population would become racially and democratically homogenous.[17]

Progressive southerners working for the socioeconomic advancement of the South echoed all of these ideas. Virginia, a state with a history of control by "enlightened" elites, embraced both the Progressive and eugenics movements. Not coincidentally, the heyday of eugenics and its southern ascendance coincided with the presidency of Woodrow Wilson, a Virginia-born Progressive, and the South's resurgence in national politics.[18] Progressive state intervention projected the visage of a benevolent southern patriarchy.[19] Wilson's southern cabinet members took steps to ensure the rehabilitation of the South through federal programs. The United States Public Health Service (USPHS) reflected this effort, as northern and southern politicians and eugenicists extolled government intervention in the name of public health. In 1920 Wilson—at the behest of Secretary of the Treasury Carter Glass, a fellow Virginian—appointed Hugh Smith Cumming, a University of Virginia alumnus and eugenics supporter, to the office of Surgeon General. In 1932 Cumming, along with Taliaferro Clark and Raymond A. Vonderlehr, who were also Virginia alumni and eugenicists, established and implemented the infamous Tuskegee Study of Untreated Syphilis in the Male Negro.[20] These three men had been taught by the University of Virginia's former chairman of the faculty and professor of medicine, Paul B. Barringer, who believed strongly in the hereditary inferiority of African Americans and established the precedent for eugenical thought at the university. Barringer's successor in the medical school, Professor of Anatomy and Histology Harvey Ernest Jordan, taught eugenics before and during Lewis's tenure. Jordan wrote extensively on eugenics, coauthoring the 1914 book, *War's Aftermath: A Preliminary Study of the*

Eugenics of War, with David Starr Jordan (a distant cousin), president of Stanford University and a preeminent American eugenicist. Harvey Jordan and Lewis became fast friends and lived as neighbors on the university campus. Together, they advised President Edwin Anderson Alderman on the hiring of three more eugenicists: anatomist Robert Bennett Bean (1916), pediatrician Lawrence Thomas Royster (1921), and geneticist Orland E. White (1927).[21] Alderman had ties to the Aristogenic Association, a group of elite Americans who believed that "[white] Race survival and advance depend much on leadership. . . . The study and understanding of the biological characteristics of leaders is therefore of importance."[22] The study of eugenics flourished in such congenial surroundings. Lewis organized the university eugenicists, and together they promoted the passage of Virginia's two eugenic laws of 1924.[23]

Between 1904 and his death in 1931, President Edwin Anderson Alderman and his confidant Ivey Foreman Lewis endeavored to modernize the University of Virginia while simultaneously conserving its distinctly southern heritage. Modernization was an ambitious undertaking, for Virginia stood—in the southern imagination if not always in fact—as the flagship university of the South.[24] Ivey Lewis joined the faculty of the University of Virginia in 1915 when, he wrote, "the strong wind from Germany, first let loose by Johns Hopkins in 1876, blew through the ancient halls of American universities, and with the emphasis on research, transformed every graduate school in the country."[25] Lewis became one of Alderman's chief advisors. Lewis's guidance combined with the larger social currents in the New South—including institutional and social conservatism, religious liberalism, and educational Progressivism—to modernize the university. Such institutional reforms implied that university research would facilitate social change; ultimately, they merely reinforced the status quo by modernizing its basis.

Born in 1882 and reared in Raleigh, North Carolina, Ivey Lewis's forebears had strong southern roots, of which he was immensely proud. One of five children of an established doctor, Lewis grew up as the South was systematically disfranchising African Americans.[26] Although Jim Crow's grip did not absolutely preclude cross-racial interaction, it sought to manage and administer such contacts and thereby taught children about racial hierarchy.[27] More significantly, Lewis matured as class tensions rocked the southern white population. Battles over voting rights increased the strain among southern whites, fracturing racial solidarity that was often assumed by earlier white supremacists. At the same time, however, systematic racism became a *national* phenomenon. America's 1898 victory in the Spanish American War merged nationalism with nativism and racism.[28] These social currents shaped Lewis's personal development before he entered college.

Lewis enrolled at the University of North Carolina, receiving bachelor's and master's degrees in biology in 1902 and 1903 respectively. Captivated by biological research, Lewis went on to Johns Hopkins University, where he studied with William Keith Brooks, a famed cellular anatomist, and Herbert Spencer Jennings, a moderate advocate of eugenics. In 1908 Lewis completed his Ph.D. in biology with a concentration in botany. His star rose rapidly as he taught at Randolph Macon College for four years and moved to the University of Wisconsin in 1913. Churning out publications, Lewis occupied the Smithsonian Table at the Stazione Zoologica, a very prestigious research post in Naples, Italy, and then was elected a fellow of the American Association for the Advancement of Science (AAAS) in 1914.[29]

In early 1914 Lewis approached President Alderman regarding an opening in the University of Virginia's biology department. During correspondence about the position, Lewis provided Alderman with advice that allowed the president both to modernize the biology department and to retain its endowment, the Miller Fund.[30] On the basis of this interaction, Alderman developed abiding respect for Lewis. "I am more and more convinced of his splendid fitness for our work," Alderman wrote Dean James M. Page.[31] Page's own research into Lewis's background corroborated the president's opinion. Samuel C. Hatcher, vice president of Randolph Macon College, wrote Page, "While with us, he [Lewis] made his department so interesting that our students were enthusiastic for classes under him. He is also a valuable asset to any faculty in that while he is alert and progressive . . . he does not project himself in an unpleasant way."[32] Lewis displayed the tact and diplomatic skill that would characterize the rest of his career and his promotion of eugenics. Moreover, Lewis's southern heritage made him an attractive candidate. "Lewis is a very fine man and being one of our own people, I think you would like him better than anybody whom you could get who is not one of us," averred Robert E. Blackwell, president of Randolph Macon. Blackwell added, "he is a man of strong religious character, and was a leader in the Episcopal Church while here. I should like very much to have him back in the state." Alderman agreed, writing of Lewis in neo-eugenic terms, "He is a gentleman by birth and breeding, and a cultivated gentleman."[33] Lewis became the Miller Professor of Biology in September 1915.[34] Offering Lewis a hefty starting salary of $3,000 per year "to be increased . . . to the maximum sum paid our oldest professors [$3,500]," Alderman also dangled the department chairmanship, complete control over the curriculum, and exemption from summer school duties to allow Lewis to focus on research.[35] "I would not want you to come unless there would be opportunity for you to do research work," Alderman wrote. He continued, "There is nothing I welcome more than the thought of someone doing real research work." On February 20, Lewis assured Alderman that he would accept the position.[36]

With this Progressive modernization of its biology department, the University of Virginia entered the race toward national preeminence. Alderman and the Board of Visitors committed Virginia to becoming a modern research institution while maintaining the university's place in the vanguard of southern higher education. C. Vann Woodward described Alderman and his contemporaries as highly principled men whose vision "included no basic alteration of social, racial, and economic arrangements."[37] Alderman wanted to move the University of Virginia into the top tier of American universities, but he was not willing to compromise the university's southern heritage. With the hiring of Ivey Lewis, Alderman gained an ally in his quest.

Many other university presidents shared Alderman's desire to mold their institutions into research centers. Indeed, the public increasingly recognized that an important relationship existed among universities, science, and society. As the Charlottesville *Daily Progress* reported, "Nothing is more evident than the fact that modern life . . . finds its basis in science. . . . The scholar versed in the great achievements of the past and possessing exact and extensive knowledge of modern science, can interpret modern life as no one else is able to do. . . ."[38] The *Daily Progress* expressed the emerging faith in the ability of university-trained experts to improve society. Alderman felt similarly: "The ultimate mission of the state university in America is to supply training" to experts, who would then study "the actual conditions of life in the state which the university exists to aid and strengthen."[39] Alderman's ideal perfectly fit the Progressive Era ethos of scientific positivism. Alderman and Lewis, however, vacillated between actually applying expertise to effect social change and merely publicizing their intention to do so. Lewis and Alderman's responses to two issues—the controversy surrounding the Scopes trial in Dayton, Tennessee, in 1925 and the value of sociological studies of the race problem—reveal this dilemma.

Lewis and Alderman defended science against fundamentalist religion's attack on the theory of evolution in the Scopes trial, and Alderman's correspondence reveals his campaign to protect the university from challenges by creationists.[40] As early as 1922 Lewis responded to a Virginian who had asked about his position by affirming that the biology department accepted the Darwinian theory of evolution. For Lewis, science was a natural extension of God's goodwill toward humanity: science and religion were complementary, not antagonistic, modes of thought.[41] He believed that God allowed humans to discover natural laws in order to improve their condition on earth. Hereditary determinism, a natural law created by God and discovered by science, could be controlled by man through the science of eugenics. Eugenic control would result in a society of "fitter" individuals who would operate intelligently and efficiently, thereby easing the strain of survival. Such an efficient society would have the time and resources for cultivating morality through religion and education, making society more humane. A eugenically improved population would be better equipped to receive moral instruction, for there would be no "moral delinquents."[42] Lewis told students that in such a society humanity could then refine the "higher things in life," such as "courage, honor, a descent [sic] reserve, gentleness, magnanimity, pride in ideals."[43] This theme of moral improvement following eugenic advance informed all of Lewis's writing. Lewis's eugenics harmonized with a Protestant ethic of introspection, upright living, and service to one's community.[44] The address celebrating his twenty-five years of service to the university effectively captured Lewis's eugenic approach: "with scientific knowledge of the laws of life you have brought to your duties as Dean of the University a broad and strong capacity to deal with the human problems present in the lives of your students."[45] Lewis regarded the university as a microcosm of America, hence fit for eugenic aid.[46]

As scientists and social theorists debated whether heredity or environment controlled human destiny, the so-called nature/nurture question, Lewis stood convinced of nature's ultimate power. While Lewis appreciated religion's "environmental" ability to improve society's morals, he remained deeply skeptical of sociology's proposed environmental interventions— settlement houses, slum clearance, and economic amelioration. Only sociologists who viewed society as the result of biological laws seemed correct to Lewis. He denied the objectivity of sociologists who believed that environmental conditions influenced social structure, dismissing such theorists with the epithet "sentimental." For Lewis, these thinkers simply could not face the cold, hard facts of biology. These views applied not only to class issues but also to considerations of race. Lewis's and Alderman's positions regarding the race problem reflected their biological, scientific, and, to their minds, objective understanding of sociology. Their Progressive "objectivity," however, did not entirely transcend their regional prejudices. In December 1915 Alderman wrote that "the right adjustment of relations between the white man and the colored man in American life, still remains perhaps our most complex and momentous public question." Although he felt that southerners had acted with "a great deal of instinctive wisdom," it was time that "patient, wise, scientific, just men should labor at the problem and seek to place it where it belongs among the great economic and sociological questions of the time." Alderman called for scientific study, not amelioration, of an intractable problem. His use of bloodless phrases like "the right adjustment" of race relations reveals his faith in control by experts. Rather than hoping for a solution, people "should be grateful for the fact that the negro has somehow gotten off the southerner's nerves and out of the northerner's imagination."[47] Although Alderman championed university reform, his studied deliberation regarding the race question protected the social status quo.

Similarly, Lewis's hereditarianism left him hostile toward environmental solutions to the race problem. As Lewis told University of Virginia students in a 1924 speech reported by the New York *Times*, "The one clear message that biological investigation has brought as its gift to the thought of the twentieth century is that the idea of environment molding something out of nothing is sheer nonsense." Lewis continued, "This disproved theory of the creative environment has been put forth in siren tones until the idea of the great American melting pot, into which one can put the refuse of three continents and draw out good, sound American citizens, has reached wide acceptance. It is simply and perilously false." Lewis, like Alderman, sought to remove racial issues from the arena of public debate, placing the race question within the purview of educated, scientific elites like himself; to do otherwise courted failure. "We [Americans] have undertaken the direction of human evolution," Lewis said. "At the present moment we are bungling the job." Decrying the notion of the melting pot as "simply and perilously false" from a biological standpoint, Lewis made the eugenical contention, "The purity of the white race in America [which] we regard as a basal necessity for the maintenance of the heritage which we have received," risked destruction.[48] Lewis staunchly maintained that heredity and racial purity, not environmental intervention, controlled human and social evolution.

Correspondence between Alderman and Lewis concerning qualifications for a professor of sociology reveals Lewis's bias and its effect on the university. Arguing against one nominee's appointment, Lewis opined, "The Social Sciences suffer in public estimation from dilettante-ism, and I think it would be a mistake to put in as full professor of sociology any man who has not been thoroughly trained in the best thought of his times in theory, principle and practice of his subject."[49] Lewis argued the skeptic's position: unsure of sociology's value, he wanted a professor with a solid empirical—and for Lewis that meant biological—background. Rather than condoning sociology's environmentalist posture, Lewis answered the call of the *Eugenical News* and joined the Virginia State Education Committee of the American Eugenics Society. This committee sought to educate Virginians about the hereditary basis of social structure.[50] Alderman ultimately concurred with Lewis and appointed Floyd N. House, a rigorously trained social scientist, to the professorship in sociology.[51]

Comparing Lewis's actions in the 1920s with the opinion he expressed in March 1948 vividly demonstrates the consistency of his beliefs. Responding to a eugenics-based query regarding race relations, Lewis stated:

> There is a lot of sap-headed thinking about it [race as it relates to heredity], mostly based on the silly notion that all men are brothers and there-

fore alike in their potentialities. Actually, there is no biological principle better established than that of inequality of races, and yet sociologists, especially the Jewish ones, are loud and effective in their denial of any racial differences, even saying there is no such thing as race. They deride and laugh to scorn such books as Madison Grant's "Passing of the Great Race."[52]

Lewis revered authors like Grant, Lothrop Stoddard, and Virginia's own Earnest Sevier Cox. These men were America's primary eugenical propagandists, sounding the racial alarm in provocative books entitled *White America, Teutonic Unity, The Rising Tide of Color Against White World-Supremacy,* and *Revolt Against Civilization.*[53] These works became texts for Ivey Lewis's course and his personal ideological guides. Lewis displayed little tolerance for individuals or methodologies that denied what he considered self-evident scientific fact. Both his teaching and his ruminations about educational policy manifest this intolerance.

Lewis became an influential figure in Virginia education, rising to become the dean of the College of Arts and Sciences at the university and traveling throughout the state speaking to educators. Two main ideas characterize all of Lewis's writing on education. First, education should "make good and useful citizens." Second, the inherent, hereditary inequality of students limited educators' ability to achieve the first goal. Regarding education's constraints, Lewis wrote:

> It seems to me that the greatest discovery of the twentieth century is the establishment of the laws of heredity as they relate to human beings. . . . Not even the most round eyed believer in the doctrine of equality, even in the nineteenth century when the doctrine ran wild, could imagine that such things as skin color or eye color can be produced by training, but it is still a comparatively new idea that the laws of heredity hold also for mental traits and that human destiny is predetermined to a much greater extent than has been supposed by hereditary factors. The very best education can do is to cultivate and intensify the natural capacities.[54]

Lewis believed that students had an inborn potential, a capacity that education could not enlarge.[55] He advocated education for its socializing aspect—it integrated individuals into society at the level determined by their heredity. In light of these beliefs, Lewis concluded: "We must reword the bold statement to read that all men are created equal only in the sense that all have a right to equality of opportunity and equality before the law. Actually all men are created unequal in their hereditary equipment and potentialities, in their natures. Given identical training, the same food, the same home environment, the fact remains that people look different, act differently, and are different."[56]

Thus, it seemed essential to Lewis that education target a student's innate potential as gauged by intelligence tests. Without such conscious direction of students, "Compulsory education laws force the offering of such a curriculum that all can, if not profit by it, at least endure it. This means that the level of achievement must be graded down to the lowest common denominator." Decades before anyone used the term, Lewis described the "dumbing down" of education and vigorously advocated "tracking"—placing students into rigid vocational, general, and college-preparatory programs based on psychometric measurements that purported to indicate inborn ability, affinity, and intelligence.[57] Applied racially, these tracks limited blacks to manual education. In his retirement address before the AAAS, "Biological Principles and National Policy," Lewis invoked Jefferson's ideal of a pyramidal educational system that reserved higher education for the elite and for a few "scholars raked from the rubbish." Jefferson, in Lewis's view, "accepted the fact that many could not or would not take an education beyond the 3 Rs, and proposed that . . . higher education be reserved for the aristoi who could profit by it. Strange doctrine for the apostle of democracy!" While Lewis advocated scientific reform of education and society, he posited changes that failed to challenge, and indeed actively reinforced, existing inequality.[58]

The three strands—educational Progressivism, religious liberalism, and social conservatism—that were wound together in eugenics created an ideological tether that anchored Ivey Lewis to contemporary social trends within Virginia and its state university. The conditions present in Virginia predisposed the state to accept eugenics. Virginia's experience differs from that which Edward J. Larson depicts for the Deep South in *Sex, Race, and Science: Eugenics in the Deep South.* The factors that Larson argues retarded eugenic development in the Deep South—religious fundamentalism, lack of higher education and of research in the biologic sciences, and low rates of literacy—applied less to Virginia.[59] Virginia's religious culture tended, as evidenced by the muted reaction to the Scopes trial, toward a more moderate strain; though deeply religious, the state was not rife with the organized fundamentalism evident further South. The University of Virginia, which historically stood atop the South's educational structure, modernized far earlier than institutions in the Deep South, which could claim only Tulane as a research university.[60] As a result of its status, the University of Virginia was an epicenter of eugenical thought, closely linked with the national eugenics movement and with the Virginia antimiscegenation movement and tied to the state mental health professionals who promoted eugenic sterilization.[61] And, coupling the lack of a strong populist impulse in Virginia's political culture with the large number of university graduates in the state assembly, elites schooled in eugenics had a distinct advantage in affecting social policy.[62] Thus, Virginia and its university provided fertile intellectual soil for the growth and propagation of eugenical seed planted by Lewis's teaching.

Lewis's course, Biology C1: Evolution and Heredity, like the man who taught it, attempted to link evolution, heredity, and eugenics together as a scientific method for social improvement. Its content is described in the university catalogue as "Evolution, the theory and its history; the principles of heredity and their application to human problems."[63] The content of the course is apparent from a few surviving lectures, two of Lewis's own notebooks—including his topical bibliography—as well as a student notebook containing lecture notes, some final exams, and twenty-seven student term papers.[64]

The course had a distinct sociological flavor, albeit a deterministic and not environmental sociology. Lewis emphasized reading, and which books and articles he considered important is evident from his topical bibliography and his notations in students' papers. The most frequently required texts for the course appear to have been Charles Darwin's 1859 *Origin of Species* and Paul Popenoe and Roswell Hill Johnson's 1918 book, *Applied Eugenics*, although by 1947 Lewis had also been using Horatio H. Newman's *Evolution, Genetics and Eugenics*, first published in 1921.[65] Surveying the books that Lewis listed in his bibliography under the topics "Birth Control," "Birth Rates," "Color Problem," "Eugenics," "Immigration Laws," "Mentally Deficient Classes," "Negro," and "Population Problem" reveals a preponderance of eugenical opinion. The few works that are not overtly eugenic tend to be neutral—in the sense that they emphasize heredity and environment as coequal determinants of human and social development. The only book listed there that might be considered anti-eugenic is W. E. B. Du Bois's *Souls of Black Folk* (1903), which appeared under the "Negro" heading—along with both Earnest S. Cox's and Madison Grant's volumes. In the bibliographies of the students' papers (and on some of the book lists in the 1953 final exams) Lewis placed a check mark next to certain books and articles. In every case, the checked entry was a eugenic or race-biased text. These works established race as both a biological category and "an explicit and eloquent expression of elitist attitudes." This deeply conservative, racist, and elitist attitude, tempered by a patronizing sense of noblesse oblige, colored Lewis's writings on education and his classroom lectures.[66]

The dogmatic character of Lewis's eugenical teaching rings out of one of his surviving lectures: "The two forces that mold the individual are heredity and environment. Both are essential but it has long been a question which is the more important. . . . In the 18th century the view was generally held that heredity played little part. . . . This thought was reflected by Jefferson when he said, 'All men are created equal.' . . . In the 20th century an abundance of experimental evidence proves that the large part ascribed to environment was mostly imaginary and that the capacity and natural bent of an individual are due to heredity."[67]

Lewis, referring to Thomas Jefferson, set up the humanistic, egalitarian reasoning of the Enlightenment for a fall.[68] Most American eugenicists agreed that Jefferson's statement was utopian and applied only in regard to man's equality before the law. In gauging the relative importance of heredity (nature) and environment (nurture) in forming the human being, mainline eugenicists like Lewis all emphasized nature. He stated later in the lecture, "Mentally, morally and physically the hand of heredity lies heavily on us all. We know now that, while education can bring out the best in the child, it cannot create ability or aptitude. In training young people therefore, parents must discover and develop those traits which a child inherits or naturally possesses and not attempt to force the growth of qualities which are not naturally present."[69] Believing left-handedness to be hereditary, Lewis cited stammering, psychoses of a severe nature, and inferiority complex as possible results of parental attempts to force a hereditarily left-handed child to use its right hand. Given Lewis's relentless hereditarian emphasis, it seems unlikely that he presented any countervailing, environmental arguments.[70]

Lewis regarded as "sentimentalists" those who viewed racial inequalities as the result of prejudice rather than biology. In a 1924 letter written to Earnest S. Cox upon the publication of *White America*, he lamented the "drag of the negro on our civilization" and criticized "the large class of the falsely sentimental . . . who see in him [the African American] one who by his cheap and willing service helps to relieve the daily burden of living." Lewis further condemned the "conspiracy of silence" that surrounded racial amalgamation, calling it "the greatest damage." Thanking Cox for "bringing home the truth to the minds of white people," he promised to bring the book to the attention of his students.[71] Lewis not only brought Cox's book to his students' attention but also had Cox address the class in 1924.[72]

The prevailing cultural atmosphere of segregation, racism, and nativism seems to have prepared students to accept Lewis's teaching. They expressed detailed opinions on race and amalgamation in their term papers, which reflect the conservative, elitist beliefs embodied in Lewis's writing on education and his teaching of eugenics. Considering the term papers alone, however, it is difficult to evaluate the degree to which the students actually held the expressed beliefs or merely dissembled, making an argument that they knew appealed to Lewis. One thing is certain: the papers' repetition of key eugenic themes, such as faith in Mendelian genetics, the scientific proof of "Nordic" superiority, the crisis faced by the white race, and the economic and social burden that inferior people placed on society all reflect Lewis's beliefs and teaching and help to provide a detailed picture of his course and its tone.

The twenty-seven term papers from Ivey Lewis's Biology C1 course cover the full spectrum of eugenics-related topics. From "Birth Control" to "Quality as a Biological Problem: Intelligence," the papers approach their subjects from a conventional eugenical standpoint. Only two papers waver in concluding that some form of eugenical reform was necessary.[73] The papers all accept that heredity, not environment, determines human potential. "Good environment will give good heredity a chance to express itself; but you cannot produce greatness from poor heredity."[74] The papers also contend that modern society, through medical intervention and humanitarian sentiment, succeeded in short-circuiting natural selection. As a result, "The superior strata of society are dying out while the lower increase causing a regression in stock which results in the downfall of civilization."[75]

A millennial tone characterizes all the papers, as if the students viewed mankind facing a choice between progress and catastrophe. Eugenics offered the solution, for "[t]he betterment of the individual [in genetic and socioeconomic terms] follows from the betterment of the group via eugenics. The eugenist has an *idealistic*, broader view of humanity than the doctor's individual, humanitarian view."[76] The papers reflect mainline eugenicists' arguments that only by placing concern for society over concern for the individual could America avoid race suicide.

In advancing the race suicide thesis, the papers reveal elitism and concern with issues of class, political economy, and race. The papers defend the notion that hierarchy in society is biologically determined by heredity. According to the students, the best hereditary stock resided largely in the upper class, proving that success was an index of hereditary gift rather than environmental conditioning. Differential birth rates—more births in the lower than the upper class—presaged dire consequences. William Bennett Bean, whose father Robert Bennett Bean, a leading eugenicist, was on Virginia's medical faculty, argued, "Sterilization is not yet general enough to be really effective. The result is that the lower classes and more especially the positively undesirable elements of our society are increasing more rapidly than the so called upper class. This points definitely to race extinction."[77] Another student expressed the most chilling affirmation of eugenics found in any of these papers: "In Germany Hitler has decreed that about 400,000 persons be sterilized. . . . The law is a result of the German ideal of a sound mind and a sound body. The wide scope of the law may permit it to be used politically, but the eugenic results will outweigh any evil practice, if any."[78] Student papers, like the eugenical propagandists' tracts, masked cultural value judgments as scientific analyses of "objective" conditions. Lewis's lectures—and the texts he recommended—lent the imprimatur of scientific authority and value-neutrality to students' prejudices. Thus, the students' papers remained congruent with leading eugenic theories, Lewis's expressed opinions, and their own interest in strengthening the segregated, stratified South.

Perhaps these responses are not surprising. After all, as college students in an era when higher education was far from universal, these students probably identified themselves as elite—whether or not their families' economic background qualified them as such—and found it more comforting to believe their social position resulted from superior genetic make-up rather than social prejudice and class control. Such a teleology provided these students with a scapegoat for social problems, particularly evident in the papers that were written during the Great Depression. Four papers strongly maintained that the economy did not fail because of reckless speculation by the worthy upper class. Rather, the economic order toppled as a result of the destabilizing effect of a massive influx of inferior European workers combined with the disproportionate procreation of indigenous lower classes and feebleminded.[79] All of the papers concerning eugenic sterilization noted its economic benefits: sterilization reduced the number of unfit under state care, thereby allowing the safe return to society of economically productive, sterilized individuals. With the source of the unfit effectively destroyed, the larger community no longer bore the economic burden of institutionalizing any but the most severely retarded and insane. However, the students contended, without eugenics society would indeed be dragged down by the "under-man," and the under-man was increasingly of swarthy complexion and feeble mind.[80] Thus, the students' perceptions of the race problem reinforced their fears of class differences and feeblemindedness. While most scholars characterize eugenics as suffering from a class bias, race remained the primary concern in America and the South, and class issues formed a significant undercurrent.

Negrophobia and a strong undercurrent of racism spurred students' facile application of eugenic theory to racial issues and the "Negro Problem." Within the category of race, some of the papers dealt primarily with the different white "races."[81] This assumption reflected both Lewis's and the authors' preoccupation with sex across the various "color lines." "The fear of Negro assimilation—bringing with it a distracting force from the standpoint of intelligence—is dreadful enough," wrote one student, but, "the prospect of recombination of poor qualities resulting from immigrant intermarriage . . . is just as bad."[82] Assimilation with inferiors—of whatever color—promised dysgenic consequences for the race. Black assimilation, however, posed the worst possibility of all. Judging from the six papers dealing with the so-called Negro Problem, these students perceived it as being "of immense importance to the future of the United States."[83] One student agreed that "gradual amalgamation" was a "great American problem" and that racial mixture "certainly injures or destroys the more specialized qualities of the white race."[84] To establish black inferiority, many students invoked traditional shibboleths. Focusing on perceived African American "laziness," another student wrote, "the negro does not have a place in the sun [a metaphor for being among the favored races] because he has always sought the shade, ostensibly, I presume to rest there."[85] Another paper used a time-honored formulation to exaggerate black inferiority and simultaneously reinforce white superiority. "The civilization of the Negro has always been possible only because of the white. The better the white civilization, the more the Negro would be benefited. Racial integrity is, therefore, not only of the greatest importance to the caucasian but also to the Negro."[86] This student thus characterized blacks as at worst parasites, at best symbiotic partners to a social organism dependent upon the eugenic purity of the white race. Miscegenation would harm the prospects of both groups.

A number of students decided that genocide was the best solution for racial problems, especially those involving African Americans. "Sentimentalist" social interventions artificially prolonged the lives of the unfit, particularly blacks. Opposition to miscegenation and the failure of natural selection to eliminate African Americans encapsulated white Virginia's eugenic fears.[87] Therefore, William Bean eschewed repatriation as "totally impractical," while total segregation, although "practical in the South," seemed "impossible as a nation-wide policy." So, Bean argued for the "wide dissemination of birth control knowledge" among African Americans.[88] Implicit in the advocacy of birth control was a eugenically motivated attempt to heighten dysgenic pressure on the African American population itself, thereby eliminating the threat to white racial purity through extinction. A number of students made this contention explicitly. "If the negro is given knowledge of contraception and access to contraceptive devices, this combined with his high death rate and present declining birth rate, aided by strict racial integrity laws as now in Virginia will cause his extinction in a comparatively short time and then insure a white America and her place in the world."[89] Whether or not factual information backed these assertions regarding birth and death rates is immaterial. What is important is the students' application of eugenics as a panacea for interracial tensions—a "final solution" that promoted inequality and segregation as precursors to extinction.

The chimerical quest for racial purity encouraged undisciplined theorizing that ignored boundaries between skeptical science and biased opinion. Students extended hereditary determinism into the murky realm of public policy through eugenics. Lewis's eugenic message had three main strengths that drew students to its policy-making potential. First, eugenics gained popularity and remained remarkably coherent and consistent over time; between 1914 and 1928 the number of colleges teaching eugenics skyrocketed from 44 to 376, with an estimated course enrollment of almost 20,000 students.[90] Second, eugenics maintained flexibility in its response to social conditions at various times. During periods of crisis—World War I, the Great Depression, and in the South during periods of civil rights militancy—eugenics offered stability in the form of various supposedly scientifically based reforms. The social order did not need to be changed; instead, people had to accept that heredity determined the social structure and use eugenics to improve the quality of individuals and society. Social improvement would necessarily follow. Any reorganization of social structure was destined to fail, for it neglected the iron rule of natural law. Finally, the major strength of eugenics stemmed from the claims that it permitted its adherents to make, regardless of their politics. Conservative eugenicists laid claim to the same legitimating apparatus that liberal social analysts, North and South, had used to advance their programs: modern, Progressive, scientific expertise. By claiming to be more objective and less sentimental and by decrying failed environmental interventions, eugenicists attempted to elevate their scientific programs above those of sociologists, cultural anthropologists, social workers, and others who upheld the efficacy of environment over heredity.

It should be noted that, for a time, eugenics expressed state-of-the-art scientific thinking.[91] Eugenicists rushed ahead because, in the words of historian Joseph F. Kett, "pseudo-science is often the matrix of science. Pseudo-science, in other words, is an attempt to seek too many scientific laws too quickly—not sub-science but super-science."[92] It is not surprising that the eugenicists' aggressive attempts to discern the hereditarian basis of society turned conservative in the South. Reinforcing the racial status quo and eliding the boundary between science and prejudice allowed southern eugenicists to justify and amplify racism. Eugenics also allowed educated white elites to avoid the choice between equally unpalatable racial liberalism and backward, antimodern thinking epitomized by the traditionalist Vanderbilt Agrarians. As a result, Ivey Lewis—a man who thought of himself as essentially southern and quintessentially modern—acted upon his eugenical beliefs in his educational administration and theorizing. His teaching acquired a dimension beyond mere complicity in the maintenance of an unjust cultural system of racial segregation. The extent to which individuals believed and acted, over the course of many years, upon the precepts taught in Lewis's class indicates the impact of eugenics on the larger society.

It is difficult to quantify the direct effect that Lewis had upon southern thinking and belief. His most immediate effect was on the thousands of students whom he taught over thirty-eight years, students who considered him a father figure, a fine teacher, and an authority on matters biological and social. An examination of the number of Lewis's students, the vocations they chose, and their correspondence with their former teacher begins to delineate his influence. Beyond his effect on students, Lewis's role as an influential scientist and educator brought him before diverse audiences—fellow scientists, university associations, alumni, teachers' associations, and even the newspaper-reading public. Evidence remains of his transregional influence. In evaluating this evidence, one becomes aware of the wide currency that eugenic ideas held for many educated Americans throughout the first half of the twentieth century. The facility with which these individuals deployed eugenic rationales to gain political and social ends allows historians to gauge the pervasive ideological power of this racialist thinking.

During Lewis's tenure, the biology department at the University of Virginia consistently produced more majors than virtually any other department in the college of arts and sciences. As Lewis noted in 1921, Biology 1 and Biology C1 "are elected by our students in considerable numbers. The enrollment in these courses this year is about 185."[93] Four years later, Lewis noted that enrollment "continues to grow at an embarrassing rate" with the classes logging 273 students, though "340 students would have registered for biology if room had been sufficient to take them."[94] As a report to the President's Committee on Research boasted in 1952, the year before Lewis retired, "Biology has from fifty to eighty undergraduate majors each year. This is the largest number found in any school in the College of Arts and Sciences with the exception of economics." The report continued, "In the last twenty years 89 M.A. or M.S. and 49 Ph.D. degrees have been awarded. During the last year 692 students were enrolled in [biology] courses." All majors took Lewis's eugenics course, as well as all graduate students. Moreover, the 210 investigators who had spent the summer at Virginia's Mountain Lake Biological Station since it opened in 1930 also encountered Lewis, his beliefs, and teaching.[95] It is estimated that more than 900 students passed through Biology C1 alone during Lewis's thirty-eight-year career.

A 1928 letter reveals the strong effect Lewis's course had upon his students. Describing Biology C1 as "a wonderful course," the student noted, "it transcends anything I have ever had or expect to have." The student even attached a characteristically millennial aspect to his praise: "The hope of the University of Virginia . . . and going further the salvation of religion" depended upon the "open minded" instruction embodied in Lewis's eugenics course.[96] Virginius Dabney, one of the South's leading "liberals," considered Lewis "one of my much admired and greatly loved teachers." While Dabney was not as virulent a racist as Lewis, he championed segregation as rational management of race relations.[97] Even a racial moderate like Dabney may have had his views influenced by Lewis's eugenics. Lewis succeeded in creating a sense of the logical relationship between science, religion, and the social order.

Charles W. Clark was another student convinced by Lewis's lessons. Clark wrote Lewis a number of letters to which Lewis apparently replied (copies of the replies are not in Lewis's files). Clark's first letter, quoted above, deserves more complete consideration. After extolling the racial theories of Lothrop Stoddard and excoriating the service record of blacks in World War II, Clark wrote:

> In some recent article either *Time* or *Newsweek* stated that all races are "genetically equal," whatever that may mean. This is, of course, flying right in the face of experience—not to mention facts known to every cattle breeder. Truly the back-swing from Mr. Hitler over to the opposite extreme is something to behold! And I know of no one to combat this foolishness except the scientist—the biologist and the psychologist, aided by the publicity man and the statistician.
>
> We are fighting with our backs to the wall and I fear that the worst is yet to come. . . . I do not pretend that the South has been wise in handling its problem. . . . But I still think we can handle it better without direction from Washington or advice from Albany, NY.[98]

Clark's letter displays an interesting blend of southern regionalism, racism, and eugenics. In a letter written five years later, Clark revealed more of his belief system, emphasizing the elevated racial consciousness of the eugenics true believer.

Writing almost nine months after the landmark *Brown* decision, Clark began, "This is partly a eugenic report, at which I hope you will be pleased." He described his family of five daughters, noting, "Oddly enough when there were only four, their coloration was in exact Mendelian proportion; one blond and three little pseudo-Italians." Clark then described his wife's heritage, remarking specifically that she is of "Irish ancestry (Protestant!), with Scottish, English, Swedish, and Polish blood." After sanitizing her eastern-European blood by claiming that "one of her D.A.R. ancestors was a Polish Colonel, one of Koscuisko's staff," Clark affirmed her superior genes by certifying her intellect, "She has a master's degree from Emory, and I consider her very intelligent." Clark's description and his need to ab-solve his mate of a hereditary taint reveal the operation of eugenical con-siderations in the way he represented his family to Lewis.[99]

Clark then returned to his racist diatribe. After stating that he was a farmer in the Mississippi Delta, Clark remarked that he was moving away from cotton production because "The latter simply requires too much nigger, and he is one gentleman of whom I am thoroughly sick and tired. I intend to write you more on this subject later. For the present, I am . . .

shifting to white labor. Ten thousand dollar machines are simply not trusted to a chimpanzee!" Clark used his eugenic, racist sensibilities to navigate his changing relation to the land, reaffirming his identity as a modern southerner. Abandoning black labor and cotton for white-operated machinery and crop diversification was a repudiation of the Agrarian impulse and an acceptance of modernity, all riding on his eugenically legitimated, racist valuation of blacks. With his estimation of African Americans in mind, Clark closed the letter saying, "After I hear from you, I intend to write you at length about a certain Supreme Court decision and its possible results. Also I shall invite all the helpful suggestions you can give," presumably toward fighting desegregation.[100] Maintaining racial segregation was of primary importance to Lewis, and he wrote in 1948, "In my opinion it would be a major calamity to try to force racial equality, and any informed citizens who love their country must realize that the color line must be maintained in spite of hell and high water."[101] Lewis promoted segregation with characteristic tact—through his letters, a few well-placed articles, and congratulatory remarks to others who opposed the civil rights movement. Throughout his career, people from the North and South approached Lewis for assistance in this matter.

Following the New York *Times'* coverage of his 1924 speech, "What Biology Says to the Man of Today," Ivey Lewis received a flattering letter from William W. Gregg, a lawyer in Elmira, New York. Gregg applauded Lewis's speech and announced that he was attempting, through his own agitation, "to make effective the segregation of the races in this country." Though "Segregation in the North at least is becoming increasingly difficult" because of the number of racially mixed "mulattoes and near whites," Gregg felt that "some new and definite policy was imperative unless the races are ultimately to amalgamate." Lewis's advocacy of immigration restriction and antimiscegenation laws appealed to Gregg's need to defend the white race. "In view of the very general interest now displayed regarding the proposed immigration law," Gregg wrote, "it would seem as if the time were ripe to advocate some definitive policy regarding our negro population." For Gregg, attempting "to preserve the race standards in this country" against inferior whites from southeastern Europe would "largely fail if ten and a half millions of negroes now here are ultimately to be absorbed into our white population, as is the declared purpose of the 'new' mulatto."[102] Lewis's speech, like similar appeals by other eugenicists, formed another filament bonding northern and southern white elites in the face of perceived racial peril and black agency.[103]

In a 1955 letter to Lewis, J. Segar Gravatt, a lawyer in Blackstone, Virginia, wrote, "I feel that we need to assemble and get before the people the biological opinion which points up the evil consequences of integration of the races." Apologizing for "imposing" on Lewis for help in this matter,

Gravatt closed promising to "find a convenient opportunity to have a personal talk with you about the integration problem generally."[104] In 1958 Lewis was still organizing segregationist resistance. The Reverend G. MacLaren Brydon reaffirmed Lewis's beliefs, "hop[ing] and pray[ing] that we will win our contention in the long run and be able to keep our separate schools."[105] To Lewis, desegregation challenged not merely his culture, but also his scientific belief that society ordered itself along lines delineated by natural law operating through heredity. Desegregation challenged the operation of these laws and by extension it challenged Lewis's view of God.

In his professional swan song, performed in 1951 on a national stage at the annual convention of the AAAS, Lewis incited a tremendous controversy. His final address as vice president of the AAAS and president of its botany section, entitled "Biological Principles and National Policy," hammered eugenical themes, outraged listeners, and caused the AAAS to break precedent and refuse to publish his speech in its journal, *Science*. Lewis argued that "[i]n general those who contribute least to the general welfare have the largest families," rehashing the race suicide argument of old. "Selection of the worst rather than the best as parents of the next generation simply flies in the face of biological law and will surely bring deterioration."[106] Avowing in private that his intent was "to try to deflate the rosy but unrealistic ideas of the social welfare enthusiasts," Lewis knew that he "caused quite a lot of disturbance among the council" of the AAAS.[107] Letters of support, many of which were racist and anti-Semitic, flooded in to Lewis. James A. Tignor wrote that "in this day of indecision, emotional instability and general unreliability, the German and his kindred races alone seem still to be dependable, honest, reliable, and willing to work." Agreeing with Lewis that the "modern trends of government and officialdom" undercut natural law and presaged degeneration, Tignor noted ominously, "The Gestapo was only the revolt of the [fit] people and I can well visualize it, if things keep on this way, as preferable. Enough is enough! Keep up the fight."[108] Lewis thanked one supporter and remarked, "there are some very powerful organizations that regard my views as heretical." By 1951 Lewis's brand of eugenics was no longer credible among the majority of scientists represented by the AAAS, even though many members of that body—and the public who otherwise followed its lead—still agreed with Lewis.[109]

In the final estimate, perhaps the most chilling legacy of Lewis and many other eugenicists was their effect on health care. Many of the students who took courses in eugenics went on to become physicians. Of the twenty-seven student term papers surviving from Lewis's classes, nine belonged to students who went on to become doctors, one belonged to a woman in the nursing school who became a practicing nurse, and one belonged to a man who became a plant geneticist.[110] Beyond the sterilization of institutional patients under eugenics laws, there was a long history of forced sterilization of unwed mothers and welfare recipients, particularly in the South. Fanny Lou Hamer, the champion of black representation at the 1964 Democratic National Convention, claimed to have undergone a "Mississippi appendectomy," as African American women termed these forced sterilizations.[111] Many of the accounts regarding such activities have links to eugenics.[112] While it is impossible to know the precise number of University-of-Virginia-trained physicians who performed these operations, it is certain that Virginia alumni performed many of Virginia's compulsory sterilizations between 1927 and 1972.[113] And, as previously mentioned, three Virginia graduates, backed by others taught by Lewis, founded and implemented the Tuskegee syphilis experiment.

Throughout his career, Lewis's influence was national in scope, although strongest in the South. This regional diversity reveals the appeal of eugenics and its capacity to forge an ideational bond between northerners and southerners. Eugenical ideology helped, for a time, to bolster the notion of the South's regional distinctiveness as a land of explicit segregation, which was justified, at least by some, on eugenic grounds. At the same time, however, eugenic ideology narrowed the gap between North and South, making the South, in the words of Grace Elizabeth Hale, "no longer distinct in its regional racial order, no better and no worse than the rest of an often racist and often segregated American union." Eugenics forged another ideological link chaining American identity to whiteness.[114]

Mark H. Haller wrote that Sir Francis Galton "preach[ed] . . . that man's character and capacities were primarily shaped by heredity. . . . In time this became for him a new ethic and a new religion." Galton once said, "An enthusiasm to improve the race is so noble in its aim . . . that it might well give rise to the sense of a religious obligation."[115] Ivey Lewis shared Galton's belief in the power of eugenics to improve mankind. As a biologist, Lewis appreciated eugenics' "logical" progression from the observation of human differences, to the systematization of differences as expressions of innate biology, to the formulation of policy based on biology.[116] As a liberal Episcopalian, Lewis did not find his religious beliefs challenged by the Darwinian principles upon which eugenics was based. Eugenicists generally, and Lewis particularly, relied on "pre-Darwinian concepts of economy in nature, the great chain of being theory, and teleology, in crafting a theory that matched religious and naturalistic views."[117] Thus, Lewis conflated his cultural biases and scientific convictions, and he did so in a distinctly southern fashion while dean of the South's most esteemed research university. In many ways, his influence shaped his institution and transcended its boundaries.

In 1952, a year before he retired, Ivey Foreman Lewis considered acquiring for the university artifacts that had belonged to Gregor Mendel.

Lewis wrote, "The interest in Mendel is, of course, widespread. As the founder of modern genetics, he takes his place with Darwin in the history of Science. It is a rare opportunity for the University of Virginia to become a sort of shrine for the geneticist."[118] Juxtaposing the religious imagery of a shrine and the southern traditionalism of the University of Virginia with modern images of higher education, science, Darwinian evolution, and genetics, Lewis underscored the tensions straining twentieth-century southern identity: the competing desires both to be modern and to maintain traditional, southern culture, which was often presumed to be antithetical to modernity. Averring the wide appeal of genetics, Lewis placed Virginia's interest in the contemporary mainstream and thereby freed it of "backward" regional parochialism. Yet, for Lewis, Mendel's artifacts represented the theories of eugenics and racial improvement, ideas that naturalized racial and class hierarchies based on Mendelian genetics. Although Lewis failed to acquire the relics, his attempt to obtain them expressed his ideal. He wanted to enshrine Mendel atop Virginia's ivory tower. Rhetorically he anchored the state university to the ninety-year-old Mendelian conception of biological destiny, not to more recent advances in genetics. Thus, Lewis's wish to commemorate Mendel cut against the notion of the university as a locus for the steady, modern, progressive advance of knowledge. Lewis taught eugenics and used the parlance of science to buttress traditional southern beliefs about the relative social positions of whites and blacks, rich and poor, men and women.

Given the symbiotic nature of culture and science during the Progressive Era, it is not surprising that the hereditary patterns observed by eugenicists conformed precisely to their biases regarding class, race, and culture. Context, of course, shaped these individuals and their approach to social problems. Their efforts defined both scientific method and the relationship of science to society. However, the durability of eugenic beliefs and their ability to unite whites through racism are surprising. When Carleton Putnam expounded white supremacy in his 1961 book, *Race and Reason: A Yankee View*, he relied on eugenic arguments by Lothrop Stoddard, Madison Grant, Earnest Cox, and Ivey Lewis. In 1994 Richard Herrnstein and Charles Murray revisited this well-trod ground in *The Bell Curve*.[119]

Ivey Lewis's true belief resulted from the dialectic between culture and eugenics. Scientists and their students believed that what they observed—stratification of society by class, gender, and, most important, race—developed from the unmediated operation of natural law. This attitude helps explain the reluctance of some eugenicists to repudiate their positions when faced with equally scientific refutation. Scientific revolutions actually occur gradually, more a changing of the guard than the flipping of a switch.[120] Eugenicists' absolute certainty that they were objective increased their staying power. This same dynamic characterizes present scientific culture:

scientists tend to dismiss the possibility of repeating the mistakes of early eugenicists because contemporary science is somehow "more objective"—and hence implicitly more moral—than the "primitive" science of the past. Present-day scientists teach their students based on their belief in the validity of their observations—which they, like Ivey Lewis, assert develop from value-neutral, objective investigations. Thus, today's geneticists teach about genes connected to alcoholism, breast cancer, sexual orientation, and aggression—in a culture that is concerned with substance abuse, epidemiology, morality, and violence. Contemporary genetic researchers, although more circumspect than the media, which often misrepresent their findings, still risk the errors made by Lewis. Understanding the relationships among Lewis, his science, his teaching, and the segregated culture in which he lived clarifies contemporary evaluations of science and its role in formulating public policy. Such an understanding may prevent the same sort of errors that insinuated racist beliefs into the educational and social structures of the United States in the first half of the twentieth century.

NOTES

The author thanks Paul A. Lombardo for suggesting this study and Lisa J. Lindquist Dorr, Grace Hale, Joseph F. Kett, Martin S. Pernick, and the anonymous readers for the *Journal of Southern History* for their helpful advice and criticism.

1. Charles W. Clark to Ivey Lewis, March 11, 1949, "C" Folder, Box 10, Dean's Papers 5119 (Special Collections, Alderman Library, University of Virginia, Charlottesville); hereinafter cited as Dean's Papers.

2. J. David Smith engages similar ideas in his book *The Eugenic Assault on America: Scenes in Red, White, and Black* (Fairfax, Va., 1993). Smith's emphasis that Virginia eugenicists sought to control the American Indian population fits well with this study; officials feared white/American Indian intermarriage because they believed that American Indians were already genetically tainted by previous intermarriage with blacks. Smith, however, claims that "[p]rejudice is a form of mental illness" and often a "shared mania" (*ibid.*, xiii). Such an explanation trivializes racism and exculpates racists; racism is taught, learned, and consciously passed on by those whose interest it serves. This paper argues that Ivey Lewis's career exemplifies this transmission, which was bound up with a self-conscious attempt to reconstruct an identity that was simultaneously white, southern, and modern. William A. Link explores these tensions throughout *The Paradox of Southern Progressivism, 1880–1930* (Chapel Hill, 1992). A most instructive interpretation of forging the modern southern identity, and its ultimate reconciliation with the modern American identity—both being predicated on whiteness—is Grace Elizabeth Hale, *Making Whiteness: The Culture of Segregation in the South, 1890–1940* (New York, 1998). Hale only obliquely considers how formal education and scientific theories shaped southern whiteness and eased the transition to modernity, preferring a cultural analysis of other phenomena, such as fiction, consumption, and spectacle lynchings. Nevertheless, the following analysis is broadly consonant with her major arguments. Paul M. Gaston explains the tensions between

modernity and tradition in southern mythology—in some ways the root of southern identity formation—in *The New South Creed: A Study in Southern Mythmaking* (New York, 1970). Jack Temple Kirby, *Darkness at the Dawning: Race and Reform in the Progressive South* (Philadelphia, 1972), notes that removing blacks from the public arena was the basis of all the rest of southern reform.

3. Steven Selden discusses the links between education and eugenics in *Inheriting Shame: The Story of Eugenics and Racism in America* (New York and London, 1999), 39–105. Diane B. Paul and Hamisch G. Spencer discuss the durability of eugenic theories among scientists in "Did Eugenics Rest on an Elementary Mistake" in Diane B. Paul, *The Politics of Heredity: Essays on Eugenics, Biomedicine, and the Nature-Nurture Debate* (Albany, N.Y., 1998), 117–32.

4. Lewis was not the only southerner teaching eugenics; he had his mates in every southern state and virtually every southern university of this period. Lewis's Virginia context, his well-preserved papers, and his students' papers make his career particularly appropriate for study.

5. Galton's first study relating genius and lineage is *Hereditary Genius: Its Laws and Consequences* (London, 1869). He defined *eugenics* in *Inquiries into Human Faculty and Its Development* (London, 1883), 24–25. See Daniel J. Kevles, *In the Name of Eugenics: Genetics and the Uses of Human Heredity,* (New York, 1985), 1–19. An excellent primer on eugenics is Diane B. Paul, *Controlling Human Heredity, 1865 to the Present* (Atlantic Highlands, N.J., 1995). See also Paul, *Politics of Heredity;* Kenneth M. Ludmerer, *Genetics and American Society: A Historical Appraisal* (Baltimore and London, 1972); Donald K. Pickens, *Eugenics and the Progressives* (Nashville, 1968); Mark H. Haller, *Eugenics: Hereditarian Attitudes in American Thought* (New Brunswick, N.J., 1963); and Allan Chase's thoroughly researched, albeit thoroughly polemical, *The Legacy of Malthus: The Social Costs of the New Scientific Racism* (Urbana, Chicago, and London, 1980).

6. Gregor Mendel, a Catholic monk who experimented with pea plants, first published "Versuche über Pflanzenhybriden" in 1866 in the proceedings of the Natural Science Society in Brúnn, Moravia, seven years after the publication of Charles Darwin's *On the Origin of Species.* Mendel's work went completely unnoticed by nineteenth-century scientists and was published in English as *Experiments in Plant Hybridisation* in 1924. Ludmerer, *Genetics and American Society,* 38–39.

7. Kevles points out this distinction. See *In the Name of Eugenics,* 75–76. Thomas F. Gossett also identifies this dynamic in *Race: The History of an Idea in America* (2d ed.; New York and Oxford, 1997), 162–75 and Chap. 15. See Selden's discussion of "rational equalitarianism" in *Inheriting Shame,* 118–21.

8. If intelligence was hereditary, and eugenicists believed that it was, then education was a mere aid to reaching one's inborn potential. As public schooling became nearly universal, eugenicists concluded that those who failed failed because of heredity, not lack of educational opportunity. This view was held by most psychologists of the period. The "scientific" differentiation of races ultimately rested on the analysis of intelligence quotient tests administered to African American and white inductees during World War I, and to Jewish immigrants in the early 1920s. Stephen Jay Gould develops the links among hereditary determinism, eugenics, and psychometry in *The Mismeasure of Man* (1981; 2d. ed. New York and London, 1996), Chap. 5. Nicole Hahn Rafter gathered the eugenic "family studies" that purported to demonstrate these phe-

nomena in her edited work, *White Trash: The Eugenic Family Studies, 1877–1919* (Boston, 1988). Eugenically minded scientists conflated the "Nordic ideal"—claiming the intellectual superiority of people with northeastern European heritage—with Mendelian genetics. Harvard-educated biologist Charles B. Davenport pushed Mendelism to its extreme, and most other early American eugenicists followed his lead. John Higham discusses Mendelism's importance in establishing the racist dimension of American eugenics in *Strangers in the Land: Patterns of American Nativism, 1860–1925* (1955; 2d ed., New Brunswick, N.J., 1992), 150–52.

9. The best expression of this negative eugenics is in Harry Hamilton Laughlin, "Report of the Committee to Study and to Report on the Best Practical Means of Cutting Off the Defective Germ-Plasm in the American Population," *Eugenics Record Office Bulletin*, Nos. 10a and 10b (Cold Spring Harbor, N.Y., 1914), 45–57 and 132–50.

10. The evolution of earlier forms of scientific racism into eugenics is covered in Gould, *Mismeasure of Man*, 51–141. See also Nicole Hahn Rafter, *Creating Born Criminals* (Urbana and Chicago, 1997), 1–34. American scientists developed agricultural and zoological laboratories to identify genetic traits—providing a "blueprint" for future breeding. Charles B. Davenport established the Carnegie Station for Experimental Evolution (1904) and the Eugenics Record Office (1910). Ivey Lewis helped the University of Virginia join this field-laboratory vogue by establishing its Blandy Farm (1927) and Mountain Lake (1930) Biological Stations and employing eugenicist Orland E. White as professor in 1927. See the "Blandy Farm" Folders, Box 4, President's Papers, RG 2/1/2.472, subseries VI (Special Collections, Alderman Library, University of Virginia); hereinafter cited as President's Papers, three-digit suffix, subseries number.

11. On increasing racism see C. Vann Woodward, *The Strange Career of Jim Crow* (3d. ed., New York, 1974), Chap. 3; Higham, *Strangers in the Land*, 170–71; and Gossett, *Race*, 155–60. For a 1920s-era discussion of the "100% American" identity see Horace M. Kallen, *Culture and Democracy in the United States: Studies in Group Psychology of the American People* (New York, 1924; 2d. ed., New Brunswick and London, 1998), Chap. 3 (quoted phrase on p. 119). Harvard, Yale, Columbia, and Princeton Universities and the American Museum of Natural History in Manhattan served as home institutions to many prominent eugenicists. See Eugenics Education Society, *First International Eugenics Congress: Scientific Papers and Appendices* (London, 1912).

12. Harry Hamilton Laughlin, the superintendent of the Eugenics Record Office, characterized poor southern whites thus before the Circuit Court of Amherst County, Virginia, during the 1925 hearings of *Buck* v. *Bell*, the case that established the constitutionality of Virginia's eugenic sterilization law. Laughlin, quoted in Paul A. Lombardo, "Three Generations, No Imbeciles: New Light on *Buck* v. *Bell*," *New York University Law Review*, LX (April 1985), 51.

13. E. A. Ross coined the phrase "race suicide" in "The Causes of Race Superiority," *Annals of the American Academy of Political and Social Science* (July 18, 1901). Two classic examples of eugenicists decrying the melting pot as race suicide are Henry Pratt Fairchild, *Melting Pot Mistake* (Boston, 1926); and Harry Hamilton Laughlin's report before Congress, *Analysis of America's Modern Melting Pot*, published in U.S. Congress, House, Committee on Immigration and Naturalization, Analysis of America's Modern Melting Pot Hearings, 67 Cong., 3 Sess., 1923, p. 7. See also Paul

Popenoe and Roswell Johnson, *Applied Eugenics* (New York, 1926), Apprendix C, "The Melting Pot."

14. In 1930 the "Vanderbilt Agrarians," in the words of Paul M. Gaston, "projected their hostility to modern industrial America into a generalized picture of the Southern past which portrayed agrarianism as the decisive factor in the region's development." Gaston, *New South Creed*, 10. The Agrarians, like most southerners, remained wedded to the traditional racial order. For the Agrarians' manifesto see Twelve Southerners, *I'll Take My Stand: The South and the Agrarian Tradition* (New York and London, 1930).

15. Edward A. Purcell Jr. identified an important corollary of the use of purportedly objective science to legitimize social beliefs. Scientists' "belief in the new objectivity opened the way for a practical role in society and possible ultimate realization of the methods of control, while at the same time suppressing any moral or social doubts about the actual consequences of their actions." Edward A. Purcell, *The Crisis of Democratic Theory: Scientific Naturalism and the Problem of Value* (Lexington, Ky., 1973), 26 (quotation) and 239–41.

16. The rise of expert authority is treated in Magali Sarfatti Larson, "The Production of Expertise and the Constitution of Expert Power" and Thomas L. Haskell, "Professionalism versus Capitalism: R. H. Tawney, Emile Durkheim, and C. S. Peirce on the Disinterestedness of Professional Communities," in Haskell, ed., *The Authority of Experts: Studies in History and Theory* (Bloomington, Ind., 1984), 28–80, and 180–225. See also the essays in Ronald G. Walters, ed., *Scientific Authority and Twentieth-Century America* (Baltimore and London, 1997). The search for social efficiency, similar to Frederick W. Taylor's scientific management, was a familiar concept in the technocratic culture of the 1910s and 1920s. Taylor invented the new specialty, the "efficiency expert," using time-and-motion studies to speed up production and increase output. In *Principles of Scientific Management* (1911; 4th ed., New York, 1967), he explicitly linked human efficiency to machine efficiency. Just as Taylor emphasized using science to make humans more efficient workers, eugenicists spotlighted using science to make humans inherently more efficient beings. Eugenicists went one step beyond Taylor in the quest for efficiency. Eugenics held appeal across the political spectrum, not just for conservatives as in this case. See Diane B. Paul, "Eugenics and the Left," in Paul, *Politics of Heredity*, 11–35. The "conservation" of America's "human capital" echoed the Progressive efforts of Theodore Roosevelt, Gifford Pinchot, and Margaret Sanger, all advocates of eugenics. Gary Brechin, "Conserving the Race: Natural Aristocracies, Eugenics, and the U.S. Conservation Movement," *Antipode*, XXVIII (Summer 1996), 236; and Pickens, *Eugenics and the Progressives*, 83. See also James W. Trent Jr., *Inventing the Feeble Mind: A History of Mental Retardation in the United States* (Berkeley, Los Angeles, and London, 1994), 135–37.

17. These conclusions differ from Edward J. Larson's study of eugenics in *Sex, Race, and Science: Eugenics in the Deep South* (Baltimore and London, 1995). Nevertheless, they tend to support Larson's regional distinctions. Unlike in the Deep South, eugenics found great support in Virginia and North Carolina, the Progressive upper South. Elites in these states readily embraced Progressive liberalism without adopting racial liberalism. While few whites, North or South, can be characterized as committed racial liberals—those favoring immediate equalization of all civil and social rights—during the first half of the twentieth century, southern liberalism had a de-

cidedly conservative cast. See Virginius Dabney, *Liberalism in the South* (Chapel Hill, 1932), for an analysis of the conservative nature of southern liberalism.

18. Wilson, too, was familiar with eugenics, having signed New Jersey's eugenic sterilization statute into law in 1911. Trent, *Inventing the Feeble Mind*, 173.

19. As C. Vann Woodward noted, "Racism was conceived of by some as the very foundation of Southern progressivism." Woodward, *Strange Career of Jim Crow*, 91. D. W. Griffith used quotations from Woodrow Wilson's *A History of the American People* (5 vols.; New York and London, 1901) as intertitles in *Birth of a Nation*. Both Wilson's history and Griffith's movie portrayed government intervention during Reconstruction as a crime against the South. In this view, national healing could occur only with the disfranchisement and subjugation of African Americans. The correspondence in time of the movie, Wilson's presidency, and eugenics was not merely a coincidence.

20. These three men maintained close ties with both the national eugenics movement and their alma mater. While Lewis taught none of these men, they all studied under Lewis's fellow eugenicists at the University of Virginia's medical school. Moreover, Virginia became a "feeder school" for the USPHS. Many junior surgeons in the USPHS corps, the men who carried out the study for forty years, did take Lewis's course and apply its teaching. A paper by the author, "Rearing Human Thoroughbreds: Eugenics, Medical Education, and Public Health," presented at the conference of the American Association for the History of Medicine, Bethesda, Maryland, on May 21, 2000, examines this issue in detail. James H. Jones, *Bad Blood: The Tuskegee Syphilis Experiment* (New York and London, 1981; 2d. ed., New York, and other cities, 1993), remains the benchmark study of the experiment.

21. Faculty members at the University of Virginia often lived in the Pavilions surrounding Jefferson's lawn at the center of the "Academical Village" on the campus of the university. Jordan and Lewis were neighbors "on grounds" (in the parlance of the university), only a couple of doors apart for many years. Harvey Ernest Jordan and David Starr Jordan, *War's Aftermath: A Preliminary Study of the Eugenics of War . . .* (Boston and New York, 1914). Among other articles, Jordan wrote "Eugenics: Its Data, Scope, and Promise as Seen by the Anatomist" in Morton A. Aldrich, et al., *Eugenics: Twelve University Lectures* (New York, 1914), 107–38. The book was "arranged for in the belief that the most necessary step to be taken towards the end of awakening a eugenical conscience, and thus paving the way to an effective operation of public opinion and to wise legislation along eugenical lines, must be that of education" (p. v). For eugenics and college education see Steven Selden, "Education Policy and Biological Science: Genetics, Eugenics, and the College Textbook, c. 1908–1931," *Teachers College Record*, LXXX–VII (Fall 1985), 35–51; and Selden, "Biological Determinism and the Normal School Curriculum: Helen Putnam and the NEA Committee on Racial Well-Being, 1910–1922," in William F. Pinar, ed., *Contemporary Curriculum Discourses* (Scottsdale, 1988), 50–65. For an account of Bean's flawed racist studies see Gould, *Mismeasure of Man*, 109–14. Bean's son, William Bennett Bean, who became dean of the University of Iowa Medical School and one of the most famous internists in America, was taught by Ivey Lewis. The younger Bean's eugenical views will be discussed below. Royster and White wrote less frequently on eugenics, but both maintained membership in national eugenics organizations.

22. Quotation is from the Aristogenic Association, "Review of Fundamentals

Leading to Aristogenic Record" (dated ca. 1930–31), in the folder cited at the end of the note. Founders of the Aristogenic Association include Lewellys Franklin Barker, a eugenicist at Johns Hopkins University, David Starr Jordan, Charles B. Davenport, director of the Carnegie Institution's Station for Experimental Evolution and of the Eugenics Record Office, both in Cold Spring Harbor, Long Island, and Madison Grant, a prominent New York lawyer, socialite, and philanthropist. Correspondence between Alderman and members of the Aristogenic Association is in "A" Folder, Box 1, President's Papers, .491, subseries I.

23. Lewis, Bean, and Jordan founded the university's chapter of the scientific honor society, Sigma Xi. Congress passed the eugenically motivated Immigration Restriction Act in 1924, the same year that Virginia enacted two pieces of eugenically motivated legislation—the Racial Integrity Act (forbidding miscegenational marriages) and a compulsory sterilization act (permitting sterilization of the feeble-minded). Lewis supported the 1924 Immigration Restriction Act (see note 48). While Lewis did not participate directly in the lobbying for the sterilization bill (probably because he viewed it as a medico-eugenic measure best handled by physicians), he supported the antimiscegenation bill through his association with its principal lobbyists, Earnest Sevier Cox, John Powell, Walter A. Plecker, and their organization, the Anglo-Saxon Clubs of America. For Lewis's compliance in enforcing this law, see W. A. Plecker to Ivey Lewis, October 29, 1926, and Ivey Lewis to Plecker, November 9, 1926, "1926 Letters" Folder, Box 1, Ivey Foreman Lewis Collection, 5119a (Special Collections, Alderman Library, University of Virginia); hereinafter cited as Lewis Collection. Lewis's teaching supported the principles and practices of both bills. J. David Smith's *Eugenic Assault on America* details the campaign for the Racial Integrity Act, but he misses Lewis's involvement (see note 72 below). Additionally, Lewis and Alderman's successor, President John Lloyd Newcomb, engaged in covert discussions with Harry H. Laughlin of the Eugenics Record Office (see note 61 below). On Virginia's eugenic acts see Paul A. Lombardo, "Miscegenation, Eugenics, and Racism: Historical Footnotes to *Loving* v. *Virginia*," *University of California, Davis Law Review*, XXI (1988), 421–52. On immigration and eugenics see Frances Janet Hassencahl, "Harry H. Laughlin, 'Expert Eugenics Agent' for the House Committee on Immigration and Naturalization, 1921 to 1931" (Ph.D. dissertation, Case Western Reserve University, 1970).

24. Virginia's preeminence was so well established that when a southerner said someone attended "the university," listeners assumed the speaker referred to the University of Virginia. The university resisted change, integrating its graduate schools only when forced by Supreme Court order in 1950. Virginia was the last major state university to admit women and did so only under the threat of litigation, by federal court injunction, in 1970. For a specific treatment of Alderman's earlier Progressive impulses see Michael Dennis, "Reforming the 'Academical Village': Edwin A. Alderman and the University of Virginia, 1904–1915," *Virginia Magazine of History and Biography*, CV (Winter 1997), 53–86; and Dennis, "Educating the 'Advancing' South: State Universities and Progressivism in the New South, 1887–1915" (Ph.D. dissertation, Queens University at Kingston, Canada, 1996). On the "Progressives'" transformation of American universities generally see Laurence R. Veysey, *The Emergence of the American University* (Chicago, 1965).

25. Ivey F. Lewis, "Address to Alumni (April 22, 1948)," in "Speeches" Folder, Box 5, Lewis Collection.

26. Lewis's father attended medical school at the University of Virginia before settling in North Carolina. Lewis's mother Cornelia Viola Battle was the granddaughter of Kemp Plummer Battle, a president of the University of North Carolina. The Lewis and Battle families have distinguished histories; Lewis's correspondence reveals his genealogical pride. See Boxes 1–5, Lewis Collection, passim; and Edwin Alderman to Ivey Lewis, January 13, 1928, "L" Folder, Box 2, President's Papers, .472, subseries VIII.

27. Edward L. Ayers, *The Promise of the New South: Life after Reconstruction* (New York and Oxford, 1992), 132.

28. Higham, *Strangers in the Land*, 170–71; C. Vann Woodward, *Origins of the New South 1877–1913* ([Baton Rouge], 1951), 321–26 and 355–56; and Woodward, *Strange Career of Jim Crow*, Chaps. 2 and 3.

29. Ivey Lewis to Edwin Alderman, January 5, 1914, "Biology 1908–1914" Folder, Box 5, President's Papers, .472, subseries I; Jane Maienschein, *Transforming Traditions in American Biology, 1880–1915* (Baltimore and London, 1991), esp. 43–47; announcement of Lewis's AAAS fellowship induction in Ivey Lewis to Dean J. M. Page, January 12, 1914, *ibid.* Lewis's scientific stature grew throughout his career. In 1929 he was appointed to the National Research Council, chairing its division of biology and agriculture from 1933 to 1936. He became president of the American Society of Naturalists in 1939, of the American Biological Society in 1942, and of the Botanical Society of America in 1949. In 1950–1951 he was president of the biology section of the AAAS. All of these positions brought him into personal contact with major figures in the American eugenics movement.

30. The deed for the Miller Fund, the trust that supported the school of biology, stipulated that the money be used to further experimental agriculture. Some trustees questioned using the fund to support academic biology. See collected letters in "Biology 1908–1914" Folder, President's Papers, .472, subseries I.

31. Edwin Alderman to Dean J. M. Page, January 29, 1915, *ibid.*

32. Samuel C. Hatcher to Dean J. M. Page, February 7, 1914, *ibid.*

33. So impressed by Lewis, Alderman asked *him* his opinion of *other* candidates for the job. See Ivey Lewis to Dean J. M. Page, May 25, 1914, and Ivey Lewis to Dean J. M. Page, June 22, 1914, *ibid.* Quotations from Robert E. Blackwell to Dean J. M. Page, January 14, 1914, and Edwin Alderman to R. T. W. Duke, Secretary of the Miller Board, January 14, 1914, *ibid.*

34. Ivey Lewis to Edwin Alderman, February 20, 1915, "Biology" Folder, Box 2, President's Papers, .472, subseries III.

35. Edwin Alderman to Ivey Lewis, February 6, 1915, *ibid.*

36. Ivey Lewis to Edwin Alderman, February 9, 1915, Edwin Alderman to Ivey Lewis, February 12, 1915, and Ivey Lewis to Edwin Alderman, February 20, 1915, *ibid.*

37. Woodward, *Origins of the New South*, 397. For an indication of the failure, over many years, of the university's leadership to alter its stand on the region's most pressing social issue, see a 1932 letter, asking Alderman if anyone at the university advocated racial amalgamation, which prompted immediate response from Acting-President Newcomb (Alderman had died a few months earlier), "you need have no fear. . . . No institution could be further from teaching that sort of doctrine than the University of Virginia." Dr. Lillian Crockett Lowder to Edwin Alderman, June 9, 1932; and John Lloyd Newcomb to Dr. Lillian Crockett Lowder, June 10, 1932, "L" Folder, Box 13, President's Papers, .491, subseries I.

38. In "The University of Virginia," Charlottesville *Daily Progress*, December 29, 1916, p. 18.

39. *Ibid.* Lewis echoed Alderman, commenting that the biology department contributed to "the teaching profession of the Southern States. We hope to encourage the spirit of research and sound scholarship in the teachers of our colleges and secondary schools." Ivey F. Lewis, "The Last Ten Years in Biology at the University of Virginia." See paper and undated clipping, labeled "Chattanooga News," in "Articles on University" Folder, Box 3, President's Papers, .491, subseries I.

40. Extensive correspondence documenting Alderman's position exists in "Evolution" Folder, Box 7, President's Papers, .472, subseries VII: 7.

41. Ivey Lewis to V. B. Harris, esquire, November 2, 1922, "1922 Letters" Folder, Box 1, Lewis Collection. Lewis lectured to various churches on "Evolution and Religion" and "Science and Religion" both before and after the Scopes Trial. See W. H. Ruffin to Ivey Lewis, February 2, 1927, "1927 Letters" Folder, Box 1, Lewis Collection; and Ivey Lewis to Tom H. Garth, Westminster Presbyterian Church, October 1, 1947, "1947 Letters" Folder, *ibid.* See also generally, Boxes 1–37, Dean's Papers, passim.

42. Lewis's views on the relation of science and religion paralleled those of his colleague and mentor, Edwin Grant Conklin. See Kathy Jane Cooke, "A Gospel of Social Evolution: Religion, Biology, and Education in the Thought of Edwin Grant Conklin" (Ph. D. dissertation, University of Chicago, 1994), especially pp. 91–105. Unlike Lewis, Conklin was a racial liberal and moderate eugenicist. "Moral delinquent" was a term developed to describe the feeble-minded during the *Buck* v. *Bell* case. Lombardo, "Three Generations, No Imbeciles," 49 and 62.

43. Lewis, "Address to New Students (September 3, 1940)," in "Speeches" Folder, Box 5, Lewis Collection (quotations). See also Ivey F. Lewis, "Ancient Wisdom and Modern Knowledge (May 5, 1935)," *ibid.*

44. Lewis echoed eugenics popularizer Alfred E. Wiggam, whose *New Decalogue of Science* (New York, 1922) married Protestant Christianity and eugenics, proclaiming, "had Jesus been among us, he would have been president of the First Eugenics Congress" (p. 110). Lewis's role as a founder and then chairman of the university's Young Men's Christian Association reveals his commitment to hands-on attempts to help people realize their genetic potential. See "1929 Letters" Folder, Box 1, Lewis Collection. Lewis, who became senior warden of his church in 1931, also occupied seats on the board of St. Anne's School and the diocesan school board. His views about the relation of natural law to man influenced his Christian commitment to help through education. See Ivey F. Lewis, "Untitled Essay (undated)," and Ivey Lewis to Bishop W. R. Mason, March 24, 1949, loosely filed, Box 24, Dean's Papers; and Ivey F. Lewis, "Address before the American Association of University Women, Wytheville, VA (April 5, 1946)," in "Dean Lewis" Folder, Box 11, President's Papers .581; document hereinafter referred to as AAUW.

45. "Address Commemorating Dean Lewis's 25th Anniversary," in "Articles and Addresses not by Ivey F. Lewis" Folder, Box 2, Lewis Collection.

46. Lewis used intelligence and personality tests to weed out students who got bad grades or behaved badly. For example see Charles M. Kauffman, Director of Personnel and Placement Office, to Ivey Lewis, May 31, 1948, "K" Folder, Box 6, Dean's Papers.

47. Edwin Alderman, "Untitled Address to Commission (December 20, 1915)," Box 8, President's Papers, .472, subseries III. Many commentators have noted southern resistance to outside intervention in the solution of southern social problems. See particularly John Egerton, *Speak Now Against the Day: The Generation Before the Civil Rights Movement in the South* (New York, 1994), 301–16; Ayers, *Promise of the New South*, 419; Dewey W. Grantham, *The South in Modern America: A Region at Odds* (New York, 1994), 3; and Link, *Paradox of Southern Progressivism*, 9.

48. "Biologist Supports Curb on Immigrants," New York *Times*, April 6, 1924, p. 3E, c. 3–4. This piece appeared the same day the *Times* ran a story about the House consideration of the Immigration Restriction Act. "Immigration Bill Taken Up in House," *ibid.*, sec. 1, p. 10, c. 1. The *Times'* coverage of Lewis was reprinted in the *Virginia Teacher*, the leading professional magazine for Virginia educators. See "Environment Cannot Mold Something out of Nothing, Says Biologist," *Virginia Teacher*, V (June 1924), 163–64. The address drew warm responses from people of both sections, as will be discussed below.

49. Alderman accepted Lewis's arguments over those of Professor Wilson Gee, the chairman of the department of sociology. Ivey Lewis to Edwin Alderman, May 18, 1926; and Wilson Gee to Edwin Alderman, May 26, 1926, "Institute for Research in the Social Sciences" Folder, Box 12a, President's Papers, .472, subseries VII. Alderman followed Lewis's recommendation regarding faculty appointments in every instance found; in each case, the result preserved the university's southern identity. Alderman dismissed a candidate whom he favored for Dean of Women (at this time there were women in the nursing school and graduate programs) as a result of Lewis's appraisal: "She is a very attractive woman of great ability. I think she would find a good deal of adjusting of her point of view necessary, and if I were charged with any responsibility in this matter, I would look first for a Southern woman." Ivey Lewis to John Lloyd Newcomb, July 18, 1927, "L–Le" Folder, Box 7, President's Papers, .472, subseries IX; and Edwin Alderman to Florence Lowther, Ph.D., July 18, 1927, "Women at the University" Folder, Box 29, President's Papers, .472, subseries VII.

50. Lewis's name first appears on the rolls of the American Eugenics Society in 1925. The *Eugenical News*, "The Official Organ of The Eugenics Research Association, the Galton Society, and the American Eugenics Society," called for the creation of education committees in May 1926. The list of chapters created appeared in the October 1927 issue. *Eugenical News: Current Record of Race Hygiene*, XI (May 1926), 72; and *ibid.*, XII (October 1927), 138–39.

51. House had been trained by Robert Park in the University of Chicago's sociology department and used statistical analysis in explaining social development. For more on House see Daryl Michael Scott, *Contempt and Pity: Social Policy and the Image of the Damaged Black Psyche, 1880–1996* (Chapel Hill, 1997), 59 and 220n7. House's personal papers at the university are found in Floyd Nelson House Papers, RG 21/77.851, Special Collections (Alderman Library).

52. Ivey Lewis to John D. Martin Jr., esquire, March 6, 1948, "M" Folder, Box 7, Dean's Papers. Lewis was a virulent anti-Semite. He tracked and controlled the number of Jewish students admitted to the university. Though he extolled Jewish efforts to defend their own racial purity, he felt that Jews as a "race" remained inferior to "Nordic" whites. Ivey Lewis to John Lloyd Newcomb, January 31, 1939, "Dean Lewis" Folder, Box 5, President's Papers, .491, subseries III. His statements in favor

of Jewish racial purity appear in "Biologist Supports Curb on Immigrants," cited above.

53. Mark Haller described racist eugenicists as propagandists. Haller, *Eugenics*, 147. Cox's books, *White America* (Richmond, Va., 1923, 1925, 1937) and *Teutonic Unity: A Basis for Peace* (Richmond, Va., 1951), mimic Stoddard's *The Rising Tide of Color Against White World-Supremacy* (New York, 1920) and *Revolt Against Civilization: The Menace of the Under-Man* (New York, 1922) and Grant's *The Passing of the Great Race or the Racial Basis of European History* (New York, 1916) in style and tone.

54. Ivey F. Lewis, "AAUW," 1; and "Address before the Roanoke Teachers Association (December 11, 1937)," in "Speeches" Folder, Box 5, Lewis Collection, 7–8. See also Ivey Lewis to John Dale Russell, Director Division of Higher Education, U. S. Office of Education, January 14, 1948, "R" Folder, Box 8, Dean's Papers.

55. Lewis scorned the Lamarckian theory that posited the inheritance of acquired traits and the increase of innate potential through training and environmental influence. See also Ivey Forman Lewis, "Biological Principles and National Policy: Address of Retiring Chairman of Section G [Lewis] American Association for the Advancement of Science (December, 1951)," p. 6, in "Speeches" Folder, Box 5, Lewis Collection.

56. Ivey F. Lewis, "The High School Program in Relation to Success in College Work (February 8, 1946)," p. 18 in "Articles and Abstracts" Folder, Box 2, Lewis Collection.

57. *Ibid.*, 19 (quotation) and 3. Lewis also sat on the boards of the Miller School for Manual Labor and the Blue Ridge Industrial School, in addition to his involvement with parochial schooling. Lewis often used IQ tests as diagnostics in his capacity as dean of students. See for example Charles H. Kauffman, Director of Personnel and Placement Office to Ivey Lewis, February 1, 1950, "F" Folder, Box 15, Dean's Papers; and Kauffman to Ivey Lewis, May 31, 1948, "K" Folder, Box 6, Dean's Papers.

58. Lewis, "Biological Principles and National Policy," 5.

59. Larson, *Sex, Race, and Science*, Chap. 1. Moreover, Virginia and North Carolina rank second and third, respectively, after California, for the total number of people sterilized under eugenical statutes. Virginia and North Carolina sterilized the most people in the country between 1950 and 1972. Phillip R. Reilly, *The Surgical Solution: A History of Involuntary Sterilization in the United States* (Baltimore and London, 1991), 94. For the most accurate compilation of statistics on eugenic sterilizations see Jonas Robitscher, *Eugenic Sterilization* (Springfield, Mass., 1973).

60. Larson, *Sex, Race, and Science*, 40. Again, the presence of well-developed research universities in Virginia and North Carolina helps to explain why these states eagerly accepted eugenics.

61. John Lloyd Newcomb and Lewis corresponded with Harry H. Laughlin, Earnest Sevier Cox, Dr. Walter A. Plecker (Registrar of Virginia's Bureau of Vital Statistics), and Colonel Wickliffe P. Draper, a prominent eugenicist. These men sought to make Virginia a leading state in eugenics. See H. H. Laughlin to JLN, February 18, 1936, "D" Folder, Box 9, President's Papers, .491, subseries II. Laughlin wrote, "I called on you last October about the desirability and possibility of work in eugenics by University of Virginia. . . . [Draper] is in position to give substantial financial support of work which he believes would definitely revive American racial ideals and would advance them substantially." Newcomb replied affirmatively. See John Lloyd

Newcomb to H. H. Laughlin, February 18, 1936; and John Lloyd Newcomb to Wickliffe P. Draper, February 21, 1936, *ibid.* Professor Paul A. Lombardo provided me with copies of letters not appearing in university files, particularly Wickliffe P. Draper to H. H. Laughlin, March 1, 1936, which describes Lewis's reaction: "Lewis especially seemed interested in my ideas and suggested that I meet with Messrs. Cox and Powell. . . ." Originals are in the H. H. Laughlin Papers (Pickler Library, Northeast Missouri State University, Kirksville); copies in my possession. See also Lombardo, "Miscegenation, Eugenics, and Racism," 432–35; and Lisa Lindquist Dorr, "Arm in Arm: Gender, Eugenics, and Virginia's Racial Integrity Acts of the 1920s," *Journal of Women's History,* XI (Spring 1999), 143–66.

62. For an account of Virginia's political culture during this period see Ronald L. Heinemann, *Harry Byrd of Virginia* (Charlottesville, Va., and London, 1996). Many Virginia graduates populated the state General Assembly during this period. Alderman regularly conducted surveys of each new legislature to determine just how many University of Virginia graduates, college graduates, and non–college graduates sat in the assembly. See for example "Legislative Survey" in "Legislative Program, 1927–1930" Folder, Box 18, President's Papers, .472, subseries VII. One such assemblyman, Lemuel Smith of Charlottesville, voted in favor of both Virginia's eugenic sterilization bill and the Racial Integrity Act. Thirty years later, in 1955, as a justice of Virginia's Supreme Court of Appeals, Smith voted to uphold the annulment of a "miscegeneous" marriage between a Chinese sailor and a white woman. See Gregory Michael Dorr, "Principled Expedience: Eugenics, the Supreme Court, and *Naim* v. *Naim," American Journal of Legal History,* XLII (June 1998), 1–41. Eugenicists teaching at the other state universities exposed many other assemblymen to eugenical theories.

63. University of Virginia Record-Catalogue, 1919 (Charlottesville, Va., 1919), 108.

64. Lewis used Paul Popenoe and Roswell Hill Johnson's text *Applied Eugenics* (New York, 1918). Lewis agreed with Popenoe and Johnson that "The science of eugenics consists of a foundation of biology and a superstructure of sociology" (p. v). Lecture notes and the "Topical Bibliography" are in "Miscellaneous" Folder, Box 1, Dean's Papers; other lecture notes in "Examinations and Lectures" Folder, Box 3, Lewis Collection; Student Notebook: Jim Putnam, "BIO C1: Evolution, Genetics, Eugenics Notes from Lectures by Ivey Lewis," undated student notebook, Box 43, Dean's Papers; and "Final Exams," Box 42, Dean's Papers. The course title changed to "Biology 102: Heredity and Eugenics" in 1947, a moniker it maintained until 1952. The course became "Biology 101: Evolution" by 1953, but the final exam shows that Lewis still taught heredity and eugenics. The twenty-seven term papers are found in Term Papers, 3567, Special Collections (Alderman Library); hereinafter cited as TP with a box number.

65. On the flyleaf of Alderman Library's copy of the 1922 edition of *Applied Eugenics,* neatly written in Lewis's hand, is "Miller School of Biology 1923." In the preface to the 1933 edition, the authors assert, "This revision of *Applied Eugenics* after fifteen years has not necessitated any significant change in the social philosophy, the science, or the technology of eugenics as presented in the first edition, 1918." Apparently Orland E. White, genetics professor and eugenicist, agreed, for he inscribed the flyleaf of his copy: "honest, clear judgment, lack of emotional exaggeration, fair,

calm." See Popenoe and Johnson, *Applied Eugenics* (New York, 1933), copy in Science and Engineering Library, University of Virginia, Charlottesville. Concerning the Newman text, first published in Chicago in 1921, see Ivey Lewis to Miss Betty K. Rudman, University of Chicago Press, December 29, 1947, "R" Folder, Box 8, Dean's Papers.

66. "Topical Bibliography"; and Haller, *Eugenics*, 150 (quotation). For examples of Lewis's approval, see NZF, "Race Mixture (June 1935)," and WCG, "A Plan of Eugenics (undated)," Box 2, TP. Of the twenty-seven term papers, only eight actually have grades indicated upon them.

67. Ivey F. Lewis, "Untitled Lecture (Handwritten Ms)," p. 1, in "Examinations and Lectures" Folder, Box 3, Lewis Collection. The back of this document also has outlines for other lectures on it.

68. Eugenicists repeatedly flayed Jefferson's statement that "all men are created equal" and the egalitarian, democratic ideal it expressed. See Popenoe and Johnson, *Applied Eugenics*, 75.

69. Lewis, "Untitled Lecture," p. 11.

70. Countervailing arguments propounded by the anthropologist Franz Boas (a Jew whom the anti-Semitic Lewis dismissed as sentimental), as well as other British and American scientists and lay people, existed almost from the beginning of the eugenics movement. See Kevles, *In the Name of Eugenics*, Chaps. 8–10; and Selden, *Inheriting Shame*, Chap. 6.

71. Ivey Lewis to Earnest Sevier Cox, February 26, 1924, "1924 Letters" Folder, Box 1, Lewis Collection. This letter appears as a blurb on the flyleaves of the book, along with testimonials from Madison Grant, Lothrop Stoddard, and John Powell.

72. Ivey Lewis to Earnest Sevier Cox, April 25, 1924, Earnest Sevier Cox Papers (Rare Book, Manuscript, and Special Collections Library, Duke University, Durham, N.C.). Lewis invited Cox to address the class on "the historical significance of the new Virginia law," the eugenic Racial Integrity Act for which Cox had lobbied. Lewis introduced Cox to other faculty eugenicists. Cox's papers preserve the correspondence between Cox and Lewis over a thirty-five-year period, also revealing Cox's close friendship with Madison Grant and Lothrop Stoddard, and his ties to the Eugenics Record Office.

73. Of the two equivocal papers, only one remains ambivalent to the end. See SR, "The Population Problem—A Summary (May 29, 1930)," TP, Box 2; and LML, "The American Race Problem (undated)," TP, Box 1. SR's name, clearly of ethnic derivation, may indicate the grounds for his objection to Lewis's judgment of immigrants from southeastern Europe. Interestingly, this is one of two papers to score "Excellent, Excellent @ 98." Of the twenty-seven papers, six deal with miscegenation or the race problem, five with sterilization, four with the inheritance of intelligence and/or feeblemindedness, four with immigration, two with the heredity/environment question, two with birth control/birth rates, two with the population problem, and one each with militarism and human evolution.

74. WD, "Heredity v. Environment as Portrayed by Identical Twins (undated)," pp. 5–6 (quotation), TP, Box 1. See also KHB, "Quality as a Biological Problem: Intelligence (undated)," p. 3, TP, Box 1; EFG, "Sterilization for Human Betterment (undated)," pp. 1–2, TP, Box 1.

75. KHB, "Quality as a Biological Problem," pp. 1–2 and 4 (quotation).

76. ESH, "Birth Control (undated)," p. 10 (emphasis in original), TP, Box 1.

77. William Bennett Bean, "Population (1930)," p. 26, TP, Box 1. Lewis rated Bean's paper "Excellent. Excellent. @ 98." The Beans lived next door to the Lewises and remained close family friends. Bean's father published numerous racist studies in physical anthropology. See Chase, *Legacy of Malthus*, 179–80.

78. HB, "Eugenical Sterilization (May 20, 1934)," p. 15, TP, Box 15. Another paper discussed the Nazi law, asserting "we can but believe that such a program [of mass sterilization of the "unfit"], carefully and conscientiously carried out in this nation, free from politics and false assumptions, would result in a few hundred years in a healthier and happier America." PH, "Sterilization and Society (June 1935)," p. 21, TP, Box 1. H. H. Laughlin and other eugenicists were impressed with Nazi racial programs. See Lombardo, "Three Generations, No Imbeciles," (p. 31*n*6 and p. 50*n*108); and Kevles, *In the Name of Eugenics*, (p. 347*n*21). Only two papers seem to acknowledge the questionable nature of equating economic success with desirable hereditary selection. ESH, "Birth Control," 14; and LML, "American Race Problem," 16–17. Both equivocate, then affirm the proposition. While Lewis did not directly lobby for Virginia's 1924 sterilization law, he clearly favored sterilization as a method for controlling the unfit. Lewis generally kept politics at arm's length, afraid that direct involvement would tarnish his status as a "disinterested and objective" scientist.

79. IB, "The Immigration Question (undated)," pp. 12–13, TP, Box 1; ROC, "Immigration from Europe (undated)" pp. 1–2, 5–6, and 12–14, TP, Box 1; ARF, "The Immigration Problem (undated)," pp. 5–7, TP, Box 2; and JP, "Immigration Statistics (undated)," pp. 10–12, TP, Box 2. Although these papers are undated, they refer directly to the Depression, and their authors graduated in 1935, 1936, 1934, and 1930 respectively. McLane Tilton, *Directory of the Living Alumni of the University of Virginia, 1931* (Charlottesville, Va., 1931); and Alumni Association of the University of Virginia, *Alumni Directory 1981* (White Plains, N.Y., 1981). Two of these students became physicians; one became a nurse. One wonders how eugenics influenced their professional practice.

80. Stoddard, *Revolt Against Civilization*. Stoddard coined the term "under-man" to describe eugenically unfit individuals who became socialist leaders or fell prey to radical appeals.

81. Mark Haller comments, "Having established the importance of heredity in general, racists could then proceed to describe, in impressionistic fashion, the major characteristics of particular races. . . . Even the word race, as some acknowledged, was often used to refer to national, language, or religious instead of biological groups." Haller, *Eugenics*, 146. Student papers reflect the eugenicists' loose conception of race.

82. ARF, "Immigration Problem," 12.

83. Bean, "Population," 5. Context could increase the attention students focused on racial problems. Reacting to the sensational Scottsboro, Alabama, rape trials, one student wrote, "At this time when the Scottsboro trial [nine black men accused of raping two white women] . . . [is] so before the public, a discussion of the problem is particularly appropriate." RNW, "The Negro Question (undated)," p. 1, TP, Box 2. The Virginia students deviated from Edward J. Larson's description of their Deep South neighbors. Larson avers that his subjects did not see eugenics as a panacea for the race problem, assuming that cultural racism and antimiscegenation laws operated so well that "Deep Southerners" did not fear black-white race mixing. Larson, *Sex, Race, and*

Science, 2, 23, 93. Eugenicists led the push for Virginia's antimiscegenation law, the Racial Integrity Act of 1924. The continued agitation for more stringent enforcement of the act, as well as students' preoccupation with the issue in their papers, displays Virginians' unease regarding compliance. See Lindquist Dorr, "Arm in Arm"; and Richard B. Sherman, "The Last Stand: The Fight for Racial Integrity in Virginia in the 1920s," *Journal of Southern History*, LIV (February 1988), 69–92. Larson notes that the paucity of resources in the Deep South limited sterilization to the white institutional population, excepting South Carolina's sterilization of African American women. Larson, *Sex, Race, and Science*, 4–17, and 155. Virginians, however, sterilized African Americans in segregated institutions. Erin Himstedt, "Not for Their Own Good: African American Mental Health and Eugenic Sterilization Programs in Virginia" (M.A. thesis, University of Virginia, 1995). Phillip R. Reilly states that sterilization rates at African American institutions in Virginia equaled rates at the various white institutions. Reilly, *Surgical Solution*, 138.

84. NZF, "Race Mixture," 1. He offered a two-part answer: laws against racial intermarriage and the application of eugenic practices to the black population.

85. RNW, "Negro Question," 8 (quotation); and LPR, "The Race Problem in America (undated)," p. 4, TP, Box 2.

86. TBH, "The Negro Problem in the U.S. (undated)," p. 11, TP, Box 1.

87. The papers disagree about the relative fecundity of "pure" and "mulatto" African Americans. Some papers argue in favor of the nineteenth-century notion of "reversions," which held that mulattos became increasingly less fertile until their progeny emerged sterile. Other papers contend that miscegenation itself raised African Americans' fertility, while some papers assert the inherent fertility of all African Americans. The continued existence of this debate demonstrates that the stance one took was largely determined by cultural outlook rather than scientific facts. Haller, *Eugenics*, 147–50.

88. Bean, "Population," pp. 21–22.

89. TBH, "Negro Problem," pp. 21–22. A number of papers recommend disseminating birth control among African Americans as a way to hasten their demise. The dissemination of birth control was illegal until after the 1936 decision in *United States v. One Package* was affirmed in 1938. After 1938 women could *legally* receive birth control from a doctor only if pregnancy placed their health at risk. David J. Garrow, *Liberty and Sexuality: The Right to Privacy and the Making of Roe v. Wade* (New York and other cities, 1994), 39–48.

90. Selden, "Educational Policy and the Biological Sciences," 42.

91. Anti-eugenic theory did not gain widespread attention until geneticist Herman J. Muller repudiated mainline eugenical beliefs at the 1932 Third International Congress of Eugenics in New York. For the ambivalence of many scientists see Paul, *Controlling Human Heredity*, 117–21. See also Robert N. Proctor, "Eugenics Among the Social Sciences: Hereditarian Thought in Germany and the United States," in JoAnne Brown and David K. van Keuren, eds., *The Estate of Social Knowledge* (Baltimore and London, 1991), 175–208.

92. Joseph F. Kett, *The Formation of the American Medical Profession: The Role of Institutions, 1780–1860* (New Haven and London, 1968), 179.

93. Ivey Lewis to Trustees of Miller Fund, June 18, 1921, "Miller Professor 1915–1925" Folder, Box A8–18D, Blandy Experimental Farm Papers, RG 6/9/2.831, Spe-

cial Collections (Alderman Library); hereinafter BEF Papers, page number (if applicable).

94. Ivey Lewis to Judge R. T. W. Duke, June 12, 1925, BEF Papers, *ibid.*

95. "Report of the Miller School of Biology to the President's Committee on Research," January 11, 1952, p. 1, "M-1947" Folder, Box A8–18F, BEF Papers.

96. R. R. Beasely to Ivey Lewis, (?) 1928, "1928 Letters" Folder, Box 1, Lewis Collection.

97. Virginius Dabney to Ivey Lewis, May 10, 1948, "D" Folder, Box 6, Dean's Papers. Dabney's racial scruples are revealed in his book, *Liberalism in the South.* For similar letters speaking in high praise of Biology C1 and Lewis as a teacher, see Joseph W. Chorlton to Ivey Lewis, June 6, 1950, "C" Folder, Box 14, Dean's Papers; Reverend William H. Laird to Ivey Lewis, September 20, 1947, "L" Folder, Box 7, *ibid.*; Dietrich von Schwerdtner to IFL, January 12, 1950, "V" Folder, Box 18, *ibid.*; and Robert B. McCormack to Ivey Lewis, (?) 1942, "Mc" Folder, Box 8, Correspondence of Dean of Students (1929–1944), RG 6/2/3299, Special Collections (Alderman Library); hereinafter cited as CDS 29–44. Four boxes of this collection, representing correspondence from 1929 through 1940, have been misplaced within Special Collections and were unavailable to the author.

98. Charles W. Clark to Ivey Lewis, March 11, 1949, "C" Folder, Box 10, Dean's Papers. Clark's first paragraph indicates that this letter is a response to an earlier letter from Lewis. See also John D. Martin Jr. to Ivey Lewis, January 16, 1948, "M" Folder, Box 7, *ibid.*

99. Charles W. Clark to Ivey Lewis, December 29, 1954, "1954 Letters" Folder, Box 1, Lewis Collection. The nationalist justification of his wife's eastern European blood is reminiscent of an earlier generation's rhetoric. See Lindquist Dorr, "Arm in Arm," 151–52.

100. Charles W. Clark to Ivey Lewis, December 29, 1954, p. 2.

101. Ivey Lewis to John D. Martin Jr., March 6, 1948, "M" Folder, Box 7, Dean's Papers.

102. William W. Gregg to Ivey Lewis, April 7, 1924, "1924 Letters" Folder, Box 1, *ibid.*

103. Lewis's reputation as a eugenicist extended beyond his classroom in other ways. Lewis assisted Dr. Walter A. Plecker, Virginia's Registrar of Vital Statistics, from 1912 to 1946, in enforcing the Racial Integrity Act. See this interaction as cited in note 23. Lewis also aided Cox and Senator Theodore G. Bilbo in promoting their 1939 "Negro Repatriation Bill" in Congress. Ivey Lewis to Earnest Sevier Cox, May 20, 1939, Cox Papers. On a similar note, see Earnest Sevier Cox to Ivey Lewis, July 2, 1949, "C" Folder, Box 14, Dean's Papers. In this letter, Cox asks for Lewis's endorsement of Senate Bill 1880, "which proposes to pay the expense of Negroes desirous of migrating to Liberia." Cox states, "In my opinion, there is no one in Virginia who would favor the ideals embodied in the bill more so than you, and no one whose character and influence would be more likely to favorably impress the committee." See also Michael W. Fitzgerald, "'We Have Found a Moses': Theodore Bilbo, Black Nationalism, and the Greater Liberia Bill of 1939," *Journal of Southern History*, LXIII (May 1997), 293–320.

104. J. Segar Gravett, esquire, to Ivey Lewis, October 3, 1955, "1955 Letters" Folder, Box 1, Dean's Papers.

105. In 1958–1959 Lewis ignited a firestorm within the "University Church," St. Paul's Episcopal, when he—as both vestryman and church warden—lashed out publicly against integration within the church. The Reverend G. MacLaren Brydon, D.D., to Ivey Lewis, September 6, 1958, "1958 Letters" Folder, Box 1, Dean's Papers.

106. Lewis, "Biological Principles and National Policy," 4. The speech argued that national policy in welfare, education, marriage, and even the provision of food all undercut biological law and threatened American civilization.

107. Ivey Lewis to Harcourt Parrish, esquire, July 1, 1952, "R" File, Box 27, Dean's Papers (letter apparently misfiled). See also Ivey Lewis to Harcourt Parrish, May 5, 1952, "1952 Letters" Folder, *ibid.*

108. James A. Tignor to Ivey Lewis, January 5, 1952, "T" Folder, Box 29, Dean's Papers. See also A. W. Wetsel to Ivey Lewis, January 4, 1952, "W" Folder, *ibid.*

109. Ivey Lewis to Clyde G. Harris, December 29, 1951, "H" Folder, Box 26, Dean's Papers. Alden A. Porter protested the decision not to publish Lewis's paper in Porter to Dr. Howard A. Meyerhoff, Chairman, AAAS Editorial Board, April 8, 1952, "R" Folder, Box 27, Dean's Papers (letter apparently misfiled).

110. Alumni directories and correspondence indicate the professions of former students. Lewis may well have taught an even larger proportion of future physicians than is indicated by the number of term papers; his annual reports frequently note the overcrowding of biology courses with pre-medical students. See "Miller Professor of Biology Reports," in "Miller Professor 1915–1925" Folder, Box A8–18D, BEF Papers.

111. Coerced sterilizations and those performed without patient consent became known as "Mississippi appendectomies" because physicians frequently misrepresented the operation as an appendectomy and not sterilization to avoid the patient's objections. Chase, *Legacy of Malthus*, 18. Hamer recalled her own sterilization and alleged those of other poor black women in "Mississippi 'Black Home': A Sweet and Bitter Bluesong," *New York Times Magazine*, October 11, 1970, p. 80 (quotation).

112. Such abuses first became well known in 1973 "when it was learned that two Alabama children, Mary Alice and Minnie Relf [who also happened to be black] as well as two South Carolina women—all receiving federal assistance—were coerced into consenting to sterilizations." The resulting lawsuit, *Relf* v. *Weinberger,* 372 F. Supp. 1196 (D.D.C., 1974), forced the U.S. Department of Health, Education, and Welfare to devise policies "to protect persons legally capable of consenting from being intimidated or coerced into sterilizations." The Health Research Group, a subsidiary of Ralph Nader's watchdog group Public Citizen, spearheaded the assault on this form of abuse. See Health Research Group, "Health Research Group Study on Surgical Sterilization: Present Abuses and Proposed Regulations (October 29, 1973)"; and Health Research Group, "Sterilization Without Consent: Teaching Hospital Violations of HEW Regulations (January 21, 1975)," 4 (quotations) (copies in author's possession); Chase, *Legacy of Malthus*, 15–17; and Reilly, *Surgical Solution*, 150–52.

113. Surgical residents from the University of Virginia Medical School and the university hospital performed many of these operations. In 1948 the university hospital and Western State Hospital, a state-supported hospital for the indigent located in Staunton, created a slush fund with the fees that the state hospital paid to residents for sterilizations. At the end of the years 1948, 1949, and 1950, this fund was split evenly among all members of the surgical staff. Thus, physicians had a pecuniary, as well as a eugenic, interest in these operations. Edwin P. Lehman, M.D., to Dr. Henry B. Mul-

holland, February 25, 1948; and Executive Committee Minutes, March 11, 1948, Hospital Executive Directors Office Papers (Wilhelm Moll Rare Book and Manuscript Room, Claude Moore Health Sciences Library, University of Virginia, Charlottesville).

114. Hale, *Making Whiteness*, 294. Philosopher Charles W. Mills reveals the operation of an implicit "racial contract" within the social contract theory of liberal western societies. The result is a society ultimately founded, in part, on racial subordination. In many ways, the efforts of Lewis and other eugenicists sought to reveal and sustain the terms of the racial contract by justifying them on the grounds of scientific natural law. Mills, *The Racial Contract* (Ithaca, N.Y., and London, 1997).

115. Haller, *Eugenics*, 10; and Galton as quoted in Haller, 17. Haller further notes, in a passage reminiscent of Lewis's rhetoric, that "[e]ugenicists . . . defended the compatibility of religion and eugenics" (p. 83).

116. Lewis also aided others interested in eugenics. He corresponded with Dr. E. S. C. Handy, who called his research area "Genethnics," a thinly veiled eugenics program, the name of which was an amalgam of "genetics" and "ethnics." Lewis wrote, "While I am not a specialist in the field of Genethnics, I am greatly interested in the possibilities it offers for a better understanding of human genetics and therefore a more intelligent approach to the utilization of modern science for people. So much is done for cattle and corn . . . that it seems to me extraordinary that there has been such neglect of the principles of genetics in dealing with human institutions and problems. I respect your [Genethnics] scientific approach and am enthusiastic as to the possible good that may come from it." Ivey Lewis to Dr. E. S. C. Handy, President, Genethnics, June 26, 1951, "H" Folder, Box 21, Dean's Papers. Lewis and Orland White assisted Handy in establishing Genethnics, even helping him obtain a room in Alderman Library. See E. S. C. Handy to Ivey Lewis, December 26, 1941, and Ivey Lewis to Handy, October 16, 1941, "H" Folder, 1941 Box, Correspondence of Dean of Students (1929–1944).

117. Pickens, *Eugenics and the Progressives*, 4.

118. Ivey Lewis to Mrs. Bertha Wailes, March 4, 1952, "W" Folder, Box 29, Dean's Papers. Lewis retired the following fall, after reaching the then mandatory retirement age of seventy.

119. Carleton Putnam, *Race and Reason: A Yankee View* (Washington, 1961); and Richard J. Herrnstein and Charles Murray, *The Bell Curve: Intelligence and Class Structure in American Life* (New York, 1994).

120. For the pace of scientific change see Thomas S. Kuhn, *The Structure of Scientific Revolutions* (Chicago, 1962).

J. DOUGLAS SMITH

"When Reason Collides with Prejudice": Armistead Lloyd Boothe and the Politics of Moderation

✻ ✻ ✻ ✻ ✻ ✻ ✻ ✻ *In* J. Douglas Smith's skillful handling, Armistead Boothe appears as a man caught in the middle of what for Virginians—as for all Americans—was the twentieth century's deepest and fiercest struggle over human rights. The 1954 Supreme Court decision in *Brown v. Board of Education of Topeka* called upon the states to end racial segregation in the schools. During the years that followed, Virginians had to confront and resolve the contradiction between the principles of human equality for which they had fought the American Revolution and the succeeding centuries of slavery and segregation. Virginians faced a stark choice. They either had to open the public schools to all citizens equally or to confront the federal government as they had in the Civil War nearly one hundred years before.

If, as Edmund Morgan has argued, the forcefulness with which Virginians defended republican ideals in the late eighteenth century devolved from the paradox of American slavery and American freedom in which their colony had developed, then the dilemma in which Boothe found himself was all the more painful because history in the 1950s provided neither ready compromises nor an acceptable way of passing the crisis on to future generations. But Boothe was heir to a bountiful heritage and could draw upon a richly storied political tradition to make sense out of this crisis. Even before the *Brown* decision, Boothe had advocated equality in educational opportunity and the end of segregation in transportation. As Smith observes, Boothe "expressed his understanding that Mason and Jefferson offered a guide to the objectives of good government." To Boothe "belief in the dignity of man and faith in an enlightened people" were the bedrock of the good society. At the same time Boothe inherited a reigning ideology of social segregation in which the "principle of opportunity for the individual which runs all through democracy . . . isn't put into practice."

In pursuing a moderate course in a state committed to massive resistance against desegregation in an era during which school and social integration loomed inevitable, Boothe emerges as both a tragic figure and a hero. His

394

tragedy lay in aligning with the losing side no matter what the resolution of the debate over race and freedom was in Virginia. His commitment to the sanctity of the individual led him to advocate educational opportunity for blacks, but only for the most talented. Many Virginians, however, simply refused to permit any taint of white supremacy to destroy their public schools. At the same time individual liberty prompted his call for partial school desegregation as a local option when other Virginians would brook no compromise in the face of racial amalgamation. Either way, however, Boothe was motivated by a heroic reading of human rights that no government could transgress. Edmund Morgan's paradox, then, was alive in Boothe's Virginia. His story of tragedy and heroism ties together narrative themes residing in Virginia history since the beginning of English colonization in the New World.   * * * * * * * *

* * * * * * * *
When reason collides with prejudice, it is not too difficult to predict the outcome.
—Robert Whitehead, November 9, 1954

The politician anywhere is helpless unless he holds office or has a following; and in most of the South today a politician who advocated school integration out of hand would soon have neither. Nevertheless, a constructive attitude, short of that, on the part of Virginia's leaders in the relatively propitious atmosphere of 1954–55 might have changed the course of Southern history.
—Benjamin Muse, 1961

In January 1948 Armistead Lloyd Boothe, a forty-year-old lawyer from Alexandria, was one of an exceptional group of new legislators who entered the halls of the Virginia General Assembly for the first time. The newcomers included future governors Albertis S. Harrison, Jr., and Mills E. Godwin, Jr.; future U.S. senator Harry F. Byrd, Jr., the son of the state's most important political leader; and George M. Cochran, later chief justice of Virginia's highest court. Of the thirty-four new members of the house of delegates, eighteen had recently returned from service in World War II. Like Boothe, most of the veterans were well-educated lawyers or businessmen. By a curious twist of fate, five of this group—Boothe, Cochran from Staunton, Julian Rutherfoord and E. Griffith Dodson, Jr., from Roanoke, and Walter A. Page from Norfolk—were assigned desks together in the far left-hand corner of the house chamber.[1]

The Byrd Organization controlled the legislature that greeted these returning veterans. J. Lindsay Almond, Jr., once said of the Organization: "It's like a club except it has no bylaws, constitutions, or dues. It's a loosely knit association, you might say, between men who share the philosophy of Senator Byrd."[2] The bedrock of Harry Byrd, Sr.'s philosophy was a low-tax, pay-as-you-go fiscal conservatism which guaranteed that state services always took a back seat to fiscal soundness. He and his followers limited capital outlays for education, highways, and health services. His machine had a reputation for honest government, but its leaders brooked no dissent. Loyalty was ensured through an almost circular process based on the strength of the Organization at the county level.[3]

The Organization derived power from an exceedingly limited electorate. During the 1901–2 constitutional convention, political boss Thomas Staples Martin and his supporters disfranchised a significant percentage of the electorate, black and white. A cumulative poll tax, which had to be paid for three years running and six months in advance of the primaries, kept the number of eligible voters to a minimum through World War II. From 1925 to 1945 an average of 11.5 percent of those of voting age participated in the Democratic primaries, which because of the strength of the Organization were the equivalent of a general election. The control of the Organization was so great that voter apathy remained high. Historian Allen W. Moger concluded that the Organization "was a political machine, highly respected, honest and genteel, which gave Virginia a long season of above-average government, but it was also increasingly a political anachronism guided by the legacy of ideas more appropriate to the postreconstruction period of poverty and racial strife which gave it birth than to the twentieth century when its power was most complete." Political scientist V. O. Key, Jr., provided a less generous assessment when he labeled the commonwealth "a museum piece" controlled by an "oligarchy."[4]

Although Key's description fit Virginia at the time, the museum clearly had acquired some new objects. For Armistead Boothe and many of the freshmen legislators in 1948, the war had awakened an awareness of inequities at home and helped shape the delegates' political agendas. Boothe and several of his compatriots resolved to work for increases in educational funding and for the elimination of the poll tax. Such efforts represented a clear departure from the Byrd Organization's policy of pay-as-you-go funding for state services as well as its reliance on a limited electorate to stay in power. These young men, however, did not consider themselves opponents of the Organization. In fact, they had every intention of working to promote change from within it. They had too many ties to the Democratic machine to be considered anything but reliable members. Dodson's father, for example, had successfully managed Byrd's 1925 campaign for governor in Norfolk and had been rewarded with the prestigious clerkship of the house of delegates. Boothe's father, Gardner, not only was a lifelong friend of the senator but had also been a member of the Democratic State Central Committee and chairman of the Eighth District Democratic Committee for most of the century. He was, according to James H. Latimer, the "main pillar of the Byrd Organization in northern Virginia."[5]

Armistead Boothe himself was born into the privileged ranks of Alexandria society. His parents' friends were lawyers and bankers, ministers and bishops. Boothe attended Episcopal High School when it was still directly affiliated with the Protestant Episcopal Theological Seminary, and there he developed a special affinity for history. After five years at the University of Virginia, three as an undergraduate and two in law school, he won a Rhodes Scholarship and spent two years at Oxford, from which he earned his legal degree in 1931. Boothe then returned to Alexandria and set out to establish himself before marrying Elizabeth Ravenel Peelle, a native of the Washington area whom he had met in England. In 1933 Senator Byrd aided Boothe in these pursuits by helping him secure a position as an assistant attorney in the Justice Department. Following a stint in his father's law firm, Boothe was elected Alexandria city attorney in 1938, a position he held until joining the navy as an intelligence officer in 1943. During a chance meeting on a Pacific island, Harry Byrd, Jr., first suggested to Boothe that he run for the state legislature.[6]

The perception of Armistead Boothe as a reliable lieutenant in the Organization was strengthened when he signed on as a patron of the anti-Truman bill during the 1948 session. State leaders, including Governor William M. Tuck, detested Harry S. Truman's proposed civil rights legislation. In late February, Tuck introduced a measure designed to keep the president's name off the ballot in Virginia. The Democratic State Central Committee supported Tuck's efforts and unanimously adopted a resolution offered by Gardner Boothe which condemned Truman's efforts to "abolish the barriers of segregation and social division recognized by the leaders of both races to be most conducive to the maintenance of peaceable and friendly relations between the races."[7]

Tuck's bill was introduced by E. Blackburn Moore, the elder Byrd's neighbor in Berryville and closest ally in the house. Moore suggested to Armistead Boothe that it would do him good to sponsor the bill, but when Boothe asked about the details, Moore replied that he did not have time to explain it because the governor was on his way into the chamber. Boothe signed on as a cosponsor. Once the bill was read on the house floor, he realized its purpose. A firm supporter of Truman, Boothe was horrified at what he had done. George Cochran recalled years afterward that Boothe considered Moore's maneuver a "dirty trick." Boothe set out to amend and in effect neutralize the bill. He joked later that in the end the Tuck bill said little more than "be it enacted that." By the time the measure passed the house on March 10, Boothe had successfully reworked it so that any candidate needed only one thousand signatures to be included on the ballot in the Old Dominion. Harry Truman appeared on the Virginia ballot in 1948 and carried the state despite the Dixiecrat challenge.[8]

The following year the dean of the University of Virginia law school,

F. D. G. Ribble, asked Boothe to prepare an article on civil rights for the *Virginia Law Review*. Working throughout the summer of 1949, Boothe examined dozens of federal and state court decisions as well as state laws. He found that Virginia's policy of "racial integrity" had resulted in far too many injustices. Specifically, he concluded that "there does not exist in Virginia, at the present time, equality in employment, in education, in housing, in health services or in public services and accommodations." He also recognized that blacks required equal educational opportunities before they could compete more successfully with whites for better jobs.[9]

Citing the 1949 bus segregation case of *Lee v. Commonwealth*, Boothe stressed the sheer folly of many of Virginia's Jim Crow statutes.[10] More importantly, his examination of Supreme Court decisions since 1935 led him to conclude that it was only a matter of time before segregation was ruled unconstitutional, even in the public schools. Boothe urged the state to begin to grapple with this possibility and to take steps to "foster equality of opportunity in employment, education, housing and health among all our citizenry, regardless of race or color." Referring to Justice John Marshall Harlan's dissent in *Plessy v. Ferguson*, he continued:

> In our public schools, we are threatened with an invasion of states' rights which we can meet and conquer legally only by counter attacks. For, some time in the not too distant future, Justice Harlan will be found to be speaking for the majority of the Supreme Court of the United States. . . . When the past's minority becomes the future's majority, the most staggering impact will be on segregation generally, more particularly on segregation in education, and most particularly on segregation in the primary and high schools of our public school system. If segregation in primary and high schools is declared unconstitutional in the near future, this declaration will be the keynote to tragedy. It will show utter disregard for certain facts of life, including health, moral and social differences, which, rightly or wrongly, do exist at this time in many places as race differences rather than as individual differences. It will usher in to the South, including Virginia, an era of chicanery, hatred, and violence.
>
> To prevent this calamity we must prove to the federal legislature, and especially to the federal courts, that Virginia intends to observe meticulously the guarantees given in the state and national constitutions, and will eliminate various phases of discrimination as fast as public opinion can be convinced that the elimination should be made. Of course in this venture, idealism must be tempered with common sense.

Specifically, Boothe advocated the establishment of a statewide civil rights commission "to recommend correction of abuses" and the repeal, "from a practical as well as a constitutional standpoint," of segregation laws affecting all modes of transportation.[11]

Boothe's efforts reflected not only a pragmatic understanding of constitutional law but also a determination to recognize the dignity of each individual. Journalist Guy Friddell called Boothe a tireless champion of the underdog who pushed and probed in a "positive and earnest and reasoned way" in order to make sure all citizens had a fair chance. From his education and experiences abroad emerged a committed belief in the value of the individual, a belief grounded in the Bible and the writings of America's Founding Fathers, most particularly George Mason. Boothe also maintained a realistic assessment of basic human nature, one that insisted that it was best to move carefully and gradually. In a speech delivered in the late 1950s, Boothe told a group of students that he considered the writings of the nation's founders to be the political counterpart of Christian teachings. He expressed his understanding that Mason and Jefferson offered a guide to the objectives of good government in which a "belief in the dignity of man and faith in an enlightened people" were the primary foundations.[12]

As a southerner born and bred, proud that his great-great-uncle, General Lewis Addison Armistead, had led Pickett's charge at Gettysburg, Armistead Boothe was not immune to the power of states' rights. Boothe, however, understood Jefferson to have believed that the rights of states operated as a shield from federal power only because they protected human rights. Mason, Boothe once said, emphasized that the "one thing more important than a nation or state is the individual, the human being." Consequently, Virginia and Virginians had every right to proclaim states' rights, but only as long as they understood that every right contained an accompanying duty to safeguard the dignity of the individual. The role of the law, therefore, was to accept these parallel duties and to enhance the rights of the individual before those of the state or nation.[13]

Boothe understood that the essence of racial problems in Virginia lay in the fact that whites looked at blacks as a race and not as individuals. Several months after the publication of his article in the *Virginia Law Review*, he told the Norfolk Women's Council for Interracial Cooperation that "a fundamental cornerstone of the whole democratic structure is that man be treated as an individual. This is not true when it comes to the race problem. That principle of opportunity for the individual which runs all through democracy . . . isn't put into practice."[14]

Boothe's comments appealed to the sensibilities of many of his younger colleagues in the General Assembly. Cochran recalled that "we had all just come through fighting a successful war and all of us one way or another had traveled on the same cars or trains or same planes and eaten maybe in the same messes with blacks, and it seemed to me that it was an unnecessary humiliation after we had gone through a successful war to relegate them back to riding in different parts of the trains and buses and so on." Dodson expressed similar views, emphasizing the impracticality of the state's segregation laws on common carriers. He noted that it "just didn't make any sense to segregate from Alexandria to Richmond and not from Washington to Richmond. It just didn't make any sense at all."[15]

In February 1950, joined by deskmates Dodson, Cochran, and Rutherfoord, as well as several other delegates, Boothe introduced legislation designed to effect the desegregation of public transportation. According to Dodson and Cochran, most of the group originally believed that a sincere effort to modify the Jim Crow laws in transportation and to establish a commission on race relations would constitute a sufficient show of progress to hold the line on education. Maintaining segregated schools, suggested Cochran, "was what was of deepest concern to people all over the South." In order not to alienate themselves from the Organization, Boothe and his copatrons stressed their dedication to states' rights and their desire to ward off federal intervention. Yet they noted that "in fifty years, except for passing Senator Byrd's magnificent anti-lynch law in 1928, the General Assembly has not enacted a single bill conferring upon the Negro any one of the many attributes of Virginia citizenship which we possess, and which he does not possess, although they are guaranteed to him by our Constitution. If we are to do justice and if we are to be the leaders of our own people, we must show that the rock of good faith in Richmond is far more solid than the political sands of false hope in Washington."[16]

Reaction to the proposed legislation, soon labeled the Boothe bills, was split. The *Richmond News Leader* tagged the measures as premature and unlikely to produce any benefit. The *Richmond Times-Dispatch*, *Norfolk Virginian-Pilot*, and *Roanoke World News* praised the leadership and sensibility shown by the sponsors. Two black newspapers, the *Norfolk Journal and Guide* and *Richmond Afro-American*, were ecstatic in their praise. The *New York Times* suggested that the connection of Boothe to the Organization signaled potentially positive consequences for Virginia and the South. The *Norfolk Virginian-Pilot* agreed and noted that "never before, in the legislature's modern history, had a desegregation measure of any kind been offered by a lawmaker in good standing with the reigning Democratic organization." Key members of the Organization, however, withheld comment. The bills were associated almost entirely with the younger wing of the party.[17]

Boothe assembled an impressive array of witnesses to appear before the house Committee on Courts of Justice; they included the Right Reverend Henry St. George Tucker, former presiding bishop of the Episcopal Church and a native of Virginia, and Colgate W. Darden, Jr., former governor and then president of the University of Virginia. An overwhelming crowd of two thousand supporters forced the hearings to be held in the house chamber. No one spoke in opposition. The delicate nature of these proceedings lay just beyond the public eye. Boothe and Darden both went out of their way to emphasize that the former governor had appeared only because he had been summoned by the committee. In fact, however, Darden had approached Boothe at a social gathering and indicated his willingness to testify if called. His reluctance to make this information public and his unwillingness to appear as more than merely complying with the committee's request reflected the ambivalence of a former Organization governor who did not want to cross old friends, particularly when they controlled funding for the university in Charlottesville. Despite Darden's and Tucker's support, both bills died in committee.[18]

The introduction of the Boothe bills was not the only significant aspect of the 1950 session. On the same day the bills were killed, state senator Harry F. Byrd, Jr., introduced an automatic tax refund bill, designed to return money to the taxpayer in the event of an expected budget surplus. Byrd presented his bill as the embodiment of the pay-as-you-go philosophy. No funds would be redirected to meet capital outlay needs. Opponents considered the proposal an enormous mistake, a wasteful bill that ignored long-neglected needs in education, prisons, and hospitals. Organization stalwarts, including Governor John S. Battle, seemed to understand. Battle reportedly referred to the bill as the dumbest piece of legislation he had ever seen. Nevertheless, the governor signed it. One legislator noted that young Harry "was hanging his reputation on the Byrd Automatic Tax Refund Bill. . . . If it hadn't been Harry Byrd's bill, it never would have gone through." The act remained a potentially explosive issue for several years to come.[19]

In the weeks following the 1950 session of the General Assembly, Harry Byrd, Sr., and Gardner Boothe exchanged letters about their offspring. Although seemingly aware that their sons had defined themselves in quite different terms, the two men remained hopeful that they might become fast friends. The elder Byrd initiated the contact, insisting, in reference to the antisegregation package, that "I took no part whatever against it nor did I authorize anyone to quote me to this effect. . . . I think Harry and Armistead have acquitted themselves very well, and, while it appeared by the newspapers that they differed at times, we, as fathers, can feel proud of them as standing for their convictions and ably advancing the causes in which they believe. I hope the same fine friendship that has existed between you and me will continue between Armistead and Harry." Boothe responded in almost identical words that he agreed with Byrd's assessment.[20]

No doubt the next session of the legislature awakened the two fathers to the realization that their sons would not become the friends that they hoped. Boothe reintroduced his desegregation bills, and they met the same fate as in 1950. In addition, he initiated a campaign to redistrict the state.

Article IV, section 43, of the Virginia constitution required that the legislature reapportion the state every ten years. When the General Assembly prepared to go home in March 1952 without having met its constitutional obligation, Boothe began collecting signatures to force Battle to call a special session to correct this dereliction of duty. The governor and Organization leadership expressed little desire to redistrict. They knew reapportionment would favor the growing urban areas of the state at the expense of the rural regions, particularly the Southside, which formed the bulwark of Organization power.

Boothe did not collect a majority of members' signatures before the legislature adjourned, but he continued his efforts into the spring and summer. In May he received a ruling from Attorney General Lindsay Almond that a failure to act was unconstitutional. Meanwhile, Boothe prepared at his own expense a handbook that he distributed to newspapers and civic organizations throughout the state. He documented the huge distortions in voting power whereby individuals in certain rural areas effectively possessed five votes in the senate and seven votes in the house to the single vote of those in northern Virginia and the tidewater. Finally, in December, Governor Battle summoned the General Assembly to Richmond to perform its constitutional duty. Boothe's efforts prompted *Washington Post* columnist Benjamin Muse to refer to him as "a clear voice of liberalism within the ranks of the conservative Byrd organization."[21]

In May 1953 Boothe returned to the issue of segregation. Anticipating a Supreme Court ruling on the *Brown* case before the end of the term in June, he accepted an invitation from C. Emerson Smith of the Virginia Council of Churches to serve on a biracial committee to consider the effect of the impending decision. Boothe, however, became uncomfortable with his involvement in this group. He soon sought official Organization sanction for such efforts and wrote to Governor Battle, urging him to convene a meeting of political, business, and religious leaders. In a tone similar to that of his law review article in 1949, Boothe stressed that "there has been an appalling absence of thought and consideration of the problems flowing from the decisions and if we get caught off guard we may be some time in recovering from the consequences." Battle refused to consider appointing any such group until after the Court announced its ruling. When the Council of Churches expressed its desire to push forward with its efforts, Boothe replied that he was still willing to participate but added the proviso that the committee's work be kept "unpublicized." In June the Supreme Court ordered *Brown* held over for reargument in the fall; soon after, the biracial committee apparently disbanded.[22]

In the fall of 1953, the growing public recognition of his efforts in the house forced Boothe to exercise greater caution. During Boothe's successful reelection campaign, his opponent attacked his efforts to eliminate segregation on common carriers and to establish a race commission. In December newspapers began inquiring whether he would introduce his desegregation measures for a third time. The Reverend Dr. W. L. Ransome, a representative of the Richmond Ministerial Association, an interracial and interdenominational organization, wrote Boothe requesting that he reintroduce the bills. Boothe replied that "the newspapers have already interrogated me about the matter contained in your letter. . . . Suppose you tell your committee that you have made arrangements for the introduction of the bills in question. Please do not mention my name or anyone else's name. I can assure you that our objective can be best obtained by complete silence on our part." Several weeks later Boothe told Emerson Smith that he did not oppose any pressure that might be applied by the ministers or the NAACP, as long as his intentions remained unpublicized.[23]

Boothe did reintroduce both of his desegregation bills, but once again they were defeated in committee. This time, because the Supreme Court was certain to rule on segregation in the near future, he took exception to the committee's actions and pleaded on the floor of the house for the Old Dominion's leaders to confront the issues. Boothe proclaimed that "as a man who is a Virginian by ancestry, birth, breeding, who loves Virginia and who has confidence in her people, I know that we have qualities of intellect and the capacities of spirit great enough to control our problems rather than to permit them to suppress our great capabilities. The Southern people will never reach their full maturity until they show the courage in peace they have shown in war and make practical applications of their wisdom to the facts, unwelcome but inevitable before them." For his efforts Boothe received commendations from two black organizations in Richmond. The Astoria Beneficial Club insisted that if the commonwealth refused to heed Boothe's call, blacks were perfectly justified in turning to the federal government for relief, precisely the outcome that Boothe hoped to avoid.[24]

Although Organization leaders had little trouble turning a deaf ear to Boothe's appeals for action on racial issues, they could not ignore his leadership of the Young Turk revolt. In 1954 another large group of young, well-educated lawmakers, most of whom were lawyers and many of whom had served in World War II, entered the General Assembly. Just before the session started, the new members toured state facilities, visiting universities, prisons, orphanages, hospitals, and mental hospitals. One participant was impressed by two things that he saw: "(a) At Western State Hospital we were shown a large one room facility for 'senile' old people. . . . The head of Western State wanted a linoleum floor covering over the wooden floor that had been defecated and urinated on for many years. I have a strong stomach but the stench almost got me before I could get outside. (b) I know that a court order to place a mentally deficient child in the Lynchburg

Colony . . . could not be carried out for four years although the order said forthwith. There were no facilities."[25]

This awareness of critical needs unmet soon brought about a natural coalition among many of the new members and those who had first won election in 1948. Led by Boothe, Page, Cochran, Rutherfoord, and Stuart Carter, who had entered the General Assembly in 1950, the Young Turks set out to address the state's shortage of services. A bill to suspend Byrd's automatic tax refund law for two years passed the house with fifty-six votes but was buried in the senate Finance Committee. At issue was a projected $7 million surplus in the two-year budget beginning on July 1, 1954. The Byrd tax law would have returned that money to the taxpayers, although it would have meant only a few dollars for each individual household. The house Appropriations Committee reported its pro-Organization budget to the full house. When the bill reached the floor, Armistead Boothe, along with thirty-six copatrons, introduced what became known as the Boothe amendment. In effect, this amendment appropriated the budget surplus for capital outlay throughout the state. After hours of heated debate, a fifty-two-vote majority adopted the Boothe amendment and sent its version of the bill to the senate.[26]

The senate, overwhelmingly controlled by old-guard Organization adherents, quickly squashed the amendment, thereby sending the budget bill to a conference committee. On what should have been the last day of the legislative session, Saturday, March 13, the conferees worked on a compromise. But on three successive conference reports, the slim coalition in the house held firm and refused to budge, as did the senate. Finally on Sunday afternoon, after nearly thirty straight hours of deliberation, the house coalition agreed to a compromise that would appropriate half of the $7 million for outlays and return the rest to the taxpayers. The senate, however, refused to concur. After 9:00 P.M. on Sunday, the house assented to a $2.2 million compromise, but once again the senate refused. When the house coalition threatened to walk out of the assembly without passing a budget bill for the biennium, the senate relented.[27]

Although the amount appropriated was less than a third of what they had originally sought, the Young Turks generally were considered the triumphant victors. Newspapers throughout the state debated whether their triumph was a sign of the Organization's weakening power. Certainly anti-Organization leaders such as Robert Whitehead of Lovingston emphasized this point. The Turks themselves, however, made every effort to stress their allegiance to the Organization, although clearly they sought an expanded role within it.[28]

Newsmen covering the General Assembly widely regarded Boothe as the leading force in the Young Turk revolt. As a result, they elected him the most outstanding member of the General Assembly for the 1954 session.

Although he was the leader of the movement, Boothe's views on other issues were not shared by all, or even many, of the Turks. In particular, the coalition included a number of legislators absolutely opposed to his efforts to desegregate buses and establish a race commission. Most of these members considered the Young Turk revolt a one-issue effort to rectify some serious unaddressed needs. They were not interested in taking power away from the Organization.[29]

Although Boothe played up his allegiance to the Organization in the wake of the Young Turk revolt, one contemporary ally suggested that by 1954 "it was well known that Army *was not* Organization. He never proposed to be to us Young Turks. I do not believe a single member of the so-called Organization would have recognized that Army was a member of such." Another Young Turk, however, believed that "on my arrival in Richmond in January 1954, Army was not anti-Organization though by the end of the term he was not in the bosom of the crowd." George Cochran pointed out that Boothe's efforts to amend the Tuck anti-Truman bill were the beginning of his split with the Organization. Harry Byrd, Sr.'s letters to Gardner Boothe suggested an acceptance of Boothe's independence up to a point. But it seems probable that after his continued efforts to desegregate the buses, reapportion the state, and develop a new fiscal policy, the Organization ran out of patience with the delegate from Alexandria. His amendment to the budget bill, no matter how small the compromise, signaled a rejection of pay-as-you-go policy. Perhaps most damaging of all, the Boothe amendment tarnished the reputation of the heir apparent of the mighty Organization.[30]

Whether in the Organization or out, Armistead Boothe found himself in a difficult position in the spring of 1954. Dr. Edward E. Haddock observed that longtime opponents of the Organization, such as Francis Pickens Miller, "had high hopes that Armistead would carry the 'anti-organization' torch."[31] Boothe, however, whether bound by political necessity or family ties, refused to declare a break. And then came *Brown*.

On May 17, 1954, the U.S. Supreme Court delivered its momentous decision declaring segregation in the public schools unconstitutional. Initial reaction in Virginia was muted. Governor Thomas B. Stanley expressed his desire that "cool heads, calm study and sound judgment" would prevail and indicated his intention to appoint a commission to begin studying the implications of the decision. Attorney General Almond, who had argued one of the companion cases to *Brown*, expressed his disagreement with the decision as a matter of both law and principle but added that "the highest court in the land has spoken and I trust that Virginia will approach the question realistically and endeavor to work out some rational adjustment." State superintendent of public instruction Dowell J. Howard noted that "the people of Virginia have settled many serious problems, and I feel they are capable of solving this one if they approach it gradually, calmly and with an open mind."[32]

Within a month of the *Brown* decision, however, voices of opposition began to reshape the debate. Governor Stanley called a meeting of prominent black leaders and urged them not to press for actual compliance, to no avail. Legislators from the Southside's Fourth Congressional District, led by state senator Garland "Peck" Gray, declared their "desire to have recorded our unalterable opposition to the principle of integration of the races in the schools." They pledged to find "some legal method whereby political subdivisions of the State may continue to maintain separate facilities for white and Negro students in schools."[33] Several days later Southside congressman Watkins M. Abbitt suggested that calling a constitutional convention would be more appropriate than appointing a commission. Finally, Stanley suggested the repeal of section 129 of the Virginia constitution, which provided that "the General Assembly shall establish and maintain an efficient system of public free schools throughout the State." The governor maintained that it was not his thought "to do anything to destroy the public school system," but he insisted that "separate schools are in the best interest of all the people of the Commonwealth."[34]

Soon after Stanley's remarks, an alarmed Boothe sent a "Turkeygram" to many of his allies in the Young Turk revolt. He expressed his belief that like it or not, the Supreme Court had settled the theoretical aspect of school segregation. What remained to be decided now was the practical application of the new theory. Boothe's formulation remained critical to him throughout the school crisis. He recognized a need to "respect and honor the feelings and facts throughout Virginia, especially in those areas where desegregation would have the most tragic consequences." He urged his fellow legislators to begin work on a plan that might prove acceptable to all sides.[35]

Although not yet ready to commit himself publicly, Boothe admonished Virginia's leaders to fill "the horrible void which seems to be existing in the State on this most important issue." He sent a questionnaire to the entire General Assembly as well as to selected state officials to solicit their views on segregation in the schools and to ask them to consider possible solutions to the implementation of *Brown*. The range of responses illuminates the difficulty of Boothe's position in appealing to the better reason of state leaders. Only one-third responded at all, suggesting an unwillingness to comment even privately.[36]

Numerous legislators expressed suspicion of Boothe's motives. Charlottesville's delegate suggested that any compliance with *Brown* was "bound to tend to the mongrelization of the white race." Another legislator echoed that theme when he insisted that the breaking of racial barriers would lead to the elimination of social barriers and ultimately to intermarriage. A

Young Turk challenged Boothe to make his own views known before soliciting those of others. "In view of your past actions," this legislator wrote, "I am inclined to the belief that you favor integration now." A delegate from the heart of the Southside exclaimed, "I am in favor of segregated schools in the state of Virginia. Are you? I do not think it is possible to integrate the schools in the state next year, five years from now, ten years, twenty-five years, nor fifty without serious results."[37]

Other lawmakers, including several prominent in the Young Turk revolt, expressed ambivalence and uncertainty. John Rixey, at twenty-seven the youngest of the Young Turks, replied that he was troubled by the issue and was unable to answer the questionnaire. Toy D. Savage, Jr., admitted that "I feel that many of us want Governor Stanley to appoint his committee, at least in part, for two selfish reasons: first, in order that we may defer to the committee's awaited opinions and thereby avoid answering embarrassing questions in our political meanderings; and second, in order that we may feel that the burden of constructive thought has been shifted from our own shoulders to those of the committee members, and that we can thereby escape to more pleasant fields."[38]

Boothe's position, particularly with the governor, was compromised when someone leaked to the press a copy of his initial letter on Stanley's statement. Boothe acknowledged to Stanley that he had become upset with the governor's call for the repeal of section 129 but denied any intent to criticize him publicly. In a letter to Stanley, Boothe outlined the results of his questionnaire and argued that there was a great deal of support for a plan of local option which would allow some areas to experiment with integration. Furthermore, he implored the governor to have a plan ready to present to the Supreme Court in October.[39]

Boothe's suggestions received a tepid reception at best. Stanley refused to discuss them. M. J. Menefee, an assistant to Senator Byrd, reported that Boothe apparently was attempting to persuade the governor to have his agents present Boothe's plan to the Supreme Court. Mrs. Michael Zodun of Highland Springs wrote to the *Richmond News Leader* that Boothe "is a 'liberal' who supports almost every 'liberal' scheme which comes down the pike. . . . I absolutely refuse even a single drop of this poisonous liberalism that can give the entire South and the nation the blind staggers for generations to come." Such criticism prompted Boothe to lament that it had become impossible to discuss desegregation without being accused of favoring intermarriage between the races.[40]

On August 28 Stanley appointed a thirty-two-member committee, composed entirely of state senators and delegates, to come up with a plan in response to *Brown*. The Gray commission, named for chairman Garland Gray, did not represent the biracial coalition mentioned in the press since June. The *Norfolk Journal and Guide* blasted the composition of the commission as serving only the needs of the Byrd Organization, and most particularly the Southside. The presence of state senators Garland Gray, Albertis Harrison, and Mills Godwin undoubtedly bolstered such opinions. Robert Whitehead and Robert Baldwin, a senator from Norfolk, expressed shock and disappointment that Boothe had been excluded, particularly in light of his efforts on the subject.[41]

Boothe did not wait for the Gray commission to act. In two speeches delivered in Norfolk and Richmond in October, he put forth "A Virginia Plan for the Public Schools." Boothe's effort developed a number of themes that he had introduced in his 1949 article in the *Virginia Law Review*. In addition, he drew heavily on the work of James C. N. Paul of the Institute of Government at the University of North Carolina at Chapel Hill. Paul had recently finished a report on the desegregation issue for the governor of North Carolina which was later implemented in that state's Pearsall plan. Boothe urged the commonwealth to develop a plan to present the Supreme Court when it held implementation hearings, set for December. The Gray commission, however, had no intention of proposing a plan until after the Supreme Court delivered its implementation decree.[42]

Boothe based his plan on the notion that the *Brown* decision actually had done two distinct things. First, he argued that the Supreme Court's ruling was based on a philosophical belief in the dignity of each individual. "Few Virginians," he wrote, "can quarrel with the theory or philosophy of the Supreme Court decision. We recognize that the great unifying factor in America is not race, religion, ethnic background or money, but the idea, born right here in Virginia, of the dignity of each individual, and of his right and responsibility to develop to the full the talents given him by the Creator." Second, Boothe noted that the Court recognized that the carrying out of its decrees presented numerous difficulties. Consequently, he believed that a great deal of latitude existed to formulate a plan that might be sensitive to all areas of the state. He suggested that a logical first step would be to convince the Court of Virginia's "good faith" by abolishing segregation in areas in which it made little difference, such as on buses and streetcars. A second key element in Boothe's plan required the recognition of individual achievement. He admitted that this acknowledgment would mean granting "permission to outstanding Negro students who have all the mental, moral and physical qualities, to attend and pass through any school of their choice whether it be white or colored." He attempted to head off criticism that such a plan would constitute an "opening wedge" or lead to the "mongrelization of the races" by stressing that only a few black students would be eligible to attend white schools.[43]

The essence of his plan was his insistence that "local governing bodies or local school boards be granted considerable local autonomy." Boothe argued that local option would allow regions of the state such as the Southside to maintain segregation, while other areas such as northern Virginia might choose small-scale integration. He later told one of his closest friends that he envisioned modest integration in some counties as a "model to other counties where no immediate change can be made." Boothe's conception of local option would have allowed local authorities to consider academic backgrounds, health requirements, and even the "personality, practices, needs and desires of individual children" before making school assignments. Finally, Boothe's plan asked for an indefinite amount of time to work gradually toward an acceptance of the Supreme Court decision. Given the content of the Paul report, from which Boothe drew heavily, it is significant that he omitted any mention of tuition grants in his proposal.[44]

Boothe presented his ideas as a rough draft and openly asked for comments and constructive criticism. Several individuals questioned the likelihood that the Supreme Court would grant an indefinite period of gradual adjustment. One also wondered if the Court would accept deficiencies in moral and cultural development as legitimate grounds for school assignment. The *Norfolk Virginian-Pilot* expressed similar doubt about the legal permissibility of an indefinite period of adjustment and the definition of "qualified" black students. At the same time, however, the editor acknowledged Boothe's efforts, particularly in comparison to the "disturbing" lack of discussion by public officials throughout the state.[45]

Several groups condemned Boothe's plan. An editorial in the *Journal and Guide*, Norfolk's black newspaper, wondered just who would determine the fitness of "qualified" black students. The paper mocked the Alexandrian's desire to see desegregation take place wherever no "social problem" existed and predicted that "in the absence of a firm resolve on the part of the State to recognize what is now the law in Virginia, . . . someone will see that a 'social problem' is created, whenever a Negro pupil is assigned to a formerly white school."[46]

Leaders of the NAACP considered *Brown* the law and not open for compromise. In a private letter to Boothe, P. B. Young, Sr., the publisher of the *Journal and Guide*, acknowledged that Boothe's willingness to accept blacks as individuals and as citizens far surpassed that of most of the state's leaders. Nevertheless, Young assailed Boothe's suggestion that local boards establish academic requirements and health standards for the admittance of blacks to formerly all-white schools. He wrote:

All of this takes us back to the beginning of the 1890's, the beginning of the reign of jim crowism, segregation, and discrimination, in every phase of life where the Negro was concerned in the southern states, including Virginia.
    That period gave birth to disfranchisement, to jim crow trains, and later to the jim crow street cars and buses, the jim crow housing

arrangements, the jim crowing of Negroes in public places, and the barring of Negroes from any place where white persons in control did not want them to be.

Those things also resulted in the very conditions of health and academic standards which you now seem to feel disqualify Negroes for integration. This reminds me of the intelligence test for voting.

I have lived through all of those years of racial oppression, suppression, discrimination, and ostracism, and I see little difference in your plan and what I have been reading in the proceedings of the Constitutional Convention of 1901–02. This is what shocks me.

A hundred years after the Emancipation, Negroes in Virginia have no more reason to hope for freedom and first-class citizenship, plus their acceptance as persons created by God with certain inalienable rights, than they had in 1865.[47]

The Alexandria League of Women Voters expressed similar objections. Certain members disagreed with Boothe's central premise that every individual "has the right . . . to prove himself worthy of and to try and attain the attributes of first class citizenship." Marion Galland, the president of the league and Boothe's neighbor, articulated a belief that all individuals were already first-class citizens. They did not need to earn such status. Some members "questioned the advisability of applying different standards to Negro students than to white students," while others wondered who would judge the "mental, moral and physical qualities" of individual blacks.[48]

In numerous letters Boothe accepted such criticism and recognized his approach as conservative but insisted that political realities dictated such a course. He expressed a desire "to stem the tide of thought which caused the Governor to issue his pronouncement advocating repeal of the constitutional guarantee of public free schools in Virginia" and to "bridge the gap between the realities of life, particularly in Southside Virginia, and the Supreme Court decision." He asked P. B. Young, Sr., to distinguish between private thoughts and public utterances tempered by political necessity.[49]

Although his request of Young suggested more liberal sympathies, Boothe recognized his own approach as inherently conservative. In the fall of 1957, at the height of massive resistance hysteria, Boothe wrote a revealing letter to his longtime friend from Oxford, Robert H. Houston, Jr. Boothe indicated that his stand in the school crisis was likely to lead to his defeat in 1959, although he believed that his was the "truly conservative" approach. He told Houston there were four key elements to resolving the race problems in the South:

1. To acknowledge, even if regretfully, that the Supreme Court decision is the law of the land.

2. To recognize the traditions and customs under which we have lived for 350 years.

3. To recognize that the Negro race, as a race, is very inferior to the white race.

4. To recognize that there are individual Negroes who have the character, intelligence and other requisites entitling them to full first class American citizenship. To my mind this is the key to the situation.[50]

Boothe continued by citing a history of slavery, drawing heavily from Kenneth M. Stampp's recently published work, *The Peculiar Institution.* Boothe clearly recognized the complicity of whites in the sin of slavery. Nevertheless, he maintained that the conditions of involuntary servitude and the subsequent treatment of blacks since emancipation had left blacks, as a race, inferior in their attainments of civilization. The problem, in Boothe's view, was that whites had become so possessed by the notion of racial inferiority that they had assigned the characteristics of the black race to all individual blacks. He suggested to Houston that it was the duty of "the leaders of the South, the thinkers, scholars, church people and other persons not in politics" to recognize that "an individual, colored man or woman, should have the right to demonstrate that he or she possesses every good quality regardless of the color of the skin." Boothe purposely omitted the politicians because he considered it unlikely they would move away from a posture of defiance.[51]

The limitations in Boothe's thinking were poignantly illuminated by Benjamin Muse, who once wrote in *Harper's:* "There are thousands of whites in the South who are as deficient in all indexes of civilized progress as any Negroes. But nobody has suggested segregating them." Boothe's willingness to recognize the abilities of individual blacks rested on a belief in the inferiority of the race as a whole. For whites, first-class citizenship was a birthright, but for blacks, it was something to be achieved. His local option plan reflected this formulation. Blacks were to be judged; not a single white child would be examined for physical and mental fitness. In addition, Boothe's plan gave more weight to the wishes and traditions of Virginia's whites than to the attainments of individual blacks. The Alexandrian sought to promote and recognize the achievements of individual blacks, but in the final analysis, such achievement would remain unrecognized in areas where whites did not agree with his thinking.[52]

Boothe, however, did not believe that black inferiority was intrinsic; rather, it was the result of the conditions of servitude foisted on blacks by whites. Consequently, nothing so infuriated him as the denial of well-demonstrated achievement. A case in point was his passionate denunciation of the Pope bill, passed by the General Assembly in 1956, which prohibited athletic contests that involved interracial mixing. To Boothe the bill represented the worst kind of discrimination. Athletes, he reasoned, already had demonstrated their abilities and deserved to compete on the same playing field with anyone else. Referring to the participation of Jesse Owens and other black athletes in the 1936 Olympics, Boothe noted that "the only real objection to their participation and the only resentment in their success was that of Adolph Hitler."[53]

Various individuals privately expressed their support for Boothe's school desegregation plan. Virginius Dabney, editor of the *Richmond Times-Dispatch*, remained confident that something could be worked out along the lines of Boothe's address. FitzGerald Bemiss, a prominent Richmond businessman who soon would become a member of the house of delegates, praised Boothe's point of view in contrast to the "sadly irresponsible and unrealistic" attitudes of most state officials. John W. Riely, a Richmond lawyer involved in the *Brown* litigation, told Boothe that his was "the only sound course for Virginia to follow." One of Riely's partners, future Supreme Court justice Lewis F. Powell, Jr., was serving as the chairman of the Richmond school board and, with Boothe, as a trustee on the board of Colonial Williamsburg. He wrote another Williamsburg trustee that "Armistead's moderate view may not be the most popular one politically at this time, but I believe it will prevail in the long run."[54]

Despite such private sympathies, no one publicly embraced Boothe's position. Although P. B. Young, Sr., and the Alexandria League of Women Voters criticized the inherent limitations in Boothe's plan, most people willing to speak publicly considered him a dangerous extremist. Referring to Boothe, Robbins L. Gates concluded in his study of massive resistance that "for a while at least, his was the rather lonely advocacy of gradual, partial, and localized integration through individual pupil assignment." John A. MacKenzie, a member of the house from Portsmouth, remembered that "by that time, . . . the Organization was completely Anti-Boothe. His plan never had a chance. And the sad part was that friends of Army's began to shy away as if he had the plague."[55]

By late fall Boothe undoubtedly began to feel the tide of opinion flowing against him. He confided to Toy Savage that his position might have damaging political consequences. In March 1955 he moved to maintain whatever political influence he possessed. A month before, the Virginia Council on Human Relations, an interracial group spawned by the Southern Regional Council to work for integration, had held its inaugural meeting in Richmond. Although Armistead Boothe missed that gathering, his name appeared as one of the original members of the organization, the only politician listed. Several weeks later, however, he wrote W. Carroll Brooke, the chairman of the group, and asked that his name quietly be removed from the council's rolls. Boothe cited the advice of several legislators who felt "that it would destroy my usefulness to a great degree if I do become associated with the Virginia Council no matter how laudable its purpose. I believe the advice is right."[56]

On November 11, 1955, just days after Alexandria voters elected Armistead Boothe to the state senate, the Gray commission submitted its findings to Governor Stanley. In essence, the report called for the empowerment of local school boards to assign pupils for a variety of reasons other than race, a proposal not unlike Boothe's plan. But the Gray report went further. It proposed that compulsory attendance laws be changed to avoid the enforced attendance of any child in an integrated school. Most significantly, the commission recommended that the governor convene a special session of the General Assembly to consider calling a statewide referendum to change section 141 of Virginia's constitution, which stipulated that no public money could be used to support private schools. Members of the Gray commission conceived of the amending of section 141 as a means of permitting tuition grants to private schools for families who did not want their children in integrated schools, for families who lived in areas where the public schools had been closed to avoid integration, or even for families who already had children attending private schools.[57]

The Gray report put white moderates throughout Virginia in a difficult bind. It seemed a modest compromise to Stanley's apparent willingness to abolish the guarantee of a public school system. Yet at the same time it left open the possibility that some schools might close; furthermore, the report advocated the use of state funds to support private schools in certain situations.[58]

When the assembly convened on November 30 for a special four-day session, nearly all of the so-called Young Turks threw their weight behind the Gray proposal and voted to call a referendum to amend section 141. For them, any deficiencies in the Gray plan were acceptable if it meant keeping public schools open. Only Boothe, Stuart Carter, and three delegates from northern Virginia opposed the plan. In his final speech on the house floor, Boothe, no doubt conscious of rising extremist pressures, attempted to shift the terms of the debate. He noted that "it is important to recognize at the beginning that the issue is public schools against private schools and is not segregation against integration. I believe in public segregated schools." Boothe pledged his support for the pupil assignment provision of the Gray plan but objected to tuition grants because of his fear that they would lead to "a degeneration of the public school system from which Virginia may not recover in our lifetime." He acknowledged that "a few outstanding negro students" would make their way into white schools but insisted that schools in the Southside could remain fully segregated so long as the rest of the state "provided evidence of good faith" in complying with *Brown.* The house remained unpersuaded; in the senate, only Republican Ted Dalton opposed the referendum, called for January 9, 1956.[59]

Having failed to sway the General Assembly, Boothe, Carter, and the others opposed to the Gray plan set out to convince the state. In December, Boothe appeared as the chairman of the Virginia Society for Preservation of Public Education, later renamed the Virginia Society for Preservation of Public Schools. Emphasizing that the real issue was the schools, and not segregation or desegregation, the group adopted much of the language that appeared in Boothe's speech. In addition, it expressed a belief that tuition grants for private education were unconstitutional and a threat to section 129's guarantee of a public school system.[60]

Pro-amendment forces, however, proved too formidable. Most moderates in the legislature as well as many public school advocates, according to historian James H. Hershman, Jr., accepted the argument that tuition grants would not constitute an assault on the system of public education. Instead, they envisioned the grants as a last alternative for those objecting to integrated schooling. In addition, former governors Colgate Darden and John Battle campaigned vigorously for all aspects of the Gray plan. Among Virginia's white press, only the Norfolk papers opposed the referendum. On January 9 voters decided to call a constitutional convention by an overwhelming majority of 304,154 to 146,164.[61]

Just two days after opponents of the convention were soundly defeated, Boothe was sworn in as a freshman member of the state senate. The prominence and influence he had achieved in eight years in the house were quickly erased. Signs of Organization disfavor were evident. The clerk of the senate assigned him a seat in the far left-hand corner of the chamber; his counterpart on the opposite side was one of the senate's three Republicans. Even more significantly, Boothe did not receive a single major committee assignment. Harry Byrd, Jr., and Albertis Harrison, by contrast, sat on three major committees as freshmen in 1948. By 1956, they each served on four. William B. Spong, Jr., another new member in 1956 and a former Young Turk, recalled that "there was a great belief in symbolism and that sort of thing." Boothe's assignments clearly reflected his poor standing with the Organization.[62]

During the 1956 regular session, the legislature did not pass the local option and pupil placement aspects of the Gray plan. This failure confirmed the worst fears of those who had opposed the calling of a convention. Governor Stanley had hesitated in December to pledge full support to the entire Gray plan and only capitulated after Colgate Darden pressured him. In mid-February, Boothe and Dalton introduced two bills to establish the pupil placement plan envisioned by the Gray commission. This was the first of three attempts they made over the next several years to pass local option legislation. Each time, opponents remained unpersuaded by the pair's stated objective, "to retain extensively and for as long as possible, within the limits of the law, the Virginia traditions and customs of segregation in our public free schools."[63]

Instead of adopting an assignment plan, the assembly focused on James J. Kilpatrick's conception of interposition. In late November, soon after the Gray report was released, the blustery editor of the *Richmond News Leader* began a barrage of editorials which maintained that Virginia, as a sovereign state, had the right to "interpose" its own power between the Supreme Court and the commonwealth. He asserted that interposition stopped just short of nullification but left little doubt about his intentions. Kilpatrick proclaimed, "*God give us men!* We resist now, or we resist never. We surrender to the court effective control over our reserved powers, or we make a fight to preserve these powers. We lie down, piteous and pusillanimous, or we make a stand." Lawyers on both sides of the segregation issue privately acknowledged the legal flaccidity of interposition. Nevertheless, it proved an exceedingly popular idea, especially among the Southside politicians in the Byrd Organization and segregationist groups such as the Defenders of State Sovereignty.[64]

In the General Assembly pressure to support interposition appeared overwhelming. The resolution passed the house of delegates with only five dissenting votes, while in the senate thirty-five of forty members sponsored the resolution. Boothe was not one of them. On the last day of January he addressed his colleagues; drawing on 175 years of constitutional history, he dissented from Kilpatrick's view that Virginia had a heritage of interposition. In fact, Boothe maintained that on January 26, 1833, the Old Dominion had rejected South Carolina's call for nullification and had sought to "interpose and mediate" the conflict between the federal government and the Palmetto state. Interposition, therefore, was not a measure of protest but of mediation. In reference to Kilpatrick, Boothe declared: "I do feel . . . that less patriotic men preaching the same doctrines would be regarded as advocating anarchy and almost sedition."[65]

Despite a clear belief in the foolishness of Kilpatrick's campaign, Boothe announced his intention to vote for interposition because it constituted a form of protest, not nullification. Furthermore, he maintained that interposition recognized *Brown* as the law of the land, "no matter how ardently we disagree with it or how much we dislike it." James Hershman has suggested that Boothe voted for interposition because he found "segregationist pressures irresistible," while Stuart Carter hinted that Boothe and others were constrained by their ambitions for higher office. Dr. Edward E. Haddock, one of only two state senators to vote against the resolution, was warned by a highly respected Virginian that public opposition to interposition was a trap that "could come back to haunt any dissenter who aspired to a political future in Virginia." He was advised to "blast it on the floor for all it was worth and then sit down and vote for it." Boothe himself expressed his desire "as a new member to go along . . . whenever the presumption exists that no violation of fundamental principles is involved." In this case he apparently concluded that no such violation occurred.[66]

Whatever factors contributed to Boothe's choice to vote for interposition, his decision stunned many moderates both inside and outside of the General Assembly and compromised his leadership. When Haddock entered the senate in 1956, he gravitated toward the group of fellow freshmen who had moved over from the house—Armistead Boothe, Stuart Carter, and William Spong. Haddock recalled that "I always looked to Army as the leader. He had an excellent legal mind, he reasoned well and was so gentle and courtly in his manner, was an excellent debater and commanded respect from both sides of the aisle." Although the tide clearly moved against those opposed to interposition, Haddock believed that "a stalwart unwavering negative posture on his [Boothe's] part would have strengthened our 'group' and might even have attracted others to our ranks." On the other hand, Omer L. Hirst, one of the few members of the house to oppose interposition, remained "completely tolerant" of Boothe's position. Hirst has suggested that Boothe may have "believed it such a ludicrous proposition that it was not worth the formal effort to oppose it and that it would be just as well to let it go through and expose its self as being a totally hollow and naked document."[67]

Toward the end of February 1956, soon after the interposition debate, Harry Byrd, Sr., first uttered the phrase "massive resistance." Several weeks later he stated that "if we can organize the Southern States for massive resistance, . . . I think that in time the rest of the country will realize that racial integration is not going to be accepted in the South." On March 12 Byrd, William Tuck, Watkins Abbitt, and Howard W. Smith joined ninety-seven other southern senators and congressmen in signing the Southern Manifesto, a joint declaration of defiance against the Supreme Court.[68]

In July, as the rest of the South watched to see what Virginia would do, Byrd huddled with Stanley and other state leaders and developed what became known as the Stanley plan, a package of bills that repudiated the local option component of the Gray report. In its place the Stanley plan proposed to cut off state funds for any local school district in which a single school allowed even a modest amount of integration. In addition, the plan authorized the governor to close any public schools in which integration actually occurred. Tuck made no effort to conceal the purpose of the new proposals. "There is no middle ground, no compromise," he declared. "We're either for integration or against it and I'm against it. . . . If they [other Virginia areas] won't stand with us then I say make 'em. We cannot compromise. . . . If you ever let them integrate anywhere the whole state will be integrated in a short time."[69]

Taking the lead from their seniors in Washington, Organization lieu-tenants, led by Mills Godwin, pressed the case for the Stanley plan during a special session of the General Assembly that convened in late August. Godwin argued that "integration is the key which opens the door to the in-evitable destruction of our free public schools; . . . integration, however slight, anywhere in Virginia would be a cancer eating at the very life blood of our public school system. . . . The [Supreme Court] decision is either right or wrong. If we think it is right, we should accept it without circum-vention or evasion. If it is wrong, we should never accept it at all. Men of conscience and principle do not compromise with either right or wrong."[70]

Godwin's tone represented that of the entire session. Massive resisters succeeded in defining the debate in terms of integration versus segregation. Opponents attempted to substitute local option amendments, but each failed. Boothe and Dalton tried to reintroduce their bill that had been de-feated in February; Boothe cited the example of North Carolina, where fed-eral courts had upheld the Pearsall plan, and insisted that a local option, pupil placement system would maintain nearly complete segregation. The *Richmond News Leader* captured the spirit of the resisters by ridiculing the proponents of local option: "In one pitiful, expedient retreat, they propose that Virginia abandon Constitution, society, schools and way of life—everything, all in one abject collapse. They would accept 'just a little inte-gration.' They would not abandon schools; they would abandon principles instead."[71]

In the end the Organization's massive resistance laws passed the house by a comfortable margin but only squeaked through the senate by a vote of 21 to 17. The narrow margin suggested that those moderates who had origi-nally supported the Gray plan would not sanction school closings. Fur-thermore, journalist Benjamin Muse noted that the twenty-one senators represented a smaller percentage of Virginia's population than did the sev-enteen, a clear reflection of the continued overrepresentation of rural Vir-ginia despite Boothe's redistricting efforts. In addition to the school-closing laws, resisters forced through a package of bills aimed at harassing the NAACP and curbing its membership.[72]

Implementation of massive resistance laws forced a shift in the political dialogue, particularly as it concerned such moderates as Boothe. In the years following, he continued to adhere to a belief in local option and pupil assignment, but his emphasis changed. In 1954, when he first introduced his plan for the schools, he had stressed the gradual integration of qualified blacks, but only in areas where whites were willing to go along. After 1956, however, his public statements emphasized his personal preference for maintaining segregation and his insistence that local option would result in keeping schools "99 percent segregated." By 1958, as the advent of the ex-treme path of massive resistance forced moderates to alter their rhetorical strategies, Boothe found himself pleading with his colleagues to understand that segregation could be maintained more effectively, for a longer period of time, under a plan of local option.[73]

The 1957 Democratic primary in Alexandria revealed to Boothe the increased difficulty of maintaining his position. Although not up for reelection himself, he saw in the contest between Albert A. Smoot and incumbent James M. Thomson a distressing signal. Smoot was a close friend and supporter of Boothe. Thomson, whose sister was married to Harry Byrd, Jr., was an ardent massive resister, a man Benjamin Muse referred to as "a leader of the most fanatic segregationists throughout the massive resistance era." In the January 1956 referendum, Alexandrians had supported Boothe's position and voted against the calling of a convention. Boothe clearly hoped for a Smoot triumph as a sign that moderate sentiment continued to dominate in Alexandria. Although Thomson's margin of victory may have reflected the advantages of incumbency more than anything else, Boothe interpreted the results to mean that roughly 1,000 voters had switched from the pro–public school side in 1956 to the pro–massive resistance side eighteen months later. In a district in which only 5,300 voters went to the polls in 1955, the size of this shift appeared significant.[74]

The following January, Lindsay Almond took the oath of office as Virginia's governor and proclaimed that "to compromise means to integrate." The new chief executive added that "I cannot conceive such a thing as a 'little integration' any more than I can conceive a small avalanche or a modest holocaust." In the light of such a mood, it is hardly surprising that the senate again rejected the Boothe-Dalton pupil assignment plan. In fact, the assembly moved further in the opposite direction by tightening loopholes in the massive resistance laws. This time, however, Boothe's pleadings assumed a new urgency. A number of cases had wound their way through the courts, and the likelihood existed that federal judges would order blacks admitted to white schools in the fall of 1958. In reference to Arlington, where seven black students were awaiting such admission, Boothe asked his colleagues:

> Do you really believe that in the shadow of the Capitol of the United States, . . . with the eyes of the world focused upon Washington, truly the capital of the free nations of the earth, do you really believe that 25,000 school children here will go unschooled? Do you really believe that these buildings built and paid for by the people of Arlington, even with all the might of Virginia thrown in to close them and keep them closed, do you really believe they will remain unopened? The question answers itself, my brothers. We shall reap a whirlwind of catastrophic proportions.

Boothe argued, to no avail, that the massive resistance laws would only lead to the closing and subsequent reopening of the schools on an uncontrolled basis. A pupil assignment plan, on the other hand, would not only keep the schools open but "maintain the separation of the races in the schools more effectively than any other plan."[75]

When federal courts ordered black students into nine schools in Norfolk, Charlottesville, and Warren County in September, Virginia's massive resistance laws went into effect, and Almond closed the schools in question. In addition, Judge Albert Bryan ordered that black students in Arlington enter white schools in January 1959. The judge's opinion indicated that local assignment plans would be acceptable, as had been the case in North Carolina since 1956. In a statement released just after Bryan delivered his decree, Boothe reiterated this point and emphasized that Bryan would have accepted precisely the sort of plan Boothe had advocated since 1954. Again citing North Carolina's experience, Boothe added that a plan similar to his would have kept more blacks out of the white schools than had just been ordered into the white schools by the courts.[76]

On January 19, 1959, state and federal courts both ruled Virginia's school-closing laws unconstitutional. The next day Governor Almond delivered a fiery address, full of hatred and scorn and derision for opponents of massive resistance. He pledged not to yield to what he knew to be wrong and to what would lead to the amalgamation of the races. Just nine days later, however, after a group of statewide business leaders apparently convinced him that further defiance would destroy the commonwealth's reputation, Almond addressed a special session of the General Assembly. He announced that he had fought as hard as anyone to maintain segregation but that it was no longer possible to "exercise power that the state is powerless to bestow." He recommended a series of emergency measures to reopen the schools and appointed a commission, named for state senator Mosby G. Perrow, Jr., to develop a concrete plan. On Monday, February 2, black students entered formerly all-white schools in Norfolk and Arlington. Delegate James Thomson of Alexandria reportedly lamented that "there's a sickness in my heart."[77]

In late March the Perrow commission recommended a proposal based on local option and tuition grants, a solution similar to the Gray plan. Although Boothe originally had opposed the tuition grants outlined in the Gray proposal, he began supporting such grants in September 1956, when the only alternative was the school-closing bill. Therefore, in April 1959, when the General Assembly met in a special session, no debate arose on the advisability of supporting tuition grants. After a close vote in committee, House Bill No. 50, the Perrow commission's assignment bill, passed the house and was sent to the senate. Supporters of the Perrow commission knew they had the votes to pass the measure in the full senate but not in the Education Committee.

Assigned to no meaningful committees, Armistead Boothe had discovered a parliamentary maneuver by which Perrow advocates could bypass the committee. After consulting Robert's *Rules of Order*, Jefferson's *Manual*, Cushing's "Elements of the Law and Practice of Legislative Assemblies," Hinds's *Precedents of the House of Representatives*, and Cannon's *Procedure in the House of Representatives*, Boothe traveled to Washington, D.C., and met with Lewis Deschler, the parliamentarian of the House of Representatives. Boothe discovered that when a bill originating in the house arrived in the senate, it was possible, but only before the bill was read, to move that a committee be discharged and the senate dissolved into the Committee of the Whole. On Friday, April 17, 1959, Perrow supporters did precisely this. The *Richmond News Leader* reported that a furious Harry Byrd, Jr., exclaimed that no precedent existed for such a maneuver. When Boothe referred to the House of Representatives, Byrd suggested that the Virginia General Assembly derived its precedents from the House of Burgesses, not the House of Representatives. Boothe acknowledged the accuracy of Byrd's statement and reminded him that the House of Burgesses derived its precedents from the House of Commons, where the Committee of the Whole was first used during the reign of James I during the debates on the union with Scotland. Proponents of the Perrow commission dissolved the senate into the Committee of the Whole by a 20-to-19 margin and adopted House Bill No. 50.[78]

Massive resisters made a final last-ditch effort to regain control of the senate in the 1959 primaries. *Time* reported that the most critical test was in Alexandria, where the Byrds personally involved themselves in the campaign of their cousin Marshall Beverly, a former mayor of Alexandria. To complete the family affair, James Thomson managed the bitter, vitriolic attack on Boothe. All too cognizant of Thomson's victory over Smoot in 1957, Boothe altered his campaign literature and speeches to reflect the nastiness of his opponent's attack. He ran on a platform of "public schools segregated to the limit allowed by law." He emphasized that for five years he had insisted that the schools could not remain open and fully segregated. In front of one group, Boothe declared that "the one political sin which I, as a Virginian and a segregationist, have committed is to tell you people of Alexandria the bitter truth." Boothe told the Alexandria Kiwanis Club that "in 1954 I was the first person in Virginia to advocate a plan of containment of integration in the public schools. Because of that I have been falsely labeled an integrationist. I am a southerner, born and bred. As a result I am a segregationist. I am not a degradationist. I have not, I do not and I shall not degrade every single American citizen who is born a Negro."[79]

Before the campaign ended Thomson asserted that in 1957 Almond had branded Boothe an integrationist. When Almond, at Boothe's request, denied the charges, Thomson released a two-page attack on the governor in which he recounted the instances when Almond had referred to Boothe as an integrationist who could not be trusted. Considering the intensity of the campaign, Boothe appeared genuinely surprised when he outpolled Beverly by a margin of almost two to one. *Time* magazine, the *New York Times*, and newspapers throughout Virginia interpreted Boothe's win as a major victory for the moderate forces now coalescing around Governor Almond. The election constituted a major defeat for the Byrd Organization's hopes of reviving massive resistance as well as a clear demonstration of the popular opposition to school closings among Boothe's northern Virginia constituents.[80]

In the wake of his 1959 victory over Marshall Beverly, Armistead Boothe reflected on the personal costs of his stand. It is significant that he chose to discuss his anguish with a group of college students in New Hampshire, far removed from the front line of Virginia politics. He told his audience that during the years of massive resistance, "all of us who were in office felt the tremendous tidal wave not only of anger and antipathy but of real ostracism." In reference to his 1954 plan, he said that although he was glad of the stand he had taken, "for four or five years I wished I had kept my big mouth shut."[81]

The personal and political wounds caused by massive resistance would be many more years in healing. In 1961 Boothe challenged Mills Godwin for the office of lieutenant governor, an election whose results indicate that pro–massive resistance sentiment did not die with the reopening of the schools in 1959. No two candidates could have stood in sharper contrast. Godwin, running with Albertis Harrison and Richard Button on what he described later as the last true Organization ticket, had the full backing of the Byrd machine at every level. Fully supported by his white constituents in the heart of the Southside, Godwin had shepherded the school-closing laws through the legislature in 1956 and remained an unrepentant massive resister long after Almond's capitulation in 1959. Boothe, on the other hand, had never wavered from his refusal to sanction defiance, preferring a little integration to closed schools.[82]

Despite the defeat of the school-closing laws in 1959, Organization influence remained strong. In a letter to Lewis Powell, Boothe wrote that he was expecting a "torrent of abuse" from Powell's friends in the Organization. He did not have long to wait. Godwin appealed to massive resistance sentiment by linking Boothe to the Supreme Court, labor unions, and the NAACP, all enemies of a segregated commonwealth. Furthermore, Boothe's late entrance into the campaign made it difficult for some influential Virginians who privately supported his position during the school-closing controversy to endorse his candidacy. Lewis Powell explained to Boothe that he had committed his support to Albertis Harrison and therefore could not endorse Boothe. Although the Alexandrian assured the future Supreme Court justice that his predicament would make "not the slightest dent or difference in our friendship," his feelings of isolation are not difficult to discern in a letter to Powell. Boothe and Godwin drew nearly equal support from urban voters, but Godwin garnered significant majorities in the Southside to win the election. Virginia's limited electorate, although in transition, assured the Organization another victory.[83]

Two years later, in 1963, Boothe retired from the General Assembly. In his final speech on the senate floor, he attempted to come to terms with his split from the Organization:

> It is not so much a difference in creed. We all believe in Virginia and her people. It is rather a difference in point of view or a difference in what we see when we look. You are content with what Virginia has done. We look forward to what she can do. You feel she is a way of life which must be preserved as nearly intact as possible. We feel Virginia is a living society who must change and grow in understanding and grow in leadership in a living world. The intellectual and moral wealth of Virginia is desperately needed by our Nation in determining, guiding, directing—not just accepting—the course of history.[84]

After his speech he turned to Harry Byrd, Jr., and jokingly asked if the Byrds would include him on their Christmas list of those who would receive apples from their orchards. Byrd responded that the request would depend on how Boothe acted between then and Christmas. Amid the laughter that followed the exchange, only those seated closest to Boothe heard him say, "Then I won't get the apples."[85]

Throughout his legislative career Armistead Boothe challenged the power of the very Organization into which he was born. Anti-Organization adherents would have liked Boothe to resist more forcefully, but he maintained a vigilant awareness of the politically possible. He once wrote that Harry Byrd, Sr., "was the most sensitive and accurate pulse feeler of his people. He did not exactly lead them. He was their listener and then their voice which called them to follow themselves. Consequently when he erred on important issues such as school closing, he had to be resisted and defeated tactfully, with gloved hands, and from within the organization."[86]

Boothe's sense of fairness, belief in the sanctity of the individual, and understanding of the role of government, however, finally forced him to part ways with the Organization. Throughout the 1950s Boothe's rhetoric shifted to reflect and counter the rising tide of extremism in Virginia. The essence of his personal and political philosophy, however, remained constant. He recognized early the changes taking place in Virginia in the years following World War II and insisted that the commonwealth's political leadership take the initiative in meeting the challenges ahead. Most state leaders instead preferred to react to circumstances. Boothe fought to increase funding for the state's schools, hospitals, and highways. He sought to ameliorate the worst injustices of Virginia's Jim Crow laws and argued for more equitable treatment of all citizens of the state. He believed fervently in the sanctity of the law, both state and federal, and took seriously the mandate in Virginia's constitution to reapportion the state.

As segregation in the public schools came to dominate public discourse in the 1950s, Boothe fought to keep the schools open at all costs. He stressed Virginia's commitment to the sanctity of the individual and emphasized a need to recognize the achievements of certain individual blacks, even if it meant allowing selected black students into white schools. But Boothe's emphasis on individual, qualified blacks depended upon a conception of the black race as inferior to the white race. Several of Boothe's more liberal contemporaries recognized the limitations of his views, but such distinctions did not register with most white Virginians in the 1950s.

Boothe's political sensitivity and personal philosophy guided his efforts to force white citizens of the Old Dominion to recognize and come to terms with the flaws in their society. He was mistaken, perhaps, to have believed that he could fashion a compromise acceptable to all Virginians. Nevertheless, he pleaded and cajoled, in a reasoned and dispassionate manner, for white Virginians to look beyond their traditions and customs. He saw no point in continuing to force unnecessary humiliations upon an entire segment of society. But in the 1950s passions and prejudice subsumed all other emotions; consequently, many white Virginians were not yet ready to accept even his inherently conservative vision. That acceptance would require a great deal more time and concerted effort on the part of many citizens, black and white, throughout Virginia and the nation.

NOTES

1. General Assembly of Virginia, *Manual of the Senate and House of Delegates, Session 1948* (Richmond, 1948), 87–89, 159–205.

2. *Time*, Sept. 22, 1958, 16, cited in Wilkinson, *Harry Byrd and the Changing Face of Virginia Politics*, 16.

3. Allen W. Moger, *Virginia: Bourbonism to Byrd, 1870–1925* (Charlottesville, Va., 1968), 346–55; Key, *Southern Politics in State and Nation*, 21–25; Wilkinson, *Harry Byrd and the Changing Face of Virginia Politics*, 9–61 (Almond quoted on p. 16); *WP*, July 29, 1951.

4. Moger, *Virginia: Bourbonism to Byrd*, 328, 353–54, 368–69; Key, *Southern Politics in State and Nation*, 19.

5. ALB, "A Virginia Plan for the Public Schools," *Virginia Journal of Education* 48 (Dec. 1954): 29; telephone interview, Guy Friddell, March 12, 1993; interview, James Latimer, March 25, 1993; interview, E. Griffith Dodson, Jr., March 28, 1993; interview, George M. Cochran, April 9, 1993.

6. ALB to HFB, Sr., Feb. 19, 1934, Harry F. Byrd, Sr., Papers, ViU; Guy Friddell, "'The Laughing Cavalier' Sided with Future," *RNL*, Feb. 15, 1990, 6.

7. *RTD*, March 7, 1948.

8. Friddell, "'The Laughing Cavalier,'" *RNL*, Feb. 15, 1990, 6; Friddell telephone interview; memo from Harry F. Byrd, Jr.'s campaign headquarters to Charles R. Fenwick, June 1, 1966, box 3, Charles R. Fenwick Papers, ViU; assorted newspaper clippings in Armistead L. Boothe Papers, acc. no. 8319-a, ViU, and Boothe Family Collection, Lloyd House, Alexandria, Va.; Cochran interview; *RTD*, Feb. 14, 1982.

9. ALB, "Civil Rights in Virginia," *Virginia Law Review* 35 (Nov. 1949): 951–52, 964–65.

10. Ibid., 958–59; *Norvell Lee v. Commonwealth of Virginia*, 189 Va. 890 (1949). Norvell Lee, an Olympic athlete and student at Howard University, had bought a ticket from Clifton Forge to Covington. Because the entire journey constituted intrastate travel, he was thrown off the train for sitting in a car designated for whites. Lee then purchased a ticket to Washington, D.C., reboarded the train, and was arrested for violating Virginia's segregation statutes. He was found not guilty because his second ticket classified him an interstate passenger.

11. ALB, "Civil Rights in Virginia," 968–70.

12. Friddell telephone interview; ALB, speech at Episcopal High School, Jan. 19, 1957, box 14, Boothe Papers.

13. ALB, "Speech to Naturalized Citizens," April 13, 1960, box 14, ALB, "Speech to Disabled Veterans Convention," June 18, 1961, box 15, ALB, book review of Dumas Malone's *Jefferson and the Ordeal of Liberty*, box 2, ALB, Law Day speech, "Law of Mason," April 30, 1965, box 15, Boothe Papers.

14. *Norfolk Virginian-Pilot*, May 10, 1950, clipping in Boothe Family Collection.

15. Cochran interview; Dodson interview.

16. Cochran interview; Dodson interview; copy of speech from files of E. Griffith Dodson, Jr., now in my possession.

17. Assorted newspaper clippings in Boothe Family Collection; *Norfolk Virginian-Pilot*, Feb. 25, 1950, 6.

18. Newspaper clippings in the Boothe Family Collection; Friddell telephone interview; *RTD*, Feb. 14, 1982.

19. *RTD*, Feb. 25, 1950; Cochran interview.

20. HFB, Sr., to Gardner L. Boothe, March 13, 1950, Boothe to HFB, Sr., March 15, 1950, Byrd Papers.

21. ALB, "A Handbook of Redistricting the Senate and House of Delegates of Virginia, 1952," box 10, Boothe Papers; *Alexandria Gazette*, May 24, Sept. 17, 1952; *RTD*, Sept. 17, 1952; Winston Bain to E. Griffith Dodson, Jr., Sept. 11, 1952, in my possession; *WP*, June 1, 1952.

22. C. Emerson Smith to ALB, April 21, 28, 1953, ALB to Smith, May 1, 1953, to John S. Battle, May 5, 1953, W. Carroll Brooke to ALB, May 12, 1953, ALB to Brooke, May 15, 1953, to Smith, May 21, 1953, box 1, Boothe Papers; Kluger, *Simple Justice*, 614–16.

23. ALB to Smith, Oct. 30, 1953, W. L. Ransome to ALB, Dec. 7, 1953, ALB to Ransome, Dec. 10, 1953, to Smith, Dec. 29, 1953, box 1, Boothe Papers.

24. ALB, notes on speech delivered on the floor of the house of delegates, March 8, 1954, ibid.; *RTD*, March 9, 1954; citation from the Astoria Beneficial Club, Richmond, to ALB, March 8, 1954, citation from the Richmond Civic Council to ALB, Feb. 16, 1954, box 1, Boothe Papers.

25. Interview, John F. Rixey, March 19, 1993; letter from "A Young Turk" to the author, April 6, 1993 (this correspondent, a former delegate, requested anonymity).

26. Newspaper clippings, boxes 10–13, Boothe Papers; *RTD*, March 16, 1954; James Latimer, "Longest Legislative Day Brought New Dawn for Virginia Politics," *RTD*, March 4, 1990, F5.

27. Newspaper clippings, boxes 10–13, Boothe Papers; *RTD*, March 16, 1954; Latimer, "Longest Legislative Day," ibid., March 4, 1990, F5; interview, Mills E. Godwin, Jr., March 19, 1993.

28. Newspaper clippings, boxes 10–13, Boothe Papers; *RTD*, March 16, 1954; letter from "A Young Turk" to the author, April 6, 1993.

29. *Roanoke Times*, March 16, 1954; "A Young Turk" to the author, April 6, 1993; interview, William B. Spong, Jr., March 19, 1993; Rixey interview.

30. "A Young Turk" to the author, April 6, 1993; John A. MacKenzie to the author, April 12, 1993; Cochran interview; HFB, Sr., to Gardner L. Boothe, March 13, 1950, Byrd Papers; *RNL*, March 13, 1954; Rixey interview.

31. Dr. Edward E. Haddock to the author, April 14, 1993.

32. *RTD*, May 18, June 22, 1954.

33. Gates, *Making of Massive Resistance*, 31; interview, Oliver W. Hill, April 8, 1993; *RTD*, June 21, 1954.

34. *RTD*, June 22, 26, 1954.

35. "Turkeygram" from ALB, box 12, Boothe Papers.

36. ALB to Colgate W. Darden, Jr., July 6, 1954, ibid. Boothe sent copies of the same letter to a number of state leaders. See ibid.

37. Henry B. Gordon to ALB, July 23, 1954, "A Young Turk" to ALB, July 13, 1954, C. W. Cleaton to ALB, July 23, 1954, box 13, ibid.

38. John F. Rixey to ALB, Aug. 25, 1954, Toy D. Savage, Jr., to ALB, July 21, 1954, box 13, ibid.

39. ALB to Thomas B. Stanley, Aug. 7, 1954, box 13, ibid.

40. M. J. Menefee to W. Moscoe Huntley, Aug. 17, 1954, Byrd Papers; *RNL*, Aug. 28, 1954; ALB to "A Young Turk," July 19, 1954, box 13, Boothe Papers.

41. *RTD*, Aug. 29, 30, 1954; *Norfolk Journal and Guide*, Sept. 4, 1954; Robert Baldwin to ALB, Sept. 4, 1954, box 12, Boothe Papers.

42. ALB to James C. N. Paul, Sept. 3, 1954, ALB to Robert Baldwin, Sept. 9, 1954, box 12, Boothe Papers.

43. ALB, "A Virginia Plan for the Public Schools," 29–31, reprinted in the *Roanoke Times*, Oct. 17–20, 1954. Boothe's two speeches followed a small statement he submitted to the *Virginia Journal of Education* in September in which he outlined his emerging views. Only Boothe and Robert Whitehead were willing to submit such declarations. Both the governor and Attorney General Almond replied that "they were not ready to make a statement," even four months after *Brown*. See "Supreme Court Decision Poses Problem for All," *Virginia Journal of Education* 48 (Sept. 1954): 15–16.

44. ALB, "A Virginia Plan for the Public Schools"; ALB to Robert E. Houston, Jr., Nov. 11, 1954, box 12, Boothe Papers; Albert Coates and James C. N. Paul, *The School Segregation Decision: A Report to the Governor of North Carolina on the Decision of the Supreme Court of the United States on the 17th of May 1954* (Chapel Hill, N.C., 1954).

45. D. Edward Hudgins to ALB, Nov. 16, 1954, Robert E. Houston, Jr., to ALB,

Nov. 11, 1954, Rufus B. King to ALB, Nov. 1, 1954, Lenoir Chambers to ALB, Oct. 21, 1954, box 12, Boothe Papers; *Norfolk Virginian-Pilot*, Oct. 21, 23, 1954.

46. *Norfolk Journal and Guide* (Virginia-Carolina ed.), Oct. 23, 1954.

47. P. B. Young, Sr., to ALB, Oct. 29, 1954, box 12, Boothe Papers; interview, Oliver Hill and Spottswood Robinson III, April 8, 1993.

48. Marion Galland to ALB, March 23, 1955, box 12, Boothe Papers; interview, Marion Galland, March 17, 1993.

49. ALB to Eileen Eddy, Sept. 23, 1954, to Hudgins, Nov. 22, 1954, to Herbert Cochran, Sept. 20, 1954, to the Rev. Robert S. Seiler, Sept. 30, 1954, to the Rev. Emerson Smith, Nov. 4, 1954, to Young, Dec. 2, 1954, box 12, Boothe Papers.

50. ALB to Houston, Sept. 30, 1957, box 13, ibid.

51. Ibid.

52. Benjamin Muse, "When and How the South Will Integrate," *Harper's Magazine*, April 1957, 54.

53. ALB, speech in opposition to House Joint Resolution No. 97, Feb.–March 1956, box 8, Boothe Papers.

54. Virginius Dabney to ALB, Oct. 15, 1954, FitzGerald Bemiss to ALB, Oct. 29, 1954, John W. Riely to ALB, Oct. 25, 1954, Lewis F. Powell, Jr., to Kenneth Chorley, Oct. 29, 1954, box 12, ibid.

55. Gates, *Making of Massive Resistance*, 57; John A. MacKenzie to the author, April 12, 1993.

56. ALB to Savage, Nov. 3, 1954, ALB to Brooke, March 11, 1955, box 12, Boothe Papers.

57. "Senate Document No. 1, Public Education: Report of the Commission to the Governor of Virginia," *House and Senate Documents, Virginia: Extra Session 1955, Regular Session 1956* (Richmond, 1956); *RTD*, Nov. 13, 1955; Gates, *Making of Massive Resistance*, 64–67.

58. Omer L. Hirst to the author, April 27, 1993.

59. *Senate Journal, Virginia: Extra Session 1955, Regular Session 1956* (Richmond, 1956), Dec. 3, 1955, 96; Hirst to the author, April 27, 1993; "Speech Delivered by Armistead Boothe . . . Dec. 2, 1955," box 11, Boothe Papers; Hershman, "A Rumbling in the Museum," 126; Gates, *Making of Massive Resistance*, 75.

60. Gates, *Making of Massive Resistance*, 75–83; Hershman, "A Rumbling in the Museum," 126–33; Hirst to the author, April 27, 1993.

61. Hershman, "A Rumbling in the Museum," 125–39; Gates, *Making of Massive Resistance*, 75–83.

62. *Senate Journal, Virginia: Extra Session 1955, Regular Session 1956* (Richmond, 1956), 2–4, 39–40; *General Assembly of Virginia: Manual of the Senate and House of Delegates, Session 1956* (Richmond, 1956), 30–46; *Manual of the Senate and House of Delegates, Session 1948* (Richmond, 1948), 20–29; Spong interview; Wilkinson, *Harry Byrd and the Changing Face of Virginia Politics*, 112.

63. Gates, *Making of Massive Resistance*, 79, 119–22; statements of ALB and Ted Dalton, March 1, 1956, box 7, Boothe Papers; Omer L. Hirst to the author, April 27, 1993.

64. *RNL*, Nov. 21–23, 28–29, Dec. 1, 1955, Jan. 18–19, 23 (quotation), 25, 31, 1956; Godwin interview.

65. ALB, "Virginia's Place in Constitutional History: Nationalism vs. States' Rights," Jan. 31, 1956, box 6, Boothe Papers.

66. Ibid.; Hershman, "A Rumbling in the Museum," 165; Gates, *Making of Massive Resistance*, 155–56; Haddock to the author, April 14, 1993.

67. Haddock to the author, April 14, 1993; Galland interview; Hirst to the author, April 27, 1993.

68. Muse, *Virginia's Massive Resistance*, 22–27; Latimer interview.

69. Muse, *Virginia's Massive Resistance*, 28–30, 170–71; Gates, *Making of Massive Resistance*, 133 (Tuck quotation); Wilkinson, *Harry Byrd and the Changing Face of Virginia Politics*, 132.

70. Wilkinson, *Harry Byrd and the Changing Face of Virginia Politics*, 132.

71. Muse, *Virginia's Massive Resistance*, 30–34; Hershman, "A Rumbling in the Museum," 173–79; *RNL*, Sept. 6, 1956.

72. Muse, *Virginia's Massive Resistance*, 30–32.

73. *Alexandria Gazette*, April 24, 1959, Feb. 4, 1958; *Alexandria Advocate* (ALB's campaign newsletter), June 15, July 4, 1959, box 3, Boothe Papers.

74. Robbins L. Gates's interview with ALB, July 20, 1957, in Gates, *Making of Massive Resistance*, 197–200; *WP*, July 11, 1957, clipping in Boothe Family Collection; Muse, *Virginia's Massive Resistance*, 33–34; interview, Helen Dewar, March 15, 1993.

75. "Inaugural Address of J. Lindsay Almond, Jr., Governor," Saturday, Jan. 11, 1958, *Senate Document 3*, 6–8; ALB, "Remarks on Senate Bill No. 337," Feb. 28, 1958, box 13, *Alexandria Gazette*, Feb. 4, 1958, clipping in box 11, Boothe Papers.

76. Statement of ALB, Sept. 18, 1958, box 14, Boothe Papers.

77. "Address of Governor J. Lindsay Almond, Jr., of Virginia, January 20, 1959," box 14, Boothe Papers; Muse, *Virginia's Massive Resistance*, 131–38; Spong interview; Latimer interview.

78. Statement of April 23, 1959, box 13, ALB speech at Colby Junior College, New Hampshire, Oct. 1959, box 15, *RNL*, April 18, 21, 1959, clippings in box 13, Boothe Papers; interview, Paul Saunier, Jr., Feb. 25, 1993.

79. *Time*, July 27, 1959, 14; *Alexandria Advocate*, June 15, July 4, 1959, box 3, ALB, "Talk to Alexandria Kiwanis Club," April 9, 1959, "Outline of Speech—Del Ray Citizens Assoc.," April 30, 1959, box 14, Boothe Papers.

80. *Alexandria Gazette*, June 16–17, 1959; *Time*, July 27, 1959, 14; *New York Times*, July 19, 1959, clipping in box 2, Boothe Papers; James Thomson to J. Lindsay Almond, Jr., June 25, 1959, Boothe Family Collection.

81. ALB speech at Colby Junior College, New Hampshire, Oct. 1959, box 15, Boothe Papers.

82. Godwin interview.

83. Powell to ALB, May 25, 1961, ALB to Powell, June 1, 1961, box 5, Boothe Papers; Wilkinson, *Harry Byrd and the Changing Face of Virginia Politics*, 239, 267.

84. *Washington Evening Star*, Nov. 21 or 22, 1963, clipping in box 11, Boothe Papers.

85. Ibid.; Friddell, "'The Laughing Cavalier,'" *RNL*, Feb. 15, 1990, 6.

86. Haddock to the author, April 14, 1993; Hirst to the author, April 27, 1993; ALB, review of *Man from the Valley: Memoirs of a 20th-Century Virginian* by Francis Pickens Miller, *Washington Evening Star*, May 24, 1971, clipping in Boothe Family Collection.

EXPANDED CITATIONS

ALB   Armistead Lloyd Boothe

HFB, Sr.   Harry Flood Byrd, Sr.

Robbins Gates, *The Making of Massive Resisitance: Virginia's Politics of School Desegregation, 1954–1956* (Chapel Hill, N.C., 1962)

James H. Hershman, Jr., "A Rumbling in the Museum: The Opponents of Virginia's Massive Resistance" (Ph.D. diss., Univ. of Virginia, 1977)

V. O. Key, Jr., *Southern Politics in State and Nation* (New York, 1949)

Richard Kluger, *Simple Justice: The History of* Brown v. Board of Education *and Black America's Struggle for Equality* (New York, 1976)

Benjamin Muse, *Virginia's Massive Resistance* (Bloomington, Ind., 1961)

RNL   Richmond News Leader

RTD   Richmond Times-Dispatch

J. Harvie Wilkinson, *Harry Byrd and the Changing Face of Virginia Politics, 1945–1966* (Charlottesville, Va., 1968)

ViU   University of Virginia, Charlottesville

WP   Washington Post

Contributors

STEPHEN V. ASH is associate professor of history at the University of Tennessee, Knoxville. He is the author of *When the Yankees Came: Conflict and Chaos in the Occupied South, 1861–1865* (1995) and other studies.

FRED ARTHUR BAILEY is professor and chair of the History Department at Abilene Christian University. He is the author of numerous books and articles in southern history, including most recently *William Edward Dodd: The South's Yeoman Scholar* (1997).

THOMAS E. BUCKLEY, S.J., is professor of American religious history at the Jesuit School of Theology at Berkeley/Graduate Theological Union. His most recent book is *The Great Catastrophe of My Life: Divorce in the Old Dominion* (2002).

GREGORY MICHAEL DORR is assistant professor at the University of Alabama, where he teaches southern history. His scholarship focuses on the eugenics movement in twentieth-century Virginia. His essay in this volume won the 2002 Fletcher M. Green and Charles M. Ramsdell Award from the Southern Historical Association.

J. FREDERICK FAUSZ is a history professor and former Honors College dean at the University of Missouri–St. Louis. He earned his Ph.D. from the College of William and Mary, specializing in seventeenth-century Chesapeake ethnohistory, and now focuses much of his research on the North American fur trades and the Lewis and Clark Expedition. He has consulted on many film documentaries involving Indians, including *Roanoak* (PBS) and Kevin Costner's *500 Nations* (CBS). His contribution to this collection won the 1991 William M. E. Rachal Award of the Virginia Historical Society.

ELNA C. GREEN is Allen Morris Associate Professor of History at Florida State University. She is the author of numerous books and articles on southern women's history including *Southern Strategies: Southern Women and the Woman Suffrage Question* (1997) and editor of *Before the New Deal: Social*

Welfare in the South, 1830–1930 (1999). Her most recent work, *This Business of Relief: Confronting Poverty in a Southern City, 1740–1940,* is forthcoming from the University of Georgia Press.

Jack P. Greene is Andrew W. Mellon Professor of the Humanities at Johns Hopkins University. He is the author of numerous books and essays in early American history. Many of his essays on eighteenth-century Virginia have been reprinted in Jack P. Greene, *Imperatives, Behaviors, and Identities: Essays in Early American Cultural History* (1992); Greene, *Negotiated Authorities: Essays in Colonial Political and Constitutional History* (1994); and Greene, *Understanding the American Revolution: Issues and Actors* (1995).

Kevin R. Hardwick is assistant professor at James Madison University, where he teaches the history of British colonial America and Virginia history. His scholarship has appeared in the *Journal of Social History*.

Warren R. Hofstra is Stewart Bell Professor of History and director of the Community History Project at Shenandoah University, Winchester, Virginia. He is author of *A Separate Place: The Formation of Clarke County, Virginia* (1986, 1999), editor of *George Washington and the Virginia Backcountry* (1998), and co-editor of *After the Backcountry: Rural Life in the Great Valley of Virginia, 1800–1900* (2000). His most recent book, *The Planting of New Virginia: Shenandoah Valley Landscapes, 1800–1900,* is forthcoming from Johns Hopkins University Press in 2003.

Woody Holton is assistant professor of history at the University of Richmond. His book *Forced Founders: Indians, Debtors, Slaves, and the Making of the American Revolution in Virginia* (1999) won the 2000 Merle Curti Award in American Social History and the 2000 Fraunces Tavern Museum Book Award.

Deborah A. Lee is a contract historian specializing in local, African-American, and public history. She recently completed an African-American Heritage Trail of Leesburg, Virginia, and a dissertation on Ann R. Page and the antislavery movement in the upper South. She directs an oral history project in Loudoun County and is an adjunct professor of history at Lord Fairfax Community College in Fauquier County, Virginia.

Jan Lewis is professor of history at Rutgers University, Newark. She is the author of *The Pursuit of Happiness: Family and Values in Jefferson's Virginia* (1983); co-author of *Making a Nation: The United States and Its People* (2002); and co-editor of several books, including *Sally Hemings and Thomas Jefferson: History, Memory, and Civic Culture* (1999) and *The Revolution of 1800: Democracy, Race, and the New Republic* (2002).

EDMUND S. MORGAN is Sterling Professor of History Emeritus at Yale University. He is the author of numerous books and articles on early America, including the seminal 1975 work in Virginia history *American Slavery, American Freedom: The Ordeal of Colonial Virginia.*

DARRETT B. and ANITA H. RUTMAN were on the history faculty of the University of New Hampshire when they wrote *A Place in Time: Middlesex County, Virginia, 1650–1750* (1984). Both subsequently moved to the University of Florida, where together they published *Small Worlds, Large Questions: Explorations in Early American Social History, 1600–1850* (1994). Darrett Rutman's most notable publications include *Winthrop's Boston: Portrait of a Puritan Town, 1630–1649* (1965) and *John Winthrop's Decision for America, 1629* (1975).

J. DOUGLAS SMITH received his Ph.D. in American history from the University of Virginia in 1998. He is now a visiting assistant professor at Occidental College in Los Angeles. Smith is the author of *Managing White Supremacy: Race, Politics, and Citizenship in Jim-Crow Virginia* (2003) and the co-editor of "World War II on the Web: A Guide to the Very Best Sites" (2002). His contribution to this volume first appeared in the *Virginia Magazine of History and Biography* in January 1994 and received the journal's C. Coleman McGehee Award.

ELIZABETH R. VARON is associate professor of history at Wellesley College. She is author of *We Mean to Be Counted: White Women and Politics in Antebellum Virginia* (1998), which argues that white, slaveholding, southern women were active participants in partisan and sectional politics. She has also written articles in the *Journal of American History, Virginia Cavalcade,* and the *Alabama Law Review.*

Index

Note: The italicized *t* following page numbers refers to tables.

Atwood, James, 84–85
Auxiliary Society of Frederick County, 212–14, 225
Aylmer, Justinian, 103n. 30

B. F. Johnson Publishing Company, 306–7
Bacon, Nathaniel, 63, 66, 89–90, 99
Bacon's Rebellion, 8, 11–12, 61, 65, 74, 89–95
Bailey, Fred Arthur, 8–9, 202, 235, 274, 296–97, 354
Bailey, John, 161n. 64
Baker, James, 212
Baldwin, Robert, 408
Bandit gangs, 282
Banks, Enoch M., 320n. 54
Banned books, 301–3, 312–13
Baptists, 109, 207
Barbados, slave codes in, 64
Barbour, Benjamin Johnson, 271
Barbour, James, 264, 267
Barbour, Lillie, 332
Barbour, Lucy: Clay monument proposal, 264–65; defended by press, 268; introductory notes, 4, 263, 322; outside historical mainstream, 271; reformers in debt to, 272; and Whig womanhood, 267–68
Barnaba (Berkeley slave): in Berkeley murder, 205–6; capture of, 208; clemency granted to, 218, 231n. 44; murder trial of, 215; sentencing of, 217
Barrett, Janie Porter, 272, 327
Barrett, Kate Waller, 328
Barringer, Paul B., 357
Bassett, John Spencer, 311
Battle, John S., 401, 402, 414
Battles: Concord, 142–43, 144, 146; Hampton, 136–37; Henrico, 14t, 15, 30–31; Lexington, 142–43, 144, 146; Manassas, 221; Nansemond, 14t, 15
Baugh, Bartlett, 249
Baugh, Thomas, 249
Bawdes, Mary, 85

Bawdes, William, 85
Bean, Robert Bennett, 358, 367
Bean, William Bennett, 367, 369
Beaver Dam, 75
Becker, Carl, 135
Beckley, John, 197n. 51
Beeman, Richard R., 236
Bell, John, 271
Bell Curve, The (Herrnstein and Murray), 376
Bemiss, FitzGerald, 412
Benevolent societies, 265, 269, 271
Bentley, Matthew, 84, 91, 92, 93, 94, 95
Berkeley, Julia Carter: about, 207; deceived by slaves, 208; disappearance of husband, 206–7; in ghost story, 223–24; marriage of, 203–4; portrayals of, 222–23; silence after husband's murder, 219
Berkeley, Nelson, 203
Berkeley, Robert: about, 203–4, 227n. 1; in Auxiliary Society of Frederick County, 214; character of, 217; confessions of murderers, 208–9; corpse burned, 205–6; as failed master, 219, 221; folklore of murder, 218; ghost story about murder, 223–24; introductory notes, 8, 106, 202–3, 235; marriage of, 203–4; as metaphor for crime of slavery, 226; murder of, 203, 204–6; neglect of Christian duties, 218; ongoing accounts of murder, 220–25, 226, 232n. 49, 233n. 56; search for, 208; slaves held by, 204, 227n. 4; trials for murder of, 211–12, 214–18; trusted by wife, 207
Berkeley, William, 61, 66, 89–90, 98–99
Berlin, Ira, 236
Beverley, Robert, 38, 90, 94, 95, 98
Beverly, Marshall, 420, 421
Bible, citations of, 214, 308
Blackford, Mary Minor, 271
Blackford, William, 92
Blacks: assimilation of, 368; contra-

Buckley, Thomas E., 4, 234–35
Buildings, 77–78. *See also* Houses
Burgh, James, 53
Burke, Edmund, 140
Burke, Henry, 88
Burke, John, 81–82, 88–89
Burnham, John, 90, 95
Burr, Aaron, 177, 178, 182, 197n. 50
Bushwhacker gangs, 279–80
Button, Richard, 420
Byrd, Harry, Jr., 395, 397, 401, 414, 420, 422
Byrd, Harry, Sr., 395–96, 397, 400, 401, 405, 416, 422
Byrd, William, 61–62
Byrd, William II, 122
Byrd, William III, 126, 150
Byrd Organization: about, 395–96; and Boothe, 396–97, 400, 402, 405, 412, 414, 422; control of state senate, 404; influence of, 421–22; on interposition issue, 415; Young Turks, 403–5, 406, 413

Cabell, Nicholas, 256n. 13
Caffrey, Charles, 237
Caffrey, Sarah, 237
Callender, James Thomson, 175–82, 196n. 42, 197n. 51
Camm, John, 112
Campbell, James, 159n. 51
Campbell, Sarah Winston, 241
Campbell, William, 147
Campbell County, 235, 237, 238, 240
Cane, Bastian, 69n. 39
Captain Peter, 149
Caribbean, English exploitation of, 57
Carpetbaggers, 309, 325
Carter, Charles, 138–39
Carter, Elizabeth Wormeley, 203
Carter, George, 205, 207, 216
Carter, John, 207
Carter, Julia. *See* Berkeley, Julia Carter
Carter, Landon: on despotism, 121; on Dunmore, 146, 150; on gentry, 109, 114; on good of community, 120; on man's imperfections, 117–18; on pa-

triotism, 123; as scholarly, 115, 116; on slavery, 55
Carter, Robert, 150, 203, 207–8, 213
Carter, Stuart, 404, 413, 414, 416
Cartmell, Thomas K., 220, 223
Cary, Archibald, 150
Cary, Mary Miller, 335
Catt, Carrie Chapman, 325–26, 341, 342
Censored books, 305
Charities. *See* Benevolent societies
Chatham Episcopal Institute, 313
Chesapeake system, 91–92, 103n. 39
Chesapeaks, 16
Chicheley, Henry, 85, 98–99
Chicheley family land, 82
Chickahominies, 14*t*, 15, 16, 27, 47n. 49
Children: aspirations of, 81–82; in compulsory labor, 52; court appearances of, 96; indoctrination with antebellum values, 297–98; influenced by Daughters of Confederacy, 304–6; labor laws, 327; mortality rates of, 86; slaves as fugitives, 149, 161n. 70; traditional outlook of, 82
Children of the Confederacy, 304–6
Chiswell's Mines, 137
Chowning, Robert, 86
Christ Church Parish, 78
Christian, George L., 297, 301, 303, 311
Christians: duties of, 226; slavery positions of, 210; spiritual instruction of slaves, 210, 214, 226
Church. *See* Religion
Churchill, William, 86
Cimarrons, 57
Civilians: in bushwhacker gangs, 279–80; under civil administration, 279; conciliatory policy toward, 277; emergency rations issued to, 288; flight from invaders, 277; guerrilla warfare of, 279–80; hostility toward Union forces, 278; poor whites, 284–85; slave patrols of, 276–77
Civil rights, 354, 397–99

Civil War: aftermath of, 8; amnesty program, 288; controversies over meaning, 296; and freedom, 4–5, 275; government restoration after, 287–88; literature on, 274; as Lost Cause, 219; monuments to heroes, 219, 232n. 51; neutrality on issues leading to, 303; in revisionist history, 307–9; slave population during, 285; societal disruption, 282–83; and states' rights, 9; Unionists after, 288–89; Union occupation of Virginia, 275–83, 285–87; violence of, 8. *See also* Civilians

Clagett, Ann, 269
Clark, Adele, 328, 345–46
Clark, Charles W., 354–55, 372–73
Clark, Taliaferro, 357
Clarke, Colin, 285, 286
Clarke, John, 94
Class conflict, and Revolution, 153, 163n. 86
Clay, Henry: death of, 270; introductory note, 4; monument to, 264–72; statesmanship of, 270; as symbol of compromise, 271; against Texas annexation, 270; as Virginia native son, 270; as Whig Party leader, 264; on women in politics, 267
Clay, Laura, 327–28
Clay Association: ceremony for Clay monument, 271; and Confederate benevolent societies, 271; Democrat Party attacks on, 268–69; formation of, 264–65; fundraising for Clay monument, 269, 270; on women's political participation, 268
Clingman, Jacob, 175
Clopton, William H., 286–87
Cochran, George M., 395, 397, 400, 404, 405
Cocke, Bowler, 139
Cocke, Maurice, 84
Cocke, Nicholas, 84, 92, 93, 95
Coke, Edward, 117
Colins, Henry, 140
Colonial expansionism, 36, 37

Colonies: anti-British sentiment, 142–45; blacks' status in, 58–59; early establishments, 57–58; molded on English model, 59
Colonists: aspirations of, 2–3; desertion of Jamestown, 45n. 37; in race war, 37; segregation from Powhatans, 26
Colonization, of free blacks, 212–13, 214, 236. *See also* American Colonization Society
Compulsory labor, 52–53, 55
Concord, battle of, 142–43, 144, 146
Confederate forces: areas held by, 276; surrender of, 287; against Unionists, 283
Confederate societies: Association for the Preservation of Virginia Antiquities, 300; defense of views, 297; Grand Camp of Confederate Veterans, 301, 302–3, 310–11, 319n. 46; in historical preservation, 301; reaffirmation of southern aristocracy, 298; Sons of Confederate Veterans, 303, 309; in textbook controversy, 312–13; United Confederate Veterans, 297, 316n. 9; United Daughters of the Confederacy, 297–301, 303–7, 312, 318n. 29
Confessions: of Berkeley's murderers, 208–9; interpretations of slaves, 218
Congressional Union, 337, 338–40. *See also* National Woman's Party
Connolly, John, 151
Conservatism, 396, 410
Constitutional Union Party, 271
Contraception, for blacks, 369
Conway, Edwin, 119
Cook, William, 211
Coolidge, Ellen, 166
Cooper, Oscar H., 302–3
Corbin, Alice Eltonhead, 99
Corbin, Henry, 99
Corbin, Richard, 144
Corn, as currency, 85
Court days, 95–99

Courts: actions involving Bacon's rebellion, 90–91, 98–99, 104n. 42; Berkeley's murderers trials, 211–12, 214–18, 231n. 37; blacks' rights, 58–59; divorce jurisdiction lacking in, 235; documents used by historians, 237; Middlesex County issues, 91, 94–95; officers in Middlesex County, 94, 95–96; paternalism of, 214–15; petition system, 97; role of motivation, 224; slave trials in antebellum era, 223; typical sessions in Middlesex County, 95–99. *See also* Law

Cox, Earnest Sevier, 363, 365, 366, 376, 388n. 72, 391n. 103

Cox, Thomas, 148, 160n. 60

Crank, Thomas, 92

Craven, Wesley Frank, 25

Creationism, 360

Crown offices, 111

Crump, James D., 336

Cumming, Hugh Smith, 357

Currency: corn as, 85; tobacco as, 78–79, 84, 85, 237; Two-Penny Acts, 120, 123

Curtis, John, 84

Cussons, John, 301–2, 303, 317n. 22

D. C. Heath and Company, 306

Dabney, Virginius, 371–72, 412

Dale, Thomas: and Devereux, 29; expiration of service term, 33; First Anglo-Powhatan War, 12–13; fleet of, 28, 45n. 35; governance of, 12; as governor, 28–29; lenient diplomacy of, 34; Pamunkey invasion, 33; peace of 1614, 34; peace quest, 32; against Powhatans, 30–31

Dallis, Dennis, 139

Dalton, Ted, 413, 414–15, 417

Dandridge, Serena, 268

Danger (British warship), 151

Daniell, Robert (brothers with same name), 84, 86, 88

Daniell, William, 84, 86

Darden, Colgate W., Jr., 400–401, 414

Darwin, Charles, 365, 376

Davidson, Polly: in adulterous relationship, 244–45; cohabitation with Robert Wright, 241–42, 253; community acceptance of taboo violation, 252; inheritance battle of, 246–47, 259n. 44, 260n. 51; pregnancy of, 260n. 46; in Robert Wright will, 246

Davidson, Samuel, 258n. 30

Davidson, William, 242

Davies, Samuel, 114, 128, 129

Davis, Caroline Preston, 336

Davis, Eliza Timberlake, 222–23, 231–32n. 47

Davis, James, 211, 212, 217

Davis, Jefferson, 222

Davis, John, 26, 222

Davis, Pauline Wright, 324, 325

Davis, Stephen, 222

Davis, Westmoreland, 341

Dawson, John, 177

Death. *See* Mortality rates

Debs, Eugene, 333

Debt, 51–52

Declaration of Independence, 165, 167, 214

Degeneracy, 126–29

De La Warr, Lord, 12–13, 24, 25, 26, 27, 28

Democratic Party: and Byrd Organization, 395–96; Clay Association attacked by, 268–69; and Clay monument proposal, 264; control over state politics, 321; election restrictions by, 326, 344; white women aligned with, 345; women ignored by, 268

Demographics: changing age structure of white population, 87; death rates, 59; early population growth, 56; gender disparities, 60, 70n. 50; immigration rates, 59; ratio of natives to immigrants, 86; servants in Middlesex County, 83; slave population during Civil War, 285; slaves in Virginia, 50; tithables ratios,

England (*continued*)
   rumors of slave insurrections encouraged by, 140, 147–48, 156n. 22; sentiment against, 142–45; against Spain in Caribbean, 57; white servants' collaboration with, 160n. 61
English common law, 119
English constitution, 118, 119–20
English explorers: abandonment by West, 22–23; aggression precluding intercultural accommodation, 36; alliances with Indians, 32; assessment of Powhatans, 42n. 18; cultural misinterpretations of, 35–36; in demise of Indian hegemony, 37; endemic enmity with Powhatans, 36–37; first contacts with Indians, 13, 16–17; intercultural cohabitation, 16–17; military confidence of, 13, 16; tensions with Powhatans, 18–21; trade with Powhatans, 19; weapons of, 17–18
Entail, abolition of, 51
Episcopal Church, 209–10
Eppes, Francis Wayles, 199n. 72
Eppes, John Wayles, 167, 170, 194n. 6
Equality: freedom's role in, 243; and Jefferson, 365–66, 388n. 68; paradox of slavery and, 49–50; of women, 207, 331
Equal Suffrage League of Virginia: activism of, 331–33; debate with opposition, 336; endorsements of, 330; establishment of, 328; and factionalism in suffrage movement, 339; lobbying activities of, 337; militancy in movement, 340; other activities of, 341; in ratification battle, 343; Valentine's leadership of, 338
Estates. *See* Inheritance
Estave, Andrew, 148, 152
Estill, Harry F., 303
Eugenics: about, 353; ascendancy of, 357–58, 369–70, 378n. 4, 380–81n. 17; and hereditarianism, 360–63, 367, 369–70; influence of Lewis, 353–54, 363–64, 370–73, 374–75;

introductory notes, 9, 202–3; literature of, 363, 365; and Negro Question, 357, 368–69, 389–90n. 83; racism of, 356–57; as state-of-the-art science, 370, 390n. 91; and sterilization, 367–68, 374–75, 379n. 12, 386n. 50, 392–93nn. 111–113; students of, 355–56, 371–73, 392n. 110; at University of Virginia, 355, 364–65, 367–70, 387n. 64
Evans, William, 98
Evolution, Genetics and Eugenics (Newman), 365
Expansionism, 36, 37
Extravagance, addiction to, 126–29

Fairfax County, 275, 281, 282, 287
Fall of British Tyranny, The (Leacock), 151
Fame, expectations of, 172, 173
Family: expectations of, 188–89; Hamilton on, 195n. 17; interracial families, 237–39; and Jefferson, 165–67, 170–71, 184–87, 190–92, 193, 235; obligation to, 186–87; press on Jefferson's, 181–83, 198n. 65; prominence of, 164; as prototype of society, 192–93; relationship to society, 181; Washington on, 195n. 17; women's obligations to, 188–90
Famine, 23–24
Fanny (Berkeley slave), 206, 208, 216
Farmers, 65–66
Farmer's Alliance, 298–99
Farrell, Richard, 85, 86
Fauquier, Francis, 126, 139
Fausz, J. Frederick, 2, 7–8, 11–12, 73, 106
Federalist press, 180–81
Ferdinando, Bashaw, 69n. 39
Ferguson, Adam, 53
First Anglo-Powhatan War: about, 12–13; acceptance as historical event, 37–38; cycle of reciprocal revenge, 38; De La Warr's entry into, 24; divide and conquer tactics, 25;

end of, 34; engagements of, 14*t*; English strategies, 26–27, 30, 32; funding, 31; guerrilla tactics, 20; as holy war, 12, 25–26, 27–28; introductory notes, 7–8, 11–12; justification by English, 43n. 27; map of engagements, 15; onset of, 22–24; Powhatan strategies, 30–31; precipitating events, 18–21; stalemate, 31, 33; veteran English reinforcements, 28–29, 44n. 28; Virginia Company's influence on, 31, 33

Fisher, Christopher, 84

Fiske, John, 302, 303, 310

Fithian, Philip, 108, 112, 150

Fitzhugh, George, 54

Fleming, Elizabeth, 247

Fleming, Samuel, 247–49, 253, 260nn. 51, 60, 61

Fleming, William, 139

Fletcher, Andrew, 53–54

Food: coercion of corn from Nansemonds, 41n. 17; Indian gifts of, 18, 19, 20; Indians deprived of, 27

Fort Algernon colony, 23–24

Fort Charles, 26

Fort James, 17–18

Fort La Warr siege, 14*t*, 15

Fort Monroe, 275, 277, 278

Founding Fathers, ideals of, 399

Fowey (British warship), 136, 154n. 5

Francisco, John, 69n. 39

Franklin, Benjamin, 185

Franklin, Lewis, 243, 245

Frederick County, 139, 207–8, 212–14, 225

Free blacks: acceptance by southern society, 236; assertion of rights, 246, 253; fear of influence of, 221; in Frederick County, 207–8, 213–14; identities constructed on factors other than race, 254; plans to colonize, 212–13, 214; as reminder to slaves of freedom, 213; removal from Virginia, 225, 236

Freedmen: as Baconians, 91–92; Cimarrons, 57; compulsory labor

for, 55; diminishing ranks of, 65; disenfranchisement of, 62–63; land acquisition by, 65, 83, 85, 88; military drafting of, 65, 72n. 74; poverty of, 63; without land, 60

Freedom: of blacks after Civil War, 275, 286; of blacks in 17th century, 58, 69n. 39; and Civil War, 4–5, 275; free blacks as reminder to slaves, 213; introductory note, 3–4; as power, 7; of press, 183

Freeholders, voting rights of, 111–13

Friddell, Guy, 399

Fugitive slaves: children as, 149, 161n. 70; collaboration with Dunmore, 148–51; punishment of, 148–49, 151, 161n. 64; Randolph (Berkeley slave) as, 208, 209

Fundamentalism, 364

Funeral rites, in Africa, 205–6

Gabriel's Rebellion, 141, 157n. 27, 236

Gage, Matilda Joslyn, 324

Gage, Thomas, 142

Galland, Marion, 410

Galton, Francis, 355, 356, 375

Gambling, 127

Gardner, John, 245–46

Garland, Maurice H., 248–49, 250

Garland, Samuel, 248–49

Garnett, Kate Noland, 297, 305–6

Garrison, William Lloyd, 308

Gates, Robbins L., 412

Gates, Thomas, 12, 20–21, 24, 25–26, 30, 33

Gaylor, Thomas F., 306

Gender: balance in slave population, 64–65, 72n. 73; disparities among colonists, 60, 70n. 50

Genetics, contemporary research, 377

Genocide, as solution to racial problems, 369

Gentry: about, 107–8; education of, 114; introductory note, 105–6; as justices, 211–12; moral decay of, 126–29; motivation for political participation, 114–16; orientation

Gentry (*continued*)
to action, 116; reviled by Baptists, 109; social duties of, 114; in social order, 110–11; stewardship of, 113–16
Ghost stories, 223–24, 233n. 56
Giles, William B., 310
Gilliam, Charles, 240, 243
Ginter, Lewis, 326
Glance at Current American History, A (Cusson), 301
Glasgow, Ellen, 328
Glass, Carter, 300, 357
Glebe houses, 78, 79, 100n. 8
Glen Allen village, 301, 317n. 22
Gloster (Johnson slave), 161n. 64
Godsey, Mary, 4, 235, 240, 241, 244, 252, 257n. 21, 258n. 28
Godwin, Mills E., Jr., 395, 408, 417, 421–22
Gooch, William, 110, 113
Gordon, John B., 306
Gordon, William, 94
Gough, William, 248, 250
Government: challenges faced by colonial system, 123–29; checks and balances on, 119–23; dependence on patriots, 121–22; Dunmore crisis, 142–46; English constitution, 118, 119–20; fallibility of, 118; fragility of, 173; gentry domination of, 111–12; harshness in Jamestown, 58; by House of Burgesses, 113–14; intervention in reform, 331–32; Intolerable Acts, 138; parliamentary maneuvering, 420; participation in, 58; and public opinion, 173; redistricting legislation, 401–2; restoration after Civil War, 287–88; "rule by the few," 300; suffrage legislation, 340–44; under Union occupation, 279
Grace, Susan, 69n. 39
Grand Army of the Republic, 299, 301–2
Grand Camp of Confederate Veterans, 301, 302–3, 310–11, 319n. 46
Grange movement, 298–99

Grant, Madison, 363, 365, 376
Grantham, Thomas, 74, 99
Gravatt, J. Segar, 373–74
Gray, Garland "Peck," 406, 407–8
Gray, James, 71n. 61
Gray commission, 407–8, 413, 414–15
Great Depression, 368
Green, Elna C., 9, 321–22, 354
Greene, Jack P., 3, 73, 105–6, 135, 164, 274, 297
Gregg, William W., 373
Griffing, Josephine S., 325
Griffith, David, 110, 111, 117, 118
Grymes, Benjamin, 126
Guerrilla tactics, 20, 279–80, 283–84
Guest, George, 85
Guiana, 68n. 33
Gunpowder magazine incident, 141–46, 158n. 44, 160n. 53
Guns, ownership among landless poor, 60–62
Guthridge, John, 92

Hackney, Samuel, 211, 217
Haddock, Edward E., 405, 415–16
Haden, Richard G., 248, 261n. 63
Hakluyt, Richard, 28, 43n. 27, 56–57, 58
Hale, Grace Elizabeth, 375
Haller, Mark H., 375
Hamer, Fanny Lou, 375
Hamilton, Alexander: and Burr, 178, 182; dueling nature of, 174, 175, 177, 197n. 50; on family, 195n. 17; and Jefferson, 51, 168, 174, 178; and Monroe, 175; press accusations against, 180; Reynolds affair, 175–77, 178, 179, 181, 196n. 46, 197n. 51
Hamilton, Mrs. Alexander, 177
Hamilton, Philip, 177, 185
Hamor, Ralph, 12–13, 34
Hampton, battle of, 136–37
Hanover County, 139, 144, 158n. 40
Hansford, Charles, 109
Happiness, Jefferson on, 167, 168, 194n. 12

Hardy, John, 98
Hardy, Margaret, 98
Harlan, John Marshall, 398
Harland, Marion, 267, 269, 272
Harman, William, 69n. 39
Harrington, James, 52
Harris, John, 84, 92, 148
Harris, Joseph, 3, 136–37, 154n. 5
Harrison, Albertis S., Jr., 395, 408, 414, 420
Harrison, William Henry, 266, 267
Harry (Berkeley slave), 205, 209, 215, 217
Hart, Joel Tanner, 269, 270
Haslewood, Thomas, 95
Hatcher, Orie Latham, 322, 346n. 2
Hatcher, Samuel C., 359
Hawke (British warship), 137
Hawkins, William, 239
Health care, and eugenics, 374–75, 392–93n. 113
Heath, William, 243
Hemings, John, 193
Hemings, Sally, 165, 179, 181–82, 197n. 54, 235
Henrico battle, 14t, 15, 30–31
Henry, Patrick, 1, 3, 106, 144
Hereditarianism, 355–56, 360–63, 367, 369–70
Herrnstein, Richard, 376
Hershman, James H., Jr., 414, 415
Hill, Thomas, 85
Hilson, John, 95
Hirst, Omer L., 416
Historians: on Civil War, 274; court documents used by, 237; criticism of revisionism, 310–12, 319n. 46; focus of, 6; paradox of slavery and equality, 49–50; on southern aristocracy, 299; on Virginia politics, 135; on women in politics, 263
History: banned books, 301–3, 312–13; from elitist perspective, 303; library selection of books, 304; northern vs. southern interpretations, 314–15n. 5, 316n. 9; preservation movements, 300–301; re-

shaped from slaves' viewpoint, 224; revisionism, 297–301, 307–12; scathing critiques of northern histories, 301–2; southern narratives of, 219–20, 232n. 49; teacher indoctrination, 305
History of Our Country (Cooper, Estill, and Lemmon), 302–3
History of the United States for Schools (Fiske), 302, 303, 310
History of the United States of America (Elson), 312–13
History of the United States (Thompson), 306
Hitler, Adolf, 312, 354, 355, 367, 372, 412
Hofstadter, Richard, 7
Hofstra, Warren R., 3, 106, 202, 297
Holton, Woody, 3, 7, 106, 135–36, 165
Home rule, 135, 136
Honor: decline of dueling, 187; and duels, 174–75, 177–78, 199n. 79; Jefferson on, 185
Hooker, Isabella Beecher, 325
Hooper, George, 83, 91, 92, 93, 103n. 37
Horrocks, James, 110–11, 126–27, 129
Hotchkiss, Jed, 326
House, Floyd N., 362
House of Burgesses: authority of, 120; election process, 111–13; emancipation rumors, 140; gentry domination of, 108; government by, 113–14; leadership in, 112–13; obligations of, 118–19; politics in, 113; power of, 119
Houses: appearances of, 79, 81; costs of, 78; illustrations of, 80; maintenance of, 78; Rock Hill (Berkeley) house, 204, 227n. 3; sizes of, 79; structural materials, 100n. 7
Houston, Robert H., Jr., 410
Howard, Dowell, J., 405–6
Howe, John, 172–73
Humanity: contradictions of slavery, 225; imperfection of, 117
Hunter, Edward, 250

Hunton, Eppa, Jr., 336
Hutcheson, Francis, 53
Hutchings, Joseph, 148
Hypocrisy, discussion of, 50

Idle poor. *See* Landless poor
Immigration: declines in, 86; in
    Middlesex County, 82; by national-
    ity, 58, 69n. 36; proposed restriction
    of, 373; rates in 17th century, 59,
    69–70n. 42
Imperialism, of England, 56–57
Indenture: extension of, 62; of landless
    poor, 58; in Middlesex County, 82–
    83; offset by increased slavery,
    63–64
Independence: and debt, 51–52; of
    public servants, 123
Independent Party, 323
Indians: alliances with English, 32,
    151, 162n. 71; alliances with slaves,
    139; firearms used by, 20; interracial
    marriage with whites, 377n. 4; Jef-
    ferson on, 201n. 97; in Pontiac's
    War, 139; threat level by tribes, 27.
    See also specific tribes
Individual, dignity of, 408
Industrial growth, 326–27
Infidelity, 235
Ingram, Joseph, 90, 92
Inheritance: division of land, 86, 88;
    internecine battles over, 246–54;
    looting by curators, 247–49,
    261n. 69; Robert Wright estate,
    246–51; Sylvia Wright estate, 250–
    52, 259n. 44; theft of documents,
    246; Thomas Wright estate, 239–41
Institutions: administration by Union
    forces, 279; resurrection after Civil
    War, 288
Integration: interposition issue, 415–
    16; Lewis on, 392n. 105; massive re-
    sistance to, 410, 412, 416–19, 420,
    421; speculation about, 373–74
Intelligence testing, 356, 364, 378–
    79n. 8, 384n. 46, 386n. 57
Intercultural cohabitation, 16–17

Intercultural marriage, 34
Intercultural tensions, 18–21, 35
Interposition issue, 415–16
Interracial families, 237–39
Interracial marriage: community ac-
    ceptance of, 252; forbidden by law,
    9, 235, 244; of whites and Indians,
    377n. 4; of Wrights, 234–35, 243
Interracial mixing, at athletic events,
    411–12
Interracial tensions, 203
Interracial violence, 138–39
Intolerable Acts, 138
Iredell, James, 151

Jack-of-the-Feathers, 30
Jackson, Andrew, 187–88, 270
Jackson, Elenor, 97
Jackson, John, 85
Jackson, Stonewall, 221, 232n. 51
Jacob (Rust slave), 208
Jamaica Land, 75, 84
James I, King, 19, 21, 27, 31, 38,
    41n. 12
James (Phripp slave), 152
James Fort, 17–18
James River, 90
Jamestown: burned in Bacon's Rebel-
    lion, 89–90; desertion by colonists,
    45n. 37; harsh government of, 58;
    martial law in, 29; siege of, 12, 14*t*,
    15, 23–24; war during winter, 23
Japazaws, 32
Jarratt, Devereux, 109
Jefferson, Maria, 166–67, 168, 170,
    182, 189, 190–91, 194n. 6
Jefferson, Martha, 166–67, 169–71,
    188, 189–90, 194n. 6, 200n. 86
Jefferson, Martha Wayles Skelton,
    164, 194n. 12
Jefferson, Thomas: admiration for,
    270, 399; as ambassador to France,
    67n. 5; aversion to debt, 51–52; on
    battle of Hampton, 137; correspon-
    dence with family, 168–72, 182,
    184–87, 200n. 86; debts of, 166;
    DNA testing on descendants,

197n. 54; in domestic society, 182; on Dunmore, 150; on education, 364; and equality, 365–66, 388n. 68; fame sought by, 172, 173; and family, 165–67, 170–71, 184–87, 190–92, 193, 235; and Fletcher, 53; on Hamilton, 178; on happiness, 167, 168, 194n. 12; and Hemings, 165, 235; on honor, 185; impact of, 164; on Indians, 201n. 97; introductory notes, 3–4, 164–65; on landless poor, 52, 54–55, 67n. 8; leadership of, 106; and Madison, 165–66; manipulative relationship with daughters, 171; on marriage, 189, 200n. 85; pamphlet attacks on, 178–80; and paradox of slavery position, 50–51; personality of, 183–84; on political life, 169–71, 172; on presidency, 193; as president, 168; against press, 183; press attacks on, 179–81, 198n. 61; on public service, 169, 170–72; public service demands on, 4, 190–92, 200; and Sally Hemings, 178–79, 181–82; scholarly character of, 116; and scientific racism, 356; on slavery, 55, 214, 309; social philosophy of, 184–85; on society, 169; as vice president, 168; on Washington, 172; weariness of politics, 168

Jennings, Herbert Spencer, 359
Jennings, J. S., 339–40
Jeremiah, Thomas, 147
Jesus Christ, 20, 26, 205, 218
Jim Crow, 203, 220, 221, 226
Johns Hopkins University, 358, 359
Johnson, Andrew, 288
Johnson, Michael P., 237
Johnson, Roswell Hill, 365
Johnson, William, 161n. 64
Johnston, Mary: efforts of, 330; and factions of suffrage movement, 337–38, 339; introductory notes, 9, 322; lobbying activities of, 334; as socialist, 333, 349n. 69; and suffrage opposition, 334, 335, 337; suffrage

propaganda by, 328–29; and Sugg, 329; and trade unions, 332; and Valentine, 322; and women's colleges, 329

Jones, Hugh, 116
Jones, J. William, 302
Jones, John, 95, 98
Jones, Rice, 84
Jordan, David Starr, 358
Jordan, German, 248–49, 253, 260n. 60, 261nn. 63, 67, 69
Jordan, Harvey Ernest, 357–58, 381n. 21
Jordan, Winthrop D., 63, 216
Jurors, pool in Middlesex County, 97–98
Justices of the peace, 111, 204, 211–12

Kecoughtans, 14t, 15, 16, 26, 27
Kemp's Landing raid, 149
Kett, Joseph F., 370
Key, V. O., Jr., 396
Kilpatrick, James J., 415
King, Henry, 136
Knight, Robert, 91
Knights of the White Camellia, 309
Knox, John, 139
Ku Klux Klan, 309

Labor force: compulsory labor, 52–53, 55; distrust of, 55–56; indenture of landless poor, 58; servitude system, 82–83; slaves as majority of, 63, 71n. 67; trade unions, 327, 332–33, 349n. 65
Ladies' Battle, The (Seawell), 335
Lancaster Parish, 75
Land: acquisition by marriage, 83, 85, 204; distribution in wills, 86, 88; freedmen ownership of, 65, 83, 85, 88; gentry holdings of, 107; headright claims, 101–2n. 18; holdings in Middlesex County, 83–86; importance vs. race in social status, 252–53; ownership and social class, 51–52, 60; patenting system, 101–2n. 18; proposed distribution to

Meredith, Charles V., 338
Meredith, Sophie, 338–39, 350–51n. 101
Mial (Bailey slave), 161n. 64
Micham, John, 84
Mickleburrough property, 75
Mickleburrough's Bridge, 77
Middlesex County: Baconians in, 90–95, 104n. 42; court officers of, 94, 95–96; court sessions, 95–99; decline of servitude, 85; education, 81; houses of, 78–81; land holdings, 83–86; legal issues, 91, 94–95; man's improvements, 77–78; map of, 76; mortality rates in, 101n. 15; population in 17th century, 74; "The Road," 74–76, 77; servitude system, 82–83; troublemakers, 91, 92
Militancy, 333–34, 339–40, 348n. 37, 354–55
Militias, formation of, 143, 157n. 35
Miller, Francis Pickens, 405
Miller, Patrick, 85, 86
Mingo nation, 141–42
Miscegenation: and fertility, 390n. 87; opposition to, 369; proposal of laws against, 373; tacit acceptance of, 236, 240, 252; Thomas and Sylvia Wright, 237–38
Mitchell, Thomas, 144
Moger, Allen W., 396
Monacans, 16
Mongum, Philip, 69n. 39
Monroe, James, 175, 177, 178, 197n. 51, 309
Montague, Andrew Jackson, 303
Monticello, 164, 165, 235
Monuments, 219, 232n. 51, 264–72
Moore, E. Blackburn, 397
Morality, 114, 126–29, 331
Moral reform, 269
Morgan, Edmund S., 155n. 9; *American Slavery, American Freedom*, 5–6, 10n. 3, 48; introductory notes, 12, 48, 74, 105, 136, 297; on land speculation, 2; on natural rights, 274; on paradox of slavery and freedom, 8,

73, 394, 395; on plantation aristocracy, 135; on union of black and white experience, 165
Mortality rates: of children, 86; in Middlesex County, 101n. 15; of servants, 101n. 16; in 17th century, 59
Moryson, Francis, 60
Mosby, Charles, 250
Mother Church, 77
Mount Vernon Ladies' Association of the Union, 263
Muhlenberg, Frederick, 175, 177
Munford, Beverly B., 303, 307, 309–10
Munford, Mary-Cooke Branch, 272, 327
Munford, Robert, 158n. 44
Murder: of Berkeley, 202, 203, 204–6; confessions of Berkeley's murderers, 208–9; interpretations of slaves' confessions, 218; of Patawomecs, 14t, 15, 22–23
Murray, Charles, 376
Murray, John. *See* Dunmore, Lord
Muse, Benjamin, 402, 411, 417
Musgrave, Michael, 96
Muskets, 18, 41n. 10
My Lady's Swamp, 75

Nansemonds, 14t, 15, 21, 41n. 17
Nash, Arthur, 2–3, 84, 86, 102n. 19
Nash, John (elder), 2–3, 84, 86
Nash, John (younger), 86
Nation, 310–11
National American Woman Suffrage Association, 325, 337, 340, 341
National Colored Republican Women, 345
National Woman's Party, 328, 337, 339–40, 341
National Woman Suffrage Association, 324–25
Native Americans. *See* Indians
Nativism, 366
Nat Turner Insurrection, 309
Nature/nurture question, 361
Needles, John, 84, 102n. 19

Negroes. *See* Blacks
Negro Question, 357, 368–69
Negro Women's League of Voters, 345
Nemattanew, 30
Newman, Horatio H., 365
Newman, John, 209, 211
Newman, Thomas, 211, 215, 218
Newport, Christopher, 17, 29
Newspapers. *See* Press
Nicholas, Robert Carter, 120, 123, 143, 158n. 37
Nichols, Henry, 93–94
Nineteenth Amendment, 322, 341, 342
Nonsuch siege, 14*t*, 15, 21
Norris, R. O., 343
Notes on the State of Virginia (Jefferson), 356

Old Dominion, The (Page), 311–12
Oliver, Thomas, 85
Oliver (Berkeley farmworker), 211, 221–23
Opechancanough, 22, 33
Oral culture, 116
Origin of Species (Darwin), 365
Otey, Elizabeth, 339
Otey, Lucy W., 269
Otter (British warship), 136
Overstreet, John, 251
Overy, Jeremy, 91, 92
Owen, Humphrey, 92
Owens, Jesse, 412
Ozlin, Thomas, 342

Page, James M., 359
Page, John, 148
Page, Thomas Nelson, 311–12
Page, Walter A., 395, 404
Paine, Thomas, 168
Pale Faces, 309
Palmer, A. Mitchell, 341
Pamphlet journalism: Callender and, 196n. 42; emancipation proposals, 140; historical revisionism, 297; on Jackson's marriage, 187–88; against Jefferson, 178–82; Reynolds affair,

175–77; on suffrage, 336, 340–41; violence stimulated by, 175
Pamunkeys, 22, 33–34
Pane, Francis, 69n. 39
Parahunt, 16, 20, 21
Parish houses, 78, 79, 100n. 8
Parker, James, 142, 143, 158n. 37
Paspaheghs, 14*t*, 15, 26–27
Pasptanzie, 32
Pasteur, William, 142, 143
Patawomecs, 14*t*, 15, 22–23, 32, 37
Paternalism, 215
Patriarchal norms, 4
Patriotism, 144–45, 150–51
Patriots, 121–23
Pattison, Thomas, 84
Peacham, Henry, 117
Peack, Henry, 218
Peake, Martha A., 267
Peculiar Institution, The (Stampp), 411
Peelle, Elizabeth Ravenel, 397
Pendleton, Edmund, 115–16, 141, 145
Percy, George, 12, 21, 22, 26, 42n. 19
Perrott, Richard, Jr., 94, 95
Perrott's Creek, 75
Perrow, Daniel B., 239–40, 244, 245, 247, 260n. 51
Perrow, Mosby G., Jr., 419, 420
Perrow, Stephen, 239, 243, 245, 246, 247, 251, 253, 260n. 51
Perrow, William, 239, 260n. 51
Petition system, in courts, 97
Pew, William, 93
Phil (Bailey slave), 161n. 64
Phillis (Rice slave), 149
Phill (Knox slave), 139
Phripp, Matthew, 141, 151
Piankatank River, 74, 75, 77
Pierce, Franklin, 270
Pierpont, Francis H., 279, 287, 288
Pillaging, by Union forces, 280–81
Pinckney, Charles Cotesworth, 180, 198n. 62
Pinkney, John, 146
Piracy, 71n. 51
Place in Time, A (Rutman and Rutman), 73–74

Plantations, 7, 75, 84, 237, 250, 256n. 11

Pleasants, John H., 264, 265

Pleasure, addiction to, 127–29

Plessy v. Ferguson, 398

Plundering: forbidden by Union officers, 277–78; during rebellion, 61–62; by Union forces, 281–82

Pocahontas: in captivity, 32–33; christening name of, 46n. 45; conversion to Anglicanism, 33, 34; marriage to Rolfe, 13, 34, 35

Pochins, 16

Point Comfort, 24

Politeness, 184

Political Disquisitions (Burgh), 53

Political machines. *See* Byrd Organization

Political parties: Constitutional Union Party, 271; Democratic Party, 264, 268–69, 321, 326, 344, 345, 395–96; distrust of, 122; Independent Party, 323; mass public created by, 187; Populist Party, 298–99; Republican Party, 323, 325, 345; Socialist Party, 333–34; Whig Party, 263, 264, 266–70, 323–24; women's alignments with, 345

Politics: dangers of, 173–74; framework of assumptions, 117–18; gentry domination of, 108, 110–12; gentry motivation for participation, 114–16; historians on, 135; in House of Burgesses, 113; Jefferson's views of, 168, 169–71, 172; leaders from Virginia, 106; popular vote, 111–13; pragmatic character of, 116; in public and private realms, 180; reform politics, 323–24; and violence, 172–73, 178, 187; women's inclusion in, 263, 265–68, 323

Polk, James K., 268

Poll taxes, 299, 396

Pontiac's War, 139

Poor whites, 284–85, 299

Pope, John, 280

Popenoe, Paul, 365

Population: gentry as small percentage of, 108; growth of, 56, 69n. 41; Middlesex County in 17th century, 74; percentages of whites, 87; plans for growth, 54–55; racial distribution in 18th century, 68n. 19; rates of growth in 17th century, 59–60; urban growth, 326–27. *See also* Demographics

Populist Party, 298–99

Porter, Robert, 84

Potter, Cuthbert, 78, 85

Poverty, of freedmen, 63

Powell, Lewis F., Jr., 412, 421–22

Power, 6–8, 118, 119, 120–21, 124

Powhatans: assessment of Englishmen, 17; attempted conversion to Anglicanism, 34; conflict with English, 2; cultural misinterpretations of, 35–36; endemic enmity with English, 36–37; first contacts with English, 13, 16–17; intercultural cohabitation, 16–17; James Fort assault, 17–18; military confidence of, 16, 22; segregation from English, 26; tensions with English, 18–21; trade with English, 19; tribute to King James demanded of, 21; *Tsenaccommacah* domain, 16; weaponry of, 20–21

Pratt, Katie D., 345

Preserving the Old Dominion (Lindgren), 300–301

Press: on Berkeley's murder, 209, 218; on Clay monument proposal, 264; defense of Barbour, 268; on desegregation, 400; duels encouraged by, 186; on Dunmore, 146; Federalists vs. Republicans, 180–81; freedom of, 183; on Jackson's marriage, 187–88; Jefferson attacked by, 179–81, 198n. 61; on Jefferson's family, 181–83, 198n. 65; on liberalism, 402, 407; on local education autonomy, 409; mass public created by, 187; Republican press, 180–81; on science education, 360; and suffrage,

327–28, 330, 331, 335; on textbook controversy, 312–13; violence stimulated by, 175; on women in Whig Party, 266, 267, 268–69

Primogeniture, abolition of, 51

Principall Navigations (Haklyut), 56–57

Private lives, of public figures, 4, 176–77, 179–81, 187–88

Progressivism, 322, 327–28, 354, 357–58, 376, 381n. 19

Prohibition, 343–44

Property. *See* Land

Pruden, C. O., 313

Public service: demands on Jefferson, 4, 190–92, 200; Jefferson on, 169, 170–72; and private life, 176–77, 179–81, 187–88; violence of, 173–74

Public transportation, desegregation of, 400–401

Publishing companies, 306–7

Purdie, Alexander, 140

Puritans, 66

Putnam, Carleton, 376

Race: Alderman's position on, 361–62; Boothe's views, 399, 410–12; and economic status, 259n. 36; genocide as solution to problems, 369; and hereditarianism, 355–56; identities not fixed by, 252; importance vs. wealth in social status, 252–53; Lewis's position on, 361, 362–63; in suffrage debate, 336–37, 338, 342, 344; and taxation, 244, 259n. 36

Race and Reason (Putnam), 376

Race suicide thesis, 356, 367

Racial integrity, 165, 234

Racism: absent in suffrage movement, 334; of eugenics, 356–57; in legal system, 64; of Lewis's supporters, 374; as national phenomenon, 358; in paradox of slavery and liberty, 50; prevailing atmosphere of, 366; reactions to black militancy, 354; scientific racism, 356; virulence of, 203

Radley, Thomas, 84, 92, 96

Rakove, Jack N., 173

Raleigh, Walter, 57, 68n. 33

Ralph (Berkeley slave), 205, 206, 209, 215, 217, 228n. 7

Randolph, Edmund, 123, 124–25, 141

Randolph, John, 174, 185–86, 199n. 79

Randolph, Nancy, 189–90

Randolph, Peyton, 142, 143, 144

Randolph, Richard, 200n. 87

Randolph, Thomas Jefferson, 184–85, 189, 192

Randolph, Thomas Mann, 185–86, 188, 194n. 6, 200n. 87

Randolph (Berkeley slave): about, 204–5; in Berkeley murder, 205–6; capture of, 211; conviction of, 217; as fugitive, 208, 209; introductory notes, 3, 202; motivation for murder of Berkeley, 217, 218, 219; murder trial of, 215, 216; sentencing of, 217; and violence of times, 225

Randolph-Macon College, 310, 359

Randolph-Macon Woman's College, 329, 330

Ransome, W. L., 403

Rappahannock River, 74, 75, 77, 90, 276

Ratcliffe, 15, 22

Real estate booms, 326

Rebellion: Baconians in Middlesex County, 90–95; Bacon's Rebellion, 8, 61, 65, 89–95; frustration as source of, 93; Gabriel's Rebellion, 141, 157n. 27, 236; interconnections of participants, 92–94; by landless poor, 61–62; plots by slaves, 139–41, 145–49, 157n. 27, 159–60n. 53; rumors of British complicity in slave insurrections, 140, 147–48

Reeves, George, 96

Reform: election reform, 326; government intervention in, 331–32; moral reform, 269; politics of, 323–24; and progressive movement, 327–28; social problem initiatives, 331–32; trade unionism, 327; urban reform,

motivation for murder of Berkeley, 216, 217, 218, 219; murder trial of, 215; sentencing of, 217; and violence of times, 225

Savage, Toy, Jr., 407, 412

Scalawags, 309

Schoepf, Johann David, 113

School History of the United States (Lee), 307–9

Schouler, James, 299

Scopes trial, 360, 364

Seager, Randolph, 75

Seawell, Molly Elliot, 335

Secession, defense of constitutionality, 303

Secessionists: allegiance oath required of, 280; coup plotted by, 279; defiance after war, 289; poor whites' defiance of, 284–85; resignation to defeat, 287; against Unionists, 6–7, 283

Sedition Act of 1798, 183

Segregation: Boothe's position on, 406–7; *Brown v. Board of Education*, 5, 394, 402, 405–9; in Jim Crow era, 220; Lewis as champion of, 371–72, 373; practicality of, 369; prevailing atmosphere of, 366

Servants: collaboration with British, 160n. 61; in Middlesex County, 82–83, 85; mortality rates of, 101n. 16; progression to freeholders, 88. *See also* Indenture

Settlement houses, 327

Seven Years' War, 123

Sex, Race, and Science (Larson), 364

Shawnee nation, 141–42

Shenandoah Valley Pioneers (Cartmell), 220

Shepherd, Frances, 79

Shepherd, John, 78, 79, 90, 94

Sheridan, Philip, 280

Sherman, William T., 308

Ships, as mobile fortresses, 18

Sicklemore, John (alias Ratcliffe), 15, 22

Simmons, John, 147–48

Simpson, John, 147

Sin, sermons against, 128–29

Slave patrols, 140–41, 142, 276–77

Slavery: absent from southern histories, 219; American reliance on, 49–50; attitudes in Frederick County, 213–14; Baptist position, 207; Barbados slave codes, 64; Christian positions on, 210; conservatism of Union forces, 285; contradiction with republicanism, 226; Dunmore's emancipation proclamation, 138, 142–46, 149–51, 152; economics of, 63; Emancipation Proclamation, 308; end of, 289; escape as protest, 205; evolution of, 7; free labor as incentive for, 54–55; guilt of owners, 231n. 43; humanitarian contradictions of, 225, 226; indenture offset by, 63–64; inept masters, 219, 221; Jefferson's posture toward, 50–51; and landless poor, 53–54; modern reshaping of history, 224; paradox of liberty and, 5–6, 48, 49–50, 394, 395; passive resistance to, 205; positions against, 125–26; in revisionist history, 307–8; tobacco's dependence on, 50, 125; as unthinking decision, 63; and Yankee invasion, 285–87

Slaves: alliances with Indians, 139; in Berkeley murder, 203, 204–6; capacity for rational actions, 225; children as fugitives, 149, 161n. 70; collaboration of fugitives with Dunmore, 148–51; fear of, 64–65, 135, 138–39, 285–86; freed individuals, 151–52; freedom after Civil War, 286; gender balance in population, 64–65, 72n. 73; gentry holdings of, 107; Jefferson's plans for freeing own, 55; as majority of labor force, 63, 71n. 67; motivations for murder, 216, 217, 218, 219; murdered by owners, 208; punishment of fugitives, 145, 148–49, 151, 161n. 64; rebellion plots of, 139–41,

Slaves (*continued*)
145–49, 157n. 27, 159–60n. 53; religious instruction of, 210, 214, 218, 226; retribution against former owners, 286–87; Revolution roles of, 136–37, 152–53, 161n. 68; rumors of alliances with British, 146; rumors of British complicity in rebellions, 140, 147–48, 156n. 22; sales of, 214, 230n. 32; on trial, 145, 148–49, 159n. 50, 161n. 64, 223; understandings of liberty, 3; vengeance of, 225; whites killed by, 139; and Yankee invasion, 285–87

Smith, Adam, 192

Smith, Alexander, 78, 94

Smith, Augustine C., 212, 213, 215, 225, 231n. 44

Smith, C. Emerson, 402

Smith, Essie Wade Butler, 305

Smith, Howard W., 416

Smith, J. Douglas, 5, 394–95

Smith, John: assessment of Wahunsunacock, 41n. 12; departure from Chesapeake, 22, 42n. 19; First Anglo-Powhatan War, 12–13; guerrilla tactics of, 20; intelligence information of, 25; introductory note, 1; Nansemond siege relief, 21; and Parahunt, 21; portrayal of James I to Wahunsunacock, 41n. 12; Powatan submission goal, 36; provocation of Powhatans, 21, 41n. 16; replacement as governor, 20–21; shortage of troops, 28; Wahunsunacock's capture of, 18–19

Smith, Josiah, Jr., 146

Smith, Laurence, 61–62

Smoot, Albert A., 418

Smyth, J. F. D., 108

Social class: blacks in middle class, 329; class struggle, 299–300; English idle poor, 57–58, 60; interaction with race, 236; intercourse among ranks, 109; landless poor, 53–56; land ownership role, 51–52, 54, 60; ranks of, 108. *See also* Aristocracy

Social Darwinism, 353

Social deference, 3

Social efficiency, 357, 380n. 16

Social elitism, 269

Socialism, 333, 349n. 69

Socialist Party, 333–34

Social order, 110–11

Social status, 252–53

Social values, 108, 126–27

Social work, 327

Society: disruption after Civil War, 282–83; distortion of collective memory, 220–23, 232n. 49; family as prototype of, 192–93; family's relationship to, 181; framework of assumptions, 117–18; Jefferson's vision of, 169, 184–85; subordination in, 110

Somerville, Nellie Nugent, 330

Sons of Confederate Veterans, 303, 309

Souls of Black Folk (Du Bois), 365

Southern Manifesto, 416

Southern States Woman Suffrage Conference, 337

Spain, 57

Spencer, Nicholas, 60, 98–99

Spong, William B., Jr., 414, 416

Spotswood, Alexander, 123

Squire, Matthew, 136–37

Squirearchy, 313

Stabler, Edward, 141, 145

Stampp, Kenneth M., 411

Stanley, Thomas B., 405–6, 407, 413, 414, 416

Stapleton, Thomas, 85

Starving Time, 23–24, 42n. 23

Statesmanship, as Whig tenet, 269, 270

States' rights, 9, 342, 352n. 125, 399

Status, social, 252–53

Statute for Religious Freedom, Virginia, 165

Steger, Mary, 266

Sterilization, and eugenics, 367–68, 374–75, 379n. 12, 386n. 50, 392–93nn. 111–13

Steward, William, 81, 85, 88
Stewardship, 105, 110, 113–16
Stingray Point, 75, 83, 85, 86
Stith, William, 110, 113–14, 122–23,
   127, 128–29
Stockton, Catherine, 241, 242, 246
Stoddard, Lothrop, 354, 355, 363,
   372, 376
Stokes, Ora Brown, 327, 329–30,
   345–46
Stone, Cornelia Branch, 304
Stone, scarcity of, 77
Stowe, Harriet Beecher, 313
Strachey, William, 12, 25, 36
Straits of Magellan, 57
Subordination, in society, 110
Suffrage: about, 322–23; activism in
   Virginia, 323–34; for blacks, 299–
   300; factionalism within movement,
   337–40; introductory notes, 9, 321–
   22; and liquor lobby, 343; opposing
   legislators, 351n. 122; opposition
   to, 334–37; ratification battles, 340–
   44; success of movement, 345–46;
   supporting legislators, 351–
   52n. 124. See also Voting
Sugg, Merrie, 329
Sunderland Creek, 75, 84
Susquehannocks, 16, 37
Swamps, in Middlesex County, 74, 75,
   78, 84
Swedenborgian Church, 207
Sweet Briar College, 336, 350n. 87

Tasker, Ann, 204
Tasker, Benjamin, 204
Tasker, Frances Ann, 207
Tawney, R. H., 53
Taxation: automatic refund law, 401,
   404; and race, 244, 259n. 36
Taylor, Alice O., 331, 333
Taylor, Zachary, 270
Terhune, Mary Virginia Hawes, 267.
   See also Harland, Marion
Thamon (Berkeley slave), 208
Thompson, Waddy, 306
Thompson, William, 95

Thompson, William, Jr., 248
Thomson, James M., 418, 419, 420
Thorstenberg, Herman J., 312–13
Tidball, Joseph, 211
Tignor, James A., 374
Tithables, 68n. 19, 70n. 43, 77
Tobacco: as currency, 78–79, 84, 85,
   237; economic dependence on, 124;
   expansion of production, 60; ex-
   ports of, 70n. 45; as lifeblood of
   economy, 109; production yields,
   69n. 41; Rolfe's experiments with,
   35; slave labor dependency of, 50,
   125; wealth generated by, 107;
   world market growth for, 124
Tobacco-cutting riots, 62
Tobacco houses, 77
Tom (Berkeley slave), 205–6, 209, 215,
   217
Toney (activist slave), 140, 141, 145
Tony, King, 69n. 39
Townsend, Jessie, 328, 331, 332, 333,
   337
Trade, with Indians, 19, 22–23
Trade unions: rise of, 327; strong-
   holds of, 349n. 65; and suffrage,
   332–33
Trials: in antebellum era, of slaves,
   223; of Berkeley's murderers, 211–
   12, 214–18, 231n. 37; of rebellion
   conspirators, 145, 159n. 50; of
   slaves, 148–49, 161n. 64
Troublemakers, in Middlesex County,
   91, 92
Truman, Harry S., 397
Tsenaccommacah domain, 16, 18,
   41n. 12
Tuck, William M., 397, 416
Tucker, James, 151–52
Tucker, St. George, 55, 175
Tuggle, Anne, 88
Tuggle, Mary (elder), 81–82, 88
Tuggle, Mary (younger), 88
Tuggle, Thomas, 81–82, 85, 88, 98,
   102n. 20
Tuggle, Thomas, Jr., 88
Turner, Edward, 4–5, 282, 286

Turner, Emmeline, 250, 251, 262n. 76
Turner, James, 241, 246
Turner, Nat, 309
Tuskegee Study of Untreated Syphilis in the Male Negro, 357
Two-Penny Acts, 120, 123
Tyler, Alice, 333
Tyler, John, 266

U.D.C. Catechism for Children (Stone), 304
Uncle Tom's Cabin (Stowe), 313
Underwood, John C., 324
Union forces: blacks in, 281; against bushwhacker gangs, 279–80; civil administration by, 279; civilian hostility toward, 278; coercion policy of, 278–79; conciliatory policy of, 277–78; conservatism toward slavery, 285; demobilization of, 287–88; destruction by, 280–81, 293n. 22; emergency rations issued to civilians, 288; occupation of Virginia, 275–83, 285–87; plundering by, 281–82; in rural areas, 279–82; Unionists organized by, 284
Unionists: after Civil War, 288–89; alliance with invaders, 283; on civilian disloyalty, 279; against Confederate forces, 283; fear of, 276; in guerrilla warfare, 283–84; organized by Union forces, 284; poor whites organized by, 284–85; sanction of state government, 279; against secessionists, 6–7, 283
Unions. *See* Trade unions
United Confederate Veterans, 297, 316n. 9
United Daughters of the Confederacy: book scrutiny bylaws, 318n. 29; and historical revisionism, 297–301; influence on children, 303–6; publishers pressured by, 306–7; and Roanoke College, 312
United States History (Cusson), 301
United States Public Health Service, 357, 381n. 20

University of Virginia: biology program of, 353, 359–60, 365–73, 383n. 30; eugenics at, 355, 364–65, 367–70, 387n. 64; ideological anchors of, 364; modernization of, 358, 359–60, 382n. 24
University of Wisconsin, 359
Upper Chapel, 75
Urban growth, 326–27

Vagrancy, severe measures against, 56
Valentine, Lila Meade: born after Whig Party demise, 272; efforts of, 330, 348n. 45; as Equal Suffrage League founder, 328; and factions of suffrage movement, 337–39; and Johnston, 322; lobbying activities of, 334; militancy of, 348n. 37; in ratification battle, 341, 343; and socialism, 333; and suffrage opposition, 336–37; and Sugg, 329; and trade unions, 332; and white supremacy, 321
Van Buren, Martin, 268, 270, 271
Van Lew, Elizabeth, 272, 323, 324, 348n. 45
Varon, Elizabeth R., 4, 7, 165, 263
Vause, Richard, 95
Venable, Abraham, 175, 177
Vengeance, of slaves, 225
Vice, among landless poor, 53–54
Violence: in acts of resistance, 106–7; and Berkeley murders, 225; of Civil War, 8; curtailment after Civil War, 288; in defense of honor, 175; interracial violence, 138–39; in politics, 172–73, 178, 187; of public service, 173–74; stimulation by press, 175; during Union occupation, 280–83
Virginia: budget issues, 404, 405; colonization efforts, 25; Gates's abandonment proclamation, 24; government restoration after Civil War, 287–88; governors of, 12, 20–21, 28–29; historical accounts, 12–13; Jim Crow statutes, 398, 400, 423; prominent public figures, 2; school

board reorganization, 301–2; school-closing laws, 419, 421; shortage of services, 404; State Education Committee of the American Eugenics Society, 362; suffrage legislation, 340–44; Union occupation of, 275–83, 285–87

Virginia Association of Ladies for Erecting a Statue to Henry Clay, 263, 264–65. *See also* Clay Association

Virginia Company: cruel treatment of subjects, 29; expectations of Indians, 18; on Indian enmity, 42n. 21; influence on First Anglo-Powhatan War, 31, 33; missionary intentions, 18, 35; rationalization of war, 43n. 27; reinforcements for colonists, 20–21; revitalization of, 24–25

Virginia Council, 207

Virginia gentry. *See* Gentry

Virginia Historical Society, 303

Virginia League of Women Voters, 345

Virginia Negro Woman's League of Voters, 330

Virginia's Attitude toward Slavery and Secession (Munford), 309–10

Virginia Suffrage News, 331

Virginia Woman Suffrage Association, 324–25

Virginia Women's Council of Legislative Chairmen of State Organizations, 346

Virtue: connection between public and private, 188; defense by violence, 175; of public servants, 122–23; republican standard of, 172

Vonderlehr, Raymond A., 357

Voting: election frequency, 119; election reform, 326; poll taxes, 299, 396; popular vote, 111–13; restrictions on, 299–300; women's party alignments, 345. *See also* Suffrage

Wahunsunacock: about, 16; Argall against, 32; assessment of English-

men, 17–18, 41n. 12; Dale against, 30–31; diplomatic efforts of, 18–19, 22, 32; holy war attitude, 27; introductory note, 2; Jamestown attack, 28; Jamestown siege, 23–24; misinterpretation of peace terms, 35–36; peace of 1614, 34; rumors about, 25, 33; Smith's capture by, 18–19; token ransom for Pocahontas, 32; underestimation of, 36

Walker, Betsey, 180, 183

Walker, John, 183

Walker, Maggie Lena, 330, 345–46

Waller, Benjamin, 144

War: definition of, 39–40n. 4; holy war, 12, 25–26, 27–28; Pontiac's War, 139. *See also* Battles; Civil War; First Anglo-Powhatan War; Revolutionary War

Warraskoyacs, 14*t*, 15, 27

War's Aftermath (Jordan and Jordan), 357–58

Washington, Booker T., 311

Washington, George: escaped slave of, 137; fame sought by, 172; on family, 195n. 17; Hamilton as aide, 174; home as public memorial, 263; introductory note, 3; Jefferson as secretary of state, 168, 172; Jefferson on, 172; and landless poor, 55; leadership of, 106; paradox of slavery position, 50; sense of obligation, 113; slander against, 180; on slavery, 309

Wealth: extremes in, 108; of gentry, 107; importance vs. race in social status, 252–53

Weaponry: English superiority, 17–18, 40–41n. 10; gun ownership by landless poor, 60–62; muskets, 18, 41n. 10; of Powhatans, 20–21, 30

Weatherby, Thomas, 91

Weber, Max, 53

Webster, Daniel, 266–67

Weekes, Abraham, 95

West, Francis, 21, 22–23

West, J. E., 342

Wright, Prudence, 237, 257n. 17

Wright, Robert: acceptance in white community, 253; birth of, 237; childhood of, 238–39; and Davidson family, 258n. 30; death of, 246; dispute with neighbor, 245; divorce petition, 235–36, 242–45; emancipation status questioned, 247; and father, 238–39; as gentleman farmer, 240–41; inheritance of, 239–40; introductory notes, 4, 234–35; legal racial status of, 244; manumission of, 238; marriage to Godsey, 240; as patriarch of family, 240–41, 253; and Polly Davidson, 241–42; provisions for Sylvia's care, 251; as slaveholder, 240, 257n. 23; son born to, 241; stature in community, 253; Sylvia cared for, 249; and Thomas Wright will, 240–41

Wright, Sylvia: about, 237–38; assertion of rights, 253; children of, 251; collusion in inheritance looting, 249; community tolerance of miscegenation, 252; death of, 250; estate of, 250–52; and Fleming, 260n. 60; in inheritance battle, 247, 248, 249, 261n. 67; inheritances of, 250; introductory note, 4; paid for care of Thomas P. Wright, 250; racial status

of, 259n. 36; relationship with Thomas Wright, 249; and Thomas Wright will, 239, 240–41

Wright, Thomas: about, 237; and Cabell, 256n. 13; community tolerance of miscegenation, 252; family of, 237–39; introductory notes, 4, 234–35; provisions for Sylvia's care, 251; relationship with Sylvia, 249, 251; repercussions of nonmarriage, 247; and Robert Wright, 238–39; slaves held by, 237; stature in community, 252

Wright, Thomas Pryor: birth of, 241; death of, 251; education of, 249–50; guardians of, 248; as hell-raiser, 250; inheritances of, 246–47, 250–51; racial status of, 259n. 36; weaknesses of, 253

Wright, William, 241, 250, 251, 253–54

Wyllie, Allen L., 250, 254, 262n. 76

Yankees: fear of, 276–77; hatred of, 280–81; stereotypes of, 276–77

Yellow Peter, 149

Yeoman farmers, 65–66

York River, 90

Young, P. B., Sr., 409–10, 412

Young Turks, 403–5, 406, 413